The Burden of Female Talent

HARVARD-YENCHING INSTITUTE MONOGRAPH SERIES 90

The Burden of Female Talent

The Poet Li Qingzhao and Her History in China

RONALD EGAN

Published by the Harvard University Asia Center
Distributed by Harvard University Press
Cambridge (Massachusetts) and London 2013

Printed in the United States of America

The Harvard-Yenching Institute, founded in 1928 and headquartered at Harvard University, is a foundation dedicated to the advancement of higher education in the humanities and social sciences in East and Southeast Asia. The Institute supports advanced research at Harvard by faculty members of certain Asian universities and doctoral studies at Harvard and other universities by junior faculty at the same universities. It also supports East Asian studies at Harvard through contributions to the Harvard-Yenching Library and publication of the *Harvard Journal of Asiatic Studies* and books on premodern East Asian history and literature.

Library of Congress Cataloging-in-Publication Data

Egan, Ronald, 1948–
    The burden of female talent : the poet Li Qingzhao and her history in China / Ronald Egan.
        pages cm. — (Harvard-Yenching Institute Monograph Series ; 90)
    Includes bibliographical references and index.
    Summary: "By re-examining the Chinese woman poet Li Qingzhao, Egan discusses the traditional manipulation of her image to mold her talent to make it compatible with ideals of womanly conduct and identity, and reveals the difficulty literary culture had in coping with her extraordinary conduct and ability"—Provided by publisher.
    ISBN 978-0-674-72669-7 (hardcover : acid-free paper)
    1. Li, Qingzhao, 1084-approximately 1155—Criticism and interpretation. 2. Women and literature—China—History—To 1500. I. Title.
    PL2682.Z5E38 2013
    895.1′142—dc23

2013009199

A portion of chapter 3 was previously published in *Hsiang Lectures on Chinese Poetry*, edited by Grace S. Fong, vol. 5, pp. 57–77 (Toronto: Centre for East Asian Research, McGill University, 2010), and is reprinted here with permission.

Index by the author

Last figure below indicates year of this printing

23 22 21 20 19 18 17 16 15 14 13

Contents

Tables and Maps

Abbreviations and Editions

Abbreviations Used in the Notes

Jianzhu Xu Peijun 徐培均. *Li Qingzhao ji jianzhu* 李清照集箋注. Rev. ed. Shanghai: Shanghai guji chubanshe, 2009.

Huibian Chu Binjie 褚斌杰 et al. *Li Qingzhao ziliao huibian* 李清照資料彙編. Beijing: Zhonghua shuju, 1984.

Note on Editions Used

Translations of Li Qingzhao's writings are based on Xu Peijun's edition of her works (in *Jianzhu*; see above). For her song lyrics, I have also consulted the texts in *Quan Songci* as well as several other recent editions and commentaries, as cited in the notes. I have generally followed Xu Peijun's preferences among the many textual variants listed in his collation notes but occasionally choose a different variant, following, for example, the *Quan Songci* version of a line, and do so without comment in a separate note. Page references for the song lyrics are given to both *Jianzhu* and *Quan Songci*. The numbering of the song lyrics is my own, as explained in chapter 3. For lists of all the pieces in my enumeration, see table 1 and appendix 1.

Introduction

This is a study of the woman poet in Chinese history that people think they know best. Li Qingzhao 李清照 (1084–ca. 1155) was famous for her literary skill in her own lifetime, nine centuries ago, and has remained so up to the present day. She is often referred to as China's greatest woman poet. She may or may not be that, but, at the least, she has name recognition that no other Chinese woman writer can match. It would also be hard to think of another woman whose most celebrated poetic lines are as widely known and quoted, even today.

For a writer so renowned and beloved in China, there is conspicuously little written about her in English. The only book-length discussion of her life and works is a slim volume that was published nearly fifty years ago. It is a sympathetic account, and one that will strike many readers today as uncritical. Li Qingzhao's poetry has fared better with translators, of whom it has attracted many. English renderings of her poems turn up regularly in anthologies of Chinese poetry. There are even some translations of her complete poems. But since only a few dozen of her works survive, even a "complete translation" yields but a small quantity of work. As effective as some of the translations are, it must be difficult for English readers to understand how this writer of so few and generally very short poems, which seem to be mostly about loneliness, nostalgia, and regret, could have won such acclaim in her native culture.

Yet it is not only the dearth of English-language writings about her life and work that this study seeks to redress. The Chinese scholarship on Li Qingzhao is vast, so much so that the quantity is overwhelming. It has been estimated, for example, that more has been written about her in Chinese since the founding of the People's Republic than about any other single poet of her dynasty (the Song dynasty, 960–1279), including such protean figures as Su Shi 蘇軾 (1037–1101), Lu You 陸游 (1125–1210), Fan Chengda 范成大 (1126–93), and Xin Qiji 辛棄疾 (1140–1207). Such is the intensity of the enthusiasm for her best-known compositions that it would be easy to find dozens if not hundreds of short articles on each one of them. But the enthusiasm is not always joined by critical acumen. The redundancy in this vast modern scholarship devoted to her writings is considerable.

Li Qingzhao has always been a great exception in Chinese literary history. She is the lone woman to have achieved canonical status among poets of her time or, as many would say, in the entire sweep of Chinese history. Yet it is not enough simply to recognize her as an exception, the one woman who has been vaulted into the inner sanctum of "great writers," and to leave it at that. It turns out that the tradition did not make an exception so readily or innocently. For a woman to be allowed into such company, who she was and what she stood for had to be changed in subtle and sometimes not-so-subtle ways. These changes are as much the subject of this book as is the task of trying to peel back the overlays, imposed on her through the centuries, to see what we can say about her once we dispense with them. The act of peeling back is itself no simple matter. Nearly everything that is ordinarily said about Li Qingzhao is a product of the refraction of what she originally wrote through the prism of elaborate interpretive schemes devised to make her acceptable to dominant cultural values. To further complicate the situation, there is every reason to think that her works, as they have been constituted since the Ming dynasty (1368–1644), are a messy hodgepodge of authentic compositions, later imitations, and outright fabrications made, in part, to reinforce conventional images of her.

Chapter 1 ("Women as Writers in the Song Dynasty") presents a survey of women's writing generally as it existed in Li Qingzhao's time. Unlike in later imperial times, women's writing was extraordinarily marginalized during the Song period. We know from anecdotes, mostly, about the occasional singing girl who could compose her own lyrics to the songs she performed. But such women were rare, and their lyrics, if they are recorded at all, survive only because they were viewed as anomalies. One also encounters reports of educated ladies, gentlewomen, who could compose poetry, although such reports are few. It turns out that one of the best known among these women, apart from Li Qingzhao, may well have been a complete fabrication and the poems attributed to her written by men. With that woman poet, Zhu Shuzhen 朱淑眞, we encounter a problem that will recur several times in later chapters and one that may be acute in Chinese literary history. Men had long since cultivated the technique of writing in the guise of women. This tradition of male writers adopting a female persona complicated the challenges for the unusual woman who came along and sought to write "in her own voice." This chapter's discussion of the paucity of women's writing at the time as well as the way such writing was often destroyed by women themselves—who were only too aware of the social taboos it violated—or manipulated by male anthologists who preserved it is intended to lay the groundwork for a historicized reappraisal of Li Qingzhao. While her status as a staple of China's literary history as written in modern times may in many ways be well-deserved and admirable, it also runs the risk of undermining a historicized appreciation of her accomplishment. In modern literary histories, Li Qingzhao has become a given: there were the great male writers, and then, oh yes, there was that one woman too. It is only when we reconstruct the social and literary world in which Li Qingzhao lived and wrote, and apprehend the gender biases applied to women writers—biases that are almost inconceivable by modern standards—that we are in a position to gauge accurately Li Qingzhao's achievement.

Chapters 2 and 3 turn to Li Qingzhao herself. The first of these ("Writing and the Struggle for Acceptance") begins by looking at references in her writings to the act of writing, which show how central the activity was to her life and self-image. The chapter then takes up the earliest critical assessments of Li Qingzhao, some written while she was still alive, which reveal an interesting disparity between praise for her writing and reservations about her conduct. The *shi* 詩 poetry that she wrote in a distinctly masculine style is examined next. Such writing was in part her reaction to the skepticism she faced as an aspiring writer and a means by which she sought to create space for herself in the male domain of writing. Finally, Li Qingzhao's audacious essay on the song lyric form (*ci* 詞) is discussed. Here she claims special understanding of the form and denigrates the work in it by the most famous writers of the preceding generations (all male). If the essay is considered from the standpoint of gender, its opening section can be seen as a veiled expression of the author's own aspiration that she be taken seriously as a writer.

Chapter 3 takes up issues that need to be discussed as preliminaries to an examination of Li Qingzhao's own output in the song lyric form, the cornerstone of her work as a writer. Foremost among these are the questions concerning the integrity of her corpus of song lyrics. More than one-half of the compositions attributed to her are of questionable authenticity. They did not appear until centuries after her death, and their provenance is unknown. Given what we know about the way famous persons in Chinese literary history "attracted" later attributions to them, and especially about the vogue of writing song lyrics "in the style" of Li Qingzhao, we have good reason to be skeptical about the authenticity of these works. It is not only the reliability of particular song lyrics that is in question. The haphazard mixing of authentic and probably inauthentic compositions together has affected the overall impression conveyed by her "corpus" as it is usually read. Another issue is the habit of reading Li Qingzhao's song lyrics autobiographically, as if they could be nothing other than simple first-person statements that reflect her personal circumstances. The effects of this way of reading Li Qingzhao are explored in conjunction with an examination of the contradictory findings of the latest Chinese-language scholarship concerning Li.

It was my initial plan to move straightaway to Li Qingzhao's song lyrics after the discussion of these knotty problems. Instead, I take up in chapter 4 ("Widowhood, Remarriage, Divorce") the momentous events that overtook Li Qingzhao when she was in her early forties and changed her life forever: the Jurchen invasion of North China, her flight southward with tens of thousands of compatriots, the death of her husband during that flight, her desperate wandering in the years that followed, and her remarriage and hasty divorce thereafter, which involved a court trial and brief imprisonment. This chapter includes discussion of a remarkable letter that Li Qingzhao wrote to the high official who intervened and secured her release from prison, in which she describes how she was tricked into her second marriage and the humiliation it occasioned her.

The following chapters (5, "Writings from the Aftermath," and 6, "The 'Afterword'") present and analyze a sudden burst of writing that followed her divorce. Li Qingzhao threw herself back into writing, producing an astonishing variety of texts in multiple forms. The writings include, in addition to the letter just mentioned, poems on contemporary politics addressed to emissaries who were about to go on a mission to the enemy Jurchen court, other poems with political themes, and a remarkable collection of writings on a board game called Capture the Horse that was conceived as a contest of military strategy. Chapter 6 is devoted to Li Qingzhao's best-known prose work, also from this period, the lengthy biographical afterword she wrote to her first husband's (Zhao Mingcheng's 趙明誠 [1081–1129]) scholarly notes on his collection of rubbings of ancient inscriptions. This afterword is analyzed not simply as a nostalgic commemoration of her marriage, the way it is usually read. Instead, it is situated in the context of the difficulties Li Qingzhao faced after her divorce. Such a reading allows us to discern new meanings and motives in this celebrated text.

Chapters 7 through 9 take up the reception of Li Qingzhao from the period right after her death through the Yuan dynasty (1271–1368) (7, "The Beginnings of 'Li Qingzhao'"), the Ming-Qing period (1368–1911) (8, "Saving the Widow, Denying the Remarriage"), and the twentieth century down to the present day (9, "Modernism, Revisionism, Feminism"). In the first of these we see the beginnings of the process whereby the historical writer and person, who was in many ways unconventional and threatening to prevailing notions of how a woman should behave, was refashioned into someone more acceptable to cultural norms. The process is one in which both identifiable literary critics and more amorphous forces of legend and hearsay played a role. In the Ming-Qing period, two separate developments affected the ways that Li Qingzhao was viewed and further reformulated. In literary circles, writing by women gradually became more widespread and acceptable, at least in certain quarters. As this happened, Li Qingzhao's stature was enhanced as a leading precedent and even inspiration for aspiring women writers. But during the same centuries, tolerance for remarriage by widows diminished, as the state-sponsored cult of "widows' chastity" gained ground. As applied posthumously to Li Qingzhao, these two developments came into conflict with each other, and by late Ming times critics begin to express dismay that such an exceptionally talented woman poet could have violated womanly virtue by marrying again after she was widowed. Scholars who could not accept such deviant behavior then took it upon themselves to undermine the several Song dynasty sources that record her remarriage. A peculiar scholarly campaign was undertaken to purify or vindicate Li Qingzhao from what were said to be slanderous Song dynasty reports that she had remarried. A newly reformulated Li Qingzhao as virtuous widow devoted to the memory of Zhao Mingcheng emerged from this campaign by the late Qing period.

It was this image of Li Qingzhao that the modern age inherited, when the first modern histories of Chinese literature were written by May Fourth era scholars. Chapter 9 follows this story of Li Qingzhao's elevation in twentieth-century literary history to the status of lone canonical woman poet. Her seemingly secure stature was abruptly jolted in 1957 by two lengthy studies by a young scholar who challenged the Qing denial of her remarriage, refuting it point by point. These studies touched off a furious controversy that raged back and forth for the remainder of the century, pitting older and more traditionally minded scholars, some of whom had a vested interest in preserving the May Fourth narrative, against those who now saw the weaknesses of the Qing scholarship. The controversy, which quickly devolved into heated arguments between the "remarriage camp" and the "anti-remarriage camp," has its own interest for what it shows about the malleability of the biographical past, the way Qing "evidential scholarship" was anything but objective, and the enormous appeal and staying power that accrues to certain fabricated images of iconic historical figures, not to mention the confounding of scholarship with perceived moral imperatives. Although there are still, today, those who hold adamantly to the earlier view, the scholarly consensus has reversed, and it is now generally accepted, especially by younger scholars, that Li Qingzhao's remarriage is historical fact.

The advantage of putting the two chapters on Li Qingzhao's song lyrics at the end of the study, after the contentious story of her reception has been told, paradoxically, is that we can read these works with certain preconceptions and images already in mind. Her celebrity in literary history has long since been transported into cultural history. As loving, long-suffering, talented, and wholly devoted wife, "Li Qingzhao" has become an essential part of modern China's sense of its cultural past and values, as one perceives from the several memorial halls dedicated to her today (three in her native Shandong and one in Zhejiang), the modern musical settings of her song lyrics, the numerous imaginary portraits of her circulating in print and digital form (which conventionally depict her as a wispy, vulnerable, and hypersensitive lady), and the endless telling and retelling of her "biography" in popular forms.

The largest of the Li Qingzhao memorial halls today is that situated in Leaping Spring Park 趵突泉公園 in the city center of Ji'nan, Shandong. It is a complex of buildings, including a "former residence." Visitors to the memorial hall are greeted by two calligraphy inscriptions displayed just inside the main entrance that read "The Poet of Her Time" 一代詞人 and "Her Works Transmitted and Recited for a Thousand Autumns" 傳誦千秋. The inscriptions are written in the calligraphy of Guo Moruo, the first president of the Chinese Academy of Social Sciences and a man who played the role of cultural czar for much of the Mao period in the People's Republic of China. Just behind the entrance, one comes upon a larger than life-size statue of our poet, standing some ten feet high, done in alabaster white. Behind the statue is the entire poem Guo Moruo wrote for the memorial hall, from which the entrance inscriptions are taken. This is the poem:

一代詞人有舊居	The poet of her time, her former residence is here.
半生漂泊憾何如	For half a lifetime she drifted haplessly about, such regrets she had!
冷清今日成轟烈	But her loneliness and neglect has today become towering fame,
傳誦千秋是著書	Transmitted and recited for a thousand autumns, the writings she composed.

In the poem and the inscriptions lifted from it, we see official government approbation of Li Qingzhao aligning itself with and reinforcing popular images of her. The memorial hall itself contains several rooms displaying "scenes" from Li Qingzhao's life. Wax statues representing her and those close to her are arranged in theatrical poses. Prominently featured in these scenes are images of Li Qingzhao's wifely devotion to Zhao Mingcheng and her courageous steadfastness as widow after his death.

The truth about Li Qingzhao is both more interesting and more elusive than such popular images. But it is so difficult to extricate ourselves from the accretion of her legend through "a thousand autumns" that it is best to deal with that accretion first, in all of its layers and internal tensions, before finally coming to the literary work for which she is best known, her song lyrics. It is naive to think that anyone who knows anything about Chinese history can come to Li Qingzhao's song lyrics free of preconceptions and assumptions about their author and what she expresses in them. It is preferable to educate ourselves first about those preconceptions, to see how they came about and what needs they cater to, many of which are certainly contrary to what Li Qingzhao sought to convey through her writing. The hope is that once we do this we will be in a better position, returning finally to Li Qingzhao's works, to give them a fairer and less prejudiced reading. For all the books and articles that have been written about Li Qingzhao's song lyrics, there is very little discussion of them as literary works independent of her biography, which is seen as a melodrama of virtue in the face of tragedy. As one of the first women writing in a poetic genre that already featured women and women's personas, Li Qingzhao produced strikingly distinctive and effective compositions, as Chinese readers have sensed for centuries. There is much to say in the final chapters about the interest of her work and her achievement as a writer without confounding these with her life circumstances in a reductive way. Chapters 10 and 11 also treat the divergences between the early song lyrics that have a strong claim to authenticity and much later attributions that do not.

The reconsideration of Li Qingzhao's life and works presented in this volume owes a substantial debt to feminist literary criticism and scholarship as it has developed in recent decades outside of Chinese studies. Discoveries about the meanings found in writings by women of Europe and America before the twentieth century, including well-known writers and those long neglected, have been valuable in clarifying gender dynamics and biases against women who write that are certainly not unique to China. Thus I have profited from reading studies by Rita Felski, Sarah Prescott, Paula Backscheider, and others. In addition, new insights developed during the past twenty-five years in the burgeoning fields of Chinese women's history and women's literary history, mostly focused on the Ming-Qing period, have also helped to shape my understanding of what questions to formulate and how to go about answering them. Still, I have tried to remain cognizant of the special circumstances and challenges that Li Qingzhao faced as a woman writer of her time, long before there emerged in China communities of women writers who mentored and encouraged each other, and I do not assume that the issues and concerns relevant to women writers in premodern Europe and America are wholly relevant or transportable to twelfth-century China. One of the goals of this study is to contribute to the fields of women's literary criticism and women's history by bringing to them a new case study with its own dynamics and circumstances, to enlarge the discussion and perhaps even to recenter it to a certain degree.

CHAPTER I

Women as Writers in the Song Dynasty

Over the past twenty-five years, scholars have uncovered a wealth of women's writing produced in the last centuries of imperial China, roughly 1500 to 1900. Before these discoveries, it was commonly thought that even into late imperial times few women in China were literate, and even those few were hardly active as writers. We now know this impression to be very inaccurate. From the late Ming onward, there were large numbers of women engaged in one way or another in literary culture, as readers, writers, editors, patrons, and anthologists. Whereas we used to think that reading and writing was the sole prerogative of men and that women in, say, eighteenth-century China lagged far behind their counterparts in Europe in this regard, many scholars now believe that there were more women writers in China at the time than anywhere else in the world.

The situation in Song dynasty China is not comparable to the Ming-Qing period as we now understand it. But the comparison breaks down in a rather complicated way. Our impression is that reading and writing were overwhelmingly male domains during the Song period. This impression too is probably an exaggeration to a certain degree. The truth must be that more women were educated and more women were active as writers and readers than we usually suppose. Some evidence suggests that women's literacy, at least, was not uncommon among the upper classes and that the act of women writing was not viewed as all that rare and remarkable. Yet two caveats are in order. First, in no way was women's participation in literary culture, as writers and readers, as widespread or common as it became in late imperial times.

There is little or no evidence of the emergence of communities of women writers in Song times, as we know happened in the late Ming and Qing. Song period women who were literate and chose to write did so almost entirely on their own, without the comfort and encouragement of other women and sympathetic men, who lent their support to literary women of later centuries. Everything we know about Li Qingzhao points to this being the case with her. She was not a member of a group of literary women.

Second, even after we acknowledge that the quantity of women's writing from the Song was both probably more than we commonly assume and far less than that produced during the Ming and Qing periods, we must face the fact that so much of that writing has been lost that the true "story" of women's writing during the period is going to remain unknown and elusive for us. With the Ming-Qing, scholars are even today uncovering large quantities of women's writing that has survived but was simply unnoticed and passed over in earlier literary histories. Such rediscovery is not happening for the Song, because most of what women writers produced was lost long ago.

Naturally, merely as a factor of Song's location so much farther back in historical time, the survival rate of Song materials, written by men as well as women, is far lower than that for writing produced in late imperial times. But women's writing from the period fared especially badly, it seems, and surely this fate must be tied to all the prejudices against it in elite male culture that was responsible, both actively and passively, for the preservation and transmission of books. Hu Wenkai 胡文楷, in his authoritative bibliography of women's writing through Chinese history, lists some thirty Song period literary and poetry collections by women that once existed.[1] That is the number of titles that he has found cited, altogether, in early sources. The actual number of literary collections produced by women must have been far larger than those thirty that attracted notice and comment in early materials. Yet, of those thirty, only three survived into modern times (compared with hundreds of literary collections by men that survived). One of the three, moreover, was produced by an empress (not exactly an ordinary woman), and the other two are, as we will see, of highly questionable provenance and authenticity.[2] Three out of thirty is a dismal survival rate, especially when we

---

1. Hu Wenkai, *Lidai funü zhuzuo kao*, pp. 40–69.
2. The empress is Empress Yang, the wife of Ningzong (r. 1195–1224), whose collection is *Yang taihou gongci* 楊太后宮詞. For a discussion of this remarkable woman's artistry in several forms, see Lee, *Empresses, Art, and Agency*, pp. 160–218.

recall that the Song was the period in which book printing became widespread in China. Actually, Li Qingzhao herself provides a revealing example. Acclaimed for her poetic talent already as a young woman, her song lyrics circulated in printed editions during her lifetime, and her other writings drew the attention and praise of prominent men of letters. Yet both of her collections, that of her song lyrics and that of her other literary writing, eventually went out of circulation and were lost. What we have of her writing today are only those pieces that were selected into anthologies or were quoted in other works. It is difficult to think of a parallel case among male writers of her day: that of a man renowned for his literary skill among his contemporaries but whose literary works were subsequently lost. That this happened to Li Qingzhao and her works has everything to do with her identity as a woman.

Let us begin with some quantitative information about women's writing during the Song. What survives today is quantitatively scant, nearly to the point of being nonexistent. For example, poems by women that are scattered throughout the *Complete Song Dynasty Poetry* 全宋詩 (completed in 1998), constitute considerably less than 1 percent of the total. My estimate, based on a sample of several hundred-page sections of the massive compilation (which runs to 45,698 pages), is that women's poetry makes up something closer to one-tenth of 1 percent of the work. Revealingly, there appear to be more pieces attributed to unnamed women or to women with pseudonyms (e.g., "courtesan of Pingjiang" or "a gentleman's wife") than to real women with real names. The situation is similar in the *Complete Song Dynasty Song Lyrics* 全宋詞.

The extreme marginality of woman's poetry during the Song period itself is suggested by the amount of space devoted to it in Hu Zi's 胡仔 anthology of poetry criticism, *Comments Collected by the Fisherman Recluse of Tiaoxi* 苕溪漁隱叢話, compiled in the mid-twelfth century. Hu Zi's work is a massive compendium that draws on dozens of miscellanies and "remarks on poetry" collections produced during the Northern and early Southern Song periods. Hu Zi's work consists of two parts, a "former collection" 前集 (completed in 1148) and a "later collection" 後集 (completed 1167). The bulk of each collection is devoted to criticism of major poets, arranged chronologically by poet. No female poet, including Li Qingzhao, is given her own section in either collection. Instead, entries on women are grouped together in a section titled "miscellaneous anecdotes about beauties" 麗人雜記 that is found at the very end of each collection, occupying the last few pages, located behind sections devoted to Buddhist monks, gods, ghosts, and song lyrics. In the former collection, the section on women consists of two and a half pages (in the modern typeset edition) out of a total of 418 pages.[3] In the later collection, the section on women takes up eight pages out of 343.[4] Apart from their brevity, the most significant feature of both sections on "beauties" is that the majority of the entries are not about women writers (unlike all other sections of the work, which are about writers and their works). To be sure, there are such entries, including a few about poems written by Li Qingzhao. But the bulk of the entries are about women who figure in poems other than as author. We read of men writing poems about alluring women, unlikely marriages, deceased wives, and talented courtesans, and of poems inspired by a concubine's clever remark, a serving girl's clumsiness, and so on. But only exceptionally do we read about a woman actually producing poetry.

Some women, those from well-to-do families, received a solid education, even a classical education, and some of these ladies cultivated skills as writers. But there were deep ambivalences in Song society about educating women, allowing women to write, and, even if they did write, preserving or circulating what they produced. In his *Family Regulations* 家範, the famous statesman and historian Sima Guang 司馬光 (1019–86) included writing "song and poetry" 歌詩 on a list of skills that young ladies should not be permitted to cultivate.[5] An early commentary on his work, possibly written by Sima Guang himself, observes even more pointedly that "today some people teach their daughters how to write poetry and perform popular songs; it is not right at all" 今人或教女子以作歌詩執俗樂，殊非所宜也.[6] These statements are interesting given that Sima Guang was strongly in favor of literacy for girls and getting them to the point that they could read the classics.[7] He insisted that such moral training, through books, was as important for girls as it is for boys. But he drew a line when it came to writing. He evidently saw no reason why a girl should write.

Nevertheless, it is also clear from his comments that many upper-class families were teaching their daughters how to write poetry as well as how to

---

3. Hu Zi, *Tiaoxi yuyin conghua*, "Qianji" 60.416–18.

4. Ibid., "Houji" 40.329–37.

5. Sima Guang, *Jia fan* 6.2b.

6. Neither this passage, nor the *Family Regulations* text it glosses, is found in present versions of Sima Guang's work. Yet it is quoted from that work in Zhen Dexiu's *Xishan dushu ji* 21.40.

7. Sima Guang, *Jia fan* 6.1b–2b.

embroider and to sing and play music. For families of a certain social stand-ing, it was evidently a point of pride to teach such polite accomplishments to their daughters. In all likelihood such accomplishments, pleasurable enough in their own right to the learner and her family, also enhanced a girl's prospects in betrothal and marriage. But how many families would have been comfortable with the prospect of their daughter's poems circulating outside the walls of the family compound? And what about the status of her literary compositions when she was no longer a budding young talent, that is, when she was married and a mother, and eventually a grandmother and perhaps a domestic matriarch? How many women's in-law relatives would want their daughter-in-law's poetic compositions or those by their late patriarch's widow to circulate abroad in the world, or would make any effort to gather one of their womenfolk's corpus of poems together and preserve them in manuscript form for posterity?

Even in the late Ming and Qing periods, when in certain circles writing by women was accepted and even promoted by men and women alike, the public circulation of such writing was problematic. For a woman's writing to be publicly available was a transgression of the boundary between "inner" (female) and "outer" (male) spheres. As Charlotte Furth has observed, even in those later centuries, "for a woman's writings to be seen or known was for her to be perceived sexually by outsiders."[8] We recall scenes from the great Qing novel *The Story of the Stone* (also *Dream of the Red Chamber*) in this con-nection, for example, the description of Tanchun's and Daiyu's dismay and, really, horror at the news that poems that they and other of the young female clan members had written within the privacy of their protected space (inside Grand Prospect Garden) had been stealthily transmitted out of the garden (by Baoyu) and that the older male members of the family were preparing to have them printed.[9] It is not surprising, then, that in accounts of Ming and Qing literary women we often hear of their writings being burned, either by the author herself (some women were said to burn each poem immediately after its completion) or by her family upon her death.[10] (Here, again, we think of Daiyu and the self-destruction of her poetry as she herself is dying.)

---

8. Furth, "Poetry and Women's Culture," p. 6.

9. Cao Xueqin, *Honglou meng* 48.500: "You really are the limit! [Tanchun and Daiyu said to Baoyu.] Quite apart from the fact that the poems aren't good enough, you have no business to go showing our stuff to people outside." Trans. Hawkes and Minford, *Story of the Stone* 2:461.

10. See Ko, "Pursuing Talent and Virtue," pp. 18–19.

For every corpus of women's writing that survived in Ming and Qing times, there must have been many that were deliberately destroyed.

The motif of destroyed manuscripts is one that we repeatedly encounter in accounts of women's writing from the Song period. Burned manuscripts, lost writings, poems that survive only in fragments or only because they are quoted in an anecdote, these sorts of circumstances are the norm with women's writing in the Song. Another recurrent problem is that of the name and identity of the writers. Most women writers we do not even know by their full names. Usually what we have instead is just a surname (Woman Xie 謝氏, Woman Wei 衛氏, and so forth). Even when we have a name, the precise identity, dates, and native place of the person in question remains unclear or is given differently in different sources. Aside from Li Qingzhao, the best-known woman poet of the dynasty is Zhu Shuzhen. Yet widely divergent versions of her dates have been given, ranging over two centuries. Multiple locations have likewise been given for her native place. Her marital history is also under dispute. Some scholars maintain that she was only married once, others say that she had an affair outside of wedlock, others say she was divorced and remarried, and so on. It is because the lives of women writers are so poorly documented in the standard biographical sources that such uncertainties and discrepancies arise. We will see that similar uncertainties also arise in the case of Li Qingzhao.

Courtesans as Poets

To establish the context in which Li Qingzhao functioned as a writer, I will briefly survey what can be gleaned from Song period sources about women writers generally, starting at the lower point in the social scale with singing girls who composed their own songs. In the Tang period (618–907), the best-known and most prolific women poets mostly belonged to the social group of women who worked in the entertainment quarters and befriended celebrated male poets of the day, or to women who alternated roles between Daoist nun and entertainer. Such were the lives of Li Ye 李冶 (Li Jilan 李季蘭), Xue Tao 薛濤, and Yu Xuanji 魚玄機. These are the Tang women poets whose verse survives in the greatest quantity. Also, they were well enough known to have certain of their works selected into poetry anthologies compiled during the Tang. None of the three were family women. Xue Tao and Yu Xuanji were both entertainers in the capital of Chang'an. Xue Tao exchanged poems with such eminent literati as Bai Juyi 白居易

(772–846), Yuan Zhen 元稹 (799–831), and Du Mu 杜牧 (803–52). Yu Xuanji, who lived in the ninth century, is said to have been a concubine who was driven from her master's home, whereupon she became an entertainer and Daoist woman. Her poems include two addressed to Wen Tingyun 溫庭筠 (ca. 812–70), and there are unconfirmed stories of a later romantic relation between the two. Li Ye, chronologically the earliest of the three, moved in the circle of the Buddhist poet Jiaoran 皎然 in the 760s and 770s. Her fame resulted in a summons to join the ranks of distinguished religious women/entertainers in the imperial palace. However, she was not kept on long in the palace, and she was eventually executed for having sent a congratulatory poem to the ill-fated usurper Zhu Ci 朱泚 (742–84).

In the Song period, most of the references to such women's writing concern the song lyric rather than *shi* poetry. This reflects the abundance of courtesans or singing girls, who performed song lyrics, in Song society. Female entertainers were a ubiquitous presence in the banquets, festival celebrations, and birthday parties given at all levels of officialdom as well as in private gatherings. Female entertainers were, indeed, an institutionalized component of the sprawling official bureaucracy. There were "government courtesans" 官妓 at the various levels of the bureaucracy (the military counterpart to this civilian office was termed "garrison courtesans" 營妓). There was also a system of private entertainers ("household courtesans" 家妓). Finally, there were a variety of professional female entertainers outside of these categories, who were found in all manner of tea houses, wine shops, and brothels in cities, towns, and villages.[11]

Generally, courtesans performed songs that men had written. Occasionally, we hear of courtesans composing their own songs, but this was not the norm, and it was generally not expected that courtesans would be able to set their own words to musical tunes.[12] Nevertheless, owing to their intimate familiarity with the musical and literary rules and conventions of the form, courtesans sometimes surprised those present by coming up with their own compositions. Occasionally, in the course of a festive gathering, a courtesan known to have this ability would even be invited to take her turn at composition, complementing the efforts of the men present.

---

11. Especially on the system of government courtesans, see Bossler, "Shifting Identities"; also Bossler, *Courtesans, Concubines, and the Cult of Female Fidelity*, pp. 20–28.

12. This point is made in Deng, *Nüxing cishi,* pp. 53–54.

For example, a government courtesan in Chengdu named Chen Fengyi 陳鳳儀 is thought to have composed the following song lyric on the occasion of the departure of the governor there, Jiang 蔣, who would have been considered her "supervisor," when he was about to return to the capital. Presumably, Chen Fengyi performed this song at a farewell banquet given in the governor's honor.

一絡索   *To the tune "On a Single String"*

送蜀守蔣龍圖   Seeing Off Jiang of Dragon Diagram Hall, the Governor of Shu

蜀江春色濃如霧	Spring gives the Shu River the appearance of thick fog,
擁雙旌歸去	Displaying a pair of flags he sets off on his return.
海棠也似別君難	The crab apple seems saddened by his lordship's departure,
一點點	Drop by drop,
啼紅雨	It weeps crimson raindrops.
此去馬蹄何處	Once he leaves where will the horse hoofs take him?
沙隄新路	The embankment newly covered with fresh sand.
禁林賜宴賞花時	When enjoying flowers in the Forbidden Garden, at an imperial feast,
還憶著	Will he still remember
西樓否	The western tower?[13]

The second stanza imagines Jiang being received by the emperor, who welcomes him at a feast. The embankment mentioned in the second line is the one that led to the palace and was covered with white sand so that officials, riding to court, did not sully their robes. This was a Tang practice and may be invoked anachronistically here. The "western tower" is a stock phrase for the residence of a beloved woman. The entertainer is wondering, understandably enough, if he will still remember her once Jiang finds himself in more elegant surroundings, where imperial "flowers" (doubling here as palace entertainers) replace her. We expect he will not and likewise expect that she knows he will not. It was the lot of such girls to be promptly forgotten, and it would be exceptional if they were not.

Chen Fengyi's song is representative of many of the song lyrics written by government courtesans.[14] Their compositions are apt to feature just such

---

13. Chen Fengyi, "Yi luosuo," *Quan Songci* 1:215.

14. See, for example, Nie Shengqiong 聶勝瓊, "Zhegu tian" 鷓鴣天; Seng'er 僧兒, "Manting fang" 滿庭芳; and Pingjiang ji 平江妓, "He xinlang: song taishou" 賀新郎: 送太守, *Quan Songci* 2:1359, 2:1391, and 4:3524.

apprehensions over the reliability of the favor they happened to enjoy. To judge from extant sources, it was often, indeed, when a ranking official was leaving his post that a resident government courtesan would write her own song, addressing it to him on the eve of his departure. However, some of these compositions were probably composed by men and promptly attributed to the courtesans who performed them.

Some courtesans showed the ability to write on other themes. Hong Huiying 洪惠英, said to be an entertainer in Kuaiji (her dates are unknown), wrote this interesting song ostensibly about plum blossoms threatened by the snow:

減字木蘭花　*To the tune "Magnolia Blossoms, Short Version"*

梅花似雪	The plum blossoms look like snow
剛被雪來相挫折	But recently they've been assailed by snow itself.
雪裡梅花	Plum blossoms amid the snow,
無限精神總屬他	No end of fortitude still resides in them.
梅花無語	The plum blossoms do not speak,
只有東君來作主	Their only hope is protection by the Lord of the East.
傳語東君	They pass word to the Lord:
且與梅花作主人	Kindly be the plum blossom's protector.[15]

There was a Song period vogue of writing song lyrics on plum blossoms, but not like this. The strangeness of the language begs for a figurative interpretation. Deng Hongmei 鄧紅梅 has plausibly suggested that this song is really about the perennial conflict between wife and concubine, a phenomenon that although ubiquitous in Chinese society of the time was rarely, for obvious reasons, broached in poetry written by men.[16] In the triplet of actors presented here, the plum blossoms are the concubine, the snow that threatens them is the wife, and the Lord of the East, the god of spring, is the husband and master of the household. The plum tree in China does often blossom early enough in the new year to encounter snow, and conventionally it is said that the presence of snow on the plum branches enhances the beauty of the blossoms. One reason it does so is because it shows how hearty the blossoms are: delicate as they appear, plum blossoms are not readily bruised or ruined by snow. Likewise, concubines were often subject to various forms

---

15. Hong Huiying, "Jianzi mulanhua," *Quan Songci* 3:1931–32.

16. Deng, *Nüxing cishi*, pp. 56–57.

of abuse by wives, but the concubine described in the song is all the more resilient for such ill treatment. Still, given her significantly inferior status, the concubine cannot afford to protest to the wife herself, and hence the blossoms "do not speak." Yet the concubine can entreat the husband to come to her rescue, so long as she conveys this message privately to him, and this is the strategy that the blossoms eventually decide on in the song. It would be interesting to know if Hong Huiying's composition grew out of personal experience. If she was a courtesan in a private household, her situation might have been very similar to that of a concubine. Naturally, even if she was not kept in a household, the sexual politics among wife, concubine, and husband would be familiar to her. The remarkable thing is that she chose to feature the subject in a song and to do so in this clever yet quite transparent way.

In trying to reconstruct an account of woman's writing among these female entertainers, we must be wary of the tendency evident in some sources to romanticize these women, attributing to some of them more charm, principle, and even literary talent than they are likely to have had. Such talent is, after all, part of the entertainer's lure and mystique, and may in certain instances be more imaginary than real. The story of the twelfth-century garrison courtesan Yan Rui 嚴蕊 is a case in point. Yan Rui, whose duty was to provide entertainment for the governor's staff in Taizhou (Linhai, Zhejiang), is said to have excelled at dance, musical instruments, and calligraphy and painting. She was also known for writing her own poems and songs. When Tang Zhongyou 唐仲友 (Yuzheng 與正, 1136–88) served as governor in Taizhou, he regularly had her entertain at official banquets. A gentleman guest at one of those banquets was so impressed by a song lyric she extemporized, using his surname as the rhyme, that he took her into his home for half a year. This would have been illegal, and so we are not entirely surprised to learn that subsequently, when no less a figure than Zhu Xi 朱熹 (1130–1200) came to Taizhou in 1182 as commissioner of the Ever Normal Granaries, tea, and salt for the Jiangxi Circuit, he charged Tang Zhongyou himself with having illicit relations with Yan Rui. In Zhou Mi's 周密 (1232–1308) account of these events, Yan Rui is imprisoned and beaten in an attempt to get her to implicate Tang.[17] Zhu Xi is even said to have taken his female prisoner with him when he proceeded next to Yuezhou on his inspection tour. Despite a protracted period in jail, with repeated beatings, Yan Rui

---

17. From Zhou Mi, *Qidong yeyu* 20.5684–85.

maintained that her conduct with Tang had never been improper. She said she would prefer to die than to slander him. Finally, Zhu Xi went on and left Yan Rui behind, still in custody. The official whose charge she became, evidently looking for a way to pardon her on the occasion of a seasonal festival, asked her to compose a song lyric explaining herself. This is what she composed, extemporizing orally again:

卜算子   To the tune "The Fortune-Teller"

不是愛風塵	I am not fond of the "wind and dust,"
似被前身誤	But find myself cast there by karma from a former life.
花落花開自有時	Flowers fall and flowers bloom, each in its time,
總是東君主	Entirely as the Lord of the East decides.
去也終須去	Departing, I must depart,
住也如何住	Staying, how could I stay on?
若得山花插滿頭	The next time you encounter flowers, pluck them until they fill your hair,
莫問奴歸處	And don't ask where I have gone.[18]

Line 1: "Wind and dust" is a euphemism for the life of a female entertainer or prostitute.

When we encounter this composition in Zhou Mi's account of the charges against Tang Zhongyou and Yan Rui's imprisonment, it is apt to strike us as exceptional. It seems a decidedly philosophical composition, informed by pathos and a fatalistic acceptance of its author's lot. Yan Rui emphasizes the lack of control she has over her life and is resigned to resembling the flowers, to which girls of her occupation were endlessly compared, in the brevity of their beauty. The second stanza appears to take up the theme of her mortality. Stoically, she counsels her listener not to let her sorry fate bear on his mind or interfere with his future diversions.

Unfortunately, this tale of the heroic, tragic, and talented courtesan seems to be largely the stuff of local legend. At least the parts about her refusal to implicate Tang Zhongyou and her composition of this song are evidently fictional. We know this from Zhu Xi's own memorials concerning his impeachment of Tang. Zhu Xi reported Tang's misdeeds at great length, in numerous denunciations of him that Zhu Xi submitted to the emperor over the course of several weeks.[19] Zhu Xi did indeed arrest Yan Rui and imprison

---

18. Yan Rui, "Busuan zi," *Quan Songci* 3:2169.

19. They fill nearly fifty pages in the modern edition of his writings, *Zhu Xi ji* 2:18.725–19.772.

her. But according to Zhu Xi's memorials she did provide incriminating testimony against Tang Zhongyou, and she did so quite elaborately.[20] Zhu Xi's memorials even broach the song lyric translated above but speak of it in a different light altogether. Zhu Xi says that Tang's confidante Gao Xuanjiao 高宣教 wrote it for Yan Rui.[21] More surprising still, Zhu Xi asserts that the piece was intended as Yan Rui's reply to Tang, after he asked her to remove herself from the rolls of the official entertainers, hide in one of his relative's homes, and await his instructions as to how to enter his household as his own concubine. (In Zhu Xi's quotation, the first line of the second stanza is different: "As for leaving, how could I ever leave?" 去又如何去.) In this version and context, the song becomes Yan Rui's rejection of Tang's plan for her, as she tells him to forget about her.

Zhou Mi's version of Yan Rui's story was written roughly a century after the events it describes. Zhou himself notes that an earlier and shorter version of the events had appeared in Hong Mai's 洪邁 (1123–1202) miscellany.[22] The inclusion of the story in Hong Mai's work should already give us pause: we know that Hong drew much of his material from tales and legends that were circulating orally. Zhou Mi's account of Yan Rui, like Hong Mai's upon which it further elaborates, is part of the lore that grew up around a certain type of person: the captivating and talented courtesan who was virtuously loyal to her male patron. In this case the drama of the events is enhanced by the confrontation between the sympathetic courtesan and the moralistic crusader Zhu Xi.

Literati Women as Poets

As we move up the social scale it becomes, if anything, more difficult to find women's poetry. This is paradoxical because surely there were more literate women and more women writing in the upper classes than among the professional female entertainers. The paradox disappears when we remember that

---

20. This point is made in Shu Jingnan, *Zhu Xi nianpu changbian* 1:739. I have followed Shu's critique of Hong Mai and Zhou Mi on this and several other points. Zhu Xi's attack on Tang Zhongyou for his affair with Yan Rui is discussed by Beverly Bossler as an example of moralists' efforts to curb the growing involvement of officials with professional entertainers during the Southern Song; see *Courtesans, Concubines, and the Cult of Female Fidelity*, pp. 163–65 and 190–96.

21. Zhu Xi, "An Tang Zhongyou disi zhuang" 按唐仲友第四狀, *Zhu Xi ji* 2:19.746.

22. Hong Mai, "Wu shuji Yan Rui" 吳淑姬嚴蕊, *Yijian zhi*, "Zhigeng" 10.1216–17.

the problems posed by women's writing were more intransigent at the upper levels of society and the impulse to preserve whatever was written probably also subject to greater ambivalence.

We recall Sima Guang's position on women's education: girls should be taught to read but not to write. (This is nearly the opposite of the goal of education for men, where one of the primary reasons wide reading was important was precisely because it honed writing skills.) Sima Guang's reasoning (following Ban Zhao's 班昭 [45–ca. 116 CE] *Strictures for Women* 女誡) is that women, like men, only know right and wrong through education in the Confucian classics. If they are not steeped in the classics, women will conduct themselves in immoral ways, and they will not even realize it. Consequently, "virtuous women of ancient times were all devoted to learning. Diagrams on their left and historical writings on their right enabled them to discipline themselves."[23] The only writing that Sima Guang even considers a woman might produce were "songs and poems," by which, probably, he mostly means song lyrics. But he brings up the possibility to disparage it, equating such literary work with "intricate and ornate embroidery." In delivering these injunctions, Sima Guang is speaking as a true conservative, for many upper-class families would have nurtured their daughters' skill at embroidery, and evidently at poetic composition as well.

Further insight into the conservative viewpoint among elite families is provided by remarks that the Confucian thinker Cheng Yi 程頤 (1033–1107) makes about his mother, née Hou 侯, in the commemorative biography he wrote for her.[24] She was educated as a child and is said to have enjoyed reading the histories. Her father was extremely fond of her and proud of her intelligence. He made a habit of asking her about issues of governance and was delighted by her answers. It was a pity, he remarked, that she was not a boy.[25] Later, when she herself was married and produced sons, she supervised their learning. To show how seriously she took the matter, she wrote out an inscription to place where they worked: "I cherish boys who exert themselves in their studies." She noticed that her two sons showed different aptitudes and promise, and so she wrote out two prophetic lines. For Cheng Hao 程顥 (1032–85), she wrote "Cheng Yanshou passes the palace examination" (using Hao's childhood name). For Cheng Yi she simply wrote "the

---

23. Sima Guang, *Jia fan* 6.2b.
24. Cheng Yi, "Shanggu jun jun jiazhuan" 上谷郡君家傳, *Henan Chengshi wenji* 12.653–57.
25. Ibid., p. 653.

scholar who resides at home" (anticipating the role he chose for himself through much of his adult life as well as the fact that he never did pass the highest examinations).[26]

As educated as she was, Hou wrote very little. Cheng Yi says in this regard: "My mother was fond of books but did not write literary compositions. She disapproved strongly of women who allowed their literary compositions and letters to circulate in the world. In her entire life, she wrote no more than thirty poems, and none of them were preserved."[27] The implication is that she destroyed the poems herself. Cheng Yi adds that only one poem she wrote survives, and he quotes it. It is a poem Hou addressed to her husband, Cheng Yi's father, when he was posted on a mission in the distant north. She writes of how much she misses him, of how she is unable to sleep alone at night, and she compares herself to the fourth-century lady Su Hui 蘇蕙, who wove a palindrome poem she composed into brocade to send to her distant husband as a token of her love. The passage continues with a description of Hou's perceptive reading of the dynastic histories and concludes with a reference to her younger brother, Hou Keshi 侯可世. He was a renowned scholar, we are told, whose talent and knowledge were exceptional. And yet he maintained that in matters of learning he was inferior to his older sister.

In Cheng Yi's portrait of his mother, we encounter attitudes and themes that are characteristic of the deep ambivalences of the time with regard to women, learning, and writing. Learning among women was esteemed, and their potential even to outshine men in this pursuit was acknowledged. But the act of writing by women was considered so problematic that the less a woman wrote, the more virtuous she was deemed to be. There were writing women, and some of them even allowed their compositions to circulate in society. But moralists (women as well as men) strongly disapproved of that practice. The best thing for educated women to do was to read but not to write. If they could not completely suppress the impulse to express themselves in writing, they should at least try to keep their writing to a minimum. Certain themes were more acceptable than others. Expressions of wifely devotion and loneliness during a husband's absence were among the most acceptable. Apart from such compositions, presumably kept to just a few, women should be prudent enough to make sure what they wrote did not survive. The worst thing, in Cheng Yi's and his mother's view, was for a

---

26. Ibid., p. 655.
27. Ibid.

women to be so indiscreet as to permit her written works to be transmitted outside the home.

One might suppose that any representation of these issues coming from such a staunch Confucian as Cheng Yi must be extreme. Yet we have already seen indications that the biases against women's writing and particularly the public circulation of the same were actually widespread, especially in elite circles. An entry in Peng Cheng's 彭乘 (fl. 1087) miscellany lends further support. The entry tells of a Woman Lu 盧氏 who accompanied her father on his posting to serve as magistrate in Hanzhou (in modern Sichuan) during the Tiansheng period (1023–32). At the end of his appointment, when father and daughter began their long journey back to the capital, they stopped at Nixi Way Station (still in Sichuan), and the daughter inscribed a song lyric on the wall there. The composition is about the hardships of travel. The two travelers had already left the comfort of Hanzhou and had hundreds of miles to go before they would reach the capital. Moreover, the circumstances were relatively unusual: a grown woman accompanying her father, an official, on a long trek. Under such circumstances, and facing the prospect of the journey ahead, it is hardly surprising that the woman would be moved to express her feelings in verse. What she says in the preface to the piece, however, is revealing: "As I climb mountains and skirt rivers, I do not neglect to chant poems. The notes and melodies I transpose are rooted in reflections on travel. Now I have written a song lyric to the tune 'The Phoenix Nests in the Paulownia Tree,' which I have inscribed on the wall. I hope that gentlemen of later times, reading it as they pass by, will not consider it an offense for a woman to have ventured to divert herself with brush and ink" 無以婦人竊弄翰墨 爲罪.[28] We must understand that this apology has nothing to do with the act of writing a poem on a public wall. That sort of thing was done all the time, and no one objected to it. The apology concerns the acts of composition and inscription being done by a woman. From what Lu says in her preface, it is evident that she regularly composed and recited poetry. She fancied herself as something of a poet. (And it is evident from the song lyric she wrote on this occasion that she was well versed in the literary language and conventions of the genre.) But this educated and literary woman anticipates that future male travelers will be of the opinion that a woman had no business leaving an original composition on the wall for all to see. She expects them to

---

28. Peng, *Moke huixi* 4.4b–5a; the preface and song are in *Quan Songci* 1:250.

say that it is a violation of female propriety for a woman to do so, and she asks in advance that they reconsider their conventional opinion and refrain from disapproval in her case. Probably, she secretly hopes that the skillfulness of her poem itself will persuade them to overlook her "offense." After Peng Cheng's miscellany, this entry was reproduced in several later encyclopedias and anecdote collections, dating from the Southern Song (1127–1279) through the Qing period (1644–1911).[29] Significantly, only in the version found in *Collected Comments from the Garden of Song Lyrics* 詞苑叢談 is the language altered.[30] In that version, the apologetic sentence from the preface is omitted, but everything else is retained. *Collected Comments* was compiled in the early Qing, when women's authorship of poetry and song lyrics was more widely accepted than in the Song. The compiler, Xu Qiu 徐釚, evidently succumbed to the temptation to alter his source in this case to bring it more into line with contemporary values, which he had an interest in furthering. By rewriting the passage this way, Xu Qiu introduces a small but telling distortion that elides historical changes in the status of women's writing between the Song and early Qing.

The act of inscribing a poem on a wall, left there for later travelers to see, accounts for a considerable number of poems by women other than professional entertainers that have come down to us. Often, the writing is done in a moment of emotional crisis, when it seems that the woman simply has to express herself. Having no other outlet or recourse, she finds a brush and writes on an available wall, presumably finding some relief in this method of telling her story. Such inscriptions are not infrequently associated with female suicide: the woman writes out her inscription and, having produced this testament of her plight and helplessness, then takes her life. Shen Kuo 沈括 (1031–95) tells of a woman born into a gentry family whose parents married her, down, to a household servant surnamed Lu 鹿.[31] A mere three days after she bore her first child, her husband, anxious that he not forfeit his monthly salary, insisted that she take to the road with him on an errand. He would delay no longer. In great pain and with no one to turn to, the woman must have sensed that her end was near. Before she died, she wrote out her story "in several hundred words" on the wall of the Shanxi Way Station in Xinzhou.

---

29. These works include Jiang Shaoyu, *Shishi leiyuan* 40.6b–7a; Cao Xuequan, *Shuzhong guangji* 104.6b–7a; and Pan Yongyin, *Songbai leichao* 17.18b–19a.

30. Xu Qiu, *Ciyuan congtan* 8.25a.

31. Shen Kuo, *Mengxi bitan* 24.182.

She was eventually buried behind the station. Her inscription was so heart-rending that it, in turn, inspired poems from passersby who read it. These poems mourned the unnamed woman and excoriated her venal husband. Eventually, those poems were brought together into a collection, which was titled *Poems on Lu the Menial* 鹿奴詩. It is revealing that, even as Shen Kuo writes about this woman, devoting a few hundred words himself to her story, neither he nor anyone else saw fit to record the inscription she wrote. We learn of its existence, and we hear how it moved later passersby. But we do not get to read what she wrote. No one thought to transcribe it. The collection of the poetry it inspired does not survive either. The two cases just described of inscriptions on walls by women have one important difference.

The new mother was driven to desperation and wrote, as she prepared to die, so that her complaint would be known to someone other than herself. As with many such women who wrote under dire circumstances in a public place, her writing was an isolated act. It served as her last testament. It would be interesting to know the degree of such a woman's literacy and whether she had ever written anything else. It is likely, even probable, that her inscription was the only thing she ever wrote intended for public view and posterity. It is also likely that she did not write regularly. In the case of Woman Lu, who traveled with her father, it is clear from what she says in her preface that she did write regularly. She thought of herself as having some talent as a poet. She composed verse all the time, even when on the road, as she says, although she knew that many men of her world disapproved of such activity on the part of a woman.

For us today, the problem is not finding references to women writers. The problem is finding what they wrote, because so little of it survives. The negative view of women's writing had two components. The first was the prevalent but not universal belief that women should not write even though they might be classically educated and well-read. The second was the feeling that a woman's writing, if it existed at all, should not be circulated because, if it were, it would fall into the hands of strangers, indeed male strangers. It was the two ways of thinking, acting together, that ensured that so little writing by women from the time would be preserved.

Writing by women that is preserved is often contingent, consequently, on some connection with a man. Chen Xiang 陳襄 (1017–80), a friend of Su Shi, is said to have had daughters with literary talent. One of them married a man named Li 李. When this Li was posted to Jinning Commandery (in modern Yunnan) as an administrative assistant, a staff member there asked for a poem on a screen decorated with a painting of geese. Li's wife was the one to provide the poem, writing in fact two quatrains.[32] The poems, thoroughly competent works, focus on the painting as an example of the regional land-scape of Xiaoxiang (modern Hunan). The screen in question was evidently the small kind that could be mounted on a bed, for privacy and protection from drafts. The poems describe the owner, unable to return to his homeland in Xiaoxiang, visiting it in dreams inspired by the painting situated near his pillow. Sometime after Li's wife wrote the poems, Huang Tingjian 黃庭堅 (1045–1105) inscribed the poems on the screen itself, in small regular script calligraphy. Huang was among the most respected calligraphers of the day, and he happened to be in exile in the distant southwest, not far from Jinning.[33] In all likelihood, the only reason the poems were recorded in a Southern Song miscellany is that the famous Huang Tingjian had inscribed them. The same miscellany, by Chen Hu 陳鵠 (early thirteenth century), also tells of a certain Mr. Xu 徐 who served on the bureaucratic staff of Lin Xi 林希 (fl. 1090s).[34] Lin was fond of engaging his staff in poetry competitions. He would write a poem on a set theme and expect each staff member to produce a matching composition, evidently giving them a few hours to respond. It happened that Xu's wife was an able poet, and whenever Xu faced a demand for a matching poem, he would copy out Lin's original poem and send it home for his wife to match. It is said that her compositions, which Xu passed off as his own, would regularly be sent back to the office before the other staff members had completed their poems. The motif of a woman ghost-writing for a man, that is, a woman's poetic compositions existing and being circulated only because they were masqueraded as a man's, bears comparison with that of a woman's poems attracting attention because a celebrated male calligrapher copied them out. Without the male involve-ment to enhance the stature of the woman's compositions, they probably would not have attracted written comment or survived.

Sometimes, even attention from a prominent man was no help in ensuring that a woman's writing would survive. Ouyang Xiu 歐陽修 (1007–72) wrote

---

32. Chen Hu, *Qijiu xuwen* 3.3b–4a.

33. I am assuming the place Jinning 晉寧 mentioned in this account is the one south of modern Kunming, Yunnan (there were others), and that the screen was subsequently brought to Huang Tingjian during his years of southwestern exile at the end of his life, perhaps when he was in Rongzhou (Sichuan).

34. Chen Hu, *Qijiu xuwen* 3.4a.

a preface to a poetry collection by Xie Ximeng 謝希孟, the younger sister of his friend Xie Bochu 謝伯初.[35] She had produced a corpus of one hundred poems. Ouyang explains her literary education and acumen as the result of the training she received from her mother. The mother, Ouyang tells us, had first educated Bochu and then saw to it that his younger sister was educated as well. Ouyang characterizes Ximeng's poetry as stylistically distinct from that of her brother but outstanding in its own quiet way. Then, in a rare moment of candor regarding the inequities faced by literary women, Ouyang observes: "Jingshan [Bochu] associates with the most worthy and celebrated men of his generation, and so he has achieved fame in his time. Ximeng, in contrast, has the misfortune of being a woman. She has no way to become prominent in the world." Ouyang goes on to cite the ancient example of the wife of Baron Mu of the state of Xu 許穆夫人, whose song lamenting the demise of her native state of Wei was selected by Confucius into the *Classic of Poetry*.[36] Ouyang expresses regret that there is no man of comparable stature to bring Ximeng's verse to prominence. By writing this kind of preface to her collection, Ouyang was attempting to do just that. But his effort had no effect. Ximeng's collection did not survive, and it is not mentioned in later Song sources.

Poets of Repute

LADY WEI

In the Northern Song period (960–1127), the best-known woman poet is Lady Wei 魏夫人 (Wei Wan 魏玩). She was the wife of Zeng Bu 曾布, a prominent court official under Zhezong who rose to be grand councilor under Emperor Huizong 徽宗 (r. 1101–25), only to fall out of favor soon thereafter. Lady Wei's reputation was such that, a century after her death, Zhu Xi identified her together with Li Qingzhao as the only two women of the dynasty who were fine writers.[37] Despite such affirmation, Lady Wei's literary collection was soon lost. What survives of her writings, one *shi* poem and thirteen song lyrics, were preserved in Song period anthologies, *Elegant Lyrics for Music Bureau Songs* 樂府雅詞 prominent among them.

---

35. Ouyang Xiu, "Xieshi shixu" 謝氏詩序, *Jushi ji* 43.608–9.
36. No. 54.
37. Zhu Xi, *Zhuzi yulei* 140.3332.

Most of Lady Wei's surviving song lyrics revolve around the conventional theme of a woman waiting for her distant husband or lover. The following two songs are examples.

菩薩蠻   *To the tune "The Bodhisattva Barbarian"*

溪山掩映斜陽裏	The hills beyond the stream turn dark in slanting rays,
樓臺影動鴛鴦起	The tower's shadow grows, mandarin ducks fly off.
隔岸兩三家	A few houses stand on the opposite shore,
出墻紅杏花	Red apricot blossoms rise over the wall.
綠楊堤下路	On the path beside the embankment of green willows
早晚溪邊去	Morning and evening I go to the stream.
三見柳綿飛	Three times I have seen the willow catkins fly,
離人猶未歸	The parted one still has not returned.[38]

It was presumably the same path mentioned in stanza 2, leading away from the tower, that the man took when he departed three years earlier. The speaker walks a short distance along that path daily, back and forth to the stream. She waits for the man to reappear on the path, but that never happens.

江城子   *To the tune "River Town Lad"*
春恨   Spring Regrets

別郎容易見郎難	Parting from him is easy, seeing him is hard.
幾何般	How many times
懶臨鸞	Have I been lazy to look in the phoenix mirror?
憔悴容儀	Haggard my face,
陡覺縷衣寬	Suddenly I feel that my clothes are too large.
門外紅梅將謝也	The red plum outside the door is about to fade,
誰信道	Who'd ever believe me when I say
不曾看？	I never even looked at it?
曉妝樓上望長安	In morning make-up on a balcony I gaze toward the capital
怯輕寒	But I fear the light chill,
莫憑欄	I must not lean on the railing.
嫌怕東風	I also begrudge the east wind
吹恨上眉端	For blowing regrets to land on my brow.
為報歸期須及早	Let someone tell him: your return must be early,
休誤妾	Don't ruin for me
一春閒	The pleasures of an entire spring.[39]

---

38. Wei furen, "Pusa man," *Quan Songci* 1:347.
39. Wei furen, "Jiangchengzi," *Quan Songci* 1:348.

All evidence indicates that such songs as these were taken to express Lady Wei's own thoughts and longing. As we will see, song lyrics written by women were regularly interpreted this way, that is, autobiographically, even though there were well-established conventions in the genre for the invention and manipulation of fictional personas. The song lyric was, after all, a literary form written for musical performance, usually by professional entertainers. The expectation of such performance, not to mention the highly sentimental subject matter, contributed to the disjunction between author and "voice" in the song. It was generally understood that the voice in these songs was that of a persona invented for performative effect.

But a change took place when the author was known to be a woman, and particularly when the composition by a woman began to circulate in written form (rather than simply be performed). The assumption of a distinction between author and speaking voice in the song was dropped, and a new assumption that equated the words of the song with the author's own voice and personal life was substituted in its place. One cannot, by the way, explain this change by supposing that the women who composed song lyrics performed their own compositions. It is extremely unlikely that someone of the stature of Lady Wei would ever have performed her own songs in front of people. That would hardly befit the madam of a highly distinguished household. No, if her songs were performed, and it is likely that they were, they would have been performed by professional female entertainers. The different way of reading women's song lyrics has its roots in other factors.

Because Lady Wei was who she was, a woman, written comment on her and her songs is extremely rare. Yet we can still discern some effort to forge a biographical account of her life that accommodates her songs about loneliness in love. The earliest Song period reference to her, found in Lu You's collection of random notes, speaks of her husband's protracted separation from her early in his career and quotes her chiding him not to allow himself to form new attachments while he is in the capital region.[40] In later iterations, this motif of Zeng Bu's separation from his wife would be exaggerated into a nearly constant absence. By Ming times a legend had developed that Lady Wei was befriended by Zhu Shuzhen, who as we will see was famously unhappy in her marriage, and the two of them drank together and exchanged song lyrics.[41] Naturally, it was assumed that the absent man

---

40. Lu You, *Laoxue an biji* 7.3521.

41. Tian Rucheng, *Xihu youlan zhiyu* 16.254; also see the annotation in Zheng Wenang, *Mingyuan huishi* (1620) 17.4b.

referred to in Lady Wei's song lyrics was none other than her husband. In his *History of Love* 情史, Feng Menglong 馮夢龍 (1574–1646) specifically assures us that "River Town Lad" (translated above) was a composition she sent to Zeng Bu, demanding that he return quickly to her.[42]

ZHU SHUZHEN

Next to Li Qingzhao, Zhu Shuzhen is the best known woman poet of the Song period. Unlike that of Lady Wei, Zhu Shuzhen's poetry collection, put together by an admirer shortly after her death, survived intact, and it is a sizable collection (by far the largest of the three that survived) consisting of 337 *shi* poems. She also has some thirty song lyrics to her credit, which survived in Song and later anthologies and are now regularly inserted into her "collected works."

The signature fact of Zhu Shuzhen's life, as it is traditionally represented, is that her parents married her, for reasons that are unclear, to a common merchant who was unworthy of her. Her husband is said to have neglected or abused her. Her marriage therefore was singularly unhappy, and she expressed her despair in poetry. She died young, a death brought on by her distress, and, when her poetry was gathered together, the collection was fittingly titled *Poetry of a Broken Heart* 斷腸集. Yet this collection also includes poems that refer to love and longing or that fondly recall love trysts. These poems have given rise to speculation that in the midst of her despair Zhu Shuzhen took a lover outside of wedlock or that she had had such a lover before her miserable marriage. Some commentators have even found evidence in her poems that she managed to get herself divorced from her husband and was reunited with her young love.

The following *shi* poems are representative of the issues and moods regularly found in Zhu Shuzhen's verse:

愁懷   *Longings in Sorrow, no. 1*

鷗鷺鴛鴦作一池	Gulls and mandarin ducks swim in the same pond,
須知羽翼不相宜	Everyone knows they don't belong together.
東君不與花爲主	The Lord of the East has failed as master of flowers,
何似休生連理枝	Why must we be intertwined branches all our lives?[43]

42. Feng Menglong, *Qingshi* 24.949; Zheng Wenang, *Mingyuan huishi* 17.4b.

43. Zhu Shuzhen, "Chouhuai," no. 1, *Zhu Shuzhen ji zhu* 9.130.

西樓寄情　　*Expressing Feelings in the Western Tower*

靜看飛蠅觸曉窗	Quietly I watch flies hit the window at dawn,
宿醒未醒倦梳妝	Not sober from yesterday's wine, I'm tired as I comb and put on make-up.
強調朱粉西樓上	Reluctantly I mix red powder on the western tower,
愁裏春山畫不長	In such sorrow my "spring hills" are not drawn long.[44]

湖上小集　　*Lakeside Collection*

門前春水碧於天	The spring river before my gate is azure like the sky,
座上詩人逸似仙	The poet in the room is aloof like a goddess.
彩鳳一雙雲外落	A pair of colored phoenixes vanishes beyond the clouds
吹簫歸去又無緣	It is not my fate to fly off with him who plays the flute.[45]

There is considerable cleverness in such poems to sustain interest, despite what is essentially a static, and hopeless, situation. The first poem is thought to have been written after Zhu Shuzhen's husband, having lost interest in his wife, took a concubine. In that reading, the two different types of birds, which are not found together naturally, stand for Zhu Shuzhen and the concubine (although at least one commentator takes them to represent the estranged husband and wife). The idea of the second couplet is that the Lord of the East (the god of spring) has not done his job properly as master of the flowers: he has allowed two plants that should not be joined to become "intertwined," that is, in an unhappy union that will last as long as they are alive. In the second poem, the speaker hardly has the energy to face the day. When she reluctantly applies make-up, she does so half-heartedly, not bothering to paint her eyebrows ("spring hills") in a drawn-out and attractive manner. In the third piece, the poet likens herself, in her aloofness, to a goddess. But she does not have the happy fate of Nongyu 弄玉, who was given in marriage to Xiaoshi 簫史, the flute player. One day phoenixes came to the tower the couple lived in, attracted by Xiaoshi's music, and carried the two of them away, into the heavens.

When we first encounter Zhu Shuzhen and her works, we may think that we have finally come upon a Song period woman who left more than a handful of compositions and that these were duly preserved and transmitted through the centuries. Unfortunately, when we look closely at the sources

---

44. Zhu Shuzhen, "Xilou jiqing," *Zhu Shuzhen ji zhu* 8.114.

45. Zhu Shuzhen, "Hushang xiaoji," *Zhu Shuzhen ji zhu* 8.113.

concerning her life and works, everything becomes uncertain. It turns out that "Zhu Shuzhen" the person and the poet is a bundle of contrary and implausible assertions, and we end up wondering what there is of substance about her and her writings that can be believed. The only fact that emerges from the numerous studies done on her in recent times is that there is no consensus on who she was, when she lived, where she was from, whom she married, and where her writings originated.

Consider the issue of when she lived. There are those who place her in the Northern Song (late eleventh century), others who say her life spanned the Northern Song–Southern Song transition, others who identify her as someone who lived entirely during the early Southern Song (mid-twelfth century), and others who say she lived in the early to mid-thirteenth century. Such a large range of possibilities is rare with Song persons. It results from two factors: the impressionistic use of internal dating indicators in Zhu Shuzhen's works to reach widely disparate and contradictory results, and the conspicuous silence regarding her in Song period sources.

The compiler of Zhu Shuzhen's poetry collection was Wei Zhonggong 魏仲恭, who is otherwise unknown. The preface he provided to *Poetry of a Broken Heart* is dated 1182. In the preface he tells us that while traveling in the Wuling area (modern Changde, Hunan), he often encountered people at inns who could recite Zhu Shuzhen's song lyrics. He was moved by what he heard, and he managed to learn something of her background:

> In her youth she was unfortunate, and her parents did not care for her properly. Unable to arrange a suitable match for her, they married her to an ordinary merchant. Consequently, her whole life she had pent-up feelings of frustration, and so her poetry is filled with expressions of sorrow and bitterness.... Reading her poetry, one imagines what she was like. For someone as elegant as she was to be joined with a vulgar fellow, her life was certainly wasted! When she died, her remains could not be buried so that at least she could have been properly mourned like the one in the green grave mound.[46] Her parents consigned her remains, together with her poetry, to fire. Today what survives is less than one piece in a hundred. This was her second misfortune. Alas, what injustice she suffered!

---

46. A reference to the grave of Wang Zhaojun 王昭君 (b. ca. 50 BCE), who died in barbarian lands in the north after being married off to a Xiongnu chieftan. Legend had it that the vegetation beside her grave remained green all year round.

Wei goes on to record how he resolved to gather together what he could of Zhu Shuzhen's poetry, in an effort to comfort her soul in the underworld so that she would not be as unappreciated in the afterlife as she was in life. He also refers anyone who wants more detail on her life to a biography of her written by Wang Tangzuo 王唐佐 of the capital, Lin'an (Hangzhou). This man is also otherwise unknown, and no one has ever seen or mentioned his biography.

Wei concludes by asserting that "aficionados of later times should know that my words are not unfounded." But there are several points about Wei Zhonggong's preface that look suspicious (including that final sentence). To begin with, the two men who are responsible for all we know about Zhu Shuzhen are themselves mysteries. Their very existence cannot be confirmed. Likewise, the physical remains and grave of Zhu Shuzhen are nonexistent so that there is no grave to visit or tomb inscription to read to confirm what Wei Zhonggong's preface tells us. Cremation was unusual, except for Buddhists. Why was it that Zhu Shuzhen "could not be buried"? Why in fact did she predecease her parents, and why was she with them rather than her husband's family when she died? The absence of an explanation is strange.

What Wei says about Zhu Shuzhen's writings provides additional cause for concern. Her writings were burned by her parents when she was cremated. Consequently, less than one in a hundred survives. Wei Zhonggong learned about her writings from locals in the Wuling region who were reciting her song lyrics. Wei never mentions any manuscript of Zhu Shuzhen's poems. Are we to believe that he transcribed more than three hundred poems from oral recitation? It was, to begin with, Zhu Shuzhen's song lyrics that he heard being recited. But the collection he compiles is her *shi* poetry. This is hardly a minor discrepancy. In the same era, there was a widow named Sun Daoxuan 孫道絢 who is said to have produced a large number of poems and prose pieces. Late in her life, the manuscripts of her poems were all destroyed when her house caught fire. After her death, her devoted son, Huang Zhu 黃銖 (1131–99), a friend of Zhu Xi, did what he could to reconstruct some of her writing. He managed only to come up with six of his mother's song lyrics.[47] Yet Wei Zhonggong, a complete stranger, was somehow able to recover over three hundred of Zhu Shuzhen's works after the originals were destroyed. This strains credulity.

---

47. Huang's account of his recovery of his mother's song lyrics is quoted in Zhang Shinan, *Youhuan jiwen* 8.1a–b.

There is another consideration. Wei claims that travelers in local inns often recited Zhu Shuzhen's compositions, which moved everyone to sighs. Presumably, the songs were being performed in taverns and tea houses too. Now, if this is true, it is extremely odd that no Song source of Wei Zhonggong's time makes mention of Zhu Shuzhen. For comparison, we might consider the case of Li Qingzhao. Her works were also well known and circulated widely. Li Qingzhao and Zhu Shuzhen were, according to Wei Zhonggong, contemporaries, or perhaps Li Qingzhao was older by ten or twenty years. By the time of her death, Li Qingzhao and her writings had been mentioned in dozens of Song miscellanies, remarks on poetry, and other works. If Zhu Shuzhen was so well known, how can it be that the same works, of which there are hundreds, are completely silent regarding her?

Neither Zhu Shuzhen's poetry collection nor her song lyric collection is mentioned in any of the standard Song period bibliographies. No printed edition of the latter collection is attested before the early Ming dynasty.[48] Regarding Zhu Shuzhen's song lyrics, there is another telling omission. None of the nine Southern Song anthologies of song lyrics contains a single song lyric attributed to her.[49] This is significant because these works collect thousands of song lyrics by hundreds of authors. And it is precisely in such works that we find the earliest occurrence of song lyrics by other Song women, including Li Qingzhao, that survive today.

Wei Zhonggong's edition of Zhu Shuzhen's poetry anthology did eventually attract some attention. In 1202 a certain Sun Shouzhai 孫壽齋, who is also unknown, added a postscript to Wei's collection. Toward the end of the Southern Song or in the early Yuan, the unidentified compiler of the influential anthology *Poems of a Thousand Poets* 千家詩 selected forty-five of Zhu Shuzhen's poems to go into his work.[50] This was a watershed event, and through the Yuan and Ming Zhu Shuzhen's fame and stature gradually became established. In the Yuan dynasty, the leading poet Yang Weizhen

48. See Rao Zongyi, *Ci ji kao* 2.74–75.

49. The song lyric anthologies are Zeng Zao, *Yuefu yaci* (1146); Huang Dayu, *Meiyuan* (1129); the anonymous *Caotang shiyu* (ca. 1195); Zhao Wenli, *Yangchun baixue* (ca. 1244); Huang Sheng's two anthologies, *Zhongxing yilai juemiao cixuan* (1249) and *Tang Song zhuxian juemiao cixuan* (1249) (these two also circulate together under the title *Hua'an cixuan*); Chen Jingyi, *Quanfang beizu* (1253); and Zhou Mi, *Juemiao haoci* (ca. 1275).

50. I refer to the earliest of the several versions of *Poems of a Thousand Poets*, whose full title is *Fenmen zuanlei Tang Song shixian qianjia shi xuan*; see the *Jiaozheng* 校證 edition, edited by Li Geng and Chen Xin, published in 2002.

楊維楨 (1296–1370) linked Zhu Shuzhen together with Li Qingzhao as the two outstanding women writers of recent times.[51] In the mid-Ming, the publisher Mao Jin 毛晉 (1599–1659) took the next logical step and brought out the song lyrics of Li Qingzhao and Zhu Shuzhen in a composite edition. Thereafter, the two would frequently be mentioned in the same breath as the most distinguished female talents of their dynasty.

Wilt Idema offered a suggestion some years ago regarding Zhu Shuzhen and her collection: "Perhaps it is safer to read the poems in *Duanchang ji* not so much as the products of a single, specific individual, but rather as a reflection of twelfth century male conceptions of what typical effusions from the inner quarters should be like. It is not inconceivable to me that a sizable portion of the Zhu Shuzhen poems should be the work of anonymous male authors impersonating the female voice."[52] Idema's doubts about Zhu Shuzhen's authorship are based on the peculiarities of Wei Zhonggong's preface and the tendency of male writers and editors to embellish legends of ill-fated women with literary compositions. He does not bring up the absence of references to Zhu Shuzhen in contemporary sources, discussed here. Consequently, I would go further: it is likely that most if not all of the poems attributed to Zhu Shuzhen were written by men. These men were attracted to the story of an educated woman who was married "down" to a man unworthy of her and who then expressed her sorrow in poetry. Certain features of the *shi* poetry in *Poetry of a Broken Heart* deserve comment in this regard. In the titles, there are virtually no biographical particulars: no names of persons being addressed, no place-names, no dates. Almost without exception the titles simply designate conventional themes, for example, "Sitting Alone on a Spring Day," "Apricot Blossoms," "Evening View in Autumn," "Unable to Sleep," "The Moon over the Lake." Such titles are strongly reminiscent of poetic exercises required of students.

There is a long tradition in China of men identifying with such women "who did not meet their time," that is, women whose virtues and talents were not properly appreciated. Such men often composed verse in the voice of the long-suffering woman, projecting the frustrations they experienced in their own careers and personal lives. Sooner or later, and regardless of how the poems were originally intended to be taken, the compositions are likely to be

---

51. Yang Weizhen, *Dong weizi ji* 7.19b.
52. Idema, "Male Fantasies and Female Realities," p. 24.

passed off as the woman's own.[53] (We have seen an example of this earlier, with the song attributed to Yan Rui but actually composed on her behalf by a man.) The appeal of Zhu Shuzhen's story is enhanced by the illusion that, in this culture where few women wrote and even fewer allowed what they wrote to circulate, in this case we have rare glimpses into the woman's anguish, expressed in her own words. A complex process of reception ensues, in which readers, mostly male, are drawn to the verse as voyeurs of female suffering that is usually hidden from view, while they also find in the verse figurative expression of their own discontent. We have it from Zhou Hui 周輝 (b. 1126) that most of the poetic inscriptions on the walls of postal stations and inns signed by women, especially those done in delicate calligraphy on the hardships of travel, were actually "entirely composed by aficionados who make a game of composing poems by 'women and girls'" 皆好事者戲爲夫人女子之作.[54] He means they were all written by men. In the case of Zhu Shuzhen, there is every reason to believe that such a process has occurred and has, through the centuries, prevented scholars from raising the questions that need to be raised about the provenance of her works. In recent decades, the surge of interest in women writers of premodern times has contributed in its own way to uncritical reception of Zhu Shuzhen's writings as authentic (Idema is the exception in this regard) and indeed the appearance of several new accounts of her writing and life that are mutually contradictory.[55]

This problem in Chinese literary history does not begin with the Song period. A recent study of "women poets" in the *Complete Tang Dynasty Poetry* 全唐詩 and other sources concludes that a substantial proportion of the poems so attributed were not in fact written by Tang women.[56] The poems were written by Tang male poets and attributed to women, or they were written by male poets in later times and attributed to historical Tang women, or they were written in later times and attributed to imaginary Tang women.

---

53. On this phenomenon, in addition to Idema's study noted above, see also Widmer, "Xiaoqing's Literary Legacy."

54. Zhou Hui, *Qingbo zazhi* 10.5122.

55. See, for example, Deng, "Zhu Shuzhen shiji xinkao"; and Huang Yanli and Wu Xihe, *Duanchang fangcao yuan*. Huang and Wu are sharply critical of Deng's findings concerning Zhu's dates and other biographical matters.

56. Chen Shangjun, "Tang nü shiren zhenbian."

ZHANG YUNIANG

The last poet considered here lived at the very end of the Southern Song and probably a few years into the Mongol Yuan dynasty. Zhang Yuniang 張玉娘 is, along with Zhu Shuzhen, the only other woman writer of the period whose poetry collection, *Orchid in Snow* 蘭雪集, survives. Like Zhu Shuzhen, Zhang Yuniang's life is shrouded in uncertainty. It is only known today from documents that were composed hundreds of years after her death.

Zhang Yuniang is said to have had a short and tragic life, whose key events centered on her inability to marry the man she loved. There are somewhat different versions of how this tragedy came about, but there is agreement that Zhang Yuniang's father reneged on the promise he had made to the family of Shen Quan 沈佺 to marry his daughter to him.[57] The earliest account of Yuniang's life, written in the Jiajing period of the Ming (1522–66), says that when Yuniang came of age she was betrothed to Shen Quan, who is said to have been a cousin, but that soon her father changed his mind and broke off the engagement. But Yuniang, who presumably already knew Shen Quan, was determined to honor the original agreement.[58] Some later accounts of Yuniang's life say that the two families had agreed on a match even before Yuniang was born but that the diminished circumstances of the Shen family during the ensuing years caused Yuniang's father to go back on his promise.[59] Soon, Shen Quan accompanied his father when he traveled to take up office. During this trip, the young Shen Quan fell ill and died. When Yuniang, back in the countryside, learned of Shen's death, she was distraught. Her father tried to marry her to another man, but Yuniang vowed to be true to Shen Quan and never to marry.

There are likewise variations in the account of Yuniang's death, which occurred when she was twenty-eight, after several years of resisting her father's will. On the Lantern Festival, when Yuniang was sitting alone at home, she suddenly had a vision of Shen Quan standing before her, and the

---

57. My summary of Zhang Yuniang's life and the following discussion of her poetry owes much to the excellent recent study of her by Wang Cicheng, "Zhang Yuniang jiqi 'Lanxue ji.'"

58. This is from the biography of Yuniang written by Wang Zhao in the sixteenth century; see "Zhang Yuniang zhuan," *fulu* 附錄, p. 1b; it is translated in Idema and Grant, *Red Brush*, pp. 262–64. Idema and Grant have an extended discussion of the life of Zhang Yuniang and her poetry on pages 257–69. Idema has a longer treatment of her in "Male Fantasies and Female Realities," pp. 25–48, where he translates several Ming and Qing accounts of her life.

59. Wang Cicheng, "Zhang Yuniang jiqi 'Lanxue ji,'" p. 406.

two renewed their vows of loyalty to each other. Soon thereafter Yuniang's illness worsened, from her longing for Shen, and before long she died.[60] Another version tells that Shen Quan appeared to Yuniang in a dream, and in the dream Yuniang announced that "everything has been settled." Thereafter Yuniang refused to eat, and before a month was over she died.[61] Soon, two of the maids in her household also died, one from grief and the other from suicide. Her pet talking parrot also died. The three of them together began to be called the "Three Purities" 三清, and they were buried beside Yuniang in her tomb, which came to be known as Parrot Tomb.

Yuniang may have had some local fame as early as the Yuan dynasty, but she was not well known, and it is unlikely that her writings were printed early on. Certain Yuan and early Ming scholars refer to her, but only as a woman of recent times with a talent for poetry about whom they know little.[62] The earliest biography of Zhang Yuniang was not written until the mid-sixteenth century by Wang Zhao 王詔, who was himself a native of Songyang 松陽 (in southwestern Zhejiang), where Yuniang had lived. Wang is said to have recovered Yuniang's poetry collection from a temple in Songyang and, moved by what he found, decided to write an account of her life. Yuniang's stature was greatly enhanced a century later, at the time of the Ming-Qing transition, by the dramatist Meng Chengshun 孟稱舜 (fl. 1629–49), who served for a time as an instructor in a local school in Songyang. Meng arranged for the publication of Yuniang's poetry collection—the earliest publication we know of—but he did much more than that. He and his friends made Yuniang into the model of a "chaste woman" 貞女 and eventually into a martyr and saint, the object of a local religious cult. He reconstructed her tomb, erected a shrine dedicated to her, which he named Shrine of Chaste Writing 貞文祠, and together with his friends wrote several eulogies for her. Eventually, Meng even made Yuniang the subject of one of his plays, "Zhang Yuniang and the Three Purities of Her Chamber in Parrot Tomb and Chaste Writing Shrine" 張玉娘閨房三清鸚鵡墓貞文記, which he printed and distributed. Owing to the efforts of Meng Chengshun, Zhang Yuniang became one of the

---

60. This is the way her death is narrated in Wang Zhao, "Zhang Yuniang zhuan," p. 2a.

61. This is from the biography of her in the early Qing gazetteer *(Shunzhi) Songyang xianzhi,* comp. Tong Qingnian, 6.58b; translated in Idema and Grant, *Red Brush,* p. 259.

62. Ye Ziqi, *Caomu zi* 4A.69; cf. the references to Yuniang made by the Yuan officials Yu Ji 虞集 (1272–1338) and Ouyang Xuan 歐陽玄 (1288–1357), as recorded in the biography of her in *(Shunzhi) Songyang xianzhi* 6.58b, translated in Idema and Grant, *Red Brush,* p. 259.

women martyrs to chastity and loyalty who became so revered and celebrated at the time of the Manchu conquest of China. These women were held up as exemplars of female fidelity in a way that evoked the parallel male ideal of political loyalty to the Ming and resistance to the foreign conquerors.

There are obvious reasons to be skeptical of the traditions concerning Zhang Yuniang. Accounts of her life have clearly been romanticized and influenced by the cult that grew up around her. For example, some of the Qing sources on Yuniang assert that she and Shen Quan were born at different hours of the very same day.[63] Her poetry collection, at least as we have it today, is also suspect, since its circulation can only be definitively traced back to Meng Chengshun, the very man who was instrumental in inspiring that cult. Nevertheless, given mid-fourteenth-century references to her poetry, there is reason to think that the legend that later grew up around her must hold some kernel of truth.

The poetry itself reveals interesting and unexpected features. Quantitatively it is substantial, although not as large as Zhu Shuzhen's collection. It contains 117 *shi* poems and 16 song lyrics. There is a certain edge or willfulness evident in much of the poetry in *Orchid in Snow* (the title of the collection is aptly chosen; it refers to the hardiness and integrity of that delicate plant). These qualities match aspects of Zhang Yuniang's biography as it has come down to us: her resistance of her father's altered intention regarding her, her pledges to her betrothed, even her willingness (in some versions of her life) to commit suicide to join Shen Quan in death. These qualities show through clearly in one of her most famous compositions, a series of poems said to have been addressed to Shen Quan after he went away with his father:

山之高，第三　　*The Mountain Is High, no. 3*

汝心金石堅	Your heart is as firm as metal and stone,
我操冰霜潔	My conduct is as spotless as ice and frost.
擬結百歲盟	We swore an oath to last a hundred years,
忽成一朝別	But one morning we were abruptly forced apart.
朝雲暮雨心去來	Dawn clouds and evening rains, our hearts come and go,
千里相思共明月	Missing each other across a thousand miles, we share the bright moon.[64]

---

63. Wang Cicheng, "Zhang Yuniang jiqi 'Lanxue ji,'" pp. 403–4.
64. Zhang Yuniang, "Shan zhi gao," *Quan Songshi* 71:44626.

This may seem straightforward enough, but when we realize that it was the two fathers who forced the couple apart, we see the resolve Zhang expresses here in a new light. Furthermore, the phrase "dawn clouds and evening rains" alludes unmistakably to sexual contact between the two lovers, whether actual or merely hoped for. Because of such language, this poem struck the early Ming moralist Ye Ziqi 葉子奇 (fl. 1379) as highly inappropriate. He denounced it as improper and depraved.[65]

Zhang Yuniang's verse treats an impressive range of subjects, venturing far beyond the conventional theme of the boudoir complaint. She writes about historical figures (male and female), paintings, and outings into nature. Yet whether writing about herself or others, she has a fondness for persons of exceptional integrity and principle, and keeps coming back to such types. Two examples are given below.

王將軍墓   *The Tomb of General Wang*

嶺上松如旗	Pines on the mountain peak stretch out like a banner,
扶疏鐵石姿	Towering and spare, they resemble metal or stone.
下有烈士魂	Beneath lies the soul of a hero,
上有青菟絲	Above grow green creeping vines.
烈士節不改	The hero's resolve never faltered,
青松色愈滋	The pines' green turns ever more lustrous.
欲識烈士心	If you want to know the heart of the hero,
請看青松枝	Gaze upon the green branches of the pines.[66]

A note attached to this poem identifies the general as Wang Yuanyi 王遠宜, a Song loyalist officer who died fighting against the invading Mongols.

川上女   *The Girl on the Riverbank*

川上女	The girl on the riverbank
行蹋蹋	Walks all by herself.
翠鬟濕輕雲	Dark hair at her temples is moist in wispy clouds,
冰肌清溽暑	Ice-like skin shines in moist sunshine.
霞裾瓊佩動春風	Her rosy collar and jade pendants sway in spring wind,
蘭操蘋心常似縷	Her orchid conduct and duckweed heart are constant as an unbroken string.

---

65. Ye Ziqi, *Caomuzi* 4A.69.
66. Zhang Yuniang, "Wang Jiangjun mu," *Quan Songshi* 71:44626.

卻恨征途輕薄兒	She despises the frivolous young man on his travels,
笑隔山花問妾期	Smiling beyond the wildflowers he questions her.
妾情清澈川中水	"My feelings are as pure as the river's waters,
朝暮風波無改時	Morning and evening, fair or foul weather, they will never change."[67]

Zhang Yuniang's poems are not always so uncompromising and extreme. But even when she moves away from moral concerns, she shows a penchant for expressing unconventional viewpoints. A poem she wrote about the famous red-dyed paper on which the Tang woman poet Xue Tao inscribed her poems describes in considerable detail the beautiful hues and scent of the paper. Then in its closing couplet Zhang Yuniang's poem takes an unexpected turn: "She scoffs at the palindrome composed by Miss Su, / Wasting her youth on all that labor!" 却笑回文蘇氏子，工夫空自廢韶華.[68] This refers to the long palindrome that Su Hui (fourth century) had stitched as brocade—a laborious task indeed—and sent to Dou Tao as a token of her love. To most romantic minds, Su Hui's act was one of admirable devotion and was not the object of derision. It is especially unusual to see Su Hui's arduousness undercut in a poem by a woman.

One of the historical figures that Zhang Yuniang wrote about was Green Pearl 綠珠, the beloved concubine of Shi Chong 石崇 (249–300), famous for her beauty and dancing, who threw herself to her death when she was about to be abducted by the soldiers of Sun Xiu 孫秀, who coveted her. This is Zhang Yuniang's poem:

綠珠　　*Green Pearl*

珠易佳人勝阿嬌	Pearls bought a beauty even prettier than Ajiao,
香塵微步獨憐腰	The dust was fragrant with each little step, her waist was irresistible.
危樓花落繁華盡	Flowers fallen by the tower, the splendor all gone,
總付春風舞柳條	Are forever bequeathed to willow branches dancing in spring winds.[69]

Line 1: Ajiao is Empress Chen of the Former Han, famed for her beauty. Shi Chong acquired Green Pearl by exchanging a small fortune in pearls for her, which presumably accounts for her name.

---

67. Zhang Yuniang, "Chuanshang nü," *Quan Songshi* 71:44623.

68. Zhang Yuniang, "Yong antou sijun: jinhua jian" 詠案頭四俊：錦花牋, *Quan Songshi* 71:44637.

69. "Lüzhu," *Quan Songshi* 71:44632.

The first couplet emphasizes Green Pearl's beauty and talent as a dancer, as we might expect. But the focus of the second couplet changes as it comments, albeit indirectly, on the stature Green Pearl earned for herself in cultural memory on account of her virtuous suicide. The third line echoes Du Mu's well-known poem on the same subject.[70] But whereas Du Mu had stressed the "disappearance" of the glories associated with Shi Chong, his mansion, and his concubine ("The splendor has vanished together with the fragrant dust" 繁華事盡逐香塵), Zhang Yuniang in her final line suggests that Green Pearl is very much still a presence in the place. The "splendor" of Shi Chong may be gone, but the example Green Pearl set lives on. It is "forever bequeathed" to the willow branches there, which, as they "dance" in the spring wind, remind us of her. Such memory, the poem suggests, owes more to the heroic way she ended her life than to her beauty.

This survey has highlighted some of the ways that writing by women was molded and contextualized in the Song period. A few of the instances are particularly revealing. Cheng Yi makes a point of telling us that his mother wrote few poems, despite all her learning, and what she wrote was not transmitted. Then he records for posterity a single poem by her and tells us that she wrote it to express her longing for his father when he was away. Xie Ximeng did produce a poetry collection, and the quality of what she wrote impressed Ouyang Xiu. Ouyang took the unusual step of writing a preface for Ximeng's collection, but even with such an imprimatur, from the most celebrated literatus of his generation, her collection did not survive. Yan Rui was a mere garrison courtesan, not anyone's wife, and she had the misfortune of running afoul of the law so that she was arrested and imprisoned. She confessed to the charges against her, implicating the local governor who had pressured her into having an affair with him. But popular stories about her transformed her into a self-sacrificing woman who heroically refused to implicate her lover in any wrongdoing. And those stories changed a song lyric associated with her into a plaint about her sorry fate, when actually it had originally been written to express her desire to break off relations with the governor.

Women, even educated women, hardly ever wrote, and if they did, what they wrote hardly ever survived. What did survive tended to be a type of

---

70. Du Mu, "Jingu yuan" 金谷園, *Quan Tangshi* 525.6013.

writing that, in one way or another, matched the needs and values of the elite culture that was dominated by men. Whether intentionally or unintentionally (no doubt there was some of both), the forces and circumstances that over time determined what writing was transmitted from generation to generation operated in a highly selective way with regard to women's writing. There was little room for diversity. For women's writing to survive, it had to fit into a narrow range of types of expression and sentiment. Consider the two women who left the largest bodies of writing, the only two literary collections believed to have survived (excepting that of Empress Yang) from the Song. Zhu Shuzhen and Zhang Yuniang were not ordinary female members of the educated class. There is nothing about their lives, as they have come down to us, that was ordinary. Their lives were dominated by a tragic love or a tragic absence of fulfillment in love. What they wrote expresses their loneliness and lack of fulfillment at every turn. Their predicaments differed, and that difference is reflected in the tone and style of what they wrote. But in their frustration in matters of love and marriage they are one.

The foregoing discussion notes many dubious points about the authenticity, provenance, and transmission history of those two collections. But regardless of whether those collections are actually what they claim to be or what is claimed for them by others, their very existence and make-up illustrate the cumulative effect of the special ways that Song, Yuan, and Ming period society shaped and transmitted women's writing from pre-Ming times. There is a lesson here to bear in mind when we turn to the writings of Li Qingzhao, which did not survive in any intact collection but only in anthologies and other random recordings. The cultural tradition favored certain types of expression by women and passed others over, relegating them to neglect and eventually to loss. It would be naive to think that those same selective forces did not have an impact on what survives today of Li Qingzhao's writings or those that are attributed to her.

CHAPTER 2

Writing and the Struggle for Acceptance

When we think of Li Qingzhao today, we think of her as the greatest woman poet in Chinese history, an iconic figure in the Chinese literary tradition, celebrated both for her poetic talent and for the combination of that talent with her identity as a woman. There is no woman before her in literary history (and few if any after) as prominent and as widely discussed.

We tend to forget that in her lifetime her situation was different. It is true that she attracted attention and considerable praise for her literary talent, even as a young lady. But to focus only on such comments or to pretend that such positive reception was the only reaction she faced is to do injustice to the realities of her day. It may not be easy to reconstruct the relevant features of the world she lived in, but we must make the effort to historicize her situation if we are to think about her accurately.

This chapter examines the problem of writing in Li Qingzhao's life and works from two perspectives: what writing meant to Li Qingzhao herself and how she was received as a literary woman by her contemporaries. We will deal with these matters by focusing on four discrete but related subjects: her own remarks about reading, writing, and learning in her life; the hostility of the early critical reaction to her; tendencies in her *shi* poetry that can be viewed as a reaction to the unwelcoming attitudes she faced as a literary woman; and her own essay on the song lyric with its critique of the male writers of her day. By exploring these we sharpen our sense of the hurdles Li Qingzhao faced in obtaining acceptance from the arbiters of literary merit and how her effort to do so affected the way she expressed herself as both poet and critic.

As we saw in the preceding chapter, there were a range of attitudes in Li Qingzhao's day concerning women and whether it was right or desirable that they be taught to read and, beyond that, if writing by them was permissible or worthy of preservation. Some well-to-do families saw to it that their daughters received an education, and these women occasionally went on to produce poetry and writing in other forms. Here and there, the sources refer to women writers, and it is evident that certain families prided themselves on having precocious literary daughters, wives who could ghost-write for their husbands, or mothers who could pass their learning and skill at writing on to their sons. But prejudices against the prospect of women writing were also widespread and more the rule than the exception. As proud as Cheng Yi was of his mother's learning, there is also a whiff of pride in his remarks when he tells us that in all her life she wrote no more than thirty poems and that none of them survive. As for the few women who dared to make their writing public, like Woman Lu, they expected to be chastised for doing so.

Li Qingzhao on Reading and Writing

Li Qingzhao occasionally comments on the roles that reading and writing play in her own life. Her references to these activities, while not numerous, are enough to make it clear that reading and literary composition, which went hand in hand, were of central importance to her. Seen in light of the strictures against women's writing, which were so widespread in her day, her commitment not just to learning but to the act of writing is truly exceptional. Li Qingzhao's references to her active engagement with writing, moreover, are remarkably free of apology or prevarication.

The best known of her references to reading is the often-quoted passage from the autobiographical "Afterword" she wrote to her husband's scholarly notes on his collection of inscriptions, *Records on Metal and Stone* 金石錄. This is what she says, as part of her account of the years the couple spent in Qingzhou 青州 (Qingzhou, Shandong), when her husband, Zhao Mingcheng, was out of office:

> It happens that I have a good memory, and, whenever we finished dinner we would sit in our hall named Returning Home and brew tea. We'd point to a pile of books and, choosing a particular event, try to say in which book, which chapter, which page, and which line it was recorded. The winner of our little contest got to drink tea first. When I guessed right, I'd hold the cup high and burst out laughing until the tea splattered the front of my gown. I'd have to get

up without even taking a sip. Oh, how I wished we could grow old living like that! So even though our lives were fraught with apprehensions and poverty, what we valued and strove for was never compromised.[1]

For all its charm, this passage broaches a motif that surfaces repeatedly in stories about Li Qingzhao and her husband: the competition between them in matters of learning and writing. It is probably significant that Li Qingzhao fails to mention her husband ever winning their little game. She makes it sound as if she is regularly the winner. Why, we may wonder, did beating Zhao Mingcheng at this game cause Li Qingzhao to burst out laughing? It is always fun to win, but there must also be some special delight and gratification in Li Qingzhao's victories. Mingcheng was the one who had attended the National University, where he was educated at the highest levels in canonical writings. It was Mingcheng whose official career depended in large part on his reputation for excellence in learning and scholarship. But it is Li Qingzhao who seems to have had a better command of the scholarly books they kept in their household. Indeed, she seems to have had something like a photographic memory of what she had read. A wife would not be expected to win this game, so winning it as Li Qingzhao does makes it all the more fun.

In writing too, there was a degree of competition between husband and wife. Not long after Li Qingzhao's death, the literatus Zhou Hui wrote this in his miscellany:

> Recently I met one of Yi'an's [Li Qingzhao's] relatives, who told me that when Mingcheng was serving at Jiankang [1128–29], whenever there was a snowstorm, Yi'an would put on a cap and cape of reeds and go out to walk on top of the city wall, looking out afar, in search of poetic inspiration. When she thought of some lines, she would invite her husband to continue the poem, but Mingcheng was invariably hard put to do so.[2]

There are many stories about Li Qingzhao and Zhao Mingcheng whose reliability is highly questionable. But the source of this one is a member of Li Qingzhao's family, perhaps a cousin or nephew, who told the story directly to Zhou Hui. The story is interesting not only for broaching the notion that Li Qingzhao's talent as a writer surpassed that of her husband. It is equally interesting for what it says about Li Qingzhao's quest for literary inspiration. It would have been highly irregular for a woman to go out for a walk on top of the city wall during a snowstorm, and that she did this

---

1. Li Qingzhao, "Jinshi lu houxu" 金石錄後序, *Jianzhu* 3.310.
2. Zhou Hui, *Qingbo zazhi* 8.5096.

precisely for poetic inspiration suggests a special commitment to poetic composition.

Another of Li Qingzhao's surviving couplets, from another lost poem, suggests something about how she worked at literary composition.

| 詩情如夜鵲 | My poetry sentiments resemble the magpie at night, |
| 三繞未能安 | Circling three times it still cannot settle down.[3] |

The lines transform celebrated ones by Cao Cao 曹操 (155–220). He had opened a song with these words:

月明星稀	The moon is bright, the stars few.
鳥鵲南飛	Magpies fly southward.
繞樹三匝	They circle the tree three times,
無枝可依	Finding no branch to rest on.[4]

In Cao Cao's song, the circling magpies are a metaphor for the talented men to whom his song is addressed. They have gone from one rival state to another and have not yet decided which they will give their allegiance to. Cao Cao is hoping that they decide to stay with him. Li Qingzhao completely changes the import of the circling birds image. It becomes a simile for the restlessness of her poetic impulse and the rigorous standards she sets for herself in choosing poetic diction. Her use of the phrase *shiqing* 詩情 is interesting. The phrase is normally used in the sense of "feelings expressed in poetry." In Li Qingzhao's usage the phrase designates feelings or thoughts that she intends to express in poetic lines but cannot yet express because she cannot "settle" on the right words. Her poetic feelings are in search of the right lines to contain them. The snowstorm story suggests that poetic inspiration for Li Qingzhao could sometimes be found in powerful and stirring natural scenes. This couplet yields a very different impression. We see her acknowledging the challenge of getting her lines right, and we glimpse as well her determination to do so.

Li Qingzhao's couplet was probably written relatively early in her life.[5] It is quoted by Zhu Bian 朱弁 (d. 1154) in his *Remarks on Poetry*, where he observes

---

3. *Jianzhu* 2.251.

4. Cao Cao, "Duange xing" 短歌行, *Weishi* 3.349.

5. This early date for the couplet is suggested by Wang Zhongwen 王仲聞, who notes that Zhu Bian left on a mission to the Jin in 1126 and stayed there over ten years, completing his *Fengye tang shihua* 風月堂詩話 shortly thereafter, so that Zhu probably knew of Li Qingzhao's poem before he left in 1126. Wang Zhongwen (Wang Xuechu), "Li Qingzhao shiji biannian" 李清照事迹編年, *Li Qingzhao ji jiaozhu*, p. 260.

that Chao Buzhi 晁補之 (1053–1110) "often spoke highly of Li Qingzhao to other gentlemen."[6] It is probable that Chao Buzhi knew Li Qingzhao from the time she was a child—Chao was a friend of Li Qingzhao's father, Li Gefei 李格非.[7] Having referred to Chao Buzhi's high opinion of Li Qingzhao, Zhu Bian then quotes the magpie couplet (as well as another one). Such lines, he says, "are greatly savored in people's mouths" 頗膾炙人口. Zhu Bian is not so much interested in Li Qingzhao's lines for what they tell us about her approach to writing. He is mostly interested in them as examples of outstanding poetic lines, which cleverly recast Cao Cao's lines. It is also worth noting what Zhu Bian, one of the earliest critics to say anything about Li Qingzhao, says about her literary talent: "she is good at literary composition, and she is particularly skillful at composing poetry" 善屬文，於詩尤工. Zhu says nothing about Li Qingzhao's song lyrics; to him her *shi* poetry is her greatest achievement.

Li Qingzhao was well aware that she had a reputation as a talented writer and was being talked about and praised for her talent by such men as Chao Buzhi. She reveals this awareness in a poem written in her thirties:

分得知字   *Upon Being Assigned the Rhyme "Zhi"*

學語三十年	I've studied language for thirty years
緘口不求知	But kept my mouth shut, not seeking to be known.
誰遣好奇士	Whoever sent a gentleman interested in the unusual,
相逢説項斯	To encounter then spread word of Xiang Si?[8]

Xiang Si was a late Tang person skilled at poetry. He was, however, completely unknown and obscure until Yang Jingzhi 楊敬之 (fl. 820) encountered him and announced his intention to "speak of [Xiang Si] to everyone he met," and then proceeded to do so. This information is recorded in Li Chuo's 李綽 late ninth-century miscellany.[9] Here, for once, we find Li

6. Zhu Bian, *Fengyue tang shihua* A.13b.

7. On the relationship of Li Gefei and Chao Buzhi, see Zhuge, *Li Qingzhao yu Zhao Mingcheng*, p. 60. Zhuge thinks that Li Qingzhao must have crossed paths with Chao Buzhi in the last years of his life, when he was living in retirement in Jinxiang 金鄉, while Li Qingzhao herself was living in Qingzhou (both places in modern Shandong), if not before, but there is no record of contact during those years.

8. *Jianzhu* 2.210.

9. Li Chuo, *Shangshu gushi*, 16b–17a.

Qingzhao sounding defensive about her literary talent and even claiming that she had tried to keep quiet and escape notice. It was other gentlemen who brought her to prominence.

Given the deep and widespread ambivalence about women's writing in Li Qingzhao's day, it is hardly surprising that she would occasionally explain that the circulation of her writings and her consequent literary repute happened in spite of her efforts to keep her writings unknown and out of circulation. This is what people would expect her to say. There are two additional considerations. The title of this quatrain indicates that it was written socially, as part of a poetic game in which each participant was assigned (or drew) a rhyme word to use. The phrase *fende* 分得 makes this clear.[10] Under such circumstances, when Li Qingzhao was presumably playing this game together with other women (sisters or friends), or perhaps men and women, it is all the more understandable that she, the only one playing that day who was known to the outside world as a literary talent, would feel obliged to downplay her special stature. Second, the very way she makes the point undercuts the point itself. The allusion to the Xiang Si story is quite ingenious. That story was not well known. It appears in a relatively obscure late Tang miscellany, *Shangshu gushi* 尚書故事. Consequently, the allusion shows off how extremely well-read Li Qingzhao was in Tang sources. Even her use of the phrase "a gentleman interested in the unusual" (or "marvelous") as well as her decision to allude to a story of a talented man being discovered suggest a keen consciousness of how remarkable she was as a woman to have developed such a talent (having worked at it for "thirty years") in what was essentially a male activity and the repute to go along with it.

Writing figures prominently in one of Li Qingzhao's best known song lyrics:

漁家傲　*To the tune "The Fisherman Is Proud"* (no. 3)

天接雲濤連曉霧	The sky joins billowing waves of clouds with morning mists
星河欲轉千帆舞	The River of Stars begins to pivot, a thousand sails dance.
彷彿夢魂歸帝所	My dreaming soul seems to have gone to where the Lord dwells.
聞天語	I hear Heaven speak.
殷勤問我歸何處	With utmost concern he asks what is my final destination?

10. This point is made by Xu Peijun in *Jianzhu* 2.210, n. 1.

我報路長嗟日暮	The road is long, I say, and the day already late.
學詩謾有驚人句	I study poetry but useless are my startling lines.
九萬里風鵬正舉	A vast wind blows, the giant phoenix will soon take flight.
風休住	Oh wind, do not slacken!
蓬舟吹取三山去	Blow my little boat all the way to the Immortals' Isles.[11]

This work stands out, both in Li Qingzhao's oeuvre and in the entire corpus of songs of her dynasty, for its unusual theme and exposition. The opening lines introduce the motif of the celestial, presenting images of a sky filled with clouds that look like waterborne waves and cavorting sails, matched by a River of Stars (the Milky Way) that is pivoting, or appearing to do so, as dawn approaches. The celestial motif is then developed in what follows, as the *hun*-soul of the speaker travels to heaven in a dream and is there questioned by the Lord of Heaven. The same notion of unworldliness is then carried over into the closing lines, where it is combined with the motifs of ocean and sails already seen in the opening. The speaker expresses the hope of being carried in a sailboat, propelled by the wind created when the mythical Peng bird flaps its wings to take flight, to the legendary Three Isles (Penglai 蓬萊), off the northeastern coast, populated by immortals.

The theme of a poet engaging in a conversation with the Lord of Heaven is not commonplace in earlier Chinese poetry. Li Qingzhao's language in the fourth line may be taken from a *yuefu* 樂府 by Li Bai 李白, where the same wording occurs.[12] But in Li Bai's poem "hearing Heaven speak" is just something that transpires during a heavenly ascent. It is a sign that the speaker has indeed arrived in the heavens. But there is no conversation, no indication that the divine comment is even addressed to the speaker. The situation is utterly different in Li Qingzhao's composition. The Lord of Heaven not only speaks, but he also asks the poet the ultimate question about the direction and, by implication, meaning of her life.

In answer to this question about her definitive aim in life, metaphorically called a "destination," the poet answers, sustaining the metaphor, that the "road" is long and that the "end of the day" is already near. Then, shifting to more direct discourse, she talks about her frustration in mastering poetry. She does not say that she has tried to become an able poet but has failed.

---

11. *Jianzhu* 1.127; *Quan Songci* 2:1202. The piece numbers for Li Qingzhao's song lyrics that follow tune titles in parentheses refer to my chronological list of her song lyrics. See appendix 1 for the complete list and chapter 3 for a discussion of how it was derived.

12. Li Bai, "Fei long yin" 飛龍引, no. 2, *Quan Tangshi* 23.303.

She says that she has studied (or learned or devoted herself to) poetry but finds that her "startling lines" seem to have no effect. This is something of an oxymoron. If they are "startling," how can they yet be "useless"? What she must mean is that as original as her poems are, they have less impact on others than she would like them to have. She is feeling the frustration of every writer who has doubts about the power and impact of his or her writing, of every artist who wonders if the final result is worth the effort required to produce it. Her line recalls Du Fu's 杜甫 (712–70) famous line on his commitment to literary excellence: "I will not rest even in death if my language is not startling" 語不驚人死不休.[13] But Li Qingzhao's problem is different: she feels she has already produced "startlingly" original lines. It is just that no one seems to care. This frustration leads to her fanciful wish that she could leave the mundane world behind. Given its lack of interest in her, she feels unsuited to the world.

The feelings of self-doubt and frustration concerning her literary output are certainly not unique to Li Qingzhao. What is more revealing is the centrality she assigns to poetry in her life. In response to the Lord of Heaven's question about the goal and purpose of her existence, she refers to her devotion to poetry and to that alone. Li Qingzhao may be unsatisfied with the results, but it is evident that she looks upon this activity as her life's work.

We will look at one last poem in which writing figures prominently. This is a poem marked by an unusual degree of bitterness, yet writing is mentioned as the one thing she has left, the one thing that brings her some relief. It was written, as she says in the preface, in 1121, soon after she arrived in Laizhou 萊州 (in eastern Shandong), where she joined her husband, who had recently taken up the post of governor there.[14]

感懷 *Stirred by Emotions*

宣和辛丑八月十日到萊，獨坐一室，平生所見，皆不在目前。几
上有《禮韻》，因信手開之，約以所開爲韻作詩。偶得「子」
字，因以爲韻，作《感懷》詩云。

---

13. Du Fu, "Jiangshang zhi shui ru haishi liao duanshu" 江上值水如海勢聊短述, *Quan Tangshi* 226.2443.

14. We do not know exactly when Zhao Mingcheng assumed his new post, but it must have been between the fourth month of 1121, when he climbed Yangtian Mountain, and the eighth month, when Li Qingzhao joined him in Laizhou; see Xu Peijun, "Nianpu" 年譜, *Jianzhu*, p. 451.

I arrived in Lai on the tenth day of the eighth month of the *xinchou* year of the Xuanhe period (1121) and found myself sitting alone in a single room. Nothing of what I was used to seeing my entire life was there before my eyes. A copy of *Rhymes for Rituals* was on the table, and I opened it randomly, having decided that I would use whatever rhyme I opened to to write a poem. By chance I opened to the character "son" and used it for my rhyme, composing a poem titled "Stirred by Emotions."

寒窗敗几無史書	A cold window, broken table, and no books,
公路可憐合至此	How pitiful was Gonglu to be brought to this!
青州從事孔方君	Qingzhou wine attendants and Lord Square Hole
4 終日紛紛喜生事	Enjoy causing no end of trouble all day long.
作詩謝絶聊閉門	Composing poetry I decline all invitations, closing my door for now.
燕寢凝香有佳思	Amid lingering incense in my room I have fine thoughts.
靜中我乃得至交	In isolation I have obtained perfect companions,
8 烏有先生子虛子	Mr. Nonexistent and Sir Vacuity.[15]

Line 2: Gonglu is the polite name of Yuan Shu 袁術, a warlord who came to power in the chaos of the last years of the Later Han. He proclaimed himself emperor and founder of a new dynasty in 195. He was then attacked by Cao Cao and other generals and suffered irreversible defeats on the battlefield, until he was isolated and running short of rations for his men. One day he asked his cooks for honey sauce to go with his ground wheat and was dismayed to hear that even that was unavailable. Sitting on his bed he cried out, "How could Yuan Shu have been brought to this!" He then collapsed and died.[16]

Lines 3–4: Because of an earlier usage in *Shishuo xinyu* 世説新語, "Qingzhou attendants" means good wine, or simply wine.[17] Lord Square Hole is a fanciful designation of coins, personified, owing to a pun on *kongfang* 孔方, which describes a Chinese coin with its "square hole" in the middle and also sounds like a plausible personal name (since Kong is a standard surname). This couplet must be a complaint by Li Qingzhao that feasting and other expenditures, possibly connected to her husband's new official position, have brought hardship upon her family.

There is also probably a secondary meaning in line 3, different in sense but not so different in import. Li Qingzhao and Zhao Mingcheng had just spent fourteen years living in Qingzhou (the same Qingzhou as in the *Shishuo xinyu* allusion), and the compound *congshi* may also function verbally as "to be in the service of": thus "In Qingzhou we subjected ourselves to money." This too is a complaint.

Line 8: Mr. Nonexistent and Sir Vacuity are imaginary persons who appear in Sima Xiangru's rhyme-prose "Zixu fu" 子虛賦, *Wenxuan* 7.17b–24b.

---

15. *Jianzhu* 2.211.

16. Wushu 吳書, quoted in Pei Songzhi's 裴松之 commentary in Chen Shou, *Sanguo zhi* 6.210, n. 3.

17. Liu Yiqing, *Shishuo xinyu jianshu* 20.9.708.

We will return to a discussion of this poem in a later chapter. With regard to writing, despite the tone of extreme forlornness presented in most of the lines, when the speaker takes up the subject of poetry composition, there is an abrupt change. Having shut herself in her room and refused all social contact, she turns to poetry writing and enjoys the "fine thoughts" that come to her as she sits in her perfumed room. There are thus some sharp dichotomies established: that between the world outside her room, which has endless troubles caused by worries over money and social engagements, which the speaker only seeks to free herself from, and the world inside her room, where she takes pleasure in writing. There is also a dichotomy between the material deprivation that she experiences even inside that room and the enjoyment she can nevertheless find there as she loses herself in poetry. The last two lines are double edged. The two fictional persons she mentions stand for the real companions she does not have. She tells us that she has obtained perfect companions, but then it turns out they are not real, stressing how utterly alone she is. But these two men are also literary creations, brought to life by a poet a millennium before her time. In her own literary life, she can create voices and entities that may indeed be a perfect antidote to her misery outside her room. She may find herself, newly arrived in Laizhou, in a dwelling with "no books," but she is still able to produce new writings of her own.

One other poem deserves attention here for the different direction it takes.

曉夢 *Dawn Dream*

曉夢隨疏鐘	A dawn dream follows the fleeting drumbeats
飄然躋雲霞	Soaring it treads upon the colored clouds.
因緣安期生	It is my fate to meet the immortal An Qisheng
4 邂逅萼綠華	By chance to encounter goddess Green Blossom too.
秋風正無賴	The autumn winds truly cannot be withstood,
吹盡玉井花	They blow all the flowers from Jade Well,
共看藕如船	Together we view lotus pods the size of boats
8 同食棗如瓜	And nibble on dates as large as melons.
翩翩座上客	How graceful, the guests at the banquet,
意妙語亦佳	Marvelous their thoughts, excellent their words too.
嘲辭鬬詭辯	Teasing each other, they vie in witty debate,
12 活火分新茶	With rekindled fire we brew fresh tea.
雖非助帝功	Although we do not assist the emperor doing good deeds,
其樂莫可涯	The joy of this gathering knows no bounds.
人生能如此	If a person could live like this,

16	何必歸故家	What need would there be of returning home?
	起來斂衣坐	Awaking, I straighten my robe and sit up,
	掩耳厭喧嘩	I cover my ears, annoyed by raucous shouting.
	心知不可見	They who know me can no longer be seen,
20	念念猶咨嗟	My thoughts dwell on this as I sigh.[18]

Lines 3–4: An Qishen is a legendary immortal who is said to have lived on the Penglai Islands. Some sources say that the First Emperor of Qin met him and later launched his unsuccessful Penglai Islands expedition to contact him again. Green Blossom was a mountain goddess who appeared in 359 to Yang Quan and presented divine gifts to him. She said that she originally lived on top of Jiuyi Mountain.[19]

Lines 6–7: Han Yu's 韓愈 (768–824) poem "Gu yi" 古意 describes a jade well on top of Hua Mountain in which grow lotus plants that have seed pods as large as boats.[20]

Line 8 harks back to An Qisheng, drawing on a description in *Shiji* of what he was once seen eating.[21]

This poem is in the rich tradition of dream or daydream flights of fantasy to immortal realms. Li Qingzhao seems to go out of her way to include a female goddess as one of the hosts of her visit. Green Blossom is not nearly so well known an immortal as An Qisheng, but she is given equal attention in Li Qingzhao's lines, where women take their place together with the men at an immortals' banquet. There is no mention of poetry or writing in the dream scene, but there is considerable attention to conversation, which often figures as the inspiration for writing, and it is clear that it is a highly intellectual and elevated type of conversation that is being conducted at the banquet. Li Qingzhao relishes this type of exchange and argumentation. Her words recall the account of her own family and upbringing found in an earlier poem:

嫠家父祖生齊魯	This widow's father and grandfather were born in Qi and Lu,
位下名高人比數	They counted men of renown among their followers.
當年稷下縱談時	In animated discussions at the Jixia Academy,[22]
猶記人揮汗成雨	Perspiration wiped from brows fell like rain, I still can recall.[23]

---

18. *Jianzhu* 2.214.

19. Tao Hongjing, *Zhengao* 1.1–2.

20. Han Yu, "Gu yi," *Quan Tangshi* 338.3789.

21. Sima Qian, *Shiji* 12.455.

22. The ancient state of Qi 齊, in Li Qingzhao's native northeast, was famed for its Jixia 稷下 Academy, which attracted scholars from far and wide and fostered lively debate on philosophical and political issues.

23. From "Shang shumi Han gong gongbu shangshu Hu gong" 上樞密韓公工部尚書 胡公, no. 1, *Jianzhu* 2.222. The entire poem is translated in chapter 5.

Later in life, she re-created the kind of family environment in which she grew up, making herself a participant in the elevated discussion, in "Dawn Dream."

The reference in line 13 of that poem to the emperor and his advisors is significant. Hers is a gathering of unemployed immortals, not high officials, and so they have nothing to do with the emperor. More to the point, hers is a gathering that includes women, and this puts even more distance between her group and those who "assist the emperor doing good deeds." The implication, though, is that the quality of the discussion matches the best of those that take place at the court and palace.

The closing lines of "Dawn Dream" draw a stark contrast between the dream vision and the reality she returns to on awakening. We can only guess at what the people in her household are shouting about. It is clear enough, however, that this is a most unwelcome denouement to what she just experienced in the dream, so much so that she claps her hands over her ears. We are left with an image of Li Qingzhao returning, on awakening, to a world in which she feels completely alone and without anyone who "knows" her. This is similar to what is expressed in "Stirred by Emotions." In complete solitude, alone in her room, she can only dream of happier circumstances and subsequently capture them in a poem, or otherwise turn to poetry to take refuge in "fine thoughts."

The Early Critics on Li Qingzhao

Li Qingzhao's deep level of engagement with writing was viewed with considerable skepticism by onlookers. They were not accustomed to a woman taking writing so seriously, much less to one doing it so well. Her writings circulated during her lifetime. Printed collections of her song lyrics were widely available and enthusiastically received.[24] The early critical reception of Li Qingzhao is interesting both for its inherent interest and in order to better understand the literary world in which she lived, wrote, and was evaluated. The nature of that environment, so foreign to us today, must be taken into account in any historicized assessment of her work.

---

24. We could infer the circulation of Li Qingzhao's song lyrics in printed editions from the widespread comment on them and imitation of her style even by the mid-twelfth century. But we also have explicit reference to the existence of such printed editions by the turn of the thirteenth century from Zhao Yanwei, *Yunlu manchao* (dated 1206) 14.245.

The great majority of early statements about her work, even the most praiseworthy, mention her gender as a woman. This is hardly unexpected, since so few writings by women were in circulation. Invariably the implication is that she is talented for a woman, or that as accomplished as her writing is, she is, after all, a woman so that her work could never rise above a certain level. An example is the comment Xie Ji 謝伋, a nephew of Zhao Mingcheng, makes on a few lines he quotes in his collection of critical notes on parallel prose ("four-and-six-syllable prose") from the prayer that she wrote for Zhao Mingzheng after he died. Xie quotes the lines and adds this terse but revealing remark: "This is a woman's well-crafted four-and-six-syllable prose" 婦人四六之工者.[25]

Another type of reaction to Li Qingzhao combines favorable remarks about her poetic talent with references to her remarriage in 1132, a few years after Zhao Mingcheng had died, and, sometimes, her quick divorce from that second husband as well. This treatment of her is found in several Southern Song and later sources. Here are three examples. Hu Zi:

> Among women of recent times who can write there is Li Yi'an, who produced many fine lines. Her little song lyric says: "Last night the rain was intermittent, the wind blustery. / Deep sleep did not dispel the lingering wine. / I tried asking the maid who raised the blinds, / She said the crab apple blossoms were as before. / 'Don't you know? / Don't you know? / The greens must be plump and the reds withered.'" "Greens plump and reds withered." Such language is highly original. Again, her "Double Ninth Song" says, "The blind is lifted by the west wind, / She's as wasted as the yellow blossoms." Such lines are likewise hard for a woman to come up with. Yi'an married a second time, to Zhang Ruzhou, but before long she had a falling out with him. Her petition to Qi Chuhou [Qi Chongli] says, "To my dismay, I realized that at an advanced age, when the sun hung in the mulberry and elm, I had married a worthless shyster of a man." There were none who spoke of this who did not laugh at her.[26]

Wang Zhuo 王灼 (fl. 1149):

> From her youth she achieved fame for her poetry. In talent, power, and richness, it approximated that of earlier masters. Her level of achievement is not often attained even by educated gentlemen. Among women of our dynasty, she should be ranked first for literary skill. After Zhao [Mingcheng] died,

---

25. Xie Ji, *Siliu tanzhu* 9a.
26. Hu Zi, *Tiaoxi yuyin conghua*, "Qianji" 60.416.

she married a certain fellow, then brought suit against him and divorced him. In her later years she drifted about haplessly and had no home to return to.[27]

Chao Gongwu 晁公武 (fl. 1151):

The Literary Collection of Li Yi'an, in twelve chapters. The author was the daughter of Li Gefei of our dynasty. She first married Zhao Mingcheng and enjoyed fame for literary skill.[28] Her father-in-law Zhengfu [Zhao Tingzhi] was grand councilor under Emperor Huizong. Li once submitted a poem to him that contained the line "[Your bearing is] hot enough to scorch the hand, but chilling to the heart." Nevertheless, she did not observe principle in her conduct, and late in life she wandered about the rivers and lakes until she died.[29]

There is a consistent pattern to these passages. First, Li Qingzhao's skill as a poet is acknowledged, and some lines exemplifying her talent may be quoted. But then the focus of the entry changes to her conduct in the latter part of her life. The fact that she remarried after Zhao Mingcheng died is noted, directly or indirectly, and her unhappy, indeed hapless last years are referred to. A change of tone accompanies the change of focus. The laudatory, admiring tone of the remarks about her poetry gives way to disparagement, even derision. Hu Zi's is the most harsh. He quotes the key lines from Li Qingzhao's letter to Qi Chongli 綦崇禮, the Hanlin official who managed to get Li Qingzhao released from prison, where she landed after bringing suit against her second husband, Zhang Ruzhou 張汝舟. (In Song times, a spouse who brought suit against his or her partner was liable for two year's imprisonment regardless of the merits of the suit and its outcome.) The lines that Hu Zi quotes culminate the section of her letter that describes how she was tricked into marrying Zhang and how shocked she was to discover that his real interest was not her but what was left of her wealth. When Hu Zi adds his final comment, that everyone who spoke of Li Qingzhao's estrangement from her second husband laughed at her (傳者無不笑之), we understand that Hu Zi condones this widespread mockery of Li Qingzhao and shares the same attitude, at least to some degree. Why else would he choose to

---

27. Wang Zhuo, *Biji manzhi* 2.88.

28. The text gives an incorrect version of Zhao Mingcheng's name (Chengzhi 誠之), which I have corrected.

29. Chao Gongwu, *Junzhai dushu zhi jiaozheng* 19.1033.

include this bit of information? With this final comment, the transformation of Li Qingzhao in the passage from venerable woman to contemptuous woman is complete.

These critics combine literary appraisal with judgment of Li Qingzhao's conduct as literary critics in premodern China were inclined to do. The analogous case with a male writer would typically be unprincipled or disloyal conduct in the political arena being seen as compromising his literary achievement. Still, one feels that special factors are at work in this peculiar treatment of Li Qingzhao if for no other reason than that literary talent among women was so rare and, indeed, so problematic.

Li Qingzhao was acclaimed for her literary talent even as a young lady (as Wang Zhuo states). Her song lyrics circulated, and even if her entire written collection did not, many of her *shi* poems and prose works were known to famous literati, who remark favorably on them. Along with the admiration, however, there was evidently a sense among many that there was something improper, even unnatural, in the phenomenon of such a talented woman writer. In the derision that Hu Zi reports we sense the backlash against her notoriety as a writer. Her existence as a woman of talent challenged the existing social and literary order in a way it had not previously been challenged. A few other woman poets had achieved a degree of repute, but none of them had nearly the fame that Li Qingzhao had, so she was the most likely target for latent, or not so latent, resentment against woman who transgressed the boundary that kept the literary world a male domain. The special feature of the derision Hu Zi reports is that it turns Li Qingzhao's writing back against her. It uses her own words to mock her. What better indication could there be of a sense that a woman ought not to write so well? By writing that letter to Qi Chongli, Li Qingzhao played into her detractors' hands. In erudite and heartfelt language, Li Qingzhao described the tragedy that had befallen her. Her critics scoffed at the decisions she had made and the language she used so effectively to recount them.

There is a distinctly opportunistic quality to the disapproving remarks. It is as if the critics were just waiting for a reason to denounce this woman of exceptional ability and ambition. In her remarriage and, even better, the quick dissolution of that second union, they found exactly what they needed. The result is that the critics have it two ways: they can acknowledge Li Qingzhao's literary skill and the popularity of her writings, then raise troubling concerns about her conduct as a woman. No one argues that she is not skillful as a writer. Apparently, that would have been too difficult an argument to make, especially in the face of popular acclaim for her writings. So they are content to retreat one step. They allow that she is a writer of real ability, deferring to popular opinion, then go out of their way to bring up an issue of character or conduct that threatens to overshadow what they have just said about her writing.

The last step that is taken by hostile early critics of Li Qingzhao is to suggest an integral connection between her skill as a writer and her lack of "virtue" as a widow. This is different from simply mentioning the two together as two aspects of her life. Now the writing is seen as a manifestation of the character traits responsible for her misconduct. Wang Zhuo takes this step as the passage examined above continues. Wang's critique, contained in his *Biji manzhi* 碧雞漫志 (1209), an important collection of song lyric criticism, is the earliest extended critical treatment of Li Qingzhao:

> Recluse Scholar Yi'an was the daughter of Li Gefei, judicial commissioner of the Dongjing Circuit, and wife of Zhao Mingcheng [Defu], prefect of Jiankang. From her youth she achieved fame for her poetry. In talent, power, and richness, it approximated that of earlier masters. Her level of achievement is not often attained even by educated gentlemen. Among women of our dynasty, she should be ranked first for literary skill. After Zhao [Mingcheng] died, she married a certain fellow, then brought suit against him and divorced him. In her later years she drifted about haplessly and had no home to return to. Her songs, in lines of unequal length, fully expressed people's feelings as the words turn this way and that. Capricious, clever, incisive, and fresh, a hundred different styles and moods are expressed. Knowing no restraint as her brush moved across the page, she included indecent language of the back streets. Among female members of officials' families who could write, never since ancient times has there been anyone so unconstrained.[30]

The passage goes on. A long digression follows in which Wang refers to three other historical examples of poets who wrote verse using indecent or erotic language: literati encouraged to do so by the dissolute last ruler of the Chen dynasty, certain poems by Yuan Zhen and Bai Juyi of the mid-Tang, and poems by Wen Tingyun. In each case, Wang quotes some lines but notes that the level of impropriety "was only" to an extent. The point is that although these earlier writings had been the object of critical disapprobation, in fact their impropriety was slight. Then Wang returns to the recent past and notes how there has developed a vogue of writing "crude and filthy song lyrics,"

---

30. Wang Zhuo, *Biji manzhi* 2.88–89.

under the influence of Cao Zu 曹組 (*jinshi* 1121), the likes of which even the earlier offending poets "would not have dared" to compose. So we are given to believe that the impropriety of the current erotic song lyrics exceeds by far anything in questionable taste ever written in earlier times. Wang concludes by noting that the deplorable vogue of such scandalous song lyrics has even spread to "women of the inner quarters" 閨房婦女, who seek to outdo each other in composing such songs and "have no sense of shame or anxiety" 無所羞畏. Wang is speaking about Li Qingzhao.

It is difficult to know what to make of Wang Zhuo's characterization of Li Qingzhao's song lyrics. None among the earliest and most reliable of the songs attributed to her seems remotely like the "indecent" compositions for which Wang castigates her. Even among the later pieces attributed to her that do, at least, feature vignettes about flirtatious women in the presence of a male lover, there is hardly anything that would strike us today as sufficient to provoke Wang's disapproval and, even by the standards of Li Qingzhao's day, nothing that goes beyond the references to romantic love found regularly in song lyrics by male writers.

Two considerations may account for Wang Zhuo's characterization of Li Qingzhao's lack of a "sense of shame." The first is that Wang's level of tolerance for compositions openly broaching romantic love may well have been particularly low when discussing pieces written by a woman. Wang Zhuo was a "conservative" critic when writing about the song lyric. He had little patience with the style of song that was more colloquial, closer to the popular tradition, and relatively unconstrained in its treatment of romance and sexual impulses. He is highly critical of Liu Yong 柳永 (990–1050) for his "shallowness and vulgarity" 淺近卑俗 and snobbishly observes that it is "people who cannot read" who are Liu Yong's biggest fans.[31] Wang is likewise incapable of accepting the notion that Ouyang Xiu could have written all the songs in his collection that treat romantic love openly. He flatly declares that Ouyang himself only wrote "one-third" of the songs that are in his collection, the others having been written by political enemies who sought to ruin his reputation.[32] Yet when it comes to evaluating the song lyric writers who were closer in time and in style to Li Qingzhao, writers such as Qin Guan 秦觀 (1049–1100), Huang Tingjian, He Zhu 賀鑄 (1052–1125), and Zhou

---

31. Wang Zhuo, *Biji manzhi* 2.84–85.
32. Ibid. 2.85.

Bangyan 周邦彥 (1056–1121), Wang Zhuo is more accepting of the romantic and sensuous components of their work. Huang Tingjian in particular wrote many song lyrics that are extremely colloquial and explicit in their treatment of sexual love. Wang Zhuo says only that "in his later years Huang indulged himself in the pleasure quarters, and so his [song lyrics] have places that are somewhat uninhibited" 黃晚年閒放狹邪，故有少疏蕩處.[33] Wang's comment on this aspect of Qin Guan's work is similarly accommodating and mild.[34] It appears, then, that Wang uses a different standard when evaluating Li Qingzhao's compositions than he employs for male writers. Given the biases against women writers, it is hardly surprising that a woman writing in a poetic form that regularly treated love and desire would provoke a harsh reaction among some critics.

It is also possible that Li Qingzhao wrote some song lyrics that treat romantic love more openly and explicitly than anything that survives among her works attested in Southern Song times and that these are what so scandalized Wang Zhuo. We will have a chance to consider this possibility in a later chapter.

Regardless, the most interesting quality of Wang's critique of Li Qingzhao is how what he says about her conduct anticipates what he says about her songwriting. The implication of the former is that after Zhao Mingcheng died she recklessly "married some fellow" 嫁某氏, only to discover that she could not get along with him, so that her last years were spent as a homeless drifter. A woman who is described as "drifting about haplessly" and "having no home to return to" 流蕩無歸 is a woman who has thrown herself away; who knows what she may have to do to support herself? The innuendo is unmistakable. First she shows herself incapable of remaining a chaste widow; then she cannot even keep her second marriage intact, so that she becomes a vagrant, a wanderer. Next Wang reports that Li Qingzhao's song lyrics have an analogous flaw: she uses indecent, back alley language to write erotic songs, which show that she has no sense of shame. In both her writings and her relations with men, there is impropriety involving sexual indiscretion. It is precisely a woman who knows no restraint and has no sense of shame who would remarry as a widow and then promptly divorce her new husband. Wang Zhuo suggests a parallel between the flawed conduct and the flawed

---

33. Ibid. 2.83.
34. Ibid.

literary compositions. Readers who accept Wang's judgment may well begin to think of Li Qingzhao's songs as bearing the seeds of the calamities that befell her later in life. Her literary work becomes inseparable from her failures as a widow and wife.

In other cultures and times as well, where the act of writing by women was likewise rare and deemed unacceptable by men, it was not unusual for such writing to be linked to female sexually aberrant conduct or promiscuity. Discussing images of the woman poet in England during the seventeenth and eighteenth centuries, Jane Spencer has surveyed the range of female types that were invoked—some to praise and justify but most to impose limits or to censure—including the woman poet as angel, Amazon, nightingale, whore, mother, amorous woman, domestic matron, virgin, and hermaphrodite: "Whether positive or negative in intention, whether created in hyperbolic praise, anxious self-justification, or satiric detraction, these images dealt in their various ways with one all-pervasive problem, recently theorized as the mismatch within patriarchal society between female embodiment and full human subjectivity. How could the poet's writing come from a woman's body?"[35] Of particular interest here is the connection made between woman poet and sexually promiscuous woman. Given the expectation, particularly ingrained in imperial China, that women should not show themselves in public, it followed that women who did were promiscuous (e.g., actresses, singing girls, or prostitutes). Inasmuch as poetry is often thought of as intensely personal, for a woman to allow her writing to circulate publicly was to expose her private self, her gendered body, in a way that violated the code of female seclusion. To the unsympathetic onlooker there was a sexual dimension to such exposure; the woman writer is considered sexually libertine and licentious. In seventeenth-century England, the linkage between woman poet and prostitute was explicitly made by Robert Gould (d. 1709) in his satire on women writers:

> . . . when their Verse did fail
> To get 'em brandy, Bread and Cheese, and Ale,
> Their Wants by Prostitution were supply'd,
> Shew but a Tester, you might up and Ride;
> For Punk and Poetess agree to pat,
> You cannot well be This and not be That.[36]

---

35. Spencer, "Imagining the Woman Poet," p. 100.
36. Quoted in ibid., p. 105.

Wang Zhuo's strategy in his denunciation of Li Qingzhao is similar. The advantage Wang Zhuo has is that he can point to conduct by Li Qingzhao that, in his mind, already serves as evidence of her sexual promiscuity. Her writing is further evidence of her moral depravity. The intriguing point about what he says about her song lyrics is how inaccurate it is: her songs are nothing like the way he describes them. It must be that, given his bias against Li Qingzhao as a female writer, he sees her songs in a very different light from that in which he views song lyrics by men. Consequently, even though her songs do not differ significantly in their language or treatment of romantic love from those of the leading male writers of her day, whose works Wang does not criticize this way, Wang Zhuo perceives them to be very different and associates them with the lowest and most vile of songs written by men. Wang Zhuo's assessment of Li Qingzhao's song lyrics is the most negative among those of early critics, but traces of the same type of bias against Li Qingzhao as a woman venturing into a realm normally restricted to men are visible in the comments of the other critics quoted earlier as well. They cannot comment on her literary work without mentioning how surprising it is to find a woman producing such effective lines, or they cannot express an assessment of her writing without referring to the unfortunate remarriage and hapless years that followed. We will see in a later chapter that the assertion Li Qingzhao spent her last years wandering the rivers and lakes, without a home, is also grossly inaccurate, but it fits these critics' logic of what should happen to a woman who acts so recklessly.

An incident from late in Li Qingzhao's life bears mention here. The great Southern Song poet Lu You relates, in the tomb inscription he wrote for the daughter of Sun Zong 孫綜, a minor court official, that when the girl was just over ten years old Li Qingzhao offered to take her on as a pupil. Lu You says that Li Qingzhao, "famed for her literary work, wanted to pass her learning on to Miss Sun" 李氏以文辭名家欲以其學傳夫人. Li Qingzhao would have been approaching seventy then.[37] But the proposal was rejected by the child herself, who observed, "Literary talent is not a woman's proper concern" 才藻非女子事也.[38] This ten-year-old girl missed the chance to be tutored by Li Qingzhao because of what she had already been taught about

37. Lu You records that the woman died at the age of fifty-three in the year 1193. She would have been ten years old in 1150, when Li Qingzhao was sixty-six. Lu You, "Furen Sunshi muzhiming" 夫人孫氏墓誌銘, *Weinan wenji* 35.2a.

38. Ibid. 35.1b.

the incompatibility of female respectability and literary skill. Quite possibly Li Qingzhao's own compromised reputation as a woman played a role in the child's decision or, more likely, in the decision her parents made for her. Interestingly enough, the irony of the child's rejection of this offer of instruction from the most gifted woman poet of the day seems to have been completely lost on Lu You, despite his own devotion to literary composition. Lu You's inclusion of this incident in Ms. Sun's tomb inscription is intended solely to redound upon the young girl's precocious worldly wisdom.

Li Qingzhao's Shi *Poetry and the Masculine Mode*

It is interesting to consider the impact that the doubts and challenges Li Qingzhao faced as a solitary woman writer, rather than a member of a group of women writers, might have had on her writing itself. Li Qingzhao must have been aware of the way that she would be perceived as a woman determined to produce literary work. The great majority of men would be unsympathetic or actively hostile to such intentions, even before the disaster of her remarriage occurred and played into the hands of those who would dismiss or chastise her for having the pretensions to write. It would be strange if her awareness of this unwelcoming attitude did not affect the way she wrote, one way or another.

The portion of her literary work that comes first to mind in this connection is a group of *shi* poems she wrote that have an unmistakably assertive or caustic import. Several of these explicitly offer criticism of officials or policies of her day. Others, which may not offer such critiques, take issues of statecraft and statesmanship as their primary subject. In either case, these poems are "masculine" either in tone or subject matter or both. They do not sound anything like what we would expect from a woman, or, for that matter, what we find from the hands of other women who wrote during the Song period. It appears that in this portion of her output Li Qingzhao set out to write in a way that would disarm those who would dismiss her, in other words, that she sought to write like a man. Knowing that, as a woman, her works would be looked on with skepticism, if not hostility, she tried to compensate for her gender by producing poetry that focuses on the very subjects that men wrote about and frequently even taking men to task for not being "manly" enough.

The earliest poem Li Qingzhao wrote in this mode, at least the earliest one that survives, is a poem on the theme of the Wuxi Restoration Eulogy Tablet

浯溪中興頌碑, which "matched" a poem that had been written in 1098.[39] (A poem that "matched" another was written on the same theme as the original work and used the same rhyme words in the same order.) It is generally thought that Li Qingzhao's poem must have been written within a year or two after the 1098 composition, when that piece was attracting considerable attention, so that Li Qingzhao's composition probably dates from the time when she was around seventeen years old. There is some confusion over the authorship of the original poem: it was written either by Zhang Lei 張耒 or Qin Guan. The two men were leading poets—like Chao Buzhi, they were associated with Su Shi—and frequently exchanged verses, causing the uncertainty over the authorship of the poem.[40] Li Qingzhao believed that Zhang Lei had written it, but scholars have long suspected that the real author was Qin Guan, who himself for a variety of reasons attributed the poem to Zhang Lei. Regardless of which man wrote it, the poem was in wide circulation soon after it was written and inspired poetic treatments of the same theme by other leading writers, including Huang Tingjian and Pan Dalin 潘大臨 (fl. 1090).[41] The Restoration Eulogy Tablet itself was a prose piece preceding a rhymed eulogy, written in 761 by Yuan Jie 元結 (719–92).[42] It celebrates the suppression of the An Lushan Rebellion and the reestablishment of peace under the new Tang emperor Suzong. The tablet was well known, largely because it was subsequently written out by Yan Zhenqing 顏真卿 (708–84), the most famous calligrapher of the eighth century, and carved on stone at Wuxi (in modern Qiyang, Hunan).

Li Qingzhao's matching poems (she wrote two compositions, both matching the original single poem) are far more ambitious and complex in their treatment of the Tang events than the work that she was matching. This is the first of Li Qingzhao's two matching poems:

---

39. Li Qingzhao, "Wuxi zhongxing songshi he Zhang Wenqian" 浯溪中興頌詩和張文潛, *Jianzhu* 2.197–98.

40. Today the poem is generally ascribed to Zhang Lei (the man Li Qingzhao refers to in her poem title as the author), but Xu Peijun argues that this is a misattribution and that the real author is Qin Guan; see *Jianzhu* 2.198–99. The original poem (attributed to Zhang Lei) is "Du zongxing song bei" 讀中興頌碑, *Quan Songshi* 20:13129.

41. Huang Tingjian, "Shu Moyai beihou" 書摩崖碑後, *Shangu shiji zhu* 20.688–90; Pan Dalin, "Wuxi" 浯溪, *Quan Songshi* 20:13437.

42. Yuan Jie, "Da Tang zhongxing song" 大唐中興頌, *Quan Tangwen xinbian* 380.4375.

五十年功如電掃	Fifty years' achievement was gone in a bolt of lightning.
華清宮柳咸陽草	Blossoms and willows of Huaqing Palace became the weeds of Xianyang.
五坊供奉鬬雞兒	Lads who trained fighting cocks in Five Imperial Pens
4　酒肉堆中不知老	Never thought of growing old amid their meat and ale.
胡兵忽自天上來	Barbarian soldiers swooped down from the heavens,
逆胡亦是姦雄才	The rebel barbarian was a master of treachery.
勤政樓前走胡馬	Barbarian steeds galloped before Diligent Governance Tower,
8　珠翠踏盡香塵埃	Crushing pearls and feathers until the dirt was fragrant.
何爲出戰輒披靡	Why were imperial armies routed so readily?
傳置荔枝多馬死	Too many horses had died transporting lychees from distant lands.
堯功舜德本如天	Yao's merit and Shun's virtue were as grand as Heaven,
12　安用區區紀文字	What need had they to record it meticulously in writing?
著碑銘德眞陋哉	To commemorate virtue in a tablet truly is debasing,
迺令神鬼磨山崖	Left then for spirits and ghosts to obliterate on a cliff.
子儀光弼不自猜	Ziyi and Guangbi had no doubts or jealousies,
16　天心悔禍人心開	Heaven regretted the tragedy, the people found ease.
夏商有鑒當深戒	The Xia and Shang are a mirror, we are sternly warned.
簡策汗青今具在	Their treated bamboo slips are still extant today.
君不見	Don't you see—
當時張說最多機	Zhang Yue had the most wiles and ruses of his day,
20　雖生已被姚崇賣	Yet Yao Chong managed to deceive him from the grave.

Lines 1–2: The several decades of peace and achievements of Xuanzong's 玄宗 reign (r. 712–56) were wiped away all at once by An Lushan's rebellion, leaving his beloved Huaqing Palace resort looking like the ruins of the Qin capital of Xianyang after it was burned by Xiang Yu 項羽 (232–202 BCE).

Lines 5–6: The barbarian soldiers are the rebel armies led by An Lushan. The phrase "hero of treachery" (or "hero among traitors") is taken from a characterization of Cao Cao found in Pei Songzhi's commentary on *Chronicle of the Three Kingdoms*.[43]

Lines 7–8: There is an intended irony in the mention of Diligent Governance Tower because it was there, despite the building's name, that Xuanzong frequently hosted feasts and indulged himself. The pearls and feathers refer to the adornments of the palace ladies.

Lines 9–10: This exaggerated claim refers to the infamous use of imperial riders to deliver fresh lychees to the palace to satisfy Yang Guifei's fondness for the fruit.

Line 15 refers to Guo Ziyi and Li Guangbi, the imperial generals credited with restoring order.

---

43. Pei Songzhi, commentary in Chen Shou, *Sanguo zhi* 1.3.

Lines 19–20: Zhang Yue and Yao Chong were grand councilors under Xuanzong. These lines allude to an anecdote found in the miscellany *Minghuang zalu* (but not in the dynastic histories) that tells how Zhang Yue was tricked by Yao Chong into writing a flattering tomb inscription for Yao.[44] When he was dying, Yao instructed his sons to present his various playthings to Zhang when Zhang came to mourn for him, and then request that Zhang compose Yao's tomb inscription. Yao knew that Zhang, delighted with the gifts, would first write a favorable inscription. But Yao also knew that within a few days Zhang would have second thoughts and return to ask to make some revisions in the text. But the sons were instructed to immediately have the text carved on stone and submitted to the court, so that no revisions were possible. When Zhang did return, just as Yao predicted, he discovered that Yao had tricked him from the grave.

The poem of 1098 that Li Qingzhao was matching is a predictable paean of praise to General Guo Ziyi, who defeated the rebel armies, and to the literary and calligraphic brilliance of Yuan Jie and Yan Zhenqing, who commemorated the military victory with their writing brushes. Li Qingzhao's poetic treatment of the theme is starkly different. The first ten lines of Li Qingzhao's poem concentrate on the disaster of the rebellion itself, rather than on its eventual suppression, and suggest that the dissoluteness and indulgence that had become rampant at Xuanzong's court helped to bring on the calamity. The last ten lines turn to the restoration tablet itself, which the 1098 poem extols, denigrating it as a "debased" and misguided attempt at commemoration. Truly meritorious deeds, Li argues, need no such self-conscious promotion. History and historiography will see to it that they are duly recorded. In her closing lines she returns to the themes of dynastic decline, benighted rule, and the inability of high ministers to subordinate their petty rivalries to their loyal service to the state. The poem is a sober reconsideration of the restoration tablet, one that refuses, unlike the poem it matches, to be caught up in enthusiasm for the restoration and its commemoration, and concentrates instead on the widespread misconduct that fostered the rebellion in the first place.

Li Qingzhao threw herself into this exercise, writing two compositions in response to the original one. More remarkable is the fact that a young lady would dare to venture into the arena of political verse at all. To write lengthy poems on the themes of rebellion, imperial misconduct, and official pettiness was a distinctly unladylike thing to do. The girl of about seventeen years turns out to have a more penetrating and unvarnished grasp of history and politics than did the career official who wrote the first poem. Li Qingzhao's

---

44. Zheng Chuhui, *Minghuang zalu* A.15–16.

two poems on the restoration tablet were quoted in entirety by Zhou Hui, which is why they survive. Noting how many poems had been written on the restoration tablet since Tang times, Zhou Hui observes: "For a woman to take her place among them could only happen if her literary thought and talent were exceptional."[45] It was presumably Li Qingzhao's intention to "take her place among" the men who had written on the theme, and Zhou Hui's remark shows that she succeeded.

Another poem on history that Li Qingzhao composed was similarly seen by her contemporaries as most unusual coming from the brush of a woman. It is, I suspect, not only the cleverness of this poem and the book learning it attests to but also its focus on issues of dynastic legitimacy, succession, and usurpation that made it so striking coming from a woman writer. The poem is this quatrain:

咏史　　*On History*

兩漢本繼紹	The two Hans continued dynastic legitimacy,
新室如贅疣	The New Reign was like a blister.
所以嵇中散	That is why Courtier Xi
至死薄殷周	To his dying day disparaged Yin and Zhou.[46]

This poem is thought to have been written soon after Liu Yu 劉豫 (1073–1143), a previous governor of Ji'nan who had defected to the Jurchen conquerors of the Northern Song, was established as the ruler of the puppet regime of Da Qi (1129–35) in 1129. The poem ostensibly concerns matters of dynastic conquest and legitimacy in ancient China, but in fact it is a denunciation of Liu Yu and his puppet state. The first couplet asserts that the Later Han (25–220) was the legitimate successor of the Former Han (206 BCE–8 CE) and that the interregnum New Dynasty (9–25 CE) founded by the usurper Wang Mang 王莽 (45 BCE–23 CE) was useless excrescence. These lines already point to the illegitimacy of Liu Yu's regime. The second couplet goes further, reminding us that Xi Kang 嵇康 (223–62), who opposed the usurpation of the Sima clan during the Wei dynasty (220–65), had said that he never approved of the dynastic conquest in antiquity of the Shang (Yin) against the Xia or the later conquest of the Zhou against the Shang.

---

45. Zhou Hui, *Qingbo zazhi* 8.5097.
46. *Jianzhu* 2.217.

It was none other than Zhu Xi who, in his *Collected Sayings*, singled this quatrain out for praise.[47] Xi Kang, Zhu Xi explains, "disapproved of the way Tang of the Shang and Wu of the Zhou came to power, and Li Qingzhao pairs his judgment with a reference to Wang Mang. Such lines as these, how could a woman ever manage to come up with them?" 如此等語，豈女子所能? Zhu Xi is reacting partly to the novelty of linking the Shang and Zhou conquests (normally thought of as justified) with the usurper Wang Mang, but he must also be thinking of how unexpected it is for a woman poet to show familiarity with these issues as well as such nimble thinking about them.

The Jurchen invasion of 1126–27 and the consequent relocation of the Song dynasty southward provided Li Qingzhao with ample opportunity to continue to write poems that grappled with politics. She expresses dismay at the weakness of the Southern Song leadership and frustration over the failure to mount a military campaign to recapture the north from the Jurchen and their greatly expanded Jin 金 empire. That a woman would express such sentiments, implicitly or explicitly chiding the leadership for being insufficiently martial and manly, was an irony not lost on her contemporaries. Several of her poems attracted attention at the time and were quoted and remarked on. Perhaps the best known among these pieces today is the following quatrain:

烏江　*Wu River*

生當作人傑	In life be a hero among men,
死亦爲鬼雄	In death be a champion among ghosts.
至今思項羽	Down to today we still remember Xiang Yu,
不肯過江東	Who refused to cross east of the river.[48]

Wu River is a tributary of the Yangzi River in He County 和縣, Anhui (just up the Yangzi River from modern Nanjing). It is the place where Xiang Yu, who contended with the founding emperor of the Han after the collapse of the Qin dynasty (221–207 BCE), met his death. Defeated and fleeing, Xiang

---

47. Zhu Xi, *Zhuzi yulei* 140.3332.
48. "Wu jiang," *Jianzhu* 2.238. The poem is preserved in two mid-sixteenth-century anthologies, which quote several of Li Qingzhao's compositions: Tian Yiheng, *Shinü shi* 11.5a; and Li Hu, *Gusu xinke tongkuan yibian* 17.16a. In the latter, which dates a few years after Tian Yiheng's anthology, the title of the poem is very different: "Quatrain Written on a Summer Day" 夏日絕句.

Yu came upon a ferryman at the Wu River who offered to take him across to the lands "east of the river." Although he would not be emperor, the ferryman suggested, he could set himself up as a regional king and live out his days in honor and comfort. But Xiang Yu would not be tempted. He reminds the ferryman that he had first arisen in revolt from that eastern region and had led thousands of young soldiers from there westward into his campaign against Liu Bang 劉邦 (265–195 BCE) and, eventually, to their death. "Even if the elders of the region took pity on me and made me their king, how could I possibly face them? Even if they did not mention it, how could I not be ashamed in my heart?" Saying this, he cut his throat and died.[49]

Xiang Yu's heroics stand in sharp contrast to the conduct of the Southern Song leadership, which had fled "across the river" (the Yangzi River) and had been content to remain there without making a concerted effort to retake the north. This poem is thought to have been written in 1129, two years after Gaozong's (r. 1127–62) flight south, when Li Qingzhao and her husband were on their way up the Yangzi from Jiankang to look for a place to settle. They evidently paid a visit to the temple honoring Xiang Yu at Wu River, because Zhao Mingcheng's *Records on Metal and Stone* lists a Tang inscription from that temple that was part of Zhao's collection.[50] In all likelihood, Li Qingzhao's poem was inspired by that visit. It is the only time in her life that she traveled through that region.

Two fragments of poems by Li Qingzhao offer similarly caustic observations about the Jurchen invasion and the inability of the Song leadership to retake the north. The fragments are couplets that must have been contained in separate poems that do not survive, also written in the early years of the Southern Song. The first couplet is

南渡衣冠欠王導   The "caps and robes" fleeing south lack a Wang Dao,
北來消息少劉琨   In news from the north there is no Liu Kun.[51]

"Caps and robes" is a common metonymy for court officials. The two persons named in this couplet were both associated with the fourth-century Jin 晉 dynasty (265–420) that, not unlike the Song, lost its northern half to invasion and withdrew southward to reestablish its capital at Jiankang (Nanjing). Wang Dao (276–339), as the grand councilor under the first emperor of the

---

49. Sima Qian, *Shiji* 7.336.
50. Zhao Mingcheng, *Jinshi lu jiaozheng* 7.125 (no. 1325).
51. *Jianzhu* 2.256.

Eastern (i.e., southern) Jin, stabilized the frantic court and chided those who gave up hope of recovering the north. Liu Kun (270–317) was a Jin loyalist general who fought valiantly for the Jin in the north, where he eventually lost his life.[52] Li Qingzhao signifies that no such heroes are evident in her own time of dynastic disaster.

The second couplet is:

南遊尚覺吳江冷   Traveling south we yet feel the Wu River is chilly,
北狩應悲易水寒   The northern expedition must grieve that Yi Stream is cold.[53]

This Wu River (a different one from that discussed earlier) is near Jiangning 江寧, where Li Qingzhao and her husband found themselves on their southern flight in 1128. "The Wu River is chilly" is a phrase drawn from a Tang poetic anecdote, but in Li Qingzhao's usage "chilly" reflects the state of mind of refugees from the north, like Li Qingzhao, who ironically find that the southern landscape is, in their eyes, cold and unappealing.[54] The second line alludes euphemistically to the capture of the two Song emperors Huizong and Qinzong (r. 1126–27) by the Jurchen and their northern captivity (their "expedition"). This line too contains a literary allusion, this time to the biography of Jing Ke 荆軻 (d. 227 BCE), the would-be assassin of the First Emperor of Qin, and the famous scene in which he bids farewell to his supporters on the banks of the "cold Yi Stream," knowing that he is going to his death.[55]

It is Zhuang Chuo 莊綽 who quotes these two fragments from Li Qingzhao's poems, in his miscellany that he completed in the 1130s.[56] The quotations appear at the end of an entry that contains several witty sayings or aphorisms concerning the Jurchen conquest. All of the quoted lines satirize the inept Song leadership for being ill-prepared for the invasion, proving unable to counterattack and win back the north, or being unable to protect the south from continued incursions even after the loss of the north. The

---

52. See the men's biographies in *Jinshu* 晉書 62.1679–93 (Liu) and 65.1745–54 (Wang).

53. *Jianzhu* 2.258.

54. For the anecdote see *Jiu Tangshu* 190A.4988.

55. Sima Qian, *Shiji* 86.2534.

56. Zhuang Chuo's *Jile bian* has a preface dated 1133 (Shaoxing 3), but as the modern editors point out, the work includes references to events that happened a few years later, in 1139, so Zhuang evidently continued to insert material after he wrote the preface. See *Jile bian*, p. i.

first lines Zhuang cites were devised by irreverent National University students (e.g., "Our court did not resist the mighty Jin [gold] but they prohibited the private minting of coins [gold]" 不禦大金禁銷金). Another utterance adapted phrases from the *Thousand Character Classic* to ridicule the ineptness of the Southern Song's defenses, which could not stop Jurchen incursions south of the Yangzi each winter so that residents had to hide in the mountains (giving new meaning to the phrase "store away [our harvest] in the winter").

Zhuang Chuo saves Li Qingzhao's lines for last in this list of witticisms, and he says this by way of introducing them: "At the time, Zhao Mingcheng's wife, Li Qingzhao, likewise composed poems to disparage the scholar-officials." Zhuang is surely thinking of the irony that this mockery of the lack of stalwart leadership and martial valor as well as the pathetic condition of the two captive emperors would have been penned by a woman, and it is probably why he saves Li Qingzhao's lines for last. He suggests that the situation is so shameful that even a woman (note that she is identified as her husband's wife) was moved to write about the humiliation of it all. Li Qingzhao's couplets must, in fact, have been widely known. They are quoted in other early Southern Song sources as well, apparently independently of Zhuang Chuo's entry.[57]

Li Qingzhao's sharp tongue in poetry extended to other topics as well. In 1132 she wrote lines that make fun of a young man who had just placed first in that year's *jinshi* examination. Again, what survives is just a couplet from Li Qingzhao, and in this case we do not know whether the couplet stood by itself or was part of a complete poem. The young man was Zhang Jiucheng 張九成, and the object of Li Qingzhao's satire was the essay he wrote that won him the top place in the exam. In response to a question put to the candidates by Emperor Gaozong himself, Zhang Jiucheng had written an ornate and fawning answer, in mellifluous prose, imagining how the emperor could not enjoy even the sweetest delights of the four seasons, the sumptuous dishes served to him, or his lavish palace rooms because, whenever a pleasure presented itself to him, he would invariably think of the hardships being endured by the former Song emperors (his father and older brother) in their harsh northern captivity. Gaozong is said to have been so impressed by the

---

57. Including *Shishuo junyong* 詩說雋永 (dated ca. 1150), which in turn is quoted in Hu Zi, *Tiaoxi yuyin conghua*, "Houji" 40.335; Ruan Yue, *Shihua zonggui*, "Houji" 48.301; and Wei Qingzhi, *Shiren yuxie* 20.460.

answer that he awarded Zhang top place in the examination. Li Qingzhao, by contrast, was unimpressed, probably feeling that the lugubrious content and sycophantic tone of the answer were inappropriate in an exam paper that was supposed to be an objective analysis of court policy.[58] One of the pleasures Zhang said that Gaozong could not enjoy was "the wafting fragrance of cassia blossoms at night" 夜桂飄香. Li Qingzhao proceeded to lampoon that line, making it part of a couplet that paired Zhang Jiucheng with Liu Yong, the songwriter notorious for his romantic song lyrics:

露花倒影柳三變　　"Dewdrops cast their shadows": Liu Sanbian,
桂子飄香張九成　　"Cassias waft their fragrance": Zhang Jiucheng.[59]

The phrase Li Qingzhao selected from Liu Yong (Sanbian) comes from a song lyric he wrote on an extravagant imperial boating party and banquet, filled with lavish displays and gorgeously dressed palace women.[60] The implication of Li Qingzhao's couplet is that the newly awarded Number One Scholar is, in fact, as frivolous and sentimental as the man who epitomized, in literati eyes, the worst of such excesses in popular entertainment songs. In fact, Li Qingzhao's parody of Zhang Jiucheng is reminiscent of her criticism of the court for its weakness in the face of the Jurchen invasion in that it is the lack of substance and backbone in Zhang's essay that she belittles. Her lines on Zhang Jiucheng must have circulated widely: they are quoted anonymously by Ye Mengde 葉夢得 (1077–1148), who says that people considered them an apt and ingenious pairing.[61] Later, it is Lu You who identifies Li Qingzhao as their source.[62]

There are even two instances of poetic lines Li Qingzhao addressed to her father-in-law, Zhao Tingzhi 趙挺之 (1040–1107), that are quoted in early sources for being outspoken and remarkable. These survive as single lines because that is the way they are quoted, and we do not know whether they originally belonged to the same poem. Zhao was an extremely prominent official in the early years of Huizong's reign. An experienced reform party member, he was one of the leaders of the new waves of attacks on the Yuanyou 元祐 party members in 1101. Partly perhaps to reward that service,

---

58. This is Xu Peijun's suggestion in *Jianzhu* 2.261.
59. Xu Peijun, in *Jianzhu* 2.259.
60. Liu Yong, "Pozhen yue" 破陣樂, *Quan Songci* 1:35.
61. Ye Mengde, *Yanxia fangyan* A.322.
62. Lu You, *Laoxue an biji* 2.2362.

he was recommended by Cai Jing 蔡京 (1047–1126) to become co–grand councilor together with Cai in 1105. The two men soon had a falling out. Moreover, a comet appeared in the sky in 1106, and Huizong, terrified by this display of Heaven's disfavor, quickly rescinded many of Cai Jing's policies. Cai's ensuing removal from the court left Zhao as the sole grand councilor. Zhao's supremacy was short-lived, however. Cai Jing found a way to return to power in the following year, whereupon it was Zhao's turn to be cashiered. The removal must have been a crushing blow to Zhao, for he died five days later.

We cannot be sure of the exact year of the poem or poems Li Qingzhao sent to her father-in-law; they must have been written between the time she married his son in 1101 and the time of his demotion and death in 1107. In other words, they were written during the years that Zhao Tingzhi was near or at the height of his towering official career. We have already glimpsed the first of these lines in Chao Gongwu's entry on her writings. It is this:

炙手可熱心可寒   Hot enough to scorch the hand, but chilling to the heart.[63]

This is apparently a description of her father-in-law's effect on those who approached him: he radiated such power and majesty that anyone who brushed up against him was liable to be scorched, and he was also intimidating enough to bring a chill to an onlooker's heart. It is an ingenious line for its pairing of hot and cold, and it is also memorable for the candor with which Li Qingzhao as daughter-in-law describes Zhao Tingzhi. As seen earlier, it is the one line from all of Li Qingzhao's writings that the bibliophile Chao Gongwu quotes in his notice on Li Qingzhao's literary collection, and he quotes it in connection with his statement that "she was famous for her literary talent" 有才藻名.[64]

The other line describing her father-in-law is this:

何況人間父子情   How much more, given the feelings between father and child.[65]

Owing to his association with Su Shi and other prominent Yuanyou party figures, Li Qingzhao's father, Li Gefei, was listed among the Yuanyou "traitors" in the expanded lists drawn up in 1104, when Zhao Tingzhi was

---

63. *Jianzhu* 2.255.
64. Chao Gongwu, *Junzhai dushu zhi jiaozheng* 19.1033.
65. *Jianzhu* 2.253.

already grand councilor, and Li was banished to distant Xiang Prefecture (near Liuzhou, Guangxi).[66] According to the source that quotes this line, it was part of a poetic appeal Li Qingzhao sent to her father-in-law requesting clemency, or at least some consideration, for her exiled father.[67] Li Qingzhao refers in the line to her own distress over her father's distant exile, hoping that this may help to persuade Zhao Tingzhi to do something to reduce her father's punishment.

Whether Li Qingzhao was writing about political history, the humiliation of the Jurchen invasion, recent degree awardees, or even family matters, time and again she produced poems marked by strong and often caustic opinions. These poems were frequently noted and quoted by her contemporaries as remarkable, and particularly remarkable coming from a woman. The voice that she affects in these poems is not what her contemporaries expected to find in writing done by a woman.

"On Song Lyrics"

There is another important piece of writing by Li Qingzhao that expresses her struggle to overcome the dismissive attitude that her aspirations encountered and to win some critical acceptance for her work in the eyes of the arbiters of literary taste and achievement. That is her essay on the song lyric form, in which she presents her views on the distinctive prosodic features of the form and offers a sketch of its history and a critique of the major writers of the Northern Song period.

"On Song Lyrics" is not ordinarily read this way. It is normally read simply as a bold critique of the leading song lyrics writers of the day. It is sometimes taken as evidence of Li Qingzhao's strong and independent character (especially by scholars with feminist tendencies), shown by her boldness in offering a negative assessment of acclaimed literati of her day. The essay is also taken as an expression of the pride Li Qingzhao took in her own understanding of the song lyrics genre and the high standards she wanted to apply

---

66. *Jianzhu* 2.255–56, n. 1.

67. Zhang Yan 張琰, in the preface he wrote in 1138 to Li Gefei's *Luoyang mingyuan ji* 洛陽名園記, *Huibian*, p. 4. Xu Peijun has another reading of the line. He suggests that Li Qingzhao is addressing a rift between Zhao Tingzhi and his son (her husband), and asking that Tingzhi consider the natural feelings between "father and son"; see *Jianzhu* 2.253–54, n. 1. But Zhang Yan's reading, being the contemporary one, has more credibility.

in its composition and evaluation. These interpretations all have validity, but I intend to suggest a different reading of the essay. I read it as a statement about the song lyric springing fundamentally from her own sense of the challenge she faced as a woman writer who wished to accomplish something in that literary form. Certainly she wanted to convey her views of the major writers of recent decades. But she is writing not simply as a critic and still less as a critic whose own creative aspirations—highly unusual ones for her gender—are irrelevant to the subject at hand. In complex ways, "On Song Lyrics" reveals at every turn its author's predicament as a woman who was determined to write in this form and to do so as well or better than any man. Earlier we have seen ample evidence of the attitudes arrayed against her. The popular enthusiasm for her work, especially in the song lyric, did little to diminish the skepticism of the educated elite toward her as a woman writer. Indeed, popular acclaim was used by elite critics as evidence of the superficiality of her output.

When she composed "On Song Lyrics," Li Qingzhao was writing within a world of ideas and attitudes against which she was pitted even as she sought to point to an alternative set of values. It is little wonder, then, that the arguments she put forth are subtle, original, and ingenious.

A translation of the essay is given below. There are difficulties with some sentences. The passage on prosody contains technical terminology, and there is disagreement among specialists today about the precise meaning of some of the terms. Nevertheless, the main points and overall import of the essay are clear.

On Song Lyrics

Music Bureau songs and poems set to music, as complementary verse forms, reached their apogee during the Tang. During the Kaiyuan and Tianbao reigns, there was a certain Li Balang, who was the most talented singer in the entire empire. Once, when those who had just passed the *jinshi* examination were being feted at Serpentine River, among the honored guests was a gentleman of renown who, before the feast, had summoned Li and told him to change his clothes and disguise his name. The clothes he wore that day were particularly tattered, and he affected a mournful and dispirited expression as he accompanied the gentleman of renown to the feast. The gentleman announced to the other guests, "My younger cousin wants to sit at the end of the table." The others paid no attention to him. After the wine was passed around and music began, the singers entered. At the time, Cao Yuanqian and Niannu were the most celebrated singing girls in the capital. When they finished singing, the assembled guests all sighed with admiration and gave shouts of approval.

The renowned gentleman suddenly pointed at Li and said, "Let's have my cousin sing." The guests looked at Li and sneered, and some even became angry. But Li cleared his throat and began to sing, and by the time he finished one song, the guests were all moved to tears. Gathering around him they bowed and exclaimed, "This must be Li Balang!" Thereafter the "music of Zheng and Wei" became more popular by the day, and ornate new musical tunes multiplied. These included the tunes "Bodhisattva Barbarian," "The Spring Scene Is Lovely," "The Katydid," "The Waterclock," "Sands of the Washing Stream," "Dreaming of the Southland," "The Fisherman," and others, too many to fully list.

During the warfare of the Five Dynasties, the empire was sliced up like a melon and peeled apart like a bean, so that culture and learning were extinguished. Yet the Jiangnan kingdom ruled by the Li clan and its ministers still prized literary elegance. They wrote songs that had such lines as "Played no more in the low tower, the jade flute is cold" and "Wind-blown ripples fill the whole pool of spring waters." The language is certainly marvelous; still these are what is known as "the sorrowfully reflective melodies of a realm going to ruin."

When our present dynasty arose, the rites, music, literary learning, and military prowess were fully restored. After some one hundred years of beneficent influence, Liu Yong, the Military Farms officer, appeared. He rewrote old songs and composed new tunes, producing his *Song Lyrics Collection*, which was acclaimed by the age. Although his works meet the prosodic rules, his diction is down in the dirt. After him there was Zhang Ziye [Xian], Song Zijing [Qi] and his brother, Shen Tang, Yuan Jiang, and Chao Ciyan; and their kind appeared one after the other. Although here and there they too produced marvelous lines, yet their works are so fragmentary that they hardly could be considered major writers. Next came Yan Yuanxian [Shu], Ouyang Yongshu [Xiu], and Su Zizhan [Shi]. Their learning plumbed the extremes of heaven and humankind. When they composed little song lyrics, it was like drawing a small gourd of water out from a great ocean. Still, what they wrote reads like nothing more than *shi* poetry that has not been properly polished, and frequently their lines violate the prosodic rules.

Why is this? It is because while *shi* poetry distinguishes between "level" and "oblique" tones, the song lyric distinguishes five notes. It also distinguishes five tones, six musical modes, and the difference between "clear" and "turgid," and "light" and "heavy" syllables. Moreover, the tunes known today as "Sound after Sound: Long Form," "Blossoms in the Rain," and "Enjoying the Darting Oriole" may, in addition to using the "level" tone rhyme, also use the "entering" tone rhyme. "Spring in the Jade Tower" originally required the "level" tone rhyme, but it may also use the "rising" or the "falling" tone rhymes, as well as the "entering" tone rhymes. Songs that originally required the "deflected" tone rhymes, may still accord with the rules if written to "rising" tone rhymes. But if a writer sets them to "entering" tone rhymes, they become impossible to sing.

The writing of Wang Jiefu [Anshi] and Zeng Zigu [Gong] resembles the style of the Western Han period. But when they write little song lyrics, people fall down laughing because their songs simply cannot be read. We can see, therefore, that this form of writing is a field unto itself, and those who understand it are few.

Later, Yan Shuyuan [Jidao], He Fanghui [Zhu], Qin Shaoyou [Guan], and Huang Luzhi [Tingjian] appeared, and they were the first to truly understand the genre. But Yan's works suffer from lack of narrative exposition, and He's suffer from inadequate substance and classical style. Qin cares only about emotions and has too few literary allusions. His works are like a beautiful girl from a poor family. Although she may be gorgeous and radiant, she will never have the bearing of a lady from an affluent and high-ranking clan. As for Huang, although he prizes literary allusions, his works have many defects. They are like jade that has blemishes, reducing its value by one-half.[68]

As mentioned earlier, it is generally thought that Li Qingzhao's "On Song Lyrics" was written relatively early, when she was in her twenties or early thirties. That dating is derived primarily from the conspicuous omission of Zhou Bangyan from her list of the latest outstanding writers, given at the end of the text. It was not until 1116 that Zhou Bangyan came to real prominence at Huizong's court, being recalled to it from the provinces. Once back at court, he was given a series of prestigious posts, including director of the Palace Library 祕書監, edict attendant 待制, and finally director of the Imperial Music Bureau 大晟府 (1122). His appointment to this last post owed something to his reputation as an authority on music and song lyric composition. Even though during these years Li Qingzhao was off in Qingzhou living "in seclusion," it is difficult to believe that she would not have heard of Zhou Bangyan's reputation, as the most prominent song lyrics writer of the day, by the early 1120s. Hence her essay is conventionally dated as belonging to the period before the 1120s.

Li Qingzhao's "On Song Lyrics" is one of several important pieces of song lyrics criticism that were written at the end of the eleventh century or in the first decades of the twelfth. The others include Huang Tingjian's preface to Yan Jidao's 晏幾道 song collection, Yan Jidao's own preface to his song collection (both probably written around 1100), Zhang Lei's preface to He

---

68. "Cilun" 詞論, *Jianzhu* 3.266–67.

Zhu's songs, and Li Zhiyi's 李之儀 colophon to Wu Sidao's 吳思道 songs (both probably dating from about 1110).[69] Taken together, these several texts constitute an important stage in the development of song lyrics criticism.[70] They advance more ambitious claims for the legitimacy and seriousness of the genre than had ever been made previously. Even as Li Qingzhao's "On Song Lyrics" is a member of this development and group of critical essays, it differs in interesting ways from the other texts.

One of the noteworthy aspects of Li Qingzhao's essay is that it embraces the notion of the song lyric as a lowly, even dissolute, form and does not attempt to argue against that characterization. We see various manifestations of this. The first is in her characterization of the song lyric as "music of Zheng and Wei" and "ornate musical tunes." Usually when language of this sort is applied to the song lyric it is heavily pejorative and meant to denigrate the form as consisting of immoral content and empty verbal ornament. In Li Qingzhao's usage, however, these phrases are used acceptingly, simply to designate the form. She does not contest the strong negative connotations they carry. This motif of the song lyric as lowly and an alternative to what is respectable surfaces again in what she says next about the song lyric during the Five Dynasties period. She calls attention to the fact that even when the Great Tradition was no longer prevalent, damaged by the warfare and political fragmentation of the period, somehow outstanding song lyrics continued to be produced. There is an opposition here between the song lyric and high literature and culture (*siwen* 斯文). Li Qingzhao has already made it clear that the song lyric stands apart from *siwen* and can thrive even when *siwen* is in recession. Though she may describe the song lyric as "melodies of a realm going to ruin," she emphasizes that these melodies nevertheless have their appeal and beauty.

There is already an important difference here between Li Qingzhao's essay and the other pieces of song lyric criticism produced at roughly the same time. The other writers argue against the lowly stature of the song lyric in one

---

69. All these pieces are reproduced in Jin Qihua et al., *Tang Song ciji xuba huibian*: Huang Tingjian, "Xiaoshan ji xu" 小山集序, pp. 25–26; Yan Jidao, "Xiaoshan ci zixu" 小山詞自序, p. 25; Zhang Lei, "Dongshan ci xu" 東山詞序, p. 59; and Li Zhiyi, "Ba Wusidao xiaoci" 跋吳思道小詞, p. 36.

70. I have discussed these essays, together with Li Qingzhao's, in the context of song lyric history and criticism in *The Problem of Beauty*, pp. 302–26.

way or another. They seek to demonstrate that the genre's disrepute is undeserved and offer new ways of connecting it with more respectable traditions.
Thus Yan Jidao connects the song lyric with the ancient *yuefu* tradition, going
so far as to claim that there is nothing in the subject matter or feelings found
in his song lyrics that was not already found in ancient *yuefu*. He has an
ingenious answer to the objection that extant *yuefu* from earlier times do not
support this claim: such *yuefu* did exist, he insists, but they were lost. Consequently, he even titles his collection *Filling in What Was Lost* 補亡集,
reiterating the connection he wants readers to make between his song lyrics
and ancient, that is, venerable, song.[71] Huang Tingjian comes up with an even
more clever line of thought in the parallel preface he wrote for Yan Jidao's
collection. Rather than connect Yan's song lyrics with ancient verse, Huang
turns them into an indicator of Yan Jidao's highmindedness and superiority
of character. Huang accomplishes this through a familiar inversion of appearance and import, whereby apparent foolishness actually signifies wisdom,
and apparent degradedness actually indicates elevation over ordinary men.
Yan, Huang states, is a man too lofty in character to bend to the sordid ways
of the world. His decision to write only in the apparently frivolous song lyric
form thus becomes a sign of his superior cultivation: unlike other men he
does not need to vent worldly frustration in serious verse. His superior character is what draws him to the literary form that others think of as lowly. It is
one of several "foolishnesses" 痴 that Huang attributes to Yan and that are
the key features of his personality. The other "foolishnesses" include his
inability to curry favor with the rich and powerful, his refusal to mimic the
writing style of recent successful examination candidates, which would have
furthered his official career, and his willingness to give large amounts of
money to friends, even though they never repay him. The reader is meant to
understand that each of these "foolishnesses," including Yan's devotion to
song lyric composition, is actually a sign of great inner virtue and cultivation.

   As Li Qingzhao's essay continues, she develops a related type of opposition. This contrast is not between the song lyric and *siwen* but between the
song lyric and learning (*xue* 學), and her focus shifts from an earlier time
period to specific writers of her own era. The comments she makes on Liu
Yong are conventional, and the next writers she takes up do not present

---

71. This is the title of his collection used in the text of the preface. But in the preface title,
the collection name is changed to *Xiaoshan ci* 小山詞.

much of an opportunity for her—they are minor figures both within *ci* history and outside it. But the cases of Yan Shu 晏殊 (991–1055), Ouyang Xiu, and Su Shi, all major writers, scholars, and statesmen, present her with an opportunity to develop the theme that is dear to her heart. For such eminent men of learning to turn their attention to song lyric composition was like taking a mere gourdful of water from a vast ocean. The ocean is their learning and their other writings; the gourd of water is their song lyrics. Yet here a contrary theme is introduced. Despite the great disparity in significance and stature between their learning and their song lyrics, it turns out that they are not adept at the minor form. They try to compose it, but what comes out is some strange hybrid that reads like poorly written *shi* poetry. A similar critique of famous writers and scholars reappears later in the essay, after the paragraph devoted to song lyric prosody. The prose writings of Wang Anshi 王安石 (1021–86) and Zeng Gong 曾鞏 (1019–83), for which they were famous, resemble the style of the Western Han (i.e., Former Han), which had long been considered the model for all Confucian, didactic prose writing. But then Li Qingzhao abruptly deflates the reference to this august learning, subjecting it to ridicule. When such weighty writers as Wang and Zeng try their hand at song lyric composition, she continues, the result is completely laughable. The opposition between the song lyric and high culture is more starkly posed than before. It now begins to sound like high achievement in learning and classical prose writing are actually impediments to song lyric composition. A scholar who has mastered the Western Han mode of expression will necessarily be unable to write song lyrics, and if he is foolish enough to try to do it, he will send people into fits of laughter. The disparities between the song lyric and accomplishment in other fields leads to the concluding assertions: the song lyric is a field unto itself, and those who understand it are truly few.

Li Zhiyi makes a point in his preface to Wu Sidao's collection that looks, at first, similar to what Li Qingzhao says about Yan Shu, Ouyang Xiu, and Su Shi. He says that Yan Shu, Ouyang Xiu, and Song Qi 宋祁 (998–1061), although they were among the finest song lyric writers of their day, were, when they composed in the form, "amusing themselves with their residual energy" 以其餘力遊戲. One of the main points of Li Zhiyi's discussion is that the song lyric is difficult to write well and requires the utmost effort, concentration, and polishing. Thus the gist of his remark about the way the three writers treated the song lyric is to fault them for not taking it seriously enough and looking upon it as a diversion from more weighty pursuits. Like

Li Qingzhao, then, Li Zhiyi is keenly aware of the distance, in the eyes of these writers, between the song lyric and the more prestigious literary forms. But his argument is the reverse of Li Qingzhao's in the sense that he wants the song lyric to be elevated to the level of the other more prestigious genres. Li Qingzhao is not arguing for such elevation. She stresses instead the incompatibility of mastery of the song lyric with mastery of other forms.

This same distance between Li Qingzhao and the other critics is evident in what they say about the generic nature of the song lyric and its relation to older song forms and *shi* poetry. Li Qingzhao emphasizes the unique prosodic features of the song lyric, which makes it an entity unto itself that few people understand. The other critics stress the affinities between the song lyric and its more venerable cousins. Yan Jidao asserts that ancient *yuefu* writers already approximated the style and content of the song lyric. Huang Tingjian praises Yan Jidao's compositions as the Major Court Songs (*daya* 大雅) of the entertainment districts. He goes on to say that the best among them are in the tradition of the ancient "Gaotang" and "Luo Goddess" rhapsodies, and that even the inferior ones are comparable to celebrated ancient songs. In a similar fashion, Zhang Lei says that the song lyrics of He Zhu are as "poignant and pure" as the rhapsodies of Qu Yuan 屈原 (4th c. BCE) and Song Yu 宋玉 (3rd c. BCE), and they are as "sorrowful and manly" as the poetry of Li Ling 李陵 and Su Wu 蘇武 (1st c. BCE). Li Qingzhao does not attempt to establish any such pedigree for the song lyric. She is content to have the form inhabit its own separate aesthetic and literary space.

The discussion here has been circling the issue of the gendering of *ci* in the thinking of Li Qingzhao and the other critics. Now it is time to face the topic head-on. Major literary genres like *shi* poetry and the song lyric are too broad and flexible to permit reduction to a simple gendered association or identity. Still, in general conception there is yet a gendered proclivity of each form. *Shi* poetry tends toward the masculine, and the song lyric tends toward the feminine. These proclivities are captured in the traditional saying "the song lyric is dainty whereas *shi* poetry is solemn" 詞媚詩莊. References to gender, both explicit and implicit, occur repeatedly in the essays under consideration and constitute an important aspect of them as a group. The opposition Li Qingzhao develops between the song lyric and high culture or learning as well as that between it and *shi* poetry has clear-cut gender implications. Rarely women may compose in the poetic forms, especially the song lyric, but "learning" remains unambiguously the domain of men, and within that domain, "Western Han writing" 西漢文章 is the most masculine of the masculine. Thus the image Li Qingzhao presents of the Western Han style writers like Wang Anshi and Zeng Gong attempting to compose song lyrics, only to make fools of themselves, is largely the image of solemn and self-important men trying to act like charming girls—no wonder others burst out laughing. Later, Li Qingzhao offers up another image of a man attempting to play the part of a woman and also being unsuccessful in the effort. This time it is Qin Guan, whose song lyrics feature romantic feelings (as Li Qingzhao notes) and who later critics dubbed a leader of the feminine, or *wanyue* 婉約, style of song lyric writing. In Li Qingzhao's eyes, Qin Guan is trying to impersonate a lady. But the lack of literary references and allusions in his songs means that he can only be a "beautiful girl from a poor family." She may be pretty, but she is unrefined. It is hard not to read this statement as a projection of Li Qingzhao's sense that such male writers, who after all couch many of their songs in the voices of women, will never really be able to affect the female voice they are after. They try to cultivate the voice of a sophisticated, well-to-do lady, but they do not know how to do so, and they end up affecting an inferior voice. Li Qingzhao, who really is a well-bred lady, does not need to pretend in order to sound like one. It is possible to recognize that these gender meanings and tensions are present in Li Qingzhao's essay without going so far as to say that she intends to claim song lyrics as a women's genre or literary domain, one that should properly "belong" to women writers (as Wilt Idema and Beata Grant have suggested).[72] The genre had for too long been dominated by male writers for Li Qingzhao to entertain such a notion. Indeed, it was male writers who created the "feminine" aesthetic and aura of the genre. But the language of Li Qingzhao's essay does suggest, time and again in different ways, that she believes that, as a woman writing in the form, she has a certain advantage over male writers.

If Li Qingzhao stresses the feminine qualities of the song lyric and claims that male writers often make themselves look ridiculous when composing in the form, male critics take much the opposite approach. They do not write about *ci* as a masculine form (that would strain credulity) but as something a man need not be ashamed to be involved with. The most memorable passage in this regard is this one from Zhang Lei's preface to He Zhu's collection:

---

72. "Li Qingzhao's (conservative) insistence on the 'feminine' characteristics of the genre, however, should perhaps be interpreted as an attempt to protect the [song] lyric from being subverted by the male-dominated *shi* genre and to ensure that women had 'a genre of their own.'" Idema and Grant, *Red Brush*, p. 235.

Among historical figures known for their prowess, ferocity, and martial valor, no one surpasses Liu Bang and Xiang Yu. When did these two heroes ever indulge in the simpering sentimentality of boys and girls? But when one of them returned to his hometown, he was overcome with feeling, and when the other bid farewell to his concubine, he wept. Their sentiments were expressed in words and poured forth as songs, the emotion in them so poignant that those who heard them were moved to their very core.[73]

This is indeed an ingenious argument. The reputation of Liu Bang and Xiang Yu as great warriors is beyond question, and yet, Zhang Lei reminds us, each one gave in to his emotions on at least one occasion and burst forth in a sentimental song. The dichotomy is clear: warriors/masculinity is juxtaposed with sentimentality/heartfelt song. Zhang Lei is arguing against the assumption that the two are incompatible or that, if a man expresses himself in sentimental song, he compromises his masculinity. In the context of a preface to a collection of song lyrics, Zhang Lei's statement about Liu Bang and Xiang Yu serves to defend the author, He Zhu, against any criticism that it is unmanly for him to be so preoccupied with this feminine literary genre. Zhang Lei is right to anticipate such criticism—it was widespread in Northern Song times—and he cleverly takes steps to neutralize it before it can be articulated. By formulating such arguments, just as by repeatedly affirming the connections between the song lyric and older and more respectable literary forms, Zhang Lei and other critics seek to overcome the bias against the form as being unmanly and consisting merely of frivolous, self-indulgent, and childish sentiments. Male critics are apprehensive over this issue and constantly construct arguments to address it. Writing as a woman, Li Qingzhao is much more comfortable with the feminine associations of the song lyric and does not try to deny or recast them.

Viewing Li Qingzhao's essay in this light, it is possible to find new meaning in the opening section of the piece. Rita Felski and others working on feminist approaches to women writers have pointed out that, when women choose to enter the textual world dominated by male writers and patriarchal values, what they express often contains both oppositional and concessive elements. There is both rejection of conventional values—the ones that subjugate them in patriarchal society—and some degree of complicity. This is practically inevitable. The women are entering into a world not of their

---

73. Zhang Lei, "Dongshan ci zu," in Jin Qihua et al., *Tang Song ciji xuba huibian*, p. 59.

own creation: the forms, vocabulary, and thought that constitute it have entirely been developed by male writers and belonged to them. On the one hand, women cannot avoid adopting the expressive media and conceptual categories that have been standardized without their input. On the other hand, it would be an unusual woman whose gendered identity as an outsider to this world would not show itself in one way or another as an implicit or explicit challenge to the patriarchal world of thought and expression. The isolation in which women wrote—there was not yet in Li Qingzhao's time anything like a community of writing women—virtually assures that whatever oppositional values a woman writer like Li Qingzhao expresses will be veiled to some degree. "The true meaning of women's writing," Felski notes, "lies beneath the surface, in covert messages and submerged clues. Because this meaning is socially unacceptable and even subversive, it is buried deep within the text."[74] This may not always be so, but we should not be surprised if we encounter such covert strategies of conveying meaning.

The story about Li Balang is, on the face of it, a strange beginning to Li Qingzhao's discussion of song lyrics. The conventional thing to do when writing an account of the song lyric and its history was to trace its origins back to ancient *yuefu* or other poetic forms. Li Qingzhao refrains from doing that. She starts instead with an anecdote set in a particular time and place (the Tang capital during its heyday) featuring a particular singer. Li Qingzhao did not make up this story; she borrowed it from Li Zhao's 李肇 Tang miscellany *Tang guoshi bu* 唐国史補.[75] But the story was not particularly famous or well-known. Indeed, Li Balang is remembered today because of Li Qingzhao's inclusion of the story about him in her essay. He has no fame outside of Li Qingzhao's reference to him. The original version of the anecdote in *Tang guoshi bu* simply narrates the events for their inherent interest. No claim is made that the disguising of Li Balang, his performance, and the eventual revelation of his true identity have any greater significance. It is Li Qingzhao who transforms the story from an inconsequential anecdote with no claim to larger import into a watershed in the history of the song lyric. "After this," she says at the conclusion of the passage, indecent songs flourished, and the number of ornate variations in the genre became larger day by day. We might want to question the logic of cause and consequence here. Why would the

---

74. Felski, *Literature after Feminism*, p. 69.
75. Li Zhao, *Xinjiao Tang guoshi bu* C.59.

sequence of events described have such a momentous effect on the popularity of entertainment songs? If the claim were a different one, for example, that thereafter male singers became more popular and widely accepted, the logic would be more persuasive. But as it stands, the conclusion seems poorly matched with the narrative itself.

Given all these oddities, we might reasonably ask if there might not be some significance to the passage beyond the surface meaning that it first conveys. Might there be a veiled meaning that, once glimpsed, would allow us better to understand why Li Qingzhao featured the passage at the opening of her essay and attributed such a telling impact to the events it describes?

A skilled male singer is brought in disguise into a gala banquet of new *jinshi* degree awardees. He is deliberately dressed to make him look out of place rather than as one who fits in (as he might have been disguised). It is a celebratory gathering of elegant and bright young men who have abundant future promise. But Li Balang is dressed in slovenly clothes and appears to be dispirited. He seems singularly ill-suited to be present. The unnamed participant who sponsors him thus refers to him diminutively as "younger cousin" and specifies that he wishes to be seated in a place befitting persons of lower stature. Naturally, then, the other guests do not deign to pay attention to him. This "younger cousin" is clearly an interloper, someone not fit to be present at such a distinguished gathering. The female entertainers who are eventually brought in are not just any entertainers but the most famous ones of the day. When the older cousin of the slovenly fellow then suggests that his morose relative be given a chance to sing, the suggestion is understandably greeted with dismay and some annoyance. But then the fellow sings and acquits himself brilliantly so that everyone is moved. The guests immediately recognize Li Balang for who he is—such talent cannot be mistaken—and bow to him in deference. The masquerade is over, and disparagement gives way to honor.

It is easy to see how this story of talent veiled under an unpromising appearance could have had special meaning for Li Qingzhao as she embarked on her essay that challenges the accomplishments of the leading writers of the day and presents an unforgiving assessment of the weaknesses of their work. The role of gender in the story is of particular interest. Entertainment songs of the day were performed overwhelmingly by women, but not exclusively so. It was still possible to have a talented male performer, although he would be a rarity, a curiosity. As a writer of song lyrics, Li Qingzhao was an interloper in a man's world. How better to open her critique than with a reminder that a talented person of seemingly the wrong station in life and the wrong gender might yet excel or even outdo those of the right appearance and right gender? Li Qingzhao could not have opened her account with the story of a woman outdoing men in something at which men were supposed to excel. That would be too transparent, and besides probably no such story existed in song lyrics lore. Instead she tells the story of a man outdoing women and lets readers draw their own conclusions. But the import is clear: a person who is perceived to have no place in such a social circle and whose offer to perform is greeted with the deepest skepticism may indeed belie the assumptions surrounding her appearance and gender. All that person needs is to be given a chance.

The changes Li Qingzhao made in the *Tang guoshi bu* version of the story provide additional support for the interpretation offered here, which was first proposed by Li Guowen 李國文.[76] This is the *Tang guoshi bu* version:

> Li Gun [Li Balang] was skilled at singing. At first he lived south of the Yangzi River, but his fame already resounded in the capital. When Cui Zhao went to the court, he brought Li with him secretly. One day, Cui hosted a grand banquet: he invited guests and specially asked the first troupe of imperial musicians to attend as well as the capital's famous singers. He falsely introduced Li as a younger cousin and bade him to sit in the place of least honor. He had instructed Li to dress himself that day in tattered clothes. Seeing him, the guests scoffed and laughed at him. After some time, offering a toast, Zhao said, "I want to invite my young cousin to sing." The guests all laughed again. But as soon as a few notes came out of his mouth, the musicians were all astonished and declared, "This must be Li Balang!" They encircled him and bowed to him from below the steps.[77]

The Tang anecdote is essentially the story of a ruse involving a great singer. It is a story of mistaken identity and how musical talent may be at odds with outer appearance.

Li Qingzhao rewrites the story, subtly altering several of its elements and hence the general impression it conveys. She dispenses with the geographic contrast in the opening between the capital and the distant south. That geographic element is extraneous to her purpose and would not match her own situation. Next, she changes the nature of the banquet. It is no longer just any banquet in the capital. It is specifically a banquet given in honor of newly

76. Li Guowen, "'Hua zi piaoling shui ziliu,'"pp. 220–21. Li simply asserts the equivalence between Li Balang and Li Qingzhao, without elaboration or argumentation.

77. Li Zhao, *Xinjiao Tang guoshi bu* C.59.

passed *jinshi* degree holders. Those in attendance are the young literary lumi-naries of the empire. It is such a gathering of literary talents who the singers will be trying to impress. The gulf between the disguised Li Balang and the other guests—and hence the inappropriateness of his presence in the dis-tinguished company—is emphasized in Li Qingzhao's account. Balang is not only dressed shabbily; his manner is morose and sullen, which makes him all the more ill-suited to be at the celebratory feast. In the earlier version of the anecdote, the other guests at least take notice of Balang upon his entrance, if only to laugh at him. In Li Qingzhao's version so great is the social and cultural distance between Balang and the others that the others simply pay no attention to him. It is as if he does not exist in their eyes.

Li Qingzhao dramatizes and develops the performance scene in the anec-dote. She specifies the names of the female singers and describes the guests' emotional reaction to their singing. Suddenly, then, the famous scholar "points to Li" and invites him to sing. Not only do the other guests laugh derisively (as in Li Zhao's account), but "some even become angry" 或有怒者. This line is particularly significant. Why the anger? Li Qingzhao has taken pains to represent how thoroughly the guests are enjoying the performance by the most outstanding female singers of the day. Now the marvelous performance is about to be interrupted by a person who looks particularly ill-suited for the occasion. It is understandable that some guests would be angry. There is also a difference in the way the Li Qingzhao presents the denouement. In the earlier version, as soon as Balang begins his song the musicians immediately recognize him for who he is. In Li Qingzhao's version Balang gets to sing an entire song. It is not so much the quality of his singing voice (apparent to in-the-know listeners after just a few notes) that is empha-sized, but rather the emotive effect his performance has. It is evident that his performance is in no sense inferior to that of the most famous female singers, as seen through the audience's reaction. Indeed, in Li Qingzhao's retelling it is all the guests, not just the musicians, who are overawed by the performance.

When we read Li Qingzhao's recasting of the anecdote in the light of the gender implications later in her essay and indeed in the context of Li Qingzhao as a rare woman poet setting out to demonstrate her own expertise concerning song lyrics, the connection between the anecdote as she tells it and her larger purpose in "On Song Lyrics" is obvious. As a woman writer, she is seeking to take her place in an arena in which she is viewed as an outsider. She is at first content to seat herself in the most lowly position, if only to gain admittance. Naturally, the others ignore her at first, not deigning to acknowledge her as someone worthy of their greeting. Her feminine dress and everything about her physical appearance sets her apart and betokens her inferior status. As a stranger in such a setting, meeting no initial support or encouragement, she is apprehensive and morose, unsure of herself. She has gained admittance to the proceedings, first as a passive listener. That was already hard enough. But when it becomes evident that she wants more, wants a chance to demonstrate her own talent, she provokes ridicule and anger. Whether as a female writer she composes song lyrics or as a critic she pronounces on the merits of other (male) writers, Li Qingzhao is interrupting the standard provenance and circulation of song lyrics as a literary form composed by men. She is keenly aware of this, and she anticipates an angry reaction on the part of those who "belong" to the literary arena and who see her as one who does not belong. But even this anticipation she can only express indirectly by, ironically enough, appropriating a Tang anecdote about a male singer interrupting female performers.

Li Qingzhao's expectation of an angry reaction to her "On Song Lyrics" by members of the male elite was borne out. Here is what the scholar Hu Zi wrote in 1167, in the earliest extended assessment of Li Qingzhao's essay:

> Yi'an critiqued the song lyrics of various gentlemen, one by one, picking out their weaknesses, and no one was spared. Her evaluation is unfair, and I do not accept it. Her intent is to say that she monopolizes the excellences of the form, that she deserves renown for her songs. Tuizhi's [Han Yu's] poem says:
>
> > I don't understand the foolishness of the young men,
> > Why do they slander and try to harm [the reputations of Li Bai and
> >   Du Fu],
> > See the ants trying to shake a giant tree,
> > How laughable, the ignorance of their own limitations![78]
>
> His words were spoken precisely for such persons as her.[79]

Hu Zi may not explicitly refer to Li Qingzhao's gender in this critique, but it is a factor in his dismissal of her views. In his mind, she fits the description of Han Yu's 韓愈 (768–824) pathetic "ants" not only because she is an inferior writer, but also because she is a woman. Hu Zi is the same critic who gave conspicuous prominence to Li Qingzhao's identity as a woman who

---

78. Han Yu, "Tiao Zhang Ji" 調張籍, *Quan Tangshi* 340.3815.
79. Hu Zi, *Tiaoxi yuyin conghua*, "Houji" 33.255.

remarried and then divorced in his treatment of her as a poet. The misogynist viewpoint becomes explicit in the comments of some later critics, such as Pei Chang 裴暢 (18th c.): "Yi'an, confident of her own talent, looked down on everyone else. Her words do not deserve to be preserved. For a mere woman to speak out so brazenly, the absurdity of it requires no explanation, and her madness is also unmatched."[80]

In the conclusion of the Li Balang anecdote in Li Qingzhao's essay, Balang finishes his song, and the audience is moved to tears. They gather round him in homage, recognizing his talent, trusting their ears to judge his talent as a singer rather than their eyes' perception of his unpromising appearance. This is Li Qingzhao's ideal for her own reception, her hope that her inherent talent will shine through, making those who hear her forget her appearance, gender, and identity as outsider to the male literary world. This is her fantasy.

Li Qingzhao's works on writing and learning, reviewed in this chapter, illustrate how central the written word was to her life. Early in her adulthood, she may have aspired to win the kind of acceptance that Li Balang, disguised as an inappropriate interloper, was given at the banquet. However, the reactions she provoked by her unorthodox devotion to writing were considerably more complicated and problematic. She did have her admirers, especially it seems among ordinary readers who were not distinguished scholars and critics. The latter groups, however, included many who reacted to her fame and literary output with skepticism or hostility, and seized on events in her personal life to call into question her achievement and talent as a writer. She would have been aware of the skepticism with which she as a woman venturing into the man's world of literary composition would be received, and she would have been aware of it long before her disastrous second marriage. Certain characteristics of her *shi* poetry, in fact, reflect a strategy adopted to avoid being dismissed as a mere woman writer. When we turn to the subject of her song lyrics in the next chapter, we will see that her act of writing in that form brought to the fore a different dynamic of issues and challenges. But the problems of being a woman committed to writing, finding her own voice when the conventions had all been established by men, and producing work that would win acceptance rather than dismissal or condescension, these remained unchanged.

---

80. Pei Chang, quoted in *Ciyuan cuibian* 詞苑萃編 9, *Huibian*, pp. 87–88.

CHAPTER 3

Song Lyrics Preliminaries

This chapter takes up issues that should be discussed as preliminaries to the sustained examination of the song lyrics of Li Qingzhao in later chapters. The first is the problem of the textual integrity and reliability of the song lyrics now attributed to her. It turns out that the corpus of "Li Qingzhao's song lyrics" as it exists today has an uneven textual history with multiple provenances, many of which are problematic. The second concerns a way of reading her works, especially her song lyrics, that is widespread but almost never critically examined. Her compositions are read autobiographically, as expressions of the moods and thoughts of the historical person Li Qingzhao. In this connection, we will also examine the issue of Zhao Mingcheng's purported frequent absences from his wife's side and see how recent scholarship on Li Qingzhao has produced starkly inconsistent conclusions concerning such absences based on autobiographical readings of her songs.

The Authenticity Question

Historically there were two collections of writings by Li Qingzhao, a collection of song lyrics, titled *Jades for Rinsing the Mouth* 漱玉集, and a larger literary collection, *Li Yi'an's Collection* 李易安集. The title of the song lyrics collection is derived from an old saying about rinsing one's mouth in a stream that flows over stones (to purify it), with "jades" substituted for "stones."[1]

---

1. The phrase invokes the purity of nature and the life of a recluse in nature. The conventional wording of "pillow the head on rocks and rinse the mouth in the streams" was mistakenly inverted by Sun Chu 孫楚 (d. 282) and thereafter became famous. Liu Yiqing, *Shishuo xinyu jianshu* 25.6.781–82; trans. Mather, *Shih-shuo Hsin-yü*, p. 402.

Both of these collections existed in multiple recensions, of varying lengths, and both were eventually lost. *Li Yi'an's Collection* almost certainly did not contain her song lyrics. In Li Qingzhao's day, song lyrics were regularly excluded from a person's literary collection, and they circulated, if at all, in a separate collection. Consequently, it is the loss of *Jades for Rinsing the Mouth* and the transmission of Li Qingzhao's song lyrics apart from that collection that concerns us here.

Some versions of *Jades for Rinsing the Mouth* were printed early on and circulated widely during the Southern Song. But at a later time, we do not know exactly when, that collection ceased to circulate, and eventually it was lost entirely. The complete loss may have happened as early as the fourteenth century, and it certainly had happened by the sixteenth century. The bibliophile and poet Yang Shen 楊愼 (1488–1559), who was a great enthusiast of Li Qingzhao's song lyrics, says that as hard as he tried, he never managed to get hold of a copy of *Jades for Rinsing the Mouth.*

In the meantime, beginning in the Southern Song, certain of Li Qingzhao's song lyrics were regularly selected into song lyric anthologies and other compilations. As new anthologies appeared, through the Yuan, Ming, and Qing periods, new pieces attributed to Li Qingzhao regularly turned up in them. Many of these were song lyrics that had formerly been attributed to other authors or that had appeared in earlier anthologies as works whose author was unknown. By the end of the Qing dynasty, the number of song lyrics variously attributed to Li Qingzhao had swelled from the 36 attributed to her in surviving Southern Song sources to 75, more than double the number of early attributions. That number continued to grow in modern times. A recent scholarly study of her song lyrics, posted on the Internet, lists 88 song lyrics that have been attributed to her.[2] In other words, song lyrics that were first attributed to other authors or those whose authorship was unknown when they first appeared "attached" themselves to Li Qingzhao through time. This phenomenon constitutes a problem for anyone who wants to study Li Qingzhao as we ordinarily study writers, distinguishing works that have reasonable credibility as authentic from those that do not.

---

2. See the entry titled "Li Qingzhao ji jiaozhu" 李清照集校注 by Xihuang shangren 羲皇上人, http://blog.stnn.cc/wbrr/Efp_Bl_1002157393.aspx. The difference between the eighty-eight works listed therein and the seventy-five in my table 1 are the works newly attributed to Li Qingzhao in the twentieth century by Li Wenqi 李文禕 (see below) and in a work referred to as "Shanghai xinji 'Shuyu ci'" 上海新輯《漱玉詞》 (unknown to me).

To get a clearer sense of the problem and what methodology we might use to deal with it, let us begin with a simple chronology of key events in the transmission of her song lyrics. The first is the compilation of *Jades for Rinsing the Mouth* and its printing in the twelfth century. We do not know exactly when it was printed or how many times, but it is likely that the earliest printed editions were circulating in the 1130s or 1140s. The earliest reference to the printing of Li Qingzhao's song lyrics is much later (1206), but the abundance of references to her songs in the mid-twelfth century suggests that they were circulating in print by then.[3] We also do not know how many pieces *Jades for Rinsing the Mouth* contained.

The subsequent loss of *Jades for Rinsing the Mouth* gives special importance to an early anthology that included Li Qingzhao works, *Elegant Lyrics for Music Bureau Songs* 樂府雅詞, compiled by Zeng Zao 曾慥 (1091–1155) in 1146. *Elegant Lyrics* contains twenty-three song lyrics attributed to Li Qingzhao. This is by far the largest number of song lyrics attributed to Li Qingzhao in any of the several Southern Song period anthologies that contain her works, and it is also one of only two such anthologies that were compiled during her lifetime. As Rao Zongyi noted in the 1960s, these twenty-three songs are "the most reliable" of all those variously attributed to Li Qingzhao.[4]

The other early Southern Song anthology to contain song lyrics ascribed to Li Qingzhao is *Garden of Plums* 梅苑, compiled by Huang Dayu 黃大輿 (early 12th c.). The work contains hundreds of song lyrics on the theme of plum blossoms, filling ten *juan*. Oddly, the great majority of the poems it contains are presented with no authorial attribution. But it does attribute six pieces to Li Qingzhao. One of those is a misattribution: it is a piece actually written by Zhou Bangyan, and it appears in Zhou's song lyric collection.[5]

Garden of Plums was compiled in 1129, as we know from Huang's preface, making it even earlier than Zeng Zao's *Elegant Lyrics*. Despite the early date, there is something suspicious about these five songs, as a group, as one can see from a glance at table 1.[6] None of them were selected into *Elegant Lyrics*,

---

3. The existence and circulation of *Jades for Rinsing the Mouth* is attested in several Southern Song sources. Zhao Yanwei attests to the printing of the collection in his miscellany of 1206, *Yunlu manchao* 14.245.

4. Rao Zongyi, *Ci ji kao*, p. 88.

5. The piece in question is no. 29, to the tune "Yuzhu xin" 玉燭新; see Huang Dayu, *Meiyuan* 3.14a.

6. Table 1 draws on an earlier table of the presence of Li Qingzhao's song lyrics in Song–Qing anthologies compiled by Huang Mogu in her *Chongji Li Qingzhao ji*, pp. 54–55. As useful as it is as a preliminary step, Huang's table is limited to anthologies and leaves out other important Ming-Qing sources that attribute works to Li Qingzhao.

compiled a few years later. Stranger still, none of them appear in any other song lyrics anthology until the late sixteenth century (except for no. 29, the one actually written by Zhou Bangyan, which appears with the correct attribution in *The Residue of Poetry from Grass Hut* 草堂詩餘 [ca. 1195]), and two of the five do not appear again until 1630. As table 1 shows, several of the twenty-three pieces contained in *Elegant Lyrics* regularly occur in later Southern Song anthologies. But none of the five *Garden of Plums* pieces do. The absence of those five pieces from the late Southern Song anthology *A Complete Genealogy of Flowering Plants* 全芳備祖 is particularly striking. *A Complete Genealogy of Flowering Plants* is devoted to literary compositions on plants and seeks, as its title suggests, to be a comprehensive collection of such pieces. It has two chapters devoted to the plum (one on the regular plum and one on the red-blossoming plum), and these contain dozens of song lyrics on the plum by other Song period writers. Moreover, the compiler, Chen Jingyi 陳景沂 (fl. 1225–64), was familiar with Li Qingzhao's song lyrics and almost certainly had access to an edition of *Jades for Rinsing the Mouth*, since his anthology includes song lyrics of hers that are not found in any earlier anthology. The pieces of hers he presents include song lyrics on the crab apple, chrysanthemum, paulownia, banana, and cassia but none on the plum. Furthermore, none of the five *Garden of Plums* compositions are contained in the fragmentary edition of *Jades for Rinsing the Mouth* that is said to date from 1370 (on which see below).

All of this suggests that Huang Dayu's source for the song lyrics on the plum he assigned to Li Qingzhao was something different from what other Southern Song anthologists worked with. Huang Dayu was not a scholar of known repute or even a song lyrics specialist. He was a plum blossom aficionado, as he makes clear in his preface. He was bent on amassing as many song lyrics on the plum blossom as he could, and that eagerness would affect his ability to reject dubious or questionable attributions he came across. Consequently, *Garden of Plums* may be the earliest anthology to contain song lyrics attributed to Li Qingzhao, but those attributions are problematic and cannot be considered nearly as reliable as those found in *Elegant Lyrics*.

Two bibliographical events belong to the early Ming period, and both are problematic. The first is the compilation in 1370 of a manuscript copy of *Jades for Rinsing the Mouth*. This was a small volume that contained only seventeen of Li Qingzhao's song lyrics, including eight pieces that had never before been attributed to Li Qingzhao. It is not clear if this manuscript was fragmentary or simply a selection of her song lyrics. Moreover, the manu-script itself does not survive, and the earliest record of its existence comes from much later, 1630, when the late Ming bibliophile and printer Mao Jin 毛晉 (1599–1659) reproduced it in his series of poetry collections, *Shici zazu* 詩詞雜俎 from Jigu Studio 汲古閣. This small collection is the one that was eventually selected into the Qianlong emperor's imperial library (*Siku quanshu* 四庫全書) at the end of the eighteenth century. Mao Jin has an uneven reputation as a scholar, and the reliability of many of his printing projects has been questioned. This manuscript of *Jades for Rinsing the Mouth* thus occupies an ambiguous place in the textual history of Li Qingzhao's song lyrics: it purportedly dates from a relatively early time (1370), but we have no firm evidence of its existence until much later (1630). The other event was the inclusion of song lyrics attributed to Li Qingzhao in the great Ming encyclo-pedia *Yongle dadian* 永樂大典 (1407). The work includes five song lyrics on plums attributed to Li Qingzhao. The encyclopedia's source for these works must have been *Garden of Plums*, although in that earlier work these particular five pieces are presented as anonymous. There is no reason to think that the encyclopedia's compilers had any textual authority for the new attributions they gave to Li Qingzhao. In all likelihood, they took their cue from the prox-imity these pieces have in *Garden of Plums* to other works that are explicitly attributed therein to Li Qingzhao, plus a vague sense that stylistically they resembled her work in the genre.

The next key event took place in 1583, with the appearance of the large song lyrics anthology *A Refined Collection of "Flowers" and "Grasses"* 花草粹編, compiled by Chen Yaowen 陳耀文 (*jinshi* 1550). (Chen's title alludes to two earlier song lyrics anthologies, *Among the Flowers* 花間集, which contains Tang and Five Dynasties song lyrics, and *The Residue of Poetry from Grass Hut*, which mostly contains Song period compositions.) Chen's work contains no fewer than 44 pieces attributed to Li Qingzhao, plus another 5 attributed to other writers (or "anonymous") that would eventually generally come to be assigned to Li Qingzhao, for a total of 49. Indeed, if we count all the song lyrics that had by then been attributed to Li Qingzhao in anthologies, includ-ing *A Refined Collection*, the number swells to 69. In other words, between 1146 and 1570, the number of song lyrics credited to Li Qingzhao, including the few that would eventually be credited to her later, grew by three times the number of pieces assigned to her in *Elegant Lyrics* (23), and this happened precisely during the time period that *Jades for Rinsing the Mouth* was lost. The increase was brought about by the appearance of numerous other song lyrics

Table 1
Song lyrics attributed to Li Qingzhao in thirty-two sources, Song through Qing dynasties

Tune titles (調名) by Song lyric number:

1. 南歌子：天上星河
2. 轉調滿庭芳：芳草池塘
3. 漁家傲：天接雲濤
4. 如夢令：常記溪亭
5. 如夢令：昨夜雨疏
6. 多麗：小樓寒
7. 菩薩蠻：風柔日薄
8. 菩薩蠻：歸鴻聲斷
9. 浣溪沙：莫許杯深
10. 浣溪沙：小院閑窗
11. 浣溪沙：淡蕩春光
12. 鳳凰臺上憶吹簫：香冷
13. 一剪梅：紅藕香殘
14. 蝶戀花：淚搵征衣
15. 蝶戀花：暖雨晴風
16. 鷓鴣天：寒日蕭蕭
17. 小重山：春到長門
18. 怨王孫：湖上風來
19. 臨江仙：庭院
20. 醉花陰：薄霧濃雲
21. 好事近：風定落花
22. 訴衷情：夜來沉醉
23. 行香子：草際鳴蛩
24. 清平樂：年年雪裏
25. 漁家傲：雪裏已知
26. 滿庭芳：小閣藏春
27. 玉樓春：紅酥肯放
28. 玉燭新：溪源新臘
29. 念奴嬌：蕭條庭院
30. 聲聲慢：尋尋覓見
31. 永遇樂：落日鎔金
32. 憶秦娥：臨高閣

date	Source title 書名	1	2	3	4	5	6	7	8	9	10	11	12	13	14	15	16	17	18	19	20	21	22	23	24	25	26	27	28	29	30	31	32	33
1150	樂府雅詞	x	x	x	x	x	x	x	x	x	x	x	x	x	x	x	x	x	x	x	x	x	x	x										
	梅苑																								x	x	x	x	x	x				
	草堂詩餘				x								x	x							x											b	x	
	花庵詞選			x	x	x							x	x																			x	
	貴耳集																															x		
1250	陽春白雪											x																				x	x	
	全芳備祖				x	x															x													x
	其他早期詞集																												b					
	截江網																																	
1300	翰墨大全																																	
	毛晉本漱玉詞			x	x	x							x	x							x											x	x	
1400	永樂大典																																	
	詩淵																																	
	詩餘圖譜												x	x							x													
	詞學筌蹄																																	
1550	詞林萬選				w																												x	
	天機餘錦																																	
	楊金本草堂詩餘																																	
	七修類稿																																	
	彤管遺編				x								x	x							x													
1583	花草粹編	x		x	x	x	x	x			x		x	x	x	x	x	x	x	x	x	x	x	x	x	x	x	x	x	x		x	x	b
	古今女史				x								x	x																		x	x	
	沈本草堂續集																																	
	詞的				x								x	x							x											x	x	
	古今詞統				x								x	x	x						x											x	x	
1630	毛晉未刻漱玉詞	x		x	x	x	x	x					x	x	x	x	x	x	x		x												x	
	沈際飛本草堂詩餘正集																																	
	林下詞選			x	x	x							x								x												x	
	詞綜												x	x							x												x	
	詞譜												x											x									x	
	御選歷代詩餘	x		x	x	x	x					x	x	x	x	x	x	x	x	x	x				x	x	x	x	x	x		x	x	
1889	王鵬運編漱玉詞	x	x	x	x	x	x	x	x	x	x	x	x	x	x	x	x	x	x	x	x	x	x	x	x	x	x	x	x	x	x	x	x	x

Notes:

x : an explicit attribution to Li Qingzhao

w: no attribution or explicit attribution to "anonymous"

b: an explicit attribution to another author

The source *Huacao cuibian* 花草粹編 (1583) follows the convention of not repeating an author's name when presenting multiple songs by the same author. So for that work "x" marks both explicit and such implicit attributions.

4	35	36	37	38	39	40	41	42	43	44	45	46	47	48	49	50	51	52	53	54	55	56	57	58	59	60	61	62	63	64	65	66	67	68	69	70	71	72	73	74	75
添字采桑子：窗前谁种／鹧鸪天：暗淡轻黄	长寿乐：微寒应候	蝶恋花：永夜厌厌	怨王孙：梦断漏悄	怨王孙：帝里春晚	浣溪沙：楼上晴天	浣溪沙：髻子伤春	浣溪沙：绣面芙蓉	武陵春：风住尘香	点绛唇：寂寞深闺	浪淘沙：素约小腰	春光好：看看腊盏	河传：香苞素质	七娘子：清香浮动	忆少年：疏疏整整	玉楼春：腊梅先报	新荷叶：薄露初零	点绛唇：红杏飘香	青玉案：凌波不过	醜奴儿：晚来一阵	浪淘沙：蹴罢秋千	木兰花令：沉水香消	生查子：年年玉镜	柳梢青：子规啼血	青玉案：征鞍不见	临江仙：……春遲	摊破浣溪沙：揉破黄金	摊破浣溪沙：病起萧萧	瑞鹧鸪：玉瘦香浓	庆清朝：禁幄低张	减字木兰花：卖花担上	瑞鹧鸪：风度雍容	如梦令：零落残红	菩萨蛮：绿云鬓上	生查子：去年元夜时	鹧鸪天：枝上流莺	青玉案：一年春事	孤雁：天然标格	品令：急雨惊秋			
																																b		b							
												w	w	w	w	w									w		w														
		w	b	b	w													w					w														w	w	w		
																									b																
x	x																																								
																		b	b									b	b												
		x																																							
			x																																						
					x	x	x	x	x	x	x																														
												x	x	x	x	x																									
															x																										
																		x	x																						
																				x	x	x		b																	
																							x																		
																					b	w	w					x													
																								x																	
										x																															
x		x	x	x		x				x	x	b						w	b					b	x	x	x	x	x	x	x	x	x								w
		x	x			x						x												x																	
				x	x			x	x									w		b														x	x						
				x	x				x	w								x	w																		x				
			x	x	x	x												w		b																x	x				
x		x	x					x			x							x							x	x	x	x	x	x	x							x	x		
				x																																				x	
		x	x	x							x							x					x																		
x		x							x									x													x			x							x
x		x	x	x	x			x			x							x							x	x	x	x	x	x	x						x				
x		x	x	x	x			x			x							x							x	x	x	x	x	x	x										

anthologies and other sources during the intervening centuries, beyond the two early Ming works discussed above (see table 1). Chen Yaowen's *A Refined Collection* is at least the eleventh anthology after *Elegant Lyrics* to present such new pieces. Typically, each of the anthologies adds just a few. Chen's own adds 9 new pieces.

The number of song lyrics attributed to Li Qingzhao after *A Refined Collection* continued to grow, but not so rapidly. By the time Wang Pengyun 王鵬運 undertook to reconstruct *Jades for Rinsing the Mouth* in the 1880s, he had 75 song lyrics to choose from. He eventually included 57, and his new version of Li Qingzhao's song lyrics collection, vastly larger than the one reproduced in *Siku quanshu* of a century earlier (with its 17 pieces), became the basis for versions of the work that have circulated in modern times.[7] An edition of Li Qingzhao's complete works published in 1930 by Li Wenqi 李文錡 contained as many as 78 song lyrics. Li Wenqi added many new attributions of his own, drawing upon anonymous works he found in *Garden of Plums*, which he reassigned to Li Qingzhao (apparently without any textual authority for doing so). The edition of *Jades for Rinsing the Mouth* compiled in 1931 by Zhao Wanli 趙萬里 was more cautious, presenting 43 pieces as authentic, with another 9 listed as "questionable" in their attribution to Li Qingzhao, and 8 more listed as "misattributions." Zhao's selection has been influential, although many of the pieces he placed in the latter two categories have been routinely assumed to be authentic in later editions and writings about Li Qingzhao.[8] Zhao's selection was the basis for the representation of Li Qingzhao in Tang Guizhang's 唐圭璋 *Complete Song Dynasty Song Lyrics* 全宋詞, with 47 pieces, as originally compiled in 1965. More recent editions of Li Qingzhao's "complete works," including those compiled by Xu Peijun 徐培均 in 2002 and by Xu Beiwen 徐北文 in 2005 are similar: just over 50 song lyrics (53 and 51, respectively) and an additional handful of "questionable" pieces (7 and 13, respectively).[9] The song lyrics in Xu Peijun's "complete works" are based on yet another recension of *Jades for Rinsing the Mouth* compiled (but never printed) by the late Ming figure Mao Jin, containing 49 pieces, although the provenance of many of the pieces is questionable. Xu acquired a manuscript of this "Never Printed Jigu Pavilion Edition of

---

7. Li Qingzhao, *Shuyu ci*, in Wang Pengyun's *Siyin zhai suoke ci*, first printed in 1881 and then reprinted with a "supplementary" section in 1889.

8. Li Qingzhao, *Shuyu ci*, in Zhao Wanli's *Jiaoji Song Jin Yuanren ci*.

9. Xu Peijun, *Jianzhu*; Xu Beiwen, *Li Qingzhao quanji pingzhu*.

Jades for Rinsing the Mouth" 汲古閣未刻本《漱玉詞》 from collectors in Japan. He supplemented Mao's 49 works with others from various anthologies, bringing his total to 53; the total grew to 59 song lyrics in the revised edition he published in 2009.[10]

This peculiar bibliographical history has serious implications for any study of Li Qingzhao and her song lyrics. Questions need to be raised about the reliability of a corpus of works more than half of which are only known from sources that postdate the author's life by several centuries and cannot be traced back through a lineage of texts to Southern Song times. Generally in Chinese bibliographical history, whenever there are uncertainties about the provenance of writings, the more famous the author in question, the more worrisome those uncertainties are. Celebrated names attract posthumous writings attributed to them. It is not simply that unscrupulous editors and printers seek to augment sales of the books by including in them previously "undiscovered" works by famous persons, although that has happened. The eleven song lyrics anthologies mentioned above were all to varying degrees commercial publications and were competing with each other in the marketplace. An anthology that included a few "new" pieces by Li Qingzhao (or any other famous songwriter) would attract attention and potential buyers. Thus, editors, compilers, and booksellers had a pecuniary interest in adding to the small number of works attributed to her, especially after her original collection of song lyrics, *Jades for Rinsing the Mouth*, was lost. Furthermore, as we saw in chapter 1, there was a vogue of writing "in imitation" of famous persons of earlier times. Not infrequently, as the decades and centuries passed, such imitations might innocently be mistaken for the work of the imitated author and then added to her or his corpus.

Different readers will have different levels of tolerance or skepticism regarding the song lyrics anthologies' attributions to Li Qingzhao. Some will be inclined to accept the attributions found in early, that is, Song period anthologies, reasoning that since *Jades for Rinsing the Mouth* was still available then, the reliability of those early attributions should be high. In that case, the number of pieces grows from the 23 found in *Elegant Lyrics* to 36 (but only 30 if we do not include the 5 suspicious *Garden of Plums* pieces and its 1 misattribution). But how many people are going to accept the attributions that appear only in the mid- or late Ming, when even bibliophiles and song lyrics

---

10. Six new pieces are found in his "Supplement" 補遺 (2009 ed.), *Jianzhu*, pp. 540–51.

aficionados say they could no longer obtain a copy of *Jades for Rinsing the Mouth*? These later anthologies do not say where they have obtained these "new" pieces, much less evaluate their source's reliability (assuming there was a written source). Consider, for example, the nine new pieces found in *A Refined Collection*. How likely is it that they are authentic and somehow survived and were transmitted through four hundred years, during which Li Qingzhao's original collection was lost, yet were never quoted or commented upon during that long period? Contrariwise, how much more likely is it that they are recent compositions (that is, inauthentic ones) that Chen Yaowen was glad to include in his anthology because he knew no earlier anthology had them? In that case, we need not conclude that Chen Yaowen knowingly passed off forgeries as the real thing. In his eagerness to lend extra appeal to his anthology, he may not have been particularly rigorous in scrutinizing the reliability of his source or its attribution. He accepted the attribution and passed it on because it was in his commercial interests to do so.

Chen Shangjun's 陳尚君 study of Tang "women poets" calls special attention to the role played by late Ming enthusiasm for women's writing and the anthologies of women's poetry that appeared then.[11] Chen concludes that the late Ming was a particularly fertile time for the composition of "Tang women's poetry." Chen's findings have implications regarding the proliferation of Li Qingzhao's works during the Ming period.

Skepticism regarding the new song lyrics attributed to Li Qingzhao in *A Refined Collection* (as well as other Ming-Qing period anthologies) is warranted even when compared with *shi* poems attributed to Li Qingzhao in anthologies that appear at roughly the same time.[12] From early on Li Qingzhao was better known for her song lyrics than for her output in any other form. It was her song lyrics that people had in mind, as early as in the generation after hers, when they spoke of the "Yi'an style" 易安體, and it was her song lyrics that they explicitly imitated with compositions of their own. Such imitations

---

11. Chen Shangjun, "Tang nü shiren zhenbian," pp. 21–22 and 23–25.

12. I am thinking of the five poems attributed to Li Qingzhao in the anthologies of women's *shi* poetry through the ages that were published in the 1550s and 1560s: Tian Yiheng's *Lady Scholars of Poetry* 詩女史 (1557) and Li Hu's 酈琥 *A New Gusu Imprint of Works Left by Red Writing Brushes* 姑蘇新刻彤管遺編 (1567; hereafter *Tongguan yibian*). The poems are "Wujiang jueju" 烏江絶句 (titled "Xiari jueju" 夏日絶句 in *Tongguan yibian*), "Fende zhizi yun" 分得知字韻, "Xiaomeng" 曉夢, "Chuncan" 春殘, and "Ganhai" 感懷 (whose preface takes the place of that title in both anthologies); see Tian Yiheng, *Shinü shi* 11.5a–b and *Tongguan yibian* 17 ("Xuji" 續集) 15b–17a. For a description of these anthologies, see Fong, "Gender and the Failure of Canonization," pp. 134–37.

could easily, with the passage of time, be interpolated into various collections including selections of her works. Second, erroneous attributions are a phenomenon particularly endemic to the song lyric generally. Owing to the largely oral nature and performance tradition of the genre during Li Qingzhao's time, individual pieces were not so firmly rooted to their original author or to a definitive textual context as were other literary forms. Multiple attributions of a single composition to several authors are common in the song lyrics field.

It makes sense to center any discussion of Li Qingzhao's song lyrics on those that have the highest degree of reliability and then to move outward from there to those of progressively less reliability. We have a body of work assigned to Li Qingzhao that we can accept with a high level of confidence. We also have writings assigned to her that are more problematic; and, at the periphery of credibility, we have many song lyrics for which the attribution to Li Qingzhao appears to be based on nothing more than the whimsy (or unscrupulous motives) of some anthologist several centuries after her life. Finally, we have particular pieces whose authorship by other Southern Song poets is well supported in early sources, but much later they came to be separately attributed to Li Qingzhao. Why not begin with those compositions we have confidence in, see what can be said about them first, then bring the other more problematic pieces into the discussion to see how consideration of the less reliable writings alters, expands, or contradicts findings regarding the core group? The purpose of proceeding this way is not to arrive at an assessment of the authenticity of the more problematic pieces. They will remain problematic: we will probably never be able to arrive at a definitive conclusion regarding their authenticity. The purpose of structuring the discussion this way is to maintain distinctions between the more and the less reliable groups so that writings from the latter are not mixed in with those from the former at the outset (which is what usually happens), muddying the waters. We are never going to recover a fully accurate picture of the writings of Li Qingzhao. Too little of her work survives, and too much of what does survive is rife with attribution questions. But by discriminating between material of different origins and different degrees of reliability, we may at least improve on the understanding of her that is commonly conveyed. This way, we introduce into our analysis the notion of a relatively reliable "core" of works, while also making allowances for the consideration of more questionable peripheral works, which may yet be authentic or at least present interesting extensions or alternatives to the core.

It is disconcerting that in most recent scholarship on Li Qingzhao, song lyrics that were first attributed to her some four centuries after her death and whose provenance is completely unknown are regularly thrown together with those assigned to her in major anthologies compiled during or shortly after her lifetime and discussed as if they are all equally revealing about her as a writer and person. To make matters worse, scholars pick and choose among the large number of questionable compositions assigned to Li Qingzhao, accepting as authentic those that suit the image of her each critic wants to emphasize and rejecting those that do not, so that the "corpus" of her works varies significantly from one scholarly discussion to another.

Given the universal assumption in Li Qingzhao scholarship that her song lyrics are autobiographical, a curious logical circularity often operates in scholarly commentary. The more her life is scrutinized, the better one is able to see how the details of a certain song (whose attribution is highly questionable, to judge from where and when it originates) can be fit into the circumstances of one or another stage of her life, and then the more apt the scholar becomes to seize upon that "fit" to eliminate doubts about the composition's authenticity. We see this happening in the recent publications of the learned Li Qingzhao specialist Xu Peijun. When he first published his edition of Li Qingzhao's complete works in 2002, Xu did not include the five song lyrics on plum blossoms first attributed to her in the Ming encyclopedia *Yongle dadian*. But by the time he published his revised edition in 2009, he had become convinced that those five pieces are authentic, and he presents them as such in a new "Supplement." Not only does he now accept the five pieces, he tells us when he believes they must have been written, assigning them in each case to a specific year in Li Qingzhao's life, based on details and references he finds in each piece that he ties to the circumstances of her whereabouts, thinking, and mood from year to year. The explicit rationale he gives for accepting the five compositions is bibliographical, based on arguments about how *Yongle dadian* and *Garden of Plums* present or do not present their authorial attributions, arguments that are not very convincing.[13] But equally influential in Xu's change of heart regarding these pieces is his new insight into how they might be inserted into Li Qingzhao's biography. I will take up this issue of the autobiographical reading of Li Qingzhao in the next section of this chapter.

---

13. Xu Peijun, "Zaiban houji" 再版後記, *Jianzhu* (rev. ed.), pp. 552–56.

I have assigned numbers to Li Qingzhao's song lyrics based on the chronology of their appearance in Song through Qing period sources. These are the numbers used in table 1 and appendix 1; they are also given in parentheses after the tune title for each piece presented and discussed in the text.[14] The core group of her song lyrics are the twenty-three pieces preserved in *Elegant Lyrics* (nos. 1–23), which I will make group 1 in my credibility groups. The next group, with a slightly reduced level of credibility (my group 2), are song lyrics found in late Southern Song (mid-thirteenth century) song lyrics anthologies, together with one attested in Southern Song miscellanies. In my numbering, these pieces are numbered 30 through 36. Group 3 consists of the *Garden of Plums* pieces (five of them, not counting the one misattribution), one that appears in a Yuan source, and eight more that appear for the first time in the early Ming fragmentary edition of *Jades for Rinsing the Mouth* that Mao Jin reprinted (altogether fourteen pieces, nos. 28, 37, and 38–45). Group 4, that with the lowest credibility, consists of pieces that are first attributed to Li Qingzhao in later Ming through Qing period sources (plus the one *Garden of Plums* piece written by Zhou Bangyan), altogether thirty pieces (nos. 29, 46–75). Many of these pieces have earlier attributions to some other author or are formerly presented as "anonymous" (i.e., author unknown).[15]

Table 2
Credibility groups of Li Qingzhao's song lyrics

Group	Song lyrics	Number of pieces
1	nos. 1–23, *Elegant Lyrics* pieces	23
2	nos. 30–36, other pieces attested in Southern Song sources	7
3	nos. 24–28, *Garden of Plums* pieces; 37; and 38–45, from Mao Jin's early Ming (1370) truncated edition of *Jades for Rinsing the Mouth*	14
4	nos. 29; and 46–75, other Ming-Qing attributions (plus the *Garden of Plums* work actually written by Zhou Bangyan), the great majority of which have earlier attributions to other writers or are earlier presented as author unknown	31
Total		75

14. The only exception I have made to the chronological ordering is to number the *Elegant Lyrics* pieces (nos. 1–23) ahead of the six works in *Garden of Plums* (nos. 24–29), since the reliability of those pieces is highly questionable based on considerations other than chronology.

15. For a full account of these alternate attributions, see the "Cunmu ci" 存目詞 notes in *Quan Songci* 2:1212–13.

The criteria I am using to distinguish degrees of credibility are based entirely on the date and reliability of the earliest attribution as well as subsequent confirmation of the same or the lack of it. I avoid using literary style or even factoring style into my determination of credibility. My practice in this regard runs counter to what is found in most Li Qingzhao scholarship, where judgments about what she is likely or unlikely to have written routinely hinge on stylistic considerations. The weaknesses of stylistic determination are evident. First, any stylistic trait in a writer's work that we today might notice would have been noticeable to imitators or outright forgers in earlier times, and they could have aped it. This objection has particular validity in that we are more distant today from the language Li Qingzhao worked with (Literary Chinese) than were the poet's potential emulators in premodern times. Second, there were long-standing traditions in the song lyric form of men writing in the personas of women and, specifically, men writing in "Yi'an's style." Third, the song lyric is a form that is short (just a few dozen characters), has a limited range of subjects, and uses highly conventionalized language and sentiments. As a literary form that exists within a relatively narrow range of stylistic and expressive boundaries, it lends itself to stylistic imitation. It is unsurprising, therefore, that no one has developed statistical analyses of diction or imagery that are sufficient to make determinations about authorship. Anyone who thinks that he or she can, by virtue of his reading experience of song lyrics, accurately assess what a given author could or could not have produced in the form, and thus can distinguish authentic works by Li Qingzhao from inauthentic ones on the basis of their literary style has, in my view, an inflated opinion of his or her acuity.

In the voluminous Chinese-language scholarship on Li Qingzhao, there is no shortage of attention given to the dating of individual pieces. Nearly every recent edition of her "complete" song lyrics, for example, presents them in what it considers to be chronological order, and several of the compilers go to great lengths to justify their dating of particular pieces. There are also specialized studies on the dating and authenticity of compositions attributed to her.[16] But such discussions have a decidedly ad hoc quality, dealing with each composition separately. Almost always, moreover, the focus is on

---

16. For example, Wang Fan, "Li Qingzhao ci zhenwei kao" 李清照詞眞僞考, in his *Li Qingzhao yanjiu conggao*, pp. 3–34.

the literary style of the piece and its affective content as the keys to determining authenticity or assigning the piece to a period of her life. A systematic discussion of the peculiar history of her writings, the accretion of attributions to her through time, and the virtually untenable gap between her life and so many of the works first credited to her in the Ming-Qing period is missing in the scholarship. Some editors, it is true, take the precaution of distinguishing between pieces they view as authentic and those that are "doubtful." But the basis for that distinction remains ad hoc and impressionistic. It does not spring from an analytical consideration of publication history and the problems it entails.

The Autobiographical Reading Problem

The other issue that must be discussed before examining Li Qingzhao's song lyrics in detail is the conventional way of reading them as if the woman's voice in them is inseparable from Li Qingzhao's own voice as a historical person. All recent Chinese critical and scholarly treatments of Li Qingzhao that I am aware of read her works this way, and the assumption that they ought to be read this way is not subjected to scrutiny.

Consider, for example, recent comments on this song lyric, one of those attributed to her in *Elegant Lyrics*:

浣溪沙　　*To the tune "Sands of the Washing Stream"* (no. 10)

小院閑窗春色深	A small courtyard and lattice window, the spring colors are vivid.
重簾未捲影沈沈	The double blinds are not lifted, shadows gather deep inside.
倚樓無語理瑤琴	She leans against the building, saying nothing, plucking a jeweled zither.
遠岫出雲催薄暮	A distant cave emits clouds, hurrying the onset of dusk.
細風吹雨弄輕陰	A light wind brings rain, jostling the sparse shade.
梨花欲謝恐難禁	The pear blossoms are about to wither, there's no preventing it, I'm afraid.[17]

This is an effective portrait of the conflicting affections and images of spring as observed by a lone woman. As such the subject matter is completely

---

17. *Jianzhu* 1.67; *Quan Songci* 2:1203.

commonplace in song lyrics, yet it is handled here with great sensitivity and cleverness that makes the piece interesting nevertheless. The most intriguing line is the last one. To say of the pear blossoms that are about to wither "there's no preventing it, I'm afraid" is to utter an absurdity. Yet the statement aptly evokes the speaker's attachment to the blossoms' beauty, which is such that it leads the speaker into hoping against hope for the impossible. There are also some other artful turns of phrase, including the notion of the clouds "hurrying" the dusk and the light breeze "jostling" patches of shade on the ground.

The Li Qingzhao specialist Chen Zumei 陳祖美 says this about the piece: "This composition must have been written when Li Qingzhao was waiting to be married in Bianjing (the capital). It is on the theme of a young girl cherishing spring."[18] She means that the romantic feelings of cherishing spring and fearing, at the same time, its departure are those the youthful Li Qingzhao would have experienced on the point of getting married and thinking about the imminent changes she faced at that stage of her life. Xu Peijun, in his annotations on the song, quotes Chen Zumei's interpretation to take issue with it.[19] He has a different idea about the date of this song, evidently from the word *xiu* 岫, "cave" or "cliff," in the second stanza. The topography around Kaifeng (the capital) is flat, he says, whereas southwest of Qingzhou (Zhao Mingcheng's native home, where Li Qingzhao lived with him from 1107 to 1121, after they were married) stands Heaven View Mountain 仰天山. Xu notes that on the mountain is found a Buddhist monastery of the same name and that near the monastery there is a Luohan Grotto 羅漢洞; he further points out that Zhao Mingcheng, who frequently went on local excursions during this period in search of historical inscriptions, left his own inscription on that grotto in 1109. Xu concludes that Li Qingzhao's line refers to this particular grotto, as she is thinking of her husband who is off on an excursion there.

Xu Peijun's reading is erudite and ingenious, yet it lends a good deal more geographical and chronological specificity to this song than we normally bring to bear on compositions in this genre. The facts that *xiu* can mean cliff as well as cave and that Li Qingzhao does not use the word "grotto" (from

---

18. Quoted by Xu Peijun in *Jianzhu* 1.68 from Chen Zumei's *Li Qingzhao juan* 李清照卷 (not available to me); cf. the similar comments on this piece in Chen's *Li Qingzhao ci xinyi zheping*, pp. 14–16.
19. *Jianzhu* 1.68.

the name of Luohan Grotto) weaken his argument. But the key point regarding the interpretations offered by Chen Zumei and Xu Peijun is that both of them assume that the song is autobiographical. They both think that the woman in the song is Li Qingzhao herself, and the thoughts and affections are Li Qingzhao's own. (The issue of whether to understand the references to that woman in the first or third person, that is, "I lean . . . I play" or "She leans . . . she plays," is a different issue. The language of Chinese poetry does not require the reader to make a choice between these two, whereas the English translator must make a choice.) Xu Peijun's reading could even be described as elaborately autobiographical in the sense that he traces correspondences between many details in the song and the details of Li Qingzhao's Qingzhou period existence. The mountain is the mountain her husband took his excursion to, the courtyard is the courtyard in Returning Home Studio in the couple's Qingzhou residence, and so forth.[20] Chen and Xu disagree over what period of Li Qingzhao's life the song should be assigned to, but they agree on identifying the woman in it as Li Qingzhao.

The following piece brings up a different type of interpretive disagreement, but the assumptions, whether spoken or unspoken, remain the same:

減字木蘭花　　*To the tune "Magnolia Flowers, Short Version"* (no. 66)

賣花擔上	A street vendor with a pole was selling flowers,
買得一枝春欲放	I bought a branch ready to send springtime forth.
淚染輕勻	Tear-stained rouge lightly brushed,
猶帶彤霞曉露痕	They still have traces of morning dew from crimson clouds.
怕郎猜道	Afraid he might say
奴面不如花面好	My face isn't as pretty as the flowers.
雲鬢斜簪	I inserted some in my cloud locks of hair,
徒要教郎比並看	So he'd be forced to look at us together.[21]

With this piece the disagreement is over whether or not to accept it as Li Qingzhao's. This song is in my group 4; it is one of those that first appears in the Ming anthology *A Refined Collection*, so that the likelihood that it is authentic is low. Zhao Wanli, the doyen of modern studies of Li Qingzhao, has doubts about the piece's authenticity and relegates it to his section of works

---

20. For the studio detail, see *Jianzhu* 1.437.
21. *Jianzhu* 1.9; *Quan Songci* 2:1210.

whose authenticity is dubious. But the basis for his doubts is stylistic rather having anything to do with the composition's late appearance: "The meaning of the words is shallow and obvious. It does not resemble her works."[22] Recent scholars are more inclined to accept the piece as authentic, saying that Zhao Wanli's judgment seems arbitrary and unnecessarily exclusive. But even as these scholars accept the work, they uniformly assign it to Li Qingzhao's early years, soon after she married Zhao Mingcheng. Zhuge Yibing 諸葛 憶兵, in his study of Li Qingzhao and Zhao Mingcheng published in 2004, says: "The youthful Li Qingzhao, having purchased flowers to enjoy them and showing her general appreciation of beauty, intends at the same time to use them to adorn herself, cherishing as she does her own youthfulness. . . . When she takes pains to adorn herself at this moment, of course she also intends to magnify her husband Zhao Mingcheng's appreciation of her. In this way, the actions of buying flowers and putting them in her hair express, on another level, the implicit meaning of her quest for good fortune in love."[23]

The possibility that Li Qingzhao could be writing about a woman other than herself has not occurred to him or to the other scholars who date this work soon after her marriage to Zhao Mingcheng. As Xu Peijun observes, the piece "fully expresses the aura of youthfulness and the joy of newly married life."[24] Zhao Wanli's rejection of the piece based on stylistic criteria is likely based on the assumption of a correspondence between style and his conception of the historical Li Qingzhao as a lady of a certain social stature and respectability. As Zhuge Yibing has observed concerning another piece that Zhao Wanli rejects for the same reasons, his doubts spring from a perception that "the conduct of the woman in the piece does not resemble that of a refined lady of a renowned family and is more like the behavior of a merchant-class woman. That is why he rejects the notion that Li Qingzhao could have written it."[25]

One might readily take issue with several of the considerations that have gone into these scholarly efforts to determine a date for such compositions. The dating is based wholly on the attempt to correlate statements in the songs with what we know, or think we know, about events in Li Qingzhao's

---

22. Quoted in Wang Zhongwen, *Li Qingzhao ji jiaozhu* 1.71.
23. Zhuge, *Li Qingzhao yu Zhao Mingchen*, p. 49.
24. *Jianzhu* 1.10.
25. Zhuge, *Li Qingzhao yu Zhao Mingcheng*, p. 36.

life. But the perspective the critics bring is a limited one. If a song expresses sadness, it must date from a period when Zhao Mingcheng was not at his wife's side constantly. Since no critic wants to date all of her sorrowful pieces to the years after Zhao Mingcheng died, much is made (as we will see below) of his temporary absences during their marriage in order to account for songs of loneliness.

The notion that Li Qingzhao could have expressed sorrow when Zhao Mingcheng was with her is not entertained. With a modern poet, we have no trouble accepting the idea that she may feel isolated, lonely, or frustrated in love even when her lover or spouse is in the next room. But somehow with Li Qingzhao that possibility does not occur to us. Likewise, a poem that mentions anxiety over the passing of spring must date from her early years, whether just before her marriage or just after it. Thus, Xu Peijun dates the first piece to the Qingzhou period, seizing upon the absence of mountains near Kaifeng to reject earlier years. Later in her life Li Qingzhao lived in many places that had mountains nearby (for example, Hangzhou, Jinhua, and others). Yet the assumption is that an older woman would not be so concerned about the passage of spring, and so places equally qualified by their topography to be the location of the song but which she lived in after the fall of the Northern Song are not considered.

The primary problem with the interpretations reviewed above is their equation of the lady in the poem with Li Qingzhao. Li Qingzhao grew up in an official family in which the performative conventions of this song form would have been known. Her father moved in circles of leading literati of the day. As a youth, Li Qingzhao must have been present at banquets and more informal parties in which song lyrics were written and performed, or heard such performances (or heard about them) even when she was not present. The songs performed at these gatherings were mostly about love (as in many cultures around the world), about lovelorn women lonely for their absent man, or even about flirtatious women in the presence of their man. Li Qingzhao is nothing if not well versed in the conventions of the song lyrics of her day, as she shows in her critical essay "On Song Lyrics." We cannot think of her as sheltered or innocent of the way men composed in the form.

Why Are Women Poets Read That Way?

The habit of reading song lyrics autobiographically is not imposed solely on Li Qingzhao or women generally. It is often applied to male poets as well, particularly certain of them. The distinction we draw today between author and literary persona was quite foreign to native Chinese readings of poetry generally in premodern times. In the dominant form of *shi* poetry, indeed, there was a strong presumption that the speaking voice in the poem was that of the historical poet. One might think that expectations would have been different with song lyrics, which after all were regularly set to musical tunes and performed by someone other than the person who wrote them; those performers, moreover, were usually of a different gender than the authors. In fact, some song lyrics by male authors were read autobiographically none-theless. Works by Li Yu 李煜 (937–78), the ill-fated last ruler of the Southern Tang in the Five Dynasties period, have traditionally been read that way, making the expressions of sadness they contain for the passage of time and the vanishing of youthful pleasures into a ruler's laments for the loss of his kingdom. Song lyrics by the Northern Song writer Liu Yong, who is said to have been a devotee of the pleasure quarters, were often taken as first-person accounts of his romantic affairs with the singing girls he found there. The political enemies of Ouyang Xiu apparently sought to exploit the lack of readerly distinction between author and persona as well as Ouyang's well-known penchant for writing songs about love by fabricating songs they circu-lated under his name that feature an older man's romantic interest in a very young girl. The enemies thus sought to lend credence to the accusation they lodged against him for having committed incest with a niece.[26] Occasionally one encounters a song lyrics author who wants us to read his compositions autobiographically. Su Shi is a well-known case in point. Su goes out of his way to make his song lyrics sound autobiographical by providing detailed prefaces to many of his pieces that anchor them in the circumstances of his career. Su had special reasons for doing this, however, and few writers after him followed his example in this regard.

Such compositions by men that lent themselves to autobiographical read-ings were offset by the many that did not. As we have seen, men regularly composed song lyrics using a female persona or with a focus on a solitary female subject, and such pieces could not be read straightforwardly as auto-biographical. That was not the case with women writing in a female persona or about a female subject. It was not only Li Qingzhao who was read this way; all female song lyrics writers were assumed to be voicing direct expres-sion of their own emotions and life circumstances. In other words, the song

---

26. See my *Literary Works of Ou-yang Hsiu*, pp. 161–95.

lyrics by women were given unequal treatment; the allowance sometimes made in the case of male writers for divergence between poet and persona or subject was not extended to women authors.

There are various ways to account for this discrepancy. We could say that with male authors the distinction between poet and persona was more naturally made, given that men's songs were often "spoken" by female personas. Women, by contrast, seldom wrote in personas that were unambiguously male. Nevertheless, women did regularly produce song lyrics that are indeterminate with regard to the gender of the speaker or person in the scene being described. Yet such compositions too were overwhelmingly taken to be autobiographical.

Surely, condescension toward women writers played a role in this unequal treatment of men's and women's writing. In the Song dynasty writing was considered the domain of men. Cultural tradition made that so, and the expanded civil service examination system during the dynasty cemented the identification of writing with the male world. Since the vast majority of persons who picked up the brush to write were male, as were the overwhelming majority of those who were classically educated, it is not surprising that a reader's expectations would be altered in the rare instance of encountering something known to have been written by a woman. In such a cultural world, it would be natural to expect women's writing to be more rudimentary and less sophisticated than that by her male counterparts. Language, erudition, and the ability to manipulate literary devices to maximize effect—a lower level of expectation would hold for all of these when the composition was known to have been produced by a woman. A woman would be assumed to be capable only of direct and simple expression in writing. It would follow that a woman writer would and could speak only in her "own" voice.

Another factor that influenced this way of approaching women's poetry must have been the appeal of voyeuristic reading. To the extent that it was considered improper for a woman's poetry to circulate outside of her home, this was partly because of the perception of a sexual component to what she expressed on the page. In the rare instances that a woman's writing was somehow allowed to circulate (with or without her permission), readers, especially male readers, would be apt to approach it voyeuristically, as something that permitted titillating or somehow illicit access to the woman's most private moments, emotions, and, indeed, her body. This perception would naturally pique the interest of many readers. In a society in which upper-class women were socially segregated and confined, even within the household, to their own "inner quarters," woman's writing would have its special appeal as an entrée into what was socially forbidden and closed off. Any denial of the connection between the woman's writing and her most intimate self would break the path of access and diminish the writing's appeal.

Another factor is that many male readers would not be comfortable with the thought that a woman was capable, as a writer, of striking a pose. It was one thing for male writers to cultivate elaborate fictional personas—as well-to-do ladies, concubines, common wineshop entertainers, or elegant courtesans, not to mention various male personas—but for a woman to do likewise would be considered dissembling and unseemly. In a society in which the stature and power of the two sexes were hardly on an equal footing, men expected women to treat them with respect. The thought that a woman might be play-acting would be disarming. It would be an appropriation of power on her part, a moving away from her assumed role as subordinate, reverent, and loyal member of the relationship, and it would risk destabilizing the established social order. It was far more reassuring simply to assume that a woman would or could not disguise herself and her self-expression.

We can find examples of song lyrics written by women from Li Qing-zhao's time in which the female speaker or the woman being described is clearly not the author. The following song is one. It was written by Lady Wei, discussed earlier, wife of Zeng Bu, who was among the most powerful and distinguished officials under three emperors (Shenzong, Zhezong, and Huizong):

定風波   *To the tune "Calming the Wind and Waves"*

不是無心惜落花	It's not that I don't pity the fallen blossoms,
落花無意戀春華	The fallen blossoms care not for spring's splendor.
昨日盈盈枝上笑	Yesterday, full of smiles, sitting there on the branch.
誰道	Who could say
今朝吹去落誰家	Today, blown away, at whose home they came to rest?
把酒臨風千種恨	Holding wine I face the wind with a thousand regrets,
難問	Impossible to ask where,
夢回雲散見無涯	Awake from dreaming, the clouds vanish, the view is endless.
妙舞清歌誰是主	Lovely dancing and clear singing, who's the host now?
回顧	I gaze back,
高城不見夕陽斜	The high wall prevents me from seeing the setting sun.[27]

27. Wei furen, "Ding fengbo," *Quan Songci* 1:347.

The woman in this song is a professional entertainer, who, like the flowers she talks about in the first stanza, drifts from one home to the next, that is, from one male patron to the next. She entertains her host by singing and dancing, and never knows how long he will remain interested in her. In writing a piece like this, Lady Wei is participating in the long tradition of writing song lyrics about a type of woman who performed such songs, a woman who was a professional entertainer and who was "kept" by one wealthy patron after another. Lady Wei is certainly not writing about herself.

We should expect Li Qingzhao similarly to compose song lyrics on traditional subjects and themes, including those outside her own life and experience. But famous as she was, readers have not allowed her such license. Whatever she wrote in the genre is assumed to be autobiographical. A song attributed to her may have its authenticity called into question, but if the work is accepted as hers, then it is immediately inserted into her biography, usually dated, and becomes part of the reconstruction of her life. If, for example, the song features a flirtatious young lady interacting with a man, rather than taken as the poet Li Qingzhao's treatment of a well-established song lyrics theme, instead it is read as an account of the wife Li Qingzhao interacting with her husband and dated to the early years of their marriage. The song is then used, circularly, as evidence of Li Qingzhao's state of mind at that stage of her life. The possibility that Li Qingzhao could be inventing, creating fictive subjects and personas, as other song lyrics writers often did, is not considered. This has been done for so long and with such regularity that it has become accepted as the correct way to read Li Qingzhao's works. The argument here is not that Li Qingzhao never incorporates autobiographical elements into her song lyrics. Certainly there are pieces of hers that do mention, for example, place-names or buildings that we know from her life, and others whose details, even if they fall short of such specificity, seem to match well with what we know about her life experiences. But we should resist the temptation to equate the literary voice with the historical author in a narrow and uncritical way. Also, we should acknowledge the role of circular reasoning in the construction of her biography in the first place. Much of what we think we know about her life and her emotional moods at various stages is based on what we perceive "Li Qingzhao" to be telling us in her songs. Moreover, the dating of her songs to periods and even particular years of her life, which has become a scholarly obsession in its own right, is based almost entirely on simplistic preconceptions about how she felt in one period or another (as if one had a single mood in a given period of his or her life) followed by highly subjective judgments about which songs best match which emotive stage of her life. Consequently, scholars come up with wildly divergent dates for particular songs. There is, in most cases, no reliable internal or external evidence for dating, nothing to go on save the vague details found in the songs themselves.

Ultimately an issue of equity or fairness is involved. We enthusiastically turn to Li Qingzhao because she offers us something we do not easily find elsewhere in her era of Chinese cultural history. She is a woman writer whose works, some of them at least, beat the odds against perdition that were stacked against a woman writer of her time. We turn to her as the nearly unique example of a well-known historical woman whose own words we can read. We are eager to see what she has to say, since where else are we going to find elite women of the time speaking for themselves? But our very enthusiasm for this exceptional woman leads us to read her works differently than we read the works of her male contemporaries. Unwittingly, we impose assumptions about the way she writes and expresses herself that deprive her of the possibility of writing with the range and imaginative power that we recognize in male writers. Is it fair to read her in this limiting way? It is going to take considerable effort and willfulness to avoid doing so because the habit of reading her this way is so ingrained in us.

Why Did Zhao Mingcheng Not Send Letters Home to Li Qingzhao?

The assumption that Li Qingzhao's song lyrics are all autobiographical has colored even the most recent Chinese scholarship and criticism on her. The highly subjective interpretations it leads to, which vary widely from one scholar to the next, yield a tangled web of contradictory readings (for a glimpse of such contradictions, on a single issue, see appendix 2). To demonstrate this, I focus on periods of separation from her husband that Li Qingzhao is said to have endured during her twenty-seven years of marriage.

《一翦梅》   *To the tune "A Single Cutting of Plum Blossoms"* (no. 13)

红藕香殘玉簟秋	The scent of red lotuses fades in jade bamboo mat autumn.
輕解羅裳	Lightly she unties her gauze skirt
獨上蘭舟	To board the magnolia boat alone.
雲中誰寄錦書來	Amid the clouds, who sends a brocade letter?

雁字回時	As the wild geese character comes back
月滿西樓	The moon fills the western tower.
花自飄零水自流	Blossoms fall on their own, the water flows by itself.
一種相思	One type of longing,
兩處閒愁	Idle sadness in two places.
此情無計可消除	There's no means to get rid of this feeling.
纔下眉頭	As soon as it leaves the brow
却上心頭	It surfaces in the heart.[28]

In the first stanza, the "wild geese character" refers to the formation of the birds in flight, likened to the Chinese character *yi* 一 or, if in a "v" formation, to *ren* 人 (or *ba* 八). By legend, geese were said to be bearers of letters from loved ones far away. Because of an allusion, a "brocade letter" specifically implies a missive from a distant spouse.[29] In song lyrics "western tower" is by convention the dwelling of a woman, and it is where we often find a solitary woman whose lover has left. Here, even though the migratory geese are returning, raising hopes for the delivery of a letter, the question in line 4 is best understood as rhetorical, meaning that no letter has come. That is the way the line is normally read.[30]

The Yuan dynasty miscellany *Langhuan ji* 瑯嬛記, by Yi Shizhen 伊世珍 (14th c.), quotes this song lyric by Li Qingzhao and provides an explanation of its origin. Not long after Li Qingzhao was married, her husband, Zhao Mingcheng, "went off on distant travels bearing a chest of books" 負笈遠遊. Li Qingzhao could not bear to see him leave, and so she found a length of brocade and wrote out this song lyric on it and gave it to Mingcheng as a farewell present.[31] Yi Shizhen identifies the source of his information as something called an "Unofficial Biography" 外傳, which presumably was a fictionalized account of Li Qingzhao's life or perhaps of the lives of Li Qingzhao and Zhao Mingcheng together. It is interesting that such an unofficial and probably romanticized account of our poet's life existed as early as Yuan times, though unfortunately it did not survive.

---

28. *Jianzhu* 1.20; *Quan Songci* 2:1204.

29. The allusion is to the famous palindrome in brocade that Su Hui 蘇蕙 sent to her distant husband; see *Jinshu* 96.2523. From *Jianzhu* 1.22.

30. See, for example, the explanation of the line in Xu Beiwen, *Li Qingzhao quanji pingzhu*, p. 7.

31. Yi Shizhen, *Langhuan ji*, *Huibian*, pp. 28–29.

Scholarly opinion of Yi Shizhen's work is not high. It is often denigrated as being full of unreliable or spurious accounts. The biography that is Yi Shizhen's source here is just such a work of low credibility. Immediately preceding the account of the origin of this song lyric, the same source records a story about a prophetic dream Zhao Mingcheng had about his future wife before his betrothal. In his dream Mingcheng was reading a book, and when he awoke he remembered three lines from it, but their meaning eluded him. When he repeated the lines to his father, the father decoded them—by splitting up and recombining graphic elements, and by identifying sound puns—reducing them to "husband to a literary woman" 詞女之夫. Soon none other than Li Qingzhao was selected to become his wife. This story is likely part of a legend that had grown up around the famous couple.

Despite the dubious character of the information in the *Langhuan ji*, the notion that Zhao Mingcheng went off on a distant journey soon after Li Qingzhao married him evidently had considerable appeal. The *Langhuan ji* passage was quoted in numerous Ming and Qing period collections of song lyric criticism and anecdotes. It is also cited and accepted as fact in the long and influential account of Li Qingzhao's life by the Qing scholar Yu Zhengxie 俞正燮.[32] It is even repeated in recent scholarship on Li Qingzhao, including Xu Peijun's authoritative annotated edition of her complete works, first published by the Shanghai Ancient Texts Publishing Company in 2002.[33]

The durability of this idea of Zhao Mingcheng's early absence from his wife is not due solely to *Langhuan ji*. It also owes something to a few words from Li Qingzhao herself, contained in her famous "Afterword" to Zhao Mingcheng's *Records on Metal and Stone*:

> Two years later [after her marriage], my husband went out to serve as an official, whereupon we ate vegetarian meals and wore clothes of coarse cloth, intent upon obtaining from every distant place and remote region as many of the world's ancient inscriptions and rare engraved words as we could.

後二年，出仕宦，便有飯疏衣練，窮遐方絕域，盡天下古文奇字之志。[34]

Mindful of these words, Xu Peijun "corrects" the *Langhuan ji*. It was not to find a teacher or pursue his general studies (which is what the phrase *fuji*

---

32. Yu Zhengxie, "Yi'an jushi shiji" 15.763; also in *Huibian*, p. 107.
33. *Jianzhu* 1.22; also in Xu Peijun's "Nianpu," *Jianzhu*, pp. 423–24.
34. *Jianzhu* 3.309.

yuanyou 負笈遠遊 implies) that Zhao Mingcheng left, but rather to collect the rubbings that would eventually constitute the contents of *Records on Metal and Stone*.

Yet the afterword passage lends itself to more than one interpretation. If the sentence above is read by itself, taken out of context, it does indeed seem to suggest that Zhao Mingcheng went off on far-flung travels to collect ancient inscriptions. But it looks different in the original context, as seen below:

> It was in the *xinsi* year of the Jianzhong period [1101] that I married into the Zhao family. At that time, my late father was serving as vice director of the Ministry of Rites, and the grand councilor [her father-in-law, Zhao Tingzhi] was vice director of the Ministry of Personnel. My husband, twenty-one years old, was a student in the National University. The Zhaos and Lis are undistinguished families that have always been poor. On the leave days of the first and fifteenth of every month, when he requested holiday leave, we would pawn some clothes to raise five hundred cash. Then we'd walk to Xiangguo Monastery to buy fruits and rubbings of inscriptions. We'd take them home, sit down together, and spread them out, savoring them. We felt that we were living in the harmonious era of Getianshi.[35]
>
> Two years later, my husband came out to serve as an official. We ate vegetarian meals and wore clothes of coarse cloth, intent on obtaining from every distant place and remote region as many of the world's ancient inscriptions and rare engraved words as we could. As the days and months passed, our collection grew. The grand councilor [Zhao Tingzhi] stayed in the imperial city, and many of our relations worked in the palace libraries and archives. They had access to lost odes, little-known histories, and such books as those recovered from the walls of Lu and the tomb of Ji.[36] When we came upon such rare works, we exerted ourselves to make copies of them. Once awakened to the flavor of this activity, we could not stop. Later, whenever we came upon a piece of calligraphy or a painting by a celebrated artist, whether ancient or recent, or a precious vessel from the Three Dynasties, we would take off a layer of clothing to pawn for it. I remember that once during the Chongning period [1102–6] someone brought a peony painting by Xu Xi [10th c.] to show us. He was asking two hundred thousand for it. In those days it would have been hard even for young persons in eminent officials' families to come up with such a sum. The man left it with us for two days, but we finally decided we could not purchase it and returned it to him. Afterward, my husband and I looked at each other dejectedly for several days.

---

35. Getianshi 葛天氏 is a legendary king whose reign was marked by harmony and peace.
36. The reference is to two famous discoveries of ancient writings. See chapter 6.

In this light, it appears that Zhao Mingcheng never left the capital, and indeed that he, with the assistance of his wife, used his proximity to the palace archives and his personal ties through his father and other high-ranking friends and relatives to build their collection of rare books, rubbings, and antiquities. The chronology is important. Li Qingzhao was married in 1101, when Zhao Mingcheng was still a student in the National University. It was, according to her, two years later (1103) that Mingcheng began his official career. We do not know in what office or capacity that career began. But we do know that in the tenth month of 1105 he was appointed vice minister of the Office of State Ceremonies 鴻臚少卿.[37] This was a surprisingly lofty court appointment for such a young man, and it surely came to Mingcheng because by then his father was so eminent in the early years of Huizong's reign (his two older brothers also received prestigious appointments at the same time).

Huang Shengzhang 黃盛璋 addressed this issue of Zhao Mingcheng's early departure from the capital in his seminal studies of Li Qingzhao and Zhao Mingcheng of 1957.[38] Huang rejected the tradition that Zhao Mingcheng ever left the capital (or his wife) during those years, and he even proposed an explanation of how the erroneous understanding had come about. The language Li Qingzhao uses in her afterword is that Zhao Mingcheng *chu shihuan* 出仕宦. Huang says that *chu* 出, which Yi Shizhen (following the "Unofficial Biography") took to mean "went out [to the provinces]" to take up office, should be understood as *chu er shi yi* 出而仕矣, meaning that Zhao "came out [from the National University, or went out (into the world)] to join officialdom." Huang finds support for this reading in the transcription of the afterword by the early Southern Song scholar Hong Mai. Hong Mai's version of the afterword text simply says that Zhao *cong huan* 從宦 (or in some editions *cong guan* 從官), "joined officialdom."[39] Huang Shengzhang goes on to find fault with the *Langhuan ji*'s claim that Li Qingzhao's "A Single Cutting of Plum Blossoms" could have been written as a farewell song to Zhao Mingcheng, noting several features of the piece that make it implausible to fulfill such a role.

---

37. See Xu Peijun's "Nianpu," *Jianzhu*, p. 427.

38. Huang Shengzhang, "Li Qingzhao shiji kaobian," pp. 317–19. See also Huang Shengzhang's companion study, "Zhao Mingcheng Li Qingzhao fufu nianpu," pp. 149–50.

39. Hong Mai, *Rongzhai suibi*, "Sibi" 四筆 5.684.

Most scholars who have published on Li Qingzhao's life and works in recent years, including Wang Zhongwen 王仲聞, Chen Zumei, Yu Zhonghang 于中航, Zhuge Yibing, and Deng Hongmei, accept Huang Shengzhang's argument and new understanding of the whereabouts of Zhao Mingcheng during the early years of his marriage.[40] As mentioned above, however, the traditional view of the early departure of Zhao Mingcheng from his wife is still accepted by some. Xu Peijun's support for it factors into his dating of two of Li Qingzhao's song lyrics (including no. 13) that refer to separation from a loved one to the period.

Yet when we look at those scholars who agree with Huang Shengzhang on this point, we find an interesting phenomenon. Most of them suggest another type of separation that Li Qingzhao and Zhao Mingcheng had to endure early in their marriage. There are two features of these alternative separations that are immediately striking. The first is the variety of them that have been suggested, all subsequent to Huang Shengzhang's publication, and most in the past ten to fifteen years. Each scholar has his or her own suggestion for a separation, and each tends to be supplanted by the next publication that posits a new one. In other words, there is no clear consensus about exactly how the young married couple was separated and for what reason. The second feature, which is probably related to the lack of a clear consensus, is that each suggestion has weaknesses and might readily be challenged. I will briefly summarize three of these suggestions and points that might be raised against them.

Chen Zumei maintains that it was Li Qingzhao who left the capital and returned to her natal home in Zhangqiu 章丘 (Shangdong). She was forced to leave because of the decrees banning Yuanyou party officials and their offspring from office and from residence in the capital in 1103, and she was not able to return for good to the capital until that ban was lifted in 1106. Yet in between, during certain periods that the political feuding subsided and the ban was relaxed, Li Qingzhao managed to come back to the capital for brief periods (e.g., in 1104), only to be forced to leave again when the political situation worsened again.[41]

----

40. Wang Zhongwen, *Li Qingzhao ji jiaozhu*, p. 25; Chen Zumei, *Li Qingzhao xinzhuan*, pp. 64–65; Chen Zumei, *Li Qingzhao ci xinshi jiping*, pp. 50–51; Yu Zhonghang, *Li Qingzhao nianpu*, p. 47; Zhuge, *Li Qingzhao yu Zhao Mingcheng*, pp. 47–49; Deng, *Li Qingzhao xinzhuan*, pp. 47–55.

41. Chen Zumei, "Li Qingzhao nianpu jianbian" 李清照年譜簡編, *Li Qingzhao xinzhuan*, pp. 274–75; cf. Chen Zumei, "Li Qingzhao nianpu" 李清照年譜, in *Li Qingzhao pingzhuan*, p. 291.

We know that Li Qingzhao's father, Li Gefei, was on all of the various lists of Yuanyou faction "traitors" issued at the instigation of Cai Jing between 1102 and 1104. That was only natural, because he had served as professor in the National University during the Yuanyou period and was associated with the literary circle of Su Shi. It is also true that some decrees in the persecution campaign of those years specified prohibitions to be imposed not only on the Yuanyou officials, but also on members of their families. A decree issued in the third month of 1102 orders that the "sons and younger brothers" of Yuanyou officials must live in the provinces and prohibits them from entering the capital.[42] A decree issued in the ninth month of the year prohibits imperial clan members from marrying the "sons and grandsons" of Yuanyou faction members, adding that if such a marriage is promised but not yet carried out, the betrothal shall be terminated.[43] It is these decrees that Chen Zumei cites as the cause of Li Qingzhao's departure from the capital.

It is not at all certain, however, that such prohibitions would have applied to the daughters of Yuanyou faction officials. Such application would have greatly multiplied the number of persons affected by the ban. The low status of daughters in clans also argues against them being included along with "sons and grandsons." It seems particularly improbable that the ban would have applied to daughters who were already married. The wording of the second decree mentioned above, which concerned imperial relatives (Zhao Mingcheng's family was not among them), implies that nothing was to be done in the case of marriages already formalized, as Li Qingzhao's had been. Besides, this particular daughter happened to have a father-in-law who in 1102 became vice grand councilor, that is, next to Cai Jing the second highest official in the empire. Even in the unlikely case that daughters were included in the ban, if an exception were going to be made for any of them, it might well be one with such lofty connections. Another consideration is that in her own narrative of her married life of this period, Li Qingzhao says nothing about separating from her husband and returning to her parents' home. Actually, as we see in the passage quoted earlier, Li Qingzhao's memory of these years (the "Chongning period") appears to be of an integral time when she and her husband were together. She represents the years as contented ones, when she and Zhao Mingcheng were busy in their leisure time assembling their collection. The only disappointment she registers from these years

---

42. Yang Zhongliang, *Xu zizhi tongjian changbian jishi benmo* 121.13a (p. 3773).
43. Ibid. 121.16a (p. 3779).

is over the Xu Xi peony painting they could not afford, even though they were "young persons in an eminent official's family." If Li Qingzhao herself was affected by the Yuanyou persecution, she gives no hint of it in her afterword, even though that narrative was written thirty years later, when that period of persecution had come to be widely condemned and its victims thought to have been vindicated by subsequent events.

Another scenario of early separation of the married couple is put forth by Zhuge Yibing. Zhuge reminds us that when the couple was first married Zhao Mingcheng was still a student in the National University.[44] As such, he points out, Mingcheng would have been obliged to reside in the dormitories at the university and would only have been allowed to return home to visit his new wife on the first and fifteenth of every month. There is a problem, again, of reconciling this account of early separation with the way Li Qingzhao herself describes the early days of her marriage ("We felt that we were living in the harmonious era of Getianshi"). Li Qingzhao does refer to the free time she and her husband had together on the first and fifteenth of every month, when they would go to the Xiangguo Monastery market to buy books and rubbings. But that might simply mean that those were the holidays on which Zhao Mingcheng had no obligations at the university. It does not necessarily mean that Mingcheng only spent two nights at home per month. One would think that the son of the vice grand councilor might have some special privileges his classmates would not enjoy. Nevertheless, Zhuge uses the purported university residence of Zhao Mingcheng to account for Li Qingzhao's song lyrics on separation that he dates to the period. In one of them, the speaker complains, as she stands on a high balcony looking out, that she is receiving no "distant letters" 遠信.[45] To accept Zhuge's understanding of the provenance of this song, we must believe Li Qingzhao is exaggerating her separation to an extreme extent.

In Deng Hongmei's *New Biography of Li Qingzhao*, published in 2005, one more early separation of the young married couple is posited.[46] This one, she argues, came after Li Qingzhao's return to the capital in 1106, at the end of the Chongning period persecution of Yuanyou partisans. At the court, these years were marked by intense rivalry and in-fighting between Cai Jing and

---

44. Zhuge, *Li Qingzhao yu Zhao Mingcheng*, pp. 38–43.
45. "Yuan Wangsun" 怨王孫, no. 39, *Jianzhu* 1.18; *Quan Songci* 2:1208.
46. Deng, *Li Qingzhao xinzhuan*, pp. 59–66.

his former assistant, Li Qingzhao's father-in-law, Zhao Tingzhi. Tingzhi had briefly been elevated to the post of grand councilor in 1105, which he shared with Cai Jing. (It is because Tingzhi finally achieved this post, the highest possible, that Li Qingzhao refers to him by this title in her afterword.) But their co-incumbency of that highest post lasted but one month, whereupon Tingzhi requested permission to resign. The emperor, evidently pitying him, presented him with an estate in the capital to reside in during his "retirement." In early 1106, the sighting of a spectacular meteor helped to change Huizong's mind. Soon, Cai Jing was removed from office, and Zhao Tingzhi was reinstalled as sole grand councilor. But this arrangement was also short-lived. Cai Jing was back in favor by the beginning of 1107 (the first year of the Daguan period, 1107–10). He then took revenge upon the man who had become his nemesis. Zhao Tingzhi was stripped of office in the third month. Five days after this humiliation, Zhao Tingzhi died at his residence in the capital. Unfortunately, we do not know the particulars of his death. Three days later, Cai Jing took action against Tingzhi's three surviving sons (including Zhao Mingcheng). They were charged with being implicated in their late father's corruption in office. A case was mounted against them, and they were eventually arrested and imprisoned. The charges proved impossible to substantiate, however, and by the seventh month they were exonerated and released.

The standard account of Li Qingzhao's life says that in the final months of 1107 she and Zhao Mingcheng left the capital to return to his late father's home in Qingzhou, where they would remain for over a decade, the first few years being spent in mourning for Zhao Tingzhi. But Deng Hongmei has discovered a poem that, she contends, requires a different scenario. The poem was written by Xie Yi 謝逸 (1068–1113), a Jiangxi poet who befriended several of the literati of the day. The poem is titled "Sending Off Zhao Defu [Zhao Mingcheng] to Accompany his Parent(s) in Huaidong" 送趙德甫侍親淮東.[47] Based on this poem, Deng Hongmei hypothesizes the following elaborate scenario: struck by the double tragedies of her husband's sudden death and the criminal charges against her sons, Mrs. Zhao (née Guo) left the capital at the time of her sons' arrest and sought refuge in the southern city of Nanjing, not far from where her husband had once served (elsewhere in the Huaidong Circuit). When the charges against the brothers were dropped

---

47. *Quan Songshi* 22:14833–34.

in the seventh month, Zhao Mingcheng left the capital to go fetch his mother and bring her back up north to Qingzhou to commence the mourning period. But he did not travel directly there or go with haste. Taking advantage of the opportunity to add to his collection of rubbings by visiting distant regions, he traveled overland southwest into Sichuan, then down the Yangzi River through the Three Gorges and on to Nanjing. Xie Yi's poem makes mention of the Qutang Gorge 瞿塘峽 and its famous Yanyu Reef 灩澦堆 as places Zhao Mingcheng will sail past. Zhao Mingcheng did not return to the capital with his mother until the summer of 1108, after which mother and son, together with Li Qingzhao, went into mourning at Qingzhou.

Deng Hongmei deserves credit for uncovering a poem addressed to Zhao Mingcheng that had never been noticed before. Yet the conclusions she draws from it are problematic in several respects. Aside from the poem, there is no reason to think that Mrs. Zhao suddenly decided to remove herself from the capital and embark on a distant southern journey to Nanjing. It seems inherently improbable that she would do so, when she was still waiting to learn the outcome of the charges against her three sons, whose fate was now tied inextricably to her own. It stretches credulity even more to suppose that, if Zhao Mingcheng did need to go south to retrieve his mother, he would have indulged himself by going hundreds of miles out of his way into Sichuan and then sailing leisurely down the Yangzi all the way to Nanjing. The family had just been plunged into mourning, coupled with tremendous setbacks in its official standing and the prospects for the sons' future careers. What son would go sauntering so far out of his way if the immediate task were to bring his mother home for mourning?

Second, Deng assumes that Xie Yi was in the capital when he wrote his poem bidding farewell to Mingcheng. In fact, it is clear that at this late stage of his life, Xie Yi had already returned to his native Linchuan (modern Fuzhou shi 撫州市, south of Nanchang in central Jiangxi), where he spent his final years. Xie Yi had been in the capital years before, when he tried without success to pass the examinations and become an official. Eventually, he abandoned the pursuit and returned to Linchuan, where he evidently supported himself by taking students. Several tomb inscriptions that Xie Yi wrote for Linchuan natives from the period 1103–9 make it clear that he was back in Linchuan both before, during, and after 1107, the year of Zhao Tingzhi's death in the capital. (In some of these inscriptions, he describes the relatives of the deceased personally coming to his house to ask him to compose an elegy.)[48] The most one can say, in other words, is that at some time Xie Yi sent off Zhao Mingcheng on a trip from Linchuan east to Huaidong (modern Jiangsu). Incidentally, for Mingcheng to have visited Xie Yi in Linchuan means that he took another detour of a couple hundred miles, southward, if he was boating down the Yangzi from the Three Gorges to Nanjing.

Finally, the poem by Xie Yi does not fit the circumstances of Zhao Mingcheng's life in 1107. The poem makes no reference to the recent death of his powerful father or the fact that Mingcheng was now in mourning. Quite to the contrary, the poem is forward-looking and buoyant. It speaks of Mingcheng as a talented young man with a splendid future, akin to legendary steeds in divine stables, who should not, as he goes off to make his way in the world, be in any hurry to "sell himself" to just any patron. The poem belongs, in fact, to a well-known type of verse: that addressed to young men, celebrating their early achievements and promise. It would be inappropriate as something written for Mingcheng when he was in the throes of the events that befell him in 1107.

The poem remains something of an enigma. Perhaps it was not written for this "Zhao Defu." (Xie Yi left no other works addressed to Zhao Mingcheng or to "Zhao Defu.") Or, if it was, it must have been written at an earlier stage of Zhao's life. The poem mentions the addressee's unusual level of maturity "before he reached twenty years of age." Perhaps the poem was written during a youthful southern tour that Zhao Mingcheng took before his marriage at the age of twenty-one and entry into the National University. At this point we cannot know. But the poem does not appear to be what Deng Hongmei would make it to be.

The three early separations of Li Qingzhao from her husband proposed by Chen Zumei, Zhuge Yibing, and Dong Hongmei differ in their particulars, but they share one impulse and design. Faced with the persuasiveness of Huang Shengzhang's rejection of the traditional account of Zhao Mingcheng's removal from the capital soon after his marriage to Li Qingzhao, these scholars feel obliged to search out another cause for the

---

48. Xie Yi, "Chen fujun muzhiming" 陳府君墓誌銘, "Gu Chengfeng lang Wang Jizhi muzhiming" 故承奉郎王及至墓誌銘, "Jiang jushi muzhiming" 江居士墓誌銘, and especially "Wu furen muzhiming" 吳夫人墓誌銘, *Quan Songwen* 2877.3.254–55, 257–58, 262, and 2878.4.268–69. In this last piece, the place-name Linru 臨汝 is the name of a former county in Linchuan.

separation of the married couple. The tenuousness and mutual incompatibility of the separations they propose reflect the tension between their determination to find such separations and what the facts, as best we know them, concerning the two persons' whereabouts during those years permit us to say with any certainty.

The scholarly preoccupation with separations during the years of Li Qingzhao's marriage is not confined to the early years of her life together with Zhao Mingcheng in the capital. It extends to the period of their forced "retirement" to Qingzhou. That period began soon after Zhao Tingzhi's death in 1107 and seems to have lasted fourteen years. So far as we know, Mingcheng was not reinstated to official service until the autumn of 1121, when he was posted as governor to Laizhou. There is some speculation that Mingcheng's reinstatement may have come a few years earlier, but there is no source confirming any such earlier appointment, as we would expect if there had been one.

The scholarly literature gives much attention to Zhao Mingcheng's absences from home during these Qingzhou years. He regularly went off, we are told, to climb distant mountains and scour the countryside in search of ancient inscriptions to add to his collection. Many of Li Qingzhao's song lyrics that speak of her lonesomeness or of parting scenes are consequently dated to these years. Such was her literary reaction, we are supposed to believe, to Zhao Mingcheng's antiquarian perambulations about the region.

Yet when we look with a more critical eye at the evidence for Mingcheng's absences, we are apt to conclude that, just as with the preceding years in the capital, scholars have stretched minimal evidence to maximum inferences. Mingcheng did indeed take several trips during these years. But there is little reason to think that he was absent often or for long periods of time. Thanks to notations Mingcheng made on certain inscriptions in his *Records on Metal and Stone*, explaining how he acquired them, or to inscriptions he left at the places he visited, which have been preserved in the original or in rubbings, we know the date and destination of several of his outings during these years. He had two favorite destinations. The place he visited most often was Heaven View Mountain 仰天山 south of Qingzhou. The mountain was known for its Luohan Grotto, a deep cave that had a crack in one part of its roof through which the moon shone on the Autumn Moon Festival. It was from this fissure that the mountain got its name. Heaven View Mountain was about forty miles from Qingzhou. We know of altogether four trips that Zhao Mingcheng made there. These took place in 1108 (on the Double Ninth

Festival in the ninth month), 1109 (on the Duanwu festival in the fifth month), 1111 (on the Mid-Autumn Moon festival in the eighth month), and 1121 (in the fourth month; perhaps this last visit was precipitated by his appointment in that year to Laizhou, which lay in the opposite direction from his favorite mountain). There is one other inscription he left there that is undated, next to the inscription of 1108, and this may have come from a fifth trip.[49]

Aside from Heaven View Mountain, Zhao Mingcheng also liked to travel to Lingyan Monastery 靈巖寺 in Changqing County 長清縣. Changqing was south of the city of Ji'nan 濟南 and was located some 108 miles from Qingzhou. Mingcheng visited this monastery three times, as he records in an inscription he left there on his last visit.[50] He went there in the ninth month of 1109, in the summer of 1113, and in the third month of 1116. On the second of these visits, he continued on to Tai Mountain 泰山, which he climbed together with friends.[51] Tai Mountain was close by. It stood another twenty-five miles to the southeast of Changqing County so that it would have been on Mingcheng's way back home.

We have, then, seven or eight trips, scattered over a period of fourteen years. The farthest of the trips was just over one hundred miles. As for their duration, we cannot be certain, but what evidence there is suggests the trips did not last long. Most of the trips to Heaven View Mountain coincided with seasonal festivals, suggesting that their duration was short. Only one of Zhao Mingcheng's site inscriptions specifies the duration of a visit. That is the one from the 1109 trip to Lingyan Monastery. Mingcheng says, "In all we stayed two days and then went home" 凡宿兩日乃歸. The schedule of the 1113 trip seems to have been similarly brief. Mingcheng was at Lingyan Monastery on the sixth day of the intercalary month (June 22). Two days later he stood on top of Tai Mountain.[52]

When we compare what is claimed by scholars about song lyrics by Li Qingzhao that are conventionally dated to these years with what can be verified about Zhao Mingcheng's actual absences, a discrepancy is apparent. It is difficult to reconcile the concentration of the songs on the problem of

---

49. On these visits to Heaven View Mountain, see Yu Zhonghang, *Li Qingzhao nianpu*, pp. 60–61 (1108), 61 (1109), 65 (1111), and 84–85 (1121).
50. The inscription, a rubbing of which is held in the Beijing Municipal Library, is recorded in full in ibid., p. 62.
51. Ibid., pp. 67–68.
52. Ibid., p. 68.

loneliness, not to mention the depth of the despondency they contain, with what we know about Mingcheng's travels. The discrepancy is not one between the song lyrics and what we can construct about Zhao Mingcheng's travels, but rather a gulf between what scholars claim the song lyrics express or react to and those travels.

Consider the following composition, one of Li Qingzhao's best known. It is assigned by Xu Peijun to the year 1109 and said to have been inspired by Zhao Mingcheng's trip that year to Lingyan Monastery.[53] That was the trip on which, according to Mingcheng's own account, he spent two nights at the monastery before going home.

鳳凰臺上憶吹簫   *To the tune "On Top of Phoenix Tower, Recalling Flute Music"*
(no. 12)

香冷金猊	Incense lies cold in the golden lion
被翻紅浪	The bedcover is tossed crimson waves.
起來慵自梳頭	Arising, she is too languid to comb her hair,
任寶奩塵滿	And lets the jeweled make-up case gather dust.
日上簾鉤	The sun climbs to the curtain hook,
生怕離懷別苦	She fears nothing more than longing for a distant one and parting pain.
多少事	How many things have happened!
欲說還休	About to speak, she stops.
新來瘦	She's grown thin of late
非干病酒	Not from sickness over wine
不是悲秋	Or from sadness over autumn.
休休	No more, no more!
這回去也	When he left this time
千萬遍陽關	A thousand verses of "Yang Pass"
也則難留	Would not have detained him.
念武陵人遠	The Wuling man is distant now
煙鎖秦樓	Mists lock shut the tower in Qin.
唯有樓前流水	There's only the flowing river before the tower
應念我	That should remember me
終日凝眸	Staring transfixed, all day long.
凝眸處	At the spot I stand and stare,
從今又添	From today will be added
一段新愁	One layer of new sorrow.[54]

---

53. *Jianzhu* 1.61.
54. *Jianzhu* 1.59–60; *Quan Songci* 2:1204.

Naturally, we cannot prove that Li Qingzhao did not write this just as Xu Peijun imagines that she did, speaking in her own voice and describing her longing for Zhao Mingcheng when he was off on his short trip to Lingyan Monastery. Yet we can readily observe that several of the statements of the composition are at variance with its purported provenance and purpose. The woman in the song, who alternates in the song between speaker and a subject who is being observed or described, seems to be enduring a distant and long-term separation, so much so that she claims to have grown thin from her longing, and the box that contains her make-up has dust accumulated on its cover. "Yang Pass" is a parting song sung when someone is going off on a distant journey rather than on a pleasure outing or excursion. Indeed, the tone of the entire song does not match well with an anticipated separation of just a few days.

Sensing, probably, the awkwardness of connecting such a composition to a local sightseeing outing, other scholars have recently suggested a different provenance for the song.[55] It was written, they assert, when Zhao Mingcheng was reinstated to official service and left Li Qingzhao behind in Qingzhou to assume a new assignment elsewhere. But this scenario brings its own set of problems. We know for certain, thanks to Li Qingzhao's and Zhao Mingcheng's own writings, that Mingcheng served as governor in Laizhou from the autumn of 1121 to the autumn of 1124, that is, he fulfilled the standard three-year stint. We also know that he next served in the same capacity in Zizhou 淄州 (just east of Qingzhou), from 1124 until 1126, when the impending Jurchen invasion changed everything. Some scholars want us to believe that Mingcheng left Qingzhou a few years before he assumed his post in Laizhou in 1121, and then these same scholars date compositions such as "On Top of Phoenix Tower" to those years. But there is no evidence of that early departure, nothing that establishes Mingcheng anywhere else or holding any other office before 1121. The only sources are the literary compositions that scholars date to this period, without external support, and then discuss as if they were "evidence" of the marital separation they posit. The circularity of such reasoning is clear.

There is a way out of this problem and indeed a way out of the problems posed by all the contradictory separations of Li Qingzhao and Zhao Mingcheng that have been proposed. The solution is to dispense with the assumption that whenever Li Qingzhao wrote song lyrics, she wrote in a

---

55. Chen Zumei, *Li Qingzhao xinzhuan*, pp. 96–97; Deng, *Li Qingzhao xinzhuan*, pp. 85–87; Zhuge, *Li Qingzhao yu Zhao Mingcheng*, pp. 91–93.

narrowly autobiographical way so that any woman we find in her compositions corresponds to the historical Li Qingzhao and anything that woman says to a beloved is a statement addressed to Zhao Mingcheng. If we understand instead that Li Qingzhao, like every other important song lyrics writer of her time, relied heavily on conventional voices and images of lonely lovers with which to present and fill her songs, then what we will be apt to hear in "On Top of Phoenix Tower" is just such a conventional persona speaking rather than the historical Li Qingzhao. We could easily find similar voices of women protesting the departure of the man they love in song lyrics by Liu Yong, Ouyang Xiu, Qin Guan, or for that matter nearly any other male song writer of the era. Viewed this way, the project of locating "On Top of Phoenix Tower" in the chronology of Li Qingzhao's life becomes quite meaningless, as does the perceived need to link it to an actual separation between husband and wife.

We could have reached this point in the argument by more direct reasoning, yet that approach would have the disadvantage of failing to engage the vast native scholarship and criticism on Li Qingzhao, which as learned and valuable as it may be is also often fraught with questionable claims. One could simply say that we should recognize in Li Qingzhao the same ability to create and manipulate literary personas and fictive subjects that we regularly accept in the works of her male counterparts. That she is female and the other important writers male is no reason for making autobiographical assumptions about her works that we would be reluctant to adopt for other writers. It is unacceptable to contend that she would have been incapable of writing in a voice other than her own, when we recognize that male authors did that regularly. Furthermore, to think that Li Qingzhao wrote solely as devoted wife to Zhao Mingcheng and was unable to write otherwise is to reduce her literary identity and self-image to that of wife to Zhao Mingcheng. It would be problematic to do this with any woman, and it seems particularly so with a woman as outspoken and talented as Li Qingzhao. Yet that is exactly what the bulk of Li Qingzhao criticism has always done.

We will return to many of these issues and have more to say on them in chapters 10 and 11, when we consider Li Qingzhao's song lyrics themselves, after first discussing the rest of her life, her other writings, and the complicated ways "Li Qingzhao" was constructed and reconstructed in the centuries after her death. As explained in the Introduction, the inseparability of issues surrounding the interpretation of her song lyrics from these other matters favors postponing the song lyrics analysis until we have further explored previous constructions.

CHAPTER 4

Widowhood, Remarriage, Divorce

The focus changes in this chapter from Li Qingzhao's writings to events that overtook and consumed her in her middle years. Li Qingzhao's biography is of considerable interest as one of the best documented lives of a woman of her period. Aside from this inherent interest, her life is inseparable from her literary writings not only for the obvious reason that her literary expression is grounded in her life experiences, but also because the way her writings have always been read compounds the connections between her life and work. The result, as we will see, is that it is nearly impossible to read her song lyrics, for example, without reference to the biographical circumstances under which we suppose or imagine them to have been written.

The preceding chapter referred to certain events in the first years of her adulthood: to her youthful marriage to Zhao Mingcheng, to the early years of her marriage, when Mingcheng was a student in the National Academy, and to their prolonged period back at Qingzhou, when for political reasons Mingcheng found himself out of favor and without an official post. In fact, we know very little about Li Qingzhao's life from these years, aside from where she was and what her husband was doing. The lack of detail available is hardly surprising. We would not expect to know anything more about a woman of her time than the essential facts of her marital status and her husband's whereabouts. It is true that Li Qingzhao's modern biographers fill out the story of these years of her life with a great many more details. But these are embellishments and are derived almost entirely from statements found in her literary works. There are two problems with this. The first is that the dates of the great majority of her literary works that are used as the basis of these narratives of her life are utterly uncertain. Works that are taken by some biographers to date from, say, the Qingzhou period of her life and that become the basis for reconstructing details of her circumstances and state of mind during that period are taken by other biographers to date from a decade before or decades after. Needless to say, each biographer can point to reasons in support of the date he or she assigns. But given that there is no internal date in most of her literary works and that the internal "evidence" for a date of composition is far from definitive, the cases made for dating individual pieces are often weak. Hence the dates assigned for particular pieces by different biographers are widely varied and contradictory. The second problem is that even what Li Qingzhao says about her life that is not fraught with uncertainty regarding when it was written and what period it refers to is complicated by other questions regarding her motives and the reliability of what she says. We will discuss these issues at length in a later chapter.

Li Qingzhao's life changed dramatically with the Jurchen invasion of the Song empire in 1126–27. She became caught up in the dynastic catastrophe occasioned by that invasion and the flight southward by thousands of her compatriots. This was soon followed by the untimely death of Zhao Mingcheng and great personal hardship for Li Qingzhao that ensued during several chaotic years afterward. Perhaps ironically, our ability to reconstruct the details of her life during this period improves. This is partly because she and Zhao Mingcheng are thrown into the dynastic crisis and so the number of references to them in standard sources increases; it is also because Li Qingzhao's datable writings from those years increase when compared to the preceding years.

Fleeing the Jurchen and the Death of Zhao Mingcheng

The Jurchen had been a vassal tribe in the Khitan empire of Liao, north of the Song border, centered on the region that would later be known as Manchuria. But the Jurchen rebelled against the Kitan and established their own state, the Jin, in 1115.[1] In the years that followed, the Song sought to form a political and military alliance with the upstart Jin against the Liao, its

---

1. For a detailed account of the Jin invasion of the Song, see Levine, "The Reigns of Hui-tsung and Ch'in-tsung," pp. 614–43.

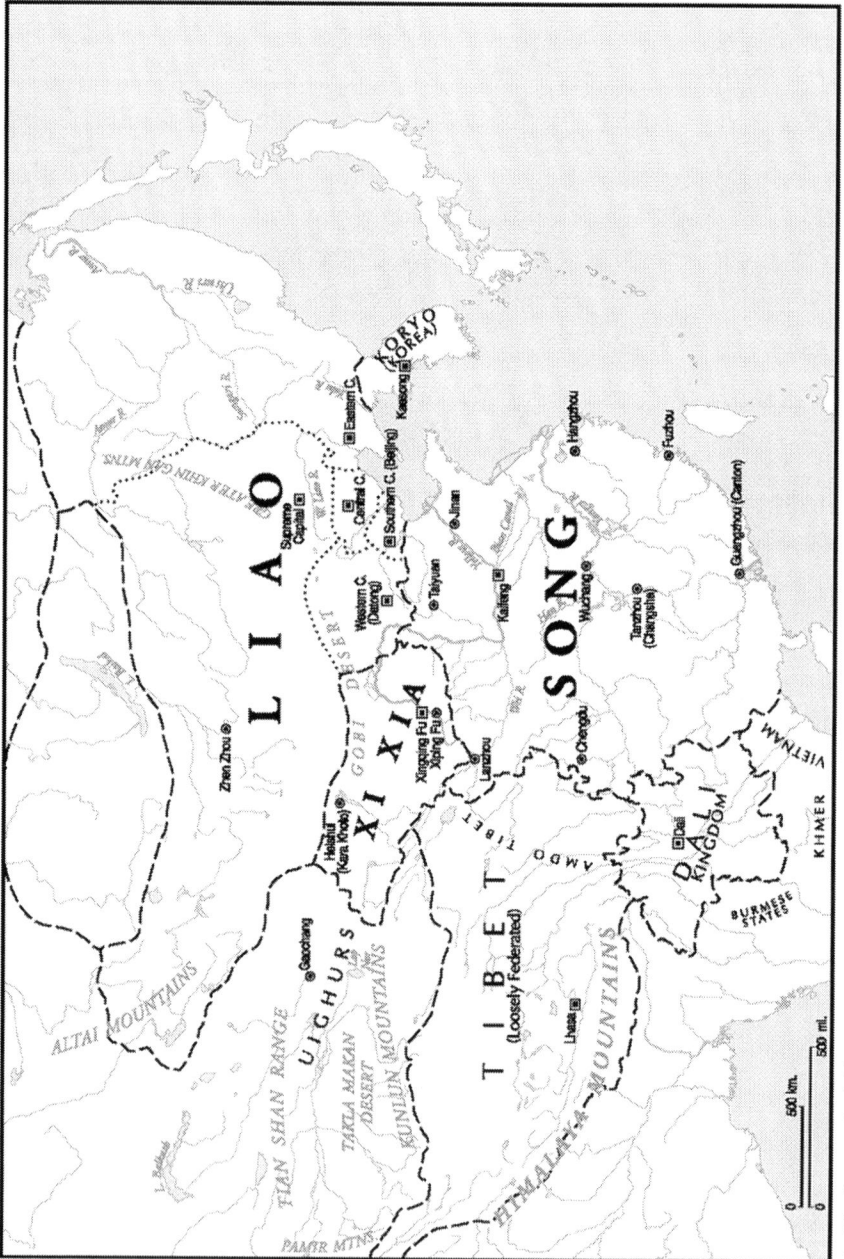

Map 1. The Song and neighboring empires, circa 1100. Reprinted by permission of the publisher from *Imperial China, 900–1800* by F. W. Mote, p. 58. Cambridge, Mass.: Harvard University Press, copyright © 1999 by F. W. Mote.

long-standing northern rival, in the hope of regaining the sixteen northern prefectures that had been ceded to the Liao during the Five Dynasties period (907–79). What transpired instead was that the Jin armies were able to drive the Liao westward from those lands by themselves. The Jin quickly established themselves as the dominant power in the north. The Jin court imposed a peace treaty on the western Xi Xia empire in 1124, then captured the last Liao emperor early in 1125, bringing that empire to an end. Buoyed by their successes and angered by what they perceived as the Song court's failure to give them the respect they had earned, the Jurchen turned their expansionist aims to the Song itself. A two-pronged campaign brought Jurchen armies to the walls of the capital of Bianliang (Kaifeng) at the end of 1125, where they laid siege to the city. By then the sense of desperation that gripped the Song court had caused Emperor Huizong to abdicate in favor of his son, Qinzong. But it was already too late to save the situation. Qinzong managed to conclude a treaty with the threatening Jurchen armies, but the terms of what the Song now promised to give to the Jin in territory and annual tribute only exposed the weakness of his position. Meanwhile, his court was torn between parties advocating appeasement and resistance. When Qinzong's policies wavered between these two in the months that followed, it was enough to provoke the Jin to launch another attack. This time they would not be pacified by treaties. After a brief siege of the capital, at the end of 1126, the Jin armies poured into the city, looting the palaces and terrorizing the people. They seized as captives the two Song emperors, Qinzong and his father Huizong, along with nearly the entire imperial clan and hundreds of palace ladies, eunuchs, officials and artisans, some three thousand prisoners in all. The prisoners were marched northward to the Jin homeland, together a long train of carts containing imperial treasure. The lone son of Huizong who was not captured, because he had fled before the siege, was quickly installed as the new Song emperor (known to history as Gaozong), presiding over a court in exile. The court and emperor fled southward, followed by thousands of officials and others who were lucky enough to escape Jin capture.

Such was the ignominious end of the glory days of Huizong's reign and the first half of the once great Song dynasty. The Chinese empire had been territorially reduced and politically humiliated in a manner that few had imagined possible. Nor was the disaster of 1126–27 the end of the hostilities. Over the next decade, Jurchen armies repeatedly made incursions southward across the Huai River into Song territory, advancing on several fronts to the

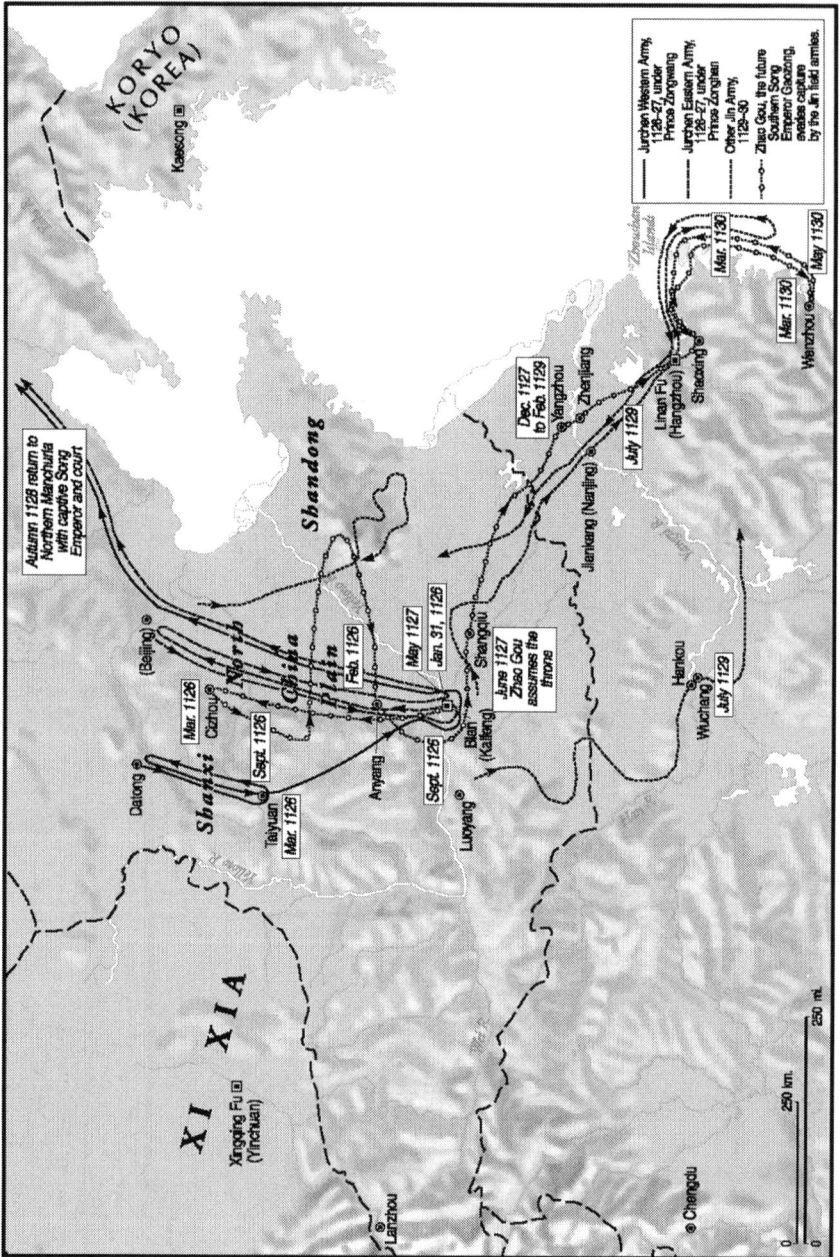

Map 2. Jin Incursions into the Song, 1126–30. Reprinted by permission of the publisher from *Imperial China, 900–1800* by F. W. Mote, p. 294. Cambridge, Mass.: Harvard University Press, copyright © 1999 by F. W. Mote.

southeast and southwest. Gaozong was forced more than once to flee from his new capital of Lin'an (modern Hangzhou), to avoid the fate that had befallen his father and older brother. There were Song campaigns of counterattack northward as well. But eventually it became apparent that neither could the Jin destroy the Song in the south, nor could the Song dislodge the Jin from occupying the Yellow River valley and North China Plain. In 1141, Gaozong concluded a treaty with the Jin that, to the dismay of the irredentist party at the court, identified the Song as a vassal of its more powerful northern conqueror. The uneasy peace and stalemate between the two empires would last nearly one hundred years thereafter.

As disastrous as the loss of the northern half of the Song empire was, that was not the only cause of the chaos of the first decades of Gaozong's reign. The foreign conquest and withdrawal southward severely undermined the central government's control over the southern lands that still nominally constituted the Song state. Uprisings by local warlords and random lawlessness were widespread throughout the southern provinces. At times, Gaozong was as occupied with maintaining a semblance of order in what was left of the Song empire as he was with defending the porous northern border from new Jurchen attacks. A recent study suggests that in the early years of Gaozong's reign (and surely through the decade of the 1130s), in the central lands of the empire, it was only the small circle of territory within roughly a hundred miles of Lin'an that was securely under central government control. The bulk of the lands outside of this circle are characterized as being prey to "endemic banditry and warlordism."[2]

When the Jurchen armies looted Bianliang at the end of 1126, Li Qingzhao and Zhao Mingcheng were in Zizhou (Zibo, Shandong), where Mingcheng was serving as governor. In the third month of 1127, when the couple must have already been preparing to flee south, they received news that Mingcheng's mother had died in Jiangning (Nanjing), and Mingcheng left first to attend to her funeral. Li Qingzhao went back to the Zhao residence in Qingzhou (near Zibo) to close the house and pack what she could to take south. She departed Qingzhou in the twelfth month, accompanied by fifteen carts of books and other belongings, having left ten roomfuls of other books behind. She rejoined her husband in Jiangning in the spring of 1128. In the ninth month of the same year, Mingcheng was appointed governor of Jiangning. But in the third month of 1129 he was removed from his new post,

2. Jing-shen Tao, "The Move to the South and the Reign of Kao-tsung," p. 663, map 23.

apparently because he had disgraced himself by abandoning the city during the night of an attempted uprising, which unfortunately for Mingcheng was suppressed by a loyalist general so that Mingcheng ended up looking like a coward.[3] Mingcheng and Li Qingzhao left Jiangning and traveled upstream by boat along the Yangzi, intending to look for a place to live on the Zhang River, east of Boyang Lake. Before they got more than halfway, in the fifth month of the same year, Mingcheng was reinstated as governor of Huzhou and invited for an audience with the emperor, Gaozong, on his way to his new post. The emperor, whose own movements were also sporadic owing to continued forays south by the attacking Jurchens, was now staying in Jiangning, the very place that Mingcheng had just left (which he had renamed Jiankang). Mingcheng must have been thrilled at his reinstatement, and, understandably, he was in a hurry to comply. He took leave of Li Qingzhao soon after he received the good news, on the thirteenth day of the sixth month, setting out by horse for Jiankang and leaving Li Qingzhao on the boat where they had stopped at Chiyang (Guichi, Anhui). By the end of the next month, Li Qingzhao received a letter reporting that Mingcheng had fallen ill en route and was now dangerously sick in Jiankang. She hurried to rejoin him, traveling as fast as her boat would allow, covering three hundred *li* per day. But by the time she arrived she found that Mingcheng was deathly ill and beyond recovery. He died on the eighteenth day of the eighth month, 1129, at the age of forty-nine.

If the events leading up to Zhao Mingcheng's death had been chaotic, what transpired in the months after it was much worse. The Jurchen armies began a new southern campaign, which lasted through the last months of 1129 and on into early 1130. This campaign brought the invading troops southward across the Yangzi River. Then one flank of the advancing army made a southeastern sweep, targeting the emperor himself, who found himself pushed farther and farther toward the seacoast. Gaozong was forced to leave Jiankang one month after Mingcheng had died there, and he proceeded downstream ahead of the foreign invaders. He reached Suzhou in the ninth month, Lin'an in the tenth month, fled to Yuezhou (Shaoxing) ten days later, and reached Mingzhou (modern Ningbo) in the twelfth month. The Jurchen army was close behind. It captured Jiankang in the eleventh month, Lin'an and Yuezhou in the twelfth month, and went on to attack Mingzhou.

---

3. Here, and throughout this section, I am following the version of events in Xu Peijun's "Nianpu," *Jianzhu*, pp. 456–94 (for Mingcheng's removal from office in Jiankang, see p. 471).

Resistance at Mingzhou caused the Jurchen to miss capturing Gaozong. The emperor escaped to sea in a ship one day before Mingzhou fell to the invaders. The Jurchen general Wanyan Wuzhu 完颜兀朮 (d. 1148) commandeered ships of his own to continue the pursuit. But he was too late. Gaozong was beyond reach, sailing southward along the coast. In the great span of Chinese history, this is said to have been the first time a reigning emperor was forced out on the ocean to elude capture.[4]

Li Qingzhao was caught up in this military action. She essentially followed the emperor in his flight from Jiankang, trailing him by half a month or so and just staying ahead of the advancing invaders. Unlike Gaozong, however, who put to sea from Mingzhou, Li Qingzhao seems to have turned south and fled south overland, at first, in a fitful series of movements through the war-torn countryside (see map 3). She too, however, was eventually forced out on the ocean from the port of Huangyan 黄巖 and then joined the emperor's flotilla as he sailed down the coast to Wenzhou, arriving there at the end of the first month of 1130. Wenzhou was the southeastern terminus of the flight for both Gaozong and Li Qingzhao. The Jurchen armies began to withdraw northward early in 1130, making it possible for Gaozong and his followers (including Li Qingzhao) to sail back northward along the coast. The imperial party disembarked from its ship at Yuezhou in the fourth month. Hoping apparently for a fresh start, Gaozong brought the disastrous Jianyan reign period to an end at the beginning of 1131, proclaiming the new Shaoxing period. He waited, however, until the start of 1132, after a renewed Jurchen threat, to take up residence again in Lin'an. Li Qingzhao followed suit, returning to the new capital sometime that spring.

Keeping herself safely ahead of the invading army was not the only problem Li Qingzhao faced during these months. She was trying not just to preserve herself, but also to keep her collection, or what was left of it, intact. No doubt the existence of the unwieldy collection complicated her life considerably at this point. But she was not about to simply throw it aside.

---

4. The relative timing of the movements of Gaozong, the Jurchen army, and Li Qingzhao are conveniently listed, in table form, in Huang Shengzhang's "Li Qingzhao shiji kaobian," p. 334. My account of Li Qingzhao's movements at this time is based on Huang's reconstruction of them, later largely adopted in Xu Peijun's "Nianpu," *Jianzhu*, pp. 456–94. For a somewhat different reconstruction of the path of Li Qingzhao's flight between 1129/8 (when Zhao Mingcheng died) and 1129/12, see Wang Fan, *Li Qingzhao yanjiu conggao*, pp. 90–107. See also Jing-shen Tao, "The Move to the South and the Reign of Kao-tsung," pp. 653–55.

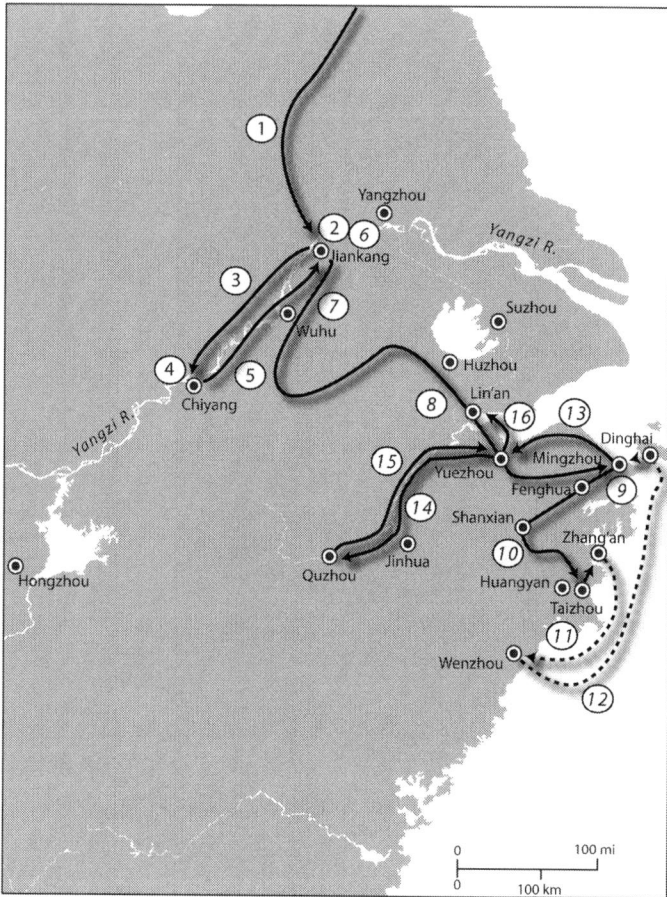

Map 3. Li Qingzhao's flight from the Jin incursions.

Quite apart from what it must have meant to her, the last time she saw her late husband in good health, when he left her at Chiyang, he had instructed her to protect the ritual vessels in the collection with her life: "live or die with them."[5] Such an injunction now must have become a heavy burden.

Her problem was not just the logistical one of moving from place to place with all these objects in a time of invasion. As a widow, traveling by herself without an adult son or anyone else to fend for her, she was an easy target for unscrupulous countrymen who sought to steal from her valuable collection. In her own narrative of this period, she mentions seeking out her younger

---

5. As she states in her "Afterword," translated in chapter 6.

	Key to Map 3
year/month	
1127	(1) Li Qingzhao's journey begins.
1128/2	(2) Li Qingzhao arrives in Jiankang (Jiangning), having fled the Jin invasion from Qingzhou (in the distant north).
1128/9	Zhao Mingcheng begins his appointment as prefect of Jiankang.
1129/3	(3) Mingcheng is removed from his post as prefect; he and Qingzhao travel westward up the Yangzi River.
1129/5	(4) The couple arrives at Chiyang. In the sixth month, Mingcheng receives a new appointment as prefect of Huzhou and sets off to the court back in Jiankang to accept the appointment.
1129/7	(5) Qingzhao learns that Mingcheng has fallen ill and hurries to join him in Jiankang, sailing back down the Yangzi.
1129/8	(6) The couple is reunited in Jiankang. Mingcheng dies on the sixteenth of the month.
	(7) Qingzhao initially intends to seek safety in Hongzhou, but when Jin armies sack Hongzhou she decides to flee to the southeast.
1129/10–11	(8) Qingzhao passes through Lin'an and Yuezhou, following the path of Gaozong's retreat from the Jin armies.
1129/12	(9) To elude capture, Gaozong puts to sea from Mingzhou and Dinghai. Qingzhao flees southward from Mingzhou, proceeding by land. She passes through Fenghua.
1130/1	(10) Qingzhao passes through Shanxian, where she left a large portion of her collection, then on to Taizhou, then to Huangyan, where she put to sea, joining the emperor's ship at Zhang'an.
1130/1	(11) Qingzhao arrives by boat in Wenzhou, following the emperor's flotilla.
1130/3–4	(12) After the Jin armies withdraw back north, Qingzhao returns by boat to Mingzhou, following the emperor, (13) then back to Yuezhou.
1130/12	(14) Another Jin advance forces Qingzhao to travel up the Qiantang River to Quzhou.
1131/3	(15) Qingzhao returns once more to Yuezhou.
1132/1–2	(16) The emperor finally returns to Lin'an, and Qingzhao soon follows.

brother to protect her. But it is unclear if, in fact, she managed to join up with him at this point or whether, even if she did, he provided any help. Her account conveys, in any case, a clear image of a woman whose vulnerability as a lone widow was exploited at every turn during a time of social chaos. She alternately seeks to travel with her collection and to find a safe place to leave it. But time and again her plans meet with failure.

Li Qingzhao's account of her actions during this time is found in a section of her "Afterword to *Records on Metal and Stone*." The narrative is disjointed and somewhat confusing, containing asides and chronological discontinuities or flashbacks. Scholars who have made the most meticulous studies of the document, noting the apparent disorder of places named, have suggested that certain lines of the text have been transposed or that some of the place-names must have been miscopied.[6] Yet it is also possible that the text as we have it is just as it was written, and the difficulties it presents mimic the illogic of the chaotic time as she experienced and later recollected it. Biographers of Li Qingzhao have tried, on the basis of this section of her afterword, to reconstruct and map the sequence of her chaotic flight. Any such attempt (as in map 3) is tentative at best and involves some arbitrary interpretations and smoothing out of the gaps and illogic of her narrative. This is the relevant section of the afterword:

> After I buried [Mingcheng], I had nowhere to go. The court had dispatched the empress and palace ladies to a separate location, and it was said that cross-ing the Yangzi River would soon be prohibited. At the time, I still had twenty thousand books, two thousand folios of inscriptions on metal and stone, and enough utensils and bedding to receive a hundred guests. My other superflu-ous things were comparable in quantity. I myself was very sick, and my breath-ing was extremely weak. I thought of my late husband's brother-in-law [Li Zhuo], who was vice minister of the Ministry of War and was then protecting the empress at Hongzhou. I dispatched two trusted clerks to him, sending along a portion of our possessions with them for safekeeping. In the twelfth month [of 1129], the Jin bandits sacked Hongzhou, and everything I had sent was lost. The books that had been ferried across the Huai River in a string of boats were turned into smoke and clouds. All I had left were a few small, lightweight scrolls of calligraphy inscriptions; manuscript copies of the works of Li Bai, Du Fu, Han Yu, and Liu Zongyuan; *A New Account of Tales of the World* and *Discourses on Salt and Iron*; a few dozen mounted rubbings of stone inscriptions from the Han through Tang dynasties; some ten bronze vessels from the Three Dynasties; and a few cases of manuscripts from the Southern Tang. From time to time I would amuse myself with these during my illness. These were the only remnants I had left, as I lay sick in bed.
>
> It was impossible to go farther up the Yangzi River, and moreover the invaders' movements were unpredictable. My younger brother, Hang, was serving as reviser in the Law Code Office, and so I decided to go seek refuge with him. By the time I got to Taizhou [1130/1], the prefect there had fled. When I got to Shan, I proceeded over land. I discarded my clothes and bedding as I hurried to Huangyan, where I hired a boat and set out to sea, hoping to catch up with the traveling court. At the time the emperor had docked at Zhang'an. I followed the imperial ship to Wenzhou and from there

---

6. Both Huang Shengzhang and Wang Zhongwen arrive at this conclusion; see Huang's "Li Qingzhao shiji kao," pp. 331–32, and Wang Zhongwen, "Li Qingzhao shiji biannian" 李清照事迹编年, *Li Qingzhao ji jiaozhu*, p. 246.

went back to Yue. In the twelfth month of *gengxu* [1130], when the officials were dismissed, I proceeded to Quzhou. In the third month of the *xinhai* year of Shaoxing [1131], I went again to Yue. In the *renzi* year [1132], I returned to Hangzhou.

Previously, when my husband was extremely ill, a certain Academician Zhang Feiqing came to see him bringing a jade pitcher, which he then took away with him. The pitcher was actually made of jadelike stone. I do not know who started the rumor, but it was falsely said that there was talk of "an imperial behest of gold." Some even said there was going to be a secret inquiry into the matter. I was terrified. I did not dare to speak out, but I also did not dare do nothing. I decided that I would take all my household's bronze vessels and other objects and present them to the traveling court. By the time I got to Yue [1129/12], the emperor had already moved to Siming. I did not want to keep those things in my house, and so I stored them all in Shan, together with the book manuscripts. Subsequently, when the imperial army was rounding up rebels, what I had stored there was all taken away. Later, I heard that it ended up in the household of the old general Li. Of "the remnants I had left," 50 or 60 percent was now lost. All that remained were some six or seven boxes of calligraphy, paintings, inkstones, and ink. I could not bear to put them anywhere else. I kept them beside my bed, where I'd open them occasionally.

At Kuaiji [Yue, 1131/3] I resided in a place owned by a local named Zhong. One night, a thief broke in through a wall and carried five of my boxes off. I was so grief-stricken I thought I'd die, and I offered a handsome reward to get them back. Two days later my landlord, Zhong, brazenly produced eighteen scrolls, asking for the reward. So I knew the thief was not far away. I tried everything I could to recover the rest, but nothing would free it up. Today I know that eventually Wu Shuo, the assistant fiscal commissioner, bought everything for a low price. At this point, 70 or 80 percent of "the only remnants I had left" was lost. What remained were just one or two random and fragmentary volumes that did not make any complete title or set, together with just a few very ordinary calligraphy manuscripts.[7]

It was not just invading troops, local military men, and opportunistic landlords who helped themselves to portions of Li Qingzhao's collection. Emperor Gaozong himself, or his agents, also had his eyes on it, and the reference in this passage to rumors that terrified Li Qingzhao probably refers to the imperial interest in her possessions. It may at first seem implausible that the emperor who was just then fleeing for his life, hoping to evade the capture by the enemy that had befallen his father and older brother, would have bothered about books, art objects, and ritual vessels. But to think this

---

7. Li Qingzhao, "Jinshi lu houxu" 金石錄後序, *Jianzhu* 3.312.

way is to fail to understand the significance that the possession of just such cultural artifacts had in imparting an aura of cultural legitimacy to the imperial institution. An imperial collection of books, art, and ancient vessels of enormous size and richness, quite possibly the largest such collection that had ever been assembled in China, had been lost a few years before when the Bianliang palaces were sacked and looted. The young Gaozong, who was his father's son when it came to his valuation of art and learning, was determined to rebuild the imperial collection, and he was not going to wait for more peaceful times. As unlikely as it seems, Gaozong was already involved in far-reaching efforts to rebuild the imperial collection even as he was evading the Jurchen armies. These efforts on his part are well attested in contemporary sources. We read, for example, "When the Exalted Emperor [Gaozong] was forced to embark across the Yangzi River southward, several times he issued decrees of procurement, and many people who donated books to him were rewarded with office."[8] And again, "Siling [Gaozong] had uncanny insight into the eight methods of calligraphy and let his spirit dwell upon the ancient and elegant. Even in the midst of warfare and turmoil, he spared no effort in searching out model calligraphy and famous paintings. . . . Consequently, men from all quarters of the empire vied in submitting such things to the court, and not a day passed when something new did not arrive."[9] The collection that Zhao Mingcheng and Li Qingzhao had built up over nearly thirty years must have been one of the largest private collections of books and artworks in the empire. It is hardly surprising that Gaozong or his attendants would have known about it and set their sights on it.

Although Li Qingzhao makes no mention of it, we know from other sources that barely one month after Zhao Mingcheng died, Gaozong's personal physician, Wang Jixian 王繼先, approached Li Qingzhao in an attempt to "buy" some ancient vessels in her collection. Wang's effort was stopped when Xie Kejia 謝克家, a maternal cousin of Zhao Mingcheng's who was then serving in the eminent office of minister of the Ministry of War, memorialized to the throne in protest. Here is the relevant passage that records these events in Li Xinchuan's 李心傳 annals of Gaozong's reign:

> Wang Jixian, grand master of Hean and retired military training commissioner of Kaizhou, took three hundred *liang* of yellow gold to try to purchase ancient vessels from the household of the late Zhao Mingcheng, senior compiler of

---

8. Wang Mingqing, *Huizhu lu* 1.3579.
9. Zhou Mi, *Qidong yeyu* 6.5495.

the Imperial Archives. Xie Kejia, minister in the Ministry of War, memorialized against it, saying, "I fear that if news of this spreads abroad, it will damage flourishing [imperial] prestige. I ask that the action be terminated." The emperor added his own note concurring with the memorial, ordering the Three Departments to question Wang Jixian.[10]

We do not know if Wang Jixian was acting on his own or if, as seems more likely, Gaozong or one of his ministers prompted Wang Jixian to thus attempt to acquire some of Li Qingzhao's ancient vessels.[11] It hardly matters. Wang Jixian was known to be especially close to Gaozong and is represented in later historiography as one of the emperor's "sycophants and favorites."[12] The perception was, as Xie Kejia's wording makes clear, that Wang Jixian was acting on the emperor's behalf and that the attempted "purchase" was damaging to the emperor's reputation.[13] Why would news of Wang's action be perceived this way? Presumably because it was a transparent attempt to take advantage of a woman who had just been plunged into mourning. The paltry sum that Wang offered in exchange for the vessels may have increased the air of impropriety of the whole affair. Nevertheless, if the powerful Xie Kejia had not objected, probably the transaction would have gone through.

In all likelihood, the frightening rumors that Li Qingzhao mentions in her account had something to do with Wang Jixian's attempt to "purchase" ancient vessels from her, and the reference she makes to a secret inquiry is the inquiry that Gaozong ordered into Wang Jixian's actions. But the connection, if there was one, between the rumors and the strange affair of Zhang Feiqing 張飛卿 and his "jade pitcher" is unclear.

The words I have translated "imperial behest of gold" are *banjin* 頒金 (literally, "to confer or distribute gold"), a phrase that is well attested in contemporary sources. Chinese emperors of the Tang, Song, and later periods

---

10. Li Xichuan, *Jianyan yilai xinian yaolu* 27.423.

11. The latter is what Nangong Bo assumes to have happened; see his *Li Qingzhao de hou bansheng*, pp. 30–31.

12. See his biography in *Songshi* 470.13686–88.

13. Deng Hongmei has a substantially different understanding of Xie Kejia's memorial. She thinks that Xie mistakenly supposed that Li Qingzhao intended to sell valuable parts of her collection to Wang Jixian, having heard of his interest in them, and memorialized to the throne to have Li Qingzhao's plan thwarted. But it is most unlikely that Xie, a relative by marriage, would have resorted to a memorial to stop the sale. This interpretation also misreads *banjin* in the afterword, supposing that it refers to Li Qingzhao's purported decision to "sell for gold" her treasures, and it assumes that the phrase "flourishing prestige" in Xie's memorial refers to the honor of the late Zhao Mingcheng rather than to the emperor, which is a forced reading. See Deng, *Li Qingzhao xinzhuan*, pp. 138–44.

frequently distributed gold (or gold and silks) as rewards to their subjects for meritorious conduct. The phrase is always used to refer to an imperial behest of this kind rather than a gift made by an ordinary person.[14] We can only guess why these rumors frightened Li Qingzhao so much. Perhaps she felt she was in danger of being perceived as demanding a higher price for her treasures than Wang Jixian had offered, in effect extorting money from the throne. Perhaps it was the rumor that there was to be a "secret inquiry" into the matter that struck her with fear. The word "secret" implies that she would not be given a chance to tell her side of the story so that it would be a perfect opportunity for anyone who had a grudge against her late husband or his family to ruin her. Perhaps what scared her was the misimpression people had that her husband had willingly given Zhang Feiqing one of his valuable vessels but that now Li Qingzhao was resisting an attempt by the emperor's attendant to acquire others of them. We also do not know if Li Qingzhao had asked Xie Kejia to memorialize to get Wang Jixian to desist or if Xie did that on his own. Suffice it to say that anyone, not just a recently widowed woman, at any time during the era, not just those months of particular social chaos, would likely be terrified to hear that he or she was about to be implicated in a secret investigation conducted at the court.

A very different interpretation of this passage of Li Qingzhao's afterword should be mentioned here, if only because it is widespread in the scholarly literature.[15] Combining the Zhang Feiqing incident with the rumor that follows it in Li Qingzhao's account and taking the word *jin* in the phrase *banjin* to refer to the Jin invaders, there are many who think that the rumor was that Li Qingzhao (either acting on her own or together with her husband in his last days) had "presented to the Jin" the jade pitcher in order to curry favor with the enemy and secure safety during the invasion. The appeal of this interpretation to those who subscribe to it is evidently that it helps to account for the severity of Li Qingzhao's reaction to the rumor, since such treachery would have been viewed as a heinous crime. This interpretation also makes it easy to argue the rumor was completely baseless, a position

---

14. This is pointed out by Xu Peijun in *Jianzhu* 3.330–31, n. 58. For other contemporary uses of the phase in this sense, see Li Yu, *Songchao shishi* 3.15b; Qian Yi, *Nanbu xinshu*, "ding," p. 46; and Kong Pingzhong 孔平仲, "Song Dong shaoqing" 送董少卿, *Quan Songshi* 16:20913.

15. This interpretation can be traced back to the Qing scholar Yu Zhengxie, "Yi'an jushi shiji" 15.768; also in *Huibian*, p. 111. It is adopted by many modern scholars; see, for example, Chen Zumei, *Li Qingzhao xinzhuan*, p. 146; and Zhuge, *Li Qingzhao yu Zhao Mingcheng*, pp. 157–58.

eagerly embraced by those who view Li Qingzhao as a "patriotic poet" who would never have considered betraying the Song state.[16] But this is to rush to a defense that is unnecessary in the first place. This interpretation ignores the way the phrase *banjin* is used in writings of the time. It also ignores the historical circumstances: Li Qingzhao (or she and her dying husband) was in no position to offer anything to the invading armies. It would have been logistically unfeasible, if not impossible, to have done so.

Regardless, the rumors about her and the report that a secret court inquiry had been launched made Li Qingzhao fear for her life. For the time being, at least, she felt that she could no longer keep possession of what was left of her collection. As an entity of great value in a time of the nearly complete breakdown of social order, the collection had come to be too large a liability for her to have with her. She now perceived that it was not just an enormous inconvenience to move about, but that having it complicated her life in other ways as well and could even put her in grave danger with the court. She says that she resolved to donate all of it to the emperor. When the emperor's flight ahead of her made this impossible, she physically separated herself from the bulk of it, sending it off for what she hoped was safekeeping in Shan (south of Yue). But what she left there was soon, she tells us, confiscated by the imperial troops and ended up in the possession of one of their generals.

Remarriage and Divorce

In the spring of 1132 (Shaoxing 2), the emperor left Yue and returned to Lin'an, where he would establish his capital. Li Qingzhao also returned to Lin'an and probably took up residence with her younger brother there. She then remarried to a man named Zhang Ruzhou. This remarriage must have taken place soon after her return to Lin'an, possibly in the third or fourth month. We can date it roughly to that time because, according to Li Qingzhao's own words, this second marriage lasted only "one hundred days," and we know from other sources that by the beginning of the ninth month of the same year, a lawsuit that she brought against Zhang Ruzhou was adjudicated. The result of the lawsuit, recorded on the first day of the ninth month, was that Zhang Ruzhou was demoted in office and exiled to distant Liuzhou (Liuzhoushi, Guangxi).[17]

---

16. Deng, *Li Qingzhao xinzhuan*, p. 140.
17. Li Xinchuan, *Jianyan yilai xinian yaolu* 58.1003.

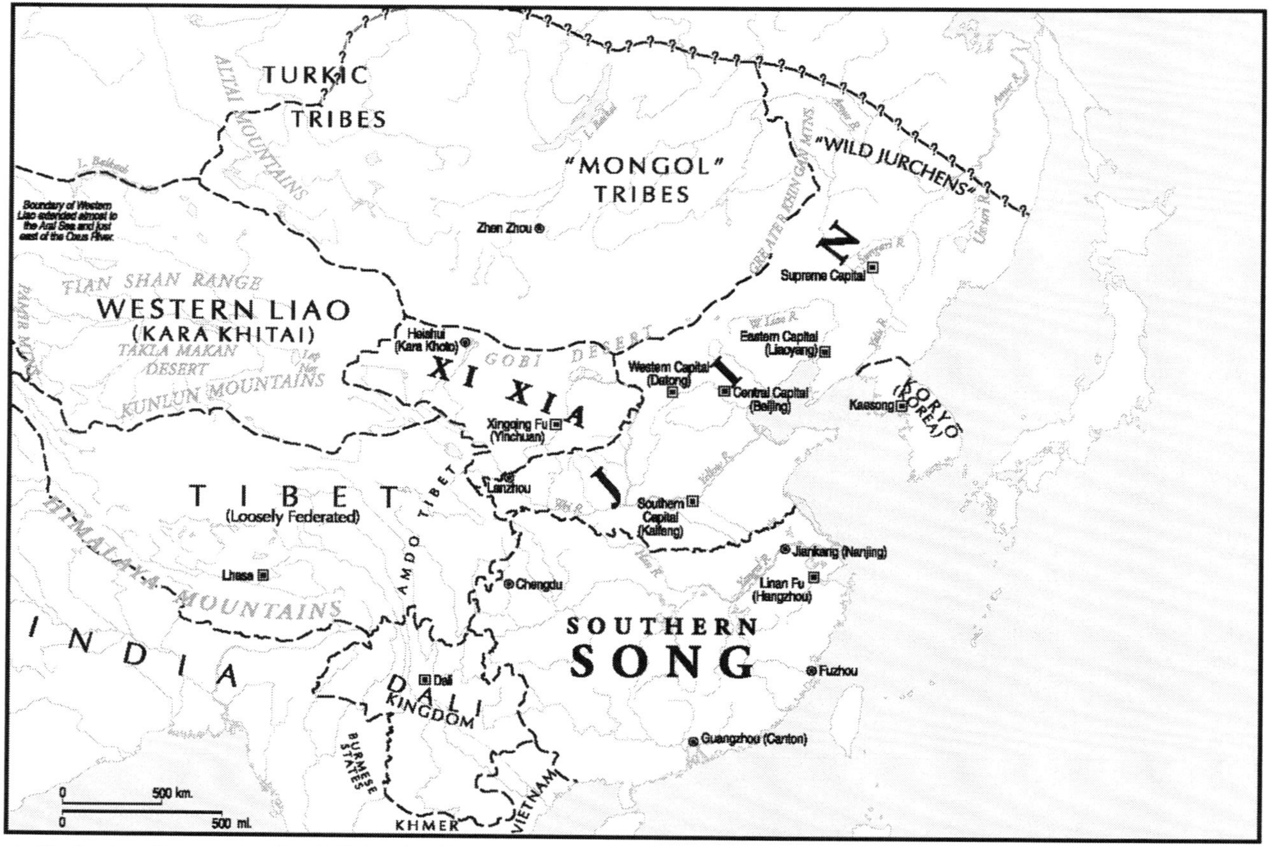

Map 4. The Southern Song empire, circa 1140. Reprinted by permission of the publisher from *Imperial China, 900–1800* by F. W. Mote, p. 230. Cambridge, Mass.: Harvard University Press, copyright © 1999 by F. W. Mote.

We would like to know more about this remarriage and divorce than we do. We would like to know exactly how it came about, what considerations prompted Li Qingzhao to agree to it, what Zhang Ruzhou's intentions were, and the precise nature of the falling out between the two of them that ensued. Unfortunately, the sources for these events are sketchy and leave many questions unanswered. They allow us to make some informed guesses about the motives of the persons involved but only that. The sources consist of passing references to the remarriage and divorce in a number of Song historical writings and miscellanies as well as a lengthy letter that Li Qingzhao wrote describing the entire event. The letter is a fascinating document and provides considerably more detail than any other source. But it has its own limitations and must be used with care. One of the upshots of the lawsuit is that Li Qingzhao herself was imprisoned. After a mere nine days, however, she was set free, apparently because a prominent official, the Hanlin academician Qi Chongli, intervened on her behalf and secured her freedom. The letter was written to Qi Chongli, who was a relative of Zhao Mingcheng by marriage, on Li Qingzhao's release from prison. In it Li Qingzhao thanks him profusely for his efforts and tries to explain how she became embroiled in the disastrous marriage to Zhang Ruzhou in the first place. The letter is hardly a disinterested account of the events it describes. It presents a version of events that suited Li Qingzhao as she expressed her gratitude to her benefactor under peculiar and humiliating circumstances. But the letter is, after all, a window on Li Qingzhao's thinking about the events that she had just experienced. Being a formal document, as the occasion called for, the letter is written in a "high" style of parallel and euphuistic prose, and the language is packed with literary and historical allusions. Yet the formality of the style does not mask the substance and emotion behind what is being expressed.

"A Letter Submitted to Hanlin Academician Qi Chongli"

Qingzhao reports: For a long time I have sought to learn right from wrong and have gained some crude understanding of the *Songs* and the *Rites*. Recently, an illness I contracted was nearly fatal. I could no longer distinguish oxen from ants, and the ashes and nails for the coffin were made ready.[18] Although I still had my brother to taste medicine for me, there was only one old soldier to answer our door. Being so hard pressed, I became imprudent. I trusted words that were as melodious as the notes of a flute and was beguiled by speech as

---

18. Yin Zhongkan 殷仲堪 (3rd c.) was once so ill and disoriented that when he heard ants crawling under his bed, he thought he was listening to oxen fighting. Liu Yiqing, *Shishuo xinyu jianshu* 34.6.914.

alluring as a piece of brocade. My younger brother was tricked into thinking that the letter of official appointment was genuine.[19] I myself was on the point of death; who would have thought it was not his jade mirror stand?[20] The quickness of it all would be hard to describe, and there was hesitancy and indecision. Then while I was still fraught and sighing, he forced me to go off with him as wife. But once my eyesight and hearing became clear, I realized it would truly be difficult to live together. To my dismay, I realized that at an advanced age, when the sun hung in the mulberry and elm, I had married a worthless shyster of a man.

Abhorring the stench that now clung to my body, I sought only to break away. But he held fast to the jade disk, determined to kill its owner.[21] He then began to abuse me freely, and his blows came down daily. It made one recall Liu Ling's chicken ribs; how could they have withstood Shi Le's fists?[22] Crouching under heaven and stepping timidly on the earth, I presumed to emulate the moving complaints of the woman who chattered to herself.[23] Advancing from the great hall to the inner apartment, I was not so eager as Li Chi.[24] With no

---

19. The allusion is to an event in the life of Wang Shi 王適 (7th c.), who tricked the family of the girl he wanted to marry into believing that he already had an official appointment. He had the matchmaker claim that the document she held, but never opened for them, conferred an official appointment upon Wang. See Han Yu, "Shi dali pingshi Wang jun muzhiming" 試大理評事王君墓誌銘, *Han Changli wenji jiaozhu* 6.436.

20. Another allusion to fraudulent betrothal. Wen Qiao 溫嶠 (288–329) tricked his aunt into accepting betrothal gifts for her daughter. Wen was supposed to be the matchmaker, but he turned out to be the suitor, and the betrothal gift of a jade mirror stand he "gave" in fact belonged to the aunt's family. Liu Yiqing, *Shishuo xinyu jianshu* 27.9.857.

21. When Duke Zhuang of Wei 衛莊公, injured in a battle, sought refuge in the house of a man named Ji 己, he offered Ji a jade disk if Ji would save him. Ji replied, "And if I kill you, where do you think your jade is going to go?" Ji proceeded to kill the duke. *Chunqiu Zuozhuan zhuzi suoyin* B.12.17.5/464/10–11 (Ai 17).

22. Once when Liu Ling 劉伶, the famous drinker, angered a brute who was about to beat him, he asked the man how his puny little frame ("chicken ribs") could ever withstand the bully's fists. See Liu Xiaobiao's 劉孝標 commentary on Liu Yiqing, *Shishuo xinyu jianshu* 4.69.250. Shi Le 石勒, founder of the Later Zhao (4th c.), was known as an avid boxer and wrestler in his younger days; see *Jinshu* 105.2739. Li Qingzhao's sentence conflates the two stories.

23. The "woman who chattered to herself" 談娘 (also known as "the woman who wobbled as she walked" 踏搖娘) was a woman whose drunken husband regularly beat her, until she came out on the street to complain to anyone who would listen. Her bizarre manner was mimicked by others, and she eventually became a stock character for farce and popular entertainment. See Cui, *Jiaofang ji*, p. 10a–b.

24. Li Chi 李赤 was beguiled by the ghost or demon of his privy, which appeared to him as his lovely wife. When he followed the ghost into the privy, he felt he was following his wife into their apartment. In the end, he fell into the privy and died. Liu Zongyuan, "Li Chi zhuan" 李赤傳, *Liu Hedong ji* 17.311–12.

one to turn to for help, it seemed best to present my own case. Never did I expect that this trivial problem would be heard so high above. The Celestial Mind received my request, and the matter was turned over to the Office for Law Enforcement. We faced each other, bound in manacles; together with the vile one I put forth my case. Was it only Master Jia who was ashamed to associate with Jiang and Guan?[25] Are Laozi and Han Feizi the only incompatibles who have circulated together?[26] I prayed only that I escape death and had no expectation of cash compensation. My companionship of the wayward and vile one had lasted one hundred days; surely it was not a calamity sent down from heaven.[27] Captivity in prison was to last nine days; who could say it was all human doing?[28] If you spend a fortune to shoot down a sparrow, where is the profit to be found? But splitting one's head against a pillar will surely bring about a loss.[29] Truly there was perversity and obtuseness; both the good and bad comingle, after all, in the courts and the marketplace.[30]

It was then that I bowed before the palace writer and recipient of edicts [Qi Chongli], he the scion of an esteemed clan of the official tablet and sash, a man of impeccable background who has the cap and carriage insignia of high position. Under the sun he has no equal; among men he is number one. The imperial victory at Fengtian was rooted in phrases drafted by Lu Zhi; the pacification at Huaicai was actually brought about by the Huichang decrees.[31]

---

25. As commentators have pointed out, Li Qingzhao seems to have confused Jia Yi 賈誼 (200–168 BCE), the early Han statesmen and writer, for the contemporary general Han Xin 韓信 (d. 196 BCE). It was Han Xin who is said to have been ashamed to associate with the Lord of Jiang 絳侯 (Zhou Bo 周勃) and Guan Ying 灌嬰, other of Han Gaozu's ministers. *Shiji* 92.2628.

26. This too is an allusion, not an invention, based on the perceived incompatibility of the Daoist work *Laozi* 老子 with the Legalist work *Han Feizi* 韓非子. When Wang Jian 王儉 (5th c.) found that he was to be seated together with a man he despised, Wang Jingze 王敬則, he exclaimed, "I never thought I would see Laozi and Han Feizi circulate together." *Nanshi* 南史 45.1130. Li Qingzhao means that she and her former husband were similarly incongruous.

27. The sense must be that it was human actions (including her own errors) rather than fate that brought the marriage about.

28. Meaning that she had Heaven or the addressee (i.e., like a divine being) to thank for the brevity of her imprisonment.

29. The meaning of these two sentences seems to be that while her insignificant life was hardly worth anyone's trouble to save, to have taken her own life was a course that made no sense to her either. The language is derived from Zhuangzi 莊子; see *Zhuangzi zhuzi suoyin* 28/82/21–22, about the wasteful acquisition of a sparrow, and *Shiji* 81.2440, about smashing one's head on a jade disk to keep from having to give up the disk.

30. The perversity and obtuseness mentioned here are not her own but those of the law court that treated her like a criminal.

31. The meaning is that Qi Chongli's own literary service to the emperor, in the capacity of Hanlin academician, is as great as that of the Tang writers Lu Zhi 陸贄 (754–805) and Li Deyu

He treated the pitiable person who had no one to appeal to with a degree of generosity like that of unbridling one of the team of horses.[32] His kindness was as lofty as the wild goose in flight, and he truly seemed to have personally accomplished the deed. So it happened that my white head was spared the vermilion writing brush.[33] How should I, Qingzhao, presume not to reflect upon my errors and feel a sense of shame, or not place my hand on my heart in acknowledgment of my disgrace? Measured against either common principles or good sense, my actions have made it impossible for me to escape the censure of ten thousand generations. My virtue ruined, my name ruined, how could I ever bear to meet gentlemen of the central court? All the bamboo on South Mountain, converted into writing slips, would be insufficient to record the insults that the crowd hurled at me. Only a wise man's words could put a stop to their baseless slander.

The towering *peng* bird soars high above, whereas the little quail sinks to the ground. The fire mouse and the ice silkworm can hardly share the same preferences. This is as obvious to little boys as it is to wise men. I ask that you confer your evaluations upon me and that you share with me your purifying influence. I swear that dressed in plain cloth and eating vegetarian meals, I shall devote myself to "knowing the new by keeping the ancient fresh in my mind."[34] If ever I get to see the old rivers and mountains, it will be as before, with a single pitcher and a single rice bowl. Should I be able to return to our ancestral home, I will be sure to bathe and perfume myself three times before proceeding in. I have brought shame upon my distant relative and have presumed to defile his name.[35]

The "distant relative" referred to in the closing sentence is Qi Chongli himself.

Based on what Li Qingzhao says, we can try to reconstruct what happened after she returned to Lin'an. Li Qingzhao had returned to Lin'an early in 1132, after having spent over two years in flight, crisscrossing the southeastern

---

李德裕 (787–849) (who drafted imperial decrees during the Huichang 會昌 period [841–46] and left a collection of them so named). It is fanciful to credit the imperial victories at Fengtian 奉天 over the rebel Zhu Ci 朱泚 (742–84) and at Huaicai 淮蔡 over the rebel Wu Yuanji 吳元濟 (d. 817) to the two drafters of decrees, as important as they might have been.

32. It was Yanzi 晏子 who untied one of his horses to buy the good man he encountered on the road, Yue Shifu 越石父, out of servitude. *Shiji* 62.2135.

33. In earlier ages criminals were often labeled as such with red ink on the face.

34. *Analects* 2/11.

35. The letter, "Tou Neihan Qi gong qi" 投內翰綦公啓, is preserved in a late twelfth-century work, Zhao Yanwei, *Yunlu manchao* 14.246–47. I have followed the text of the letter in *Jianzhu* 3.309–13 and have profited from Xu's annotations as well.

Jiangnan region. It was two and a half years since her husband had died suddenly in Jiankang. During the months of flight, she had watched her possessions, especially her huge collection of books and art objects, shrink steadily as one after another plan she devised to safeguard them proved a failure.

In her description of her decision to remarry, Li Qingzhao stresses her sickness, her isolation from everyone except one brother and a lone servant, and the suitor's duplicity. By the springtime of 1132, Li Qingzhao would have completed the twenty-seven months of mourning that was expected of a widow. Her experiences between Zhao Mingcheng's death and that spring had shown that as a single woman with at least some possessions left of value, her situation was precarious, if not completely untenable. Her need for some relative—a man—to look out for her had forced her to seek out her younger brother. Now, by her own words, that brother was, together with her, duped by her suitor. There may be a suggestion in Li Qingzhao's language that her brother pressured her into accepting the marriage proposal. Such pressure would hardly be surprising, especially if the brother had his own wife and family to look after. This was, after all, a younger brother who in the normal course of things would not be expected to take his older sister into his household. Indeed, relatives of widows often encouraged them to remarry in order that the relatives themselves would not end up having to provide for them.

The remarriage of widows was not unusual in Li Qingzhao's day. Widows were expected to observe the "three-year" (actually twenty-seven-month) mourning period for their first husband, but after that they were free to remarry, and many did. It is true that the acceptability of a widow's remarriage varied with social class. Generally speaking, the practice and acceptability of a widow's remarriage was more widespread among the lower classes. Among the elite there was greater resistance to the practice, owing to ingrained patriarchal Confucian values. Nevertheless, during Shenzong's 神宗 reign (1068–75), the long-standing prohibition against the remarriage of "titled wives" (*mingfu* 命婦), which is what Li Qingzhao was by virtue of Zhao Mingcheng's past appointments as governor (*taishou* 太守), had been lifted, and we find in Song sources many examples of elite women remarrying.[36]

---

36. For a detailed discussion of widows' remarriage in the Song, contrasted with the Tang and Yuan periods, see You, *Song Yuan zhiji funü diwei de bianqian*, pp. 268–87 (esp. 277–79) and 345–50.

Yet what was legal did not necessarily coincide with what was deemed laudable. Viewed as a whole, Song society embodied contradictory values and positions on the matter of widows' remarriage, especially among the elite. Certain leading intellectuals, including Sima Guang, Cheng Yi, and Zhu Xi, took strong positions harshly criticizing the remarriage of widows. The most celebrated (or infamous) pronouncement on the issue is that made by Cheng Yi:

> Someone asked, "If a widow is alone and impoverished and has no one to rely on, may she then remarry?"
>
> Cheng Yi replied, "It is because people in recent times fear being cold and starving to death that there is this idea. Actually, starving to death is a matter of little importance. Losing one's chastity is matter of the gravest importance."[37]

The word translated "chastity" is *jie* 節, which is a blanket term for integrity, principle, and so forth. For the Confucian moralist, nothing could be worse for a man than to "lose his integrity." Applied to the lives of women, who show their "integrity" through loyalty to their husbands, the same word becomes "chastity," or that component of a woman's integrity that is considered fundamental.

Cheng Yi's statement is an extreme formulation, but there were many who agreed that it was best if widows refrained from remarrying. The Song government regularly publicized the virtuous conduct of widows who chose not to remarry, commemorating their conduct in proclamations, banners, and stele inscriptions. Officials even rewarded such women with gifts of grain or tax exemptions. These women were treated as moral heroes, their conduct seen as analogous to that of filial children.[38] Indeed the two virtues converged. The widow who chose to remain in her late husband's household and care through the years for his aging parents was in effect fulfilling the filial duty that her husband could no longer perform. Such behavior was seen as exemplary in its selflessness, especially in comparison with the widow who abandoned her husband's family to enter into a new marriage. However, some widows were encouraged to remarry by their late husband's relatives, if their continued presence in the family was seen as a burden (one more mouth to feed) or if the relatives believed such remarriage would force the woman

---

37. Cheng Yi, *Henan Chengshi yishu* 22B.301.
38. Ebrey, *Inner Quarters*, pp. 194–98.

to give up whatever claim she had on her husband's property or even the dowry she had brought into the family. Some women put up a fight, resisting the pressure to remarry, thus achieving reputations as moral exemplars, while others simply acquiesced and gave up whatever possessions they were legally entitled to.

Li Qingzhao was free from certain of the constraints that helped to keep many widows from remarrying. Both of Zhao Mingcheng's parents had died before he did, so that there was no question of the widow having to care for elderly in-laws. Nor did Li Qingzhao have any young children who had been designated Mingcheng's heirs, the prospect of whose continued upbringing within the Zhao clan might have been another reason against remarriage.

We have already seen evidence that Li Qingzhao's existence as a widow with no grown children made her vulnerable to predatory affronts. This is exactly what we would expect, even without the added complications of foreign invasion, the breakdown of lawful social order, and this particular widow's exceptional material wealth. Writing about widows generally in Song times, that is, in predominantly peaceful times, Patricia Ebrey observes:

> Widows who tried to maintain some degree of independence did not have an easy life. . . . Widows in Song China undoubtedly would have liked clearer legal claims to their dowries and to their husband's estates. But keeping what they were legally entitled to was enough of a problem. Men would try to wrest property away from them by means they would not have used against other grown men. . . . A reading of cases in the Judicial Decisions provides an abundance of evidence that men assumed widows without adult sons were easy targets. They were, after all, women; they had been brought up to be agreeable, to yield to others, to defer to men regarding "outside" matters, and to be embarrassed to be seen in public. . . . Widows needed protection from relatives as much as from bullies.[39]

We do not know much about Zhang Ruzhou. His only known appointments were low-ranking ones associated with military units. In 1131 he served on the staff of an army supervisor in Chichou, and in 1132 he is referred to as an accounts officer in an army unit (*jian zhujun shenjisi* 監諸軍審計司). He had a prestige title of gentleman for attendance (*chengfeng lang* 承奉郎), which was very low ranking (twenty-ninth out of thirty in the administrative class of officials).[40] In some scholarship about Li Qingzhao it is said that

---

39. Ibid., p. 190.
40. See Lo, *An Introduction to the Civil Service of Sung China*, p. 72, table 6.

Zhang Ruzhou had a considerably more distinguished career, having served as governor of various prefectures and also as examiner (*jianzheng* 檢正) in the Secretariat. But it is now generally thought that this was a different man with the same name, not the Zhang Ruzhou that Li Qingzhao married.[41]

In her letter to Qi Chongli, Li Qingzhao emphasizes Zhang Ruzhou's duplicity in how he represented himself to her, suggesting through literary allusions that he misrepresented his official status and even that he fraudulently presented engagement gifts. She stresses her own illness and confusion at the time, and her reluctance even despite her ill health and his dishonesty to agree to the marriage. Then, once it took place, it quickly became clear to her that she had made a grave mistake. These are the words of someone who is deeply mortified by what she had done.

We have no way of knowing exactly what transpired once the marriage took place. But Li Qingzhao's letter implies that Zhang's real motive in marrying her was to take possession of her wealth, that is, her collection. Given what Li Qingzhao says in her afterword about how much of her collection she had lost by this point, we might wonder what was left to tempt Zhang Ruzhou. But there are reasons to think that Li Qingzhao overstates how little she had left, as we will see, so that it is not implausible that Zhang sought to gain materially from the marriage. Yet Li Qingzhao resisted his effort to wrest her belongings away from her. "I sought only to break away. But he held fast to the jade disk, determined to kill its owner." Li Qingzhao couches her narrative in learned allusions, but in a way that leaves little doubt as to what was happening. "He then began to abuse me freely, and his blows came down daily." This is one sentence that she writes straightforwardly, without the ornament of literary allusion. It is followed by two sentences that contain allusions to beatings: one about a strapping bully taking out his wrath on a man with a puny little frame ("chicken ribs") and the other specifically about a woman driven to madness by her drunken husband's repeated thrashings of her. What is striking about these allusions is that, in both cases, as Li Qingzhao has tailored the references, the two persons concerned are grossly mismatched in physical strength. In reading literary Chinese, one does not often encounter allusions to such stories about physical abuse; yet Li Qingzhao somehow managed to get these into her letter.

---

41. See Deng, *Li Qingzhao xinzhuan*, p. 149, n. 1; and Nangong, *Li Qingzhao de hou bansheng*, pp. 62–64.

Even in recent times and among Li Qingzhao's most fervent and learned admirers, there are those who think that she is exaggerating when she suggests in the letter that Zhang Ruzhou beat her.[42] Taken to an extreme, this refusal to believe that such abuse could have happened becomes one reason, among others, for casting doubt on the authenticity of the letter itself.[43] Younger (and especially female) scholars who have written in recent years about Li Qingzhao's life are more apt to accept the assertion as credible. Indeed, the way Li Qingzhao broaches the beatings in the letter and the space she devotes to expanding on them leave little doubt that she intended her words to be taken literally and to be seen as describing a key part of the events she narrates.

Song dynasty law specified multiple reasons for which a husband might divorce his wife. But wives were given no legal grounds on which they could initiate a divorce of their husbands.[44] Court cases show that some judges might grant a wife a divorce if the husband or his family had committed a serious crime against her, including incest between father-in-law and daughter-in-law.[45] But Li Qingzhao must have felt that whatever she could point to would be considered inadequate. Wives who simply left their husbands of their own accord were liable for two years' penal servitude.[46]

Consequently, Li Qingzhao did not bring suit for divorce. She brought suit against her husband for malfeasance in office, evidently hoping that his conviction for wrongdoing would bring with it dissolution of the marriage, which is what finally happened. She charged him with having "entered into office by having wantonly exaggerated the number of times he had qualified [for the palace exam]" (*wang zeng jushu ruguan* 妄增舉數入官).[47] There were provisions in Song bureaucratic policy for allowing men who reached a certain advanced age or those who had taken but not passed the palace or other high-level exam a certain number of times to have "their names specially submitted" (*tezou ming* 特奏名) to the emperor for official

42. Nangong, *Li Qingzhao de hou bansheng*, p. 57.

43. This is implicit in Yu Zhengxie's remarks on the letter and, in particular, on the passage in question; see "Yi'an jushi shiji," 15.777–78; also in *Huibian*, pp. 119–20.

44. Ebrey, *Inner Quarters*, p. 258.

45. See McKnight and Liu, trans., *The Enlightened Judgments*, pp. 377–78.

46. Ebrey, *Inner Quarters*, p. 258.

47. As recorded by Li Xinchuan, *Jianyan yilai xinian yaolu* 58.1003.

appointment.[48] Sometimes a specific age (e.g., forty) was combined with a specific record of examination attempts (e.g., six). These were exceptions allowed in the system, and they were applied flexibly and irregularly. Men who were lucky enough to encounter them thus managed to enter official-dom without ever passing the highest exam. Because the number of times a candidate had sat for the exams could be used this way, all men admitted to take the palace exam were required to report the number of their previous attempts in their registration documents together with the details of their age and family background, and strict punishments were specified for anyone who exaggerated that number. Occasionally, individuals did lie about the number of their previous attempts and get away with it. Zhang Ruzhou was evidently one such person. Unfortunately for him, it seems that he was also foolish enough to brag about his ruse to his new wife, Li Qingzhao. Zhang was eventually convicted of wrongdoing, stripped of office, and banished to faraway Liuzhou. Presumably, the marriage was annulled in tandem with this finding of guilt and banishment.

Why, then, was Li Qingzhao, the one who brought the suit against Zhang Ruzhou, imprisoned for nine days, and indeed what specifically she is thank-ing Qi Chongli for in her letter? The conventional wisdom, following the interpretation of Wang Zhongwen, is that by bringing a suit against her husband, Li Qingzhao exposed herself to the Song period law that specified two years' imprisonment for persons bringing suit against a higher-ranking member of their own family (e.g., parents, grandparents, maternal grand-parents, or husband). The two-year imprisonment was required regardless of the merits of the suit or its outcome.[49] That is why Li Qingzhao was impris-oned. It happened that Qi Chongli, a friend and relative of the late Zhao Mingcheng, had just recently been appointed Hanlin academician. Qi used his eminence and influence to obtain special consideration for Li Qingzhao, securing her release from prison. The sentence in her letter that says "so it

---

48. Here I am following Chen Zumei's understanding of the phrase *zeng zhushu* and her illuminating discussion of this exception policy in the Song selection of officials; see "Guanyu Yi'an zhaji erze," pp. 87–91. Deng Hongmei has a different understanding of *zeng zhushu*, supposing that it refers to exaggerating the number of men who recommended Zhang Ruzhou for official appointment (or to take the highest exam); see her *Li Qingzhao xinzhuan*, p. 153. But the Song sources clearly show that Chen Zumei's understanding of the phrase (which Deng does not refer to) is the correct one.

49. Wang Zhongwen, "Li Qingzhao shiji biannian," *Li Qingzhao ji jiaozhu*, p. 252.

happened that my white head was spared the vermilion writing brush" must refer to the consequence of Qi Chongli's intervention, which is that Li Qingzhao was pardoned from incrimination and released from prison. If this understanding of the event is correct, it puts Li Qingzhao's decision to bring suit against Zhang Ruzhou in an interesting light. It seems most unlikely that Li Qingzhao could have known in advance that any such attempt by Qi Chongli would succeed. Someone else, after all, had to approve of Qi Chongli's request that she be pardoned. Li Qingzhao must have initiated the suit against her husband knowing that it would likely cause her to face two years of incarceration. This is an indication of how desperate and determined she was to end her marriage.

The preceding understanding of the trial, imprisonment, and release has recently been questioned in an unpublished paper by the song lyrics specialist Wang Xiaoli 王曉驪.[50] Referring to Song law regarding domestic lawsuits, Wang argues that Li Qingzhao's imprisonment could not have been part of a two-year confinement from which she received early release because Li Qingzhao would not have qualified for such a sentence reduction.[51] Wang says that the nine-day imprisonment must instead have been a temporary incarceration imposed on wife (and husband) for the duration of the trial, and that is why it ended so quickly. This sounds plausible; but if it is taken to eliminate any intervention on Li Qingzhao's behalf by Qi Chongli, it raises a new question. It is clear from Li Qingzhao's letter to Qi that he did something for her in the course of the episode, and it was evidently something of great consequence for which she was profoundly grateful. If Li did not intervene to somehow secure an early release for her from prison, he must have done something else of great effect, but at our remove we do not know what it was.

In either case, the tone of the letter to Qi Chongli suggests that Li Qingzhao's humiliation over the remarriage was profound. This sense comes through even though the language is highly formal. Several phrases are striking, even in the grandiloquent style, for the depth of feeling they convey:

---

50. Wang's paper, which she kindly shared with me, is titled "Li Qingzhao weishenme zhi ruyu jiutian?" 李清照爲什麼只入獄九天. Dr. Wang teaches in the Humanities School of East China University of Politics and Law.

51. Wang supports this point by considering various means by which one could qualify for pardon in such a case and concludes that Li Qingzhao did not qualify for any of them.

"my virtue ruined, my name ruined"; "impossible for me to escape the censure"; "place my hand on my heart in acknowledgment of my disgrace." Naturally, it was her decision to initiate the lawsuit that opened up the failure of her remarriage to public view. In her letter she anticipates the reaction that Hu Zi so callously records two decades later: "there were none who spoke of this [her remarriage and divorce] who did not laugh at her" 傳者無不笑之.[52] Yet it was Li Qingzhao's decision to subject herself to this public humiliation rather than to continue in the marriage.

Larger Issues

Several centuries after the events narrated above, starting late in the Ming and continuing through the Qing and the twentieth century, the version of Li Qingzhao's life that has her marrying a second time and getting divorced soon thereafter was called into question and, ultimately, vigorously rejected. One by one, the numerous Southern Song period sources that refer to her remarriage were challenged and their accuracy or reliability denied. The letter that Li Qingzhao wrote to Qi Chongli was drastically reinterpreted or dismissed as having been tampered with or fabricated outright. Replacing a widow's unfortunate choice in a second husband, followed by lawsuit and divorce, Qing scholars posited instead a wicked plot on the part of Li Qingzhao's enemies to create the false impression that such events had occurred, a plot whose intent was to ruin her reputation. Those who believed the Song sources had been duped by her enemies' scheme. The Qing scholars, who took great pride in having exposed the treachery and set the record straight, were said to have expunged the "shame" of remarriage that Li Qingzhao had unfairly borne.

The Qing and twentieth-century scholarly campaign to "save" Li Qingzhao's reputation is fascinating in its own right for what it tells us about rewriting history, attitudes toward widows' remarriage in later times, and the nature of Li Qingzhao's iconic image as premodern China's most celebrated woman poet. Although the scholarly consensus has now been reversed, with more and more scholars during the last twenty years accepting the remarriage and divorce as historical fact, the legacy of the Qing and twentieth-century denial of those events is still in evidence today. Certain scholars continue

---

52. Hu Zi, *Tiaoxi yuyin conghua*, "Qianji" 60.417.

to accept the denial as valid or refuse to take sides in the "remarriage controversy." Furthermore, in popular Chinese culture there is conspicuous avoidance of the subject on the part of those who officially or unofficially have responsibility for constructing and managing popular images of Li Qingzhao. Three of the four Li Qingzhao Memorial Halls in the People's Republic of China make no mention of her remarriage and divorce, even in the detailed chronological biographies that are displayed on their walls. I will return to these issues in later chapters on Li Qingzhao's reception history.

Granted that Li Qingzhao's remarriage and subsequent divorce was for her a traumatic experience, what if any greater significance do these events have in helping us to understand her life? What do they tell us about Li Qingzhao and the society in which she lived? The remarriage and divorce came to be thought of as an essential part of her life, mentioned over and over even by the earliest persons who wrote about her. The way the events are mentioned by the early critics is by juxtaposing them with her unusual talent as a woman poet and implicitly using them to undermine admiration for that talent.

Perhaps there are other ways of discerning meaning in these events. Do they, for example, tell us anything about Li Qingzhao's character? It is occasionally asserted by modern scholars that Li Qingzhao's decision to remarry shows her independent spirit, in the sense that she made the decision to do something that was only marginally acceptable in elite society. Some have even suggested that Li Qingzhao's remarriage shows how happy she was in her first marriage to Zhao Mingcheng; she could not imagine continuing in an unmarried state and acted hastily in an attempt to regain conjugal happiness.[53] My own understanding of her remarriage is that it probably tells us more about the towering difficulties she faced as a widow than about her character or the satisfaction of her first marriage. Reading her own account of what happened to her after Zhao Mingcheng's death, who could be surprised that before long she decided to marry again? In explaining to Qi Chongli her decision to accept Zhang Ruzhou's proposal, Li Qingzhao stresses how she and her younger brother were tricked by him. It is hard not to think that the desperation of her circumstances played a role in the success of Zhang's deceit.

---

53. Zhuge, *Li Qingzhao yu Zhao Mingcheng*, pp. 163–64.

It is more plausible to find Li Qingzhao's decision to divorce the man as revelatory of something about her personality. It was highly unusual for a wife to bring suit against her husband. Everything that a wife was supposed to be would have discouraged such an action, not to mention the disincentive of two years' imprisonment with which Song law reinforced the culture of wifely submission and passivity. Zhang Ruzhou underestimated his new wife. And he certainly expected an easier time helping himself to her belongings than what actually transpired. Again, the language of Li Qingzhao's letter to Qi Chongli is revealing. As she describes it, Li Qingzhao is nothing if not horrified by the true nature of her new husband, once she sees him for what he is. "Abhorring the stench that now clung to my body, I sought only to break away." She is also very forthcoming about the physical abuse she suffered at his hands. As we have seen, she dwells on the motif of bullies beating up weaker persons, almost as if unwilling to relinquish it in her narrative. This was not a woman who was going to stay quiet about what happened behind closed doors. We can attempt to account for Li Qingzhao's behavior by recalling that this was, after all, a woman who had a privileged upbringing. She was given an education and apparently allowed to socialize with her father's friends. As a wife she made a practice of competing with Zhao Mingcheng in games that tested memory and learning, and she bested him regularly. But does anyone doubt that in this society there were women similarly privileged and educated who, thrown together with a physically abusive husband, suffered in silence rather than take action that was certain to expose herself to ridicule and shame?

Perhaps the greatest significance of these events is that, for once, they permit us to glimpse Li Qingzhao's world through the experience of a woman. We study Song period society, literature, and institutions, and we have considerable understanding of them. But we have never quite seen them in this light before because the sources are so unbalanced in favor of male experience and accomplishments. We write about the male members of elite society—the political leaders, the poets, the philosophers—and we are barely aware of who their wife is at any time or how they are affected by losing a wife to untimely death (this happens regularly) and taking a new one. And we know precious little about their concubines. Did any of the eminent men of the Song experience divorce? We hardly think to ask the question, so accustomed are we to the silence of the sources on such matters. The poet Lu You, a younger contemporary of Li Qingzhao, was forced by his mother to divorce his first wife. Prolific writer though he was, he did not write about the experience. When by chance he encountered the woman years later, he wrote a song lyric about her sadness through the years.[54] This is exactly what we would expect: the male writer suppressing the event in his autobiographical writing but quite content to appropriate a woman's voice and speak on her behalf. But his representation of her experience is itself distinctly male.

We find plenty of comment on divorce from men engaged in moralizing. Yet these are generalizations about the practice rather than personal observations about experiencing it. Both Sima Guang, in his *Family Instructions*, and Cheng Yi, in discussions with his disciples, express the opinion that husbands are overly reluctant to divorce their wives.[55] Divorce should occur more often than it does, they assert. That is how numerous are obstreperous wives and timid husbands. One of Cheng Yi's disciples sees in his master's call for more divorce the chance that the practice will be abused:

> Someone asked, "In ancient times, there were husbands who divorced their wives for scolding a dog in front of her mother-in-law and for serving a steamed pear that was undercooked.[56] Although the offense was not great, still the husband divorced his wife. Why?"
>
> Cheng Yi replied, "This was the way the ancients practiced generosity and loyalty. In their personal relationships, the ancients never spoke hateful words. A gentleman could not bring himself to identify the vile behavior for which he divorced his wife. He divorced her using the pretext of some minor infraction. This was how he showed his generosity and loyalty. The woman who scolded the dog in front of her mother-in-law must have been guilty of some great wrongdoing. It was because the husband already had a just cause from prior days that he divorced her when this incident occurred."[57]

Cheng Yi's high opinion of husbands contrasts sharply with his assumptions about wives. He evidently believes that no husband ever divorced his wife for unfounded or opportunistic reasons.

The experiences of Li Qingzhao are valuable to us for how clearly they illustrate the difficulty of remaining a widow in Song times. It would have been difficult even in peaceful times and even with a grown son or sons to look out for her. We might expect that Li Qingzhao, as a well-connected

---

54. Lu You, "Chaitou feng" 釵頭鳳, *Quan Songci* 3:1585.

55. Sima Guang, *Jia fan* 7.20b–21a; cf. 3.6a–b.

56. For the dog incident, see Fan Ye, *Hou Hanshu* 29.1017. The husband in the steamed pear incident was none other than Confucius' disciple Zengzi; see *Kongzi jiayu zhuzi suoyin* 38/67/2–4.

57. Cheng Yi, "Yichuan xiansheng yu" 伊川先生語 4, *Henan Chengshi yishu* 18.243. This passage is also translated and discussed in Ebrey, *Inner Quarters*, p. 257.

member of the privileged elite, would have considerably more security and independence than most widows of her time. Yet her material wealth, in the form of what was left of her collection of books and art, seems if anything to have made her more vulnerable, especially during a period of the break-down of civil order, and may well have exacerbated the crisis of widowhood for her.

We also see through Li Qingzhao's experiences what a tragedy it was for a woman to make the wrong decision when faced with a marriage proposal. Sima Guang and Cheng Yi, who advocate that husbands should have a lower threshold for divorce, were probably incapable of thinking about marital unhappiness from a woman's point of view. Once she discovered the true nature of her new husband, Li Qingzhao faced a dilemma. If she stayed in the marriage, she would face physical abuse and probably, sooner or later, the loss of whatever material wealth she still had. If she decided to terminate the marriage, she would expose herself to public humiliation and ridicule—for what kind of woman remarries at an advanced age only to bring a lawsuit against her husband after three months? This was a woman who, owing to her social eminence and the enthusiastic reception of her writings, enjoyed a public renown that was unequaled by any other woman of her time. Now, her notoriety would be cast in a harsh new light, as admiration for her writings would turn to ridicule of her judgment and character. Her feeling of public humiliation and consciousness of how much her reputation had suffered are clearly expressed in her letter to Qi Chongli.

These events in Li Qingzhao's life permit us a glimpse of a side of elite Song society that is seldom seen. The marital state, the loss of a spouse to untimely death, remarriage, and divorce—all these have vastly different meanings in the lives of women than they had for men. The convention that men do not write about such personal affairs surely complicates the issue: there must have been considerably more male anxiety, reflection, and emo-tion about marriage, a wife's early death, and divorce than is expressed in the writings of men. Still, men had more freedom and options in these matters. What a wife meant to her husband and what a husband meant to his wife were not, generally speaking, comparable. We think back, again, to the charge that Zhao Mingcheng gave his wife as he was leaving her in Chiyang: to safeguard the sacrificial vessels they owned with her life. Within a few weeks he was dead, having made, in Li Qingzhao's words, "no provision" for her once he was gone. In what ensues, we see Li Qingzhao trying to cope with her greatly altered circumstances, which plunged her into an abyss from which she was lucky to emerge, even though not unscathed.

CHAPTER 5

Writings from the Aftermath

The years immediately after Li Qingzhao's remarriage and divorce continued to be difficult ones for her. The capital of Lin'an, to which she had returned in 1132 just before marrying Zhang Ruzhou, was threatened by a new southern attack of the Jin armies in 1134. There was again massive flight and dislocation in the face of this onslaught. Li Qingzhao removed herself from Lin'an to Jinhua 金華, some one hundred miles southwest. She stayed there a year or two before returning again to the capital after the invading armies withdrew.

Despite the turmoil, the years immediately following her divorce were extremely productive years for Li Qingzhao as a writer, almost certainly the most productive of her entire life. In addition to continuing to write poems and song lyrics, she turned now to prose and to the rhyme-prose form (*fu* 賦). In just over two years, she produced several major compositions, the best known of which is her "Afterword to *Records on Metal and Stone*" (which I will take up in chapter 6).

A striking feature of these compositions is their public orientation. Whether, as often, she addresses political and military issues of the day or she writes about pastimes and games, in these writings Li Qingzhao speaks to a presumed audience that knows her. She writes herself into these pieces, referring to her own background and aims. This is a new mode of expression for her. We see it first in her letter to Qi Chongli of 1132. In the months and years that followed, as a writer Li Qingzhao moved beyond the crushing sense of humiliation found in that letter to develop new ways of projecting herself as a woman of self-confidence and principle.

Poems Addressed to Emissaries

The most explicitly political—and public—compositions from this period are two poems that Li Qingzhao submitted in the summer of 1133 to the court officials Han Xiaozhou 韓肖胄 (1075–1150) and Hu Songnian 胡松年 (1087–1146), who were about to depart on a diplomatic mission to the Jin empire. These are lengthy compositions (the first especially) that were written as commentary and advice concerning Song relations with its invader. The fact that a lady would inject herself into the raging debates about how to deal with the Jin, now that it occupied the northern half of the Chinese empire, directly addressing the commissioner of military affairs (Han) and the minister of works (Hu) as they were about to set off on their difficult mission, was itself astounding and almost certainly unprecedented in Song politics. It turns out that what she says in the poems is nearly as remarkable as her decision to address the two officials in the first place.

Even as it was engaged in nearly constant military confrontations with the Jin, trying to resist wave after wave of Jurchen onslaughts southward, the Southern Song court continuously dispatched envoys to its northern enemy. The stated purpose of these missions was often to deliver gifts to the two former Chinese emperors (Huizong and Qinzong) and the dozens of other imperial relatives held captive by the Jin in the distant north. Each envoy also presumably had instructions to try to negotiate with the Jin for the release of the imperial captives. The mission of 1133 had special significance. It was initiated upon the return of the previous emissary, Pan Zhiyao 潘致堯, who informed the Southern Song court in the fifth month of the year that the Jin wanted the Song to send a high-ranking official to negotiate a peace treaty.[1] Five days later, Emperor Gaozong selected Han Xiaozhou, military affairs commissioner and a seasoned official who had previously been sent as envoy to the Liao empire, to undertake the task. He was assisted by Hu Songnian, minister of the Ministry of Works.[2] Up until this point, the Song court had been divided on the issue of whether or not to negotiate a peace with the Jin that would make the loss of the northern half of the empire permanent. But this is what Han Xiaozhao intended to do, a course that Emperor Gaozong favored at the moment in the hope of securing the return of the two former

---

1. Li Xinchuan, *Jianyan yilai xinian yaolu* 65.1102; Xu Mengxin, *Sanchao beimeng huibian* 155.11b–12a. The latter has the Jin message refer specifically to the prospect of a peace treaty.
2. Li Xinchuan, *Jianyan yilai xinian yaolu* 65.1103–4.

emperors and other relatives. In the memorial he submitted to the court on the eve of his departure, Han Xiaozhou takes note of the contentiousness of the factions at court advocating peace and continued fighting, but then says that peace is "the proper expedient of the moment," given all the internal difficulties the Song court was facing.[3] He adds that the court can resort to military efforts at some future time to recover the north and thus "expunge the humiliation we have suffered." As he set out, Chinese armies that had been dispatched to attack the puppet state of Qi north of the Huai River were withdrawn from the field so as not to jeopardize Han Xiaozhou's efforts as peace negotiator.[4] When Han Xiaozhou returned to Lin'an in the eleventh month of the year, he was the first of the Chinese envoys to be accompanied southward by Jin officials offering their respects to the Song court.[5] Nevertheless, by the time of Han's return, the Qi ruler Liu Yu, to whom Han had paid his respects in Kaifeng, had sent his armies across the Huai River border and attacked and taken the city of Xiangyang, beginning another round of military attacks and counterattacks between the rival empires. It was not until eight years later that a permanent treaty between the Southern Song and the Jin would be concluded. This was the agreement, notorious in Chinese historiography, that formally recognized Jin control of the northern half of the empire.

Li Qingzhao had heard of the commissioning of Han Xiaozhou and Hu Songnian in the summer of 1133, and she responded with two poems, the first a lengthy eighty lines long, directly addressed to the two emissaries. The poems survive because they were quoted in entirety in a late twelfth-century miscellany by Zhao Yanwei.[6] In introducing the poems, Zhao observes that Li Qingzhao's song lyrics are widely available in printed editions but that her other writings are seldom seen and little known. Zhao clearly admires Li Qingzhao's talent as a writer and is doing what he can to bring her writing in other forms to people's attention. Later in the same entry Zhao quotes, without comment, Li Qingzhao's letter to Qi Chongli. Here are the two poems:

---

3. Ibid. 66.1112.
4. Ibid. 65.1108.
5. Ibid. 70.1180.
6. Zhao Yanwei, *Yunlu manchao* 14.245–47.

上樞密韓公工部　　*Presented to Lord Han of the Military Affairs*
尚書胡公　　　　　*Bureau and Lord Hu of the Ministry of Works*

紹興癸丑六月，樞密韓公，工部尚書胡公使虜，通兩宮也。有易安室者，
父祖皆出韓公門下，今家世淪替，子姓寒微，不敢望公之車塵。又貧病，
但神明未衰落。見此大號令，不能忘言，作古，律各一章，以寄區區之
意，以待採詩者云。

In the sixth month of the *guichou* year of the Shaoxing reign [1133], Military Commissioner Han and Minister Hu of the Bureau of Works were sent as emissaries to the northern barbarians, where they were to carry messages to the Two Palaces.[7] Here is the woman Yi'an, whose father and grandfather were disciples of Lord Han's ancestors. Their family is in decline, and she as its younger member is lowly and insignificant. She would not presume even to look upon the dust from their lordships' carriages. Yi'an suffers, moreover, from poverty and ill health, yet her spirit and understanding are not the least bit diminished. Hearing of this august imperial commission and command, she could not fail to speak out. She has composed two poems, one each in the ancient and regulated styles, to convey her humble views, awaiting, now, the official Poetry Collector.[8]

三年夏六月	In the summer, the third year, the sixth month,
天子視朝久	The Son of Heaven examined his court carefully.
凝旒望南雲	He gazed at southern clouds through jade cap tassels that did not sway,[9]
4　垂衣思北狩	Thought of the northern excursion, his robes hanging down.[10]

---

7. The text actually says "fifth month," but the poem that follows specifies the "sixth month," and this is supported by Li Xinchuan's account, so I have changed the wording in the preface accordingly. Two Palaces refers to the two captive former emperors, Huizong and Qinzong.

8. *Jianzhu* 2.220–22. My reading of the poems that follow has profited from the annotations in that work as well as those found in Wang Zhongwen, *Li Qingzhao ji jiaozhu*, pp. 109–20, and Xu Beiwen, *Li Qingzhao quanji pingzhu*, pp. 195–205. Qing scholars, in quoting the two poems, divide them differently, supposing that lines 1 through 46 constitute the first poem, addressed to Han Xiaozhou, and lines 47 through 80 plus what I give as the second poem (eight lines) are the second poem, addressed to Hu Songnian. Wang Zhongwen argues convincingly against this understanding. The previous English translation adopts the Qing division, failing to take note of what Li Qingzhao says in her preface, that she has composed one poem in the ancient style and one in the regulated form (i.e., the eight-line second poem); see Rexroth and Chung, *Li Ch'ing-chao*, pp. 59–65.

9. The jade cap tassels that are not swaying shows the depth of his concentration.

10. "Northern excursion" (or "hunting expedition") refers euphemistically to the northern captivity of Gaozong's father and older brother. They had, indeed, "traveled" north but not by choice or for pleasure. The robe "hanging down" evokes a ruler who rules like a Daoist sage by "not interfering" (*wuwei* 無爲).

如聞帝若曰	It seemed that His Majesty spoke these words:
岳牧與群后	"Titled lords, governors, and myriad officials:
賢寧無半千	A worthy man appears every five hundred years.[11]
8 運已遇陽九	Our time has witnessed calamities for an eon.
勿勒燕然銘	Let us not celebrate victories with a Yanran Mountain stele,[12]
勿種金城柳	Nor need we plant willows at Golden City.[13]
豈無純孝臣	Is there no perfectly filial subject,
12 識此霜露悲	Who understands this frost-and-dew grief?[14]
何必羹捨肉	Why must I set meat aside from the broth?[15]
便可車載脂	Let us grease the carriage axels to quicken them.
土地非所惜	Our lands, we do not cherish them,
16 玉帛如塵泥	Jade and silk are like dirt to us.
誰當可將命	Who is fit to convey our message?
幣厚辭益卑	Gifts increase as our words become more humble."
四岳僉曰俞	The feudal lords together said, "Yes,
20 臣下帝所知	Your Majesty knows his subjects well.
中朝第一人	The best man in the central court,
春官有昌黎	Is a Han Yu among the rites officials.[16]
身爲百夫特	His person stands out among one hundred,
24 行足萬人師	His conduct makes him teacher to ten thousand.
嘉祐與建中	During the Jiayou and Jianzhong periods
爲政有皋夔	His ancestors managed policy as did Gao Tao and Kui.[17]

---

11. So it says in *Mencius* 2B/13, although there it refers to the appearance of a sage king.

12. This line and the next allude to ancient northern campaigns, in which heroic Chinese generals attacked and beat back northern enemies. It was the Han general Dou Xian 竇憲 (d. 92) who erected a stele at Jiluo Mountain 稽落山, celebrating his defeat of the Xiongnu; see *Hou Hanshu* 23.814–15.

13. It was the Jin period figure Huan Wen 桓溫 (312–73) who planted willows at this place on a northern campaign and then returned years later to find them fully grown; see Liu Yiqing, *Shishuo xinyu jianshu* 2.55.114.

14. The appearance of frost in the autumn and dew in spring reminds the gentleman of the passing of the seasons and hence the aging of his parents, that is, Gaozong's mother and father in their northern captivity; see "Ji yi" 祭義, *Liji zhuzi suoyin* 25.1/123/24.

15. When feasted by his duke, Ying Kaoshu 穎考叔 (d. 712 BCE) took the meat out of his soup, setting it aside for his mother, who had never had the chance to eat such a meal; see *Chunqiu Zuozhuan zhuzi suoyin* B1.1.4/2/25–26 (Yin 1).

16. That is, Han Xiaozhou is as great a statesman as the Tang figure Han Yu, with whom he shared a surname.

17. The lines refer to Han Xiaozhou's great-grandfather Han Qi 韓琦 and grandfather Han Zhongyan 韓忠彥, who were grand councilors during the named reign periods of the Northern Song. Gao Tao 皋陶 and Kui were high officials under the sage kings Yao and Shun.

	匈奴畏王商	The Xiongnu fear this Wang Shang,[18]
28	吐蕃尊子儀	The Turfan revere this Guo Ziyi.[19]
	夷狄已破膽	The barbarians have already lost their courage,
	將命公所宜	He is the one to receive the command."
	公拜手稽首	The lord made obeisance with hands and head,
32	受命白玉墀	He accepted the appointment below the white jade steps,
	曰臣敢辭難	Saying, "How dare I shrink from hardship
	此亦何等時	When we live in a time like this?
	家人安足謀	What thought do I have of my family?
36	妻子不必辭	I need not take leave of wife and children.[20]
	願奉天地靈	I yearn to hold the spiritual power of Heaven and Earth
	願奉宗廟威	I yearn to hold the majesty of the ancestral shrine.
	徑持紫泥詔	Grasping the decree sealed with purple powder
40	直入黃龍城	I shall proceed straight into Yellow Dragon City.[21]
	單于定稽顙	The Khan will kowtow in receiving me,
	侍子當來迎	His hostage sons will come to welcome me.[22]
	仁君方恃信	Our benevolent ruler relies on trust,
44	狂生休請纓	Hot-blooded men need not ask for ropes.[23]
	或取犬馬血	Perhaps we shall use the blood of horse and dog,
	與結天日盟	To sign a treaty bound by an oath to the sun in the sky."
	胡公清德人所難	Lord Hu's pure goodness is rare among men,
48	謀同德協必志安	Of shared aim and virtue, his resolve is firm.
	脫衣已被漢恩暖	The jacket shed, he is warmed by Han's beneficence,[24]

---

18. Wang Shang was a Han dynasty grand councilor. His appearance and reputation intimidated the Xiongnu chieftan when he came to the Han Court. *Hanshu* 82.3370–71.

19. Guo Ziyi was a Tang dynasty general of great distinction in campaigns against northern enemies. His biography in *Xin Tangshu* contains a passage in which his fearsome reputation as warrior frightens a Huihe 回紇 general, so it appears that "Turfan" here names the wrong northern people; see *Xin Tangshu* 137.4604.

20. According to Han Xiaozhou's biography, when he was about to depart, his mother urged him to think only of his mission and not concern himself with her welfare. When the emperor heard of this, he granted the mother an official title. See *Songshi* 138.11691.

21. The Jin capital, near modern Harbin, Jilin.

22. That is, the princes whom the poem fancifully imagines the Jin ruler will send back with Han Xiaozhou as tokens of his submission to the Song Court.

23. Cords would be used to tie up the enemy chieftain and deliver him back to the Chinese court as prisoner. This is what the Han general Zhong Jun 終軍 (d. 112 BCE) boasted he would do to the king of the Southern Yue. *Hanshu* 64B.2821.

24. It was Han Xin who said that the future founder of the Han dynasty, Emperor Gaozu 高祖 (r. 206–187 BCE), was so solicitous of him and his service that he shared food with him and took off his own jacket to clothe him. *Shiji* 92.2622.

	離歌不道易水寒	His farewell song complains not of the Yi River's chill.[25]
	皇天久陰后土濕	Lord Heaven has long been clouded over and Consort Earth wet,
52	雨勢未回風勢急	The driving rain does not abate, the wind increases.
	車聲轔轔馬蕭蕭	Carriage wheels creak and horses whinny sadly,
	壯士懦夫俱感泣	Men of valor and cowards are both reduced to tears.
	閭閻嫠婦亦何知	A widow of the inner apartments, what do I know?
56	瀝血投書干記室	I write this in blood to submit to the Imperial Archives.
	夷虜從來性虎狼	Barbarians have long had the nature of tiger and wolf,
	不虞預備庸何傷	What harm is there in preparing for the unexpected?
	衷甲昔時聞楚幕	Armor was concealed under clothing in the ancient tent of Chu,[26]
60	乘城前日記平涼	We know about defending the wall at Pingliang in days of old.[27]
	葵丘踐土非荒城	Aren't Kuiqiu and Jiantu no more than ruins?[28]
	勿輕談士棄儒生	Do not belittle advising gentlemen or reject scholars.
	露布詞成馬猶倚	A victory report was written leaning against a horse,[29]
64	崤函關出雞未鳴	Xiaohan Pass was left behind before the cock crowed.[30]

---

25. As he set off on his suicide mission to assassinate the First Emperor of the Qin, Jing Ke 荊軻 (d. 227 BCE) sang a sad farewell song that mentioned the cold waters of the Yi River, where his farewell scene took place. *Shiji* 86.2534.

26. Although they said that they were to sign a treaty with the Jin 晉, men of the rival state of Chu in ancient times went to the ceremony wearing armor under their clothes, planning a surprise attack on the Jin representatives. *Chunqiu Zuozhuan zhuzi suoyin* B9.27.3/293/16–25 (Xiang 27).

27. A Turfan official treacherously ambushed the Tang official Hun Jian 渾瑊 at Pingliang in 629, when the two met supposedly to sign a treaty; see *Jiu Tangshu* 134.3700. This must be what Li Qingzhao has in mind by "climbing the wall" since no mention is made of such an action in the account of the ambush.

28. Kuiqiu and Jiantu are both places where famous treaties were signed during the Spring and Autumn period; see *Chunqiu Zuozhuan zhuzi suoyin* A5.9.2/81/12 (Xi 9) and A5.28.8/109/31 (Xi 28). The only way I can make sense of this line is to turn it into a question. In this reading, the line means that the treaties concluded at those places had no lasting value or effect, and the places themselves have fallen into neglect and ruin.

29. The Jin writer Yuan Hu 袁虎 had been disciplined and stripped of office while accompanying Huan Wen 桓溫 (312–73) on a northern campaign. But when Huan needed a victory report drafted, it was Yuan Hu who did the job brilliantly, filling seven pages without pausing one time to think and doing it while leaning back against his horse. Liu Yiqing, *Shishuo xinyu jianshu* 4.96.273.

30. This alludes to a well-known Lord of Mengchang 孟嘗君 story. When the Lord, famed for the number of retainers he kept, reached Xiaohan Pass (Hangu Pass 函谷關), he managed to obtain passage through it before dawn and thus elude capture by forces sent by the king of Qin only because one of his most lowly retainers knew how to mimic the cock's crow and thus

	巧匠何曾棄樗櫟	A skillful carpenter does not reject even inferior timber,
	芻蕘之言或有益	Kindling gatherers sometimes supply sage counsel.[31]
	不乞隋珠與和璧	We do not seek Sui's pearl or He's jade disk,[32]
68	只乞鄉關新信息	All we want is fresh tidings of our homeland.
	靈光雖在應蕭蕭	Lingguang Palace still stands but must be desolate,[33]
	草中翁仲今何若	How fares the stone statuary, engulfed by weeds?
	遺氓豈尚種桑麻	Do our abandoned subjects still plant mulberry and hemp?
72	殘虜如聞保城郭	Do the routed barbarians still guard the city walls?
	婺家父祖生齊魯	This widow's father and grandfather were born in Qi and Lu,
	位下名高人比數	They counted men of renown among their followers.
	當年稷下縱談時	In animated discussions at the Jixia Academy,[34]
76	猶記人揮汗成雨	Perspiration wiped from brows fell like rain, I still can recall.
	子孫南渡今幾年	Their descendant crossed the river south years ago,
	飄流遂與流人伍	To drift aimlessly now as a refugee.
	欲將血淚寄山河	Take my blood-stained tears to those hills and rivers,
80	去灑東山一坏土	And sprinkle them on a clod of East Mountain soil.[35]

The second poem is this:

	想見皇華過二京	We imagine the envoys' splendor as they pass the two capitals,
	壺漿夾道萬人迎	Vats of liquor line the highway as thousands rush to welcome them.

---

tricked the guards into thinking that dawn had arrived, when travelers were allowed through the pass. *Shiji* 75.2354. In this couplet, the poet is urging Han Xiaozhou to accept the assistance and counsel of lowly inferiors. Possibly she means herself as well as attendants who will accompany him on his mission.

　31. This couplet continues the theme of the preceding one. The language is drawn from *Zhuangzi* (see *Zhuangzi zhuzi suoyin* 1/3/4) and the *Classic of Poetry* 254/3.

　32. The line names two legendary treasures.

　33. Lingguang Palace, belonging to Prince Yu of Gong 恭王餘, of the Former Han, was said to have survived the strife at the end of the Former Han, while the imperial palaces in Chang'an did not. The line implies that the disasters of 1126–27 and the Jin invasion were even worse than those that brought about the end of the Former Han. Nevertheless, the palace still survives and beckons the Chinese in the south to return northward.

　34. The ancient state of Qi 齊, in Li Qingzhao's native northeast, was famed for its Jixia 稷下 Academy, which attracted scholars from far and wide and fostered lively debate on philosophical and political issues.

　35. East Mountain 東山 is a place in the northeastern state of Lu 魯 (i.e., Li Qingzhao's homeland) mentioned in *Mencius* 7A/24.

連昌宮裏桃應在	Peach trees must still blossom in Lianchang Palace,
4　華萼樓前鵲定驚	Magpies are startled before Flower Calyx Tower.[36]
但說帝心憐赤子	Say only that our emperor cherishes his little children,
須知天意念蒼生	Heaven is mindful, they must know, of our commoners.
聖君大信明如日	His Majesty's great trust is as bright as the sun,
8　長亂何須在屢盟	Why must it be that frequent treaties prolong the strife?[37]

Li Qingzhao knew that the "peace" party was then ascendant at the court and that Han Xiaochou was selected to lead the delegation because he was an outspoken advocate of such a peace. Li Qingzhao, like many, strongly disagreed with this policy, which its critics viewed as spineless appeasement. The two poems above convey Li Qingzhao's disapproval with great tact and ingenuity, while ostensibly praising Gaozong's intentions in dispatching this mission, and also seem to praise Han and Hu, while suggesting that their impulses need correction. It is a delicate undertaking that Li Qingzhao has set herself in these compositions: to address high officials hand-picked by the emperor to pursue a controversial policy, conveying her disagreement with the officials' and the emperor's intent, which she views as unprincipled and foolish. She carries off her task with great skill.

In the first section of the first poem (lines 1–18), Li Qingzhao emphasizes the filial devotion of Gaozong to his parents and older brother (and other clan members), who were prisoners of the Jurchen in the distant north. She makes it sound as if the entire purpose of the upcoming mission is for Han and Hu to convey Gaozong's, and the empire's, solicitations to his captive relatives and perhaps even to secure their release and return to the south. Gaozong is described as being forever mindful of the relatives' plight (line 4): he searches for a perfectly filial subject to dispatch on a mission of filial intent (line 11), his grief is that of an exemplary son (line 12), and he does not understand why he should have been fated to be separated from his mother in her advanced years (line 13). So overwhelming is his sorrow regarding his parents' plight that territory no longer means anything to him (line 15), and he cannot give enough gifts of jade and silk to the Jurchen court in his effort to

---

36. The two buildings were both part of the Tang palace complex in Chang'an, used here as substitutes for the Song palace in Bianliang. Lianchang was known for its abundant peach trees.

37. The language and the idea of a connection between too many treaties and protracted unrest derives from the *Classic of Poetry* 198/3.

safeguard them or perhaps win their release (line 16). But many of these lines seemingly admiring of Gaozong evoke a secondary sense, often readily apparent, that runs in a counter direction as soon as we recall that the loss of the north was not only a personal tragedy for Gaozong and the imperial clan, but also an empirewide dynastic calamity of almost unprecedented proportions. To have Gaozong say, in the poem, that he no longer cares about land or that he is willing to give up any amount of jade and silk echoes the arguments against the peace party used by those who advocated a military campaign to recover the lost north. Given the ferocity of the debate just then between the opposing sides, the secondary meaning of such lines, contradicting the flattering portrait of Gaozong as filial son, would have been unmistakable to any reader. Going still further, Li Qingzhao has Gaozong explicitly reject any interest in achieving the kind of victorious northern campaign that had been led by heroic generals in earlier times (lines 9–10). What could possibly be the rationale not for not trying a northern counterattack, but for rejecting the prospect of military victories in the north? In these lines Gaozong's thinking broaches the absurd. Equally transparent is the censure contained in the closing, climactic line of this section: "Gifts increase as our words become more humble." The perception of the peace policy as one of national abasement and humiliation, carried out at great financial cost to the Song state, was precisely what outraged its critics.

In the next two sections (lines 19–72), Li Qingzhao tones down her criticism. This is possibly because of her family connection to Han Xiaozhou and possibly because she genuinely respects him. Still, for all Han's loyalty and good intentions evoked here, there remains in these lines an undercurrent of skepticism and criticism. Li Qingzhao uses the rhetoric of Chinese superiority when referring to the northern enemy. The "barbarians" have already lost their courage; they are intimidated by Han Xiaozhou; their leader will bow in receiving him; and so forth. This may be the stock language used when writing about the nations to the north, but under the circumstances, when the Jurchen were occupying the northern half of the Song empire and were holding dozens of members of the imperial family captive, it is patently false and would be perceived as such. Even more telling is the contrast she hints at between Gaozong's "reliance on trust" (line 43) and the fact that the enemy is nothing if not untrustworthy (lines 57–60). Gaozong's policy of trusting the Jurchen is made to look foolhardy and dangerous by her stress on the history of northern tribes' treachery in their dealing with the Chinese. Then we understand that the boast she has Han Xiaozhou utter that "hot-blooded men need not ask for ropes" (i.e., to tie up the barbarian leader and bring him as captive back to the Song, line 44) is, in her eyes, exactly the wrong attitude and strategy to adopt. Lines 62 through 66 urge the two emissaries to be open to suggestions of alternative approaches to their mission coming from lowly persons. She may be thinking of lesser officials who will accompany Han and Hu as their assistants. She may also be thinking of herself. She has already asked rhetorically what she, a mere widow sequestered away, could understand of such matters (line 55). Now, when she refers to lowly men and "inferior timber," she may mean to warn the emissaries against rejecting her advice out of hand because of who it comes from.

She unambiguously brings the focus back to herself in the closing section of the poem (lines 73–80). She may be a widow, but she reminds us that her father and grandfather were steeped in the proud tradition of the ancient Jixia Academy of the Shandong region, famed for attracting learned scholars and fostering debate on issues of philosophy and governance. Li Qingzhao grew up listening to those heated discussions (line 76). Can we doubt that she feels qualified to weigh in with her own opinions, especially now in a time of national crisis? In lines 77 and 78 Li Qingzhao refers to herself obliquely, as the "descendant" of that father and grandfather she remembers so proudly. She, as the representative of the family, has, however, suffered a drastic decline. Geographically displaced, she has been brought down to the level of wandering refugee. This is nearly the only place in the poem that the rhetoric emphasizing the grandeur and power of the Song state is dropped and a bit of the reality of the situation is allowed to show through. As the contemporary reader would realize, it is not only Li Qingzhao who has been reduced to the status of refugee. Hundreds of thousands of her compatriots, including the newly installed emperor himself, were now in effect displaced persons. The thought about her identity as refugee then leads to the injunction of the closing couplet and its image of making an offering to the soil on East Mountain, in the homeland she can no longer visit. "Blood-stained tears" of the penultimate line echoes the earlier image of her pricking her own blood with which to write these poems (line 56). One writes in blood that way as a show of loyalty to a higher cause, as a display of selflessness, and often in taking a principled stand against something one cannot agree with or condone. The phrase she uses in the poems' preface, saying that when she heard of the mission she "could not fail to speak out" 不能忘言, has a similar import. It is used to evoke the obligation to speak out in opposition to policies that one believes to be misguided. Almost always it applies to men, but not here.

If the first poem mostly uses the rhetoric of the august Song state to suggest that the present policy of negotiating with the invaders is cowardly and foolhardy, the second poem focuses on the plight of those who still remain in the north and are living under foreign occupation. The poem opens with the imagined scene of welcome, as the former subjects of the Song rush to greet the emissaries from the south. This is pure fantasy, and nothing of the kind would have been allowed by the Jurchen, even if the Chinese would have really wanted to greet with such enthusiasm representatives of the court that had disgraced itself and abandoned them.[38] The second couplet refers to two palace buildings in the Tang dynasty capital of Chang'an and by implication to the Song palace in Bianliang, which the emissaries will pass on their trip farther north to the Jin capital. The first of these palace buildings, constructed by Gaozong of the Tang, is known to have had a garden filled with peach trees, and that garden is already said to have been deserted in a mid-Tang poem.[39] Li Qingzhao's line evokes the deserted Song palace building, though the reasons for its abandonment were dramatically more calamitous than in the case of the Tang building actually named. Line 4 goes a step further. It too names a Tang palace building, but one specifically associated in Tang sources with imperial feasting and frivolous gaiety.[40] The ill-fated Emperor Xuanzong built Flower Calyx Tower on a site that adjoined the palaces of several princes, and the emperor frequently entertained the princes in the tower. Owing to other literary allusions, we are probably to understand that the magpies are startled with delight when they see that the emissaries from the south are passing by. Li Qingzhao had no shortage of other palace building names available to her when she composed this line. That she chose a building associated in Tang sources with frivolous imperial partying carried out by an emperor who, though he was celebrated early in his reign, lost his empire to rebel armies swarming down from the north and eventually had to abdicate is certainly no coincidence. The parallels with the "frivolity" of Huizong, as it was perceived after 1126, if not before, as well as his demise and abdication are too close to be accidental. This line, then, implies the author's criticism of Huizong, the reigning emperor's father, and blame of him for the dynastic calamity.

38. Cf. Qian Zhongshu's comments to this effect on a similar scenario presented in a poem by Fan Chengda 范成大 (1126–93), *Songshi xuanzhu* 宋詩選註, p. 224.
39. Yuan Zhen, "Lianchang gong ci" 連昌宮詞, *Quan Tang shi* 419.4613.
40. Zheng Chuhui, "Yiwen" 逸文, *Minghuan zalu*, p. 56.

Lines 5 and 6 enjoin the emissaries to convey messages to the Chinese subjects living under foreign subjugation about their emperor's concern for them and, indeed, Heaven's concern for them. The lines sound like vapid reassurances and are probably intended to sound that way. Li Qingzhao's position is that all such expressions of concern are quite meaningless if the Southern Song state is actually pursuing a policy of appeasement with the conquerors. Line 7 harks back to the theme broached in the first poem of Gaozong operating on the basis of trust. Here, the ostensible meaning is that the northerners should put their faith in Gaozong, knowing that he will never forget them. But the underlying implication is that, as before, Gaozong's policy toward the Jurchen is based on his trust in them—hence his decision to dispatch high-ranking emissaries to negotiate with them. But the first poem makes it abundantly clear that Li Qingzhao believes such trust to be misplaced. The concluding line is a fitting capstone to these poems that consistently say one thing while meaning another. A couplet in the *Classic of Poetry* attributes protracted civil strife and disorder in a certain kingdom to the fact that the ruler there negotiates one treaty after another with the forces causing the unrest rather than taking definitive steps to eliminate them. The literal meaning of Li Qingzhao's line calls this assertion into question: why must repeated treaties necessarily have this result? But inasmuch as the source for this assertion of causation between treaties and protracted strife is the ancient classic, and the reality of Li Qingzhao's day was that multiple treaties with the invaders had done nothing to stop their further incursions (much less to wrest the north back from their control), the inverse implication over-shadows what the line says. Readers are meant to understand that the classic was right, and the situation it describes is a good match for the disastrous circumstances that they were living through. Li Qingzhao cannot say this directly to the two imperial emissaries on the eve of their departure, but the way she phrases her observation makes the inverted meaning unmistakable, as recent commentators on these poems have pointed out.[41]

Writings on Capture the Horse

The northern mission of Han Xiaozhou and Hu Songnian in 1133 accomplished nothing of substance. No treaty was agreed upon, and no progress was made toward winning the release of the imperial captives. By the year's

---

41. For example, Wang Yingzhi, *Li Qingzhao ji*, pp. 137–38.

end, Liu Yu of Qi initiated a new southward campaign that attacked and took control of Xiangyang, on the Han River (in northeastern Hubei). This was a serious incursion because a further southern push from Xiangyang could have cut the Song empire in half. Song armies led by Yue Fei 岳飛 (1103–42) counterattacked and retook Xiangyang in the summer of 1134, but in the ninth month of that year, Jin and Qi forces launched a new southern invasion farther east in the Huai River valley, threatening to cross the Yangzi River again and putting the capital of Lin'an at risk. Li Qingzhao herself describes the ensuing chaos this way:

> This year on the first day of the tenth month, winter, we heard that military emergencies were reported on the Huai River. Those who live in the Yangzi River and Zhe River regions fled westward from the east and southward from the north. Those who live in the hills and forests made plans to flee into cities, while those who live in cities made plans to flee to hills and forests. In this protracted flight, with everyone hurrying this way and that, ultimately there was no one who was not displaced.[42]

There was discussion of having the emperor flee southward again for safety. But this time, at the suggestion of grand councilor Zhao Ding 趙鼎 (1085–1147), Gaozong decided to stay and face the threat, saying that he would "lead the army" in its resistance of the invasion. Gaozong proceeded westward to Suzhou. The invading armies advanced southward from the Huai River but suffered a major defeat near Hefei at the hands of Song forces led, again, by Yue Fei. Late in 1134 news reached the invading generals that the Jin ruler, Taizong 太宗 (Wanyan Sheng 完顏晟), had become seriously ill (he would die in the first month of 1135), and they began to withdraw, hurrying back north to pick his successor. Taizong's failing health effectively ended this southern invasion, and the weakened Song state was spared again.

When the new invasion began in 1134, Li Qingzhao evidently decided that it was too dangerous to stay in the capital. Knowing how quickly the invaders had advanced just four years before, this time she wanted to seek refuge early. She traveled by boat up the Fuchun River from Lin'an and proceeded southwest to Jinhua (in central Zhejiang), where she rented a place to live in the residence of a certain Chen family. We do not know how long she remained at Jinhua. She stayed there at least into the next year and probably returned to Lin'an later in 1135 as soon as she determined that it was safe to do so.

---

42. Li Qingzhao, "Dama tujing xu" 打馬圖經序, *Jianzhu* 3.340–41.

Toward the end of 1134, after arriving in Jinhua, Li Qingzhao produced a remarkable series of writings on a gambling game called Capture the Horse 打馬. These writings consist of (1) a preface, written in parallel prose, to "diagrams and text" 圖經 she wrote about the game. The "diagrams and text" do not survive. The preface consists of general remarks on the game, provides details of the circumstances under which Li Qingzhao wrote the work, and compares Capture the Horse with other board games. (2) A *fu*, or "rhyme-prose," that offers a rhapsodic account of the game, linking it especially to the tradition that connects such board games with real-life military strategy. (3) A series of thirteen short entries or paragraphs, called "Instructions" 命辭, which give poetic descriptions of various moves, strategies, and configurations of "horses." It is possible that these "Instructions" were part or all of the text of the "diagrams and text." Taken together, these writings reveal a different side of Li Qingzhao as a person and writer: the avid gameswoman, wit, and strategist. The writings also complement the poems addressed to the emissaries. Capture the Horse was a game conceived of as a military confrontation. The game's participants—usually three to five persons played at one time—were thought of as commanders of armies facing each other on the battlefield and trying to outmaneuver each other with their armies, represented by "horses." Li Qingzhao's writings about the game are full of implicit and explicit references to the actual military plight of the early Southern Song. It is this aspect of her writings on the game that complements the poems just discussed, and these references shed further light on the aspirations and frustrations that she as a lone woman, recently divorced, and still fleeing from Jurchen incursions eight years after being forced from her homeland, experienced at the time.

Capture the Horse was a Song period gambling game; money played an important part in the game as players were continuously "rewarded" or "fined" with funds from a central purse or bank. Capture the Horse was one of many such games that were played at the time, and like several of the others, Capture the Horse went out of fashion after the Song period and was not transmitted to later times. Consequently, there is much we do not understand about the rules and actual conduct of the game, although it is clear enough that the rules were elaborate and the game complicated. Our ignorance of the particulars of the game makes some of what Li Qingzhao says about it impossible to understand. This is particularly so with her "Instructions." But what Li Qingzhao says in the preface and rhyme-prose is tolerably clear, as it is revealing.

Preface to "Capture the Horse," Diagrams and Text

"Insight leads to penetrating understanding, and with penetrating understanding there is nowhere to which the mind cannot reach";[43] concentration leads to refined skill, and with refined skill everything one does will be at a level of marvelous excellence. Therefore, whether it be Cook Ding's carving of oxen, the man of Ying's wielding of the ax, the hearing of Musician Kuang, the eyesight of Lilou, matters of such great import as the humaneness of Yao and Shun or the wickedness of Jie and Zhou, or matters of such little import as throwing beans and catching flies or moving chess pieces with the corner of a handkerchief, they all arrived at the ultimate principle of things.[44] Why? Because each attained marvelous excellence at what he did. But as for people of later ages, not only did they fail to reach the level of the sages in their learning of the sagely Way, even in amusements and games, most of them gave up their cultivation before ever achieving even a semblance of what earlier men had achieved. Now, board games can be reduced to this: techniques for striving to win. Anyone who gives them his concentration can master them. By nature I am fond of board games. I can lose myself in any of them so that I can play all night long without thought of food or sleep. My whole life I have won most of the contests I have played. Why? Because of my level of refined skill.

Since crossing the Yangzi River southward, I have been separated from loved ones and forced to wander here and there. I have seen my board games lost and scattered, and so seldom have I had any chance to play. But in my heart I have never forgotten them. This year on the first day of the tenth month, winter, we heard that military emergencies were reported on the Huai River. Those who live in the Yangzi River and Zhe River regions fled westward from the east and southward from the north.[45] Those who live in the hills and forests made plans to flee into cities, while those who live in cities made plans to flee to hills and forests. In this protracted flight, with everyone hurrying this way and that, ultimately there was no one who was not displaced. I myself, the Resident Scholar of Yi'an, traveled upstream from Lin'an. I crossed the river amid the high terrain of Yan Rapids and proceeded to Jinhua, where I found a place to live in the home of the Chen family. Having recently exchanged the comforts of verandas and windows for the hardships of boat and oar, I feel

---

43. From Ling Xuan's preface to *Zhao Feiyan waizhuan*, p. 8b.

44. It was Cao Pi 曹丕 (187–226), Emperor Wen of the Wei, who is said to have used his handkerchief to flip the playing pieces in the game Pellet Chess. Liu Yiqing, *Shishuo xinyu jianshu* 21.1.712.

45. I have emended the text here, which originally says "northward from the south," which makes poor sense under the circumstances.

quite content. But "the night watches are slow and the lamp burns bright";[46] how can I pass the long night? So I resolved to write an account of board games.

Now, Long Walk, Leaves, Borderlands, and Pellets, these games are no longer known. Strike and Lift, Big and Little Pigpen, Ghost Clans, Barbarian Drawings, Storehouse of Numbers, and Fast Bets, these kinds of game are vulgar and not often seen. Storing Ale, Clutch the Reed, and Double Alert have been abandoned and forgotten in recent times. Pick the Immortal, Add and Take Away, and Insert the Flame are simple, dull games that depend on luck and leave no room for people to apply their knowledge or ingenuity. Large and Small Ivories and Weiqi can only be played by two persons at a time. It is only Selecting Colors and Capture the Horse that can be considered elegant games of the women's inner quarters. But I dislike how complicated Selecting Colors is, requiring so much looking up. Few people can really master it, and so it is difficult to find an able opponent. Capture the Horse, by contrast, is simple and straightforward, although it is somewhat lacking in color and style.

I note that there are two versions of Capture the Horse. One version uses one general and ten horses. It is known as Horses West of the Passes. The other version has no general but uses twenty horses. This one is known as Horses According to Texts. Having been around for a long time, both versions have diagrams and texts and rules that can be consulted. The two have some different moves, rewards, and punishments. There is also another version developed during the Xuanhe reign period [1119–25] that uses two types of horses in different quantities. This version depends more on luck, and the ancient flavor of the game is completely lost. It is known as Xuanhe Horses. The version I like is Horses According to Texts. Here, I have made estimates of some scenarios for reward and punishment, and have composed a few lines on each one, which are appended to each of the named arrangements of the pieces on the board. And I have had a youngster draw a diagram of each. This work may be transmitted not only to players of the game, but also to other interested persons so that a million generations hence everyone who hears of Capture the Horse will know that [writings about the game] began with the Recluse Scholar Yi'an.

The twenty-fourth day of the eleventh month of the fourth year of the Shaoxing period [1134], by Lady Yi'an.[47]

There are several themes and layers of meaning in this piece. In the opening paragraph Li Qingzhao asserts a connection between trivial amusements and weighty matters of governance. The connection is that in all activities,

---

46. From Du Fu, "Jin xi xing" 今夕行, *Dushi xiangzhu* 1.59.
47. Li Qingzhao, "Dama tujing xu," *Jianzhu* 3.340–41.

regardless of their import, concentration leads to skill, and skill leads to a high level of performance. By putting the matter this way, Li Qingzhao is linking the trivial activity she is going to write about with ones that are in no need of a defense. This is an apologist strategy, yet it is not only that. The idea that "ultimate principles/truths" could be glimpsed through protracted study and mastery of seemingly inconsequential activities was current among literati of the time. Su Shi wrote about this theme a few different times.[48] That Li Qingzhao alludes to this notion is the first indication that she is not simply writing about a board game. She is writing about a board game but intends to use it to approach or intimate issues of greater importance than mere gaming. At the end of the first paragraph, she returns the subject to herself, telling us how enamored she is of these games. Then she mentions that she nearly always wins. This is strikingly immodest for anyone to say, and especially so for a woman. It is all the more surprising given that she has just reduced board games to a single impulse: "striving to win." This is hardly the type of behavior that was normally expected of women.

The second paragraph presents a long digression away from her subject, in which she describes the Jin invasion, its consequences, and her removal to Jinhua. As students of her life, we would like to know even more. Did she make this trip alone or with her brother and his family? Why exactly did she end up at Jinhua? Did she have friends or benefactors there? There is speculation that she chose Jinhua because Zhao Mingcheng's brother-in-law, Li Zhuo 李擢, to whom Li Qingzhao had turned for help once before (see her afterword, below), was then serving as prefect there.[49] But if that were so, it is odd that upon arriving in Jinhua she finds lodgings for herself in some apparent stranger's house.

Nevertheless, the passage is quite unnecessary in this preface. Her personal circumstances surrounding the composition of this piece are off subject. That she explains them at such length must be for a reason. She writes not only about her own removal from the capital and trek to Jinhua, but also about the destabilizing effect that news of the new military attack has had on society generally; this is someone who is not just thinking about her own hardship. She concludes the section by noting how pleasant her current situation is in contrast to the arduous boat journey to get to Jinhua.

----

48. See my *Word, Image, and Deed in the Life of Su Shi*, pp. 279–80.
49. See Xu Peijun, "Nianpu," *Jianzhu*, p. 490.

The line about the slow night watches and bright lamp is a quotation from a Du Fu poem. It is a nice touch, which reminds us of her learning and cleverness.

The following paragraph lists in encyclopedic fashion all the board games she knows of, including those that survived into the Song dynasty in name only. If we had any doubt, we now know how knowledgeable she is about the subject. Her purpose here is not only to list, but also to eliminate from consideration. All the games she names have one or another drawback. They have been lost long ago, or are so vulgar that they are seldom seen among the elite (like Li Qingzhao), or they have recently fallen into obscurity, or they depend on luck rather than ingenuity, or they can only be played by two persons at a time. Even among the final two games, she faults the first (Selecting Colors) for being too complicated. If we at first think this means it is too complicated for Li Qingzhao, we later understand her to mean that its inherent difficulty makes it hard for her to find a worthy opponent!

Narrowing her focus even further, in the final paragraph she describes different versions of Capture the Horse. I suspect that what she says about the Xuanhe period variation on the game has a deeper meaning. In the early years of the Southern Song, any mention of the Xuanhe reign invariably caused a strong reaction: revulsion at the extravagance of Huizong's court coupled with outrage over its inability to defend the empire from Jurchen attack. When Li Qingzhao complains that the Xuanhe variation of the game put too much emphasis on luck and lost its "ancient meaning," the reader would naturally connect this with the blindness of Huizong's court, which counted on little more than luck to sustain it, only to see that luck run out, and its departures from hallowed principles of governance. Two interesting points are made in the closing lines. First, what Li Qingzhao has composed may be of interest not only to board game enthusiasts, but also to other "interested persons." This is a clear indication that, as she writes about the game, she has matters beyond the game itself in mind. Then there is the extravagant concluding claim: people of countless generations hence will think of her when Capture the Horse is mentioned, crediting her as the first to write an authoritative treatment of the subject.

Li Qingzhao refers to Capture the Horse as an "elegant game of the women's inner quarters" (paragraph 3). She also makes it clear that this is one of the only board games that depends on intelligence and ingenuity, while disparaging other games as lowly and the Xuanhe variation as dependent only on luck. An irony of gender runs through the preface: here we have a woman writing about a game that is conceived of as a mock military contest. She tells us that she is obsessed with such contests of strategy, claiming that she always wins, and predicting that future generations will know of this game from what she writes about it. Meanwhile, she goes out of her way to remind readers of the military weakness of the Song empire and the social havoc that this weakness has brought about even in the current year. She also includes a pointed reference to a debased version of the game associated with the emperor who was blamed for the loss of the north. Then she ends by implying that "other interested persons" aside from those who are fond of playing board games may find her remarks of value. Li Qingzhao is clearly thinking about more than Capture the Horse. She is treading a fine line, here and there drawing close to ridicule of the reigning emperor and court. It is only acceptable for her, as a woman, to write about "elegant games of the women's inner quarters," if she writes at all, but she wants to broach matters of national policy and defense. Reading this preface, we sense both the pride and the frustration she feels, rooted in the contradiction between what she believes she understands about current military and political issues, and the restricted scope that she has for airing those views.

In the rhyme-prose she wrote on the game, around the same time, Li Qingzhao goes deeper into issues of strategy used in the game. Everything she says in her "Rhyme-Prose on Capture the Horse" resonates with the military situation of her day and her sense that the Song leaders need to be instructed how better to manage the ongoing conflict with the Jurchen. The most telling passage is the closing section, translated below:

> Moreover, to enjoy winning is human nature, and playing games is a trivial talent of the gentleman. Mentioning the plum alleviated thirst; so too may this relax the mind bent on rushing wildly ahead.[50] Drawing the pancake satisfied hunger; likewise may this curtail an intent to beat out all others.[51] If you want to get real results, then you must face danger unflinchingly. But to repay great

---

50. Virtually every phrase in this passage has some literary antecedent or reference. Here I am simply glossing those allusions necessary to establish the meaning that Li Qingzhao has in mind. When Cao Cao was leading a campaign and his soldiers were suffering from thirst, he falsely told them that close ahead there was a grove of plum trees and that the sweet-sour taste of the fruits would quench their thirst. Hearing this, the soliders' mouths began to water, and so they were able to keep marching ahead until they came upon a spring. Liu Yiqing, *Shishuo xinyu jianshu* 27.2.851.

51. Emperor Wen of the Wei decried unsubstantiated fame as akin to drawings of pancakes, which could not satisfy anyone's hunger. Chen Shou, *Sanguo zhi* 22.651.

favor bequeathed to you, you must understand what is imminent and first withdraw. Sometimes you need to advance cautiously with a gag in the mouth in order to get past the obstacles at mountain passes. Those who "peddle their valor," vying to be first, fall into a trap before they see it.[52] Such calamities come from not knowing when to stop or what is enough; thus the greedy bring on their own blame and remorse. You must know how to regulate the chariot properly and must not forget the superior man's injunctions inscribed on the sash. Is this pastime not better than doing nothing at all, the truth of which is asserted in the classic itself?[53] If the pieces are used with forthrightness, the significance of the game will match divine virtue. The mare accords with the constancy of earth, and as for "going back," we recall the method employed with the lady from Lu.[54] A lesson is taken from the wife in the Liang clan with pendant hair-knots.[55] We retrace the curving riverbank followed in the state of Qi. Encircling the couch, [Liu Yu] shouted and all five "woods" came up black. Sprinkling wine on the ground, [Liu Xin] cried out and six dice all came up red.[56] All his life [Huan Wen] never lost at board games, and thus his victory in

---

52. In antiquity, an officer in the army of Qi, Gao Gu 高固, after displaying heroics in battle, boasted to his fellow soldiers that he would "sell" his surplus of valor to anyone who needed more. *Chunqiu Zuozhuan zhuji suoyin* B.8.2.3/187/15 (Cheng 2).

53. In *Analects* 17/22 Confucius rails against people who are content to fill their bellies all day long and never use their minds. He goes on, "Isn't there chess? Playing that is at least better than doing nothing."

54. "The mare accords with the constancy of earth" is derived from the language applied to Hexagram no. 2, Kun (pure *yin*), in the *Classic of Changes*. Judgment: "Kun consists of fundamentality, and prevalence, and its fitness is that of the constancy of the mare.... Should the noble man set out to do something, if he were to take the lead, he would go astray, but if he were to follow, he would find a master." The commentary adds, "The mare is a metaphor for the Earth, for it travels the Earth without limit." The "going back" associated with the lady of Lu refers to the etiquette observed when Shuji 淑姬 was given as bride to the nobleman Gao Gu of Qi. The carriage in which she was brought to Qi was sent back immediately, but the horses that pulled the carriage were kept in Qi for a three-month period in case the marriage did not work out and the bride had to return to her parents in Lu. See the subcommentary on the *Zuozhuan* 左傳 passage *Chunqiu Zuozhuan zhuzi suoyin* B7.5.3/162/31–B7.5.4/163/1 (Xuan 5) found in *Chunqiu Zuozhuan zhushu* 22.2a.

55. This sentence and the next must refer to movements or dispositions of the pieces on the board. The drooping hair-knots (lit. "fallen horse hair-knots") of Sun Shou, wife of Liang Ji, is thought to refer to horse pieces that "fall" into traps the opponent has set. *Hou Hanshu* 34.1179–80. Retracing a curving riverbank is thought to describe a circuitous or flanking forward movement of one's own pieces.

56. These two sentences refer to two military leaders, Liu Yu 劉裕 of the Eastern Jin, and Liu Xin 劉信 of the Southern Tang (10th c.), who beat rivals at board games by staking their fate on a single risky throw, which turned out favorably for them. *Taiping yulan* 754.5a–b and Zheng Wenbao, *Nantang jinshi* 2.223.

the campaign against Jiangge was assured.[57] [Xie An] had not gambled away his mountain villa when the invaders at Huai and Fei were already defeated.[58] Today how could we lack a Yuanzi [Huan Wen]? Our enlightened age is not short of an Anshi [Xie An]. Why must we be like Tao Changsha [Tao Kan] when he hurled the chessboard in the river?[59] We should instead emulate Yuan Yandao [Yuan Dan] who threw down his cloth cap.[60]

The concluding verse says:

佛貍定見卯年死　　Foli will definitely die in the *mao* year,[61]
貴賤紛紛尚流徙　　Our high-ranking officials and commoners still flee in all
　　　　　　　　　directions.

---

57. When the Jin general Huan Wen was about to start his campaign against the Cheng-Han kingdom in Sichuan (Jiangge) in 341, many predicted that he would be unable to succeed. Liu Tan 劉惔 disagreed, saying that Huan was certain to be victorious: "I have observed his gambling habits. If he's not certain of winning, he won't play." Liu Yiqing, *Shishuo xinyu jianshu* 7.20.401.

58. This line combines two chess stories about Xie An 謝安, the Jin military leader who defeated Fu Jian 符堅 at the famous battle of Fei River in 383. On the eve of the battle, Xie An bet his mountain villa on a game of chess and won the game, even though he was playing against Xie Xuan 謝玄, his nephew, who ordinarily beat him. But Xie An was confident of victory in the upcoming battle, whereas Xie Xuan was apprehensive and so could not concentrate on the game. Later, when news came to Xie An of the victory, he was also playing chess. He received the news without showing any reaction and continued to play the game as if nothing had happened. *Jinshu* 79.2074–75; cf. Liu Yiqing, *Shishuo xinyu jianshu* 6.35.373–74.

59. Tao Kan 陶侃, another Jin dynasty general, was a stickler for discipline. When he saw that his subordinates were spending their time drinking and gambling, he gathered up their wine cups and chess implements and threw them all in the river. *Jinshu* 83.2170.

60. Yuan Dan 袁耽 (Yuan Yandao) was another Jin period chess master. He agreed to help extricate Huan Wen from his creditor by gambling at chess, even though he was then in mourning for his parent. Yuan Dan first disguised himself and hid his mourning cap inside his shirt. When he finished winning thousands of cash, he took out his cap and threw it on the floor, demanding of his opponent, "Now do you recognize Yuan Yandao?" Liu Yiqing, *Shishuo xinyu jianshu* 23.34.748–49.

61. The language is borrowed from a children's ditty predicting the death in 451 of Foli 佛貍, that is, Emperor Taiwu 太武 of the Northern Wei (r. 424–52), whose armies were then threatening the southern Song dynasty. *Songshu* 74.1912. Here Foli stands for the Jurchen ruler, Emperor Taizong. The original line in the children's song was a prediction, and Li Qingzhao's usage is probably also a wishful prediction (as I have translated it). She is believed to have written this piece in 1134 (Shaoxing 4) because the companion piece "Diagrams and Texts on Capture the Horse" is dated to that year in its preface. The following year was in fact a *mao* 卯 year (1135, Shaoxing 5, *yimao* 乙卯), and Taizong did indeed die in 1135, although his death hardly ended the Song problems with the Jurchen. To have written this line, it seems likely that Li Qingzhao had already heard about Taizong's illness. It is also possible that this rhyme-prose was written in 1135 rather than in the preceding year, and this line is simply reporting the news of the death by way of the fifth-century children's song.

滿眼驊騮雜騄駬	The great steeds Hualiu and Lu'er fill my eyes,[62]
時危安得眞致此	In dangerous times where can we find real horses like these?[63]
木蘭橫戈好女子	Mulan holds her lance crosswise, a fine warrior woman![64]
老矣誰能志千里	Aged now, who still has ambitions that stretch a thousand miles?[65]
但願相將過淮水	All she wants is to cross with others the Huai River once more.[66]

There are a few key ideas in this passage of "Rhyme-Prose on Capture the Horse." One is the validation of board games such as Capture the Horse. This is broached already in the opening sentence and elaborated thereafter. The references to the fictitious plums and the drawn pancakes (appearances that are not reality) are justifications for gaming. Capture the Horse may be just a game, not a real military encounter, but the game has beneficial effects on the players nonetheless. Although the pancakes allusion is usually taken the opposite way to evoke a false appearance that has no practical value, Li Qingzhao turns the meaning around. Later in the paragraph, we are likewise reminded that Confucius himself referred to chess in a positive way, as a useful means for exercising the mind. Toward the end of the paragraph, we encounter a string of references to officials and military leaders who are known to have been fond of and skilled at board games like Capture the Horse. Their fondness for the game is not incidental. It is precisely because they were gifted military strategists that they were devoted to such games. Chess allowed them to hone their mastery of military tactics or even to gain new insights. This connection between skill at chess and skill as a commander is particularly clear in the cases of Huan Wen and Xie An, two Jin period

---

62. Hualiu 驊騮 and Lu'er 騄駬 were names of famous horses of ancient times.

63. This line is borrowed verbatim from Du Fu's song on Wei Yan's 韋偃 painting of horses, in which Du Fu expresses the wish that in his "dangerous times" war horses as magnificent as those Wei Yan had painted could be obtained to aid the imperial cause. Du Fu, "Ti bishang Wei Yan hua ma ge" 題壁上韋偃畫馬歌, *Dushi xiangzhu* 9.754.

64. Mulan was the celebrated woman warrior said to have disguised herself as a man and joined the Northern Wei's fifth-century campaigns against northern tribes.

65. The language is taken from Cao Cao's song "The old steed lies in the stable / But has ambitions one thousand miles away. / The heroic man is in his twilight years, / But his virile heart is unchanged." "Buchu xiamen xing" 步出夏門行, *Weishi* 1.354.

66. The Huai River was the boundary, a porous one to be sure, between the Southern Song and the Jin puppet kingdom of Qi to the north. Li Qingzhao, "Dama fu" 打馬賦, *Jianzhu* 3.355–56.

generals. Indeed, Xie An is described in anecdotes as so absorbed in his board game that he shows little interest in the outcome of the battle he is directing that rages a few miles away. Or is it that he is so skilled at chess that he knows in advance how the battle will end? In such stories we are close to the Chinese archetype of the commander as sage-mystic, and it is on the chessboard, as microcosm of the battlefield, where he learns, refines, and displays his divine insight.

This way of writing about chess and its connection to warfare may be largely conventional, but when a woman invokes this trope it takes on special meaning. As Li Qingzhao keeps reminding us (yet again in the opening of this rhapsody), Capture the Horse is an "elegant game of the women's inner quarters." In real life, women were not military leaders, but they could be chess players (just as military leaders were), and as such they too could have insight into real military strategy. Li Qingzhao acts as if she wants a voice in the clamor of the day over the latest military humiliations the dynasty was undergoing. At the very least, she wants to show her concern and has cleverly found a way, through her knowledge of and skill at this board game—which seem indisputable by this point—that what she has to say might not be dismissed out of hand because she is a woman.

Another feature of this passage is the stress placed on the virtues of restraint and cautiousness in battlefield strategy. We read about the advantages of withdrawing first, advancing cautiously, and driving the chariot according to prescriptions. We likewise hear of the calamities suffered by those who boast of their valor or do not know when to stop. If military strategy is divided into *yin* and *yang* components, what is emphasized here is the *yin*. The sentence about the mare makes this especially clear. Li Qingzhao draws on lines explaining the Kun hexagram in the *Classic of Changes*, which represents the *yin* principle in its purest form, pointedly neglecting to balance it with any reference to the Qian (*yang*) hexagram as we might expect. The docility and constancy of the mare, which the classic characterizes as one who follows and accords with circumstances rather than striking out on her own, thus becomes the strategist's prudence and wisdom. The matching reference to the lady from Lu and the way that the horse who pulled her bridal carriage is detained at her husband's place, and not sent directly back with the empty carriage, must similarly point to the virtue of taking precautions and developing expediencies rather than taking risks when devising battlefield strategies.

The concluding verse is memorable both for its ingenious borrowings and for the way it presents Li Qingzhao's self-image as a writer on this subject. The borrowing in the opening line, from a children's song predicting the imminent death in 451 of Taiwu, ruler of the Turkic Northern Wei empire, and in line 4, from a Du Fu poem on a horse painting, help to situate Li Qingzhao's composition in the long tradition of expressions of apprehension and indignation concerning military strife (e.g., foreign invasions or rebellions) that threatened the Chinese state. The Du Fu borrowing is particularly clever. The great Tang poet was gazing at a mural of horses (two of them, apparently) and thinking of the rebellion still raging back in the heartland of the empire. Li Qingzhao is imagining herself staring at (or perhaps is actually staring at) a game board on which dozens of "horses" are deployed, and these game pieces all have the names of famous steeds of historical times written on their top side.[67] This assemblage of celebrated steeds "fills her eyes," making her all the more conscious of the weakness of the imperial armies that have yet again suffered a string of defeats at the hands of the invading Jurchen troops in recent months.

The image of Mulan in line 5 confirms the reader's sense that, throughout these writings on the board game, Li Qingzhao is thinking of herself as would-be woman warrior and, indeed, wrote these compositions in large part to offer her own reflections on the military events of the day. The analogy between Li Qingzhao and Mulan may seem so incongruous that some readers will understand it to be made tongue-in-cheek. Li Qingzhao must be joking or poking fun at herself by casting herself in this role, they will think. But the surrounding lines argue strongly against such an interpretation. When she refers to the "dangerous times" and her wish, in her old age, simply to be able to cross the Huai River northward again, she is certainly not joking or being coy. Of course she has not lost sight of the fact that she is writing about a game. But her claim to have singular insight into this game, with all that implies for her understanding of the plight of the Song state at the time, does not sound like something uttered lightly. It is interesting to notice that the line about Mulan stands alone prosodically; it is not matched by another, forming a couplet. The lines before and after it are all members of couplets,

---

67. This naming and labeling practice is described in the preface to Li Qingzhao's "Xiama" 下馬, "Dama tujing mingci" 打馬圖經命辭, no. 3, *Jianzhu* 3.376. The naming practice is also attested in the Southern Song encyclopedia *Shilin guangji* 事林廣記; see Chen Yuanjing, *Zuantu zengxin qunshu leiyao Shilin guangji*, "Xinji shang" 辛集上, p. 7a–b.

as we would expect them to be. Only the line that mentions Mulan stands by itself. Such an unusual structure gives the line special prominence and force.

We get a better sense of at least one of Li Qingzhao's motives in writing so extensively about this game from the thirteen short "Instructions" she wrote on the game. These are by far the most concrete and detailed of her writings on Capture the Horse. They reveal a great deal about the actual conduct of the game. At the same time, they are the most challenging to make sense of today, since we cannot fully reconstruct the game. As imperfect as our understanding of these entries may be, there is at least one cluster of closely related themes in them that is very suggestive regarding Li Qingzhao's special interest in writing about the game at this time.

If the rhyme-prose counsels caution and discretion rather than brazen valor in developing military strategy, the "Instructions" teach that losses may be only temporary, and weaknesses can be turned to an advantage, leading ultimately to victory. There are references to Meng Mingshi 孟明視 of the ancient state of Qin, who continued to be trusted by the Qin ruler despite suffering repeated defeats in battles with the state of Jin. Eventually, Meng Mingshi led the Qin armies to a victory over Jin.[68] There is likewise a reference to the famous story of the "old man of the border who lost his horse" 塞翁失馬, the first in a series of events that befell the old man, each of which turned out to have consequences, fortuitous or unfortuitous, that were the opposite of people's initial expectation.[69] The lesson is clear: a defeat may be a blessing in disguise, if dealt with the right way. Thus, we read, "success and failure each have their time, what is there for me to regret [when things don't go my way]?"[70] Besides, when the right strategy is employed, even the enemy's overwhelming numbers are no guarantee of success: "If you occupy a steep, narrow pass, one soldier can hold off a thousand; then you will have success, the few a match for the many."[71] Given this way of thinking, it is not surprising that Li Qingzhao gives special attention to one facet of the game known as "falling into a ditch" 落塹.[72] When this happens to a player's horse (probably when it is caught in the midst of a particular configuration of

---

68. The multiple *Zuozhuan* references to Meng Mingshi are listed in *Jianzhu* 3.381, n. 4. He is referred to in Li Qingzhao's "Xiama" 3.376 and "Dama" 打馬, no. 1, *Jianzhu* 3.380.

69. "Dama," no. 1, *Jianzhu* 3.380.

70. Ibid.

71. "Xingma," no. 1, *Jianzhu* 3.377.

72. "Luoqian," *Jianzhu* 3.387.

opponents' horses), it can no longer be moved. This is certainly a setback. Yet a horse thus trapped in a "ditch" may also suddenly be liberated so that it "flies out"—just as Li Qingzhao says Liu Bei's horse did when he called to it beneath the waves—depending on certain rolls of the dice or new movements by other players. Not only does the player get his or her horse (or horses) back; the player is also handsomely rewarded with the entire contents of the bank so that the apparent misfortune abruptly turns into a great windfall.

One of the thirteen entries concerns a player who has lost everything but still is determined to play again.[73] The verse is put into the words of one of his horses, which has been taken off the board.

打馬，之三　　*Capture the Horse, No. 3*

Having lost all his horses, one player wanted to join the game again. The words say:

被打去全馬，人願再下。詞曰：

虧于一簣	For lack of one bucket of dirt [the mound is incomplete],
敗此垂成	Failure and success are that closely aligned.
久伏鹽車	Long was I yoked to a salt cart,
4　方登峻坂	Before climbing a high slope.
豈期一蹶	Who would have thought a single misstep
遂失長塗	Would cause me to lose the long road?
恨群馬之皆空	I regret that all the horses have disappeared,
8　忿前功之盡棄	Am angry my former achievements have come to naught.
但素蒙剪拂	I received my master's grooming and training,
不棄駑駘	He did not reject me as an inferior steed.
願守門闌	I shall wait patiently behind the gate and fence
12　再從驅策	Until once again I gallop as he directs.
溯風驤首	In the north wind I proudly lift my head
已傷今日之障泥	Though I've already stained the mud guards he had me wear,
戀主銜恩	Devoted to my master and mindful of his kindness,
16　更待明年之春草	I await the spring grasses of the coming year.

Line 1: Originally, this classic statement from "Lüao" 旅獒, *Classic of Documents* 33/10, refers to the importance of diligence even in minor actions and is offered as an injunction to the ruler. Li Qingzhao alters the meaning, making the statement exemplify the proximity of success and failure.

---

73. "Dama," no. 3, *Jianzhu* 3.383–84.

Line 3: The idea of a great horse unable to display its talent because it has been yoked to a salt cart is from Jia Yi's "Rhyme-Prose Lament for Qu Yuan" 弔屈原賦, *Shiji* 84.2493.

Line 7: Han Yu had said that when the legendary horse trainer Bo Le passed through Jibei, he emptied the region of all outstanding horses, taking them all with him. Li Qingzhao uses Han Yu's language but changes the meaning: the horses have disappeared from the board because they have been captured by an opponent.[74]

Line 14: In early times, Wang Wuzi was good at understanding horses. He was riding one outfitted with cloths that hung down to prevent mud from splattering the rider, and that horse balked at crossing a stream. Wang surmised that the animal did not want to ruin the mud guards—so devoted was he to his master. Wang had the cloths taken off, and then the horse promptly crossed the stream. Unlike Wang Wuzi's horse, the horse speaking in this verse confesses to having done damage to its cloths.[75]

Line 16: When Wei Wuzi was old and about to die, he ordered his son, Ke, to marry his favorite concubine off after he was gone; but later he changed his mind and ordered Ke to bury her alive with him. When Wuzi died, Ke married the woman off, explaining that he would not follow the latter order uttered when his father was no longer thinking clearly. Later, when Ke was fighting against Qin, an old man entered the battlefield and tied grasses into knots that tripped up the Qin officer Du Hui so that Ke was able to capture him. The old man subsequently appeared in Ke's dream, explaining that he was the father of the former concubine, who had repaid the kindness Ke showed to his daughter. The horse in this line is promising to repay his master's kindness in the future.[76]

The themes featured in this and other of the "Instructions," such as determination to keep striving, loyal devotion to one's master, insistence that setbacks can be overcome and that losses are temporary rather than permanent, all have implications for the Song state that was, just as this was written, facing a new Jurchen invasion. Although the "Instructions" are ostensibly about the game Capture the Horse, no one at the time would have failed to see how they could be applied to the political and military circumstances of the day. In that application, the "Instructions" look toward the future and offer hope that the seemingly dire military situation might be reversed if only the leaders do not give up.

---

74. Han Yu, "Song Wen chushi fu Heyang jun xu" 送溫處士赴河陽均序, *Han Changli wenji jiaozhu* 4.164.

75. See Liu Yiqing, *Shishuo xinyu jianshu* 20.4.704.

76. *Chunqiu Zuozhuan zhuzi suoyin* B7.15.2/180/20–23.

CHAPTER 6

The "Afterword"

The "Afterword" that Li Qingzhao wrote to her husband's scholarly notes on his collection of rubbings, *Records on Metal and Stone*, deserves its own chapter in this study, first for its well-deserved fame and second for the knotty set of problems that it raises. However, it belongs to the group of writings examined in the foregoing chapter both because it dates from the same period, the few years immediately following Li Qingzhao's remarriage and divorce, and because it should be read in the context of what she was striving to do as a writer during that period: to reestablish herself, to reassert her voice as a writer, and to regain her stature and respect.

Here is a short chronology of the events surrounding this group of writings:

year/month	
1132/2–3	Li Qingzhao returns to Lin'an from the southeast
1132/6–7	marries Zhang Ruzhou
1132/9	brings suit against Zhang Ruzhou, is briefly imprisoned, and writes her letter of gratitude to Qi Chongli
1133/6	addresses poems to Han Xiaozhou and Hu Songnian on the eve of their mission to the Jin
1134	writes the afterword to *Records on Metal and Stone*
1134/10	in response to a new Jurchen invasion, leaves Lin'an to seek refuge in Jinhua
1134/11–12	writes her Capture the Horse compositions

To say that her afterword should be read in the context of these events of her life and the other writings she produced in these years may seem like stating the obvious, but it is already a sharp departure from the way the composition is usually read. It is typically read by itself, without reference to the other writings Li Qingzhao produced during those years and also without reference to the remarriage and divorce that preceded them. If the afterword is read together with anything else that Li Qingzhao wrote, it is normally read together with her song lyrics, especially the ones that are traditionally interpreted as expressions of her devotion to Zhao Mingcheng. The long prose text and the group of song lyrics readily seem to complement and reinforce each other: in the afterword Li Qingzhao appears to be presenting a narrative account of the years of blissful marriage she shared with Zhao Mingcheng, and her song lyrics seem to be expressions of her loneliness for Zhao when he was absent and her inconsolable despair after he died.

But what happens when we question this conventional reading? The first step is to place the afterword in the context of the other works that Li Qingzhao produced during the exceptionally prolific years following her remarriage. To take this single step immediately has the effect of enabling us to view the afterword in a new light. We are then less likely to read the work naively—as it tends to be read—that is, as if it were nothing more than a straightforward reminiscence of her marriage to Zhao Mingcheng and the hardship she suffered after he died, a narrative springing entirely from innocent nostalgia tinged with loneliness and grief. Once we place the afterword in its chronological and circumstantial context, we are more likely to discern writerly aims and motives behind the text beyond that of unreflective nostalgia. Moreover, among the other writings of the period, the afterword is a singularly personal text. It is in fact intensely personal. It is the most likely among all of Li Qingzhao's writings of the period to have direct connections with the wrenching personal experiences of her immediate past.

We have seen pieces of this remarkable composition in earlier chapters. Here is a translation of the complete text:

Afterword to *Records on Metal and Stone*

What is this book, *Records on Metal and Stone*, in thirty chapters? It is work written by Zhao Defu [Zhao Mingcheng]. Taking as his subject two thousand inscriptions carved on bronze vessels and stelae dating from the Three Dynasties of high antiquity all the way down to the Five Kingdoms of recent times, including both interior and exterior inscriptions on bells, *ding* tripods, steamers, *li* tripods, basins, water vessels, wine beakers, and grain containers, as well as those concerning the lives of both eminent officials and obscure scholars found on rounded or rectangular stelae, he corrected their errors, distinguished the authentic from the spurious, and evaluated their historical value. He composed colophons on all those inscriptions that suffice either to affirm the Way of the sages or to emend mistakes in the historiographical record. The contents are rich indeed. The calamities suffered by Wang Ya and Yuan Zai show that there is no difference between hoarding works of art and hoarding pepper.[1] Likewise, both Changyu and Yuankai were sick men. What does it matter that one was obsessed with money and the other with the *Zuo Commentary*?[2] Their sicknesses went by different names, but their delusion was the same.

It was in the *xinsi* year of the Jianzhong period [1101] that I married into the Zhao family. At that time, my late father was serving as vice director of the Ministry of Rites, and the grand councilor [her father-in-law, Zhao Tingzhi] was vice director of the Ministry of Personnel. My husband, twenty-one years old, was a student in the National University. The Zhaos and Lis are undistinguished families that have always been poor. On the leave days of the first and fifteenth of every month, when he requested holiday leave, we would pawn some clothes to raise five hundred cash. Then we'd walk to Xiangguo Monastery to buy fruits and rubbings of inscriptions. We'd take them home, sit down together, and spread them out, savoring them. We felt that we were living in the harmonious era of Getianshi.

Two years later, my husband came out to serve as an official.[3] We ate vegetarian meals and wore clothes of coarse cloth, intent upon obtaining from every distant place and remote region as many of the world's ancient inscriptions and rare engraved words as we could. As the days and months passed, our collection grew. The grand councilor stayed in the imperial city, and many of our relations worked in the palace libraries and archives. They had acess to lost odes, little-known histories, and such books as those recovered from the

---

1. Wang Ya 王涯 (correcting Wang Bo 王播) and Yuan Zai 元載 were both grand councilors during the Tang dynasty, and both suffered disastrous ends. Wang Ya was a great art collector who safeguarded his paintings in vaults behind double walls. But when he met his end, his house was ransacked and his paintings discarded in the street. *Xin Tangshu* 179.5319. When he was forced to commit suicide by imperial decree, Yuan Zai was found to have stored away some eight hundred piculs of pepper in his house. *Xin Tangshu* 145.4714.

2. Changyu 長輿 is He Jiao 和嶠, who was so parsimonious that he was said to have "an obsession with cash" (*qianpi* 錢癖). It was none other than Yuankai 元凱 (Du Yu 杜預) who said this, the man who by his own admission had "an obsession with the *Zuo Commentary*," which he spent his life annotating. *Jinshu* 45.1284 and 34.1032.

3. On the meaning and significance of this line, see the discussion of it in chapter 3.

walls of Lu and the tomb of Ji.[4] When we came upon such rare works, we exerted ourselves to make copies of them. Once awakened to the flavor of this activity, we could not stop. Later, whenever we came upon a piece of calligraphy or a painting by a celebrated artist, whether ancient or recent, or a precious vessel from the Three Dynasties, we would take off a layer of clothing to pawn for it. I remember that once during the Chongning period [1102–6] someone brought a peony painting by Xu Xi [10th c.] to show us. He was asking two hundred thousand for it. In those days it would have been hard even for young persons in eminent officials' families to come up with such a sum. The man left it with us for two days, but we finally decided we could not purchase it and returned it to him. Afterward, my husband and I looked at each other dejectedly for several days.

Later, we lived in seclusion in our hometown for ten years.[5] By managing our expenses carefully, we had more than enough for food and clothing. Then my husband served successively as prefect in two separate places, and we devoted all of his salary to purchasing books and writing materials.[6] Whenever we obtained a new book, the two of us would collate it together, comparing other editions, then produce a corrected copy with a new title page. When we obtained a calligraphic scroll, painting, or ritual bronze, we would also pore over it to amuse ourselves, identifying any defects we could find. Our custom was to limit ourselves to the duration of one candle per night. In this way, we were able to gather works with a quality of paper and completeness in their texts and brushwork that were superior to those of other collectors.

It happens that I have a good memory, and whenever we finished dinner we would sit in our hall named Returning Home and brew tea.[7] We'd point to a pile of books and, choosing a particular event, try to say in which book, which chapter, which page, and which line it was recorded. The winner of our little

---

4. The reference is to two famous discoveries of ancient writings. The first took place in the second century BCE, when walls in the former residence of Confucius (in Lu 魯) were found to contain texts long hidden there, and the second took place in the third century CE, when the *Bamboo Annals* 竹書紀年 and other works were recovered from a Warring States period tomb in Ji Prefecture 汲郡 (Ji County, Henan).

5. This setback in Zhao Mingcheng's career was brought about by the fall from power and death soon thereafter of his father, Zhao Tingzhi, in 1107. The hometown was Zhao's ancestral home in Qingzhou (Qingzhou, Shandong).

6. From 1121 to 1126, Zhao Mingcheng held appointments as prefect of Laizhou and Zizhou (also Zichuan 淄川), both in modern Shandong.

7. Returning Home Hall 歸來堂, named after Tao Qian's 陶潛 (365–427) famous rhapsody, was in the Qingzhou ancestral home. Thus with this sentence Li Qingzhao apparently reverts in her narrative to the time before Zhao Mingcheng's two provincial appointments in the early 1120s.

contest got to drink tea first. When I guessed right, I'd hold the cup high and burst out laughing until the tea splattered the front of my gown. I'd have to get up without even taking a sip. Oh, how I wished we could grow old living like that! So even though our lives were fraught with apprehensions and poverty, what we valued and strove for was never compromised.

When our books were complete, we built a library in Returning Home, with large cabinets marked with numbers. We arranged the books accordingly inside. Whoever wanted a book to read would have to get a key and record the book's number in a log before taking it out. If the borrower made the slightest mark or smudge on a page, it was his or her responsibility to repair or clean it. We were no longer as easygoing as at first. In this way, what had started as an amusement turned into a source of vexation. I couldn't stand it, so I decided that we would eat no more than one meat dish per meal and dress in no more than one colored garment at a time. I wore no pearls or feathers in my hair and kept no gilded or embroidered article in my household. Whenever we came across a book of any kind whose text had no lacunae and was free of misprints, we would buy it on the spot to use as a back-up copy. Our family specialized in the study of the *Classic of Changes* and the *Zuo Commentary*, and so our collection was particularly complete with regard to scholarship on those two works. Eventually, books were scattered all over our desks and were stacked in piles on our pillows and mats. Our thoughts met with those in the books, and our minds communicated with their authors. Our eyes went forth among their pages, and our souls were enriched by them. Certainly the joy that they gave us was superior to that of dancing girls or raising dogs and horses.

In the *bingwu* year of the Jingkang period [1126], when my husband was serving as prefect of Zichuan, we heard that the Jin bandits had attacked our capital. We had no idea what to do. We gazed at our overflowing boxes and brimming trunks with both fond attachment and distress. We knew they would not be ours for long.

In the third month of the *dingmo* year of Jianyan [1127], we hurried south for my mother-in-law's funeral. Realizing that we could not take all those superfluous things with us, we first set aside the large printed books, then we set aside the paintings with multiple panels, and then we set aside the ancient vessels with no inscriptions. Finally, we set aside books in National University editions, ordinary paintings, and all heavy vessels. But even after these many reductions, we still traveled with fifteen carts of books. When we reached Donghai, we crossed the Huai River in a string of boats. Then we crossed the Yangzi River and arrived at Jiankang [Nanjing]. We had left under lock and key more than ten rooms of books and other items at our old residence in Qingzhou. We planned to return the following year and transport them south by boat. But in the twelfth month, the Jin sacked Qingzhou. The more than ten rooms of belongings were reduced to ashes.

In the ninth month of the *wushen* year of Jianyan [1128], my husband came out of mourning and was appointed prefect of Jiankang. His appointment ended in the third month of the following year. We prepared a boat to take us to Wuhu and into Gushu, intending eventually to find a new place to live along the Gan River.[8] But in the fifth month, when we had reached Chiyang, my husband received an imperial command appointing him prefect of Huzhou and was summoned for an audience before the imperial throne.[9] So we decided to make our home in Chiyang, with my husband going on by himself in response to the summons. On the thirteenth day of the sixth month, he was packed and, having left our boat, sat on the bank. Dressed in coarse clothes with a kerchief around his head, his mood that of a tiger on the prowl, his eyes darting and flashing, he looked toward our boat and bid farewell. I was in a terrible state of mind and shouted to him, "What shall I do if I hear the town is threatened?" He pointed at me and answered from afar,[10] "Go with the crowd. If you must, discard the household belongings first, then our clothes, then the books and paintings, and then the ancient vessels. But the ritual vessels, be sure to take them with you wherever you go. Live or die with them. Don't forget!" With this, he galloped off.

Hurrying toward his destination, he paid no attention to the summer heat and, as a result, fell ill. By the time he reached the traveling court, his sickness was serious.[11] A letter from him at the end of the seventh month informed me that he was confined to bed. I was frightened, knowing that, as he was high-strung by nature, any illness would be dangerous. If he developed a fever, he was bound to take cooling medicines, and then his condition would become worse. I had our boat untied and sailed day and night to be with him, covering three hundred *li* a day. By the time I arrived, he had in fact taken large doses of bupleurum and scutellaria.[12] His fever was constant now, and he had also developed dysentery. His condition was beyond treatment. I wept bitterly and was too upset to ask what plans he had made for me after he was gone. On the eighteenth day of the eighth month [of 1129], he could no longer get up. He picked up a brush and wrote out a poem. When he finished the poem, he

---

8. That is, they planned to settle on the Gan River 贛江 in modern Jiangxi. Li Qingzhao and her husband sailed up the Yangzi from Jiankang 建康 (Nanjing) and got as far, as we learn in the next sentence, as modern Guichi 貴池, Anhui.

9. Her husband was summoned back to Jiankang, where the emperor then was.

10. For *ji shou* 戟手 in the sense of "point at," see the explanation of Wang Shuizhao 王水照 quoted in Xu Beiwen, *Li Qingzhao quanji pingzhu*, p. 222.

11. That is, by the time he arrived back in Jiankang.

12. Both herbal medicines were used in treating fevers.

died. He had no final instructions regarding "dividing up the incense or selling sandals."[13]

After I buried [Mingcheng], I had nowhere to go. The court had dispatched the empress and palace ladies to a separate location, and it was said that crossing the Yangzi River would soon be prohibited. At the time, I still had twenty thousand books, two thousand folios of inscriptions on metal and stone, and enough utensils and bedding to receive a hundred guests. My other superfluous things were comparable in quantity. I myself was very sick, and my breathing was extremely weak. I thought of my late husband's brother-in-law [Li Zhuo], who was vice minister of the Ministry of War and was then protecting the empress at Hongzhou.[14] I dispatched two trusted clerks to him, sending along a portion of our possessions with them for safekeeping. In the twelfth month [of 1129], the Jin bandits sacked Hongzhou, and everything I had sent was lost. The books that had been ferried across the Huai River in a string of boats were turned into smoke and clouds. All I had left were a few small, lightweight scrolls of calligraphy inscriptions; manuscript copies of the works of Li Bai, Du Fu, Han Yu, and Liu Zongyuan; *A New Account of Tales of the World* and *Discourses on Salt and Iron*; a few dozen mounted rubbings of stone inscriptions from the Han through Tang dynasties; some ten bronze vessels from the Three Dynasties; and a few cases of manuscripts from the Southern Tang. From time to time I would amuse myself with these during my illness. These were the only remnants I had left, as I lay sick in bed.

It was impossible to go farther up the Yangzi River, and moreover the invaders' movements were unpredictable. My younger brother, Hang, was serving as reviser in the Law Code Office, and so I decided to go seek refuge with him. By the time I got to Taizhou [1130/1], the prefect there had fled. When I got to Shan, I proceeded over land. I discarded my clothes and beddings as I hurried to Huangyan, where I hired a boat and set out to sea, hoping to catch up with the traveling court. At the time the emperor had docked at Zhang'an. I followed the imperial ship to Wenzhou and from there went back to Yue. In the twelfth month of *gengxu* [1130], when the officials were dismissed, I proceeded to Quzhou. In the third month of the *xinhai* year of Shaoxing [1131], I went again to Yue. In the *renzi* year [1132], I returned to Hangzhou.[15]

---

13. The language is taken from Cao Cao's deathbed instructions to his wife and concubines, the latter of whom were told they should, if they had nothing better to do, content themselves with making sandals and selling them to support themselves. Cao Cao's words are quoted in Lu Ji 陸機, "Diao Wei Wudi wen" 弔魏武帝文, *Wenxuan* 60.7b.

14. The identification of the brother-in-law as Li Zhuo 李擢 comes from Xu Peijun, "Nianpu," *Jianzhu*, pp. 474–75.

15. For the timing of the movements of Gaozong, the Jurchen army, and Li Qingzhao, see Huang Shengzhang, "Li Qingzhao shiji kaobian," p. 334.

Previously, when my husband was extremely ill, a certain Academician Zhang Feiqing came to see him bringing a jade pitcher, which he then took away with him. The pitcher was actually made of jadelike stone. I do not know who started the rumor, but it was falsely said that there was talk of "an imperial behest of gold." Some even said there was going to be a secret inquiry into the matter. I was terrified. I did not dare to speak out, but I also did not dare do nothing. I decided that I would take all my household's bronze vessels and other objects and present them to the traveling court. By the time I got to Yue [1129/12], the emperor had already moved to Siming. I did not want to keep those things in my house, and so I stored them all in Shan, together with the book manuscripts. Subsequently, when the imperial army was rounding up rebels, what I had stored there was all taken away. Later, I heard that it ended up in the household of the old general Li. Of "the remnants I had left," 50 or 60 percent was now lost. All that remained were some six or seven boxes of calligraphy, paintings, inkstones, and ink. I could not bear to put them anywhere else. I kept them beside my bed, where I'd open them occasionally.

At Kuaiji [Yue, 1131/3] I resided in a place owned by a local named Zhong.[16] One night, a thief broke in through a wall and carried five of my boxes off. I was so grief-stricken I thought I'd die[17] and offered a handsome reward to get them back. Two days later my landlord, Zhong, brazenly produced eighteen scrolls, asking for the reward. So I knew the thief was not far away. I tried everything I could to recover the rest, but nothing would free it up. Today I know that eventually Wu Shuo, the assistant fiscal commissioner, bought everything for a low price.[18] At this point, 70 or 80 percent of "the only remnants I had left" was lost. What remained were just one or two random and fragmentary volumes that did not make any complete title or set, together with just a few very ordinary calligraphy manuscripts. Yet I still treasured them as if they were my life itself. How foolish I am!

Today when I chance to open one of my books, it is like meeting an old friend. I remember when my husband sat in Quiet Governance Hall in Donglai.[19] Each folio of an inscription was mounted on scented paper and tied with a silken cord. Ten folios were bound together as a single volume. Every day in the evening, after the clerks had gone home, my husband would add editorial collations to two inscriptions and would write a colophon for one.

---

16. Kuaiji 會稽, which Li Qingzhao refers to earlier as Yue 越, is the modern Shaoxing 紹興. The incident described in this paragraph took place during the author's third stay in Yue, in the spring of 1131.

17. Reading the textual variant *bu de huo* 不得活 in place of *bu yi* 不已.

18. Wu Shuo is known as an accomplished calligrapher; see Tao Zongyi 陶宗儀, *Shushi huiyao* 書史會要 6.46a.

19. Donglai 東萊 is Laizhou, where Zhao Mingcheng served as prefect in the early 1120s.

Of the total of two thousand inscriptions, only 502 have colophons. Today the brush strokes in his colophons still look freshly made, but the tree trunks beside his grave are already thick. How sad it is!

Formerly, when Xiao Yi was conquered at Jiangling, he did not regret the loss of his kingdom, but he did destroy his books and paintings [so that they would not fall into his conqueror's hands].[20] When Yang Guang was overthrown at Jiangdu, he did not bemoan his own death, but he did arrange to take his books and paintings with him into the afterlife.[21] Isn't it so that what a person by nature treasures he will never forget, even in death? In my case, is it that heaven considers me too insignificant to possess these alluring things? Or is it that my husband has consciousness in the afterlife and still prizes these things so tenaciously that he won't let them remain behind in this world? Why else would they be so difficult to acquire but so easy to lose?

From the time I was two years younger than Lu Ji when he wrote his rhapsody until I was two years older than Qu Yuan when he perceived the error of his ways, that is, in thirty-four years, how numerous have been the worries and losses I have suffered![22] Nevertheless, possession is always followed by loss, just as the act of gathering always gives way eventually to dissolution. It is a fundamental principle of things. One man loses a bow; another man finds it.[23] What does it matter? The only reason I have taken the trouble to record all this here is to warn persons of later generations who are learned and fond of ancient things.[24]

This is a remarkable document, and few readers will fail to feel sympathetic toward the author for all that she has been through. The earliest recorded reactions are of this kind, even from Southern Song critics who could be so harsh in their comments about Li Qingzhao and her remarriage. Hong Mai, who records the entire text in his scholarly miscellany completed just a few decades after Li Qingzhao's death, adds these comments: "After Zhao Mingcheng died, she grieved that all the things they had collected could

---

20. Xiao Yi 蕭繹 is Emperor Yuan of the Liang dynasty. See *Suishu* 49.1299.

21. Yang Guang 楊廣 is Emperor Yang of the Sui dynasty. "Yang di" 煬帝, *Taiping guangji*, 280.2229.

22. Li Qingzhao means from the time she was eighteen, when she was married, to the time she was fifty-one, when she wrote this afterword. Lu Ji 陸機 (261–303) was twenty when he wrote "Wen fu" 文賦, and Qu Yuan 蓬瑗 (6th c. BCE) was fifty when he realized that everything he had done in the preceding forty-nine years was in error. On this way of inclusive counting of the thirty-four years, see Huang Shengzhang, "Zhao Mingcheng Li Qingzhao fufu nianpu," pp. 156–57.

23. From *Kongzi jiayu zhuzi suoyin* 10.6/17/17.

24. Li Qingzhao, "Jinshi lu hou xu" 金石錄後序, *Jianzhu* 3.309–33.

not be kept intact and wrote this afterword, giving a full account of all the difficulties and deprivations she encountered, from beginning to end. . . . She managed to record her own history like this; reading what she wrote I feel sorrow for her."[25] Readers in later times, up to the present, have had similar reactions.

In recent years, Stephen Owen has suggested a reading of the afterword that moves beyond simple empathy.[26] In several of Li Qingzhao's statements about the collection and her relationship to her husband, Owen finds hints of estrangement and references to the imbalance of power and authority in their marriage. Owen's is a perceptive and important step in reconsidering this text. Yet he does not take into consideration a number of other facts and issues that lie outside the text and yet are relevant to it.

Looking beyond the Text

We may begin by stressing the singularity of this document. There is nothing like it in earlier Chinese literature, especially nothing like it written by a woman. The writing is intensely personal, emotional, and nostalgic. The portrait it gives of Li Qingzhao's married life is striking in part because people of the time by and large did not write about domestic life with such candor, especially not in prose. This deeply personal document was part of Zhao Mingcheng's scholarly study when Li Qingzhao submitted that work to the court at some point in the Shaoxing era. We do not know what year Li Qingzhao made this presentation; yet certainly the afterword was already attached to the text when she submitted it, which raises the likelihood that she wrote the piece fully intending that it would be made public this way. If that is so, we have the confluence of an unusually personal document with a very public display. It is a most striking combination.

If there are many unusual features of the afterword, there are also some conventional ones. The comments about the folly of attachment to material things, the inevitability that large collections would not survive, and the idea that the ultimate dispersal of the collection should serve as a warning to would-be collectors of future times, these are all ways of thinking that are common in Song period writings about "things" in general or art collections in particular. In the preface that Ouyang Xiu had written to his scholarly

---

25. Hong Mai, *Rongzhai suibi*, "Sibi" 5.684–86.
26. Owen, *Remembrances*, pp. 80–98.

notes on his collection of inscriptions (which was the most important precedent for Zhao Mingcheng's project), Ouyang acknowledges that such collections are bound to be broken up and says that onlookers consider him foolish
to expend such time and energy in amassing it.[27] Su Shi wrote frequently
about the delusion of thinking that one could possess things, and he specifically criticizes art collectors of his day for becoming slaves to their collections.[28] Even the apologist's strategy of belittling the worth or import of the
very activity to which one has devoted oneself for years and written about
lovingly is a convention of its own. Li Qingzhao's father, Li Gefei, had
employed this strategy in the afterword he wrote to his *The Gardens of Luoyang*,
in which the splendor of those gardens becomes a negative measure of the
condition of the state: the more lavish the Luoyang gardens become, the
more they show the empire to be in a downward spiral of "decline" 衰.[29]

It is probably best to assume, as a working hypothesis, that in such a
lengthy, original, and complex text Li Qingzhao has multiple motivations and
aims. The text is usually read basically on one level and assigned a simple
purpose: to express nostalgia for the days of her marriage to Zhao Mingcheng and her sorrow over the sudden and violent end to those golden days,
the early death of Zhao, and the subsequent loss of their collection. This
reading of the text has, over the centuries, been used together with many of
Li Qingzhao's song lyrics to canonize the Zhao-Li union as an ideal marriage
in Chinese history, an ideal made all the more poignant because it was cut
short and gave way to all the loss and suffering that the afterword describes.
But reflection on the larger circumstances and challenges that Li Qingzhao
faced at the time she wrote the afterword suggests that such a reading fails to
take notice of some issues that were of crucial importance to her soon after
her remarriage and divorce. The acute humiliation of those recent experiences, which comes through so clearly in her letter to Qi Chongli, hangs
like a specter behind the afterword and everything it tells us about her first
marriage and what ensued after it was abruptly terminated. To put it plainly,
Li Qingzhao had more on her mind in 1134 than merely any urge she may
have felt simply to commemorate her first marriage with a moving narrative.

27. Translated and discussed in my *Problem of Beauty*, pp. 12–13.
28. For Su Shi's thinking on these matters, see ibid., pp. 165–88.
29. Ibid., pp. 144–61.

One of her interests at the time must have been to fend off any more predators on her and her collection. The second half of the afterword makes it clear that such predators were in abundance, whether they were invading armies, avaricious Chinese military leaders, or thieving landlords. By the time of her divorce, Li Qingzhao had come to look upon her second husband as one more predator. As she remarks about him in her letter to Qi Chongli, "Abhorring the stench that now clung to my body, I sought only to break away. But he held fast to the jade disk, determined to kill its owner. He then began to abuse me freely, and his blows came down daily." Furthermore, as discussed in chapter 4, even Gaozong, or at least one of the emperor's agents, had his eyes on Li Qingzhao's collection and approached her offering to buy some of it less than one month after Zhao Mingcheng had died. Xie Kejia, a maternal cousin of Zhao Mingcheng, considered this attempt so brazen and offensive that he memorialized to the emperor to stop it, and it apparently was stopped. But soon a rumor reached Li Qingzhao's ears involving imperial interest in her collection; there was talk of a secret investigation. She became so terrified that she decided to donate the bulk of her treasures to the court, but it was impossible for her to do so when everyone, including the emperor, was fleeing from the invasion.

In this connection, it is interesting to learn that at least one calligraphy scroll by the great Northern Song calligrapher Cai Xiang 蔡襄 (1012–67) that had been part of the Zhao-Li collection did end up in the imperial collection within a few years after Zhao Mingcheng's death. We do not know how it went from Li Qingzhao's possession to the Imperial Archives, whether directly or indirectly. Perhaps it was among the works that she stored in one place or another and never recovered, or part of what was stolen directly from her. In any case, we know that by 1133 it was in imperial possession thanks to a colophon that the same Xie Kejia wrote about it, which is reproduced along with other colophons in several sources: "In years past, my younger cousin, son of my mother's sister, Zhao Defu [Mingcheng] repeatedly brought this scroll out to show me. Today, not long after he has departed this world, his family has been unable to keep it in their possession. As I examine it, I am filled of sorrow. Written at Fahui Temple in Lin'an, on the eleventh day of the ninth month of the *guichou* year [1133]."[30]

---

30. Bian Yongyu, *Shigu tang shuhua huikao* 10.2b–3a.

The identification of the place Xie Kejia viewed this scroll is significant. Fahui Temple 法慧寺 (also written 法惠寺) was a Buddhist temple in Lin'an, just inside the Yongjin Gate 湧金門 (also known as the Fengyu Gate 豐豫門) on the eastern side of the city wall.[31] Known for having a well that never went dry even in the worst of droughts, the temple had long been used by palace officials to pray for rain.[32] When the court was relocated to Lin'an, it initially appropriated the temple as well as a vacant piece of land beside it for imperial needs. Implements used in elaborate court rituals were stored there.[33] Then, early in the year that Xie Kejia wrote his colophon, the temple became the home of the Korean Relations Institute 同文館, in anticipation of the arrival of a delegation from Korea to the Southern Song court. But the delegation never arrived, having been shipwrecked on the coast.[34] Three months after Xie Kejia wrote his colophon, the temple was designated the new home of the Imperial Archives.[35] It remained the site of the archives for ten years, until a more suitable building was constructed nearby. The Imperial Archives had its own collection of ritual vessels, famous calligraphic scrolls, and paintings, in addition to its holdings of books and documents.[36] In fact, the decision in 1143 to construct a new building for the archives was based on the argument that the former temple was unsatisfactory because it was located amid commoners' residences. In such a location, the danger of fire was high, and it was imprudent to expose the valued treasures to such a risk.[37] Indeed, as soon as the new building was completed in 1144, Emperor Gaozong led a group of distinguished officials to view its "calligraphic works, paintings, and

---

31. The location of the temple is clear from references to it in two sources: Tian Rucheng, *Xihu youlan zhi* 14.195–96; and Su Shi, "Shen sansheng qi qing kai hu liutiao zhuang" 申三省起請開湖六條狀, *Su Shi wenji* 30.868.

32. See Tian Rucheng, *Xihu youlan zhi* 14.196; and *(Xianchun) Lin'an zhi* 80.17b.

33. Lou Yao, *Gongkui ji* 54.6b–7a.

34. Li Xinchuan, *Jiannian yilai xinian yaolu* 63.3a–b.

35. The date of this action, coming in the first month of 1134, comes from Li Xinchuan, *Jiannian yilai xinian yaolu* 72.2b. Other sources provide the same information but without so precise a date, referring to the use of the temple as the Imperial Archives as something that began "early in the Shaoxing period." See *(Xianchun) Lin'an zhi* 7.1a; Chen Kui, *Nan Song guan'ge lu* 2.1a; and Tian Rucheng, *Xihu youlan zhi* 15.206. These citations, incidentally, clearly show that the two forms of the temple's name were interchangeable.

36. Tian Rucheng, *Xihu youlan zhi* 15.206.

37. See the memorial by Yan Yi 嚴抑 quoted in Li Xinchuan, *Jianyan yilai xinian yaolu* 150.17b–18a.

ancient vessels."[38] Even though the formal designation of the site as the Imperial Archives came three months after Xie Kejia's colophon, it is probable that the scroll he saw was located there in the ninth month of 1133 because preparations were already under way to effect this conversion. (Otherwise, we must suppose that the scroll had been moved to the building for the edification of the Korean envoys who had never shown up, and this seems less likely.) In other words, as Huang Shengzhang concludes, the presence of the scroll in the building that would soon be formally named the Imperial Archives must mean that the scroll had already entered the imperial collection.[39]

The same man who had intervened five years earlier, right after Zhao Mingcheng's death, to stop the emperor's physician, Wang Jixian, from acquiring ancient vessels in the Zhao-Li collection, now came upon one of Zhao Mingcheng's favorite calligraphy scrolls in an imperial building in the Southern Song capital and proceeded to write a colophon expressing his regret that the scroll in question was no longer in the the Zhao-Li collection. Xie Kejia's outspokenness is surprising; perhaps his prominence at the court gave him what he felt was the license to speak his mind. He had in recent years been minister of the Ministry of War and the Ministry of Rites; he also served briefly as assistant councilor of state.[40] When he wrote this colophon, the year before he died, he was academician of Zizheng Palace, a position that would have given him access to the Imperial Archives. Xie must have been distressed to see that his previous effort to safeguard his cousin's collection from imperial designs upon it had fallen short, in this instance at least. Consequently, he expresses his frustration in this remarkable colophon that is a tacit denunciation of imperial avarice, although he couches his comment as a lament for the legacy of a deceased relative, which would have made it more palatable. He also takes care to refer to the present location of the scroll anachronistically, identifying the building by the name it had before it was taken over as imperial property, veiling his criticism, but only thinly. If Xie Kejia actually inscribed his colophon on the scroll itself, the fact that others who had viewed it in recent decades had already added several

---

38. *(Xianchun) Lin'an zhi* 7.1a–b. See also the source cited in note 36 above.
39. Huang Shengzhang, "Zhao Mingcheng Li Qingzhao fufu nianpu," p. 177.
40. For Xie's offices, see *Songshi* 213.5550 and 5551 and Li Xinchuan, *Jianyan yilai xinian yaolu* 27.549.

colophons to it must have made it seem more permissible for Xie to add his own.[41]

In her afterword, Li Qingzhao emphasizes how much of the collection has been lost and how many times such losses have been suffered. Her narrative presents a process of inexorable diminishment of these books and artworks that the couple had assembled over three decades. With each successive subtraction, it seems that Li Qingzhao grows more attached to what is left. Toward the end of the account, it is clear that the few remaining items are treasured not just for their inherent value and merit; they have also become cherished mementoes of her late husband and of their marriage.

The reader of Li Qingzhao's afterword will be surprised to learn that when she relocated to Jinhua in 1134, well after all the losses chronicled in the afterword, Li Qingzhao still had in her possession a copy of the *Veritable Records of Zhezong* 哲宗實錄. This work had two parts, the "Former Records" in one hundred *juan* and the "Later Records" in ninety-four *juan*.[42] We know about Li Qingzhao's possession of this work because the court, which had lost its copy during the removal southward of 1127, requisitioned it from her there in 1135. The language of the decree concerning this requisition is this: "It is commanded that the *Veritable Records of Emperor Shenzong* be sought out where it is kept in Wu [i.e., Jinhua] in the home of Zhao Mingcheng, the former academician of Dragon Diagram Hall."[43] This is clearly a reference to Li Qingzhao and her residence in Jinhua. It makes good sense that a copy of this work would have been in the Zhao-Li library, because Zhao Tingzhi (Zhao Mingcheng's father) had been one of the compilers of the work in the 1090s. Incidentally, this was not the first time that the court had tried to locate a copy of this important work that bore upon contemporary court politics and history. Three years earlier, in 1132, the court had tried to recover a copy of the work from the home of "the former chief councilor" Zhao Tingzhi in Quanzhou (in southeastern Fujian).[44] We know that two of Zhao Mingcheng's brothers, Zhao Cuncheng 趙存誠 and Zhao Sicheng 趙思誠, resided in Quanzhou at that time, and so it must have been from them that

---

41. The earlier colophons, including one by Mi Fu 米芾 (1051–1107), are also reproduced in Bian, *Shigu tang shuhua huikao* 10.2b.

42. See Chao Gongwu, *Junzhai dushu zhi* 6.233. A later recension of the work existed in a single part of 150 *juan*; see the following entry in *Junzhai dushu zhi*.

43. "Chongru" 崇儒, *Song huiyao jigao* 4.24a (p. 2242).

44. "Chongru," *Song huiyao jigao* 4.22a (p. 2241).

the court hoped to retrieve a copy.[45] But the brothers did not have the work. Li Qingzhao had it. Consequently, the court's renewed efforts directed toward her in 1135 were successful, and the work was duly installed in the imperial library, where soon a somewhat abbreviated new version of it was prepared.[46]

At the end of the afterword, Li Qingzhao says of the books she had left, "What remained were just one or two random and fragmentary volumes that did not make any complete title or set, together with just a few very ordinary calligraphy manuscripts." We would not have supposed from this language that in fact she still possessed a complete copy of the "veritable records" of one of the longest and most contentious reigns of the Northern Song. The work in question, consisting of nearly two hundred *juan*, would have been of considerable bulk and size. It would have been a manuscript copy, not an imprint.

Based on this alone, the modern scholar Nangong Bo 南宫搏 draws the conclusion that Li Qingzhao exaggerated the extent of her losses.[47] The point is not to deny that the losses she had suffered were considerable but simply to suggest that she had more remaining than she allows in her afterword. There is one other indication of this. Some eighteen years later, in 1152, Li Qingzhao showed up one day at the home of Mi Youren 米友仁 (1074–1153) in Lin'an. She brought with her that day two calligraphy scrolls she owned by Youren's father, Mi Fu, and she requested that Youren write colophons on them. He did, and the colophons survive.[48] It is clear from what the colophons say that the purpose of Li Qingzhao's house call that day was to have Mi Youren vouch for the authenticity of the calligraphy scrolls as the calligraphy of Mi Fu. Mi Fu, who had died in 1107, was one of the most celebrated calligraphers of the day. Scrolls by him would have been extremely valuable, especially after the authenticating colophons were added by his son. In her afterword Li Qingzhao had said that she had only a few "very ordinary" calligraphy manuscripts left. This statement too seems at odds with the facts.

---

45. See Xu Peijun, "Nianpu," *Jianzhu*, pp. 487–88.

46. The fact that the requisition attempt of 1135 was successful is recorded in Li Xinchuan, *Jianyan yilai chaoye zaji* 4.109.

47. Nangong, *Li Qingzhao de houban sheng*, p. 103.

48. Mi Youren, "Lingfeng xingji tieba" 靈峰行記帖跋 and "Xianren shou shi tieba" 先人壽詩帖跋, *Quan Songwen* 143:183.

Why might Li Qingzhao have exaggerated the extent of her losses in the afterword? We have seen that once Zhao Mingcheng died a whole range of persons—the emperor, an unscrupulous landlord, a greedy second husband, and so forth—tried to help themselves to portions of the Zhao-Li collection. Emphasizing how much she had lost might be partly a strategy to safeguard whatever she had left. It would have been in her interest, as a lone widow, to have people think that everything had already been lost, that there was nothing left to tempt another opportunistic man.[49] After all, the items she still possessed from the Zhao-Li collection were not only mementoes of her happier years and first marriage. They were also a form of wealth, and she had to be concerned about having the means to support herself through the rest of her life now that remarriage, yet again, was hardly an option. This way of describing her situation might also have helped her attract some sympathy, something in the interest of any widow living in her world.

Other Aims and Considerations

After the personal disasters of 1132—the remarriage, lawsuit, imprisonment, and divorce—Li Qingzhao needed to reconstitute herself. She needed to regain her respectability, to rehabilitate her reputation. We recall the keen sense of humiliation that she conveys in her letter to Qi Chongli ("My virtue ruined, my name ruined. . . . All the bamboo on South Mountain, converted into writing slips, would be insufficient to record the insults that the crowd hurled at me.") Moreover, we have seen ample evidence that the reaction many had to what had happened to her was one of bemused derision and even misogynist delight in her misfortune. Li Qingzhao would eventually be able to do, at least to a certain extent, what she considers unthinkable when writing her letter to Qi Chongli: to circulate in elite society and be welcomed as a woman of learning and talent (we have just seen how she would pay a call on a high court official, Mi Youren). But it is a long climb from the self-perception evident in the lines above to the self-confidence needed to emerge again in high society. The writing of the afterword was an important part of that climb back to respectability.

We can identify three goals that Li Qingzhao must have had in rehabilitating herself, ranging from the very concrete and legal to the more abstract and social. First, she would have wanted to regain her status as the late Zhao Mingcheng's "titled wife" 命婦, which provided a monthly government

---

49. Nangong Bo also makes this point; see *Li Qingzhao de houban sheng*, p. 85.

stipend, which she would have lost upon her remarriage to Zhang Ruzhou.[50] Second, she would have wanted to repair her relationship with the brothers and other relatives of Zhao Mingcheng, which would have suffered upon her remarriage, because they were well-connected and politically powerful. As such, they might well have been in a position to assist her in regaining her status as a titled wife; at the least, she would have wanted to keep the Zhaos from intervening to thwart her in that goal. Third, she would have wanted to recoup the favorable image she had previously enjoyed generally in high society, which knew her as a singularly talented woman poet. Naturally, these three aims overlapped and did not necessarily need to be pursued independently of each other.

We do not know when or through what agency Li Qingzhao regained her status as titled wife, but it is clear that she did manage to do so. To regain this status, her remarriage to Zhang Ruzhou would probably have had to be not just annulled but struck from the record of her legal history, as if it had never happened. This likely would have required some special consideration, perhaps from the court or the emperor himself, beyond matters covered by general statutes, but we have no record of how or when it was done. A work completed in 1141 specifically refers to her as "Zhao lingren Li" 趙令人李 (Lady Li, Zhao [Mingcheng's] titled wife), and we know that *lingren* was one of the designations used for titled wives at the time.[51] The work is a critical study of parallel prose, and it was compiled by Xie Ji, who was none other than the son of Xie Kejia (Zhao Mingcheng's maternal cousin), who certainly knew about Li Qingzhao's status. What is quoted by Xie Ji in his study is, fittingly enough, a couplet from a prayer to Zhao Mingcheng that Li Qingzhao wrote after his death. Xie Ji adds that the couplet shows Li Qingzhao to be "a talented master of parallel prose among women."[52] Apart from this, Li Qingzhao's actions of submitting seasonal verses of felicitations to the emperor, empress, and imperial consorts in 1143 as well as her submission of Zhao Mingcheng's *Records on Metal and Stone* to the throne are further evidence that she had somehow regained the status of titled woman (specifically, that of *wai mingfu* 外命婦, a titled woman outside the palace, as contrasted with those inside it). A commoner woman without such status in all

---

50. On the monthly stipends for titled wives, see *Songshi* 132.4351, discussing the temporary suspension of such stipends because of the fiscal crisis brought on by war.

51. Ji Huang et al., *Qinding Xu tongdian* 38.15a, cited by Nangong, *Li Qingzhao de hou bansheng*, p. 61.

52. Xie Ji, *Siliu tanzhu*. p. 9a.

likelihood would not be asked or permitted such access and privilege.[53] Even the wording of the decree of 1135, directing that the *Veritable Records of Zhezong* be retrieved from the home of the late Zhao Mingcheng, implies that her status as Zhao's widow had already been restored by then. And we saw earlier that in her poems of 1133 addressed to Han Xiaozhou and Hu Songnian, she pointedly refers to herself twice as "widow."

Perhaps Li Qingzhao's afterword played some part in regaining her status as widow and titled wife. It seems more likely, though, that the crucial moment affecting that restoration would have been the lawsuit and trial of 1132. Again, according to the statutes, we would have expected Li Qingzhao to be liable for two years imprisonment for bringing suit against her husband. That she was released after nine days shows that her case must have been handled as an exception to the law. We do not know what testimony she gave in the trial, but we recall that in her letter to Qi Chongli, she describes Zhang Ruzhou's marriage proposal as fraudulent and also says that while she was still undecided about accepting his proposal, "he forced me to go off with him as wife" 強以同歸. It seems possible that either the fraudulent proposal or the forcible removal may have been enough to get the marriage annulled in a way that would restore her status as Zhao Mingcheng's widow. Wang Xiaoli's recent study proposes another reason Li Qingzhao's former status was restored: the upshot of the lawsuit Li Qingzhao brought against Zhang Ruzhou was that their marriage was annulled because Li Qingzhao had violated the regulation that widows wait three years before remarrying.[54] She had married Ruzhou just thirty months after Zhao Mingcheng's death, short of a full three years. This argument has its own problems, however, because Song statutes make it clear that the "three year" waiting period was usually considered fulfilled after twenty-seven months.[55] Wang Xiaoli maintains that officials had the prerogative of interpreting the "three years" literally and must have done so in Li Qingzhao's case (as a convenient way to declare the marriage illegal and thus void). But this is speculation, and we have no way of affirming that such reasoning was used.

---

53. On the participation of *wai mingfu* in court and palace rituals and ceremonies, see the ritual treatise compiled during Huizong's reign, Zheng Juzhong, *Zhenghe wuli xinyi;* numerous references to such activities are found in *juan* 170, 188, and 190. Nangong Bo also makes this point in *Li Qingzhao de hou bansheng*, pp. 109 and 119.

54. Wang Xiaoli, "Li Qingzhao weishenme zhi ruyu jiutian?" pp. 6–8.

55. Dou Yi, *Song xingtong* 30.242.

We cannot know what if any role the afterword played in getting Li Qingzhao's status restored, but the composition was apparently part of her effort
to tell her side of the story of recent events in her life, with a view toward
deflecting some of the "insults" and mockery that now converged upon her.
We can identify four aims of the piece, in this regard. First, she intends to
show how devoted a wife she was to Zhao Mingcheng, how companionable
the two of them were, and how they were bound together as husband and
wife with common interests and values. Second, she wants to make it clear
that after his sudden and untimely death she remained true to him. She did
not forget him. She even did everything humanly possible to protect the
books and artworks that he so treasured. She was not successful in safeguard-
ing them, but as the collection shrank in size, what was left came to mean
more and more to her as tangible reminders of her years together with Zhao
Mingcheng and all that he prized and stood for. The problem posed by her
remarriage, naturally, was that it cast doubt on her devotion to her first husband. It is true that widows often remarried. But they did so at some cost to
their reputation. The higher the status of the woman, the more she would be
expected to be above "base" considerations of finances and loneliness (not
to mention sexual desire). Furthermore, Li Qingzhao was not just another
widow. She was among the most renowned women of her day, possessing a
kind of fame or notoriety that was probably unequaled by any other woman.
For such a woman to remarry when she was nearly fifty years old and then
quickly to take steps to dissolve the new union she had just formed would
have done great damage to her credibility and repute. It is little wonder that
the literary critics of the time, writing ostensibly about her poetry, could not
keep from referring to her disastrous remarriage. It had become an essential
feature of her life and now greatly compromised reputation. To get out from
the shroud of disapprobation that surrounded her, she quite naturally would
have wanted to persuade people in general and perhaps the Zhaos in particular that she was, indeed, a loving wife to Zhao Mingcheng.[56] At that point,
before the afterword began to circulate, people would not have had much of
any impression of the quality of her marriage to Zhao Mingcheng. They
certainly would not have the idealized image of that marriage that later
became widespread (thanks, in large part, to the afterword). Assuming that
they read her song lyrics autobiographically, they might have concluded that

---

56. Again, it was Nangong Bo who first suggested this as one of Li Qingzhao's purposes
in writing the afterword; see *Li Qingzhao de houban sheng*, p. 85.

she deeply missed Zhao Mingcheng when he was not with her. But they would not have in their heads the image of like-minded husband and wife thoroughly devoted to each other that proved to have such powerful appeal in later times. What they would know about her personal life was simply that she had been married to Zhao Mingcheng and then soon after his death, at an age when most widows would have resigned themselves to remaining single, she remarried. People thinking this way might then question her devotion to Zhao Mingcheng and his memory. Li Qingzhao herself must have been deeply cognizant of this.

The third aim of the afterword is to suggest that after Zhao Mingcheng died, Li Qingzhao as a single woman fleeing from invasion combined with local banditry faced an impossible situation. Her life was further complicated by the collection she strove to keep intact, because it attracted thieves and opportunists to her. In her letter to Qi Chongli, Li Qingzhao had explained her decision to remarry as the result of illness, confusion, her suitor's misrepresentation of himself, and her brother's encouragement. The afterword, while making no explicit reference to the remarriage whatsoever, adopts a different approach, suggesting that it was simply unfeasible for her to remain alone. We perceive through the afterword that widowhood for her was not a viable option. Any reader who reflects on what she tells us of her experiences after Zhao Mingcheng's death is likely to draw this conclusion. The fourth aim, which is closely linked to the third, is to hint that Zhao Mingcheng himself was partly responsible for the impossible situation she found herself in by making unreasonable demands on her and by doing less to plan and provide for her future without him than he might have done. The key passages in which these matters are broached are the parting scene at Chiyang ("I was in a terrible state of mind and shouted to him. . . . He . . . answered from afar, '. . . But the ritual vessels. . . . Live or die with them. Don't forget!'") and the death scene ("When he finished the poem, he died. He had no final instructions regarding 'dividing up the incense or selling sandals.'"). As others have remarked, in the Chiyang scene Zhao Mingcheng is made to look quite like a madman. The description of his manner, dress, and eyes is remarkably unflattering. Then, in response to her question, he delivers a command that shows that he has come to value portions of his collection as much as he values the life of his wife. It is a shocking revelation. This command became a kind of curse that Li Qingzhao had to live with after he was gone.

The death scene, as she narrates it, shows a breakdown of any communication between the dying husband and his wife. She has no idea how he expects her to carry on after he dies and cannot even bring herself to ask. He appears, meanwhile, to be completely self-absorbed. Rather than show any interest in her needs and apprehensions, his final act is to try to express his feelings one last time in poetry. The final sentence, with its allusion to incense and sandals, has been much discussed in scholarly literature for what it may indicate about the presence of a concubine in the household. That issue can be argued different ways. What is beyond question, however, is that Li Qingzhao is emphasizing how poorly Zhao Mingcheng attended to the prospect of her welfare as a widow. We see in the afterword how close Li Qingzhao was to Zhao Mingcheng in life and how much she cherishes his memory. But we also see Zhao Mingcheng as a man obsessed with his possessions to such an extent that he fails to fulfill certain responsibilities to his wife, leaving her with burdens virtually impossible to bear as a widow.

Above I have suggested reasons for reconsidering the traditional reading of Li Qingzhao's afterword. The conventional interpretation of it as loving testament to the memory of Zhao Mingcheng does not do justice to the complexity of the contents of the text and also ignores the circumstances under which Li Qingzhao wrote the work, as it ignores the connections with the other works she wrote in the same period of her life. Oddly, for all the intensely personal material it contains, this too was a very public piece of writing. The afterword must have been attached to Zhao Mingcheng's *Records on Metal and Stone* when she presented that work to the court, and probably she wrote the afterword with a view to making it public in that way.

If the afterword yields up new meanings and implications when read critically, perhaps it is time to reconsider as well what we thought we knew about the marriage of Li Qingzhao and Zhao Mingcheng. Admittedly, we are on more speculative ground when we do this than when we scrutinize a single text. No doubt there is much about the private life of this husband and wife that we can never know. Yet our reading of the afterword, which has always been the primary source for impressions of the Zhao-Li marriage, has pointed to aspects of that relationship that, while having been noticed by some insightful scholars, have generally been passed over in the effusions of enthusiasm over an idealized projection of the marriage. Li Qingzhao's feelings toward Zhao Mingcheng, as conventionally imagined, lie at the center of the way her song lyrics are ordinarily read. Conseqently, to raise questions about the validity of that impression is not irrelevant to the task of rethinking our literary analysis of her poetry, a task that awaits us in later chapters.

CHAPTER 7

The Beginnings of "Li Qingzhao"
Reception during the Southern Song and Yuan

The process of trying to accommodate Li Qingzhao to dominant cultural values was set in motion when she was alive. Those values, shaped over centuries primarily by men, needed to find a way to accommodate such an unusual woman who had proven to be successful and celebrated in the man's world of literary composition. Thus began a protracted and complicated dynamic of engagement between Li Qingzhao, as represented by her writings and what was generally known about her conduct, and the critics and others who would mold and modify images of her. More than any other woman of her day, Li Qingzhao alternately constituted an affront and an inspiration to ideals concerning women and literary talent.

The Misery of Her Later Years

Hu Zi is one of the few critics to have expressed opinions about Li Qingzhao while she was still alive. Hu Zi's 1148 comment on Li Qingzhao is important both for its substance and for its early date. As we have seen, Hu Zi opens his entry with praise for Li Qingzhao as an outstanding woman poet and quotes lines from two of her well-known song lyrics, ending with the observation that "such lines are likewise hard for a woman to come up with." The conclusion of his entry is this: "Yi'an married a second time, to Zhang Ruzhou, but before long she had a falling out with him. Her petition to Qi

Chuhou [Qi Chongli] says, 'To my dismay, I realized that at an advanced age, when the sun hung in the mulberry and elm, I had married a worthless shyster of a man.' There were none who spoke of this who did not laugh at her."[1]

Hu Zi wrote this only some eighteen years after Li Qingzhao's remarriage and divorce. His final sentence reveals that Li Qingzhao was already a "topic" among Hu Zi and his peers. Hu Zi even knows about the letter of gratitude Li Qingzhao sent to Qi Chongli, and he knows it well enough to quote the lines in it that best epitomize the humiliation that Li Qingzhao felt as she tried to explain to Qi Chongli how she had gotten herself into such a degrading situation. But to Hu Zi and the others who chatted about these events, the lines are not poignant or pitiable. They are cause for derision.

Critics like Hu Zi knew of Li Qingzhao from her writings. A woman who could write so well was already likely to be a conversation topic. When it turned out that she behaved in an extraordinary manner as well (but not an exemplary manner), she would have been spoken and gossiped about extensively, a fact not lost on Li Qingzhao herself. That her letter to Qi Chongli was also circulating, or at least famous lines from it were circulating orally, is an indication of widespread fascination that such a humiliating series of events could befall such a celebrated woman. Li Qingzhao's song lyrics were available in printed editions. If her letter to Qi Chongli circulated, it probably did so in an entirely different way, as a scandalous topic of conversation.

In the way Hu Zi formulates his entry, there is a discrepancy and tension between Li Qingzhao's excellence as a poet who exceeds expectations about what a woman is capable of and her conduct as a widow and remarried woman. This discrepancy is found in remarks about her in other Southern Song sources as well. In addition to Wang Zhuo and Chao Gongwu, who were quoted in chapter 2, Zhu Yu 朱彧 offers:

> The correctness and richness of her poetry did not pale before the ancients, and her song lyrics were even more lyrical and beautiful, often surpassing the boundaries of conventional thought. In recent times she has no equal. Her works are contained in a literary collection of twelve chapters and *Jades for Rinsing the Mouth* in one chapter. Nevertheless, she was unable to maintain her chastity in her later years, and she drifted about until she died. Heaven gave her such an abundance of talent but scrimped on her fate. What a pity it is![2]

---

1. Hu Zi, *Tiaoxi yuyin conghua*, "Qianji" 60.416–17.
2. Zhu Yu, *Pingzhou ketan*, a nonstandard edition, quoted in Wang Zhongwen, *Li Qingzhao ji jiaozhu*, p. 310.

As observed in chapter 2, there is a common shape and movement in such passages. They proceed from admiring comments about her poetry to reference to her misfortune or misconduct in her remarriage and the ensuing unhappy consequences. (In this respect Hu Zi's entry has the same structure.) It was because Li Qingzhao married "a certain fellow" then divorced him,[3] or was unable to maintain her chastity (as a widow), or did not observe principle in her conduct that she ended up a forlorn wanderer, homeless.

This common refrain in the sources appears all the more remarkable when we realize that there is little factual basis for it. Quite to the contrary, all the evidence suggests that Li Qingzhao lived for nearly the last twenty years of her life in the capital of Lin'an, where she had at least a degree of contact with eminent persons and even the imperial court. It is true, as we have seen, that she removed herself from the capital in 1134, going southwest to Jinhua. But this was not aimless wandering. It was a flight from the new Jurchen invasion of that year. Tens of thousands of persons were displaced by the invasion, not just Li Qingzhao.

We do not know how long Li Qingzhao remained in Jinhua. She was still there in the summer of 1135, when the court requisitioned her copy of the *Veritiable Records of Zhezong*. After 1135, there is a hiatus in the sources concerning Li Qingzhao, and it is impossible to know where she was for the next few years. But it is certain that she had returned to Lin'an by 1143, and most scholars believe that she returned to the capital well before then, probably within months after Gaozong found it safe to return there in 1135. In 1143 Li Qingzhao composed and submitted to the palace several seasonal congratulatory poems for the imperial clan and palace ladies. To celebrate spring (i.e., the New Year), she submitted poems to the empress and the honored consort (*guifei* 貴妃). To celebrate the Duanwu Festival in the fifth month of the same year, she submitted poems to the emperor, the empress, and imperial consorts (*furen* 夫人). The Bureau of Academicians was responsible for soliciting such poems (presumably a considerable quantity of them) and elaborately preparing them for presentation—each written out on silk decorated with golden thread and each packet distinguished by certain features appropriate to the rank of the addressee.[4] The collection and submission of them in 1143, however, was anything but routine. That was the first year since

---

3. Wang Zhuo, *Biji manzhi* 2.88.
4. Zhou Mi, "Li chun" 立春, *Wulin jiushi* 2.11a (quoted in *Jianzhu*, p. 505).

the dynastic disaster of 1126 that the old custom of submitting such poems had been reinstituted.[5] We can be sure that particular care was taken in the preparation of poems for that year.

Merely from the fact that Li Qingzhao participated in the presentation of these poems in 1143, we might surmise that she must have returned to the capital by this time. Zhou Mi, who quotes each of her Duanwu Festival poems, confirms this by specifically noting that she was in Lin'an at the time.[6] Equally important, that Li Qingzhao was asked to submit poems and that the poems that she composed were permitted to be presented to the imperial clan show that in all likelihood she had already regained her status as titled wife and was, in any case, hardly the socially disgraced woman, wandering the "rivers and lakes," who is described in the sources quoted above. If she had been, no one would have been able to contact her to ask her to write these poems, much less have been inclined to do so.[7]

There are other indications that Li Qingzhao was living in the capital in the 1140s and on into the 1150s. As mentioned earlier, at some point after 1134, she formally submitted Zhao Mingcheng's *Records on Metal and Stone* to the court. We do not know when she did this except that it was sometime during the Shaoxing reign.[8] She also paid at least one house call to Mi Youren in Lin'an in 1150, inviting him to add colophons to scrolls of his father's calligraphy that she owned.

We see, then, that not only did Li Qingzhao reside in the capital in the 1140s, probably remaining there until her death in the mid-1150s, but she was socially active and visible. She submitted congratulatory poems to the emperor and the palace ladies. She presented Zhao Mingcheng's scholarly

---

5. Li Xinchuan, *Jianyan yilai xinian yaolu* 148.2375 (quoted in Yu Zhonghang, *Li Qingzhao nianpu*, p. 132).

6. Zhou Mi, *Haoranzhai yatan* A.12b.

7. There is an interesting detail concerning Li Qingzhao's submission of the poems noted in Zhou Mi's account. He tells us that at the time Qin Zi 秦梓 (Qin Chucai 秦楚材), the older brother of the controversial grand councilor Qin Gui 秦檜 (1090–1155), was a member of the Bureau of Academicians and that he bore a grudge against Li Qingzhao and consequently blocked or diminished the imperial gift she was to receive in response for writing the Duanwu Festival poems. Why did Qin Xin bear a grudge against Li Qingzhao? Wang Zhongwen, noting first that Li Qingzhao was related by marriage to the Qins, speculates that Qin Zi had hoped that she would allow him to present the poems as his compositions, and when she refused and submitted them as her own, he became angry. Wang Zhongwen, *Li Qingzhao ji jiaozhu*, p. 261.

8. It is Hong Kuo 洪适 (1117–84) who reports this; *Li shi* 隸釋 26.17b.

notes on ancient steles to the court. She paid social calls to one of the leading painters and calligraphers of the day. She even offered her services as tutor to the young daughter of the eminent Sun family (as discussed in chapter 2). Admittedly, we cannot reconstruct Li Qingzhao's life from these years in great detail. But from what we do know, she did not spend her last years wandering the countryside, homeless and destitute, as the early sources report.

We might ask how the inaccurate reports came about. It is evident from the remarkable consistency of them that they had a certain currency and circulation, despite their inaccuracy. What purposes might they have served? Two come readily to mind. The men who wrote these accounts, men whose sense of their social place and identity was likely to be threatened by the behavior of widows who chose to remarry, would have viewed the purported misery of her last years as the natural and fitting consequence of her misconduct in remarrying after Zhao Mingcheng's death. Knowledge was widespread that this remarkable woman not only remarried but chose badly when she did, so that the second marriage was a disaster. What followed could only have been what such an "unprincipled" woman deserved, a steady descent into misery and ignominy. The idea that after this double disaster Li Qingzhao might still have retained respectability and visibility in elite society would have been, to many persons, so discomforting as to seem quite implausible. Consequently, an alternate scenario was developed.

Second, the notion that Li Qingzhao's last twenty or so years were spent in abject loneliness provided a seemingly fitting background for many of the song lyrics that were attributed to her. So long as readers insisted on reading her songs autobiographically, it was handy to have the conviction that miserable circumstances dogged her after her remarriage and divorce, just as it was handy to understand that, even when he was alive, Zhao Mingcheng was frequently away on distant travels, leaving his wife alone.

Devotion to Zhao Mingcheng

Another way of thinking about Li Qingzhao that is evident in early comments is rooted in her afterword to *Records on Metal and Stone* and reflects, based on that narrative, on the nature of the union between Zhao Mingcheng and Li Qingzhao. We have just a handful of these early comments on the afterword, but they are enough to demonstrate that her account of the marriage attracted attention and consistently inspired a particular type of reaction. I translate four of them below. The first is from Hong Mai:

Zhao Mingcheng of Dongwu was the middle son of Chief Councilor in State Qingxian [Zhao Tingzhi]. He composed *Records on Metal and Stone*. Taking as his subject all inscriptions from the Three Periods of antiquity down to the Five Dynasties of recent times, whether they be colophons found on tripods, bells, or vessels and goblets of the *yan, ge, pan, yi, zun,* or *que* type, or records concerning eminent officials or obscure gentlemen preserved on great rectangular or large rounded steles, he corrected what was spurious and mistaken and sorted out the praise and blame. In all, he collected and commented on two thousand inscriptions.

His wife, Yi'an, Recluse Scholar Li, shared his intent with him throughout her life. After Zhao Mingcheng died, she grieved that all the things they had collected could not be kept intact and wrote this afterword, giving a full account of all the difficulties and deprivations she encountered, from beginning to end. Today, the *Records* has been printed by the archives in Longshu Prefecture, but the afterword was not included in the work. Recently, I saw the original manuscript of the afterword, possessed by Wang Shunbo, and so here I copy out the gist of the text. [Here the complete text of the afterword is reproduced.]

This work was composed in the fourth year of the Shaoxing period, when Yi'an was fifty-two years old. She managed to record her own history like this; reading what she wrote I sorrow for her and have added this colophon to Zhao's book.[9]

Zhao Shihou 趙師厚 (fl. 1205) writes in his postface:

Zhao Defu's [polite name of Zhao Mingcheng] *Records on Metal and Stone* was engraved on printing blocks in Longshu Prefecture long ago, but that edition has many lacunae and misprints. Now, I have had the good fortune to be able to borrow and consult a manuscript from magistrate Zhang Huaizu, of Zhao Mingcheng's native place, which Zhao had personally copied out and which has corrections done by that prefecture's literary scholar Wang Yushi of Shanyin. Feeling it a pity, moreover, that Yi'an's afterword was not appended [to the Longshu edition], I have had it engraved as an appendix. In this way I hope to satisfy the cherished hopes of Defu and to fulfill Yi'an's intention.[10]

Chen Zhensun 陳振孫 (fl. 1211–49) writes regarding *Records on Metal and Stone* and Li Qingzhao's afterword:

---

9. Hong Mai, *Rongzhai suibi,* "Sibi" 5.685–86.

10. Zhao Shihou, "Postface" to the Yayu tang edition of *Records on Metal and Stone, Huibian,* p. 13.

I always laugh at [other] scholarly works on ancient inscriptions. Their excesses in devising forced attributions and explanations, even with their detailed and wide-ranging use of sources, regularly fall short of credulity. It is only the scholarly notes in this book that are different, because [Zhao Mingcheng] was a more discerning man among those devoted to antiquity. His wife, the Recluse Scholar of Yi'an, composed an afterword for his work that is quite worth looking at.[11]

And an anonymous thirteenth-century author notes:

The Recluse Scholar of Yi'an, Li, was the wife of Mingcheng, the son of Chief Councilor of State Zhao Tingzhi. Her talent was lofty and her learning extensive. Few in recent times could compare with her. Many of her poems and song lyrics circulate in the world. Once I saw the "Afterword to *Records on Metal and Stone*" that she wrote for her husband. Reading it, men of later generations can only sigh with deep feeling. Today I record it here.[12]

A few salient and shared features of these entries stand out. One recurrent idea in these early comments is that the afterword demonstrates that Li Qingzhao was of one mind with her husband. Readers familiar with the afterword will view this reaction as reasonable. Li Qingzhao's level of education, highly unusual in a woman, made the cooperative nature of the collection project possible. Most wives, even those who may have been interested in such matters, would not have been as qualified as Li Qingzhao to take an active part in building the collection, collating and recopying books, and doing the research for the notes on the inscriptions. As testament to this unusual extent of mutual interest and undertaking by husband and wife, the afterword serves to commemorate the happy marriage. Thus, in the anonymous passage above, Li Qingzhao is said to have written the afterword "for" her late husband, as if to console him in the afterlife. In this reading, the aim that Li Qingzhao explicitly articulates in the afterword itself—that she wrote the work as a warning to future would-be collectors about the uselessness and folly of assembling such collections—is completely overlooked. In Zhao Shihou's formulation, his act of correcting mistakes in an earlier printed edition of *Records* and reprinting it, this time adding Li Qingzhao's afterword, has the double benefit, in his eyes, of in effect fulfilling both the husband's and the wife's wishes now that they are gone. Again, the two are paired together as an ideal couple, even in death as they were in life.

---

11. Chen Zhensun, *Zhizhai shulu jieti* 8.233.

12. From the anonymous work *Ruigui tang xialu* 瑞桂堂暇錄, thought to date from the late Southern Song, *Huibian*, p. 25.

Despite all the enthusiasm these writers express for the joint involvement of husband and wife in building the collection, and by extension the ideal marital harmony they enjoyed, there is still a clear gendered hierarchy in the Zhao-Li relationship as described. Zhao Mingcheng wrote the massive collection of scholarly notes on two thousand inscriptions. Li Qingzhao added a short afterword whose distinctive feature is how moving it is. Zhao Mingcheng went out into the world at large and collected and brought home its treasured antiquities. His colophons on them belong to the world of scholarship and history, that is, the realm mostly of men. Li Qingzhao stayed at home, longing for her absent husband, and eventually contributed an afterword to Zhao's work that is distinctly domestic, personal, and nostalgic. Chen Zhensun's comment epitomizes this disparity when, after describing in considerable detail the strengths of Zhao Mingcheng's *Records* compared with other epigraphical studies, he says simply that Li Qingzhao's afterword is "quite worth looking at" (*po keguan* 頗可觀). This hardly does justice to the originality and effect of what Li Qingzhao's work achieves, but it is as much as Chen Zhensun is willing to concede. That Li Qingzhao was, after Zhao Mingcheng's death, unable to preserve the collection they had worked so hard to assemble also shows her weakness once she was left by herself. As a widow, she was not a viable custodian of such a vast collection, as the afterword clearly shows. This revelation must have had its own peculiar appeal to male readers, as wittingly or unwittingly the afterword confirms their sense of male superiority by documenting Li Qingzhao's powerlessness. How sad it is, they say. But as they say it, they are aware that if Zhao Mingcheng had remained alive things might have gone differently.

These early enthusiasts of Li Qingzhao's afterword may appreciate its moving account of the happy years of the marriage, the portrait it provides of Li Qingzhao's devotion to Zhao Mingcheng and his values, and the sorrowful story of the eventual loss of the collection. But they do not seem to be able to probe the deeper ramifications of what Li Qingzhao says. It is not until Ming times that a critic appears who notes that Li Qingzhao shows greater wisdom about the nature of collecting and loss than her husband did by describing a process of growing possessiveness, obsession, and covetousness and reflecting, toward the end of her afterword, on the folly of what she and her husband did.[13] Only in modern times do we begin to explore the

---

13. Cao An, *Lanyan changyu*, p. 39b; also in *Huibian*, p. 31.

hints Li Qingzhao drops in the composition about the unequal access she and her husband had to the precious collection as a reflection of the disparity in authority between husband and wife.[14]

Yet perhaps the most telling aspect of these early comments on the afterword is that they do not mention Li Qingzhao's remarriage and quick divorce. So taken are these critics with Li Qingzhao's account of her marriage and the building and loss of the collection that they, unlike other early critics, do not think to condemn Li Qingzhao for her "misconduct" as a widow. It is unlikely that these writers do not know about her remarriage, since knowledge of that event and its untoward consequences was widespread in the Southern Song. It is more probable that this group of critics has simply lost sight of those events, choosing as they do to focus on the sanguinity of Li Qingzhao's first marriage as she represents it.

Stories in the Unofficial Biography

A third thread can be distinguished in early images of Li Qingzhao. It is apparent that lore and eventually something like a legend concerning this singular woman and her first husband began to evolve early on. In these early stories we discern some effort to come to grips with the anomaly that Li Qingzhao was, to acknowledge it, and at the same time to begin to refashion her into something that is less strange and consequently less threatening to the literati and critics of the day. There need not have been a conscious attempt to accomplish this for it to have happened. The existence of such literary talent in the person of a woman would have been culturally disorienting enough to set all sorts of impulses in motion among men to somehow correct the situation. One of the most effective ways of recasting someone is to use that person's own words to do so. Li Qingzhao provided plenty of material that lent itself to the task.

By the fourteenth century, if not before, there had appeared an "Unofficial Biography" 外傳 of Li Qingzhao (or possibly of Li Qingzhao and Zhao Mingcheng together) that recorded anecdotes about her marriage and probably much more. An unofficial biography is a biography of someone that consists of hearsay, fictionalized accounts, and other tales that would be considered too unreliable or trivial to be included in an "orthodox (or official) biography" 正傳. The form is called "unofficial" not only because it was not

---

14. Owen, *Remembrances*, pp. 80–98.

part of official imperial historiography, but also because its contents typically stand outside, *wai* 外, of what is deemed legitimate historiographical material. Labeling the work "unofficial" puts the reader on notice that this is a biography that presents popular lore about its subject, which many readers prefer to sober history. Telltale signs in Southern Song sources suggest that stories about Li Qingzhao circulated from early on, probably while she was still alive, and gave rise to persistent popular images of her. It is hardly surprising that a woman like Li Qingzhao would inspire such stories. They were a way of fitting her strikingly original songs into a biographical framework. They thus functioned to help make this most unusual writer understandable to a culture lacking conventions or preparation for dealing with a woman like her.

It is Yi Shizhen (14th c.) who quotes the otherwise unknown "Unofficial Biography" in his *Langhuan ji*. The *Langhuan ji* itself does not have high scholarly repute. It is dismissed by the *Siku quanshu* editors as consisting "entirely of baseless exaggerations and trivial tales," and consequently it was excluded from the imperial library. Such material is invaluable, however, in reconstructing images of persons as developed in the popular imagination. The two Li Qingzhao anecdotes that Yi Shizhen quotes from the unofficial account of her life are translated below (I have referred to them in chapter 3 but here present them in their entirety). The first is as follows:

> Yi'an sent the song lyric "Double Ninth Festival, to the tune 'Drunk in the Blossoms' Shade'" to Mingcheng in place of a letter. Mingcheng exclaimed with admiration and was ashamed that he himself had never written such a fine composition. He vowed to attempt to outdo her. He refused all visitors and for three days and nights had no thought of food or sleep. He managed to compose fifty songs, and he showed them to his friend Lu Defu, having first slipped Yi'an's composition in among them. Defu pored over them for two or three days and eventually came to Mingcheng and said, "There are only three good lines in the entire group." Mingcheng asked which they were. Defu recited, "Don't say she's not heartbroken, / The west wind lifts the blinds, / She's as wasted as the yellow flowers" 莫道不銷魂／簾捲西風／人似黃花瘦. They were precisely lines from Yi'an's composition.[15]

---

15. Yi Shizhen, *Langhuan ji*, *Huibian*, p. 28. Standard versions of the song have *bi* 比 instead of *si* 似 in the last line so that the line reads, "She's more wasted than the yellow flowers." The song is my no. 20, *Jianzhu* 1.52–53; *Quan Songci* 2:1205–6.

The second anecdote is this:

> When Zhao Mingcheng was young and his father was about to select a wife for him, one day Mingcheng napped in the morning and dreamed of reciting some writing aloud. When he awoke, he could only recall three lines: "'Word' combines with 'office,' / 'peace' loses its top, / 'Grass' is taken off 'mushroom' and 'hibiscus'" 言與司合，安上已脫，芝芙草拔. He quoted these to his father. His father explained them this way: "You shall have a wife who is able to compose literary works. 'Word' combines with 'office' yields the character 'literary works' (*ci* 詞); 'peace' loses its top leaves the character 'woman' (*nü* 女); and 'grass' is taken off 'mushroom' and 'hibiscus' produces the characters 'the husband of' (*zhi fu* 之夫). Isn't it clear that you will be the husband of a literary woman (*cinü zhi fu* 詞女之夫)?" Subsequently, Mr. Li gave Mingcheng his daughter to be his wife. She was Yi'an, who was indeed favored with literary talent.
>
> Not long after Yi'an was married, Mingcheng went off on distant travels carrying a chest of books. Yi'an could not bear to see him leave, and so she found a brocade kerchief and wrote a song lyric to the tune "A Single Cutting of Plum Blossoms" as a parting gift. [The words follow.]

These two anecdotes are all we have from the unofficial biography of Li Qingzhao. It is a pity we do not have the entire work. Presumably it contained a wealth of such stories that had grown up around Li Qingzhao and her husband.

Still, even these small tidbits of the biography are interesting and revealing. To start with, in both of them the song lyric attributed to Li Qingzhao is taken to be autobiographical and to be addressed to Zhao Mingcheng. These anecdotes are the clearest indications that the tradition of reading Li Qingzhao's song lyrics autobiographically was in place from very early on. In the first anecdote, the song lyric takes the place of a letter. Obviously, it was addressed to Zhao Mingcheng, and the woman who figures in it, pining away for him, losing weight and her vitality, is Li Qingzhao. Likewise, in the second anecdote, even though Zhao Mingcheng has not left yet, Li Qingzhao composes the piece in question as a soon-to-be solitary wife, longing for her absent husband. We will return to this way of reading the song below.

The first story concerns the problem of a wife who surpasses her husband in literary talent. In this telling, the problem is broached in a mildly humorous manner. Mingcheng's determination is described in an exaggerated, parodic way, so that he becomes a caricature of an upright and self-respecting gentleman scholar. This makes the denouement all the more effective, for the reader, and embarrassing for Mingcheng. Mixed in anonymously among

Mingcheng's fifty compositions, the superiority of Li Qingzhao's three lines still stood out.

This story is reminiscent of the statement from the presumably more reliable source Zhou Hui appended to Li Qingzhao's poem on the Tang restoration tablet in his miscellany: "Recently I met one of Yi'an's relatives, who told me that when Mingcheng was serving at Jiankang, whenever there was a snowstorm, Yi'an would put on a cap and cape of reeds and go out to walk along the city wall, looking out afar, in search of poetic inspiration. When she thought of some lines, she would always invite her husband to continue the poem, and Mingcheng invariably was hard put to do so."[16] Zhou Hui's preface to his miscellany is dated 1192. That puts it some sixty years after the events in question, but it is not impossible that a second- or third-generation descendant of Li Qingzhao would have related this to him, just as he says. It is reassuring for the credibility of Zhou Hui's account to notice that although Zhao Mingcheng and Li Qingzhao were in Jiankang, where Mingcheng was serving as governor, for only half a year, their time there was in fact during the winter of 1128 to 1129 (from the ninth month of 1128 through the third month of 1129). Zhou Hui's report, in turn, reminds us of what Li Qingzhao says in her afterword, describing the way she and her husband amused themselves in the evenings during their years in Qingzhou. Having prepared tea, they would look at a pile of books and play a game of guessing in which volume, chapter, page, and line a certain passage could be found. The person who guessed correctly got to sip his or her tea. Li Qingzhao had opened this section of the afterword by saying, "It happens that I have a good memory," and now, describing the game, she says: "When I guessed right, I'd hold the cup high and burst out laughing until the tea splattered the front of my gown. I'd have to get up without even taking a sip." The implication is that she was regularly the winner in this contest as well.

Describing Mingcheng's frustration when asked to contribute his own lines, Zhou Hui's wording is "*Mingcheng mei kuzhi*" 每苦之, literally, "Mingcheng always suffered over it" or "was hard put to do so." This is presumably the language that Li Qingzhao's descendant used when telling Zhou Hui the story; the descendant must have wanted Zhou Hui to know this detail as evidence of Li Qingzhao's superior talent. Since the point of Zhou Hui's entry is to call attention to the excellence of Li Qingzhao's poetry, the

16. Zhou Hui, *Qingbo zazhi* 8.5096–97.

relative's report perfectly supports his aims. In the unofficial biography anecdote, however, Mingcheng's frustration has been multiplied to excessive and comic proportions. This is no longer a proud descendant's recollection; much less Li Qingzhao's own self-satisfied memory. Now the wife's superiority drives her husband to desperation, locking himself in his room for three days and nights, and even then he fails. The tone of the presentation is humorous, but there is an issue underlying the humor that is serious. A husband does not want to be upstaged by his wife, especially in a society as patriarchal as this one was. The thought that she is doing so may well lead him to take desperate measures to try to restore the proper hierarchy of accomplishment. The popular image of Li Qingzhao we glimpse here recognizes that her very talent has a destabilizing effect. It is liable to make her husband insecure and threaten his role as the member of the marriage who should have distinctly superior learning and skill in writing. The anecdote is funny precisely because things should not be this way between husband and wife. The reader may be amused, but he (if he is male) is probably not going to wish that he were Zhao Mingcheng, who had a wife who constantly reminded him of his inferiority.

The second anecdote consists of two parts. The first relates a dream prophecy of the marriage of Li Qingzhao to Zhao Mingcheng, and the second explains the provenance of one of Li Qingzhao's well-known song lyrics. Both parts concern Li Qingzhao's relation to her husband, as does the first anecdote. Mingcheng's dream belongs to a story type that is widespread in China. Perplexing words are seen in a dream and remembered, but not understood, when the dreamer awakes. Another person, with greater understanding, decodes their meaning, using the method of splitting and recombining graphic elements to form new characters (a practice Joseph Needham dubbed "glyphomancy"). Chinese script lends itself to this type of encoding, and so such phrases of scrambled script became a standard way that prophecies are presented in Chinese culture.

What does it mean that the marriage of Li Qingzhao to Mingcheng was foretold in his dream? It means that it was fated, to begin with. This belief is part of the rosy romanticization of the couple's marriage that was an essential part of the lore concerning Li Qingzhao. The matching of this woman with this man was not their parents' doing, as normally was the case. It was arranged in heaven, fated before the parents even took the first steps toward betrothal. Behind this conviction about how the marriage came about is the unspoken assumption that this husband and wife were uniquely suited for each other. As a modern, scholarly account of their lives says, once married, "husband and wife shared the same aspirations and had matching principles, as together they took delight in cultural relics" 夫婦志同道合, 共賞文物.[17] This image of their marriage derives from the account of its early years that Li Qingzhao gave in her afterword. So powerful is her account, and so unusual was it to find a pairing of a husband and a wife that were so like-minded in a society where parental arrangement of marriages was the rule, that popular belief, going further than anything Li Qingzhao herself says, concluded that the marriage must have been arranged by divine forces, and this perception found its way into the unofficial biography.

The second part of this anecdote describes how Li Qingzhao came to write one of her song lyrics, "A Single Cutting of Plum Blossoms" (which was discussed in chapter 3). It is significant that this song lyric was especially well known in Song and Yuan times. It is one of the most frequently anthologized of her compositions in Southern Song collections of song lyrics, and its popularity lasted through later dynasties and, indeed, right up to the present. As we saw, this passage reflects a belief that Zhao Mingcheng went off on distant travels soon after marrying Li Qingzhao in 1101. That belief was universal among scholars until Huang Shengzhang challenged it in 1957 (as discussed in chapter 3), arguing that the language Li Qingzhao used in her afterword about her husband joining officialdom after finishing at the National Academy had been misunderstood, giving rise to a popular belief about Mingcheng departing the capital on distant travels. It is impossible to know if the unofficial biography passage gave rise to this misunderstanding or if the passage simply reflected an understanding about the couple's early separation that was already widespread.

Actually, the song lyric does not match the purported circumstances well at all, as Huang Shengzhang pointed out. The song does not read like something written at a parting scene. In the song the male lover is already distant, and the person in the western tower (by convention, a solitary woman in song lyrics of the period) is waiting for letters from him, hoping that they will be delivered by migratory geese. But the letters never come. If Zhao Mingcheng were really about to depart, would Li Qingzhao present him a song describing how he never sends letters home on his distant travels? It seems an unlikely thing for her to do.

---

17. From *Jianzhu*, p. 419.

If the song does not fit the circumstances well, perhaps that is because the circumstances are made up, just as the idea of Mingcheng going off on distant travels soon after the two were married was made up. Fabricating the anecdote concerning Mingcheng's travels and the provenance of this song accomplishes a few different purposes. First, it attempts to explain why a wife fortunate enough to find herself in an ideal marriage (this is the tie-in with the first half of the anecdote) could write such a sad song. It is because the two are so well matched that, naturally, when he must go away she is overcome with sorrow. Why else would she be sorrowful? It must be because her husband is going away. Again the assumption is that whenever Li Qingzhao writes, she writes as herself; she cannot be speaking as anyone else. The conviction that she must be writing as herself overrides the awkwardness that the song does not fit the circumstances very well. Second, the story reinforces the image of a devoted Li Qingzhao. "Yi'an could not bear to see him leave." She is completely focused on Mingcheng. The prospect of being separated from him is quite intolerable to her. Third, the story indirectly addresses the problem broached in the first anecdote by suggesting that whatever Li Qingzhao writes springs from her devotion to her husband. It is her impulse to express her love and longing for him that causes her to write. This notion corrals her talent. In fact, it subordinates her poetic talent to her marriage and role as wife. It goes a long way toward neutralizing the problem of a wife who is better than her husband at the male task of literary composition. This image of Li Qingzhao, channeling her greater talent wholly into expressions of devotion to Mingcheng, is very different from the image of Li Qingzhao venturing out in snowstorms for poetic inspiration and coming up with lines that gave Mingcheng fits when he tried to match them, as it is different from the image of Li Qingzhao bursting out in laughter when she bests him in their literary guessing game. This subtle transformation in how Li Qingzhao's talent is directed has in fact already taken place in the first unofficial biography anecdote. Mingcheng could not equal what she wrote, but at least what she wrote about was how she was pining for him.

The Epitome of the Lonely Woman

Two groups of early critics have been distinguished above by the divergent images they embrace of Li Qingzhao. One group cannot think of her without thinking of her disastrous second marriage and chastising her for it, despite their recognition of her talent as a poet. The other group could picture her only in the context of her devotion to Zhao Mingcheng, as seen especially in her afterword. Related to this second group are anecdotes about Li Qingzhao and Zhao Mingcheng that idealized their marriage as a match made in heaven, even though some of the stories broach the awkwardness occasioned for Mingcheng by having a wife who regularly outshone him. Yet that awkwardness is made more palatable by showing that it was wholly channeled into expressing her affection for Mingcheng.

We could characterize these ways of thinking about Li Qingzhao as contradictory, but it is more accurate to see them as alternatives held by different readers and critics. There is a contradiction between the two images of Li Qingzhao as devoted wife (and nostalgic widow) and disloyal widow. But we have seen no evidence in Southern Song sources that this surfaces as an internal contradiction within the thinking of any particular critic. Perhaps because the two images are so contradictory, the sources suggest that critics simply opted for one or the other, rather than face the troubling prospect of holding the two simultaneously in mind. We will have ample occasion to return to this problem of incompatible images and interpretations of Li Qingzhao in later chapters, which trace the later history of thinking about her.

Whichever aspect of her life a Southern Song critic chose to focus on, it provided him with a biographical setting for sadness and sorrowful literary expression. To be sure, the circumstances and emotions of the two are distinguishable. In one view Li Qingzhao was a devoted wife who shared with her husband his passion for antiquities. When he left on travels (to add to his collection of rubbings) or, even more so, after he died prematurely, she could express her longing and loneliness for him in exquisite and poignant song lyrics. In the other, Li Qingzhao's later years are filled not only with sadness over Zhao Mingcheng's early death, but also with shame and remorse over her remarriage and divorce. The humiliation of these events compounds the sorrow of her loss of Zhao Mingcheng and adds a deeper layer of grief to her literary expression.

So complete and compelling is this conception of Li Qingzhao that, soon after her death, if not before it, and continuing throughout the Southern Song, there developed a vogue among male authors of writing song lyrics "in the manner" of Li Qingzhao in an effort to try to replicate her sorrow. This may sound strange, but it seems less so when we recall that male poets had always enjoyed writing about or in the voice of lovelorn women. Occasionally, a certain historical woman captured writers' imaginations, and they proceeded to compose poems using her persona. This is probably what had happened with "Zhu Shuzhen"; it had certainly happened with other famous women, be they actual (e.g., Wang Zhaojun) or imaginary (e.g., Su Xiaomei 蘇小妹). What was new with Li Qingzhao is that she provided an example of a real woman who actually had written her own poems, which could now be aped and emulated in literary expression.

Here is the way the thirteenth-century poet Liu Chenweng 劉辰翁 (1232–97) responds to Li Qingzhao's song lyric on the Lantern Festival, which contrasts the speaker's current melancholy with recollected youthful gaiety on the same festival years earlier. Ironically, the song (translated later in this chapter) is set to the tune "Always Having Fun" 永遇樂. Liu wrote this preface to the song lyric he composed to the same tune "in the style of Li Yi'an": "The Lantern Festival of the *yihai* year [1275] was the first time I recited Li Yi'an's 'Always Having Fun,' and it moved me to tears. Three years have passed since then, and still, whenever I hear that song lyric, I cannot bear it. Using the same tune, I have now composed a piece in the persona of Yi'an to indirectly express my own feelings. Although the language falls short of her song, the sorrow and bitterness surpass it."[18] There is an interesting mixture of feelings here. Liu Chenweng may be so moved each time he hears Li Qingzhao's composition that he "cannot bear it" (*bu zikan* 不自堪), yet he also cannot restrain himself from imitating her song (he did this twice, actually), writing as if he were her and even priding himself on having exceeded her song in sadness. He thinks nostalgically of her nostalgia, and her deprivation has become an attraction to him as he thinks about his own reduced circumstances. Liu Chenweng, we know, lived through the Mongol invasion, which was taking place in the years that he began to match Li Qingzhao's composition. Watching his dynasty collapse, he identified with the chaos that Li Qingzhao lived through when the Northern Song fell. His poem celebrates her sorrow, as a metaphor for his own, and specifically her ability to capture in scintillating phrases the diminishment of circumstances she felt when recalling the glories of the Lantern Festival as she had known it in the Northern Song capital. Her later condition, as Liu imagines it:

此苦又誰知否	Who could ever understand such suffering?
空相對	Uselessly sitting before
殘釭無寐	A dying lamp, unable to sleep,
滿村社鼓	The village filled with the sounds of shrine drums.

---

18. Liu Chenweng, "Yongyu le bing xu" 永遇樂並序 (the first of two), *Quan Songci* 5:4087; also in *Huibian*, p. 22.

The image of a Li Qingzhao who was reduced in her later years to "wandering the rivers and lakes" until she died in destitution has powerful appeal and utility for Liu Chenweng.

Actually, the literary emulation of this image of Li Qingzhao had begun in the twelfth century. The literatus Hou Zhi 侯寘, who must have been born while Li Qingzhao was still alive, wrote the following song lyric, subtitled "Imitating the Style of Yi'an":

眼兒媚　　*To the tune "Charming Eyes"*

花信風高雨又收	The flower-bringing wind is strong, the rain ended,
風雨互遲留	But winds and showers linger.
無端燕子	Foolish, the swallows,
怯寒歸晚	Fearing the cold, return in the evening,
閒損簾鉤	Idly I lower the blinds from the hook.
彈棋打馬心都懶	Feeling too languid for chess or Capture the Horse,
擷掇上春愁	The mood only exacerbates early spring sadness.
推書就枕	Pushing books aside I go to my pillow.
鳧煙淡淡	The duck censer's smoke grows faint,
蝶夢悠悠	The butterfly dream is distant and hazy.[19]

The swallows, which nest in pairs, are unwelcome reminders of the woman's solitary condition. She lowers the blinds both because it is dusk and because she does not want to be reminded anymore. The reference to the board game Capture the Horse indicates that this song lyric is not only written "in the style" of Li Qingzhao; the woman speaking (or being described—the song can be read in the first or the third person) is Li Qingzhao. Spring brings her, consequently, nothing but sadness. This Li Qingzhao cannot even divert herself with books and writing. She pushes aside her books to go to bed early. Clearly, we are in the realm of contrived images of the celebrated woman poet. The works reliably attributed to Li Qingzhao sound nothing like this. She never mentions books and writing as an ineffective antidote to loneliness. The scene ends with the imagined Li Qingzhao lying awake, watching the censer's smoke, and unable even to clearly recall the dream of the vanished past (with her beloved husband) that haunts her waking moments.

------

19. Hou Zhi, "Yan'er mei," *Quan Songci* 3:1862; also in *Huibian*, p. 13.

In Early Anthologies

From early on an image of Li Qingzhao circulated that depicted her as a woman consumed by longing for the husband she loved so deeply, feelings that she expressed in heartfelt and moving literary compositions. This image was vague enough to admit certain variations. In the minds of some, Li Qingzhao's misery was connected with her remarriage and quick divorce. In that case, the conviction that she spent the last twenty-five years of her life in miserable circumstances, wandering the rivers and lakes, has an element of righteous chastisement in it. She brought her suffering on herself, or heaven punished her for losing her "principle" as a widow. Other readers and critics attributed her sadness primarily to Zhao Mingcheng's frequent absences and then his untimely death.

Li Qingzhao's own writings contributed to this image of her, particularly when read autobiographically. Likewise, the afterword Li Qingzhao wrote attracted attention from early times and provoked both admiration and pity.

This widespread image of Li Qingzhao probably affected the way she was represented in song lyrics anthologies in the Southern Song (and later). Male literati culture of the time had a pronounced interest in women depicted as dependent on their man and miserable in his absence. The male writers in that culture endlessly described many variations of this female stereotype in their own literary compositions, especially the song lyric. When the male anthologists encountered the exceedingly rare example of a woman who wrote her own song lyrics, they would have gravitated toward those compositions among her works that presented an image consistent with the dominant motifs of women presented by the overwhelming majority of writers, male writers. We saw other examples of this in chapter 1 with historical and, probably, imagined women poets. Such poetry of female loneliness and dependency would not only have its own appeal to male instincts; implicitly it would serve to validate the conventions of representing women in works written by men.

Two points about the argument put forward here should be emphasized. First, although Li Qingzhao's own compositions contributed to this image of her, that image took on a life and a momentum of its own as male readers and critics, whose interests it served, elaborated and romanticized it, emphasizing it through the way they selected her own works in anthologies and further elaborating it with fictionalized anecdotes. It is not inconsistent to say that Li Qingzhao herself contributed to this image but that the final elaborated and exaggerated version of it was created over time by processes and persons that had no direct connection with her and were, indeed, beyond her control. Second, it is important to bear in mind that we are speaking here of a writer whose complete literary collection seems not to have circulated widely and was eventually lost sometime after the Song anthologists were re-creating their own image of her. Consequently, the anthologies' representation of her was particularly influential. Once her song lyrics collection (*Jades for Rinsing the Mouth*) together with her literary collection were lost, the possibility of returning to an unfiltered presentation of her writings was gone forever.

We can watch the process of selective emphasis of particular themes in Li Qingzhao's work by examining the compositions that later Southern Song anthologies, which postdate the earliest one, *Elegant Lyrics for Music Bureau Songs* (1146), chose to include. The anthologies are *The Residue of Poetry from Grass Hut* (ca. 1195), *Flower Cottage Song Lyrics Anthology* 花庵詞選 (1249), *Bright Spring and White Snow* 陽春白雪 (ca. 1250), and *A Complete Genealogy of Flowering Plants* (ca. 1250). Each of the four presents significantly fewer compositions by Li Qingzhao than did *Elegant Lyrics*. The earlier anthology selected 23 of Li Qingzhao's song lyrics. The four later anthologies have altogether 14 pieces (5 in *Grass Hut*, 8 in *Flower Cottage*, 3 in *Bright Spring*, and 6 in *A Complete Genealogy*, respectively, with some overlap). It is highly likely that the compilers of the latter four anthologies had access to *Elegant Lyrics*, since that anthology was well known and apparently in wide circulation. But it is also clear that the compilers of *Grass Hut* and *A Complete Genealogy* had access to some other source as well (perhaps Li Qingzhao's song lyrics collection), since some of their selections are not found in *Elegant Lyrics*.

It is striking how much redundancy there is both among the four later anthologies and between the four and *Elegant Lyrics*. Certain "favorite" songs appear in multiple anthologies. And these favorites display certain common features. The most frequently anthologized compositions are the following, which occur in three of the four later anthologies.

如夢令   *To the tune "As If in a Dream"* (no. 5)

昨夜雨疏風驟	Last night the rain was intermittent, the wind blustery.
濃睡不消殘酒	Deep sleep did not dispel the lingering wine.
試問捲簾人	I tried asking the maid who raised the blinds,
却道海棠依舊	She said the crab apple blossoms were as before.
知否	"Don't you know?
知否	Don't you know?
應是綠肥紅瘦	The greens must be plump and the reds withered."[20]

---

20. *Jianzhu* 1.14; *Quan Songci* 2:1202.

醉花陰　　*To the tune "Drunk in the Blossom's Shadows"* (no. 20)

薄霧濃雲愁永晝	Light mist, thick vapors, sad for an endless morning.
瑞腦銷金獸	Auspicious Brain turns to ash in the gold beast censer.
時節又重陽	Again it's the Double Ninth Festival
寶枕紗廚	The precious pillow, the gauze netting,
半夜涼初透	At midnight a chill enters in.
東籬把酒黃昏後	Holding wine after sunset by the eastern fence,
有暗香盈袖	A subtle fragrance fills the sleeves.
莫道不銷魂	Don't say she's not heartbroken,
簾捲西風	The west wind lifts the blinds,
人比黃花瘦	She's more wasted than the yellow flowers.[21]

Line 2: "Auspicious Brain" (also "Dragon Brain") is a type of incense (borneol), imported from Borneo.

A few characteristics of these songs stand out. In both of them, there is a clear sense of a person being described, and that person is female. The gender of the subject may have fewer explicit markers in the first song, but the interest the person shows in flowers and the tone of the speech would have suggested a woman to readers of the time. There was a well-established tradition that preceded Li Qingzhao of writing song lyrics that either had no strong sense of a personal subject in them or had a subject whose gender was deliberately left indeterminate. Neither of those traits is found in these songs. The way they are written, presenting such a tangible sense of a woman, would have made it easy for readers to identify that person with Li Qingzhao herself.

A feature of this female subject in the first piece is that not only does she speak but she exclaims. This is a woman given to strong emotion, which shows itself in verbal outbursts. In the second piece, there is no such outburst. Yet the conceit in the closing line has much the same effect as the exclamations in the preceding song. (To understand this line, it helps to recall that chrysanthemum blossoms do not fall still fully formed to the ground. They shrink and wither on the branch.) The line is hyperbolic, intended to indicate that this woman is one who feels and suffers deeply. That is perhaps the most salient common thread between these two compositions. The

---

21. *Jianzhu* 1.52–53; *Quan Songci* 2:1205–6.

woman being described is one of acute sensibility. She is keenly distressed by phenomena that ordinary persons do not even notice (the first piece). Readers are even cautioned (the second piece) not to miss the fact that she is grief stricken, and a glimpse of her, conveniently provided by the autumnal wind that lifts the blinds, demonstrates the extent of her suffering. This woman is supremely sensitive and uniquely fragile.

It is not entirely coincidental and certainly not insignificant that the word *shou* 瘦 ("withered," "wasted," or "grown thin") occurs in each piece. It is a key word in each, the final word. These compositions are carefully crafted to present the reader with a lasting image of the woman being described as wasting away. In the first piece, it is literally the blossoms that are wasting away. But because of the well-established convention of reading blossoms as a trope for women, readers know to take the expression of despair over the fading and buffeting of the "reds" as a metaphor for the aging of the woman speaker who is so distressed by this withering.

We might say that of course these pieces were favorites of the Southern Song anthologists: they are extremely well written and effective vignettes, and they are among the most beloved and anthologized of Li Qingzhao's songs even today. But when we evaluate them this way, how objective are we being? How can we be sure we are not being influenced by the Li Qingzhao legend, which makes us see the songs as effective partly because they conform to and reinforce an image of Li Qingzhao that suited the male literary culture that embraced and propagated it, an image still with us today?

By way of contrast, we might look at some of Li Qingzhao's compositions in *Elegant Lyrics* that were not selected in any of the four subsequent Southern Song anthologies. These pieces must have been known to the compilers of those anthologies because of their presence in *Elegant Lyrics*, but they chose to avoid or deselect them in their compendia. Again, two examples are given below:

怨王孫   *To the tune "Resenting the Prince"* (no. 18)

湖上風來波浩渺	Wind comes across the lake, waves stretch endlessly.
秋已暮	At the end of autumn
紅稀香少	The red flowers are few, the fragrances slight.
水光山色與人親	They befriend me, the water's light and hills' colors,
説不盡	Impossible to describe,
無窮好	The infinite appeal of the scene.

蓮子已成荷葉老	The lotus pods are formed, the leaves droop.
清露洗	Pure dew washes
蘋花汀草	Duckweed flowers and islet grasses.
眠沙鷗鷺不回頭	Gulls and egrets napping on the sand do not turn to look
似也恨	As if they begrudge me
人歸早	Going home so early.[22]

鷓鴣天　　*To the tune "Partridge Sky"* (no. 16)

寒日蕭蕭上鎖窗	The cold sun looks bleak, as it climbs the lattice window,
梧桐應恨夜來霜	The paulownia must resent last night's frost.
酒闌更喜團茶苦	After wine, the tea's bitterness is even more to my liking,
夢斷偏宜瑞腦香	My dream interrupted, the camphor's fragrance is just right.
秋已盡	Autumn has ended,
日猶長	But the days are still long.
仲宣懷遠更淒涼	Missing his homeland made Zhongxuan more dispirited.
不如隨分尊前醉	Better to get tipsy beside the wine jug whenever you want,
莫負東籬菊蕊黃	Don't be untrue to the east fence chrysanthemums' yellow blossoms.[23]

Line 7: Zhongxuan is Wang Can 王粲 (177–217), the poet who was driven to the south from his homeland in Shandong. Upon climbing a tower in Jingzhou and gazing in the direction of his home, he composed a rhapsody expressing his longing to return.

There may be various reasons behind the omission of these pieces from the four Southern Song anthologies after *Elegant Lyrics*. But among those reasons was probably a sense that these pieces do not fit well with what was already becoming the prevalent image of Li Qingzhao. That is, these works are difficult to reconcile with the assumption that Li Qingzhao's primary literary impetus was to give expression to her longing for Zhao Mingcheng, to vent her sorrow during his travels or after his death. The woman in the first piece above, apparently on an outing to a lake and seemingly alone, is completely absorbed by the beauty of the natural scene she finds at lakeside on a late autumn day. She has no thought for a distant or deceased husband. As she starts home, she imagines that the birds find it odd that anyone could leave such an attractive place.

---

22. *Jianzhu*, "Buyi," p. 540; *Quan Songci* 2:1205.
23. *Jianzhu* 1.101; *Quan Songci* 2:1205.

In the second song, there is something untoward in the speaker's situation, but even that does not quite match what readers "expect" from Li Qingzhao. To begin with, the speaker's mood in the first stanza is quite sanguine. Her dream may have been interrupted, but the tea and incense she finds herself with upon awakening are delectable. In the second stanza she is still enjoying the long days of autumn. Her mind turns to the subject of homesickness but only to reject it as something best kept at bay. Readers would have seen a parallel between Zhongxuan (Wang Can) of ancient times and the author, since both hailed from Shandong and found themselves displaced to the southland. But the speaker in this song resolutely decides against permitting herself to follow Zhongxuan's example. She will not indulge herself in homesickness. Instead, she will follow the lead of Tao Qian, drinking a bit to console herself whenever she pleases. The chrysanthemums beside the fence, from Tao's famous poem, call to mind steadfastness and also contentment in isolation and even transcendence of one's immediate circumstances. This piece ends with yellow chrysanthemums like number 20 above, but they are invoked in a very different way. This time they are an image of fortitude and of principles, embodied in Tao's poetry of reclusion, that the speaker is determined "to be true" to. It is also rather unexpected that a woman poet would explicitly adopt a male model this way.

There is, momentarily, a sense of displacement from home in the second song, but in neither of these examples is there any suggestion of an absent or deceased husband. The lack of that element makes it hard to reconcile these compositions with an image of Li Qingzhao as a fragile and sentimental woman whose poetic expression revolves around her devotion to Zhao Mingcheng. The Southern Song anthologists were, knowingly or not, engaged in the process of refining and reinforcing certain assumptions about the poetic inspiration of Li Qingzhao, and since pieces like these did not match well with those assumptions, they passed over them.

CHAPTER 8

Saving the Widow, Denying the Remarriage
Reception during the Ming and Qing

This chapter will trace developments in Li Qingzhao's reception and reputation through the later imperial period, that is, through the Yuan, Ming, and Qing dynasties. Interesting transformations in opinions and images of Li Qingzhao took place during these dynastic periods that reveal much about changes in Chinese society, new attitudes toward women, and the problématique of women and talent in this period. New views of Li Qingzhao that emerged during this era also laid the groundwork for the further refashioning of her image in modern times. We will focus on two major themes. The first is the gradual growth of Li Qingzhao's repute as woman poet, culminating with her being firmly established by the late Ming among the preeminent women writers of earlier times. The second, contrary, trend is growing hostility to her conduct as a widow who remarried, seen in the context of the cult of the "chaste" widow in the Ming and Qing. A great tension arose between these two ways of thinking about Li Qingzhao, a tension that begged for resolution, and resolved it was, in an intriguing way, by the late eighteenth or early nineteenth century.

The Ming-Qing Rise of Women's Writing

To follow and understand Li Qingzhao's growing stature as woman poet, we must take note of the dramatic increase during Ming and Qing times in women's involvement with writing, especially poetry and the song lyric. As text producers, readers, anthologists, editors, and literary critics, women during the later imperial period came to constitute a significant and influential presence in the literary world. During the past twenty-five years, seminal studies in this area by a host of North American and Chinese scholars have transformed our understanding of women and writing in late imperial China. The traditional view that writing continued to be the domain solely of men, that women were content to remain distant from the written word, and that at most they were readers but not writers is no longer tenable. New attention to previously overlooked sources, many of which are preserved only in rare book collections in China or elsewhere, reveals that especially from the seventeenth century on women across a broad social range were extremely active as producers and transmitters of literary texts. This activity has been thoroughly documented and discussed in several recent scholarly monographs.

A few aspects of this involvement of women with writing deserve special comment. Although women had been writing in China since ancient times, as far as we know that happened as isolated, individual acts. Even Li Qingzhao wrote, so far as we can tell, as a solitary woman writer. If she received any reaction to her works from others, they were men and not women. From the late Ming and on through the Qing, however, there arose communities of women writers, especially among the privileged and educated class of *guixiu* 閨秀, or "gentlewomen." By the nineteenth century, there were female poetry clubs, literary salons made up exclusively of women or of men together with women, women who mentored other women as writers, and even women who, though they seldom if ever met, maintained a long correspondence with each other, discussing each other's writings. As Ellen Widmer has recently discussed, Qing period novels, especially *The Story of the Stone* (*Honglou meng*), were avidly read by women and elicited an outpouring of poetic comment from them.[1] The images of talented young women so vividly conveyed in the pages of that novel evidently helped to effect a rethinking of the possibilities of literary women among male and female readers alike.

There were men who took an interest in the promotion of women's writing. During the mid- and late Ming, a number of anthologies of women's

---

1. Widmer, *The Beauty and the Book*, pp. 30, 154, 225–47.

poetry appeared, compiled by men. These anthologies signal a new awareness of the gendered differences in poetry by men and by women, and a new curiosity regarding women poets who stood outside the established canon of recognized writers.[2] In the Qing, we find examples of men who actively promoted women's literacy and assembled female disciples and students around them, mentoring them and encouraging them to write. Yuan Mei 袁枚 (1716–98) is the best known of such men, or most notorious in his own time, but he was not alone. One hundred years earlier, there were already men who took it upon themselves to publish women's poetry. They began to develop justifications for women expressing themselves through writing, and they even broached the ideas that poetry came more naturally to women than to men and that women's verse contained a kind of spiritual beauty not found in the works of men.[3]

Women themselves took an active role in the preservation, transmission, and critical discussion of women's writing, not content to leave these matters solely in the hands of men.[4] In letters and in the well-established form of poems about poetry, late Ming and Qing women began the project of developing ways of thinking and criticizing women's poetry that place it in a discursive space distinct from that conventionally assigned to poetry by men. One of the strategies was to actively confront and reject the old notion that among women lack of talent is, or ensures, virtue. Gentlewomen of the period insisted on the compatibility of *cai* 才, "talent," and *de* 德, "virtue," boldly asserting that they themselves embodied both qualities.[5] Female anthologists, too, emerged to gather together, comment on, and transmit women's poetry. These anthologists show themselves to be keenly aware of the fragility of women's writing and its tendency to be lost. Beyond preservation, however, some of the anthologists are also motivated by the conviction that women's poetry anthologies compiled by men are flawed in one way or another. The anthologist Ji Xian 季嫻 (1614–83), for example, complains in her "Principles of Selection" that men tend to have low standards when dealing with women's verse, and consequently their anthologies include much mediocre or jejune poetry that actually does harm to the image of the woman

---

2. See Fong, "Gender and the Failure of Canonization."
3. Chang, "Ming-Qing Women Poets," pp. 252–53.
4. On this subject, see Fong, *Herself an Author*, pp. 121–58.
5. Chang, "Ming-Qing Women Poets," pp. 250–56.

poet.[6] The implication is that her own anthology, *Guixiu ji* 閨秀集, has higher standards.

Li Qingzhao had lived centuries before these Ming-Qing developments, but she was an important presence in them nevertheless. It was crucial for advocates of women's writing in late imperial China, both men and women, to have an earlier precedent to point to. More than any other female writer, Li Qingzhao served as that precedent. Her existence and example is adduced time and again as forerunner of the engagement with writing to which so many women in late imperial times aspired. There are a few reasons that, among all earlier writers, Li Qingzhao was thus singled out. The revival of the song lyric in the Ming and Qing was one of them. Although women composed in all the verse forms, the song lyric, with its feminine associations, held special appeal for women writers, and in this genre Li Qingzhao had no rival among earlier women. Li Qingzhao was important not simply because she had written in the song lyric form but because it was generally acknowledged that the quality of her work did not pale before that of the best male writers of her time. She was not just a known writer, she was a major writer (*dajia* 大家), a level of achievement accorded to only a handful of men.[7]

The Iconic Woman Poet

Although in her own time Li Qingzhao was recognized as an outstanding literary talent, the vast majority of comments about her qualify their praise by noting that she is, after all, a woman. The great philosopher Zhu Xi is typical in this regard. After quoting a poetic quatrain by Li Qingzhao on historical events that drew a parallel between the two dynastic conquests of high antiquity (the Shang of the Xia and the Zhou of the Shang) and Wang Mang's usurpation at the end of the Former Han, which implicitly condemned the puppet regime of Liu Yu in the north, Zhu Xi remarks, "Such lines as these, how could a woman be capable of producing them?"[8] Later in the Southern Song, in a work dated 1248, Luo Dajing offers a similar remark. In a discussion of the use of duplicated characters in poetic lines, he concludes, fittingly enough, with a reference to the opening lines of Li Qingzhao's

---

6. Fong, *Herself an Author*, p. 135.

7. On this point, see Zhang Hongsheng, "Jingdian queli yu chuangzuo jian'gou," pp. 280 and 297.

8. Zhu Xi, *Zhuzi yulei* 140.3332.

"Note by Note, Long Version" with its striking string of seven duplicated characters. "She was a woman," he observes, "and yet was able to be so creative and come up with lines as original as these."[9]

Occasionally one encounters a critic who feels compelled to elaborate on the shortcomings of women's verse, even at its best. Such a critic is the Yuan poet Yang Weizhen 楊維楨 (1296–1370), who has this to say about women poets:

> Among women who recite texts and compose literary works, the histories praise Venerable Madam Cao [Ban Zhao] of the Later Han. In recent times there have been such women as Yi'an [Li Qingzhao] and Shuzhen [Zhu Shuzhen]. They wield their literary brush, and each poem and page they compose causes their readers to be moved. Nevertheless, what they write is rooted in little knowledge and narrow intelligence, as it is hampered by a crudeness of manner. Their writing never reaches what is correct and orthodox in human sentiments and character. Women writers could never be discussed together with great masters, with all their talent and good conduct, whose writings may serve to instruct the ladies of the palace and, as the finest literature of their age, bring glory to their fathers and elder brothers.[10]

It is likely that Yang's perceptions represent those of the Song critics who keep reminding us that, for all her talent, Li Qingzhao is still a woman writer.

As we move into the Ming dynasty, however, the situation begins to change. Gradually a different type of remark begins to appear, and by the late Ming the dominant sentiment expressed concerning Li Qingzhao is that Li Qingzhao is just as good as the best of male poets. In this formulation, the idea that she is merely talented for a woman or even that she is the best among women writers is dropped. She is fully accepted as a talent that can match or rival the most talented male writers.

This development must be connected to the increased acceptance of women's writing during the late Ming and Qing. Quite apart from delivering an assessment of Li Qingzhao, such remarks were made with contemporary writing of Ming-Qing times in mind. By asserting that Li Qingzhao equaled the achievement of the best male poets of her day, the critics were fostering new views of the legitimacy of women's writing in their own literary world. Their remarks would have had dual effects: both to encourage women to

---

9. Luo Dajing, *Helin yulu*, "Yibian" 乙編 6.5308.
10. Yang Weizhen, *Dong Weizi ji* 7.19a–b; also in *Huibian*, p. 26.

write and to encourage men to be open-minded when encountering works composed by women.

The Ming literatus Yang Shen 楊慎 (1488–1559) says of Li Qingzhao: "Among writers of the song lyric in Song times, Li Yi'an is known as one of the finest. If she had worn a cap and robe (i.e., if she had been a male of the official class), she would have competed for supremacy with Qin Qi [Qin Guan] and Huang Jiu [Huang Tingjian]. It is not just that she is supreme among the women's inner quarters."[11] The determination to move Li Qingzhao and evaluations of her into the arena of male writers is perfectly clear. As it turns out, Yang Shen's second wife, Huang E 黄峨, was herself well known as a writer of song lyrics. The compositions she exchanged with her husband circulated during the couple's lifetime. The Qing critic Wang Shizhen 王士禎 (1634–1711) adds this: "Zhang Nanju divided the song lyric into two styles: delicate restraint (*wanyue* 婉約), and heroic abandon (*haofang* 豪放). In my view, Yi'an [Li Qingzhao] is the progenitor and standard-bearer of the delicate restraint style, whereas Youan 幼安 [Xin Qiji] is the leading practitioner of the heroic abandon. They are both natives of Ji'nan, my native place. It would be hard for anyone to follow in their footsteps."[12] One could argue, on the one hand, that this comment still reflects a gender bias, that by associating Li Qingzhao with the obviously more "feminine" of the two styles, Wang Shizhen is persisting in the tradition of viewing her apart from male poets. On the other hand, the delicate restraint style was a fully legitimate and respectable style of the song lyric and was not reserved exclusively for women poets. By identifying Li Qingzhao as the standard-bearer of that style, Wang Shizhen is elevating her to a preeminent position. Wang's formulation, cleverly matching the two polite names each of which contains the character *an* 安, came to be well known and influential. In later times it was referred to as the "two *an*" view of song lyric history.[13] Qing critics went so far as to assert that Li Qingzhao was actually superior to outstanding male practitioners of the song lyric. This viewpoint may be related to the notion occasionally found in Qing poetry criticism that women have a special natural endowment for poetic composition that is not found in men. Here is what the scholar, publisher, and bibliophile Li Tiaoyuan 李調元 (1734–1803) says about Li Qingzhao:

---

11. Yang Shen, *Ci pin* 詞品 2, *Huibian*, p. 35.
12. Wang Shizhen, *Huacao mengshi* 花草蒙拾, *Huibian*, pp. 75–76.
13. Shen Zengzhi 沈曾植, *Junge suotan* 菌閣瑣談, *Huibian*, p. 158.

Among the various lady writers of the Song period, Yi'an stands alone, having developed a distinctive style. Nor is she in any way inferior to Qin Qi [Qin Guan] or Huang Jiu [Huang Tingjian]. There is not a single one of her song lyrics that is not skillfully written. The refinement of her language steals the mat from underneath Mengchuan [Wu Wenying], and the splendor of her lines partakes of that achieved by Pianyu [Zhou Bangyan]. The fact is, she does not merely look down upon other women; she is able to overpower the whiskered men as well![14]

Wang Shizhen's Matching Song Lyrics

Aside from his high critical evaluation of Li Qingzhao, Wang Shizhen also wrote some sixteen of his own song lyrics matching songs by Li Qingzhao. That is, he wrote pieces that used the same rhyme words in the same order as the original piece by Li Qingzhao.[15] These matching poems were well known in Qing times. Given Wang's stature as a leading poet, anthologist, and literary critic of his day, his project of matching Li Qingzhao's song lyrics did much to enhance her stature as a writer and, indeed, to establish her as a seminal author in the genre, just as Wang had described her. Wang's matching compositions are of special interest for what they reveal about how Wang perceived and shaped the early Qing reception of Li Qingzhao. The piece that follows is perhaps the best known among Wang's matching compositions:

蝶戀花　*To the tune "Butterfly Loves Flowers"*
和漱玉詞　Matching a song lyric in *Jades for Rinsing the Mouth*

涼夜沈沈花漏凍	The chilly night drags on and on, the ornate water-clock must be frozen.
攲枕無眠	Leaning on my pillow, unable to sleep,
漸聽荒雞動	Gradually I hear the cocks in the wilds begin to stir.
此際閒愁郎不共	He shares it not, my idle sorrow in this place.
月移窗罅春寒重	The moon moves to the slit in the window, springtime chill is heavy.

---

14. Li Tiaoyuan, *Yucun cihua* 雨村詞話 3, *Huibian*, p. 97.

15. These are found in his song lyrics collection *Yanbo ci* and in another collection of song lyrics that Wang coauthored with Zou Zhimo, *Yisheng chuji*.

憶共錦裯無半縫	We shared the embroidered bedcover, not half a seam between us,
郎似桐花	He was like the paulownia blossom
妾似桐花鳳	I was the phoenix nesting in the paulownia tree.
往事迢迢徒入夢	Distant events of bygone days uselessly enter my dream,
銀箏斷絕連珠弄	The silver zither's string has broken, "Joined Pearls" plays no more.[16]

As is the norm in his matching compositions, Wang Shizhen here adopts the persona of Li Qingzhao. He is not just writing his own work that prosodically echoes hers. Nor is he content to write a work describing her as a third-person narrative. Instead, he casts his work in the first person, writing as if he were her. Wang Shizhen's admiration for the woman poet who lived so many centuries before takes this interesting form, in which he impersonates her and tries to re-create her voice.

Li Qingzhao's original poem describes a woman enduring what is evidently a temporary separation from her absent lover.[17] In the closing line, she fingers the snuff of the lamp wick, which is a conventional portent of an auspicious event, presumably the early return of the absent man. Wang Shizhen has changed the situation to one of hopeless loneliness. Wang is writing about a Li Qingzhao who has already been widowed, as we can see from his closing lines. Her memories of distant happiness "uselessly" enter her dream because it is impossible to experience them again in waking moments. The "melody" of her marital bliss with Zhao Mingcheng cannot be played again.

Wang Shizhen does not always change the circumstances this way, but he does regularly concentrate his "imitation" on the problem of Zhao Mingcheng's absence, whether temporary or permanent. Here is another of his compositions:

如夢令，其二　*To the tune "As If in a Dream," No. 2*
和李清照詞　Matching a song lyric by Li Qingzhao

簾額落花風驟	Blossoms fly past the top of the blinds in blustery winds
春思慵如中酒	Springtime longing makes me languid as if with wine.
久待不歸來	I've waited long, still he does not return.
解識相思如舊	Does he know to miss me as before?

---

16. Wang Shizhen, *Yanbo ci* 2, in *Shiwen ji* 詩文集 7, in *Wang Shizhen quanji* 2:1495; also in *Huibian*, p. 77.

17. Li Qingzhao, "Die lian hua," no. 15, *Jianzhu* 1.84; *Quan Songci* 2:1204.

堪否	How can it be endured?
堪否	How can it be endured?
坐盡寶爐香瘦	I sit until smoke from the precious censer grows thin.[18]

In this poem Li Qingzhao is waiting for her absent husband and clearly expects him to return. She is not yet widowed. But readers who recall the original poem ("Don't you know? / Don't you know? / The greens must be plump and the reds withered") will realize that Wang Shizhen has substantially altered the theme. The original work presents a woman who suddenly realizes that a storm the previous night must have beaten down most of spring's blossoms. Wang Shizhen is not content to write on such a theme. His "Li Qingzhao" song lyrics revolve entirely around the speaker's relationship with her husband. In this matching poem, the "thinness" or "sparseness" of the red blossoms in Li Qingzhao's original now becomes the thinness of the smoke from the censer, which signifies how long she has sat there, waiting in vain for her husband's return. For many readers that last word would also call to mind the frailness of the poet herself, as invoked in what had long since become Li Qingzhao's most famous line, comparing her withered frame to shriveled chrysanthemum blossoms.

Although female loneliness is central to Wang Shizhen's poems, there are a few that provide relief from this predicament, featuring instead vignettes of Li Qingzhao as a flirtatious wife united with her husband. One of Wang's matching songs, for example, ends with Li Qingzhao coyly asking her husband if he knows how to draw her eyebrows.[19] Here is another of the compositions in this mode:

浣溪沙・其二   *To the tune "Sands of the Washing Stream," No. 2*
春閨   Inner Chambers in Spring
和漱玉詞   Matching a song lyric in *Jades for Rinsing the Mouth*

漸次紅潮趁靨開	A blush spreads across her face as dimples form,
木瓜香粉印桃腮	Fragrant papaya powder dabs peach-hued cheeks.
爲郎瞥見被郎猜	Glimpsed from the corner of his eye, he dotes on her.
不逐晨風飄陌路	Do not chase the morning wind floating over the path,
願隨明月入君懷	I want to follow the bright moon into your embrace.
半床孋夢待郎來	On my side of the bed, half in dream, I wait for you.[20]

---

18. Wang Shizhen and Zou Zhimo, *Yisheng chuji* 2.4a; also in *Huibian*, p. 79.
19. "Huan xisha" 桓溪沙 no. 1, *Yisheng chuji* 3.13a; also in *Huibian*, p. 79.
20. "Huan xisha" no. 2, *Yisheng chuji* 3.13b; also in *Huibian*, p. 79.

In such a song lyric, Wang Shizhen is imitating the few compositions attributed to Li Qingzhao that offer images of female flirtatiousness, even though the attribution of those pieces, none of them attested before the Ming, is highly problematic. The late appearance does not concern Wang Shizhen. For him the flirtatious and the forlorn are complementary aspects of the Li Qingzhao he envisions. His emphasis is on the latter, yet the former goes with it in the sense of anticipating it. Both are expressions of Li Qingzhao's wholehearted devotion to her husband, which is what Wang Shizhen takes to be the beginning and the end of Li Qingzhao's literary expression.

Wang Shizhen's portraits of Li Qingzhao as flirtatious woman even broach sexual relations between husband and wife. We see hints of this in the image of Li Qingzhao waiting for her husband to join her in bed. Here is a more explicit example:

浪淘沙   *To the tune "Waves Scour the Sand"*

和漱玉詞   Matching a song lyric in *Jades for Rinsing the Mouth*

硯匣日隨身	The inkstone case accompanies her daily,
檢點殘春	As she closely inspects the late spring scene.
橫雲斜月鬪鮮新	Stretching clouds and setting moon vie in freshness.
昨夜相思曾入夢	Last night love longings entered my dream,
香雨香雲	Fragrant rain and fragrant clouds.
記得齧丹唇	I remember lips being nibbled,
似喜還嗔	Feigning pleasure then pouting.
醒來惆悵隔仙津	Awake, I sorrow that the celestial ford separates us.
欲識迴腸千萬轉	I know the feeling of innards churning, in countless revolutions,
日日車輪	As day after day the wheels turn.[21]

"Rain and clouds" (more commonly "clouds and rain") is a standard reference to sexual intercourse, so we know what kind of dream the speaker had the night before. One might ask if such a poem does not go too far, violating a certain decorum and restraint expected when "matching" a work by an earlier poet of the stature of Li Qingzhao. But again her identity as woman poet helps to explain the great license that Wang Shizhen has assumed for himself. I think it is not simply that Wang can take this kind of liberty when writing about Li Qingzhao because she is a woman—it is hard to imagine

21. "Lang taosha," *Yisheng chuji* 9.7a; also in *Huibian*, p. 79.

that he would write such lines when "matching" a male poet's composition—but, to him, "Li Qingzhao" is wholly a wife to her husband. Mostly this means she is the wife who is irrepressibly disconsolate when the husband is absent from her side, but occasionally it means that her sexual desires and dependence on him may also be allowed to show. This poem goes further than Wang's others in this regard. But it is significant that the sexual act here is not actual or in the present. It is an erotic dream instead, a dream occasioned by memories of the past. Sexual intimacy must itself be subsumed under the rhetoric of longing and nostalgia for an unrecoverable past. Sexual love is suggested but seen through the filter of the lonely widow. There is nothing remotely like this in reliable Li Qingzhao compositions.

The Multitalented Woman, "Genuine" Words

A related development that took place, particularly it seems during the Ming, was that Li Qingzhao's accomplishments were growing in breadth. She came to be thought of as skilled not just in writing but in other fields as well, including calligraphy, painting, and even music. We saw in the preceding chapter that by Yuan times her life had become the subject of lore. The Yuan and Ming multiplication of her talents was part of the growing lore concerning her. By the late Ming, the ideal of the multitalented woman, as courtesan especially or even as wife, became well established in certain circles.[22] The new image of Li Qingzhao as a woman of many talents was largely a response to and a projection of this development.

The earliest reference to Li Qingzhao as painter and calligrapher is apparently that by the Yuan figure Yuan Huai 元淮 (fl. 1335). In a poetic quatrain, "Upon Reading Li Yi'an's Writing," he refers to a painted fan and also to calligraphy in the draft script that she wrote (and which may be the "writing" in his poem title).[23] He goes so far as to say that a few of her characters are superior to those of Wang Xizhi 王羲之 (303–61), the sage of calligraphy. The painting critic and connoisseur Xia Wenyan 夏文彦 (fl. 1365), writing about a certain Lady Hu, notes that she is skilled at the zither and at calligraphy, and that her paintings of plum blossoms, bamboo, and small landscapes are also excellent. Her contemporaries, Xia reports, compared her to Li Qingzhao.

---

22. Chang, "Ming-Qing Women Poets," pp. 249–55.
23. Yuan Huai, *Jinyuan ji* 金囦集, *Huibian*, p. 27.

By the late Yuan or early Ming, a calligraphy manuscript of Bai Juyi's famous narrative poem "Song of the Pipa" 琵琶行, supposedly copied out by Li Qingzhao, was circulating. The literati Chen Fuliang 陳傅良 (1137–1203) and Song Lian 宋濂 (1310–81) had inscribed colophons on the manuscript, expressing radically different opinions of Li Qingzhao and the significance of Bai Juyi's poem in her life (to be discussed later).[24] By the late Ming, artworks attributed to Li Qingzhao had evidently become more numerous. The painter Mo Shilong 莫是龍 (fl. 1596) claimed to have purchased an ink bamboo painting done by Li Qingzhao. The poet and painter Chen Jiru 陳繼儒 (1558–1639), who was something of a champion of women's writing, reports this acquisition and expresses regret that he never saw the painting.[25] The calligraphy and painting catalogue by Zhang Chou 張丑 (1577–1643), the art collector and connoisseur, makes reference to several works attributed to Li Qingzhao.[26] There are, first, colophons in her small regular style calligraphy inscribed on a painting by the Five Dynasties artist Zhou Wenju 周文矩 (10th c.) of scenes from the life of Su Hui 蘇蕙, the fourth-century woman famous for the long palindrome poem she embroidered on silk to win back the heart of the husband who had abandoned her. Li Qingzhao's calligraphy reproduces Su Hui's poem and the "preface" to that poem subsequently written by Empress Wu Zetian. Zhang Chou also refers to a painting (or paintings) of bamboo and rocks by Li Qingzhao. Finally, Zhang Chou catalogues a manuscript copy done in Li Qingzhao's calligraphy of her song lyric "To the tune 'A Single Cutting of Plum Blossoms.'" Zhang notes that this manuscript had formerly been in the collection of the Yuan painter Ni Zan 倪瓚 (1301–74).

Sources of her own time do not refer to Li Qingzhao as a calligrapher, painter, or musician. It is a century or more after her death that such comments begin to be recorded and later still that artworks attributed to her begin to appear and circulate. Yet by Ming-Qing times, it was apparently widely believed that she had these accomplishments. She has been transformed, in other words, into the later ideal of the "multitalented lady" (*cainü* 才女 or *caifu* 才婦) of Ming courtesan culture and "scholar and beauty" (*caizi jiaren* 才子佳人) romantic fiction. Indeed, Li Qingzhao apparently had

---

24. Song Lian, "Ti Li Yi'an suoshu 'Pipa xing' hou" 題李易安所書《琵琶行》後, *Song xueshi ji* 宋學士集 32, *Huibian*, p. 30.

25. Chen Jiru, *Taiping qinghua* 太平清話 1, *Huibian*, p. 45.

26. Zhang Chou, *Qinghe shuhua fang* 清河書畫舫, *Huibian*, pp. 52–53.

her own biography in a Ming work, now lost, titled *Records of Talented Women* 才婦錄.[27] Amid the spread of this enhanced image of Li Qingzhao, I have encountered only one person in premodern times who voiced skepticism. That is the art critic Gu Wenbin 顧文彬 (1811–89). Writing about the ink bamboo paintings attributed to Li Qingzhao and the chrysanthemum paintings attributed to Zhu Shuzhen, Gu wisely asks whether these works do not come "from manly fellows who had adorned themselves with powder and eyebrow liner," that is, men impersonating the celebrated women. If we persist in believing the unlikely attributions, Gu goes on to say, probably the women themselves will be "holding back their laughter in the grave."[28]

Another persistent theme in Ming and Qing comments on Li Qingzhao is the genuineness of sentiment and circumstances found in her song lyrics. Consider the song (no. 10) that opens with these lines: "In the small courtyard outside an idle window the spring colors are vivid, / Double blinds are not lifted, the shadows are heavy, / I lean against the sill, not speaking, and pluck the jeweled zither." The great painter and calligrapher Dong Qichang 董其昌 says of them: "In these few phrases [Li Qingzhao] captures the heart and feelings of a woman of the inner quarters."[29] Similarly, commenting on another piece (no. 30) set to the tune "Remembering Her Charms," the late Ming anthologist Shen Jifei 沈際飛 (fl. 1621–34) observes, "This is the sound of the genuine" 眞聲也. "She does not 'imitate the frown' of Han and Wei period poets, or emulate the walking of the High Tang. The lines respond to the circumstances she encountered to convey her thoughts to others."[30] Responding to the same piece, Shen's contemporary, Lu Yunlong 陸雲龍, says, "It is a scene of suffering, and it is also a real scene" 苦境，亦實境.[31]

The genuine (*zhen* 眞) and the true or real (*shi* 實) had long been fundamental values in literary work, especially in *shi* poetry. But the move from that older genre to the song lyric created a problem regarding these ideals because of the very nature of the latter as an entertainment song. Song lyrics were generally not written according to the occasional and autobiographical model

27. Comments on Li Qingzhao from this work are quoted in Zhang Chou, *Qinghe shuhua fang*, *Huibian*, p. 53.

28. Gu Wenbin, *Guoyun lou shuhua ji* 過雲樓書畫記, *Huibian*, pp. 152–53.

29. Dong Qichang, *Biandu caotang shiyu* 便讀草堂詩餘 1, *Huibian*, p. 45.

30. Shen Jifei, *Caotang shiyu zhengji* 草堂詩餘正集 4, *Huibian*, p. 48.

31. Lu Yunlong, *Ci jing* 詞菁, *Huibian*, p. 58.

that dominated *shi* composition. The song lyric was written to be performed. Its nature is that the persona in the piece will be adopted by singer after singer, each one naturally striving to give a "persuasive" performance, while everyone knows that the singing is just that, a performance rather than a unique individualized expressive act. To make matters worse, male authors of song lyrics frequently wrote their compositions in the voice of women, since they would be sung by women. Consequently, the genre had a credibility problem. Spokesmen could not readily make the claims of "sincerity" and authentic emotion for it that were fundamental to the valorization of *shi* poetry. This was a major reason that the song lyric struggled to achieve the respectability accorded to *shi* and why it never enjoyed quite the repute of the older poetic form.

With Li Qingzhao, however, the problem that had dogged the song lyric genre disappeared. Critics simplistically assumed that she was speaking as herself. There was no "persona" in her compositions and certainly no calculated manipulation of a voice distinct from her own nonliterary voice. Her songs were taken to be the unmitigated expression of her true and direct response to events in her life, and they were admired for this "genuineness."

Today we find much to be dissatisfied with in this way of reading Li Qingzhao's works. It strikes us as naive and, worse still, condescending. It is something done to her works because she was a woman. Yet as we try to reconstruct the history of Li Qingzhao's reception in premodern times, we cannot pretend that this approach to her works did not exist or deny that it contributed to the appeal her writings had. Coming upon Li Qingzhao's song lyrics among the vast corpus of Song period works in that genre, Ming and Qing period critics were convinced that they were, for once, reading the sincere expressions of a twelfth-century woman. Her works were different in this aspect from those by male writers, which so often adopted voices that clearly could not be identified with the author himself. This perception that Li Qingzhao's compositions stood by themselves in this regard in song lyric history gave them special power and authority. In an era when men and women alike were looking for new means to validate women's writing, the belief that Li Qingzhao's works had this special trait fulfilled a contemporary need.

Not surprisingly, then, women song lyrics writers in Ming-Qing times felt a special affinity for Li Qingzhao. They openly imitated her famous lines, or they reworked them in ways that made their source and inspiration obvious. They "matched" individual song lyrics by Li Qingzhao, using the same rhyme words, and announced that they were doing so in prefatory notes.[32] One late Qing woman, Xu Depin 許德蘋 (d. 1861), matched each of the fifty-four song lyrics she thought Li Qingzhao had written and even named the resulting collection after Li Qingzhao's, calling it *Matching Jades for Rinsing the Mouth* 和漱玉集. An interesting intimation accompanied this canonization of Li Qingzhao as the premier woman poet of earlier times. It became commonplace to refer not just to Li Qingzhao but to her distinctive style, dubbed "the style of Yi'an" 易安體. The implication of this phrase is that Li Qingzhao wrote in a style that was her own. From this it is easy to entertain the notion that women's writing might indeed be different from men's, that women poets might by virtue of their different experience of life be able to explore subjective and affective experience different from that explored by men. This possibility itself could then serve as a strong encouragement and legitimation for aspiring literary women of later times. To the thousands of women poets of late imperial times, Li Qingzhao became the standard by which all others were judged. The highest praise that could be given a woman poet was that her compositions were in no way inferior to those of Li Qingzhao. Rarely it might even be claimed that the later woman surpassed Li Qingzhao. Whichever way the comparison was made, Li Qingzhao was the benchmark of excellence, the canonical figure of the great woman poet, the epitome of the "woman of talent" (*cainü*).

The Remarriage of Widows, Yuan through Qing

The concurrent development that affected the conception of Li Qingzhao during the later imperial period comprised changes in attitudes toward widows and the possibility of their remarriage. In the Song period, as we have seen, the remarriage of widows was not unusual, at all levels of society, yet there was already some stigma attached to the practice, stemming from the old Confucian belief that a woman who served two husbands was analogous to a man who served two rulers. According to this way of thinking, remarriage after a first husband's death showed lack of principle and loyalty to that first husband. In Li Qingzhao's time, the preservation of a widow's "chastity" by not remarrying was an ideal or precept that was often not followed in practice. In her new study Beverly Bossler discusses the increased

---

32. Numerous examples of all manner of imitation, borrowing, transformation, and matching are given in Zhang Hongsheng, "Jingdian queli yu chuangzuo jian'gou," pp. 289–304.

emphasis on notions of female fidelity, including that of a widow remaining "loyal" to her late husband, that appeared in the Southern Song. She traces this to the political crises and betrayals as well as the violence against women and female martyrdom that were widespread upon the fall of the Northern Song. Still, she finds that "overall the topic of female fidelity remained a relatively minor theme in Southern Song social and moral discourse."[33] But in the centuries that followed, through the late imperial period, the widow's faithfulness to the memory of her husband came to be viewed as more and more important, the remarriage of widows was viewed with less tolerance, and the ideal of the rigidly faithful widow was more stringently applied in day-to-day life, as the central government eventually became actively involved in the promotion of a cult of widow's chastity.

The history of this gradual hardening of attitudes regarding widows and their ability to remarry is long and complex, involving political, legal, institutional, and ideological factors. Three critical historical moments contributed to the process, between Li Qingzhao's time and the late Qing dynasty. The first occurred during the Yuan dynasty, when the Mongol rulers introduced legal changes that had major effects on marriage law, women's property rights, and women's marital condition more generally.[34] Soon after the Mongols conquered China, the ruler Khubilai issued a decree stating that upon a man's death his younger brother or even his son (provided, of course, that she was not his own mother) had the right to marry the wife of the deceased. This was an imposition of levirate marriage practices, an old Mongolian custom, on the newly conquered Chinese. In the Chinese view, this was a horrific practice, since for a son or younger brother to marry the wife of an older male in the family was considered incest. The Chinese had long been aware of this custom among the northern nomadic peoples and considered it clear evidence of their barbarism. Within just five years, the law was relaxed. Levirate marriage was still permitted, but a widow could escape it by declaring that she would remain chaste. A public vow of chastity would be required, and a woman could be prosecuted if anyone showed that she had violated her vow.

---

33. Bossler, *Courtesans, Concubines, and the Cult of Female Fidelity*, p. 252.

34. I am summarizing here the findings in Birge, *Women, Property, and Confucian Reaction in Sung and Yüan China*, pp. 200–282.

Within a few years, another crucial change was made in property law. It had always been the case in China that the dowry a woman brought into a marriage was considered her own property. If subsequently she was widowed or divorced and left her husband's family, either to remarry or to return to her natal family, she took her dowry with her. But in 1303 the Ministry of Rites issued a directive that stipulated that a woman who left her husband's family, whether as a widow or as a divorcee, forfeited her possession of all property she had brought into the marriage. Her dowry became the property of her in-laws. Soon, other regulations were issued that further compromised a widow's ability to control her life. Traditionally, a widow had been free either to remarry or, if she chose, to leave her in-laws and return to her natal family. But under the next Yuan emperor, Wuzong (r. 1307–11), it was decreed that if a woman chose to remain chaste, she must do so in her in-laws' household. Moreover, if she were to remarry, the remarriage would be arranged by her in-laws, and the betrothal gifts would become the property of the in-laws. These regulations altered in key ways the legal status of widows, transferring the right to arrange a new marriage from widows and their own parents to their in-laws.

These Yuan developments reflect a perhaps unexpected convergence of Mongolian steppe customs with Confucian ideals promoted by the Learning of the Way school of Zhu Xi and Huang Gan 黄榦 (1152–1221). It was Mongol custom for a widow to remain in her in-laws' family, with that family controlling her marital future and taking over her possessions. Yet these practices coincided ideologically with the patrilineal ideals of the Learning of the Way school. When these ideals were first articulated in the late Southern Song, they marked a radical shift from Chinese traditions concerning women, property rights, and remarriage. Zhu Xi's follower Huang Gan, in the early thirteenth century, had advocated that widows avoid remarriage and remain chaste, remain in their in-laws' home, and relinquish control of their personal property and share it with their husband's family. Now, thanks to foreign conquest and the ascendancy of Learning of the Way scholars at the Mongol court, the Yuan institutionalized Huang Gan's ideals, making them law. Moreover, many of these Yuan developments persisted through later imperial times. The law that prevented a widow from taking her dowry with her when she left her husband's family was written into Ming and Qing legal codes.

Complementing the changes it introduced in remarriage and property law, the Yuan government began actively to promote widows' chastity. It did this by directing local officials to identify and report the names of "meritorious"

widows, whose virtue would then be officially recognized by the issuance of
an insignia to be displayed on their doors and rewarded with exemption from
corvée labor. The criteria for such rewards were spelled out: the woman had
to have been widowed before the age of thirty, to have made a public vow
of chastity, and to have kept her vow until she was fifty. This was the first
time in Chinese history that widows' chastity was systematically promoted
throughout the empire. The Yuan criteria for identifying virtuous widows
were carried over into Ming and Qing times.

Quite apart from the lure of official recognition and corvée labor exemption, the reforms that the Yuan introduced gave widows new reason to avoid
remarriage. Women had to come to terms with a drastic diminishment of
control over their property and marital fate. The only way a widow could
retain possession of whatever property she had brought into her marriage
was to vow chastity and remain in her in-laws' family. That was also the only
way she could avoid having a second husband not of her own or her parents'
choosing forced upon her. Also, levirate marriage was eventually (in 1330)
banned altogether for Chinese women. So a woman who chose to remain in
her husband's family knew that she would not be forced to marry a brother-
in-law. Faced with greatly curtailed rights and other options, it is not surprising that many widows yielded to the pressures of the new regulations and
chose to take a vow of lifelong chastity.

The second critical moment occurred during the latter part of the Ming
dynasty. The resurgence of the School of the Way movement in the fifteenth
century has been explained by scholars as an attempt by literati, in reaction to
early Ming imperial despotism, to reaffirm a basis for their involvement in
and ultimately control over state governance and policy. Philosophers and
literati alike stressed the importance of the Five Relationships in an effort to
re-Confucianize the bureaucracy. A wave of shrine building ensued, beginning in the late fifteenth century and gaining momentum through the sixteenth, carried out mostly by local officials who were eager to show that they
embraced the new moralism. Shrines were built to commemorate the lives
and sacrifices of persons who lived up to Confucian ideals. The great majority of these shrines were dedicated to men, not women, who had distinguished themselves through exemplary conduct or self-sacrifice. There were
Shrines to Local Worthies 鄉賢祠, which honored local men of virtue,
and Shrines to Eminent Officials 明宦祠, which extolled men who had
served as officials in the locale but were not natives of the place. At the same
time, a smaller number of shrines were established honoring women who

were considered exemplars of Confucian virtue. Extending such recognition to women made the revivalist enterprise more comprehensive and complete. The men thus commemorated had distinguished themselves by virtuous conduct in or out of office. In the case of women, the great majority celebrated with shrines were martyrs—women who died to preserve their virginity or their chastity as widows.

In her study of shrines dedicated to chaste widows of the mid-Ming period, Katherine Carlitz traces the growth of shrine construction in the Jiangnan region through an examination of local gazetteers.[35] During the Song and Yuan periods, local gazetteers generally do not give attention to faithful widows, and there are nearly no shrines dedicated to their memory listed in Song sources. But lists of such women regularly appear in gazetteers from the late fifteenth century onwards, and by the sixteenth century memorial arches and shrines dedicated to these women could be found in every county. Ming society was in the grip of a fervor for female "fidelity." T'ien Ju-k'ang has documented an unprecedented number of lifelong widows commemorated in Ming local histories.[36] A peculiar feature of this fervor was the valorization of the practice of widows' suicide, that is, a widow takes her life to follow her husband in death (*xunsi* 殉死). Although this practice was viewed with great ambivalence by many at the time, including some Ming emperors and intellectuals, in some quarters it was considered the ultimate demonstration of a woman's devotion to her late husband. Widows' suicide, not merely their refusal to remarry, accounts for a large percentage of the mid- and late Ming shrines dedicated to widows. Such suicide was also prominently featured in poetry and drama of the period. In fact, as Carlitz points out, the cult of the widow as *lienü* 烈女, or martyr, has connections to the Ming interest in *qing* 情, "emotions, sympathy, passion." There is more than moralistic impulse at work in this celebration of the martyred widow. There is also poetic appeal in the figure of the suffering woman, often widowed while still young, an outpouring of sympathy and commiseration for her heroic frailty and suffering, culminating in her decision to join her husband in death. As Carlitz shrewdly observes, in treatments of this new poetic subject, we often find the *lienü*'s vulnerability described with overtones of sexual vulnerability.[37]

---

35. Carlitz, "Shrines."
36. T'ien, *Male Anxiety and Female Chastity*, pp. 39–69.
37. Carlitz, "Shrines," p. 636.

The third moment in the evolving attitudes toward widows was reached during the Qing dynasty, which culminated during the High Qing reigns of Yongzheng 雍正 (1723–35) and Qianlong 乾隆 (1736–95). The state promotion of the ideal of widows' chastity during this period is a well-known phenomenon. The Qing government took a far more activist role than had either its Yuan or Ming predecessor in encouraging and rewarding faithful widows who did not remarry. Whereas in earlier periods government recognition of chaste or martyred widows was primarily a local matter, or at most a central government response to local requests for such recognition, during the Qing the central government itself took the lead in mandating an empirewide program that systematically searched out and conferred imperial honors, usually posthumously, upon such widows and provided funds for the construction of shrines or arches commemorating them.[38] The numbers alone are impressive. As Susan Mann has noted, between 1644 (the start of the dynasty) and 1736, some 6,840 widows in the Jiangnan region received imperial honors for their fidelity. In 1733, 120 widows were so recognized in Suzhou alone.[39] If we could calculate the number of honors given for the entire eighteenth century through the end of the Qing empire, it would certainly be in the tens of thousands. As some early foreign visitors to the Qing remarked, by the nineteenth century these shrines and arches were a ubiquitous feature of the Chinese landscape.

Why was the Manchu dynasty so interested in promoting chastity among widows, causing it to embark on such a far-reaching campaign? In her recent study of the phenomenon, Janet M. Theiss argues that the Qing government's obsession with widows' fidelity was part of its larger commitment to *jiaohua* 教化, or the instruction and improvement of the moral fiber of its populace. In fact the government regularly addressed itself to what it considered problematic social issues and behaviors, including what it considered the erosion of filial piety and family unity, extravagant marriage and funeral observances, heterodox religious sects, rowdiness at operas, female infanticide, and wanton mixing of the sexes in public places. A steady stream of imperial edicts and court directives, statutes, and substatutes exhorted magistrates and other local officials to adopt an extremely proactive stance and, first, to tour their locale and inform themselves of the conduct of its

---

38. These issues are discussed at length in Theiss, *Disgraceful Matters*, pp. 25–54.
39. Mann, *Precious Records*, p. 24.

residents and, second, to find ways of mobilizing the local bureaucracy to intervene and actively moralize and improve the lives of the people. This was a substantially new vision of the role of the imperial bureaucracy in the civilizing mission. The Qing rulers were no longer content to think of the official class as moral exemplars, in the old Confucian sense, who themselves set a high moral standard that inspired others to follow suit. The Qing rulers envisioned a morally activist state bureaucracy that directly intervened to enhance the virtuous conduct of the populace.

As it extolled faithful widows, the Qing introduced an important break with the past. Manchu emperors unequivocally rejected widows' suicide, which had been a key part of the cult of widow chastity in the Ming. Yongzheng and Qianlong after him denounced this practice as depraved and refused to allow imperial honors for any woman who had opted for it. Interestingly, the Qing continued to honor woman martyrs who died resisting rape or forced remarriage. But they rejected the practice of following one's husband in death as irresponsible. Indeed, one can readily imagine the destabilizing effect the custom had on society. Who would take care of the young children or care for the elderly in-laws? Imperial edicts also inveigh against the practice as cowardly. It was far more difficult and heroic, they argue, for a woman to sustain herself through, possibly, decades of widowhood than to end her life in one reckless act.

This rejection of widows' suicide served the interests of the Manchu rulers in more than one way. It made it easier for them to fit their state cult of chaste widows into their larger claim of *jiaohua* intent. They characterized widows' suicide as a popular perversion of Confucian values. By labeling it as dishonorable, they could say that they were helping to educate, purify, and civilize the people. In the first decades after the Manchu conquest, moreover, suicide by widows was largely seen as analogous to the martyrdom of Ming officials who killed themselves rather than live under Manchu rule. The fidelity of widows who ended their lives was a reminder of the single-minded devotion of Ming loyalists who killed themselves, or simply of Ming loyalism generally. For political reasons, therefore, in addition to whatever moral high ground they claimed, the Manchu rulers were not inclined to accept widows' suicide, much less to glorify it.

A widow's ongoing acceptance of her lot, however, and the preservation of her fidelity to her deceased husband, matched well with the social (and political) values of loyalty, stoic resignation, self-denial, and subjugation of personal interest to those of the larger social unit that the Manchu rulers sought to cultivate in the people they ruled over as foreign conquerors. In this light we are able to understand why, among all the moral values and exemplars they promoted, the Manchu rulers seem to have given primacy to that of the faithful widow. This type of woman, who patiently abided in difficult circumstances, who was content to manifest her integrity through dutiful acquiescence, became an apt epitome of the personality and values it was in the interest of the Manchu rulers to propagate among the Chinese over whom they ruled.

Moral Condemnation of Li Qingzhao

In the comments on Li Qingzhao made by Ming critics, we can see the influence of the hardening of attitudes regarding widows' faithfulness to their deceased husbands. Li Qingzhao's decision to remarry begins to be denounced in a way we do not find in Song period sources. In those early sources, as exemplified by Hu Zi's remark about those who laughed at her for marrying Zhang Ruzhou and then quickly divorcing him, it was more apt to be the unhappy outcome of the second marriage that provoked criticism rather than the fact that it took place at all. That is because widows' remarriage was widespread in Li Qingzhao's day, if already perceived as falling short of an ideal. But by Ming times, and even more so during the Qing, remarriage itself is enough to incite harsh criticism.

An example is found in a colophon the Ming literatus and moralist Song Lian wrote on a copy of Bai Juyi's "Song of the Pipa" that was attributed to Li Qingzhao, that is, believed to have been copied out by her in her own calligraphy.[40] The scroll that Song Lian saw already had a colophon that had been added to it by the Southern Song literatus Chen Fuliang. Chen's colophon does not survive, but it evidently expressed commiseration for Li Qingzhao and her remarriage. This prompted Song Lian to add his own colophon, taking issue with Li Qingzhao's conduct and Chen's sympathy.

Song Lian thinks that Li Qingzhao had special reasons for copying out Bai Juyi's poem. He supposes that she did so because she identified (after her remarriage and divorce) with the melancholy merchant's wife in the poem, who had formerly been a celebrated performer in the capital but, as she aged and lost her good looks, found herself less in demand and eventually married a traveling merchant, who often left her living on their houseboat alone

---

40. Song Lian, "Ti Li Yi'an suoshu 'Pipa xing' hou," *Song xueshi ji* 32, *Huibian*, p. 30.

(where Bai Juyi encountered her) as he went off to trade his goods. In short, Song Lian thinks that the lonely and abandoned merchant's wife functions in Li Qingzhao's mind as her own self-image. If Song Lian has in mind Song period reports that after her divorce Li Qingzhao spent her remaining years "wandering the rivers and lakes," which seems likely, the parallel between the two women would seem all the more plausible to him. The key passage of Song Lian's colophon is a poem he wrote expressing his reservations about what Chen Fuliang had said and about the way Li Qingzhao had conducted herself. This is the poem:

佳人薄命紛無數	Ill-fated beautiful women have always been many,
豈獨潯陽老商婦	The aging merchant's wife of Xunyang is hardly unique.
青衫司馬太多情	The black-robed military officer had too much emotion,
一曲琵琶淚如雨	Writing his pipa song his tears flowed like rain.
此身已失將怨誰	You've discarded your body, whom can you blame?
世間哀樂常相隨	Joy and sorrow in this life often follow each other.
易安寫此別有意	Copying this out, Yi'an had her special meaning,
字字似訴中心悲	Word after word seems to tell her own heart's sorrow.
永嘉陳侯好奇士	Master Chen of Yongjia, an outstanding gentleman,
夢裏謬爲兒女語	Composed foolish and childish words in a dream.
花顏國色草上塵	A pretty face and fatal beauty are but dirt on the grasses,
朽骨何堪污唇齒	Why defile our lips with talk of decaying bones?
生男當如魯男子	A boy should grow up to be like the fellow of Lu,
生女當如夏侯女	A girl should grow up to be like Xiahou's niece.
千年穢跡吾欲洗	I wish to wash away the pollution of a thousand years,
安得潯陽半江水	How can I get half the Yangzi River at Xunyang?

The first four lines concern Bai Juyi and his excessively emotional poem about the pipa player who had become a merchant's wife. But I suspect that line 5 is already meant to apply to Li Qingzhao as well as to the merchant's wife. The notion of "throwing one's body away" would seem to be more in line with Ming ideas about unchaste widows than with a former professional entertainer entering into her first marriage. The fourth couplet refers to Li Qingzhao's identification with the merchant's wife. The fifth couplet expresses disapproval of Chen Fuliang's sympathy for these women.

Song Lian puts his most trenchant criticism in his closing lines. The conduct of Li Qingzhao is characterized as so unclean that it is defiling even to speak of it. The legacy of what she did needs to be cleansed (it has already lasted hundreds of years and threatens to last one thousand), but so sullied is her conduct that it is going to require half the Yangzi River's waters (at Xunyang, where Bai Juyi's poem is set) to wash it away. The penultimate couplet alludes to two exemplars of virtue, the first known for his resistance to sexual temptation and the second for her familial loyalty. The fellow of Lu, referred to in *Family Sayings of Confucius*, is someone who refused to give shelter to a neighbor widow whose dwelling collapsed during a storm. When she pleaded to be let into his house, he refused, speaking to her through the window, because he feared that if he allowed her in he might be tempted to do something that would compromise his "virtue." Confucius is said to have praised this conduct.[41] Xiahou's niece is the woman known in history as the wife of Zhang Fei 張飛 (d. 221) of Three Kingdoms fame. She had been raised by her uncle, who served the Wei kingdom, but was kidnapped and eventually married to Zhang Fei, a key Shu-Han kingdom general. Years later, Xiahou was killed by troops under Zhang Fei's command. Although her uncle was a military enemy, the niece requested permission to give him a proper burial, out of a sense of indebtedness and family loyalty.[42] Song Lian's meaning is that Li Qingzhao failed on two counts. Unlike the Fellow of Lu, she succumbed to sexual temptation when she remarried. And unlike Zhang Fei's wife, who had much more compelling reasons to spurn her deceased uncle, she was "unfaithful" to her former husband.

A similarly harsh assessment of Li Qingzhao is given early in the Ming by the bibliophile Ye Sheng 葉盛 (1420–74). An entry in his diary begins by quoting one of Li Qingzhao's song lyrics (no. 43), which contains the line "The things are right, the person wrong, everything is over" 物是人非事事休, and ends with the speaker wondering if the little boats found at Twin Streams, where the spring scene is said to be lovely, could possibly bear the weight of such a load of sorrow as she feels. Ye Sheng then adds this comment:

> Teasing out the meaning of her words, we wonder if they were written subsequent to her afterword to *Records on Metal and Stone*? Or was it after she remarried, to Zhang Ruzhou? Wenshu [Li Gefei] was unlucky to have such a daughter, and Defu [Zhao Mingcheng] was unlucky to have such a wife 文叔不幸有此女，德夫不幸有此婦. Are not her words and writings truly what is known as the tools of inauspiciousness, which will ensure ridicule of her for a thousand ages?[43]

---

41. *Kongzi jiayu zhuzi suoyin* 10.16/18/29–19/4.
42. *Wei lue* 魏略, quoted in Pei Songzhi's commentary, in Chen Shou, *Sanguo zhi* 9.272; cf. Bamanzi, "Guanyu Zhang Fei qizi."
43. Ye Sheng, *Shuidong riji* 水東日記 21, *Huibian*, p. 31.

Looking at the way Ye Sheng's entry is structured, opening with a quotation of the full text of one of Li Qingzhao's best-known song lyrics, followed by this extreme condemnation, one suspects that he is greatly bothered by the acclaim given to Li Qingzhao's song lyrics by enthusiastic readers and critics. Ye Sheng wants to register a dissenting opinion. He insists on relocating her admired song lyric in a version of her biography that does not overlook the fact of her remarriage even after she proclaimed her lasting affection for and devotion to Zhao Mingcheng in her afterword. The snide trick he pulls of turning her words against her ("the person is wrong") is reminiscent of the ridicule that Hu Zi recorded back in Li Qingzhao's own day. But the pronouncements Ye Sheng goes on to deliver about Li Qingzhao as a disgrace to her father and Zhao Mingcheng go far beyond what anyone said in the Song dynasty. In pre-Ming times, no one ever condemned Li Qingzhao's conduct so categorically or with such moralistic certainty. It seems that in Ye Sheng's mind a widow's remarriage is no longer a defensible option.

Ye Sheng was not alone in this assessment. It becomes commonplace in Ming sources for Li Qingzhao to be compared with other infamous "fallen women" of Chinese history, that is, other women who compromised their integrity by violating social and sexual taboos. Dong Gu 董穀 (fl. 1516) pairs her with Cai Yan 蔡琰 of the late Han, as two women of literary talent who "lost their virtue."[44] (The fact that Cai Yan's first remarriage to a Xiongnu chieftan followed her abduction by invaders is overlooked in this assessment of her.) The late Ming literatus Jiang Zhihuai 江之淮 compares Li Qingzhao unfavorably with another Han dynasty lady, Zhuo Wenjun 卓文君, who eloped with Sima Xiangru 司馬相如.[45] Years later, when Xiangru fell in love with a younger woman, Zhuo Wenjun vented her disappointment and anger in poetry and thus won back Xiangru's affection. To Jiang Zhihuai, although Wenjun had disgraced herself by eloping, her later humiliation, though temporary, made her worthy of pity. He has no such sympathy for Li Qingzhao. He says this of her remarriage to Zhang Ruzhou: even peach blossoms fallen into a river and carried away with it are no comparison. He means that the fallen peach blossoms may be wanton in their direction and "conduct," but one could not expect any more of them. Li Qingzhao's wantonness was deliberate and consequently far more deserving of condemnation.

---

44. Dong Gu, *Bili zacun* 碧里雜存 A, *Huibian*, p. 40.
45. Quoted in Zhao Shijie 趙世傑, *Gujin nüshi* 古今女史 1, *Huibian*, p. 56.

This negative opinion of her, when the focus is on her conduct rather than exclusively on her literary work, can be found in the "inner quarters" as well. An intriguing mix of admiration for her literary talent and disapproval of her conduct, with the latter being given the final say, occurs in a quatrain by the late Ming woman poet Zhang Xianjing 張嫻婧:

讀李易安《漱玉集》   *Upon Reading Li Yi'an's* Jades for Rinsing the Mouth

從來才女果誰儔	Among talented women since earlier times, who could compare?
錯玉編珠萬斛舟	Her carved jades and strung pearls could fill a large boat.
自言人比黃花瘦	She claimed she was more frail than the withered yellow blossom.
可似黃花奈晚秋	But at least the yellow blossom can endure late autumn.[46]

This is, again, an instance of someone turning Li Qingzhao's own words against her. Zhang Xianjing means that although Li Qingzhao claimed she was more frail and withered than the wilting chrysanthemum, the flower can yet withstand the harsh weather of the autumn in which it blooms, whereas Li Qingzhao could not endure the "autumn" of her later years as a widow and decided to seek the comfort of remarriage even though doing so compromised her integrity. We should not be surprised to find such a sentiment being expressed by a Ming period woman, even a woman writer. Attitudes that we perceive today to be restrictive to women's control over their lives were widely accepted by women of Ming and Qing times, even as some of them explored latitudes within those confines.

Disbelief and Exasperation

A slightly different note is sounded in a few Ming and early Qing sources. It combines the two contrary attitudes toward Li Qingzhao: growing admiration, on the one hand, for her stature as a woman of literary talent and precursor of latter-day female poets, and, disapproval, on the other, for the widow who proved unable to fulfill her obligation to remain loyal to her deceased husband. The potential for conflict between these two ran deep because Li Qingzhao's most admired literary works were those believed to embody her devotion to Zhao Mingcheng, both when he was alive and when

---

46. Zhang Xianjing, *Cuilou ji* 翠樓集, *Huibian*, p. 64.

he was dead. Many of the comments examined above have been focused predominantly, if not exclusively, on one of the two topics or have privileged the importance of one (usually the failed widow) over the other, as did Zhang Xianjing. The comments below explicitly call attention to the contradiction between the two and express puzzlement over how the two sides could possibly be combined in one person.

This is what the Ming book collector Lang Ying 郎瑛 (1487–1556) writes about her:

> Zhao Mingcheng, whose polite name was Defu, was the middle son of Lord Qingxian [Zhao Tingzhi]. He composed *Records on Metal and Stone* in [thirty] chapters.[47] His wife, Li Yi'an, was a hero among literary women. She too was broadly learned about antiquity and mastered arcane knowledge. Her literary works are limpid and delicate, and her *Jades for Rinsing the Mouth* circulates in the world. The various sources concerning her all say that she was of one mind with her husband, and so they were extremely close to each other and deeply in love. When I read her afterword to *Records on Metal and Stone*, I knew that it was true. But as for her remarrying Zhang Ruzhou, that one event, I simply do not understand how she could have done so. Alas, there is little to separate her from Cai Yan. This is how readily sexual desires can lead a person astray. Even the palace gentleman [Cai Yong] was not spared![48]

Lang Ying's entry is found in a chapter in his miscellany devoted to "Morality and Principle," and in this chapter he discusses many historical examples of conduct that raises troubling moral issues or questions about human nature. He is familiar with Li Qingzhao's literary works, and he has read various sources that assert the deep intellectual and romantic bond between Li Qingzhao and Zhao Mingcheng. He finds confirmation of this bond in Li Qingzhao's own afterword. All of this leaves him at a loss to understand how her remarriage to Zhang Ruzhou ever could have happened. Confronting the inexplicable contradiction between Li Qingzhao's affection and her remarriage, Lang Ying takes recourse in the concept of the power of sexual desire to substitute lust for reason. Lang Ying cannot think of any way that reason, by itself, could account for Li Qingzhao's remarriage. This is the crux of the dilemma. Ideological and sociological changes between Li Qingzhao's time and the mid-Ming blind literati like Lang Ying to the good reasons that a

---

47. I have corrected Lang Ying's wording. He actually says "one thousand" chapters, which is clearly an error.

48. Lang Ying, *Qixiu leigao* 17.252; also in *Huibian*, p. 32.

woman in Li Qingzhao's situation might have had to choose remarriage—quite apart from how she had felt about her first husband—as a rational decision rather than as a surrender to irrational sexual impulses. Cai Yan again is unfairly used as the negative exemplar of a woman overwhelmed by lust. The reference to her father, Cai Yong 蔡邕 (133–92), means, I believe, that even such an upright and accomplished gentleman as Cai Yong could not avoid having such a daughter—that is the corrupting power of sexual urges.

We find much the same type of bewilderment in the first part of Jiang Zhihuai's entry on Li Qingzhao: "Among husbands and wives who have, since ancient times, become the best of friends, none could compare with Li Yi'an and Zhao Mingcheng. As beautiful young lady and talented young man, for a thousand ages no couple can match them. But when Defu [Mingcheng] died she married Zhang Ruzhou. What could she possibly have been thinking?"[49] We clearly see here the projection of the Ming period "scholar-beauty" romantic ideal on the Song period husband and wife. But Li Qingzhao's remarriage after Zhao Mingcheng's death is a stark violation of those ideals, and as such Jiang Zhihuai simply cannot understand it. This perception of something gone grossly wrong in Li Qingzhao's conduct, something that defies logic and understanding, is crucial to the next critical step in the Ming-Qing reception history of Li Qingzhao.

Denying the Remarriage

Something had to give. Somehow the conflict between the radically different ways of thinking about the most famous of earlier literary women had to be resolved. Ultimately, the solution was to deny that she had ever remarried, and this denial, which was not easily accomplished given the range of Song sources that refer to her remarriage, eventually became the scholarly and popular consensus. This consensus was achieved only after a lengthy period of increasingly elaborate (and contradictory) scholarly inquiry into the nature and meaning of the Song sources. The denial became a kind of scholarly project, even a cause célèbre, in Qing scholarly circles.

It seems inevitable that the resolution would have taken the path it did, not just because it is easier to exonerate a sympathetic person than to consign

---

49. Jiang Zhihuai and Zhao Shijie, *Gujin nüshi* 1, *Huibian*, p. 56.

her to unending castigation, but also because literary works (her writings) have an ongoing living presence, whereas historical sources (the Song period biographical materials) seem to grow older and mustier with time. Readers and critics of the Ming and Qing could readily avail themselves of Li Qing-zhao's song lyrics in anthologies and, eventually, in reconstituted editions of her works. Meanwhile, the seven or eight Song period historiographical sources that referred to her remarriage became increasingly obscure in the sea of historical literature, which grew exponentially with the passage of each new century. Finally, literary works, especially when perceived to be written in the first person, have an advantage over historiographical literature. One picks up a poem or song lyric attributed to Li Qingzhao and one has the distinct sense of a voice speaking, quite without mitigating filters, directly and unabashedly. This is the power of poetry. It is different from historiographical writings, in which the gulf between the narrative voice and the many subjects being covered, even when the author lived at roughly the same time as the persons and events he is writing about, is all too obvious.

The resolution of the growing conflict seems to have been entirely one-sided. That is, no one sought to resolve it by arguing that Li Qingzhao was not a good poet after all—that her writings were trivial and that nothing would be lost by rejecting them on the grounds of her moral failings as a widow. The high regard for her literary talent made this an untenable position.

Instead, then, the solution was to assert that she had never remarried. The first person to make this claim appears to have been the late Ming literatus Xu Bo 徐燉 in his miscellany *Xushi bijing* 徐氏筆精.[50] Xu seems to have been something of a maverick scholar, given to offering unconventional views, often borne of misunderstandings of historical fact (according to the notice on his work in the *Siku quanshu* catalogue).[51] Regardless, what he had to say about Li Qingzhao anticipated what much more eminent and learned scholars would argue during the next dynasty.

His entry on Li Qingzhao, boldly titled "Yi'an's Remarriage," opens by quoting Hu Zi's account of her, including references to her remarriage and quick divorce. Then Xu Bo repeats Hu Zi's quotation of the lines from her letter of gratitude to Qi Chongli. These, Xu Bo, announces, are unreliable

---

50. Xu Bo, *Xushi bijing* 7, *Huibian*, p. 52.
51. Ji Yun et al., *Siku quanshu zongmu tiyao* 23.2499–500.

slander, something that Li Qingzhao could not have written. Xu Bo thinks
that he knows something about Li Qingzhao that no one else knows. He goes
on to quote the passage near the end of Li Qingzhao's afterword, in which
she specifies the period of "thirty-four" years from the time of her marriage
to the time of the afterword's composition. Xu Bo then continues in his
own words:

> She composed this afterword in the second year of the Shaoxing reign [1132],
> when she was fifty-two. She was already old! The daughter-in-law of Lord
> Qingxian [Zhao Tingzhi] and the wife of a prefectural governor [Zhao
> Mingcheng], there certainly would have been no reason for her to remarry.
> Today, the versions of the "Afterword to *Records on Metal and Stone*" found in
> other sources are all incomplete. It is only the old copy kept in my house that
> has the complete text. We do not know who first came up with the notion that
> she remarried, but it is nothing but baseless slander of a virtuous lady.

Xu Bo's dates are slightly off—his text contains the 1132 date of the preface—but this does not substantially affect his argument. His point is that at
age fifty-two (or forty-nine, as most would now have it) Li Qingzhao would
not have even considered remarriage, much less since she was the daughter-
in-law and former wife of such high-ranking officials. Xu Bo must know that
a widow of such status would have been entitled to a government stipend.

Xu Bo points to the superiority of his version of the afterword as the basis
for his revisionist assertion about Li Qingzhao's life. There is something
intriguing about this. Scholarly arguments often stand or fall on claims of
access to a superior version of a text. There is, in fact, some basis for Xu Bo's
claim. He goes on, in his entry, to identify three other "versions" of the afterword, quotations of it, actually, in widely circulating sources that he is aware
of: Hong Mai's *Rongzhai suibi* (Southern Song), Hu Yinglin's miscellany (late
Ming), and a prose anthology edited by Chen Jiru (late Ming).[52] He adds that
none of these contains a complete version of the text. What he really means
is that none of them contains the passage in which Li Qingzhao says that
thirty-four years had passed between the time of her marriage and her
writing of the afterword. Xu Bo is right about this. So he is, in a sense, correct
to claim that he has special knowledge of Li Qingzhao's situation. Unfortunately for his argument, however, Xu overlooks the fact that although the key
sentence is indeed omitted in Hong Mai's version of the text, at the end of

---

52. Hong Mai, "Zhao Defu jinshi lu" 趙德甫金石錄, *Rongzhai suibi* 5.684–86; Hu Yinglin,
Shaoshi shanfang bicong 4.69–70; and Chen Jiru, *Guwen pin wailu* 23.11a–12b.

his quotation of the afterword, Hong Mai mentions when it was written (1134) and that Li Qingzhao was then fifty-two (fifty-one we now believe; Hu Yinglin also dates it to 1134). So Xu Bo is not uniquely privy to this information about the author's age. It had been widely known since Song times; indeed, the lines from Li Qingzhao's letter to Qi Chongli, which Xu Bo refuses to accept, point to her remarriage as taking place at just such an "advanced" age. It appears that in his eagerness to claim he has access to a superior text, Xu has misrepresented what is clearly stated in the earliest quotation of the work.

Xu Bo's refusal to accept the standard accounts of Li Qingzhao's remarriage must be rooted in what he takes away from his reading of her afterword, not just the lines about her age, but also the general impression it conveys of her devotion to her first husband. Xu Bo says that the slander has been directed at a "virtuous lady." How does he know she is so virtuous? From her afterword, of course. Xu Bo does not posit a motive for the slander (that would be done by later scholars); nor does he give any attention to the problem posed by the variety of Song sources that record Li Qingzhao's remarriage or their historiographical reliability. But in many other respects, Xu Bo anticipates the arguments to come.

The next scholar to take up the remarriage issue was Lu Jianzeng 盧見曾 (1690–1768). Lu's treatment would have been roughly a century after Xu Bo, and it is not clear that Lu was aware of Xu Bo's opinion. Lu was an important scholar, educator, and book printer of the Qianlong era. In fact, the occasion of Lu Jianzeng's consideration of the subject was his printing of a new edition of Zhao Mingcheng's *Records on Metal and Stone* in 1762. He appended Li Qingzhao's afterword to Zhao Mingcheng's work. It is in the preface he wrote to his new edition of *Records on Metal and Stone* that Lu Jianzeng takes up the question of Li Qingzhao's remarriage.[53] Surprisingly, Lu devotes more space in his preface to the issue of Li Qingzhao's remarriage than he does to his description of Zhao Mingcheng's work and how he has edited and corrected errors in earlier editions.

As with Xu Bo, Lu Jianzeng's conviction that Li Qingzhao could never have remarried is based entirely on his reading of her afterword. "People say that after Defu died, Yi'an remarried. . . . When I consider this in light of the afterword she wrote to this book, I know that it definitely never happened."

---

53. Lu Jianzeng, "Chongkan *Jinshilu* xu" 重刊《金石錄》序, Yayu tang 雅雨堂 edition of *Jinshi lu* 金石錄, *Huibian*, pp. 94–95.

Lu goes on to offer this reflection: Li Qingzhao composed the afterword six years after Zhao Mingcheng died (he dates the composition to 1135), when she was still so attached to his memory that she could not bear to keep her grief to herself and expressed her ongoing love for her late husband, and sorrow over his passing, in the afterword. How could a woman who felt like that ever, in the meantime, have given herself in marriage to another man? "Even an ordinary woman would have been incapable of such conduct," Lu declares. "How much less a woman as intelligent and accomplished as Li Qingzhao!"

Like Xu Bo, Lu Jianzeng believes that the reports of Li Qingzhao's remarriage are slander spread by her enemies. Also like Xu Bo, Lu stops short of explaining why the remarriage is referred to in numerous Song sources. Aside from his complete reliance on the afterword to resolve the question of Li Qingzhao's remarriage, the most significant aspect of Lu Jianzeng's treatment of the issue is the identity of Lu Jianzeng himself. Lu was a major figure in scholarship and publishing during the High Qing. He was the complier of the collectanea *Yayu tang congshu* 雅雨堂叢書, a friend of the eminent scholars Ji Yun 紀昀 (1724–1805) and Wang Chang 王昶 (1724–1806), and the founder of numerous academies in diverse prefectures where he served as official. For such a figure to take up the issue of Li Qingzhao's remarriage and to declare that the received wisdom was not just wrong but a malicious lie brought the issue to a new level of prominence. Much remained to be done, but in Lu Jianzeng the Ming-Qing scholarly campaign to refashion the biography of Li Qingzhao found its first major spokesman.

There must have been a lingering discomfort with the new opinion, however, despite the stridency with which Lu Jianzeng had made his pronouncement. There was too much respect in the Qing scholarly world for the importance of received texts for the remarriage issue to be dealt with in so cavalier a manner. In order to make the revisionist opinion truly persuasive, sooner or later someone needed to marshal a more specific argument against the credibility of the Song sources on Li Qingzhao's life. That argument would be even stronger if it could delve into the particulars of the case and explain the process by which the Song sources came to say what they did. In other words, a detailed textual deconstruction was needed to accompany the higher-level categorical denial of the remarriage event.

The first person who tried to fulfill that need was Yu Zhengxie, who was born just a few years after Lu Jianzeng died. Yu Zhengxie was an even more accomplished scholar than Lu Jianzeng. Known as the founder of the Lichu

理初 school of historical geography (named for him), he made valuable contributions especially to the geography of borderland regions, including the Sino-Russian border, Taiwan, and Tibet.[54] He was one of the compilers of a revised edition of the famous *Essentials of Geography for Reading History* 讀史方輿紀要. But he also worked in a range of other fields, including institutional history, legal history, classics, philology, astronomy, mathematics, and medicine. His scholarly research in these fields is contained in two collections, *Guisi leigao* 癸巳類稿 and *Guisi cungao* 癸巳存稿, works that are generally considered among the most learned and valuable reading notes collections from the Qing dynasty. Liang Qichao 梁啓超 (1873–1929), for example, included Yu's *Guisi* volumes among the ten finest such scholarly works of the period.[55] Today, Yu Zhengxie is also remembered as an early advocate of equal treatment for women.[56] He spoke out against the belief that widows should not remarry, objected to the legal and ritual subjugation of wives to husbands, and railed against the custom of foot-binding. The twentieth-century educator and social reformer Cai Yuanpei 蔡元培 (1868–1940) praised Yu as a visionary spokesperson for the emancipation of women.[57] Yu also had special expertise in Song period legal documents, having reconstructed a portion of the lost *Collected Statutes of the Song* 宋會要.

Yu Zhengxie's research on Li Qingzhao, titled "Collected Materials on the Recluse Scholar Yi'an" 易安居士事輯, is a long essay, nearly ten thousand characters in length, that comes at the very end of *Guisi leigao*.[58] Preceding it in that work are several of his iconoclastic essays on women and women's issues, and it is probably fair to view his work on Li Qingzhao in the context of his general sensitivity to the inequitable treatment of women in Chinese society. It is obvious that Yu Zhengxie is a great admirer of Li Qingzhao. His long essay is mostly a great pastiche of quotations from her works (song lyrics, the critique of others' song lyrics, the afterword, the long poems, the rhyme-prose on Capture the Horse, and so on) and early anecdotes concerning her. Yu interjects his own comments between these quotations, noting how talented she was, how ingenious and outspoken her poetic lines are, and

---

54. In addition to the entry on Yu Zhengxie in Hummel, *Eminent Chinese of the Ch'ing Period*, pp. 936–37, on his geographical studies see Shu Xilong, "Lichu xuepai de lishi dili yanjiu."

55. See Chen Donghui, "Zhongguo jindai qimu qianxi de yiwei renjie."

56. Xu Shiduan, "Yu Zhengxie de renquan yishi jiqi funüguan pingshu."

57. Ibid., p. 144.

58. Yu Zhengxie, "Yi'an jushi shiji" 15.763–79; also in *Huibian*, pp. 107–20.

how apt her political and literary critiques of others were. Eventually, in the final pages of his review of her life and works, he turns to the issue of her remarriage. "I have always loathed the claim that Yi'an remarried Zhang Ruzhou" 余素惡易安改嫁張汝舟之説, he says, and he recalls that when Lu Jianzeng reprinted *Records on Metal and Stone*, "based on his feelings he figured that Yi'an could not have done such a thing" 以情度易安不當有此事.[59] Yu Zhengxie may be an early advocate for more liberated views on the remarriage of widows, but he was still a man of his time in certain respects. When it came to the historical woman whose life he championed and whose talent he revered, he could not abide the thought that she had compromised herself by remarrying a lowly fellow. Being the scholar he was, however, Yu was not content simply to deny Li Qingzhao's remarriage on the basis of his intuition. He was determined to make a scholarly-sounding argument against its historicity. Yet we see the origins of his conviction: "I have always loathed the claim that . . ." It is Yu's sentiments that set him off on this path. Given his world view, he could not accept the idea that an iconic woman could have behaved this way, even while in other contexts he argued for greater tolerance of widows' remarriage. At one point he insists that to clear Li Qingzhao's name of the slander that has attached itself to her is simply a matter of "fairness" and that he is not motivated to do so simply because he wishes that she had not remarried (非望易安以不嫁也).[60] Many readers will feel that in proclaiming this denial he has inadvertently revealed the truth.

At the center of Yu Zhengxie's explanation of what happened is a new understanding of Li Qingzhao's letter to Qi Chongli. To a certain degree, it is to Yu Zhengxie's credit that he feels obliged to address the existence of this letter, rather than simply to dismiss it or ignore it as had been done by earlier scholars intent on denying the remarriage. This is what he says: there was, originally, a letter that Li Qingzhao sent to Qi Chongli. Certain sentences from it may still be found in the present letter. But the present letter is a document that has been tampered with, drastically altering the original intent and meaning. This is clear, Yu asserts, from the inferior literary style of the present letter, which nevertheless still contains some "fine phrases" (left over from the original). Unfortunately for the strength of his argument, Yu never

---

59. Yu Zhengxie, "Yi'an jushi shiji" 15.777; also in *Huibian*, p. 119.
60. Ibid.

identifies the passages that he finds "inferior in literary style" 文筆劣下, and some recent scholars have specifically challenged his judgment in this regard.[61]

Li Qingzhao originally wrote the letter, Yu says, to thank Qi Chongli for intervening and clearing her name in the incident involving Zhang Feiqing and the jade pitcher, after the malicious and erroneous rumors that Li Qingzhao and Zhao Mingcheng had kept the vessel and offered it to the invading armies to assure the couple's safety. (Chapter 4 discusses the problems with this way of reading the relevant passages of Li Qingzhao's afterword.) Some person or persons who wanted to do further damage to Li Qingzhao's reputation subsequently changed several elements in the original letter (e.g., "Zhang Feiqing" to "Zhang Ruzhou," "jade pitcher" to "jade mirror stand," and so forth) and rewrote other parts to make it seem that Li Qingzhao had remarried a man named Zhang Ruzhou. Originally, there had indeed been a court case and trial, but it had to do with the investigation into the alleged traitorous offering of the jade pitcher and had nothing to do with charges against a second husband.

Yu Zhengxie goes on to undermine some of the Song sources that report Li Qingzhao's remarriage. Li Xinchuan's *Important Records since the Jianyan Reign Arranged by Year* 建炎以來繫年要錄, he says, is full of hearsay and unreliable records. Li and others who record Li Qingzhao's remarriage, Yu states, were simply duped by the malicious rumors that had been spread. In fact, Li's *Important Records* is highly regarded and considered an indispensable and accurate source for the history of the period. Yu also quotes passing mention of Li Qingzhao in sources toward the end of her life that refer to her as "[the late] Zhao Mingcheng's husband," believing these to be further evidence that she never remarried. Recent scholars are more likely to take such references as evidence that after her remarriage and divorce Li Qingzhao eventually regained her status as Zhao Mingcheng's widow. It has been pointed out, for example, that one source that refers to elderly Li Qingzhao as Zhao Mingcheng's wife also mentions her remarriage not long after Zhao died, suggesting that Yu's point has no validity.[62] Finally, Yu discusses selected passages from the letter that he believes was tampered with. He finds that these passages are at odds with Song practice or historical fact and claims that these

---

61. See, for example, Nangong, *Li Qingzhao de hou bansheng*, p. 54. For Yu Zhengxie's statement about the style of the letter, see "Yi'an jushi shiji" 15.777; also in *Huibian*, p. 119.

62. Huang Shengzhang, "Li Qingzhao shiji kaobian," p. 345.

"lapses" are additional evidence that the letter, as we have it, is not authentic or credible. Yet in his discussion of these passages, Yu himself repeatedly misunderstands the gist of what is being said. For example, he thinks that the "jade mirror stand" and the "letter of official appointment" are meant to refer to a wedding gift and official permission given to Li Qingzhao to remarry, which he asserts she would not have needed. He does not realize that neither of these were actual; they are both literary allusions to fraudulent marriage proposals.[63] Yu likewise thinks that the court trial, including imperial involvement, mentioned by the letter concerned Li Qingzhao's request for a divorce. In this regard he belittles the idea that a high court, much less the emperor, would bother with such trivial domestic matters: "The failure of Song emperors to act like emperors did not sink that low!"[64] Yet our understanding is that the testimony and trial Li Qingzhao refers to concern the charge of official malfeasance she brought against Zhang Ruzhou rather than a divorce suit (for which she had no legal basis). Such an accusation of official misconduct would have been a matter of import and would have necessitated a trial.[65]

Yu Zhengxie's article on Li Qingzhao draws on an impressive number of sources and, bringing up a multitude of particular points in no particular order, is both difficult to read and seemingly authoritative. It was not directly challenged until the second half of the twentieth century, as we will see in the next chapter. Although many of Yu's Qing dynasty readers credited him with having "expunged the humiliation" from Li Qingzhao's life and legacy, others were not so sure. Some scholars were still uneasy over the discrepancy between what the Song sources said (Yu Zhengxie had not dealt with all of them that report Li Qingzhao's remarriage) and the "solution" that Yu had proposed. One of those still unpersuaded was Lu Xinyuan 陸心源 (1834–94), the great Qing book collector and scholar who specialized in epigraphy and Song period editions (one of his libraries was named Two Hundred Song Imprints Hall 皕宋樓). Lu said that he was particularly bothered by two weaknesses in Yu Zhengxie's argument: it pretended that Zhang Ruzhou was a fiction, and it failed to acknowledge the historicity of Li Qingzhao's lawsuit

---

63. This point is discussed in Nangong, *Li Qingzhao de hou bansheng*, pp. 55–57; cf. Huang Shengzhang, "Li Qingzhao shiji kao," pp. 229–30.

64. Yu Zhengxie, "Yi'an jushi shiji" 15.778; also in *Huibian*, p. 119.

65. Nangong, *Li Qingzhao de hou bansheng*, pp. 57–58; Huang Shengzhang, "Li Qingzhao shiji kao," p. 229.

against Zhang for official misconduct.[66] We see that Lu Xinyuan takes Li Xinchuan and his *Important Records* seriously: he cannot bring himself simply to dismiss that key historical source and what it says about Zhang and Li Qingzhao. But Lu Xinyuan is also aware of several other Song sources that mention Zhang Ruzhou, and so he cannot accept the idea that "Zhang Ruzhou" is simply a made-up name intended to substitute for Zhang Feiqing. There is an irony in this opinion of his, which is that most of the other Song references to Zhang Ruzhou, some of which Lu refers to, are believed by modern scholars to refer to another Zhang Ruzhou, not the man of the same name Li Qingzhao married, and a man who was in fact considerably higher ranking than Li Qingzhao's second husband.[67] This other Zhang Ruzhou held several prefectural governorships, a level of office Li Qingzhao's Zhang Ruzhou never came close to.

Lu Xinyuan concedes to the Song sources more credibility than Yu Zhengxie had done. His problem is how then to balance this fairer assessment of the early sources with his conviction that Li Qingzhao could not have remarried. It is clear that Lu never considered the possibility that what the Song sources say could actually be what happened. It is when he tries to explain away what the sources say, stopping short of discrediting them outright as generally unreliable, that his argument becomes truly bizarre.

There was indeed such a person as Zhang Ruzhou, Lu Xinyuan proceeds. In fact this man was none other than Zhang Feiqing (who had brought the jade pitcher). "Ruzhou" was the formal name (*ming* 名); "Feiqing" was the polite name (*zi* 字). Zhang brought the jade pitcher to Zhao Mingcheng to be assessed, but Zhao lost it. Angered, Zhang spread the rumor that Zhao and Li Qingzhao had presented it to the invading Jurchen. In the meantime Zhao Mingcheng died, but Li Qingzhao responded to the slander by charging that Zhang had obtained office by exaggerating the number of his recommenders. Hence a trial was held and Zhang was found guilty and demoted. The text of Li Xinchuan's *Important Records,* reporting these events presently says, "Zhang Ruzhou, the gentleman for attendance of the right and army accounts officer, was given in custody to the officials after Ruzhou's wife, née Li, brought suit against him for having obtained office by wantonly exaggerating

---

66. Lu Xinyuan, "'*Guisi leigao*: Yi'an shiji' shuhou" 《癸巳類稿：易安事輯》書後, *Yigu tang tiba* 儀顧堂題跋, *Huibian*, pp. 138–39.

67. Deng, *Li Qingzhao xinzhuan*, p. 149, n. 1; and Nangong, *Li Qingzhao de hou bansheng*, pp. 62–64.

the number of times he had qualified [for the palace exam]" 右承奉郎監諸軍審計司張汝舟屬吏，以汝舟妻李氏訟其妄增舉數入官也.[68] But Lu Xinyuan insists that the original version, before it was maliciously altered, had the three characters Zhao Mingcheng 趙明誠 before the word "wife"; thus: "after Ruzhou was sued by Zhao Mingcheng's wife, née Li, for having . . ." Lu does not say how this change was made in the text. Regardless, furious at having his official misconduct exposed by Li Qingzhao, Zhang somehow tampered with the letter of thanks that Li Qingzhao had sent to Qi Chongli at the trial's end, making it appear not just that she had remarried but that she had married Zhang himself (now a criminal). Such was Zhang's desperation and impetuousness that he schemed to defame Li Qingzhao by claiming she had married such a "worthless shyster" and wife-beater as himself!

It did not take long for the obvious objections to Lu Xinyuan's speculation to be raised. Lu's contemporary Li Ciming 李慈銘 (1830–94) wrote a long rebuttal of virtually every point in Lu's argument.[69] Li, a scholar and poet who is perhaps best known for his diary, *Yueman tang riji* 越縵堂日記, is adept at poking holes in Lu's scenario. The two names "Ruzhou" 汝舟 and "Feiqing" 飛卿 do not go together well as *ming* 名 and *zi* 字, he points out. Moreover, according to Li Qingzhao, Zhang Feiqing took the jade pitcher away with him; Zhao Mingcheng did not lose it. Also, Li Qingzhao says that she does not know who started the rumor about "presenting" the pot to the Jurchen (in that way of reading her phrase); if Zhang had started the rumor, she would have known it and said so. Li Ciming is particularly impatient with the suggestion that Zhang could have tampered with Li Qingzhao's letter to Qi Chongli, making it seem that she had married him. Who would impugn himself that way, calling himself a shyster and describing how he beat his wife? No one would have such little self-regard. Li Ciming also objects that the wording of the *Important Records* passage is perfectly clear as it stands. There is no need to rewrite it and no grounds for supposing that it ever said anything different. The crime of misreporting the number of recommenders for office is something that only a wife could know. How could Li Qingzhao know this detail about Zhang? Li Ciming's summary view of Lu Xinyuan's scenario is that it is "entirely of his own creation and has no basis in reason" 殊臆決不近理.

---

68. Li Xinchuan, *Jianyan yilai xinian yaolu* 58.1003.

69. Li Ciming, "Shu Lu Fangfu guancha 'Yigu tang tiba' hou" 書陸剛甫觀察《儀顧堂題跋》後, *Yueman tang yiji* 越縵堂乙集, *Huibian*, pp. 139–42.

Li Ciming is good at debunking Lu Xinyuan's explanation, but when it comes to proposing his own alternative, it likewise sounds highly speculative. The letter of thanks that Li Qingzhao sent to Qi Chongli was, he claims, not occasioned by any remarriage or the jade pitcher incident but rather by Wang Jixian's attempt to "buy" the ancient bronzes in the Zhao-Li collection right after Zhao Mingcheng died. As for Zhang Ruzhou, it was probably some other woman in Li Qingzhao's clan who married him and then divorced him. Subsequently, Li Qingzhao's enemies conflated the two events and rewrote her letter to Qi Chongli, making it look like Li Qingzhao had married the man. Or, he goes on, perhaps Zhang Ruzhou's wife was an unrelated woman, also named Li, who also happened to be a gifted writer. She was the author of the letter (as it presently stands), describing her abuse by Zhang and her divorce trial, and eventually the letter came to be attributed to the more famous Li Qingzhao in order to damage her reputation.

In all of this, it is obvious that Li Ciming, for all his dissatisfaction with Lu Xinyuan, shares with Lu the a priori conviction that Li Qingzhao could not have remarried. Indeed, referring to the claim that she did, he offers such comments as "it does not deserve argument" 不待辨 and "the truth is clear without analysis" 不辨而明. To mention just a couple of problems with Li Ciming's explanation, Li Qingzhao's letter to Qi Chongli was, based on internal and external evidence, written in the autumn of 1132. If she were writing to thank Qi for helping her in the matter with Wang Jixian, why did she wait a full three years before sending this letter? Or, if we choose to adopt Li's other suggestion that another woman named Li composed the letter just as it is, how many women of Li Qingzhao's day do we suppose there were who could have written such a letter? And is it not odd that such a talented woman is completely forgotten in Song sources? Li Ciming was not humble about what he came up with. He boasted that he had "filled in what was missing in Yu Zhengxie's research and corrected the errors in Lu Xinyuan's explanation; mine can be called a definitive version that will stand for all time." Actually, no scholar after Li Ciming has found his version of events particularly compelling. It is, finally, interesting to note that Li Ciming was an ardent admirer of Li Qingzhao's afterword. He reports that he used to love to recite it from memory and that he considered it the finest piece of women's writing from the Song and later times.[70] Li Ciming, like so many before and after him, had come under the afterword's spell.

---

70. Li Ciming, *Yueman tang dushu ji* 越縵堂讀書記 9, *Huibian*, p. 142.

Considerable space has been given here to an account of several of the most important Qing arguments intended to establish that Li Qingzhao never remarried. They illustrate the great difficulty the Qing scholars had advancing their contention, given their respect for received texts and scholarly standards for "evidential research." The scholars are torn between what the Song sources, including the crucial letter written by Li Qingzhao herself, tell them happened and what their values concerning widows' virtue and their beliefs concerning Li Qingzhao's devotion to Zhao Mingcheng allow them to deem plausible and acceptable. It is a struggle for them between texts several centuries old and the social and ideological values of their own day, a struggle further complicated by Li Qingzhao's rise in Ming-Qing times to the stature of canonical writer and, indeed, paragon of women's writing. One after another learned gentleman comes forward to make his case, advancing ever more ingenious solutions to the problem. Each is well aware of the flaws in the preceding arguments and even feels obliged to point them out. But no one can manage to make a case that will really stand up to scrutiny. The Song sources resist their efforts. The truth is that the sources cannot readily be manipulated or recast to yield a scenario that the Qing scholars can be comfortable with. That is the crux of the scholars' problem. Indeed, the intractability of the Song sources is even greater than we might think, reading the Qing scholars. No Qing scholar ever gives a comprehensive list of all the Song references to Li Qingzhao's marriage, much less manages to explain them all away. We witness in these Qing contentions the depth of the psychological and emotional commitment these scholars have to the task at hand. The recasting of the Song historiographical record that they are trying to accomplish is no simple matter. They know that and yet are determined to succeed nevertheless.

Was there no one, we may wonder, who managed to rise above this struggle and who spoke candidly and objectively about what was going on? We do, rarely, come upon such a person. Liang Shaoren 梁紹壬 (b. 1792) is an example. Far less eminent than the other Qing scholars discussed above, he nevertheless perceived the situation accurately. Writing jointly about the scholarly effort to deny Li Qingzhao's remarriage and that to clear the other Song woman poet, Zhu Shuzhen, of the charge that she had an extramarital affair, based on some lines in one of her poems, he observed: "Latter-day scholars have vigorously argued that Yi'an never remarried and that Shuzhen did not write this poem. Such arguments are nothing more than attempts to exonerate talented women [from improper conduct]. In fact, the ancient sages never forbid the remarriage of widows."[71] But such a voice of reason was drowned out by more passionate opinions.

The Reconstituted Li Qingzhao in the Late Qing

Looking back on the Qing campaign to deny Li Qingzhao's remarriage, we may feel the weaknesses in the arguments to be transparent and the ulterior motives all too obvious, and Qing scholars may likewise have been aware of the flaws in each other's explanations, but among nonspecialists, scholars and general readers alike, the new view became widespread. That is to say, despite the shortcomings of the arguments themselves, so frequently were the arguments reiterated, so prestigious were the scholars making them, and so ardently were they advanced that eventually their acceptance became the general consensus. The Qing campaign to deny Li Qingzhao's remarriage was a success. There may have been some skeptics, but they kept quiet. What we find instead is an outpouring of affirmations of the conclusions of the remarriage denial and praise for those who had brought it about. This chorus grows in volume through the nineteenth century and into the early twentieth. The scholars discussed above are celebrated for finally having "expunged the disgrace" that had wrongfully attached itself to Li Qingzhao for so many centuries. It was not until 1957 that this consensus was challenged, and even then it took several decades before the remarriage became generally accepted as historical fact.

To give a few representative examples, in his *Remarks on Song Lyrics*, Lu Ying 陸鎣 (19th c.) refers to Li Qingzhao as a talented woman who, because of her talent, attracted defamation.[72] Nevertheless, he observes, Lu Jianzeng had taken the initiative to set the record straight in the preface to his edition of *Records on Metal and Stone*. More recently Yu Zhengxie had delved into Li Qingzhao's "complete collection" (Lu is overstating the case here; the "complete collection" had long been lost) and determined the year and month of each piece, and then, reexamining the traditional sources on her life, had "vigorously exonerated her" 力爲昭雪 from any wrongdoing. Consequently, "the origins of the slander Yi'an had suffered first became known to the world" 易安被謗之由，始白於世. In a colophon she wrote on Lu Jianzeng's edition of *Records on Metal and Stone*, the mid-nineteenth-century

---

71. Liang Shaoren, *Liangban qiuyu an suibi* 兩般秋雨庵隨筆 2, *Huibian*, pp. 122–23.

72. Lu Ying, *Wenhua lou cihua* 問花樓詞話, *Huibian*, p. 132.

woman poet Huang Youqin 黄友琴 similarly lauded Lu's outspokenness in defense of Li Qingzhao. In the poem she appended to her colophon, Huang characterizes Lu as Li Qingzhao's "understanding friend" across the centuries and says that, because of what Lu had done, Li Qingzhao could now stop shedding tears in the afterlife. Huang's colophon and poem are included in the important nineteenth-century anthology of women's poetry *Correct Beginnings: Women's Poetry of Our Dynasty* 國朝閨秀正始集.[73]

A seminal event toward the end of the century (1881) was the publication by Wang Pengyun 王鵬運 of a new edition of Li Qingzhao's reconstituted collection of song lyrics, *Jades for Rinsing the Mouth*, ushering in the start of Li Qingzhao studies in modern times. In a significant sense, Wang's decision to devote himself to this task as compiler, editor, and publisher shows that "the problem" of Li Qingzhao and her questionable conduct had been overcome. Now that it had, it was acceptable for a scholar of high standing to bring out her works again. Whatever we today may think of the Qing scholars who "expunged the humiliation" that Li Qingzhao had suffered, with regard to preserving her works and making them a worthy subject of scholarly study again, we owe those scholars a considerable debt. The erudite and ornate preface that the poet Duanmu Cai 端木埰 (1816–92) wrote for Wang Pengyun's edition is primarily about the slander that Li Qingzhao had endured and how finally the untruths about her had been exposed by Yu Zhengxie, preparing the way for Wang to return to her writings. Duanmu is no longer making a case for Li Qingzhao's innocence. He considers that already to have been done. He is reviewing for the reader's benefit the history of how Li Qingzhao was misrepresented and how that error came to be undone. What he says about the situation that existed when the "slander" was rampant and before her name was cleared is revealing: "men of principle clutched their hearts with grief, and chaste women wrung their hands with disbelief."[74]

It was not simply that Li Qingzhao had her name cleared in the Qing campaign launched on her behalf and emerged as a fully respectable woman who had never, it was now believed, compromised herself by remarrying. The final result of all the defenses marshaled for her was something more than this. In the course of arguing the case for a new conception of her, the

---

73. Huang Youqin, "Shu Yayu tang chongkan Jinshi lu hou," in Yun Zhu, *Guochao guixiu zhengshi ji* 19.1a–b; also in *Huibian*, p. 134.

74. Duanmu Cai, "Shuyu ci xu" 漱玉詞序, *Huibian*, p. 148.

Qing scholars established her as something of a moral paragon. She was now, in many persons' perception, more than just a talented woman poet. She was a woman whose moral uprightness had been vindicated after centuries of undeserved ignominy. She began to be viewed as a moral hero whose stature was all the greater for having endured mistreatment and recently emerged from it. She had, it was now believed, suffered twice. She suffered once in life when her husband was first frequently absent and then died young, leaving her widowed and unprotected. Then she suffered again in the afterlife, when disgruntled and envious persons spread malicious lies about her. This second ordeal had lasted centuries, through which her spirit in the afterlife had no recourse and was stricken with grief. References to her torment in the afterlife, one of which we have seen above, become common in the late Qing, even as it is affirmed that finally her spirit has now found relief.[75] In this image of Li Qingzhao, suffering not only in life but in the afterlife too, we detect the influence of the widespread fascination with vulnerable and afflicted women (both fictional and real), which figured in the cult of the chaste and long-suffering or martyred widow.[76] "Li Qingzhao" now acquired a meaning and identity larger than that which could be contained within literary history.

The 1841 edition of the *Prefectural Gazetteer of Ji'nan* gives a biographical notice on her in its section on "exemplary women" 列女傳, the section reserved for female heroes of virtue.[77] Li Qingzhao is given considerable prominence in that section of the gazetteer, lifted out of the subsection devoted to women of Zhangqiu 章邱 (Li Qingzhao's native county) and promoted to the head of the chapter, where she is placed second, after the notice on a Tang woman. Li Qingzhao's notice, the only one in that category for a Song dynasty woman, is twice as long as nearly any other entry in the three chapters devoted to exemplary women, over six thousand of them. The notice has dual foci: Li Qingzhao's literary talent, including her essay on the

---

75. See, for example, the reference to her "eight hundred years of tears" in the closing lines of the long poem that Fan Zengxiang 樊增祥 (1846–1931) inscribed on a portrait of her, "Ti Li Yi'an yixiang" 題李易安遺像, in Xu Zonghao 徐宗浩, *Shixue zhai shiji* 石雪齋詩集 3, *Huibian*, p. 156.

76. Katherine Carlitz has written perceptively about the poetic appeal of the long-suffering widow and heroines of fidelity in connection with the Ming cult of widow chastity; see "Shrines," pp. 616–20. See also Chang, "Ming-Qing Women Poets," pp. 256–57.

77. *Ji'nan fu zhi* 濟南府志 (1841) 57.2a–b.

song lyric, and her devotion to Zhao Mingcheng. Not one word is mentioned about her remarriage or even about "slanderous" rumors concerning it. Significantly, the compilers of the gazetteer note that they have moved the biographical notice on her from the "literary persons" 文苑 section, where it appeared in earlier editions of the *Zhangqiu County Gazetteer* 章邱縣志, to the "exemplary women" section. Actually, the shift had already been made in versions of the *Zhangqiu County Gazetteer* compiled in 1755 and 1833.[78] But in still earlier versions of the county gazetteer, a Ming edition of 1596 and a Qing edition of 1691, the entry on Li Qingzhao is indeed found in the "literary persons" chapter, appended to the notice on her father.[79] The relocation of her biographical notice in the mid-eighteenth-century gazetteer coincides with the early stage of Qing scholars' active campaign to deny her remarriage. The two events reflect the emergence during the High Qing of the conviction that commendable virtue was a key component of Li Qingzhao's life and legacy, and that she could not have compromised herself by remarrying.

We see this emphasis on Li Qingzhao's moral integrity also in an act of homage paid to her in 1911 by the artist Xu Zhonghao 徐宗浩 (1880–1957). Xu had purchased a small portrait of Li Qingzhao in Beijing and used the occasion to put together a little album in honor of her. He wrote out several of her song lyrics, added the portrait, and further asked his fellow artist Yu Difan 俞滌煩 (1884–1935) for a painting titled *Looking at Bamboo* to mount on the cover. Xu then inscribed his own poem on the bamboo painting. Xu's poem concerns the conventional notion of bamboo as exemplar of steadfast elegance, purity, and moral intrepidity, and it is clear that the painted bamboo is intended to stand for these qualities in Li Qingzhao herself:

高節凌雲自一時	The lofty joints rise to the clouds, all at once,
嬋娟已有歲寒姿	Its tender beauty may yet endure winter's cold.
霜竿特立誰能撼	The frost-touched trunk stands firm, who can shake it?
寄語西風莫浪吹	Tell the west wind not to bother blowing wastefully.[80]

The poet is thinking of the reemergent Li Qingzhao, who has withstood centuries of harsh treatment but is now all the stronger for it. *Jie* 節 in the opening line refers to the joints in the trunk of the bamboo, but it also refers

---

78. *(Qianlong) Zhangqiu xianzhi* (1775) 10.25a, in the "Cai nü" 才女 subsection; and *(Daoguang) Zhangqiu xianzhi* (1833) 12.91b, also in the "Cai nü" subsection.

79. *(Wanli) Zhangqiu xianzhi* (1596) 28.53a; and *(Kangxi) Zhangqiu xianzhi* (1691), 6.72a.

80. Xu Zonghao, "Ti Li Yi'an kanzhu tu xiaoxiang" 題李易安看竹圖小像, *Shixue zhai shiji* 石雪齋詩集, *Huibian*, p. 161.

to the "integrity" of the plant (which bends but never breaks), so that the line could also be translated "Its towering integrity reaches to the clouds, all at once." This same character *jie* in the sense of a woman's "chastity" takes us back to the criticism made in the twelfth century, by Zhu Yu and many others after him, that Li Qingzhao had been unable to preserve her "chastity" after Zhao Mingcheng's death. We have come full circle. In the poem of 1911, Li Qingzhao exemplifies perfect integrity.

Perhaps the most extreme instance of the veneration of Li Qingzhao in the Qing period was her installation as a goddess in a Ji'nan lakeside shrine sometime during the Tongzhi 同治 reign (1862–73). A group of literary men had the idea of elevating Li Qingzhao to this special status in Ji'nan, the prefectural seat of her native place. At Daming Lake in the city there had formerly been a Lotus Goddess Shrine 藕神祠, but that shrine had fallen into neglect, and no one knew any longer the exact identity of the goddess it was dedicated to. The literary men, led appropriately enough by the song lyrics poet Fu Zhaolun 符兆綸, came up with the idea of refurbishing the shrine and "installing" the spirit of Li Qingzhao as the new resident goddess there. In the long and somewhat rambling account that Fu Zhaolun gives of this process, several motives for the enshrinement are mentioned. This is the key passage:

> Considering her fragrant and lovely literary talent, together with her deep, wide, and peerlessly attractive learning, how could we not cherish and admire her? Someone may say, "It is fine that you cherish and admire her. But cherishing and admiring her, then to go on to worship her, that is not acceptable." This is incorrect.
>
> Long ago the recluse scholar lived beside Willow Catkin Spring. Her former residence has long since become ruins, so that passersby pace back and forth sadly there and cannot bring themselves to leave. The recluse scholar left the world long ago. If she were alive today, someone as talented as she, having fallen on hard times and being without a husband, we would build a home of several columns beside this lake and mountain to be her dwelling. This is something that anyone who values persons of talent could not help but do. . . .
>
> The few of us here are low-ranking officials posted to distant lands. Bearing long halberds, we are mere retainers for other men. How could we presume to esteem someone as distinguished as the retired scholar? It is simply that we would cleanse ourselves in her lingering fragrance and thereby transform our vulgar bones. Thus the improvement we receive from the recluse scholar becomes ever more profound, and the cherishing of her in our hearts becomes ever more pronounced. At the same time, we use Thousand Buddha Mountain

to exorcise her lifetime of anguish, and we borrow the waters of Daming Lake to wash away the innumerable slanders that she endured. On future days, when we seek poetic inspiration along the lake, who is to say we will not envision her, dressed in lotus skirt with orchid sash, moving gracefully across the waves toward us?

Respectfully, on a certain day in a certain month we pour out water from Willow Catkin Spring as a libation and offer up a segment of verdant lotus as we install the recluse scholar's spirit in this ancient shrine.[81]

There is an interesting mixture of sentiments and impulses here, including admiration, commiseration, the urge to protect, pride in recognizing talent, hope of receiving purification, righteous anger at Li Qingzhao's detractors, and confidence that her spirit can serve as their own poetic muse. The accompanying poem that one of Fu Zhaolun's colleagues composed on the occasion draws a parallel between Li Qingzhao and the ancient water goddesses the Consorts of the Xiang 湘妃 (wives of the legendary Emperor Shun) and the Luo River Goddess 洛神.[82] Li Qingzhao had become a goddess in these men's eyes.

81. Fu Zhaolun, "Minghu oushen ci yisi Li Yi'an jushi ji" 明湖藕神祠移祀李易安居士記, in Mao Chenglin, *Minguo xuxiu Licheng xianzhi* 51.18a–b; *Huibian*, p. 144.

82. Wang Dayu 王大堉, "Oushen ci shi" 藕神祠詩, in Mao Chenglin, *Minguo xuxiu Licheng xianzhi* 51.18b; *Huibian*, p. 145.

CHAPTER 9

Modernism, Revisionism, Feminism

Reception in Modern Times

T he publication of a new edition of *Jades for Rinsing the Mouth* in 1881 by
Wang Pengyun can be thought of as ushering in the "modern" era of Li
Qingzhao studies. Wang's edition of her song lyrics, with the moralizing and
self-righteous preface by Duanmu Cai, was the bibliographical culmination
of the Qing campaign to clear her name from slander. Li Qingzhao's reputation was now fully restored. Doubts about her integrity had been overcome,
and she could be read and studied again now not just as a great woman poet,
but also as a virtuous woman. Having been re-created as Zhao Mingcheng's
devoted wife and widow, she became even more admired and more of a sympathetic figure, because it was now perceived that she had posthumously
endured centuries of injustice and abuse.

May Fourth Period Histories of Chinese Literature

When the project began a few decades later to create a history of Chinese
literature that answered the needs of the new nation and social order, as part
of the May Fourth Movement, Li Qingzhao was given a prominent if special
place. She began to be acclaimed as the greatest woman poet not only of her
dynasty, but also of Chinese history.[1] Her critique of other song lyrics writers

---

1. Zheng Zhenduo, *Chatu ben Zhongguo wenxue shi* (1932) 2:31.

of her day was singled out for its incision and boldness.[2] At the least, she was regularly given her place alongside the finest male writers of the song lyric in the many general literary histories and histories of song lyrics that appeared during the Republican Period.[3]

Li Qingzhao was one of only a handful of women writers who received notice in the newly devised literary history. Hu Yunyi 胡雲翼, in his edition of her song lyrics published in 1931, mentions her along with Cai Yan of the Han dynasty and Xue Tao of the Tang.[4] But immediately he qualifies the comparison, noting that Cai Yan only has one famous poem to her credit, and Xue Tao's works, while more numerous, could never be considered the equal of those of any of the major Tang poets. That leaves Li Qingzhao as the only woman poet who is as talented or even more talented than the outstanding male poets of her era. It is true, he goes on to say, that her achievement was limited to the field of the song lyric, but the nature of that achievement ensures that her fame in literary history will be as enduring as that of Qu Yuan, Tao Qian, or Du Fu.

In this way, Li Qingzhao takes her place beside the great male poets, but she is the only woman so privileged. Her presence among the men shows that a woman was indeed capable of rising to the highest level among literary luminaries. This is an inclusive gesture; it involves women in the national history of literary composition, showing that they have their role and claim to fame. Writing was not exclusively a male domain after all. There was an international aspect of this canonization in addition to the national one. Zheng Zhenduo 鄭振鐸, in his *Illustrated Edition of A History of Chinese Literature* 插圖本中國文學史, first published in 1932 and republished many times throughout the twentieth century, compares Li Qingzhao to Sappho, noting that the two women shared the same fate of having most of their writings lost.[5] Many May Fourth intellectuals, and Zheng Zhenduo in particular, were well-read in world literature and knew that other national traditions included some women as major writers. If China was going to have a literary history comparable to that of Japan and Western nations, it would

---

2. Liu Yupan, *Cishi* (1930), pp. 105–6.

3. In addition to the works cited in notes 1 and 2 above, see Xie Wuliang, *Zhongguo funü wenxue shi* (1916), part 3A, pp. 4–22; Hu Shi, *Guoyu wenxue shi* (1927), pp. 144–45; Lu Kanru and Feng Yuanjun, *Zhongguo shishi* (1930) 3:1116–20; Wang Yi, *Ciqu shi* (1930), pp. 164–66; and Wu Mei, *Cixue tonglun* (1933), pp. 109–10.

4. Hu Yunyi, *Li Qingzhao yu qi Shuyu ci*, pp. 1–2.

5. Zheng Zhenduo, *Chatu ben Zhongguo wenxue shi* 2:31.

need to have great women writers in addition to the men. The canonization of a woman writer would also have the effect of encouraging education and literacy among modern women, making them more "competitive" with women in other modern nations, another important goal of the May Fourth Movement.[6] In the larger context, the canonization of Li Qingzhao as one of China's "great writers" was part of the complex process that took place through the late Qing and Republican Period of rethinking the place of women in Chinese cultural history and searching for new ways of reconciling the old tensions among women, beauty, talent, and virtue that fit the needs of the emergent modern nation.[7] It was a complicated rethinking that gave rise, particularly outside literary history, to some most unlikely women as exemplars.[8]

Yet at this stage of the literary historiography there was only one woman poet, Li Qingzhao, who was recognized as truly great. The implication was clear. Literary history did not exclude women, but their greatness was severely limited. The field of writing remained overwhelmingly male. Li Qingzhao was the exception that proved the rule. Her canonization had dual utility. It showed that women were not excluded from literary greatness, but it also reminded everyone how exceptional it was for a woman to rise to the highest level in the field. Interest in exploring the widespread involvement of women in literary history was still decades away. That did not emerge until nearly the end of the twentieth century.

The way of reading Li Qingzhao was also peculiar. She was read differently from male poets. Here is an excerpt from an article on Li Qingzhao that Zheng Zhenduo published in a literary journal in 1923:

> It is very difficult for us to find within the field of Chinese poetry writing that which is the outpouring of genuine emotions. Poets write for amusement or they write to exchange social verse, and most of them produce compositions in which "they moan although they have no illness." Poets who are truly sincere, those whose feelings truly force themselves out to be written on the page, are no more than three or four out of a thousand. Li Qingzhao is one among the very small number of genuine poets.[9]

---

6. This goal is broached in Xie Wuliang's introduction to his *Zhongguo funü wenxue shi* (pp. 1–3), one of the earliest (1916) systematic histories of women's writing in China.

7. For the history of this process at the turn of the twentieth century, see Judge, *The Precious Raft of History*.

8. See Shenqing Wu, "Gendering the Nation."

9. Zheng Zhenduo, "Li Qingzhao."

No doubt the admiration here is real, yet this type of praise cuts two ways. The emotions thus imagined to be "genuine" are also unmitigated by intelligence or artistry. This kind of genuineness is thus often associated with the primitive or childlike. At the same time that it is valued for its directness and authenticity, it is perceived as simple and uncomplicated. There is little room or need in this type of expression, so perceived, for writerly skill or talent. This point is brought out in the contrast Zheng draws later in the same article between Li Qingzhao and her contemporaries Qin Guan and Huang Tingjian. Those two writers relied entirely on their skill with words when they composed song lyrics. Li Qingzhao was different, even superior to them, because her song lyrics "flowed forth from the bottom of her heart." One wonders which other few poets Zheng Zhenduo would group together with Li Qingzhao as poets of "genuine emotion." It is interesting that he does not name any others. It is, after all, a very special type of poet that he is envisioning, one who hardly needs the expertise we usually expect of a great writer.

An idea that goes together with this reputed genuineness of expression is that Li Qingzhao's literary work is connected seamlessly with her life. The speaking voice in her poems is identical with that of Li Qingzhao herself. Zheng Zhenduo, again, calls attention to her uniqueness in this regard in his *Illustrated Edition of A History of Chinese Literature*: "Innumerable poets and song lyrics writers have written innumerable poems featuring lonely boudoir complaints. Most of these writers speak in the voice of the female protagonist. All such poems and song lyrics, before Li Qingzhao, are like so much manure and defy evaluation."[10] Li Qingzhao is different because when she speaks, also as a woman, it is in her very own voice that she utters her words. Zheng Zhenduo goes on to describe Li Qingzhao's marriage and her joy living together with Zhao Mingcheng (drawing on Li Qingzhao's afterword). He also notes that not long after she was married, Zhao Mingcheng left her to embark on travels (and official appointments). During this period of separation, he asserts, Li Qingzhao "sent to him a great many song lyrics" that she wrote. Zheng is imagining that her surviving song lyrics are precisely these works, but we know that there is no internal or external evidence for such a provenance or use of her songs.

There is one other interesting thought in Zheng Zhenduo's account of Li Qingzhao in his influential *History of Chinese Literature*. She is not simply

---

10. Zheng Zhenduo, *Chatu ben Zhongguo wenxue shi* 2:32.

described as China's greatest woman writer; she is also said to stand completely apart from other writers (i.e., male writers). Indeed, the place that she occupies stands outside of literary history: "As for the song lyrics that she wrote, whether one considers the ideas they express or their style and tone, one can truly say of them that 'no one among the ancients came before her, and no later writer came after her.' She created her own unique style, and she stood alone among all other song lyrics writers. She was not influenced by other writers, and other writers were not influenced by her."[11] This curious insistence that Li Qingzhao stood outside of literary history and owed nothing to other song lyrics writers must be related to her singularity as the only celebrated female writer in Zheng's perception of the period. One senses here the difficulty that the literary historian is having accommodating this writer in his account. She is given a place, but it is a unique place, with no ties diachronically or synchronically to other writers. Even as she is being written into literary history, she is also being separated out from it.

Li Qingzhao did not fare even this well in all literary histories written during the Republican Period. Some scholars were unable to accommodate her. So it was with Qian Jibo 錢基博 (father of Qian Zhongshu). The Song dynasty chapter of Qian's *History of Chinese Literature* was written during the War of Resistance against Japan, between 1939 and 1942.[12] The Song chapter is very detailed, with copious information on books and authors as well as numerous examples of their literary compositions. The chapter is just short of three hundred pages long. Despite its considerable length and detail, there is no mention in the chapter of Li Qingzhao whatsoever. From this omission we begin to appreciate what a big step it was for a scholar like Zheng Zhenduo to include Li Qingzhao in his literary history. And we can better understand the tenuous nature of her inclusion.

The other conspicuous attribute of Li Qingzhao in Republican Period accounts is that her remarriage is not mentioned, or if it is brought up, it is denied as malicious slander. That is what Hu Yunyi does in the introduction to his edition of Li Qingzhao's song lyrics. He notes that the Qing scholar Yu Zhengxie already "proved" that the reports of her remarrying late in life are completely baseless.[13] Zheng Zhenduo and others simply do not broach

---

11. Ibid. 2:31–32.

12. See Qian Zhongxia, "Houji," no. 3, in Qian Jibo, *Zhongguo wenxue shi* 3:1144.

13. Hu Yunyi, *Li Qingzhao yu qi Shuyu ci*, p. 10.

the issue at all. For such scholars, Li Qingzhao is the Li Qingzhao they inherited from the late Qing: a woman who was completely devoted to Zhao Mingcheng, in life and after his death, and one who never would have considered remarriage during her widowhood.

As we have seen, that perspective makes it all the easier to read her song lyrics on loneliness as expressions of her longing for Zhao Mingcheng when he was off traveling or after his death. With that reading also comes the perception of the special "sincerity" of her work as a poet. In other words, the suppression of Li Qingzhao's remarriage from her biography, which was the norm throughout the Republican Period, leads to views of her and readings of her writings that would hardly be possible if the remarriage were restored and accepted. Restoring the remarriage to her biography would complicate the situation considerably. It might raise questions about her love and devotion, not to mention her judgment. It might also have the effect of undermining the authority of her afterword. People might begin to wonder, if she had just recently remarried but suppressed that information from her autobiographical afterword, whether or not other aspects of the afterword should be accepted at face value.

Finally, removing the remarriage from Li Qingzhao's biography makes it easier, ultimately, to accept her into the pantheon of China's greatest writers, the rest of whom are male. Li Qingzhao may be the lone female in the group, but she is less threatening and recalcitrant because it turns out that the entirety of her literary output is focused on her husband. In the standard reading of her in the Republican Period, the inspiration for her greatness as a poet comes from her husband and her feelings of dependency on him.

The Remarriage Controversy, 1957–2010

The field of Li Qingzhao scholarship was changed dramatically in 1957 with the publication of the two lengthy studies by Huang Shengzhang, his chronological biography of Li Qingzhao and Zhao Mingcheng, and his "Events in the Life of Li Qingzhao."[14] Together, Huang's studies marked the first serious challenge to the Qing period denial of Li Qingzhao's remarriage. As radical as Huang's thesis was at the time, the argumentation in his studies was rigorous and the documentation solid so that his conclusions could not

---

14. Huang Shengzhang, "Zhao Mingcheng Li Qingzhao fufu nianpu" and "Li Qingzhao shiji kaobian," respectively.

be ignored even by those who were most reluctant to accept his findings. Huang's work initiated a scholarly controversy concerning the historicity of Li Qingzhao's remarriage that raged—that is not too strong a word—for the next forty years and even today has not been laid completely to rest. Hundreds of scholars and aficionados have published on the topic. An entire book, published in 1990, is devoted to gathering together and reprinting the more important scholarly treatments of the controversy, on all sides, and the material it reprints from the modern period (most of which appeared after Huang Shengzhang's articles) runs to over three hundred pages.[15] And that is a selective collection of what had been written on the topic. Huang Shengzhang's "Events in the Life of Li Qingzhao" was truly, as one of his disputants admitted early on, "an article that had an influence."[16]

The bulk of Huang Shengzhang's "Events" is devoted to refuting the Qing scholar Yu Zhengxie's efforts to discredit the Song period sources that refer to Li Qingzhao's remarriage to Zhang Ruzhou. As we have seen in chapter 8, Yu Zhengxie was among the earliest of the Qing scholars to write a detailed study of Li Qingzhao's life whose purpose was to deny the historicity of her remarriage. Much of what he wrote was aimed at undermining the Song period sources on the event. Yu Zhengxie maintained that all the Song references to the remarriage were unreliable, either because they had uncritically accepted contemporary efforts to slander her or because they themselves were composed (or had been tampered with) by detractors who were determined to malign her reputation. Huang Shengzhang takes up Yu Zhengxie's categorical denigration of the Song sources that refer to the remarriage one by one, arguing that Yu Zhengxie had grossly misrepresented their reliability or their essential nature and intent. Huang discusses, for example, the reference in Hong Kuo's *Explanations of Clerical Script* 隸釋 (mid-12th century) to Li Qingzhao's remarriage.[17] Hong Kuo's work, Huang reminds us, is a scholarly study of inscriptions in the ancient script form, a work that is in the tradition of Zhao Mingcheng's own *Records on Metal and Stone*. Hong Shi's entry on Zhao and his wife mainly concerns Zhao's *Records*, and what it adds later about Li Qingzhao's misfortunes after Zhao's death is said by way of explaining the loss of Zhao's collection of inscriptions. The

---

15. He Guangyan, *Li Qingzhao gaijia wenti ziliao huibian.*
16. Huang Mogu, "Weng Fanggang 'Jinshi lu' ben duhou," p. 58.
17. Huang Shengzhang, "Li Qingzhao shiji kaobian," pp. 335–48.

tone with which Hong refers to that loss is one of regret for the disappearance of something of antiquarian value. It is implausible that Hong means to do anything more than register his regret over that loss. His reference to Li Qingzhao's remarriage should be read in this light, Huang suggests, and to do anything else is to lose sight of the very nature of Hong Kuo's text.

More egregious still, Huang points out, is the way Yu Zhengxie has misrepresented what is said concerning Li Qingzhao's remarriage in Li Xinchuan's *Important Records since the Jianyan Reign Arranged by Year*.[18] Yu quotes an early negative assessment of the reliability of another work by Li Xinchuan, his *Miscellaneous Accounts of Court and Countryside since the Jianyan Reign* 建炎以來朝野雜記, taking it as a criticism of *Important Records*, which it is not.[19] We do not know whether Yu Zhengxie misapplied this criticism deliberately or out of carelessness. Yu goes on to attribute to the Southern Song writer Xie Fangde 謝枋得 (1226–89) a charge that Li Xinchuan "fabricated" unflattering reports about Xin Qiji 辛棄疾 (1140–1207) (the implication being that he did the same or uncritically accepted similar baseless reports concerning Li Qingzhao), when in fact Xie does not name Li Xinchuan in his reference to such fabricated comments.[20] The conclusion that Yu Zhengxie draws from these misattributions is that what Li Xinchuan says about Li Qingzhao's letter to Qi Chongli cannot be considered credible, when actually Li Xinchuan's reference to Li Qingzhao's remarriage makes no mention of her letter to Qi Chongli. Yu Zhengxie's "defense" of Li Qingzhao is thus shown by Huang Shengzhang to be full of inaccuracies and distortions.

As damaging as such revelations are to the credibility of Yu Zhengxie's argument, Huang Shengzhang goes one step further, taking his critique of Yu Zhengxie to a higher level. The fundamental problem with Yu Zhengxie's case, Huang points out, is not the carelessness with which he treats the Song sources but rather the highly subjective state of mind with which he approaches the entire subject.[21] Yu Zhengxie is committed to the view that it is morally wrong for widows to remarry, and, admiring Li Qingzhao as a

---

18. Li Xinchuan, *Jianyan yilai xinian yaolu* 58.1003; Huang Shengzhang, "Li Qingzhao shiji kaobian," pp. 339–40.

19. The negative assessment is found in Zhou Mi, *Qidong yeyu* 3.5468; Yu Zhengxie, "Yi'an jushi shiji," 15.777; also in *Huibian*, p. 119.

20. Xie Fangde, "Song Xin Jiaxuan xiansheng muji" 宋辛稼軒墓記, *Quan Songwen* 355: 8218.119.

21. Huang Shengzhang, "Li Qingzhao shiji kaobian," pp. 347–48.

woman of superior talent and character, he cannot accept the prospect that a woman like her could be guilty of such a failing. Yu Zhengxie is trapped, Huang would say, in the biases of the late Qing concerning widows' "chastity." The values and morality in which he was immersed prevent him from viewing the relevant sources and, indeed, the historical events they record in an objective way.

Huang Shengzhang's studies, appearing as they did during the Hundred Flowers campaign, pointed to a radically new way of thinking about China's foremost woman poet. The rigor and persuasiveness of Huang's arguments quickly won over a few leading scholars. Wang Zhongwen, a specialist in poetry of the Five Dynasties and Song periods (and the son of Wang Guowei 王國維 [1877–1927]), was completely convinced. In support of Huang's findings, Wang published a supplement to Huang Shengzhang's studies in 1963.[22] Wang elaborated on several of the points that Huang had made and came up with his own new criticisms of many of the assertions made by the Qing scholars who had denied the remarriage. Wang identifies several mistakes those scholars had made in their discussion of Li Qingzhao's letter to Qi Chongli, as they tried to turn it into one or another kind of document. They took certain phrases at their literal sense, then argued that the sense was at odds with Song law and institutions, when in fact the meaning of the phrases hinges upon literary allusions. Or they found evidence in specific terminology used in the Song sources that refuted, they maintained, the remarriage view. For example, sources that date from late in Li Qingzhao's life or soon after her death refer to her as Zhao Mingcheng's wife, and in her long poem to the departing emissaries to the Jurchen court, Li Qingzhao calls herself a widow. Wang Zhongwen points out the logical flaws of these scholars' reasoning.[23] After she was divorced from Zhang Ruzhou, there was no reason for her not to be referred to as the late Zhao Mingcheng's wife or for her to call herself "widow." In fact, most of the points made by Wang Zhongwen against the Qing scholars turn on issues of terminology, logic, knowledge of Song institutions, and word usage in the Song documents. We must recall that the Qing scholars themselves were already several centuries removed from the Song texts, and it is little wonder that their understanding of key phrases might be questionable, especially since they were caught up in a moral

---

22. Wang Zhongwen, "Li Qingzhao shiji zuopin zakao."
23. Ibid., p. 172.

campaign and cause. Wang Zhongwen tries to bring a superior understanding of Song writing and history to the subject. One of Wang's final points is that widows' remarriage was more widely accepted in Li Qingzhao's day than it was in the time of the Qing scholars who labored to rescue her from disgrace. This leads into Wang's concluding paragraph:

> From the standpoint of the society of Li Qingzhao's day, the act of remarriage would not have damaged her moral standing. Today it should be even less of a problem. Starting with Yu Zhengxie, numerous scholars have exhausted themselves in an attempt to clear Li Qingzhao from slander, but their efforts have not effected any increase in her repute. As Huang Shengzhang wrote, "What this case brings up are the twin issues of how we evaluate the reliability of historical sources and how we access the veracity of historical events." Then he went on to cite the statements of [the Song period writers] Hu Zi, Wang Zhuo, Chao Gongwu, Hong Kuo, Chen Zhensun, and others as proof that Li Qingzhao truly did remarry. With that, the arguments of the earlier scholars intended to clear Li Qingzhao from slander were completely demolished and rendered empty. Deeply worried as I am that others will still try, one after another, to reverse the verdict on Li Qingzhao's remarriage, I have dared to add my own words to the subject, addressing issues that Mr. Huang did not bring up or filling out those he merely touched on, supplementing his study in a small way as a further reference for those who would study and reconstruct the life of Li Qingzhao.[24]

Yet not everyone was so readily persuaded. There were, especially among senior scholars, who had been publishing for decades on Li Qingzhao and Song literary history, men who had inherited the Qing consensus about the "injustice" that had been done to Li Qingzhao and were heavily invested in perpetuating it. In 1962, the eminent literary scholar Xia Chengtao 夏承燾 added a note to an essay he had written in the 1930s on Yu Zhengxie's study.[25] Although he did not refer to Huang Shengzhang by name, Xia Chengtao must have been aware of Huang's iconoclastic work on Li Qingzhao and felt impelled to reaffirm his belief that she could never have remarried. He comes up with new "ancillary evidence" against the remarriage view, thinking of a point that no prior scholar had made. Li Qingzhao is believed to have written her satirical couplet about the new *jinshi* graduate Zhang Jiucheng in 1132. If she had really remarried in that year, and divorced soon after, bringing shame

---

24. Ibid., p. 175.
25. Xia Chengtao, "Houyu er," pp. 222–23.

and humiliation upon herself, how could she possibly have chosen to expose herself to even more notoriety and denunciation by writing such snide lines? This reasoning overlooks the fact that Li Qingzhao's couplet is thought to date from early in the year, in the third month, when the *jinshi* examinations were held, whereas Li Qingzhao is not thought to have remarried until a few months later. More important, the way Xia frames the question shows that his thinking has not broken free of Qing dynasty treatments of these events.

In 1961 the single most eminent authority on Song period song lyrics, Tang Guizhang, also expressed his continued commitment to the denial of the remarriage.[26] Although his statement of the case is essentially a reiteration of the Qing position, Tang ingeniously introduces his own reversal of Huang Shengzhang's point about the Qing scholars being trapped in a "feudal mentality." Li Qingzhao was slandered in her day, he asserts, by men who could not abide such a talented, strong-willed, and outspoken woman. Tang thus redirects the opprobrium of backward thinking from the Qing scholars to the Song sources on Li Qingzhao. It was precisely because Li Qingzhao violated Song period norms for womanly behavior that she offended so many people, especially those officials who favored the "peace policy" with the northern invaders, which Li Qingzhao seemed to belittle in several of her poems. Li Qingzhao had no means to defend herself against the well-coordinated campaign to disparage her. No one came to her defense. She became a "sacrificial victim" of the backward thinking of her time.

Not long after these reactions to Huang Shengzhang in the early 1960s, the onset of the Great Proletarian Cultural Revolution in the People's Republic of China would bring to a halt for over fifteen years the yet unresolved scholarly controversy concerning Li Qingzhao's remarriage. It was not until the early 1980s that the debate concerning her remarriage resumed in academic books and journals.

Outside of the People's Republic, however, one significant publication on the controversy during this hiatus deserves attention. That is Nangong Bo's thin but important book of 1971, *The Second Half of the Life of Li Qingzhao* 李清照的後半生, published by the Commercial Press in Taipei. The remarriage question is the focal point of Nangong Bo's volume, and he is adamant in his conviction that the remarriage is historical fact. It is true that there is considerable overlap between Nangong's study and the earlier work of

---

26. Tang Guizhang, "Lun Li Qingzhao de houqi ci," pp. 135–37.

Huang Shengzhang, which Nangong had read. But Nangong's discussion goes further than Huang had done in his examination of Song laws on remarriage and divorce, and particularly the involvement of courts and even the emperor himself in the annulment of marriages.[27] This research on Song law and institutions is relevant to Nangong's discussion of Li Qingzhao's letter to Qi Chongli, which he, unlike the Qing scholars he criticizes, sees as absolutely consistent and credible as an explanation of how she got into and out of her marriage to Zhang Ruzhou. Like Huang Shengzhang, Nangong Bo also gives sustained attention to the nature and content of the eight Song sources on Li Qingzhao's remarriage. His conclusion about them, collectively, is that the Qing scholars' contention that they can only reflect a widespread campaign of slander against Li Qingzhao is completely untenable. Nangong Bo also devotes considerable space to discussing Li Qingzhao's plight after Zhao Mingcheng's death—her hapless wandering and largely unsuccessful efforts to keep their collection intact—as the context in which to view her ill-fated decision to remarry to Zhang Ruzhou.[28]

However, the most memorable aspect of Nangong Bo's study is one of a more personal nature concerning the history of his involvement with Li Qingzhao as an enduring subject of interest. Nangong Bo is known as a Taiwanese novelist specializing in historical fiction. As he explains in the introduction to his scholarly study of Li Qingzhao, he had written a historical novel about her some ten years before.[29] He confesses that he was deeply dissatisfied with that novel because he had based his account of her life on the understanding of the Qing scholars and had rejected the idea of her remarriage as untrue. Over the years, the existence of the Song sources nagged at him, and he came to see the Qing rejection of those sources as more and more problematic. He finally decided to undertake a thorough scholarly reconsideration of the second half of her life, focusing on the remarriage question, and came to the conclusion that the Qing position was a projection of Qing social morality and values, and had no basis in historical fact. We see in Nangong Bo, then, the interesting example of a man switching sides on this most divisive issue and recognizing quite on his own the shortcomings of the view he had inherited from late imperial China's most esteemed scholars.

---

27. Nangong, *Li Qingzhao de hou bansheng*, pp. 57–68.
28. Ibid., pp. 35–44.
29. Ibid., pp. 1–7.

The decade of the 1980s was a period of heated debate and disagreement among P.R.C. scholars concerning Li Qingzhao's remarriage. A number of biographical and literary studies devoted to Li Qingzhao that appeared early in the decade accepted Huang Shengzhang's viewpoint and incorporated it in their accounts of the poet's life. These included *Li Qingzhao* 李清照 by Xu Peijun (1981), *A Critical Biography of Li Qingzhao* 李清照評傳 by Wang Yanti 王延梯 (1982), and another biography, *Li Qingzhao* 李清照, by the esteemed scholar Cheng Qianfan 程千帆, in collaboration with Xu Youfu 徐有富 (1982). But those opposed to Huang Shengzhang, Wang Zhongwen, and their acceptance of the remarriage remained outspoken in their rejection of the new view.

Perhaps the most persistent critic of the remarriage viewpoint was Huang Mogu 黄墨谷, a professor at Hebei Normal Academy. During the eighties and nineties Huang published numerous articles on the remarriage issue, as well as a new edition of Li Qingzhao's works, and became something of a spokesperson for those who refused to accept Li Qingzhao's remarriage. Her earliest articles, which appeared in 1980 and 1981, marshal several arguments in an effort to undermine Huang Shengzhang's conclusions.[30] Among Huang Mogu's many points, the more plausible ones, at first glance, include the following: that Huang Shengzhang derived his conclusions from Southern Song *biji* and other writings that had no direct connection with Li Qingzhao and in many cases only appeared decades after her death, while at the same time he completely disregarded the evidence from Li Qingzhao's own hand, including her afterword and her poems and song lyrics, and he also failed to give adequate attention to the political controversies of the day, especially the bitter rivalry between the peace and irredentist factions at Gaozong's court.[31] Second, she points out that several reputable Southern Song figures, including Zhu Xi, Lu You, Zhao Shihou, and Hong Mai left comments on Li Qingzhao and her afterword without any trace of disapproval, which, she says, could never have happened if Li Qingzhao had remarried.[32] The weakness of the first point is that it assumes that documents composed by Li Qingzhao are inherently more reliable concerning the historical circumstances of her life than those composed by others, and it also overlooks the

---

30. Huang Mogu, "Weng Fanggang 'Jinshi lu' ben duhou," pp. 56–60; and "'Tou neihan Qigong Chongli qi' kao."
31. Huang Mogu, "Weng Fanggang 'Jinshi lu' ben duhou," pp. 57–58, 59.
32. Ibid., p. 60.

possibility that Li Qingzhao or any writer might repress from her writings references to biographical events that were unpleasant or a source of embarrassment. The problem with the second point is that it assumes that a widow's remarriage was as unacceptable in Li Qingzhao's time as it later became in the Ming-Qing period, and it also construes the absence of a reference to a biographical event as evidence that the event never took place. Huang Mogu also tries to bolster her attack on Huang Shengzhang with claims whose logic is likely to strike most readers as problematic. For example, she quotes Song critics who praise Li Qingzhao's afterword for the detailed and moving portrait it gives of the Zhao-Li marriage as evidence that Li Qingzhao could not have remarried; if she had, Huang Mogu says, those critics would not have been such sympathetic readers of the afterword.[33] In a separate article, Huang Mogu takes up Huang Shengzhang's reading of Li Qingzhao's letter to Qi Chongli.[34] She rejects this reading, contending instead that the letter was originally written to thank Qi Chongli for helping clear her name from the charge of currying favor with the invaders (i.e., the jade pot incident). She says that the original letter was subsequently tampered with by Li Qingzhao's enemies to make it look like a document concerning remarriage. This is a reading of the letter that can be traced back to the Qing dynasty scholar Yu Zhengxie (as we saw in the preceding chapter) and one whose shortcomings had already been discussed at length by Huang Shengzhang and Nangong Bo. Huang Mogu adds nothing of substance to Yu Zhengxie's interpretation of the letter.

In a peculiar way, the Cultural Revolution that had wreaked such havoc in the People's Republic in the 1960s and 1970s, and was particularly destructive for the intellectuals there, served to strengthen the sense among those who clung to the denial of Li Qingzhao's remarriage that they were right. Writing before the outbreak of the Cultural Revolution, Huang Shengzhang had argued that the Qing scholars' contention about an elaborate campaign mounted in Li Qingzhao's day to slander and discredit her by her enemies (including members of the peace faction and others she had satirized in poems) was not believable. Such a campaign would have required a degree of coordination and, ultimately, a record of success in overturning the truth about her life that were simply implausible. After the experience of the

---

33. Ibid., pp. 59, 60.
34. Huang Mogu, "'Tou neihan Qigong Chongli qi' kao."

Cultural Revolution, it became rather easy to attack Huang Shengzhang's view as naïve, for had not countless upright and virtuous figures seen their good reputations completely destroyed during Mao's "lost decade" by vicious and baseless campaigns of slander? Huang Mogu repeatedly makes reference in her articles to such lessons of the Cultural Revolution and the implications they have for understanding the Song sources on Li Qingzhao's remarriage.[35]

Later in the 1980s, one notices a hardening of the positions of the two camps of scholars, who begin to be referred to as the "remarriage" and "anti-remarriage" groups. The rhetoric also becomes more harsh and more intolerant of the other side's position, especially among the "anti-remarriage" group, who must have sensed that they were losing the argument in the scholarly world generally, as Song social history and remarriage practices became better understood and the biases of the Qing scholars began to be more accurately perceived. The divide was largely, if not entirely, generational, with the older scholars resisting the remarriage idea and the younger ones accepting it. Of course the older scholars had been writing about Li Qingzhao from long before the time that Huang Shengzhang's studies appeared, and it was more difficult for them to change their thinking.

In 1983, 1984, and 1985 the doyen of song lyric studies, Tang Guizhang, weighed in repeatedly on the issue.[36] In his "Notes on Reading Song Lyrics" (1983), he refers approvingly to Huang Mogu's published articles on the subject and reiterates his view that Li Qingzhao's letter to Qi Chongli concerned the jade pot incident and was subsequently tampered with. He also quotes the late Qing scholar Kuang Zhouyi 況周頤 (1859–1926), who argued that the respective locations of Li Qingzhao and Zhang Ruzhou during the years in question made it impossible that they could have married, because they were never in the same place at once (although the "Zhang Ruzhou" he writes about is a different person from the one late twentieth-century scholars identify as Li Qingzhao's second husband). There is nothing new in the substance of what Tang Guizhang says or in the evidence he brings to bear. What is new is the tone of his remarks, exemplified by the heading he gives to this section of his article: "Li Qingzhao Absolutely Did Not Remarry" 李清照絶無改嫁之事. Here is a representative passage:

---

35. Huang Mogu, "Weng Fanggang 'Jinshi lu' ben duhou," pp. 58–59.

36. Tang Guizhang, "Duci zhaji"; "Du Li Qingzhao ci zhaji"; and "Li Qingzhao ping-zhuan."

When mean-spirited men of the marketplace slander virtuous persons for their own laughter and amusement, such an activity is hardly worth discussing. What is surprising is when educated persons do not accept Li Qingzhao's "Afterword to *Records on Metal and Stone*" as a truthful account of her life and accept instead rumors spread by mean-spirited men of the marketplace, so that they turn right and wrong upside down, fail to distinguish black from white, and cause Li Qingzhao to be subjected to an everlasting injustice. What could be more regrettable than this?

I consider Li Qingzhao to be someone who would not change her principles because of poverty and lowliness, could not be seduced by wealth and eminence, and was a heroic stalwart among women who could not be intimidated by might and military power. Her love for Zhao Mingcheng was constant from beginning to end, and was unchanging in life and death. She absolutely could not have remarried.[37]

Such remarks, coming from the compiler of the *Complete Song Dynasty Song Lyrics* in addition to dozens of other authoritative scholarly editions and studies on song lyrics, could not be readily dismissed.

One of the 1984 issues of the journal *Qilu xuekan* 齊魯學刊, published in Qufu, Shandong, not far from Li Qingzhao's native place, contained several articles devoted to the remarriage debate. Zheng Guobi 鄭國弼 and Liu Yixuan 劉憶萱 wrote against the historicity of the remarriage;[38] Rong Bin 榮斌, unpersuaded, wrote an article in response titled " 'Qingzhao's Remarriage' Is Difficult to Deny."[39] One gets some idea of how polarized the two sides had become and how far apart their thinking and assumptions were by looking at the disagreement over a single line in Li Qingzhao's afterword. Unlike the case of the letter to Qi Chongli, there was no disagreement about the authenticity of Li Qingzhao's afterword or the integrity of its text. Yet the significance of particular lines could be understood in completely different ways by the two groups of scholars. Describing the ten years that she had lived in Qingzhou with Zhao Mingcheng, when he was out of office and his future career uncertain, she had stressed their self-sufficiency and the pleasure they took in each other's company, concluding this way: "So even though our lives were fraught with apprehensions and poverty, what we valued and strove for was never compromised" 雖處憂患困窮而志不屈. In her 1980

---

37. Tang Guizhang, "Duci zhaji," p. 259.
38. Zheng Guobi, "Li Qingzhao gaijia bianzheng"; Liu Yixuan, "Li Qingzhao yanjiu zhong de wenti."
39. Rong, " 'Qingzhao gaijia' nanyi fouren."

article, Huang Mogu had cited this line as evidence that Li Qingzhao could never have allowed herself to be "untrue" to Zhao Mingcheng after his death.[40] Zheng Guobi had reiterated the point in his article of 1984.[41] Rong Bin, however, finds this reasoning completely unacceptable. The line only applies, he insists, to the period of the marriage that Li Qingzhao is describing in her afterword. To interpret it as relevant to whatever Li Qingzhao may have done after Zhao Mingcheng's death is unwarranted. "I do not understand how Comrade Huang could be so inattentive," he observes, as to interpret the line the way she does.[42] But Huang Mogu, far from being chastened by Rong Bin's criticism, became even more adamant. She cites Rong Bin's remark in an article published later in 1984 only to reaffirm her position. Li Qingzhao's statement in the afterword deserves, she insists, to be considered an important piece of evidence against her remarriage.[43] Li Qingzhao would never have written those words in 1134, no matter that they ostensibly apply to her life with Zhao Mingcheng years before, if she had remarried in 1132. Scholars who subscribed to the two different schools of thought were reading the crucial texts in mutually incompatible ways.

What had transpired was that Li Qingzhao had been transformed into a cultural icon that embodied ideals that were fervently admired. For many scholars and readers, it was all but impossible to question the historical validity of the icon because to do so was seen as an assault on the ideals themselves. There is a revealing account of an incident in Tang Guizhang's later years. One of Tang's younger colleagues at Nanjing Normal University, Zhou Xunchu 周勛初, reported that in the early 1980s he once accompanied a visiting Japanese scholar when he went to call on Tang. At one point the conversation turned to Li Qingzhao, and the visitor from Japan asked Tang if he thought she had ever remarried. "All at once, [Tang's] expression became very severe. 'Never!' he said." Zhou goes on to explain that, in his view, Tang Guizhang (who was then in his eighties) had long since projected his own life experiences and principles into his thinking on this issue. Tang himself had been widowed early on, had never remarried, and had raised three children by himself. Zhou says this not to criticize Tang Guizhang but to praise him for

---

40. Huang Mogu, "Weng Fanggang 'Jinshi lu' ben duhou," p. 59.
41. Zheng Guobi, "Li Qingzhao gaijia bianzheng," p. 111.
42. Rong, "'Qingzhao gaijia' nanyi fouding," p. 115.
43. Huang Mogu, "Wei Li Qingzhao gaijia zai banwu," p. 107.

the kind of man he was, quite beyond his scholarly achievements. The incident is described in eulogistic remarks that Zhou made during a conference commemorating the one-hundred-year anniversary of Tang's birth, which was held at Nanjing Normal University in 2001.[44]

The divide between scholars on the remarriage issue continued through the 1980s and 1990s, even as acceptance of Li Qingzhao's remarriage became more widespread within academia. Those who refused to accept the view now became the dissenters, and when they spoke out, they were likely to attract the support of prominent senior scholars who had spent their careers subscribing to the view that Li Qingzhao would never have remarried. However, the issue had become so contentious that it was often tactfully avoided, as it is in a 1999 summary of scholarship on Li Qingzhao of "the last fifty years," or only broached indirectly.[45]

In 1990 Liu Ruilian 劉瑞蓮, a teacher at People's University in Beijing, published a volume titled *A New Discussion of Li Qingzhao* 李清照新論. Her study stresses Li Qingzhao's singularity among literary women of her time for being so outspoken in expressing her views on politics and poetry, so ardent in her loyalty to her nation, and so unwilling to accept conventional ideas about the limits of womanly talent and behavior. Liu Ruilian rejects the notion that Li Qingzhao ever remarried, basing her judgment primarily on her assessment of Li Qingzhao's character and her feelings toward Zhao Mingcheng: "My own view is this: whether she remarried or not is a question that should not influence our evaluation of her [as a poet]. But based on her character and the affection between her and Zhao Mingcheng, she absolutely could not have, at that [advanced] age and time of her life, remarried a man like Zhang Ruzhou."[46] Liu Ruilian goes on to remind the reader of other Southern Song cases in which persons were slandered by their enemies. She believes that this is what the "remarriage" comments amount to in Li

---

44. Zhou Xunchu's remarks are reported in the unsigned article "Yunshan cangcang, Jiangshui yangyang, xiansheng zhifeng, shangao shuichang—Tang Guizhang xiansheng danchen yibai zhounian jinianhui zhaiyao" 雲山蒼蒼，江水泱泱，先生之風，山高水長—唐圭璋先生誕辰一百週年紀念會摘要, *Nanjing shida bao* 南京師大報, November 30, 2011, section 4.

45. Wang Kean 王克安, "Jin 50 nian Li Qingzhao yanjiu zongshu." The issue is likewise avoided in a summary of one hundred years of Li Qingzhao scholarship published in 2007: Lu Yuan, "Jin bainian Li Qingzhao yanjiu zongshu."

46. Liu Ruilian, *Li Qingzhao xinlun*, p. 86.

Qingzhao's case and says that the letter to Qi Chongli was altered to defame Li Qingzhao accordingly.

There is really nothing new in what Liu Ruilian says on the remarriage issue. What is of interest is the endorsement her volume received from elder scholars. No less a figure than Zhou Ruchang 周汝昌, the eminent *Honglou meng* specialist, wrote a preface to the book, in which he gives fulsome praise to its insights and value. Zhou's preface emphasizes the special acumen that Liu Ruilian, a woman, brings to the study of China's greatest woman poet. And he refers the reader to the celebrated appreciation found in that novel of female talent and the courage of women to stand their ground in a patriarchal society.

Zhou Ruchang makes no explicit comment on Liu Ruilian's position regarding Li Qingzhao's remarriage. But it is clear enough that he has a special interest in that aspect of the study, as we see in the paragraph translated below:

> The Recluse Scholar Yi'an titled her song lyrics collection *Jades for Rinsing the Mouth*. From this we can discern the way she conducted herself and her principles. The phrase "jades for rinsing the mouth" is derived from the statement "to rinse the mouth with stones and pillow the head on streams," but "jades" is substituted for "stones."[47] The phrase expresses the high-minded purity of Li Qingzhao's desires and the goodness of her personality. Chinese culture since early antiquity prized jade and applied the highest aesthetic ideals to it, identifying its essential characteristics this way: it is extremely warm and smooth yet is also very hard and durable; it has color and elegance but also seems endowed with spirit and sentience. (The ancients differentiated jade and stone by saying that jade is spirited but stone is obtuse; that is the great difference between the two.) Because jade has these four attributes, it embodied Li Qingzhao's ideals and came to symbolize what she strove to be. How could a person who produced "jades for rinsing the mouth" ever associate herself with that which is filthy and defiled? Unfortunately, the archaeology of later ages only knew to focus its attention on bronzes and colored ceramics and did not appreciate the great significance and uses of jade in Chinese cultural history. No one studied it seriously so that a true understanding of the substance was nearly lost. Consequently, the title *Jades for Rinsing the Mouth* came to be taken as something quite ordinary.[48]

---

47. See chapter 3, note 1.
48. Zhou Ruchang, "Xu."

In his own ingenious way, Zhou Ruchang is here restating Liu Ruilian's point about how Li Qingzhao's character rules out the possibility that she remarried to Zhang Ruzhou. In addition to Zhou Ruchang, Liu's study was also warmly received by the eminent literary historian Zhou Zhenfu 周振甫. In her postface Liu thanks Zhou for his encouragement and for suggestions he made for improving her manuscript.[49] The abstract of the volume that is printed in front of the table of contents also quotes remarks of praise for the book that Zhou Zhenfu contributed.[50]

Even among those who recognized the substance and importance of Huang Shengzhang's and Wang Zhongwen's studies, there were some scholars who were still reluctant to accept their conclusions. One of the better recent accounts of Li Qingzhao's life is the chronological biography published by the Commercial Press in Taiwan in 1995. Its author, Yu Zhonghang 于中航, a Shandong scholar and official of the Ji'nan Municipal Museum, credits Huang and Wang with making many discoveries about Li Qingzhao's life and correcting long-standing errors.[51] But when it comes to the question of her remarriage, Yu steers something of a middle path. When he gets to the year 1132 in her chronology, he simply notes that there are two schools of thought regarding the historicity of the remarriage.[52] It sounds, at first, as though Yu Zhonghang is going to be completely noncommittal, recognizing the points in favor of each view. But then he goes on to discuss at considerable length the case of Ouyang Xiu and the two instances during his life when he was accused of sexual misconduct, only to have the formal charges brought against him eventually dropped in both cases. The implication that Yu Zhonghang leaves is clear: slander was widespread in Song times regarding personal conduct, especially when it came to matters of sexual conduct, and we should be skeptical of contemporary sources that may have recorded it, whether knowingly or unwittingly.

The divide in Chinese scholarship on the remarriage issue is mirrored in what little work is available on Li Qingzhao in English. Her early biography in the Twayne's World Author Series (which has remained the only full-length study of her in English up to now), written by Hu Pin-ching in 1966, summarily dismisses the episode, observing that "the rumor about her remarriage

49. Liu Ruilian, *Li Qingzhao xinlun*, p. 187.
50. Ibid., p. ii.
51. Yu Zhonghang, *Li Qingzhao nianpu*, pp. i–ii.
52. Ibid., pp. 116–17.

to Zhang Ruzhou has never been proved."[53] The reader would hardly suspect, from this language, that the "rumor" is something recorded as fact in several reputable Song period sources. On the other side of the issue is the short biography of Li Qingzhao by Ling Chung contained in the complete translation of her poems by Kenneth Rexroth and Ling. That biography deals adroitly with the issues at hand, recognizing the Qing scholars' denial as a projection of their own values ahistorically back upon Li Qingzhao's period and personal situation, adding, "The writings of these scholars must have been motivated by their wish that the private life of the greatest *ci* poetess be stainless."[54] Unfortunately, however, these insights had little impact, since the volume presents itself primarily as literary translation rather than as a scholarly study. More recently, the divide has been perpetuated in two influential anthologies devoted to Chinese women writers. The entry on Li Qingzhao by Eugene Eoyang in *Women Writers of Traditional China* echoes what Hu Pin-ching had said, glossing over the problem with minimal attention: "A legend (inspired perhaps by envy) has her marrying a low-ranking military man and divorcing him soon thereafter."[55] By contrast, Wilt Idema and Beata Grant, in their anthology, *The Red Brush: Writing Women of Imperial China*, accept the remarriage as fact. They even include an abbreviated translation of Li Qingzhao's letter to Qi Chongli and correctly describe the Qing denial of the remarriage as springing from Qing expectations and values.[56]

Back in the People's Republic, there is no question that the scholarly consensus has gradually shifted over the past twenty to thirty years. Scholars who have published major studies of Li Qingzhao since 2000 generally accept her remarriage as fact. Conspicuous among this group are the leading Li Qingzhao scholars in China, including Chen Zumei, Deng Hongmei, and Zhuge Yibing. It took nearly half a century, since the publication of Huang Shengzhang's studies in the late 1950s, for this scholarly consensus to emerge. The protracted time involved and the resilience of the anti-remarriage view should not surprise us any more than should the intensity of the rhetoric generated in this controversy. All are signs of how important Li Qingzhao had become by the twentieth century as a cultural icon of the talented woman who was also singularly devoted to her first husband. That the historical

---

53. Pin-ching Hu, *Li Ch'ing-chao*, p. 40.
54. Rexroth and Ling, *Li Ch'ing-chao*, p. 93.
55. Chang and Saussy, *Women Writers of Traditional China*, p. 89.
56. Idema and Grant, *Red Brush*, pp. 214–17.

person and her lived experience might have been considerably more complicated than the iconic perception of her, that remarriage after being widowed might not be at odds with devotion to one's first husband, and that literary talent in a woman might be quite unrelated to personal conduct, these were new ways of thinking about Li Qingzhao that could not readily replace the image of her, evolved over many centuries, that was so appealing and satisfied so many cultural values and needs.

Although the denial of Li Qingzhao's remarriage is now, among specialists at least, a minority viewpoint, it continues to exist and will, no doubt, crop up from time to time even in academic publications for the foreseeable future. Moreover, at the level of popular culture, the relative balance of viewpoints seems to be reversed. In the People's Republic today, there are four separate Li Qingzhao memorial halls and museums. Three are in Shandong: in Ji'nan, the provincial capital (her native region), Zhangqiu (her birthplace), and Qingzhou (where she lived for so many years with Zhao Mingcheng); the fourth is in Jinhua, Zhejiang (where she sought refuge in 1134, fleeing a new Jurchen invasion).[57] The largest and most prominent of these, by far, is the one in Ji'nan, which is found inside that city's centrally located Leaping Spring Park and graced with inscriptions by Guo Moruo, as mentioned in the introduction to this volume.

All of the four memorial halls display detailed chronologies of the life of Li Qingzhao in addition to portraits, statues, and calligraphy of Li Qingzhao's poems. Three of the four chronologies make no mention of Li Qingzhao's remarriage or even of the possibility that it occurred. The only chronology that does refer to the remarriage is the one in the Jinhua memorial hall, which happens also to be the memorial hall that is most distant from Li Qingzhao's native place, the most modest of the four, and surely the least visited by the public. It would be interesting to know why those who built the Jinhua hall felt obliged to mention Li Qingzhao's remarriage. Perhaps the level of scholarly involvement with that project was unusually high. Whatever the reasons, reference to the remarriage is apparently deemed inappropriate and unacceptable, even today, in the memorial halls that stand in Li Qingzhao's native region of Shandong Province.

---

57. The Chinese names of these are as follows: 李清照紀念堂 (Ji'nan), 清照園 (Zhangqiu), 李清照紀念館 (Qingzhou), and 李清照紀念堂 (Jinhua).

Li Qingzhao's image as it exists in contemporary popular culture seems to extend upward rather higher than one might expect. In my experience speaking with recent university graduates from China and Taiwan, including some who majored in Chinese literature, a large percentage of them have at best a hazy idea of a controversy concerning Li Qingzhao's remarriage. Among those who have heard of there being a controversy (and not all have), many believe that it is still lingering and unresolved.

The Concubine or Other Woman Question

A more recent development in Li Qingzhao scholarship, one that began only in the 1990s and has gained considerable momentum since, is a line of inquiry that posits domestic disharmony between Li Qingzhao and Zhao Mingcheng, and seeks to account for this disharmony by asserting that Zhao Mingcheng had taken one or more concubines during his married life or that he was having romantic affairs outside his household altogether. Upon first hearing of this argument one might think it must be deliberately provocative or simply crackpot, since it so utterly contradicts the traditional image of the Zhao-Li marriage, like the claim recently discussed abundantly on the Internet that Li Qingzhao was addicted to gambling and drinking. In fact, unlike that claim, which likely was calculated primarily to attract attention, the idea of other women in Zhao Mingcheng's life is put forward by responsible scholars and deserves serious consideration. This supposition about another woman or women coming between Zhao Mingcheng and Li Qingzhao is not something that stands by itself; rather it is invoked to serve a larger purpose or utility: it is seen as a way to account for much of the sorrow and anxiety that can readily be seen in Li Qingzhao's literary work. In what follows I will trace the development of this idea, suggesting some reasons why it has recently come into favor, and then discuss its ramifications for our understanding of the great poet.

The first thing to notice about this idea is that it is not present in the resurgence of Li Qingzhao scholarship in the early 1980s after the end of the Cultural Revolution. That period of scholarship was dominated by the remarriage controversy, and neither side in that debate gave any sustained attention to the question of the marital happiness of Li Qingzhao's first union. That was universally assumed to be a nonissue. For example, the scholar who first raised the question in the mid-1990s, Chen Zumei, had written in the early 1980s about the Zhao-Li marriage as one that had no internal conflict or disharmony. Whatever hardship Zhao and Li faced in their lives, according to the early scholarship by Chen, was imposed from outside, especially by the politics of Li Qingzhao's father-in-law, which pitted him against her own father.

But in 1995 Chen Zumei published *A Critical Biography of Li Qingzhao*, which argued at considerable length that Zhao Mingcheng had concubines, mistresses, or both.[58] This point was one of the most prominent in Chen's new book and made it highly innovative. Chen followed suit with a revised biography in 2001, *A New Biography of Li Qingzhao*, that went even further, devoting more space to this facet of Li Qingzhao's life and using it to discuss and explain even more of her poems.[59] Chen's new understanding of the problematics of the Zhao-Li marriage was taken up by Deng Hongmei in her book of 2005, also titled *A New Biography of Li Qingzhao*. Although many of the details of Deng's argument differed, and the poetic "evidence" she cites varies considerably from that cited by Chen, the general gist of her argument is the same: that Zhao Mingcheng took concubines while married to Li Qingzhao, and this action was a major source of tension in their marriage and of grief personally for Li Qingzhao.[60] In the meantime, Zhuge Yibing had published in 2004 his joint study of the couple, *Li Qingzhao and Zhao Mingcheng*. Even though that volume is part of a series titled *Literary Lovers* 文人情侣, it too reflects the new scholarly trend to discern periods of neglect and disaffection between husband and wife.[61] Yet Zhuge Yibing does not go nearly as far in emphasizing this theme or in using it to analyze Li Qingzhao's poems as do Chen Zumei and Deng Hongmei.

Two factors come to mind by way of explaining why this new approach to Li Qingzhao appeared when it did. The first has to do with the remarriage controversy. By 1990 the consensus among scholars who work on Song literature had already shifted, with most, especially those among the younger generation, now accepting her remarriage as historical fact. In other words, a key aspect of the traditional image of Li Qingzhao had already been altered. For those who accepted her remarriage, Li Qingzhao was no longer the woman who could not have even considered being "untrue" to her first husband after his death, as she was constructed during the Qing dynasty and

---

58. Chen Zumei, *Li Qingzhao pingzhuan*, pp. 64–76.
59. Chen Zumei, *Li Qingzhao xinzhuan*, pp. 77–82, 96–111, 126–29, 215–17.
60. Deng, *Li Qingzhao xinzhuan*, pp. 56–66, 69–70, 80–100.
61. Zhuge, *Li Qingzhao yu Zhao Mingcheng*, pp. 106–20.

Republican periods. After decades of heated debate, the scholarly community gradually came to understand that its own leading authorities of the preceding generations had been wrong on this crucial aspect of her life. This realization quite naturally opened the door for a reconsideration of other aspects of the received wisdom about her.

The second is the raised consciousness regarding feminism, women's studies, and women's history that swept through intellectual circles in the People's Republic in the 1990s and after. It is generally recognized that it was not until the 1990s that feminist thinking and the challenges it brings to traditional reconstructions of the present and the past became widespread in China.[62] We are speaking here of a large-scale introduction of new issues and debates, with a great range of influences, and it is not possible to delineate a highly specific trajectory of cause and effect with regard to Li Qingzhao studies. We can only point to a few hallmark events and manifestations. One was the United Nations Fourth World Conference on Women, convened in Beijing in 1995, which brought together for the first time in China feminist scholars and activists from all over the world. In conjunction with the official UN conference, which had some five thousand participants, a much larger NGO forum on women was concurrently held, and that forum attracted some thirty thousand participants. In Chinese academia, the new awareness of women's studies and women's history can be seen in a spate of conferences, courses, and publications that began to appear later in the nineties and on into the first decade of the twenty-first century. Western scholars who had been working since the 1980s on the history of women in China certainly had their impact. A conference held at Peking University in 2001 on "Research on Women's History and Historiography of the Tang and Song Dynasties" is a case in point. The conference was attended by leading American scholars working on Chinese women's history, including Dorothy Ko, Patricia Ebrey, Bettine Birge, and Beverly Bossler.

A feminist-influenced inquiry into the life and writings of Li Qingzhao would be reluctant to accept uncritically conceptions of her life and marriage formed in imperial times. The assumed emotional dependency on Zhao Mingcheng, the ready subordination to her husband in everything but poetic composition, the construction of her identity as loving wife and faithful widow, all these would naturally be called into question and subjected to

---

62. For a general overview of women's studies and its impact on Chinese studies, inside and outside the People's Republic, see Barlow, "The Direction of History and Women in China."

reexamination by scholars open to new ways of thinking about women and gender in premodern Chinese society. We recognize premodern Chinese society as a patriarchal and Confucian society. The ways that such a society would receive and represent a woman of extraordinary talent, molding her to its own needs and interests, would be subjected to critical reconsideration by scholars influenced by feminism, as well as other modern and postmodern modes of inquiry. Specifically, such scholars would consider Li Qingzhao's life and work from a standpoint that is informed by what we now recognize as inequities of power and prerogative, in marriage as well as social life generally, that women experienced on a daily basis in twelfth-century China.

I am looking here primarily at Chinese-language scholarship, but it would be remiss not to credit Stephen Owen with making a substantial contribution to the impulse and willingness to reconsider Li Qingzhao's marriage in a new light. "The Snares of Memory," a chapter on Li Qingzhao's afterword in Owen's *Remembrances: The Experience of the Past in Classical Chinese Literature*, published in 1986, was important for suggesting a new reading of that famous narrative that detected tension in the account of their marriage. Owen does not raise the question of a concubine. But what he does say about the inequities of the husband-wife relationship, which he deftly perceives in several of the passages of the afterword, helped to open the way to a different way of thinking about the marriage. Owen's analysis may have been resisted by many scholars in China, but it did, on balance, contribute to the willingness in China in the 1990s and later to rethink the traditional image of the marriage.[63]

An examination of Li Qingzhao's life cognizant of gender roles in premodern Chinese society is not going to be content to take only passing notice of the fact that Li Qingzhao never gave birth to a child, let alone a son. In traditional accounts, this lack of offspring is typically referred to only to emphasize her loneliness after Zhao Mingcheng's death. In the later scholarship on the remarriage controversy, her lack of a son is sometimes invoked to explain why she may have agreed to Zhang Ruzhou's marriage proposal at the age of forty-nine. More recent scholars, however, are committed to exploring the implications Li Qingzhao's lack of progeny may have had during her first marriage, not just subsequent to it.

---

63. See, for example, Zhuge Yibing's discussion of Owen's chapter in *Li Qingzhao yu Zhao Mingcheng*, pp. 111–12.

The lack of a son after several years of marriage would have put tremendous pressure on any husband who had the stature and means of Zhao Mingcheng to acquire one or more concubines to ensure that he had an heir. So important was it in Song society to continue the family line through a son that whatever disadvantages there might be to bringing a concubine into the household (e.g., the expense of acquiring and supporting her, the distaste a wife might have for such a course) paled by comparison. Indeed, Song sources tell of some wives who, after failing to produce a son after several years, on their own initiative purchased a concubine for their husband so that he could have an heir. Sima Guang's wife is said to have done this, although her husband, being the exceptional man he was, showed no interest in the woman.[64] Actually, whether or not a son had been produced, the practice of bringing one or more concubines into a well-to-do household was commonplace in the Song period. In her recent study of the phenomenon, Beverly Bossler speaks of the "nearly ubiquitous presence of concubines in Northern Song elite families."[65] Our understanding of Song society makes it difficult to imagine that Zhao Mingcheng would have been reluctant to acquire a concubine after several years of childless marriage to Li Qingzhao.

The problem is with proving that he actually did acquire one. There is no explicit reference in any Song source to the entry of a concubine into the Zhao-Li household. Yet the lack of any such reference is exactly what we would expect and cannot be taken as evidence that there was no concubine. Her presence would have been so unremarkable and her status so low, especially compared to the celebrated Li Qingzhao, that her existence in the household would probably not have occasioned any written record or comment.

There is no explicit mention of a concubine in any written source, but there are hints or indirect suggestions of a concubine in Li Qingzhao's own writings, as interpreted in recent scholarship. The most often cited such hint is a line from Li Qingzhao's afterword. It will be recalled that in describing the death of Zhao Mingcheng she says: "His fever was constant now, and he had also developed dysentery. His condition was beyond treatment. I wept bitterly and was too upset to ask what plans he had made for me after he was gone. On the eighteenth day of the eighth month [of 1129], he could no

---

64. Zhou Hui, *Qingbo biezhi* C.186–87; cf. Ebrey, *Inner Quarters*, pp. 220–21.
65. Bossler, *Courtesans, Concubines, and the Cult of Female Fidelity*, p. 115.

longer get up. He picked up a brush and wrote out a poem. When he finished the poem, he died. He had no final instructions regarding 'dividing up the incense or selling sandals.'"[66] It is the last line of this passage that many have seized upon as evidence that there was a concubine (or concubines) in the Zhao-Li household. The quotation is from Cao Cao's deathbed instructions to his wife and concubines, found in a dirge that Lu Ji wrote for Cao, included in the great anthology *Wenxuan*.[67] Cao Cao ordered that his remaining incense be divided among his various concubines and that, if they had further needs, they should learn to make sandals with tassels and sell them to support themselves. It is possible to read this line simply as a literary allusion to a deathbed scene and final instructions: Li Qingzhao is saying that her husband's death came so quickly that he had no time to give such instructions. In this reading, the original reference to concubines in Cao Cao's words is irrelevant. We know that allusions often work this way, with only a portion of the original meaning and context bearing on the derivative text. The argument against that simpler reading is that Li Qingzhao was too learned and careful a writer to take such a large liberty with an earlier and well-known text: she would not have drawn on Cao Cao's language unless Zhao Mingcheng had a concubine in addition to a wife. Ultimately, it is not possible to choose with certainty between the two readings of the line. There is good reason to think that the wording implies the presence of a concubine in the household, but it is impossible to be certain that that is what it means.

Scholars who believe that Zhao Mingcheng had a concubine or other lovers outside the household find support for that belief in other of Li Qingzhao's writings as well. Two poems that she wrote during the period that Zhao Mingcheng was prefect of Laizhou from 1120 to 1122, at the end of his period of unemployment in Qingzhou, are frequently cited in this regard. The first is the *shi* poem "Stirred by Emotions" that was discussed in chapter 2 in connection with Li Qingzhao's writings about writing. We look at it again, now, from a different point of view (for notes on the allusions, see the earlier translation). The poem is remarkable, even among Li Qingzhao's works, for its mood of abjection and despair. It is true that the speaker eventually finds solace in the act of writing this very poem, but what stands out is the sense of destitution of her general situation.

---

66. "Jinshi lu hou xu," *Jianzhu* 3.311; see also the translation of the entire afterword in chapter 6.

67. Lu Ji, "Diao Wei Wudi wen" 弔魏武帝文, *Wenxuan* 60.17b.

感懷 *Stirred by Emotions*

宣和辛丑八月十日到萊，獨坐一室，平生所見，皆不在目前。几上有《禮韻》，因信手開之，約以所開爲韻作詩。偶得「子」字，因以爲韻，作《感懷》詩云。

I arrived in Lai on the tenth day of the eighth month of the *xinchou* year of the Xuanhe period (1121) and found myself sitting alone in a single room. Nothing of what I was used to seeing my entire life was there before my eyes. A copy of *Rhymes for Rituals* was on the table, and I opened it randomly, having decided that I would use whatever rhyme I opened to to write a poem. By chance I opened to the character "son" and used it for my rhyme, composing a poem titled "Stirred by Emotions."

寒窗敗几無書史	A cold window, broken table, and no books,
公路可憐合至此	How pitiful was Gonglu to be brought to this!
青州從事孔方君	Qingzhou wine attendants and Lord Square Hole
終日紛紛喜生事	Enjoy causing no end of trouble all day long.
作詩謝絕聊閉門	Composing poetry I decline all invitations, closing my door for now.
燕寢凝香有佳思	Amid lingering incense in my room I have fine thoughts.
靜中我乃得至交	In isolation I have obtained perfect companions,
烏有先生子虛子	Mr. Nonexistent and Sir Vacuity.[68]

Since this is a *shi* poem, we can be more comfortable reading it as a first-person statement than with Li Qingzhao's song lyrics. Chen Zumei, Zhuge Yibing, Deng Hongmei, as well as other recent scholars all try to account for the extreme despair by speculating that Zhao Mingcheng had taken a concubine with him to Laizhou, had acquired one there, or was having extramarital affairs there when Li Qingzhao arrived from Qingzhou to join him.[69] Consequently, they argue, when Li Qingzhao did arrive, Zhao Mingcheng, who was not necessarily expecting her, lodged her in a room all by herself. It was in that room, and in a state of rejection by her husband, that she wrote this poem.

It does seem clear that Zhao went first to Laizhou, on being appointed prefect there in autumn of 1120, and that Li Qingzhao joined him there, as she says in the preface to this poem, one year later. Aside from the general mood and situation of the composition, a few details in what Li Qingzhao

---

68. *Jianzhu* 2.211.

69. Chen Zumei, *Li Qingzhao xinzhuan*, pp. 108–10; Zhuge, *Li Qingzhao yu Zhao Mingcheng*, pp. 107–15; and Deng, *Li Qingzhao xinzhuan*, pp. 94–95.

has written seem particularly significant. One is her statement "Nothing of what I was used to seeing my entire life was there before my eyes." Chen Zumei asserts that Li Qingzhao would not have said this if her husband were staying with her.[70] Another is what she says about opening the one book in the room, a ritual handbook, and "randomly" turning to the rhyme "son." If Zhao Mingcheng had acquired a concubine, the ostensible or actual reason for doing so was Li Qingzhao's inability to produce a son. If he was neglecting his wife at this time in favor of a concubine, Li Qingzhao's inability to bear a son might well be weighing heavily on her mind. The fact that "son" in Chinese (zi 子) is a particularly difficult rhyme word to write a poem to makes us suspect all the more that her choice of the word was not random at all. In addition, line 2 conveys a sense that the speaker was now confronted with a situation worse than any she ever anticipated, and the closing couplet stresses that her only "companions" are fictional literary characters.

The other piece that is cited in reference to the idea of marital disharmony and a concubine during the Laizhou period is the following song lyric:

蝶戀花   *To the tune "Butterfly Loves Flowers"* (no. 14)
晚止昌樂館寄姊妹   In the evening at Changle Station, sent to my sisters

淚搵征衣脂粉暖	Tears were wiped from the traveling coat, my rouge and powder felt warm.
四疊陽關	The four stanzas of "Yang Pass"
唱了千千遍	Were sung thousands and thousands of times.
人道山長水又斷	"The hills stretch far and rivers block the way," we said,
蕭蕭微雨聞孤館	In the lone way station we listened to soughing rain.
惜別傷離方寸亂	My heart was in turmoil, pained by our separation,
忘了臨行	Now I forget, as I made ready to set out,
酒盞深和淺	How deep the wine cup was.
若有音書憑過雁	Letters you write can be given to the passing geese.
東萊不似蓬萊遠	Donglai is not as distant as Penglai.[71]

Here is the way this song is read in recent scholarship: when Zhao Mingcheng went to take up his new post in Laizhou in 1120, he left Li Qingzhao behind in Qingzhou, but he took his concubine with him to his new post, or he acquired a concubine there, or he became romantically involved

---

70. Chen Zumei, *Li Qingzhao xinzhuan*, p. 109.

71. *Jianzhu* 1.86; *Quan Songci* 2:1204.

with other women there. Rejected and alone, Li Qingzhao decided on her own in 1121 to go join her husband and try to regain his affection. This song was written at a parting scene when Li Qingzhao had already set out for Laizhou, when she was bidding farewell to her "sisters" who had accompanied her as far as Changle Station, part way to Laizhou. (Li Qingzhao did not have any real sisters; the addressees of this poem are thought to have been other female relatives or close friends from Qingzhou.) Since Li Qingzhao was on her way to rejoin her husband, one might expect this to be an occasion filled with joy and anticipation. But it was not such an occasion, as we can see from what she wrote. The reason for all the emotion we find in this composition is that Li Qingzhao was deeply apprehensive about how she would be received by her husband in Laizhou. Her "sisters" were, at this point in her life, her only source of support and comfort, and now she was leaving them, taking a chance that she would be able to regain Zhao Mingcheng's love but worried that she might not succeed. That is why she is so reluctant to leave her female friends and implores them to stay in touch with her.[72]

There are some problems with this reading of the song, as plausible as it may sound at first. The most serious one is that the prefatory note ("In the evening at Changle Station, sent to my sisters") is not found in the earliest text of the song (in the early anthology *Elegant Lyrics*). The prefatory note, which has only been discovered in recent times, is from a text of the song included in the Yuan dynasty encyclopedia *Shiwen leiju hanmo daquan* 事文類聚翰墨大全, compiled by Liu Yingji 劉應李.[73] What if the prefatory note is a later, spurious addition? We have seen that Li Qingzhao's compositions attract biographical readings, and it is not unlikely that some editor added the note as a way of anchoring the song in Li Qingzhao's life. If read without the note, the composition can be understand in a very different way. It could be construed as a farewell piece addressed to Zhao Mingcheng when he was setting off for Laizhou. In that reading, the tears of the opening line are still Li Qingzhao's tears, but the traveling coat on which they fall is Zhao Mingcheng's garment. And in the closing lines, Li Qingzhao is imploring Zhao Mingcheng to write often to her from Laizhou, reminding him that

---

72. For this reading or slight variations on it, see Chen Zumei, *Li Qingzhao xinzhuan*, pp. 103–5; Zhuge, *Li Qingzhao yu Zhao Mingcheng*, pp. 106–16; and Deng, *Li Qingzhao xinzhuan*, pp. 92–93.

73. Cited in Wang Zhongwen, *Li Qingzhao ji jiaozhu* 1.28. The work is not available to me.

Laizhou is not, after all, as far away as the legendary Penglai. In fact, this is the way the composition was often read before the recent discovery of the prefatory note in the Yuan encyclopedia.[74] Even this reading assumes that the composition is autobiographical and directly reflects some event in Li Qingzhao's life. What if it is a literary exercise instead?

The degree of speculation concerning these two works is considerable—though not as great as in much recent scholarship on Li Qingzhao's works—and the conclusions drawn are problematic. We cannot be certain, for example, that it was another woman who was the cause of Li Qingzhao's unhappiness in the poem "Stirred by Emotions." The only things she names in that poem as sources of annoyance are drinking parties and expenditures of money. Anything identified beyond that as a root cause of her despair is a guess. It might also be incorrect to read significance into the choice of "son" as the poem's rhyme. The word might really have come to her randomly, just as she says. One modern commentator, writing before the idea of a concubine interfering in the marriage had circulated, explains that the reason for the vexation in this poem is that the Zhao-Li collection of rubbings and other artworks was not with the couple in Laizhou, and this is what Li Qingzhao is thinking of when she says that nothing she was used to was with her then.[75] The elaborate scenario scholars develop around the Changle Station song lyric is even more precarious. Stripped of its prefatory note, whose authenticity is uncertain because of its late appearance in a single source (no later anthology in premodern times repeats it), that song lyric sounds very different. The story that scholars weave around the piece may be ingenious, but it is still an invention, with roots in the long and questionable tradition of trying to situate everything that Li Qingzhao wrote in her biography and basing the meaning of her work on her identity as Zhao Mingcheng's wife.

Once the notion took root in the mid-1990s that Zhao Mingcheng must have had a concubine or other women in his life, reading Li Qingzhao's poems in light of this discovery became something of a new scholarly cause or even an obsession. Songs that had been read for centuries as simple expressions of loneliness or poetic elaborations on images of neglected beauty were now subjected to wholesale reinterpretation as expressions of despair over her husband's unfaithfulness in love. Many of these new readings are apt

---

74. This information comes from ibid. Wang is the one who first discovered the subtitle in the Yuan encyclopedia and accepts it as authentic.

75. Liu Ruilian, *Li Qingzhao xinlun*, pp. 60–61.

to strike a reader who is not committed to finding new evidence of a rival woman as strained or, at least, highly speculative. Consider, for example, a song lyric Li Qingzhao wrote in the long song form on the white chrysanthemum. This piece figures prominently in the efforts of Chen Zumei and Deng Hongmei to establish the presence of a romantic rival in Li Qingzhao's marriage:

多麗　*To the tune "Gorgeous"* (no. 6)
咏白菊　On the White Chrysanthemum

	小樓寒	The low tower was cold,
	夜長簾幕低垂	The night long, blinds and curtains hung down.
	恨蕭蕭	How unwelcome, soughing on and on,
	無情風雨	The uncaring wind and rain
5	夜來揉損瓊肌	That bruised their jadelike skin.
	也不似	They do not resemble
	貴妃醉臉	Guifei's face flushed with wine
	也不似	Nor do they resemble
	孫壽愁眉	Sun Shou's sorrowful eyebrows.
10	韓令偷香	The perfume that Director Han stole,
	徐娘傅粉	The powder that Lady Xu wore,
	莫將比擬未新奇	Were not nearly so fresh and marvelous.
	細看取	When we look closely
	屈平陶令	It is Qu Yuan and Tao Qian
15	風韻正相宜	Whose graceful bearing befits theirs.
	微風起	As a slight breeze stirs
	清芬醞藉	Their pure fragrance and refinement
	不減酴醾	Equal those of the briar rose.
	漸秋闌	As autumn reaches its end
20	雪清玉瘦	Their spotless snow and slender jade
	向人無限依依	Gaze with endless longing toward us.
	似愁凝	They seem filled with sorrow:
	漢皋解佩	The pearl pendants untied on Han'gao Mountain.
	似淚灑	They appear to be shedding tears:
25	紈扇題詩	The white silk fan inscribed with a poem.
	明月清風	With bright moonlight and chill winds
	濃煙暗雨	Heavy mists and dark rains
	天教憔悴度芳姿	Heaven makes their fragrant beauty look haggard.
	縱愛惜	No matter how much we cherish them
30	不知從此	It's impossible to know, from this moment on,
	留得幾多時	How much longer they will last.

人情好	If a person truly cares for them,
何須更憶	Why must one always think back to
澤畔東籬	Qu Yuan's marsh and Tao Qian's eastern hedge?[76]

Line 7: Stories about Yang Guifei, the Tang emperor Xuanzong's beloved concubine, include the emperor's special fondness for her face when flushed with wine.[77]

Line 9: "Sorrowful eyebrows" was one of the seductive expressions cultivated by Sun Shou 孫壽, the beautiful wife of Liang Ji 梁冀 of the Later Han.[78]

Line 10: The allusion is to the illicit romance between Han Shou 韓壽 (d. 300) and the daughter of his supervisor, Jia Chong 賈充. The daughter had access to a gift of imperial perfume, the smell of which stayed on Han Shou's person after his secret nighttime visits to her room, so that the affair came to light.[79]

Line 11: Lady Xu 徐娘 was the beautiful and eccentric concubine of Emperor Yuan of the Liang dynasty.[80] Extant sources, however, contain no reference to any powder that she used. White facial powder is often associated with the courtier He Yan 何晏 (d. 249).[81] Li Qingzhao may have mistakenly substituted Lady Xu for He Yan, or perhaps the text was corrupted in transmission. Another possibility is that Li Qingzhao was privy to a story about Lady Xu and powder that does not survive.

Line 23: In ancient times, Zheng Jiaofu 鄭交甫 encountered two goddesses on Han'gao Mountain. They were wearing pendants with large pearls, which they took off and presented to him. Soon, both the women and the pendants disappeared.[82]

Line 25: After Concubine Ban 班婕妤 lost the favor of the Han emperor Cheng (r. 32–7 BCE), she inscribed a poem on a fan, hoping that the presentation of the fan to the emperor would rekindle his love for her.[83]

Apart from the several song lyrics on plum blossoms, whose authenticity is uncertain, this is the only "song lyric on an object" (*yongwu ci* 詠物詞) among the early songs attributed to Li Qingzhao. Song lyrics on objects often present interpretive challenges. While the literal sense may be clear enough, it is frequently difficult if not impossible to be sure of any deeper level of meaning that may be intended.

---

76. *Jianzhu* 1.36–37; *Quan Songci* 2:1202–3.
77. See Li Jun, *Songchuang zalu*, p. 7a.
78. *Hou Hanshu* 34.1180.
79. Liu Yiqing, *Shishuo xinyu jianshu* 35.5.921.
80. *Nanshi* 12.341–42.
81. Liu Yiqing, *Shishuo xinyu jianshu* 14.2.608.
82. See *Taiping yulan* 803.6b, quoting *Biographies of Immortals* 列仙傳.
83. Concubine Ban's poem is "Yuange xing" 怨歌行, *Wenxuan* 27.17a–b; trans. Idema and Grant, *Red Brush*, p. 78.

The key to this composition would seem to be in the contrast between the two stanzas and the distinctions they present between what the chrysanthemum blossoms are said not to resemble and what they finally are said to resemble. But that contrast itself is complicated by a change in the latter resemblance that is developed in the second stanza.

The allusions in the first stanza are all to what would be considered frivolous and shallow types of feminine beauty, certain of which are also connected with scandal or impropriety. The mention of Yang Guifei's face flushed with wine calls to mind the disastrous effect that Emperor Xuanzong's infatuation for her had on his empire. Sun Shou was a coquette, and Director Han was involved in an illicit affair. These are allusions about feigned appearances, perfume, and powder; nothing is substantial or deeply felt in them. Such comparisons would, nevertheless, conventionally be made in poetic descriptions of a flower's beauty. Li Qingzhao insists on rejecting the comparisons for the flowers she is writing about. Having offered these negations, at the end of the stanza Li Qingzhao turns to the cultural icons Qu Yuan and Tao Qian as exemplars of the qualities she finds in the blossoms. Both men were, in fact, conventionally associated with the chrysanthemum owing to references to the flower in their poems.

But the second stanza introduces a new way of thinking about the flower. The allusions in lines 22 through 25 are two stories that have nothing to do with chrysanthemums and so are unlikely to turn up in a *yongwu ci* on the subject. This is precisely the novelty of what Li Qingzhao is doing. Yet the color white does figure prominently in each allusion: the Han'gao goddesses were wearing pendants with large white pearls, and the fan on which Concubine Ban inscribed her poem was made of white silk. The color makes the allusions permissible, even though they are not chrysanthemum allusions.

What the second stanza does is to substitute a new cluster of images for those mentioned in the first stanza. These are, first, images of feminine beauty that have no associations with frivolity or scandal. The goddesses are images of unearthly beauty and romantic love, and Concubine Ban is a sympathetic woman of talent. They represent a new way to anthropomorphize the white chrysanthemum, an alternative to both the images of coy or seductive females and those of the principled and long-suffering banished minister and recluse poet of the first stanza. The ending is particularly clever. Having concluded the first stanza with endorsement of the flower as the embodiment of male virtues of perseverance in a hostile world, the poet now poses this question: if one truly appreciates the delicate beauty and grace of this flower, what need is there always to connect it back to those celebrated men of ancient times? Li Qingzhao has put forward a new way of thinking about and savoring the flower's appeal, one that replaces its male associations with feminine ones.

Scholars who are looking for evidence of Zhao Mingcheng's meandering affections find it in the allusions in stanza 2. The reference to Concubine Ban's loss of favor is a projection of Li Qingzhao's own plight, they argue. It is more difficult to explain the Han'gao goddesses this way, and so there is disagreement on how to fit them into this interpretation of the song. Chen Zumei suggests that they are a reference to Zhao Mingcheng's dalliance with other women.[84] That way, we have a couplet devoted to Zhao Mingcheng's new love followed by a couplet on Li Qingzhao's abandonment. Deng Hongmei suggests instead that both allusions are to love that ends unhappily (the goddesses disappeared; Concubine Ban was cast aside) and that, indeed, the women involved in both stories, as ladies of beauty, elegance, and talent, are perfect parallels for Li Qingzhao herself.[85] But then this interpretation must still deal with the meaning of the song's closing lines. The solution is to read them this way, Deng says: If a person truly did cherish the flower, there would be no need to connect it always with the spurned minister and poet who could only live in isolation. Unfortunately, the "person" does not cherish the flower (i.e., Zhao Mingcheng does not care for our poet anymore), and so there is no choice but to think of the flower (i.e., Li Qingzhao) in terms of the ancient ministers who had been cast aside.

Needless to say, this song lyric had not been read this way in earlier times. Even among those who believe that there was another woman in Zhao Mingcheng's life, moreover, there are those who do not accept this interpretation of the song, evidently thinking it too unnatural. Zhuge Yibing is one such scholar. He discusses the song simply as an ingenious and highly original treatment of the white chrysanthemum, suggesting that it is a product of Li Qingzhao's poetic competitions with Zhao Mingcheng during their Qingzhou period, and adds that it stands out among her works, meaning that it does not have the burden of personal sadness that we so often encounter in her writing.[86]

---

84. Chen Zumei, *Li Qingzhao xinzhuan*, p. 77.
85. Deng, *Li Qingzhao xinzhuan*, pp. 57–58.
86. Zhuge, *Li Qingzhao yu Zhao Mingcheng*, pp. 62–63.

For an even more extreme example of imposing an "other woman" reading on Li Qingzhao's songs, we turn to Chen Zumei's interpretation of the opening stanza of one of Li Qingzhao's most famous song lyrics:

聲聲慢　*To the tune "Note after Note, Long Song"* (no. 31)

尋尋覓覓	Searching, hunting, seeking, looking,
冷冷清清	So chilly and yet so clear.
悽悽慘慘戚戚	Distressed, dismal, and forlorn.
乍暖還寒時候	Warm awhile then cold again, it's that season,
最難將息	The worst for taking care of oneself.
三杯兩盞淡酒	How can two or three cups of weak wine
怎敵他	Hold up against
晚來風力	The strength of the evening wind?
雁過也	The wild geese have flown past,
正傷心	Truly saddening the heart,
卻是舊時相識	What's more I recognize them from years past.[87]

There is a textual variant in the eighth line, *xiaolai* 曉來 "morning" (or "since morning"), instead of *wan*, "evening." Adopting this variant and combining it with the "dusk" mentioned in the second stanza of the piece causes the time frame of the song to stretch through an entire day. Many commentators prefer this variant because the extended time it yields up seems a better match for the intensity of the distress expressed in the song.

Chen Zumei does not just prefer this textual variant; she insists on it. That is because a wind "since dawn" (and lasting until dusk) allows her to argue that the line (and indeed the entire song) alludes to poem 30 in the *Classic of Poetry*, said to have been composed by Wei Jiang 衛姜, wife of Duke Zhuang of the state of Wei 衛莊公, after her husband rejected her. That poem opens with the line "All day the wind is violent" 終風且暴. The "Preface" to the *Classic of Poetry* as well as the *Zuo Commentary* explain the cause of Wei Jiang's plight: Duke Zhuang favored one of his concubines, and Wei Jiang had produced no offspring.[88] Chen Zumei thus derives an elaborate allusive frame for Li Qingzhao's composition, fitting the piece into her reconstruction of the tragedy of Li Qingzhao's childlessness and the dire consequences that had for her relationship to Zhao Mingcheng. To my knowledge, Chen is the

---

87. *Jianzhu* 1.161–62; *Quan Songci* 2:1209.
88. *Chunqiu Zuozhuan zhuzi suoyin* B1.3.7/6/12–13.

first commentator to perceive this additional meaning in Li Qingzhao's composition. Hers is a radically new reading of a piece that had been acclaimed for other characteristics through the ages.

To sum up, concerning this new line of inquiry into the likelihood that Zhao Mingcheng had other women in his life, it adds a new dimension to our consideration of the biography of Li Qingzhao. It brings a new candor to our reconstruction of the circumstances of her life. It is, indeed, likely that Zhao Mingcheng took one or more concubines when, after several years, his marriage to Li Qingzhao was still childless. To fail to recognize the probability of such a course is to fail to situate the Zhao-Li marriage in the context of Song dynasty social history. Yet such was the appeal of the idealized image of that marriage that no one wrote about this possibility until the last twenty years. The new thinking has the effect of freeing our impression of the marriage from the romanticized vision of it that had evolved through the centuries. That is no small achievement.

This new awareness of the pressures that would have exerted themselves on the couple may also affect our reading of Li Qingzhao's literary work. Here, however, we must be cautious. We still cannot be certain that there was "another woman" in Zhao Mingcheng's life. Consequently, any reading of Li Qingzhao's works that assumes there was such a woman is not logically justifiable. We may, by virtue of the new light in which her marriage is seen, suppose that we have found new ways to account for certain features of her writing, for example, her persistent loneliness, her characteristic refusal to specify the causes of her distress, and so on. But this type of reading remains speculative because we cannot be sure that our supposition about a marriage complicated by another woman is correct. Furthermore, if we use a conviction about the presence of a concubine in the marriage as the basis for interpreting Li Qingzhao's song lyrics, we are repeating the old error of failing to distinguish between her biography and her literary works, and reducing the latter to mere projections of her biographical circumstances.

Recently, new evidence has come to light that Zhao Mingcheng did, after all, produce offspring. A previously overlooked passage in certain editions of the Ming gazetteer *Bamin tongzhi* 八閩通志 refers to the "sons" 諸子 of Zhao Mingcheng living with their uncle in Quanzhou 泉州 (in Fujian) after their father died.[89] The wording of the passage is somewhat unclear, and the

---

89. Huang Zhongzhao et al., *Bamin tongzhi* 68.3b.

sons referred to might conceivably belong to another of Mingcheng's brothers, but the most natural reading would identify them as Mingcheng's sons. At the time of this writing, the paper that makes this finding has not yet been published.[90] It is too early to say how the scholarly community will receive this argument, which is likely to be viewed as highly controversial. If, in due course, it generally becomes established that Zhao Mingcheng did father children with a concubine, it will then be time to reconsider Li Qingzhao's writings with that fact in mind.

The pitfalls that this new way of thinking about Li Qingzhao and her marriage may lead to are apparent. Scholars who are committed to the idea of a concubine or other woman in Zhao Mingcheng's life ransack Li Qingzhao's writings, looking for veiled references to substantiate their speculation. Song lyrics that are undatable in the first place, and are probably best not read as narrowly autobiographical, are then interpreted as expressions of sorrow or anger over Zhao Mingcheng's fickleness in love, when in fact the song may have been composed before Li Qingzhao's marriage or after Zhao Mingcheng's death, and have nothing to do with any sort of marital infidelity. Allusions are perceived where they may not have been intended, or allusions are interpreted to support the concubine theory, while other equally plausible interpretations are ignored. It is no wonder, then, there is little agreement among the proponents of the "other woman" idea concerning how particular compositions by Li Qingzhao support the interpretation. The readings of the compositions offered are subjective and highly arbitrary as seen in the foregoing discussion. For a more comprehensive listing of the disagreements among the interpretations, see appendix 2.

---

90. Qian Jianzhuang, "Weirao Zhao Mingcheng 'zhuzi.'"

CHAPTER 10

Song Lyrics, Part 1

We finally turn now to Li Qingzhao's song lyrics, the portion of her writing for which she is best known. We have delayed taking up the subject until now in order to delve into her other writings and her biography as well as the complicated history of the way her image and reputation have been transformed and manipulated through time. All of these matters are inextricably linked to the ways her song lyrics are usually read today. In trying to go beyond standard treatments of her song lyrics, which tend quickly to conflate her poetry with her marriage and widowhood, it is best to do so with full knowledge of the whims and vicissitudes of her reception history. Given their long history and weight, it is difficult to break free of traditional images of her. It would be even more difficult to do so if their provenance, function, and change through time were not first explicitly addressed and understood.

We are now in a position to propose new ways of dealing with the problem of reading Li Qingzhao's works autobiographically, discussed in chapter 3. Consider the following song lyric, one attributed to her in the early anthology *Elegant Lyrics*:

訴衷情 *To the tune "Telling My Deepest Feelings"* (no. 22)

夜來沈醉卸妝遲	Drunk last night, I was slow to take off my make-up.
梅萼插殘枝	Plum blossoms in my hair have withered on their stem.
酒醒熏破春睡	Sobering up, their scent interrupts my spring sleep,
夢遠不成歸	My distant dream did not carry me home.

人悄悄	No sounds of people now,
月依依	The moon hangs longingly in the sky.
翠簾垂	The green blinds are lowered.
更挼殘蕊	Again, I finger the withered flowers,
更撚餘香	Again, pinching out their remaining fragrance,
更得些時	Again, to get a little more time.[1]

First, a comment about the voicing in the original language as opposed to the translation. In the original, we might understand this poem as written either in the first person (as translated) or in the third person, that is, spoken by a narrator who is observing the woman being described. There is nothing in the Chinese that precludes either reading. This is often the case with Chinese poetry, though not always the case. The Chinese poet often has the luxury of not having to commit to one or the other; the English translator must make a commitment, and different translators will choose different options.

I have deliberately translated the poem in the first person to facilitate the question I want to ask. How do we read this poem; specifically, how do we understand the relationship between the speaking voice in the poem and Li Qingzhao, the historical person? The immediate response of most readers is that of course the speaker is Li Qingzhao. The woman in this poem fits well with the conventional image of "Li Qingzhao," the hypersensitive, distraught, and long-suffering female that the tradition for various reasons has made her out to be. The poem, read this way, is an affirmation of the conventional image of her, and the conventional image is immediately available to provide a way of interpreting the poem.

In chapter 3 I have explained why such a reading is problematic. It is not the way we read song lyrics written by Li Qingzhao's male contemporaries. It is condescending to assume that a woman is incapable of creating and manipulating poetic personas when we recognize that ability in male writers. It may be that the poem is less effective for us, less moving and revealing, when we remove the author from it, separating her and her life from the woman who is a literary creation in the poem. That is a different matter, a matter of literary effect and appreciation, and need not be entangled with the issue of putting Li Qingzhao's literary work on an equal footing with that by male writers. When we allow ourselves to hear the historical Li Qingzhao in such poems, we are surrendering clear thinking about her situation and talent

---

1. *Jianzhu* 1.111; *Quan Songci* 2:1206.

to the weight of centuries of romanticization of her as loving wife and long-suffering devotee of Zhao Mingcheng. If the history of Li Qingzhao's reception in the centuries after her death teaches us anything, it shows how adroitly different groups in different periods, each with its own values and conscious or unconscious agendas, have manufactured a "Li Qingzhao" to suit its own needs. We emerge from our examination of that history with a new humility regarding the question of what, after all, is knowable about the person behind the hauntingly engaging and elusive poetry.

There are various possibilities regarding the voice we hear in the song lyric. At the two extremes, it could be, first, a complete invention, having no meaningful connection with the person Li Qingzhao or her situation and feelings. Second, it could indeed be the historical person speaking to us as herself, as Li Qingzhao. I take the likelihood of either of these extremes to be very low. Literary expression inevitably draws, at some level, on the life experience of the author. But those experiences are shaped as they are given expression by literary genre, history, and whatever "artistry" the author brings to her task. No writing is entirely free of mediating influences of form and convention. If it were, it would probably not be intelligible.

Another possibility is that Li Qingzhao is deliberately exploiting her identity as a woman in cultivating a woman's literary persona. Of course she was very cognizant of her singularity as a woman poet. The men around her would not let her forget this singularity for a minute, and her awareness of it shows clearly through in her essay on the song lyric form, as argued earlier. We can never know at what level or degree of consciousness it may have occurred to her that, as a woman, she had an advantage when writing in a literary form that featured images of women and "feminine" sentiments. We do know that in her song lyrics, at least those that survive, she refrains from cultivating the voice of a woman who obviously could not be she herself. That is, she does not project the voice of a palace lady or, at the other end of the social scale, a female entertainer or low-class singing girl. The women who "appear" in her song lyrics occupy much the same social status and space that Li Qingzhao herself occupied in upper-class society. She even occasionally allows into her songs details from her biography, mentioning, for example, actual places such as town, lakes, and buildings that she moved among. It is entirely possible that, competitive person that she was, she sensed that she as a woman could cultivate an aura of sincerity or authenticity in this special literary genre and took advantage of it. But if that is so, the persona who speaks in her songs is still a cultivated voice, an artful one, and should be distinguished from Li Qingzhao the person. To allow the possibility of such artistry, such artifice, is a more responsible approach than simply to assume, without reflecting on the implications of the assumption, that whenever she writes, she can only write as the historical Li Qingzhao.

In what follows I will attempt to discuss the distinctive traits of Li Qingzhao's song lyrics, treating them as literary works and not as windows onto the private life and emotions of the author. The question of how the voice we hear in her songs is related to the thoughts and feelings of Li Qingzhao the historical person is ultimately unanswerable. Recognizing it as unanswerable, it is best to put it aside, to resist the temptation to suppose that through her songs we can be privy to her "true, heartfelt" sentiments and that it is these that are the keys to her effectiveness as a writer. My departure point, by contrast, is to suppose that her literary works do not need to be read that way to appreciate their effectiveness or to identify the features that set them apart.

As we proceed to examine her song lyrics, we must do so bearing in mind what has been said in chapter 3 regarding the problems of the reliability of many of the compositions attributed to her. Consequently, I will concentrate on what I have designated as groups 1 and 2 of her songs, those with the earliest (Song period) attributions to her.

There are several ways that Li Qingzhao's output in song lyrics might be presented and analyzed. This chapter will treat them according to a few discrete features and thematic groupings: her habit of rewriting earlier poetic lines, a subset of songs unusual for being about a woman's outings into nature, and the peculiar mood or psychology of the woman presented in many pieces. It is my aim in structuring the chapter this way to discuss her best-known song lyrics as well as several usually overlooked, and also to take up, one by one, the key aspects of her corpus that make it so distinctive. In chapter 11, two clusters of later songs attributed to Li Qingzhao will be discussed for what they tell us about the ways Li Qingzhao was imagined in later times and how such songs depart from what we find in the earlier, more reliable attributions.

Rewriting Earlier Lines

One of Li Qingzhao's favorite techniques is to adapt or rewrite lines from earlier poetry. The earlier lines may be in *shi* poetry or song lyrics, but when Li Qingzhao draws on them, she effects changes. To rewrite earlier lines in this way is not a practice unique to Li Qingzhao. Employed by many song lyrics writers of her time, it is a technique known as *yinkuo* 檃括, "to straighten," that is, "to adapt" a previous phrase to one's own purpose. Probably the most common form is to borrow an entire line from an earlier *shi* poem and incorporate it unchanged into a song lyric. Zhou Bangyan is particularly known for doing this. It is a tour de force that inevitably alters the literal meaning or import of the line, and the educated reader enjoys hearing the "echo" of an earlier poetic line (e.g., lifted from a Tang *shi* poem) now placed in a new setting. Another common practice was to recast an entire earlier piece, originally written in another poetic form or even in prose, into a song lyric. Su Shi famously did this several times, for example, setting Tao Qian's "The Return" 歸去來兮辭 and Han Yu's descriptive *shi* poem on a zither performance to song lyric tunes. Huang Tingjian also did it, setting Ouyang Xiu's prose piece "Inscription on a Drunken Old Man's Pavilion" 醉翁亭記 to the tune "Lucky Crane Immortal" 瑞鶴仙.[2]

What Li Qingzhao likes to do is somewhat different. She is fond of borrowing one or more lines from an earlier poem and changing the wording at the same time, in effect rewriting the original and giving it a decidedly new thrust and direction. It is tempting to posit a connection between her fondness for doing this, which has been remarked on before, and her special identity as a woman writer. In chapter 2, we saw abundant evidence of her self-consciousness as a writer, her keen awareness of herself as a woman writer, and her sense of competing with male writers, especially in this particular genre that was so heavily associated with female subjects, voices, and sentiments. One way to think of her fondness for rewriting earlier poetic lines is to see it as one small but telling manifestation of her competitiveness with men as a woman writer. There is something forward and apparent about the way Li Qingzhao borrows and rewrites earlier lines. She does it in a way that advertises or calls attention to itself. In one instance, as we will see, she even goes out of her way in a preface to a song lyric to announce what she is doing. Such an announcement was a most unusual thing for a song lyrics writer to make, yet it is in keeping with the forwardness of Li Qingzhao's borrowings.

We begin with this topic, in any case, both because it is a feature of her song lyrics, found in many of her compositions, and because it is suggestive about the self-consciousness and meticulousness of her approach to writing

---

2. On this technique in song lyrics generally, see Uchiyama, "Liang Song yinkuo cikao"; and Wu Chengxue, "Lun Songdai yinkuo ci."

in this form generally. In her critical essay "On Song Lyrics," Li Qingzhao took some major writers of the preceding generation to task for having a cavalier attitude toward the genre, for not taking it seriously enough or putting earnest effort into composing in it. The ways that Li Qingzhao rewrote earlier poetic lines in her song lyrics points to a writerly attitude and approach that was anything but nonchalant.

Here is the first example, in one of her most widely anthologized compositions:

如夢令　　*To the tune "As If in a Dream"* (no. 5)

昨夜雨疏風驟	Last night the rain was intermittent, the wind blustery.
濃睡不消殘酒	Deep sleep did not dispel the lingering wine.
試問捲簾人	I tried asking the maid who raised the blinds,
却道海棠依舊	She said the crab apple blossoms were as before.
知否	"Don't you know?
知否	Don't you know?
應是綠肥紅瘦	The greens must be plump and the reds withered."[3]

This song lyric is derived from the last four lines of a *shi* poem by the late Tang poet Han Wo 韓偓 (842–923). Han Wo's entire poem is this:

懶起　　*Too Lethargic to Arise*

百舌喚朝眠	The shrieks awake her with their calls,
春心動幾般	How many feelings stir her amorous heart!
枕痕霞黯澹	Stains on the pillow are somber evening clouds,
淚粉玉闌珊	Tear-streaked powder is speckled jade.
籠繡香煙歇	Incense no longer shrouds the embroidered bed curtain,
屏山燭燄殘	The candle's flame flickers weakly on the painted screen.
煖嫌羅襪窄	For warmth, she begrudges her thin gauze stockings,
瘦覺錦衣寬	Grown thin, the brocade robe feels too large.
昨夜三更雨	Last night, rain at midnight,
今朝一陣寒	This morning, a barrage of chilly air.
海棠花在否	Are the crab apple blossoms still there or not?
側臥捲簾看	She turns on her side to open the blinds and look.[4]

---

3. *Jianzhu* 1.14; *Quan Songci* 2:1202.
4. Han Wo, "Lanqi," *Quan Tangshi* 683.7832.

It is useful to read the entire Han Wo poem, not just the lines that were Li Qingzhao's immediate inspiration. First, there can be no question that Li Qingzhao draws on the Tang poem. There are too many elements common to both works for this to have been a coincidence.

That said, Li Qingzhao's transformation of what Han Wo had written is striking. In Han Wo's poem the last four lines read almost like an afterthought. Before we get to them, we already know as much as we need to know about the female subject. However, after all the conventional language of the first eight lines, toward the end the woman is finally permitted a relatively spontaneous thought, wondering if the crab apple blossoms have survived the previous night's rain and chilly air. Li Qingzhao seizes on this moment in the poem and makes an entire song lyric out of it. She dispenses, in other words, with all of the stock language and imagery of the preceding lines and develops the least conventional element in Han Wo's poem into a separate composition. While doing this, she enhances considerably the interest of this moment by dramatizing it and especially by introducing another person into the room, presumably a maid performing the task of lifting the blinds in the morning. This menial person is the perfect foil to the oversensitive mistress of the room because the maid, going about her daily routine, is either oblivious of the diminished condition of the blossoms outside the window or does not care. To her the flowers are just the same as yesterday or may as well be. This lackadaisical attitude is what provokes the lady's outburst: "Don't you know? Don't you know?" Li Qingzhao has even lifted the key word in her piece, *shou* 瘦, "thin, withered," from Han Wo's poem, although it occurs outside of the last four lines of his work and is applied to the woman rather than to the flowers. Whereas *shou* in Han Wo's usage is clichéd, Li Qingzhao's usage of it is highly original; indeed, it is what the song is remembered for.

Another example of a conspicuous borrowing and transformation involves a song lyric's opening line: "Deep, the deep courtyard, how deep is it?" 庭院深深深幾許. Li Qingzhao thought that the song this line opens had been written by Ouyang Xiu, but in fact the piece (and the line) was written by the Southern Tang poet Feng Yansi 馮延巳 (903–60). Here is Feng's entire song:

鵲踏枝　　*To the tune "Magpie Steps on the Branch"*

庭院深深深幾許	Deep, the deep courtyard, how deep is it?
楊柳堆煙	Willows pile up the mist,
簾幕無重數	Countless layers of blinds and curtains.

| 玉勒雕鞍遊冶處 | Jade bridle and carved saddle are in the pleasure quarters. |
| 樓高不見章臺路 | Zhangtai Road cannot be seen from the high tower. |

雨橫風狂三月暮	Wild winds drive slanting rain, sunset in the third month.
門掩黃昏	The gate shuts in the dusk,
無計留春住	But there's no way to detain spring.
淚眼問花花不語	Tear-filled eyes ask the flowers, the flowers do not speak.
亂紅飛入秋千去	A whirl of red petals flies past the garden swing.[5]

Line 4: "Jade bridle and carved saddle" evokes the horses of elegant young men who roam about the pleasure quarters. Presumably the woman's lover is among these young gallants.

Line 5: Zhangtai Road is another name for the pleasure quarters.

Li Qingzhao was attracted to the opening line and, appropriating it, composed several pieces of her own with the same opening line, rewriting, in effect, what followed it. She announces in a preface to one of her songs: "Mr. Ouyang composed a song lyric to the tune 'Butterfly Loves Flowers' that contains the line 'Deep, the deep courtyard, how deep is it?' I am terribly fond of the line (予酷愛之). I have used his wording in composing several verses that begin with the same words, set to the tune 'Immortal by the River.'" Although she says she has written "several" pieces using this line, only one survives in an early attribution. It is this piece:

臨江仙   *To the tune "Immortal by the River"* (no. 19)

庭院深深深幾許	Deep, the deep courtyard, how deep is it?
雲窗霧閣常扃	Cloudy windows and misty halls are forever locked.
柳梢梅萼漸分明	Willow tips and plum buds can gradually be seen.
春歸秣陵樹	Spring returns to the trees of Moling,
人客建康城	This person is a sojourner at Jiankang city.

感月吟風多少事	Moved by the moon, chanting in the wind, so much has happened!
如今老去無成	Today I'm old and have accomplished nothing.
誰憐憔悴更彫零	Haggard and declining too, who pities me?
試燈無意思	Trying the lanterns holds no interest for me,
踏雪沒心情	And I've no enthusiasm for treading on the snow.[6]

There are textual and other problems with this song. Different versions of the song in different anthologies contain many textual variants. The version

5. Feng Yansi, "Que ta zhi," *Quan Tang Wudai ci* 1:3.656.
6. *Jianzhu* 1.105 (adopting some of the textual variants in *Yuefu yaci*); *Quan Songci* 2:1205.

given here is essentially the earliest one, from *Elegant Lyrics*. The place-name in line 5 exists in at least three variants: Yuanan 遠安, Jian'an 建安, and Jiankang (as above). Commentators choose among these on the basis of how they reconstruct Li Qingzhao's travels and when they imagine this poem to have been composed. It probably makes more sense to choose among the three the place that best matches the preceding line's "Moling," an alternate name for Nanjing. In that case, Jiankang (another alternate for Nanjing) is preferable.

Despite all the uncertainties concerning the meaning of this song, we can still offer a tentative reading. The person in the song feels confined, trapped almost, in a locked building and the deep enclosure she looks out on. Spring has come to the place where she is, but the arrival of the season only intensifies her awareness of how much she has undergone and her feeling that she is not where she would like to be. She is near Moling (a site associated in song lyrics with parting scenes), which is somewhere near Jiankang. The speaker is a writer and thinks of herself primarily in that capacity. Furthermore, despite how much poetry she has written (line 6), she feels that it amounts to nothing (line 7). Depressed by this thought, she is keenly aware of her aging. Consequently, activities such as hanging paper lanterns or going for a walk in the snow, which might have brought her pleasure or diversion at other times, now hold no interest for her.

Furthermore, we can see how much distance Li Qingzhao has put between her composition and the song by "Ouyang Xiu" (actually Feng Yansi) that inspired it. Li Qingzhao says that she is inordinately fond of the earlier song's opening line, but we now see that she has substantively rewritten the song that followed from that opening. Her song still presents a woman who is secluded or trapped, but she is a very different sort of woman. She is not the stereotypical woman of song lyrics (as in the earlier song) who has been left alone because her philandering man is off looking for professional entertainers and who is presented with tear-filled eyes and no thoughts of her own beyond her longing for the man who has abandoned her. The woman in Li Qingzhao's poem may also feel sorry for herself, but she is not wholly focused on an absent man. Even her rejection of possible diversions (the last two lines) implies her ability, in other times and moods, to sustain herself with a kind of self-sufficiency. It is just that that possibility does not exist in the present moment of despair.

There is another type of rewriting evident in Li Qingzhao's song lyrics that operates on a smaller scale, involving just a line or two rather than an entire composition. Yet it is just as interesting, despite the more localized effect, and equally revealing of her distinctive genius as a writer. The two examples discussed above both show Li Qingzhao radically altering the female subject in an earlier poem from which she borrows. The following examples display a wider range of changes, yet some shared tendencies can be noted among them. Consider the closing lines of the second stanza of the following song by Li Qingzhao, discussed in another context in chapter 3:

一翦梅　*To the tune "A Single Cutting of Plum Blossoms"* (no. 13)

. . . .

花自飄零水自流	Blossoms fall on their own, the water flows by itself.
一種相思	One type of longing,
兩處閒愁	Idle sadness in two places.
此情無計可消除	There's no means to get rid of this feeling.
纔下眉頭	As soon as it leaves the brow
却上心頭	It surfaces in the heart.[7]

The last two lines, as Xu Peijun has pointed out, are derived from lines in a song lyric by the Northern Song statesman Fan Zhongyan 范仲淹 (989–1052).[8] Here is his song:

御街行　*To the tune "Walking on the Imperial Road"*

紛紛墮葉飄香砌	Leaves fall everywhere, drifting over the fragrant steps.
夜寂靜	The night is quiet,
寒聲碎	They sound brittle in the cold.
眞珠簾捲玉樓空	The pearl blinds are raised, the jade tower is empty.
天淡銀河垂地	In the pale sky the Silver River hangs over the earth.
年年今夜	Year after year this night,
月華如練	The moonlight as white as boiled silk,
長是人千里	The person always a thousand miles distant.
愁腸已斷無由醉	The sad heart broken, there's no way to get drunk.
酒未到	Before the wine is tasted
先成淚	Tears already flow.
殘燈明滅枕頭欹	The dying lamp flickers, the pillow lies askew.
諳盡孤眠滋味	She's tasted fully the flavor of sleeping alone.

---

7. *Jianzhu* 1.20; *Quan Songci* 2:1204.
8. For Xu's comment on the borrowing, see *Jianzhu* 1.23, n. 8.

都來此事	This matter, she figures,
眉間心上	Not for the brow or the heart
無計相迴避	Is there any way to avoid it.[9]

It is not just the shared wording (*mei* 眉, *xin* 心, *wuji* 無計) plus the synonymity of *xiaochu* 消除 and *huibi* 迴避 that points to conscious borrowing and transformation by Li Qingzhao. It is also the placement of the lines at the very end of both compositions. On top of that, given Fan Zhongyan's fame (plus the fact that he seems to have composed very few song lyrics), it stands to reason that Li Qingzhao would have known his song.

The change that Li Qingzhao has made in Fan Zhongyan's formulation may be linguistically simple, but its implications are far-reaching. Fan's lines mean simply that the woman cannot "get away" from the loneliness that plagues her and that it is present in her face and her heart alike. Li Qingzhao's lines introduce a hierarchy of "brow" and "heart." The woman may be able to banish the appearance of sadness from her face, but it will then surface in her heart, and from there, the implication is, she will be unable to banish it. This way of putting the matter gives attention to the subject's inner life and indeed suggests a contrast between superficial exterior and substantive interior. Whereas Fan Zhongyan treats "brow" and "heart" as equals, Li Qingzhao suggests that there is something far "deeper" about the latter. This quality of the heart, in fact, is so profound that it lies beyond the capacity of the person concerned to control it, while she can control or mask her face.

The last instance of creative borrowing we will discuss here involves a river and boat motif. The analogy between the water flowing in a river and a great quantity of human sorrow was famously evoked in the closing lines of a song lyric by Li Yu, the last ruler of the Southern Tang: "I ask how much sorrow can one have? / Just like the entire volume of the swollen Yangzi River in spring as it flows east" 問君能有多少愁 / 恰似一江春水向東流.[10] Perhaps with Li Yu's lines in mind, the early Song poet Zheng Wenbao 鄭文寶 (953–1013) came up with a new formulation of the idea of rivers and sorrow as physical quantity or capacity, suggesting that the boat on which a traveler was departing carried in addition to that man a heavy "freight" of sorrow:

---

9. Fan Zhongyan, "Yujie xing," *Quan Songci* 1:14.
10. Li Yu, "Yu meiren" 虞美人, *Quan Tang Wudai ci* 1:3741.

絕句三首·其一   *Three Quatrains, No. 1*

亭亭畫舸繫春潭	Graceful, the painted ship tied at the cove in spring,
直到行人酒半酣	Waits until the traveler is half tipsy with wine.
不管煙波與風雨	Heedless of misty waves and wind-blown rain
載將離恨過江南	It will carry parting sadness through the Southland.[11]

Zheng Wenbao's idea proved to be a favorite with later poets, as Qian Zhongshu has pointed out, and was repeated with slight variations time and again.[12] On his way up the Grand Canal ("Bian River") in 1084, Su Shi opened a song lyric he presented to Qin Guan with these lines:

波聲拍枕長淮曉	Waves lap at my pillow, dawn on the long Huai River,
隙月窺人小	Through a crack a tiny slice of moon peeks at me.
無情汴水自東流	Heartless, the Bian River flows toward the east
只載一船離恨	It carries an entire boatload of parting sadness
向西州	On toward the western districts.[13]

Here it is the river that "carries" the boat, but the boat is still bearing a burden of parting sadness. The interest of these lines is increased by the contrary movement to which Su calls attention: the canal is flowing eastward, but he will be sailing westward, against the current. Su probably intends this as a metaphor for the opposition between his desire to remain with his friend and his duty to proceed to his new post in Ruzhou.

Since Su Shi was far more famous, once he had adapted Zheng Wenbao's lines, the formulation "became" his and was, in turn, imitated by his admirers. Using the same tune pattern and clearly echoing Su Shi, Chen Yuyi 陳與義 (1090–1138) wrote, "Tomorrow when I sober up from wine, the great Yangzi flowing / Will carry an entire boatload of parting sadness / On toward Hengzhou" 明朝酒醒大江流 / 滿載一船離恨 / 向衡州.[14] Zhou Bangyan ingeniously worked Su Shi's lines into the first stanza of a much longer song lyric, while expanding upon the lines themselves:

---

11. Zheng Wenbao, "Jueju sanshou, qi yi," *Quan Songshi* 1:640.

12. Qian Zhongshu, *Songshi xuanzhu*, pp. 3–4.

13. Su Shi, "Yu meiren" 虞美人, no. 4, *Quan Songci* 1:395.

14. Chen Yuyi, "Yu meiren" 虞美人, *Quan Songci* 2:1387.

尉遲杯　*To the tune "Yuchi's Wine Cup"*

隋堤路	Along the Sui Dike road
漸日晚	Gradually dusk gathers.
密靄生深樹	Thick mist forms in the deep woods,
陰陰淡月籠沙	Dimly a pale moon veils the sand,
還宿河橋深處	I return to sleep at a secluded spot beside River Bridge.
無情畫舸	Heartless, the painted ship
都不管	Is heedless of all the
煙波隔南浦	Misty waves from here to the south bank,
等行人	Awaiting this traveler,
醉擁重衾	Drunkenly clutching his lined quilt,
載將離恨歸去	Carrying parting sadness on the journey back.[15]

Line 1: Sui Dike was on the bank of the Bian River near Bianliang, from which the speaker is departing.

After these several iterations of the motif, we come to Li Qingzhao's handling of it:

武陵春　*To the tune "Spring in Wuling"* (no. 43)

風住塵香花已盡	The winds stop, the ground is fragrant, the flowers gone,
日晚倦梳頭	As the day wears on I'm too lethargic to comb my hair.
物是人非事事休	The things are right, the person wrong, everything is over,
欲語淚先流	About to speak, tears first flow.
聞說雙溪春尚好	I've heard spring is still lovely at Twin Streams
也擬泛輕舟	I'd like go boating in a light skiff there
只恐雙溪舴艋舟	But fear the tiny grasshopper boats they have there
載不動	Would not carry
許多愁	Such a quantity of sorrow.[16]

---

15. Zhou Bangyan, "Yuchibei," *Quan Songci* 2:790.

16. *Jianzhu* 1.140; *Quan Songci* 2:1208. This is the only piece from my group 3 that I discuss in this chapter as credibly coming from Li Qingzhao. It does, by date of first attribution, belong to group 3, but there are some mitigating circumstances. First, the existence of the song is attested in the Southern Song because it appears in *Caotang shiyu* (ca. 1195), "Qianji" A.509. Second, although in that work it is given no attribution, it appears immediately after a piece that is explicitly attributed to Li Qingzhao (no. 5). As others have pointed out, early anthologies do not necessarily repeat an author's name when it is the same in consecutive pieces. So although we cannot say that the work is explicitly attributed to Li Qingzhao in the anthology, there are grounds for believing that the compiler thought it was hers.

Consider how Li Qingzhao's situation, as a woman, is connected to what is different about her use of this motif. This is the first time we encounter the motif outside of a parting poem. Earlier, the boat in question was a traveler's boat, and the assertion was that the boat would be weighed down not just with the traveler, but also with the burden of melancholy he took with him as he went away from those he would rather stay with. It was, of course, men who traveled by themselves, crisscrossing the territory of the vast empire, often in response to an official posting or other assignment. Li Qingzhao did her share of long distance travel, but unlike the men of her day, she was not constantly forced to pick up and proceed to a new place by a bureaucratic career. She was, however, very fond, as we will see, of writing about daytime outings, especially outings in small pleasure boats. Here, the persona in the song considers such an outing but ends up rejecting the prospect because on this particular day she is feeling too out of sorts. To evoke this feeling of hopelessness, Li Qingzhao draws on the tradition of parting poems and songs and their conceit of a boat carrying a heavy load of sadness. No one had ever used the conceit to say that the boat could not carry the emotion. Such a statement would have no place in a parting poem, because the parting always happened, no matter how reluctant the traveler was to leave. But Li Qingzhao's afternoon outing is something that need not take place. The prospect can be rejected as ill-suited to the mood of the speaker. A brief outing on some stream, moreover, does not call for a large boat. A small craft, the kind that could be paddled by a single woman, would be adequate. Such a small craft, then, lends itself aptly to the idea of a quantity of emotion overwhelming it, making for a truly creative reworking of what had become a stock poetic figure.

The Outdoors

We are accustomed to thinking of women of Li Qingzhao's era as living almost exclusively indoors, and not only indoors but secluded in "inner quarters," that is, sections of the residence set aside exclusively for women. The writings of Li Qingzhao do not entirely fit this stereotype. There is, to be sure, plenty of attention in her works to women living in sequestered rooms in seclusion. But there is also a surprising amount of writing about a woman roaming about outdoors, not just in the family courtyard or garden but in the unbounded outdoors, beyond any enclosure. It is difficult to say if Li Qingzhao herself was singularly unconstrained in this respect or if our assumptions about the seclusion of educated women in this period—before more restrictions were placed on their movement and also before foot-binding became widespread—need to be reconsidered. The anecdote mentioned earlier about how Li Qingzhao liked to go out in snowstorms and walk along the city wall in search of poetic inspiration favors the first possibility. One of the points of that story is to emphasize how atypical her behavior was for a woman.

Here is one of her song lyrics about an outing into nature, presented in chapter 7 as an example of pieces that most Southern Song anthologies chose to exclude:

怨王孫　　*To the tune "Resenting the Prince"* (no. 18)

湖上風來波浩渺	Wind comes across the lake, waves stretch endlessly.
秋已暮	At the end of autumn
紅稀香少	The red flowers are few, the fragrances slight.
水光山色與人親	They befriend me, the water's light and hills' colors,
說不盡	Impossible to describe,
無窮好	The infinite appeal of the scene.
蓮子已成荷葉老	The lotus seeds are formed, the leaves droop.
清露洗	Pure dew washes
蘋花汀草	Duckweed flowers and islet grasses.
眠沙鷗鷺不回頭	Gulls and egrets napping on the sand do not turn to look,
似也恨	As if they begrudge me
人歸早	Going home so early.[17]

As many have pointed out, given the tradition of "sorrowing over autumn" (*beiqiu* 悲秋) in Chinese poetry, a song like this that insists on the beauty of a late autumn scene, without any reference to remorse or regrets, is very unusual. In this respect alone the song is already most original. Owing to the fond description of the scene in the first stanza, when we read the closing lines, we quite naturally think that Li Qingzhao has transposed onto the birds the persona's own feelings about leaving such a scene. It is really this transposition of feelings, from the speaker to the birds, that makes the ending so effective. Since the woman is going home at the end of the song, we conclude that this has been a single day's outing. It was a day's outing that brought her to this place, the result of a calculated decision to spend the day outside,

---

17. *Jianzhu*, "Buyi," p. 540; *Quan Songci* 2:1205.

away from the home. It sounds like this is an outing in a boat. Several of the details in the poem suggest this, including the mention of lotus plants (once in each stanza) and all the other aquatic imagery; indeed, some Ming anthologies present this piece with the subtitle "Enjoying Lotuses" 賞荷. As we will see, Li Qingzhao frequently writes about a woman going boating. One other noteworthy feature is that there is nothing in the entire piece that suggests the woman has anyone accompanying her on this outing. The wording seems deliberately crafted to call attention to the speaker's solitary state. Indeed, what "befriends" her is not human companions but selective elements of nature. First, it is the water and the mountains, and then it is the birds that do not want to witness her departure. When the woman leaves the scene to return home to society, she is leaving, reluctantly, an unpeopled natural scene that has welcomed her into it.

Li Qingzhao's best-known outdoors poem is the following one:

如夢令　　*To the tune "As If in a Dream"* (no. 4)

常記溪亭日暮	I often recall one sunset in the pavilion by the river.
沈醉不知歸路	Having drunk too much, I lost the way home.
興盡晚回舟	My enthusiasm spent, I started back in my boat at dusk
誤入藕花深處	But drifted by mistake into a thick patch of lotuses.
爭渡	Paddling hard to get through,
爭渡	Paddling hard to get through,
驚起一灘鷗鷺	I startled a whole sandbar of egrets into flight.[18]

The situation in this song shares several features with that of the previous piece. Again the woman is on a daylong outing in a boat, and she seems to be alone. There is no hint that even an attendant or servant accompanies her. She is the one who has to struggle to propel the boat through the towering clump of lotus plants she had strayed into.

Unlike in the previous song lyric, this time there is no explicit acknowledgment of the beauty of the natural scene. Yet the speaker has clearly enjoyed her outing, staying there too long, long enough to consume a bit too much wine, so that she is unsure of the way home, and dusk is already gathering. But instead of being about the afternoon's enjoyments, this song is about what happens as she turns her boat homeward. The image of the final line is as unexpected (to us as it was to her) as it is vivid. A flock of white egrets

---

18. *Jianzhu* 1.40; *Quan Songci* 2:1202.

suddenly flies up against the darkening sky. The entire event is framed and enhanced by the opening words, "I often recall" 常記. We infer from this phrase that the experience, particularly its climactic and beautiful ending, held special meaning for the woman, even if the song does not attempt to put that meaning into words.

In the generation before Li Qingzhao, Ouyang Xiu had written a song lyric about women boating, which likewise ends with a surprising twist:

漁家傲   *To the tune "The Fisherman Is Proud"*

花底忽聞敲兩槳	Beneath the flowers, suddenly the sounds of two oars,
遶巡女伴來尋訪	In a moment her girlfriends have come to find her.
酒盞旋將荷葉當	Lotus leaves serve as wine cups,
蓮舟蕩	As the lotus boat sways,
時時盞裡生紅浪	Red waves bob in the cups.
花氣酒香清廝釀	Flowers' fragrance and wine's perfume blend,
花腮酒面紅相向	Crimson flower petals and wine-flushed faces draw close.
醉倚綠陰眠一餉	Tipsy, they nap a short time in green shade,
驚起望	Then are startled awake.
船頭閣在沙灘上	The boat has run up on a sandspit![19]

Here we have a boating woman who starts out alone but soon is joined by girlfriends. She is also a member of an easily recognized social type (the lotus-picking girl) that is often romanticized in popular lore and literature. These lotus-picking girls have, somewhat implausibly, wine to drink and time on their hands. The poet toys with the similarity between the beauty of the girls and the beauty of the flowers before ending their idyll with a gentle jolt. Li Qingzhao's account of solitary boating is utterly different in tone and import from Ouyang's quixotic portrait of the lotus girls. Yet to appreciate the originality of what Li Qingzhao has written, it helps to remind ourselves of the way women out boating were conventionally portrayed.

We have seen earlier the other two songs by Li Qingzhao that make reference to a woman going boating. One reference was in number 13: "The scent of red lotuses fades in jade bamboo mat autumn / Lightly she unties her gauze skirt / To board the magnolia boat alone." The other was in number 43: "I've heard that spring is still lovely at Twin Streams / I'd like to go boating in a light skiff there / But fear the tiny grasshopper boats they have there / Would

---

19. Ouyang Xiu, "Yujia ao," *Quan Songci* 1:164.

not carry / Such a quantity of sorrow." The first of these specifies that the woman is boarding the boat by herself. This gives us more confidence that it is valid to infer that the woman is alone in the songs discussed immediately above.

Although boating or the prospect of it is not the main event or primary interest in songs 13 and 43 (unlike in no. 4), still, the mention of boating in these songs reinforces the prominence of boating and the outdoors in the lives of the personas in Li Qingzhao's songs. Not only is boating alone a possibility for these ladies; it is a favorite diversion. Boating appears to be something the women to do to get away from their sadness and apprehension. It hardly matters that, in number 43, the speaker eventually decides that she is feeling too despondent on the occasion even for boating to help her. The point is that an outing into nature, undertaken in a boat rather than by carriage or horse or on foot, serves to relieve these women of the stress of daily worries that they face when secluded in their rooms. Also, it does not seem important what season it is. What would normally be represented, in poetry, as a dolorous autumnal scene may be perceived to be as beautiful and welcome as any springtime vista.

Since the personas in these poems are female, there are limits to how much they may indulge their enjoyment of nature. They must start home at sunset, no matter how reluctant they are to do so. Unlike Su Shi, they cannot gallop out into a spring landscape and, finding a particularly endearing spot beside a stream, decide on the spur of the moment to spend the night there, sleeping under the stars.[20] Still, the amount of freedom they have to go out by themselves into nature for the day, at least, may be more than we would have anticipated. Nature and its comely sights are figured, in these songs, as an alternative to the pent-up concerns of inner rooms, and, surprisingly enough, that alternative is depicted as being quite accessible for solitary female excursions.

A Peculiar Mood

The song lyrics about excursions outdoors are, for all their interest, quantitatively few in Li Qingzhao's corpus. More common are songs set indoors or near a building, perhaps mentioning an enclosed courtyard or a garden. Such

---

20. Su Shi, "Xijiang yue" 西江月, no. 11, *Quan Songci* 1:367; trans. in my *Word, Image, and Deed*, p. 334.

a physical space was, after all, where women spent the greater part of their lives, even adventuresome women like Li Qingzhao. Here I will first discuss a subset of these home-bound compositions, saving another set for the next chapter. This subset features a mood that is much the opposite of the freedom, abandon, and exhilaration that we find in the outdoor poems. Barriers and impediments are prominently mentioned. The overall feeling is one of seclusion bordering on the claustrophobic. The person featured in these poems is female and alone. There is scope in these poems for some variation of emotion, but the dominant emotion is unhappiness. Often the cause of the unhappiness is left unexplained, but sometimes it is obliquely hinted at.

A representative selection of these poems follows. As the first selection suggests, this type of song is predominantly set to the short song form:

憶秦娥　*To the tune "Remembering Qin E"* (no. 33)

臨高閣	From a high balcony,
亂山平野煙光薄	Jumbled hills, a level plain, bright mist drifts.
煙光薄	Bright mist drifts.
棲鴉歸後	After the roosting crows have gone back,
暮天聞角	In the evening sky, the sound of a horn.
斷香殘酒情懷惡	The incense is out, some wine remains, my mood is foul.
西風催襯梧桐落	West wind hurries the paulownia leaves to fall,
梧桐落	The paulownia leaves fall.
又還秋色	Again, an autumn scene,
又還寂寞	Again, loneliness.[21]

The following song sometimes has the alternate tune title "Picking Mulberries" 采桑子:

添字醜奴兒　*To the tune "Vile Charmer, Long Version"* (no. 34)

窗前誰種芭蕉樹	Who planted a banana tree in front of the window?
陰滿中庭	Its shade fills the central courtyard,
陰滿中庭	Its shade fills the central courtyard.
葉葉心心	Leaf after leaf, heart after heart,
舒卷有餘情	Folding and unfolding with an excess of feeling.

---

21. *Jianzhu* 1.51; *Quan Songci* 2:1207.

傷心枕上三更雨	Despondent, midnight rains heard from my pillow.
點滴霖霪	Dripping, a steady downpour,
點滴霖霪	Dripping, a steady downpour,
愁損北人	Overwhelms a northerner with sadness
不慣起來聽	Who's not accustomed, sitting up, to hearing this sound.[22]

Another on late night reflections:

南歌子　　*To the tune "Southern Song"* (no. 1)

天上星河轉	In the sky the River of Stars pivots,
人間簾幕垂	In the mortal world blinds and curtains hang down.
涼生枕簟淚痕滋	A chill is felt on pillow and mat, tear stains are many.
起解羅衣	I arise to undo my silken robe
聊問夜何其	And ask about the progress of the night.

翠貼蓮蓬小	Turquoise that stitches the lotus pods is slight,
金銷藕葉稀	Gold that outlines the lotus leaves is delicate.
舊時天氣舊時衣	The weather of times past, the clothes of times past.
只有情懷	It's just that my feelings
不似舊家時	Are unlike those of times past.[23]

Also:

好事近　　*To the tune "A Happy Event Draws Near"* (no. 21)

風定落花深	The wind settles, fallen flowers are deeply layered.
簾外擁紅堆雪	Outside the curtains clusters of red and mounds of snow.
長記海棠開後	I always recall, after the crab apples blossomed
正是傷春時節	Truly it was the time to feel the poignance of spring.

酒闌歌罷玉尊空	Drinking finished, singing over, the jade goblet is empty.
青缸暗明滅	The bronze lamp flickers darkly.
魂夢不堪幽怨	My soul in a dream cannot stand the hidden resentment,
更一聲啼鴂	What's more, the sound of the shrike's cry.[24]

And finally:

---

22. *Jianzhu* 1.97; *Quan Songci* 2:1207.
23. *Jianzhu* 1.35; *Quan Songci* 2:1201.
24. *Jianzhu* 1.132; *Quan Songci* 2:1206.

菩薩蠻   *To the tune "Bodhisattva Barbarian"* (no. 7)

風柔日薄春猶早	The wind is delicate, the sun pale, it's still early spring,
夾衫乍著心情好	Putting on a lined jacket, my mood was pleasant.
睡起覺微寒	Arising from sleep, I feel the chill in the air,
梅花鬢上殘	The plum blossom in my hair has withered.
故鄉何處是	My homeland, where is it?
忘了除非醉	I can't forget it unless I'm drunk.
沉水臥時燒	Aloeswood incense burned as I rested.
香消酒未消	The fragrance has dissipated but the wine has not.[25]

There is an insistence in these poems on the woman's emotional distress that is remarkable; it is found throughout these examples and in poems we have seen before (e.g., nos. 13, 19, and 43 in this chapter; nos. 5 and 20 in chapter 7; and no. 12 in chapter 3). Often it is quite directly expressed. Chinese male poets had for centuries been perfecting techniques of indirection in their description of lonely women. The aesthetic of such indirection became dominant in Southern Dynasties (420–589) "palace-style poetry" and had been widespread in Tang poems about lonely women as well. In the song lyric, a similar aesthetic was the rule in the earliest literati collection, *Among the Flowers*. It was through evocation and oblique inference, rather than direct statement, that the courtiers of the Five Dynasties (and the Song literati after them) distinguished their composition from the popular romantic song, which they would have considered unrefined, unlearned, and bawdy. While not reverting to the brashness of the popular song, Li Qingzhao often violates the expectation that emotional states be conveyed only through indirection. "My mood is foul"; "tear stains are many"; "overwhelms a northerner with sadness"; "again, loneliness": these lines are striking in their candor. We do not expect such lines in song lyrics from elite authors.

Yet it is not just the directness of statement but rather the combination of that with reluctance or even refusal to identify the source of the distress that makes these pieces so unusual. It is almost as if the emotion is a given, a foregone conclusion, requiring no explanation. We saw earlier an example of an explicit decision by the female subject against explaining what is on her mind: "About to speak, she stops" (no. 12). Next, conventional explanations for her poor condition are explicitly ruled out ("She's grown thin of late / Not

---

25. *Jianzhu* 1.131; *Quan Songci* 2:1203.

from sickness over wine / Or from sadness over autumn"). The women being described in the songs above are similarly reluctant to put into words exactly what is on their minds, why they are so miserable, and what are the larger and crucial circumstances of their lives. Rarely, in Li Qingzhao's songs, a woman will burst out in agitated, angry speech: "No more, no more! / When he left this time / A thousand verses of 'Yang Pass' / Would not have detained him" (also no. 12). But such outbursts are quite rare. More common is the insistence on not speaking that we find here. Perhaps the silence can only be maintained just so long, and then it erupts in exasperated speech. But behind both the outburst and the silence, there is the implication that words are not going to help. The woman is trapped in her situation, and there is little or no point in analyzing or explaining it.

Beyond these features there is something else that runs through these songs and makes them effective. Compositions that present images of lonely women are legion in song lyrics before, during, and after Li Qingzhao's time. The challenge of continuing to write in this subject area is to find novel things to say, innovative ways of presenting such a standard type of figure. Li Qingzhao succeeds in doing this with remarkable consistency. Every one of the songs under discussion has one or more elements that make it fresh and interesting.

In number 33 the woman being described hears the sound of a horn in the evening sky. Li Qingzhao's readers would have immediately associated this with the military: horns in combination with drums were sounded in military camps to mark time.[26] In cities and towns, it was the beating of a drum that marked the hours of the night. The mention of a horn's sound in a song by someone who lived through the fall of the Northern Song calls to mind the fortified northern border regions of the Southern Song empire, which were repeatedly invaded by Jurchen armies after the fall of the north. The woman in the song, then, seems to be living in such an area and might well be thinking of the homeland she left behind. The reference to the horn thus introduces a social and political element into the poem. This larger concern would help to account for the insistent disconsolation of the closing lines. In those lines, the use of *you* 又 is effective. It has a double meaning, probably deliberately so, because it suggests both "on top of this" and "one more time."

---

26. See *Weigong bingfa*, a work that dates from at least as early as the Tang, as quoted in the Qing encyclopedia compiled by Chen Ying, *Yuanjian leihan* 228.12a (quoted by Xu Peijun, *Jianzhu* 1.104, n. 6).

Therefore, the lines suggest that the person has endured multiple autumns with this feeling and that she feels that multiple aspects of her situation reinforce her loneliness.

Song 34 also indirectly invokes the fall of the north by referring to the woman as a displaced northerner unaccustomed to hearing the sound of rain dripping on the broad leaves of the banana tree. As simple as this idea is, it is not one often found in earlier song lyrics. Chinese poets had long written about listening at night to rain dripping on leaves (usually of the paulownia tree), being kept awake by the sound, and then reflecting in their sleeplessness on some beloved but distant person or place. An earlier song lyric by Wen Tingyun, which Li Qingzhao surely knew because of its inclusion in *Among the Flowers*, features just such a scenario:

更漏子　　*To the tune "The Clepsydra"*

玉爐香	The jade censor is fragrant,
紅臘淚	The crimson candle weeps,
偏照畫堂秋思	Lighting a painted room full of autumn melancholy.
眉翠薄	Her dark eyebrows are faint,
鬢雲殘	Cloud-locks of hair disheveled.
夜長衾枕寒	The night is long, the blanket and pillow cold.
梧桐樹	A paulownia tree,
三更雨	Rain at midnight,
不道離情正苦	Heedless are they of the bitterness of parting sorrow.
一葉葉	Leaf after leaf,
一聲聲	Sound after sound,
空階滴到明	Dripping on the vacant steps until dawn.[27]

Because of the shared words and phrases ("rain at midnight," "leaf after leaf," "dripping"), it is likely that Li Qingzhao had Wen Tingyun's song in mind when she composed hers. In fact, Wen's piece had already been "rewritten" by a poet somewhat older than Li Qingzhao, Moqi Yong 萬俟詠.[28] Moqi had already substituted the banana tree for Wen Tingyun's paulownia tree, a substitution that makes good sense if one needs broad leaves to catch dripping raindrops. But in neither earlier song is the essential element of Li Qingzhao's work found: the tree and the sound it makes in the rain are

---

27. Wen Tingyun, "Geng louzi," *Huajian ji zhu* 1.15.
28. Moqi Yong, "Chang xiangsi" 長相思, *Quan Songci* 2:1050.

foreign to the listener because the listener has been displaced from her native land. Once we understand the situation—and Li Qingzhao does not reveal it until the final line of her piece—in retrospect the opening line of her song with all of its brashness and annoyance becomes all the more effective. The speaker is acting like her space has been violated by someone who thoughtlessly planted the tree outside the window where she sleeps. Eventually, we understand that the speaker herself is the one who does not belong in that place.

In the next song, number 1, it is late at night, when the Milky Way is said to turn, and the woman is cold in her bed. She has been weeping. Unable to sleep, she gets up to ask what time it is, apparently impatient with how long the night is lasting. The first two lines of the second stanza describe her garment: we do not know if it is the one she has just laid aside or one she is still wearing. At least one commentator thinks that the lines refer obliquely to the woman's loneliness, by way of well-established puns on the two words for lotus *lian* 蓮 (= *lian* 憐, "to love") and *ou* 藕 (= *ou* 偶, "match, mate").[29] By wording the lines the way she does, Li Qingzhao, according to this interpretation, is suggesting that the love the woman receives and her time together with her lover are slight. But she never says this outright. The closing three lines continue the preceding references to clothes and weather. All the lines say is that, despite the continuities with the past, the woman's feelings are not like in the past. We are meant to infer that she feels vastly worse than she used to.

In song 21, some commentators think that the mention of the blossoming crab apple is a reference to Li Qingzhao's famous song lyric on those blossoms (no. 5, "The greens must be plump and the reds withered"). Such an interpoetic reference would be extremely unusual. The line makes perfectly good sense without imposing this reading: now that the blossoms (of all the plants) are fallen and spring is truly over, the woman recalls how she anticipated this regrettable brevity of spring even as the crab apple tree first opened in blossom. This is the only poem in the group that mentions socializing. There was a party, earlier in the evening, but now it is over and the woman is solitary again. Moreover, the party did not relieve her loneliness. The next to last line is complicated. Souls in dreams are commonplace in song lyrics. Usually, the soul travels in the dream to visit a faraway person or place that

---

29. Cai Yijiang, "Liang sheng zhendian leihen zi," p. 151.

an individual is dreaming of. Just as often the dream is interrupted, or sleep itself will not come for all the distress, or it does come but the dreaming soul finds the distance too great to traverse. There may also be the realization, on waking, that even though the beloved has been visited in a dream, it was just a dream and is poor consolation in wakeful moments. Li Qingzhao's dreaming soul is different. The soul, although it has entered a dream, finds that it is still tormented by "hidden resentment" and finds that it "cannot stand" it. It is as if the soul's distress, in the midst of its dream, has awakened it from that dream. This is a most unexpected use of the familiar motif. What happens next, in the final line, only adds to the misery. Now that the speaker is awake, she hears an unwelcome sound. The shrike was known to call at the onset of summer, thus marking the end of spring and its blossoms. Thus, the bird's call in this line marks the definitive passing of the season, signs of which already fill the first stanza. In addition some commentators equate the shrike with the cuckoo.[30] If Li Qingzhao intended this equivalence, there is another likely meaning: the cuckoo's call was often said to sound like the words "best to return home" 不如歸去 so that its cry here would be a reminder of the inability of the persona and other displaced northerners to return to their captive homeland.

The last song above (no. 7) is unusual for the abrupt change of mood it conveys. In the opening stanza the speaker is enjoying the early spring scene and tells us so. But as soon as she awakens and remembers her dislocation from her homeland, sadness reasserts itself. The opening lines of the second stanza are remarkable for their directness and the desperation that they reveal. To drive the point home, the closing lines hint at how much wine she had consumed, so that its effects last long after the last trace of incense has dissipated and after her respite in sleep has come to an end.

Women in Song Lyrics by Male Writers

It may help to pinpoint the nature of Li Qingzhao's achievement in such songs if we read them against some portraits of female sadness and solitude in song lyrics by earlier, male writers. Here is one by Yan Shu:

---

30. See, for example, *Jianzhu* 1.133, n. 5.

浣溪沙   *To the tune "Sands of the Washing Stream"*

淡淡梳妝薄薄衣	So delicate her make-up, so sheer her clothes.
天仙模樣好容儀	Looking like a goddess, lovely in deportment.
舊歡前事入顰眉	Old pleasures, past events enter her knit eyebrows.
閒役夢魂孤燭暗	Idly she relies on a dreaming soul, the single candle burns out.
恨無消息畫簾垂	Regretting no letter comes, the painted blinds hang down,
且留雙淚說相思	She leaves a pair of tears on her face to express her longing.[31]

This piece is very much in the tradition of *Among the Flowers*, as are many song lyrics by Yan Shu. We are gazing in upon a solitary woman in her room. She is blessed with unearthly beauty, but also with an unbearable sense of loss. A former love is now gone from her life, and she receives no news from him. Nearly every element here is taken from the stock inventory of song lyric language.

The next example is by Qin Guan:

菩薩蠻   *To the tune "Bodhisattva Barbarian"*

蟲聲泣露驚秋枕	Droning cicadas weep dew, startling the autumn pillow.
羅幃淚濕鴛鴦錦	Inside the gauze bed curtain tears moisten a pair of brocade mandarin ducks.
獨臥玉肌涼	Lying alone her jade skin is chilled,
殘更與恨長	The waning night stretches as far as her regrets.
陰風翻翠幔	A chill wind tosses the green drapes,
雨澀燈花暗	Rain splatters, the lamp wick goes dark.
畢竟不成眠	In the end, she's never able to fall asleep.
鴉啼金井寒	Crows call, the golden well is cold.[32]

The language of this song is more innovative than in Yan Shu's piece, but there are certain continuities with the tradition as well. We are still looking in on this woman. The natural reading is to take the lines as third-person narrative description. It cannot be taken as first-person statement: the phrase *yuji* 玉肌, "jade skin," rules that out, since a speaker would not refer to her body

---

31. Yan Shu, "Huan xi sha," *Quan Songci* 1:113.
32. Qin Guan, "Pusa man," *Quan Songci* 1:591.

that way. But this is privileged third-person narrative. The narrator has the
authority to speak of his subject's emotional state even as he is observing her
as an onlooker.

It is worth considering the distinction between first- and third-person
voice in these songs. It is not unusual for the two to coexist in a single piece,
with the voice alternating between one and the other as the account unfolds.
But what makes readers perceive or "hear" a line one way or the other? "Jade
skin" sounds like it has to be the narrator's voice. What about *hen chang* 恨長,
"regrets stretch far," or *bucheng mian* 不成眠, "never able to fall asleep"? In
fact, such phrases are indeterminate with regard to voice: they might occur in
either third-person or first-person lines. The more unconventional, distinctive, or personal the semantic content, the more apt we are to feel that the
line is first-person: an individual voicing her individual perception. Thus, it is
easy to accommodate *hen chang* to the assumption of ongoing third-person
narrative ("her regrets stretch far") because narrators make this kind of
observation about the emotional state of women in song lyrics all the time.
But when in Li Qingzhao's song we encounter the phrase *qinghuai e* 情懷惡,
we immediately hear it as first-person speech ("my mood is foul") because
this is intensely personal and is not the type of narrative description we are
accustomed to seeing. One of the developments in song lyric history during
the decades before Li Qingzhao was the more frequent use of the female
speaking voice in compositions by male writers. In the earlier song lyric, for
all the abundant description of women, the subjects were seldom allowed to
speak in lines that are unambiguous as speech. This situation changes with
Ouyang Xiu and the generation of writers after him. But this change may be
linked to another, which is willingness to allow the women being depicted to
be unmistakably marked as professional entertainers. Poets, in other words,
become more apt to drop the pretense that the women they write about
belong to elite society. They begin to freely represent them, sometimes as
professionals who sing and dance for a living and may also enter into romantic liaisons with their customers, or as merchant-class women who are somewhat less constrained by the strictures against meeting men before marriage
that ruled the lives of their elite sisters. It is these new types of women who
are most given to speech in songs. And what they say is usually related to their
love affairs outside of marriage. Often, their speech is an expression of anger
or regret over the inconstancy of the man with whom they became involved.
Here is an example by Ouyang Xiu:

卜算子　　*To the tune "Fortuneteller"*

極得醉中眠	Often I've been going to bed drunk,
迤邐翻成病	After a while it gradually made me sick.
莫是前生負你來	I bet I wronged you in a former life
今世裡	So that in this life
教孤冷	I'm made so alone and cold.

言約全無定	Your promises all mean nothing,
是誰先薄倖	Who was it who first proved unfaithful?
不慣孤眠慣成雙	I'm not used to sleeping alone, I'm used to a partner.
奈奴子	But you, my wretched darling,
心腸硬	Have a hard heart.[33]

This does not sound like a married woman, and it is not supposed to. It sounds like a woman who lives outside the conventions of elite society, probably an entertainer, or at least one who is free to enjoy love affairs outside of marriage and to have her heart broken by the experience. Among the early attributions to Li Qingzhao, there is no female persona who sounds anything like this.

Aside from this voice, speech or even internal thinking by women—save for the simplest kind of statement—is quite rare in song lyrics of the era. Consider the following piece by Yan Jidao:

南鄉子　　*To the tune "Southerner"*

花落未須悲	Falling flowers need not bring sorrow,
紅蕊明年又滿枝	Red petals will fill the branches again next year.
惟有花間人別後	It's only, in flower season, after he has left,
無期	There's still no set time for his return.
水闊山長雁字遲	Rivers and mountains stretch afar, geese formations are delayed.

今日最相思	Today she misses him sorely,
記得攀條話別離	Recalling when they plucked a willow frond and talked of parting,
共說春來春去事	They spoke of spring arriving and spring ending,
多時	So much time passes!
一點愁心入翠眉	A piece of her sad heart enters her dark eyebrows.[34]

---

33. Ouyang Xiu, "Busuanzi," *Quan Songci* 1:195.
34. Yan Jidao, "Nanxiangzi," *Quan Songci* 1:296.

Of interest here, again, is the question of voice or point of view. The first stanza will be taken by most readers as a narrator's (i.e., third person) representation of what is going through the woman's mind. This is what she is experiencing and thinking, but the language does not convey a sure sense of her speaking. It feels more like the narrator is relating her perceptions. It is tempting, when we get to the second stanza, to say that the voice has changed to first person: "Today, I miss him sorely / I recall when . . . " No doubt some readers will take these lines that way. But notice what happens at the end. The viewpoint reverts unmistakably to the third person: we watch her face take on a sad expression and we imagine, or know (because the privileged narrator has told us), that the expression reflects what is going on in her heart. The shift from what might be first person to what is definitely third person is significant because it exemplifies the difficulty that most poets of the time have in sustaining a female first-person voice. The earlier song lyric tradition had overwhelmingly favored third-person observation of female subjects. Even as alternatives to this became more developed during the eleventh century, including songs about men in the throes of love and female personas who spoke for themselves, the convention of the narrator's observation and description of female subjects remained formidable. It kept reasserting itself.

The comparison with other poets helps pinpoint what is distinctive about Li Qingzhao's works. It is often the subjective element in Li Qingzhao's songs that is the most original and memorable. She excels at writing about the way the persona in her songs is thinking and feeling, and in doing so she usually takes leave of the conventions male poets rely on when writing about such women. "I arise to undo my silken robe / And ask about the progress of the night"; "My mood is foul"; "Don't you know? Don't you know? / The greens must be plump and the reds withered"; "Again, I finger the withered flowers, / Again, pinching out their remaining fragrance, / Again, to get a little more time"; "I can't forget it unless I'm drunk": these are not the kind of stock lines we find in song lyrics by other writers about how women think and speak and feel. They are largely responsible for what make Li Qingzhao's song lyrics on conventional subjects unconventional.

The argument is not that there is any lack of interest or originality in other poets' compositions. There is plenty of both, even when they choose to write on well-established themes. Consider this song, also by Qin Guan:

浣溪沙 *To the tune "Sands of the Washing Stream"*

漠漠輕寒上小樓	A pervasive light chill ascends the low tower,
曉陰無賴似窮秋	The murky spring dawn oddly feels like late autumn.
淡煙流水畫屏幽	Faint mist on the river, deserted, the scene on the painted screen.
自在飛花輕似夢	Falling flowers, uncaring, are as weightless as her dream.
無邊絲雨細如愁	Threads of rain, boundless, are as delicate as her sorrow.
寶簾閒掛小銀鉤	Idly it hangs from the ornate blinds, a small silver clasp.[35]

The wording of each line is carefully wrought and intriguing. There is a woman in this room, sleeping or trying to sleep behind that painted bed screen, but she is never referred to explicitly. Nevertheless, her presence and her emotional state are amply evoked by everything else that is described around her. The first two lines of the second stanza are particularly acclaimed by critics for their ingenuity and the unlikely metaphors they present of a "weightless" dream and "delicate" sorrow. Yet throughout the song, even in those two lines that tell us about her inner life, we are looking in on her as observers from the outside. She is presented to us, by not being explicitly described, as someone to contemplate and empathize with. But the poet is not interested in letting her do, say, or feel anything on her own beyond what is conventional for this type of poetic subject. The women in Li Qingzhao's song lyrics are presented differently.

We conclude this section with two of Li Qingzhao's best-known song lyrics. They manifest several of the traits of voice and mood we have been examining, each in its own way.

永遇樂 *To the tune "Always Having Fun" (no. 32)*

元宵 The Lantern Festival

落日鎔金	The setting sun is molten gold,
暮雲合璧	The clouds congeal at dusk as a circular disk of jade.
人在何處	Where is he now?
4 染柳煙濃	The willows dyed with dark mist,
吹梅笛怨	"Plum Blossom" flutes are sorrowful,
春意知幾許	How much springtime feeling is there?
元宵佳節	The lovely season of the Lantern Festival

35. Qin Guan, "Huan xi sha," *Quan Songci* 1:594.

8	融和天氣	The weather balmy,
	次第豈無風雨	But any moment there could be wind and rain.
	來相召	They come to invite me out,
	香車寶馬	In fragrant carriages drawn by precious horses,
12	謝他酒朋詩侶	But I turn them down, drinking buddies and poetry friends.
	中州盛日	In those halcyon days in the central provinces,
	閨門多暇	There was much leisure in the women's apartments.
	記得偏重三五	I remember how important this Fifteenth was to us.
16	鋪翠冠兒	We wore kingfisher feather caps,
	撚金雪柳	And snowy willows of plied gold,
	簇帶爭濟楚	Multiple hair ornaments, glistening, gorgeous.
	如今憔悴	But today, gaunt and haggard
20	風鬟霜鬢	Hair disheveled by wind and temples touched with frost,
	怕見夜間出去	I'm embarrassed to go out at night.
	不如向	Best to sit behind
	簾兒底下	Lowered blinds
24	聽人笑語	And listen to the talk and laughter of others.[36]

It is easy to understand why this song has so often been praised, even early on. Combining personal nostalgia with sadness over the loss of the north (the "central provinces" of the song), the composition rises above narrow subjective sorrow to epitomize the plight of the displaced northerners who, as they lived out the remainder of their lives in the south, felt so keenly the dynastic diminishment and longed to recover the glories of their younger years in the northern capital of Kaifeng.

The opening lines are surely an expression of loneliness, but they are also an echo of earlier poetic lines, including those by the sixth-century poet Jiang Yan 江淹: "At sunset the azure clouds join together / The fair one still has not arrived" 日暮碧雲合，佳人殊未來.[37] The speaker's thought that even in the midst of fine warm weather a storm might occur reflects her state of mind, one of discomfort and wariness, rather than being an accurate meteorological observation.

It is not unusual in the long song form for the immediate setting of the first stanza to give way to an extended reminiscence in the second. What sets this one apart is, first, the specificity of the details recalled (her description of

---

36. *Jianzhu* 1.150; *Quan Songci* 2:1208.
37. Jiang Yan, "Xiushang ren yuanbie" 休上人怨別, *Liangshi* 4.1580.

women's hair ornaments is collaborated by accounts found in contemporary sources on urban festivals) and, second, the way that fond reminiscence returns to the chillingly candid lines about her diminished current condition and conviction that the pleasures of the festival are no longer for her.

It is commonplace to find, in song lyrics written by men, depictions of lonely women who are painfully aware of the passage of time and the gradual loss of their youthful beauty. But it is rare that we find the voice of a woman who is already elderly and still more unusual to find an extended and concrete passage of reminiscence about feminine youthfulness that is now hopelessly and irrevocably lost, as seen in the following song, whose first stanza we have seen in chapter 9:

聲聲慢　　*To the tune "Note after Note, Long Song" (no. 31)*

	尋尋覓覓	Searching, hunting, seeking, looking,
	冷冷清清	So chilly and yet so clear.
	悽悽慘慘戚戚	Distressed, dismal, and forlorn.
4	乍暖還寒時候	Warm awhile then cold again, it's that season,
	最難將息	The worst for taking care of oneself.
	三杯兩盞淡酒	How can two or three cups of weak wine
	怎敵他	Hold up against
8	晚來風力	The strength of the evening wind?
	雁過也	The wild geese have flown past,
	正傷心	Truly saddening the heart,
	卻是舊時相識	What's more I recognize them from years past.
12	滿地黃花堆積	The ground is covered with piles of yellow blossoms.
	憔悴損	I'm so haggard and weakened now,
	如今有誰忺摘	Who bothers to pick them anymore?
	守著窗兒	I sit beside the window
16	獨自怎生得黑	All by myself, how could it have gotten so black?
	梧桐更兼細雨	Paulownia trees and fine rain,
	到黃昏	Until dusk has fallen, I listen to
	點點滴滴	Drip after drip and drop after drop.
20	這次第	Facing such a scene and circumstances,
	怎一箇愁字了得	How could the word "sorrow" ever suffice?[38]

Traditional critics center their remarks on the duplicated characters in the opening lines of this song. No earlier poet in any poetic form had put

---

38. *Jianzhu* 1.161–62; *Quan Songci* 2:1209.

together such a long string of duplicated characters. Li Qingzhao's daring-
ness in doing so is rightly admired. It is not just the duplications themselves
that account for the arresting effect of the lines. It is the blending of dupli-
cate pairs that describe the weather and scene (line 2) with those that describe
an affective state (line 3) that is presumably both engendered by the weather
and preexisting in the speaker's mind. But the key is the opening line, which
so effectively anticipates and sets the tone of desperation and despair that
fills the poem. We know that the speaker is missing something and searching,
but she refrains from telling us what. The "what" is far better left unidentified, because leaving it that way magnifies the possibilities and deepens the
emotion that readers will find in the words.

   We have seen this refusal to specify the source of the speaker's distress in
several earlier songs; here, again, it is sustained throughout the composition.
The season is autumn, as we know from several details ("clear" in line 2, the
geese flying past, and, especially, the yellow blossoms—chrysanthemum
blossoms—in the second stanza), so this cannot be conventional spring
sadness. Lines 9 through 11 provide one clue: wild geese in poetry are not
merely bearers of letters; they are also reminders of a distant homeland.[39]
When the speaker sees the migratory geese fly southward past her, she thinks
of her homeland in the far north, where the geese began their journey,
and she realizes, moreover, that it has been several years that she has been
watching the flight of these birds overhead.

   Surely there is more than southern displacement on the speaker's mind,
but she is not going to tell us what so distresses her. Instead, we watch her
and listen to her thoughts as she sits by the window at dusk.[40] But her reflections contain some strikingly unconventional thoughts. One is her wondering
how the sky could have turned so black.[41] "Black" is an ominous word here,

---

39. This point is made by Xu Peijun in *Jianzhu* 1.163, n. 3.

40. If the textual variant *xiao* 曉, "morning," is adopted in line 8 in place of "evening," it
makes the time frame of the song stretch through the entire day. Many scholars prefer this
version of the line; see, for example, Chen Zumei, *Li Qingzhao ci xinshi jiping*, pp. 110–11, as
discussed in chapter 9.

41. Most commentators and translators pass over this line without comment, but in fact the
language presents problems, and the line is open to various interpretations. Many take it to
mean "All by myself, how can I wait (last, make it) until it turns black?" In that sense, the
speaker is wondering how she can endure the rest of the day, until nightfall finally comes. This
reading is possible, and it also makes for a strikingly unconventional line, given that what we
find so often in melancholy song lyrics is a speaker wondering how she can make it through a

all the more so for being used in an isolated position rather than as a modifier (e.g., black sky, black clouds). It is extremely unusual to find the word used this way in poetry, and several commentators have noted how peculiar it is here. But the odd usage thoroughly befits the dark mood of the speaker. The second striking formulation is the idea presented in the closing lines, nicely culminating what precedes, that the word ordinarily used to describe and express emotional distress is, in this instance, wholly inadequate for the job. This is not simply some platitude about the limitations of language. The speaker has singled out the one word most often used poetically to designate the emotional state she is in, already anticipated in the synonyms for it in the opening line, only to tell us that now it will not do, that it falls short of the expressive power she needs to epitomize her mood. Recall the concluding lines of Li Qingzhao's number 43, where she decides against going boating at Twin Streams because it occurs to her that the little boats there could not bear such a burden of "sorrow" as she currently feels. That is already an ingenious transformation of stock language about boats and parting sorrow. Here, featuring the same word, we see a transformation of conventional statements about the inadequacy of language, which have been narrowed and focused now, almost accusingly, on the shortcomings of that single weighty word.[42]

---

long lonely night. The crux of the problem is that the phrase *zenshengde* 怎生得, which is amply attested in song lyrics, does not appear to be used in its normal sense of "how can [subject] be able to/cause . . . ?" It almost seems that a word or words have dropped out. Ding Qizhen 丁啓陣 presents a candid discussion of the difficulties presented by the line. See http://user.qzone.qq.com/120308730/static_blog/1258043504, November 13, 2009 (71).

42. Some recent scholars read considerably more into certain lines of this composition, finding allusions in them that lend support to the view that the unspoken subject of the piece and the real source of its sorrow is Zhao Mingcheng's death. These readings come from scholars who are determined to date the piece to a particular period of Li Qingzhao's life and to read it autobiographically. The purported "allusions" are apt to strike as unconvincing a reader who does not share those scholars' assumptions and purposes. See Zhu Jinghua, "Wujing yu xinjing jiaohu ranse," pp. 120–23; Chen Zumei, *Li Qingzhao ci xinshi jiping*, pp. 111–12.

CHAPTER 11

Song Lyrics, Part 2

A small group of song lyrics attributed to Li Qingzhao have a distinctive tone that binds them together and distinguishes them from other pieces attributed to her. These compositions feature flirtatious women or girls who are speaking or acting coquettishly to attract a man's attention.

Songs of Flirtatiousness

We today might not consider these poems erotic or sexually titillating, but they would have been considered so in their own day. Three of the five such songs are translated below. First:

點絳唇　*To the Tune "Dabbing Crimson Lips"* (no. 54)

蹴罷鞦韆	Getting down from the swing
起來慵整纖纖手	Languidly she arises and straightens her clothes, her fingers slender.
露濃花瘦	Dew is heavy, the blossom frail,
薄汗沾衣透	Patches of perspiration stain her dress.
見客人來	Seeing someone coming
襪鏟金釵溜	In stocking feet, her gold hairpin drooping,
和羞走	She runs off shyly.
倚門回首	At the door she pauses, turns her head,
却把青梅嗅	And sniffs the green plum in her hand.[1]

---

1. *Jianzhu* 1.1; *Quan Songci* 2:1212, "Cunmu" 存目.

Second:

醜奴兒   *To the tune "The Vile Charmer"* (no. 55)

晚來一陣風兼雨	This evening a storm of wind and rain
洗盡炎光	Has washed away the blazing heat.
理罷笙簧	Having finished playing the flute,
却對菱花淡淡妝	Facing a caltrop mirror she applies make-up lightly.
絳綃縷薄冰肌瑩	Beneath thin silk of deep red her skin of ice glimmers,
雪膩酥香	Luster of snow, milky and fragrant.
笑語檀郎	Smiling, she tells her beloved,
今夜紗廚枕簟涼	"Tonight the pillow and mat behind the gauze curtain will be cool."[2]

And finally:

浣溪沙   *To the tune "Sands of the Washing Stream"* (no. 42)

繡面芙蓉一笑開	Her colorful face, a lotus blossom, opens in a smile,
斜飛寶鴨襯香腮	A duck censer's rising incense brushes her fragrant cheek.
眼波才動被人猜	As soon as her eyes move others can guess her mind.
一面風情深有韻	Her face full of feelings, with irresistible charm,
半箋嬌恨寄幽懷	Coy sadness and secret longing are revealed on half a page:
月移花影約重來	"When the moonlight moves the blossoms' shadows, you promised you'll come back again."[3]

The two other songs that belong to this group are numbers 66 and 45.[4] Number 66 features a woman who, worried that her man will say that the flowers she has newly purchased are prettier than her face, inserts some blossoms in her hairdo so that the man will have to look at the two of them together. Number 45 presents a "small-waisted" woman who sings to entertain her male admirer and strikes a pose of "coy anger" 嬌嗔 as she enunciates the words of the song. The five compositions (nos. 42, 45, 54, 55, 66) figure prominently in modern selections and biographies of Li Qingzhao, where most if not all of them are accepted without discussion as authentic

---

2. *Jianzhu* 1.181; *Quan Songci* 2:1212, "Cunmu."

3. *Jianzhu* 1.11; *Quan Songci* 2:1211.

4. "Jianzi mulanhua" 減字木蘭花 (no. 66), *Jianzhu* 1.9 and *Quan Songci* 2:1210; and "Lang taosha" 浪淘沙 (no. 45), *Jianzhu* 1.187 and *Quan Songci* 2:1213, "Cunmu."

and unproblematic. The compositions are usually treated in these modern studies as youthful compositions of hers. The woman in them is assumed to be Li Qingzhao herself, and the man Zhao Mingcheng, either as her fiancé or young husband. In fact, these song lyrics raise several interesting points concerning the perception and representation of Li Qingzhao in premodern and modern times.

Concerning their provenance and credibility, the first thing to say about them is that they appear late. Three of them belong to my group 4, that with the lowest credibility and the misattributed songs, and two of them (nos. 42 and 45) belong to group 3, that with the next lowest. None of them are attested in any extant Song or Yuan source; indeed, it is not until the late Ming that their existence, one by one, gradually becomes established. Yet the late appearance of these compositions and all that it implies about their authenticity are routinely overlooked in modern treatments of Li Qingzhao and of these compositions in particular.

Yet it is not simply that these works appear late. When they do appear there are also, for three out of the five, attributions to other authors. Song lyric 54, in one of its earliest appearances, in Yang Jin's 楊金 edition of *The Residue of Poetry from Grass Hut* (compiled in 1554), is attributed to Su Shi.[5] In Chen Yaowen's *A Refined Collection of "Flowers" and "Grasses"* (compiled in 1583), number 54 is presented without any attribution, meaning that in the compiler's opinion the authorship was unknown. It is presented this way in multiple later Ming and Qing anthologies.[6] Only considerably later did the piece begin to be attributed to Li Qingzhao.[7] It was otherwise attributed to Zhou Bangyan.[8] As for song lyric 55, both *A Refined Collection* and *Huixuan lidai mingxian cifu quanji* 彙選歷代名賢詞府全集 (ca. 1600) attribute the composition to the early Southern Song songwriter Kang Boke 康伯可. In yet another anthology, the song is attributed to Wei Dazhong 魏大中.[9] Song lyric 45 is attributed in its earliest appearance, also in *A Refined Collection*, to the early Southern Song writer Zhao Zifa 趙子發.

---

5. Wang Zhongwen, *Li Qingzhao ji jiaozhu* 1.83.

6. For the piece's attribution in *Huacao cuibian* and the later anthologies, see ibid.

7. If we understand the attribution in *Cilin wanxuan* 詞林萬選 to be that of Mao Jin 毛晉 (on which see n. 10 below), then Mao's is the earliest attribution of the piece to Li Qingzhao, in circa 1630. After that, the next work that attributes the piece to Li Qingzhao is in Zhou Ming's *Linxia cixuan* (compiled in 1670) 1.2a.

8. It is the anthology *Cidi* 詞的, compiled in 1620, that attributes the piece to Zhou Bangyan.

9. For these alternate attributions, see Wang Zhongwen, *Li Qingzhao ji jiaozhu* 1.82–83.

In all three cases (nos. 45, 54, and 55), then, the earliest attribution is not to Li Qingzhao.[10] But something interesting happens. Over time, the attribution of each piece to Li Qingzhao gains acceptance. We can see this happening through the late Ming and Qing, in the nearly twenty different song lyrics anthologies that survive from the time. The songs gravitate toward Li Qingzhao. By the late Qing, the anthologies that attribute the songs to Li Qingzhao outnumber those that do not, and the works become generally accepted as hers. An example of this gradual transformation can be seen in the ways different editions of *A Refined Collection* handle song 54. The original edition (1583) gives no attribution. But in a later version, reedited by Jin Shengwu 金繩武 in 1857, the attribution is changed to Li Qingzhao.[11] At the same time that these pieces are becoming more and more firmly linked to Li Qingzhao, the other two compositions (nos. 42 and 66), that do not have alternative attributions, become more and more widely accepted as authentically hers, despite having only appeared several hundred years after her lifetime.

---

10. Songs 54 and 55 appear to have earlier attributions to Li Qingzhao, but the date of those attributions is problematic. In fact, they should not be considered earlier than those found in *A Refined Collection*. At issue is the dating of attributions found in the anthology *Cilin wanxuan*, said to have been compiled by Yang Shen (1488–1559), the Ming scholar and dramatist, and first printed in 1543 (forty years before *A Refined Collection*); see Yang Shen, *Cilin wanxuan*, and Zhang Huiyan 張惠言, *Cixuan* 詞選, ed. Liu Chongde 劉崇德 et al., 4.87–88.

In recent times, Wang Zhongwen has pointed out that *Cilin wanxuan* is full of misattributions and wrong tune titles, making it, on the whole, quite unreliable; see Wang's *Li Qingzhao ji jiaozhu* 1.83. Actually, the inaccuracies in the anthologies' annotations had already caught the attention of the *Siku quanshu* editors, who, deselecting it from the imperial library, concluded that the original work was lost and that the present version is a later compilation, done probably in the early seventeenth century and falsely attributed to Yang Shen; see *Siku quanshu zongmu tiyao* 40.4480. These critics have not mentioned, apropos of the songs in the anthology attributed to Li Qingzhao, that Yang Shen, who edited and annotated other works on Song period song lyrics, wrote elsewhere that as much as he admired Li Qingzhao's song lyrics and tried to obtain a copy of her *Jades for Rinsing the Mouth*, he was never able to do so—a statement that is widely taken to indicate that the collection had been lost by the mid-sixteenth century; see Mao Jin, "Shuyu ci ba" 漱玉詞跋, *Huibian*, p. 59. It would be odd indeed if Yang Shen somehow had managed to find works by her that had never appeared in any earlier anthology (or anywhere else, for that matter). In any case, the present version of *Cilin wanxuan* was reedited by Mao Jin in the mid-seventeenth century, and from what Mao Jin says in his postface, it sounds like he freely added attributions where the version he was working from had none and altered others as he saw fit. Wang Zhongwen also says that the attributions in *Cilin wanxuan* should be considered Mao Jin's; see Wang's *Li Qingzhao ji jiaozhu* 1.8.

11. *Jianzhu* 1.2.

It is clear enough why this movement of attributions toward Li Qingzhao takes place. It happens as a result of late Ming and Qing period values and needs, which are projected back upon the Song dynasty poet. Much has been written in recent years about "the cult of *qing* 情" (love) in the late Ming, its connection to elegant courtesans and their romantic liaisons with literati then, the spread of the ideal of marriages between likeminded husbands and wives, and the concurrent blossoming of women's writing and male acceptance of the same. In literature of the period, this new fascination with romantic love is reflected in the dramas of Tang Xianzu 湯顯祖 (1550–1616), including *The Peony Pavilion* 牡丹亭 and *The Purple Hairpin* 紫釵記; the story collections of Feng Menglong and that same writer's *A History of Love*; and the "talented man and beautiful woman" 才子佳人 literature. In life, the celebrated romances of Chen Zilong 陳子龍 and Liu Rushi 柳如是, and that of Dong Bai 董白 and Mao Xiang 冒襄 epitomized the new valuation of love between literati and well-educated courtesans.

Perceptions of Li Qingzhao were directly affected by these developments, as we have seen in chapter 8, for example, in the song lyrics written by Wang Shizhen matching those by Li Qingzhao. It was precisely because a new feminine image and ideal was evolving in Ming-Qing times, in which a woman was admired not simply for beauty but also for talent, which often meant literary skill, that Li Qingzhao proved to be such a beacon from the past. Li Qingzhao's own writings could readily be used to provide support for this vision of her and her marriage to Zhao Mingcheng, but it was Ming period thinking that provided the impetus for reconceptualizing the couple this way. In his entry on Li Qingzhao, the Ming literatus Lang Ying begins with Zhao Mingcheng and his *Records on Metal and Stone* then moves on to Li Qingzhao and her own writings. He pauses to add this aside: "The various sources all say that she was of one mind with her husband; that is why they were intimate and loved each other to such an extreme!" 諸書皆曰與夫同志，故相親相愛之極.[12] The first half of this statement is reminiscent of what at least one Song period source does say (apropos of her collaboration with Zhao Mingcheng on *Records on Metal and Stone*).[13] The second half is a seventeenth-century formulation and is reminiscent of what Dorothy Ko calls the ideal of "companionate marriage" that became widespread then. The union

---

12. Lang Ying, *Qixiu leigao* 17.252; also in *Huibian*, p. 32.

13. Hong Mai, "Zhao Defu 'Jinshi lu'" 趙德甫《金石錄》, *Rongzhai suibi*, "Sibi" 5.684; also in *Huibian*, p. 9.

of Li Qingzhao and Zhao Mingcheng was often invoked in writings of the time as the prototype of this ideal.[14]

When Mao Jin obtained an abbreviated manuscript copy of *Jades for Rinsing the Mouth* in 1630 and proceeded to make a woodblock publication out of it, he appended Li Qingzhao's "Afterword to *Records on Metal and Stone*" to show readers that, in his words, "she was not only the most heroic of talented ladies of her time; she also purged clean the rotten stench of all those men of learning in the decades after the withdrawal south" 非止雄於一代才媛，直洗南渡後諸儒腐氣.[15] Romantic love, patriotic loyalty, and notions of personal virtue converged in late Ming thinking, as Kang-i Sun Chang has pointed out.[16] Indeed, late Ming courtesan-poets, who distinguished themselves by displays of loyalty to the fallen dynasty, were often invoked as foils to less principled men.[17] In addition to appending Li Qingzhao's afterword, Mao Jin also appended a handful of early appraisals of Li Qingzhao's writing and anecdotes. Among all the passages that he might have added, it is significant that he chose the anecdote about Zhao Mingcheng's abject failure in his attempt to outdo his wife in poetry composition (when his friend picked Li Qingzhao's lines out as the only good ones from among the fifty compositions that Zhao had written). That anecdote fit perfectly with emergent late Ming admiration of female talent. It calls to mind Feng Menglong's story about how the talented Su Xiaomei (the fictitious younger sister of Su Shi) tested Qin Guan's literary skill on their wedding night and in the process showed her superior learning, wit, and poetic skill.[18] Mao Jin's edition of *Jades for Rinsing the Mouth* packaged Li Qingzhao in a way that was congenial to late Ming ideals.

The preponderance of attention to the love between Li Qingzhao and Zhao Mingcheng as it came to be imagined in late Ming times was focused on how much his wife missed him when he was separated from her and how she grieved for him after his untimely death. But there was also some allowance, in this perception of the couple and their relationship, for passing attention to the pleasure they took in each other when they were together and even to Li Qingzhao's willingness to be playful and flirtatious toward Mingcheng

---

14. Ko, *Teachers of the Inner Chambers*, pp. 180–85.

15. Mao Jin, "Shuyu ci ba," *Huibian*, p. 59.

16. Chang, *The Late-Ming Poet Ch'en Tzu-lung*, pp. 3–19.

17. Wai-yee Li, "The Late Ming Courtesan."

18. Feng, "Su Xiaomei san nan xinlang."

(before they were married or as a young wife). Such moments provided some moments of lightheartedness to counterbalance the burden of sorrow attributed to her.

The five songs of love and flirtation only appeared in print in the last decades of the Ming, and when they first appeared, there was a good deal of disagreement concerning their authorship. But anthology editors, and presumably readers too, were evidently attracted to the idea that these songs were written by Li Qingzhao, and gradually this attribution gained momentum. We know that poems exchanged between the husband-wife couple Yang Shen and Huang E 黄娥, written in the mid-sixteenth century, enjoyed great popularity among late Ming readers. Those poems include playful exchanges between the two, in which they tease, pretend to scold, and flirt with each other.[19] Such actual husband-wife exchanges may have given encouragement to anthologists at the time to attribute similar poems to the canonical poet Li Qingzhao, poems that she could be imagined to have written for her husband, Zhao Mingcheng.[20] Readers would naturally be interested to see them. The idea that these songs originated from the brush of Li Qingzhao has also proven to be attractive to scholars and editors working on her in recent years. While more cautious scholars express doubts about the authenticity of some of the five, most of these works' acceptance is remarkably widespread among Li Qingzhao's most recent editors and biographers. We want her to have written these compositions.

There are, it turns out, some reasons after all to think that Li Qingzhao may have written song lyrics in the style of the five we have been discussing, if not those five in particular. There are two sources or statements in favor of this possibility.

The first is something we know from Mao Jin and his edition of *Jades for Rinsing the Mouth*. Mao Jin's edition, which he published soon after 1630, was based, he says in a colophon, on a manuscript copy of the work, which was one of more than twenty song lyrics collections in manuscript form he acquired that had been prepared in 1370, the very beginning of the Ming

---

19. On these poetic exchanges, see Ch'en and Mote, "Yang Shen and Huang O." On a later instance of husband-wife poetic exchange, which usually maintains a more serious tone, see Xiaorong Li, " 'Singing in Dis/Harmony.' "

20. I am grateful to one of the publisher's anonymous readers of the manuscript of this book for suggesting this point.

dynasty.[21] And this manuscript, which Mao Jin edited and printed, contains two of the five song lyrics under consideration, numbers 42 and 45. This is significant because it pushes the attestation of those compositions and their attribution to Li Qingzhao back some 240 years, considerably earlier than the late Ming period, when these songs begin to appear in anthologies.

Mao Jin's claim is not without its own problems. Mao Jin was a prolific editor and publisher, and the reliability of his assertions regarding the provenance and date of the works he published has often been called into question. His credibility as a scholar and bibliographer is not high. In putting together a new edition of *Jades for Rinsing the Mouth*, he was catering to late Ming tastes. It is not impossible that, despite what he says about his edition being based on a 1370 manuscript, he added some compositions to that manuscript to give his imprint more appeal. We know that he added other material, drawing on diverse sources, to the seventeen songs in his edition of *Jades for Rinsing the Mouth*. Perhaps he added some song lyrics too, drawing on recent anthologies, especially since the selection of Li Qingzhao's works was so small. Even if we take Mao Jin at his word and accept that the two songs really were in the 1370 manuscript he acquired, that does not prove that Li Qingzhao actually wrote them. They could have been misattributed to her in 1370, just as they could have been misattributed to her at the end of the Ming. Still, if what Mao Jin says is true, and he did not insert the two compositions into the collection, the reliability of their attribution gains some ground. They would have a much earlier attribution to Li Qingzhao than so many of the pieces newly attributed to her in the late Ming.

The second relevant statement is contained in Wang Zhuo's stinging critique of Li Qingzhao's song lyrics, written around 1200, quoted in part in chapter 2. The relevant section is this:

> [Li Qingzhao's] songs, in lines of unequal length, fully expressed people's feelings as the words turn this way and that. Capricious, clever, incisive, and fresh, a hundred different styles and moods are expressed. Knowing no restraint as her brush moved across the page, she included indecent language of the back streets. Among female members of officials' families who could write, never since ancient times has there been anyone so unconstrained.
>
> When the later ruler of Chen [r. 583–89] entertained himself with feasting, he had his lady poets and male lackeys exchange poems with each other. He selected the most sensually provocative and scintillating among them to set to

---

21. Mao Jin, "Shuyu ci ba," *Huibian*, p. 59.

new tunes, but they contained nothing more than such lines as "The jade disk moon is full night after night, / The bejeweled tree is renewed morning after morning."[22] Later, Li Kan rebuked Yuan Zhen and Bai Juyi for "recklessly writing tender and provocative poems. Unless the reader was a stalwart fellow or cultured gentleman, he was likely to be led to ruin by such verses. Subsequently, these compositions began to circulate among the commoners, where they were passed by word of mouth from fathers to sons and mothers to daughters. Once their lewd language and wanton expressions, like the chill of winter or the heat of summer, got under your skin, you couldn't get them out. . . ."[23]

Among the gentlemen of today there are those who imitate the crude and foul song lyrics of Cao Zu and his kind. They compose works that the lady poets and male lackeys of Chen, for all their sensual provocativeness; that Yuan and Bai, for all their unrestrained tenderness, lewd language, and wanton expressions; and Wen Tingyun, for all his illicit lyrics and sensual songs, would never have dared to write. The vogue of writing this way has even reached to women secluded in the inner quarters. Giving free rein to it with their brushes and ink, they are ashamed of nothing and have no fear. We'd better not let Li Kan see their works![24]

Cao Zu was infamous for writing "lewd" song lyrics. His writings were eventually ordered destroyed by Emperor Gaozong, and only a few compositions by him survive. Since Li Qingzhao is the explicit subject of Wang Zhuo's entry, it is clear that in his closing lines, when he refers to women secluded in inner quarters who know no shame and who allow themselves to be influenced by Cao Zu, he is thinking of Li Qingzhao, even though he does not refer to her by name.

If we think of Li Qingzhao as someone intensely interested in the song lyric; well versed in its range, its variety of styles, and its expressive purposes; and eager to demonstrate her own skill in composing in the form (we know all of this from her essay "On Song Lyrics"), it does not seem implausible that she might have experimented from time to time with compositions openly about lovers and romantic dalliance. Her father's friends did this; why

---

22. *Nanshi* 12.348.

23. Li Kan's 李戡 (*jinshi* 827) remarks are quoted by Du Mu in the grave inscription Du wrote for him, "Tang gu pinglu jun jiedu xunguan Longxi Li fujun muzhiming" 唐故平盧軍節度巡官隴西李府君墓誌銘, *Fanchuan wenji* 9.137. Wang Zhuo's quotation is nearly identical with that found in the grave inscription. On these controversial poems by Bai Juyi and Yuan Zhen, see Shields, "Defining Experience."

24. Wang Zhuo, *Biji manzhi* 2.88; also in *Huibian*, pp. 4–5.

should she be incapable of doing it? It is true that the earliest selection of her songs, that found in *Elegant Lyrics*, does not give any evidence of songs by her written in that style. But we would not expect it to, given the biases of that anthology. That same anthology systematically excluded Ouyang Xiu's more colloquial and "risqué" compositions. It would hardly be surprising if it did the same with similar compositions by Li Qingzhao.

Several modern scholars go even further. Wanting to credit Li Qingzhao with being capable of writing such "bold" and "open-minded" compositions, they quote Wang Zhuo's critique as proof of the authenticity of one or more of the five songs we have been discussing. To do so is to lose sight of all the uncertainties regarding the provenance of those five song lyrics. Li Qingzhao may have written songs about lovers openly enjoying each other's company, inciting Wang Zhuo to attack her for doing so, but that possibility cannot serve as evidence for the authenticity of any particular song attributed to her.

The two types of information that point to a possibility that Li Qingzhao wrote compositions about romantic or flirtatious encounters must be weighed against all the reasons we have to doubt the authenticity of the five songs of this type often ascribed to her since the late Ming and down to today. In the end, there is no way to make a definitive judgment about her authorship of these songs. Nevertheless, their late appearance, centuries after Li Qingzhao's death, together with the emergence at that time of new ideals concerning women, writing, and love that would have been well served by bringing Li Qingzhao into line as a precedent for them are a caution against readily accepting the compositions as authentic.

Yet there is one more point to make. If Li Qingzhao did write any of those five song lyrics, or others similar to them that do not survive, it is likely that their import and meaning were not what they were construed to be in late Ming times and thereafter. If she wrote such songs, probably she did so as exercises in a style of song lyric that was in wide circulation and was enthusiastically received in many quarters (but not universally so received). It is considerably less likely that she wrote such songs to capture or epitomize her relationship with Zhao Mingcheng. Why? Because there was no tradition of writing song lyrics that way about one's spouse (husband or wife), whereas many song lyrics writers indulged their imaginations, surely in some cases drawing on their own experience, to create vignettes about love outside of marriage between recognizable social types: the romantic, educated male and a lady (often a professional entertainer) whom he patronized.

It is useful here to go back to Wang Zhuo and reconsider what he says. Wang accuses Li Qingzhao of allowing lewd language of the streets and alleys into her compositions, asserting that this element in her song lyrics was picked up from Cao Zu and others like him. Wang Zhuo thinks that Li Qingzhao's willingness to allow this element into her compositions shows terrible judgment on her part and is, indeed, symptomatic of the moral degeneracy of her generation. It is symptomatic, but at the same time Li Qingzhao exceeded others—he certainly means she exceeded other women—in demeaning herself this way. What Wang Zhuo says is completely different from what the late Ming critics say about Li Qingzhao not only in its value judgment, but also in the way he characterizes this element in Li Qingzhao's songs. Wang Zhuo does not connect the way Li Qingzhao writes with Zhao Mingcheng. Nothing he says posits any link between her relationship to Zhao Mingcheng and the way she wrote the song lyrics that he decries. Wang Zhuo does not personalize the element in Li Qingzhao's songs that he objects to in that way. Furthermore, Wang Zhuo's remarks about Li Qingzhao omit any reference to her "Afterword to *Records on Metal and Stone*." It is entirely possible that Wang Zhuo, writing around 1200, was unaware of that afterword. As wary as we may want to be regarding Wang Zhuo's condemnation of Li Qingzhao's way of writing, nevertheless, the earliest critic to make reference to the bold treatment of romantic love in some of Li Qingzhao's songs did not see it as having anything to do with her marriage or personal life. She wrote that way because she allowed herself, regrettably, he thought, to come under the influence of a style that was already current and widely circulating.

Another way to put the matter is that when Wang Zhuo wrote his critique, the popular love story about Li Qingzhao and Zhao Mingcheng had not yet been created, or at least he had not come under its influence. Consequently, looking at Li Qingzhao's songs about lovers together, Wang Zhuo sees something utterly different from what late Ming critics and anthologists saw looking at the same songs.

If Li Qingzhao did write any or all of those five songs, or others like them, there was an interesting turnabout in their reception history. In her own time, that subset of her compositions was completely suppressed in the earliest anthology that included her works (*Elegant Lyrics*), and it was singled out for harsh censure in the earliest extended critical assessment of her writings in the form (that by Wang Zhuo). But over four centuries later, in the late Ming, owing to new developments in literary and cultural history, this component of her output was enthusiastically embraced and read in a completely new way. Today, it continues to be read that way by many scholars, even if the reasons for doing so have shifted.

Other Late Attributions

The group of songs examined above is small, and the individual pieces are readily identifiable. Apart from these there is a larger and more amorphous group of ten to fifteen compositions, depending how one counts, that is generally distinguished by a late appearance (groups 3 and 4) and a certain tone and emotion featured in the works.[25] The speaker (or person featured, at least) is clearly female and is longing for her man, who is either distantly away or perhaps deceased. Several of these compositions are mediocre in literary quality, in the sense that they are predictable and full of conventional lines. Yet they are regularly confounded together with Li Qingzhao's more reliable compositions. The effect of this mixing is to obscure Li Qingzhao's distinctive marks as a poet and to dilute the impression conveyed by her most reliable songs of a sure and steady talent that, in whatever mood it composes, produces striking work. The habit of reading these late songs together with the early ones conveys the impression that Li Qingzhao was notably inconsistent in the quality of what she wrote, capable sometimes of brilliant compositions and other times of unremarkable ones. This impression is as unfortunate as it is unfair to her.

Two of these poems will be discussed below to give a sense of the issues involved. One of the interesting aspects of these poems is the effusive praise they inspire by those critics who are convinced that Li Qingzhao wrote them. Here is the first example:

點絳唇　*To the tune "Dabbing Crimson Lips"* (no. 44)

寂寞深閨	Lonely, in the secluded women's quarters,
柔腸一寸愁千縷	Every inch of my fragile innards has a thousand threads of sorrow.
惜春春去	I cherish spring, but spring departs,
幾點催花雨	Amid a few droplets of rain that hasten the blossoms.

---

25. It includes nos. 40, 41, 44, 56, 58, 59, 61, 63, 68, 69, 70, 72, 73, and 75.

倚遍闌干	Having leaned everywhere on the balcony's railing,
祇是無情緒	I have no enthusiasm for anything.
人何處	Where is he now?
連天芳樹	Fragrant trees stretch to the horizon,
望斷歸來路	I gaze to the end of the road back home.[26]

A woman, alone in springtime, is longing for the man in her life. To escape the ennui of her own room, she goes to the balcony to gaze out into the distance, as if she could will the man back by looking expectantly for his return. In fact she has no idea where he is or when he will return.

From beginning to end, this song displays a directness of expression and reliance on stock diction that is not found in the early songs attributed to Li Qingzhao. Consider the opening line. That alone is enough to give one pause. *Gui* 閨, "women's quarters," is not a word that Li Qingzhao uses in her early songs, except once when she is reminiscing about the "women" (*guimen* 閨門) of her younger years.[27] "Secluded" makes the use of the word in this line even more conventional, and to further precede the phrase with *jimo* 寂寞 brings us into the realm of cliché. Recall how Li Qingzhao maneuvered carefully to get to the phrase *jimo* in a song we saw above (no. 33, translated in chapter 10), saving it for the very end ("Again, an autumn scene / Again, loneliness"). The opening line here is completely different. A similar penchant for unsubtle expression is evident in nearly every line that follows. What is lacking in this song is the kind of deft evocation of the speaker's emotional state through deflected, first-person statements or observations seen in numerous earlier examples.

Somehow, the conventional quality of this song lyric has not kept it from being read with great enthusiasm by respected critics. This was one of the pieces that inspired Wang Shizhen to write a matching composition. The late Ming poet and dramatist Mao Ying 茅暎 selected this piece in his song lyrics anthology and added this comment in the margin above it: "Yi'an has left us, and we will never have another like her. Whenever I compose a song lyric, I toast her with a cup of wine."[28] The late Qing critic Chen Tingzhuo 陳廷焯 (1853–92), a leader of the Changzhou School of song lyrics criticism, says of the piece: "It is superior in both feeling and language. Its 'spirit resonance' is

---

26. *Jianzhu* 1.73; *Quan Songci* 2:1209.
27. See no. 32, translated in chapter 10.
28. Mao Ying, *Cidi* 詞的 1.15a; quoted in *Jianzhu* 1.74.

effortlessly conveyed."[29] Perhaps the most revealing comment is that found in another late Ming anthology, compiled by Qian Yunzhi 錢允治 (1541–1624): "Grasses cover the long road and her lover does not return, churning in vain every inch of her viscera."[30] This is intended as high praise.

The second example follows:

浪淘沙   *To the tune "Waves Scour the Sand"* (no. 56)

簾外五更風	Outside the blinds, the wind at the fifth watch
吹夢無蹤	Blows my dream away, leaving no trace.
畫樓重上與誰同	Again I climb the painted tower, to share with whom?
4 記得玉釵斜撥火	I recall using a jade hairpin to tap the incense clean
寶篆成空	The precious seal character became nothing.
回首紫金峰	Looking back toward the purple-gold peaks,
雨潤煙濃	As rains soak and the mist is heavy,
8 一江春浪醉醒中	An entire spring river, between drunkenness and sobriety.
留得羅襟前日淚	The tears of former days still left on my silken lapel,
彈與征鴻	I would send aloft to the migrating geese.[31]

This is a more interesting poem than the preceding one, with more original language and lines. Yet there are serious questions about its attribution to Li Qingzhao.

The existence of this song lyric is not attested before 1550, when it appeared in the anthology *Cilin wanxuan*. Not only did the piece appear late; its authorship is under dispute. Ming sources record at least four attributions for the work. *Cilin wanxuan*, whose attributions are known to be questionable, as discussed earlier, assigns it to Li Qingzhao but notes that it is also attributed (in unidentified sources) to Ouyang Xiu. Mao Jin's unpublished edition of *Jades for Rinsing the Mouth* (1630) says that a Song source attributes it to Liu Yong.[32] Several other Ming anthologies perpetuate the attribution to Ouyang Xiu, whereas others further complicate the question by giving no attribution

---

29. Chen Tingzhuo, *Yunshao ji* 雲韶集 10, quoted in *Jianzhu* 1.75.

30. Qian Yunzhi, *Xuxuan caotang shiyu* 續選草堂詩餘, quoted in *Jianzhu* 1.74.

31. *Jianzhu* 1.121; *Quan Songci* 2:1212, "Cunmu."

32. If this were true, then the existence of the piece would be attested three centuries earlier than 1550. But, as Xu Peijun points out, Mao Jin's statement that Wu Zeng's *Nenggai zhai manlu* quotes the work and attributes it to Liu Yong is itself incorrect. It is another of Liu Yong's song lyrics, not this one, that *Nenggai zai manlu* cites. *Jianzhu* 1.121.

(implying their editors thought the author was impossible to identify).[33] Among recent scholarship, in his critical edition of Li Qingzhao's works, Wang Zhongwen relegates the piece to his group of "doubtful" song lyrics and says that it is probably best to accept the author as unknowable.[34] Xu Beiwen, in his edition of her works, likewise puts the piece in his group of "doubtful" compositions.[35] But these cautious approaches have not stopped others (e.g., Zhuge Yibing) from accepting the piece as Li Qingzhao's.[36] One respected scholar (Xu Peijun) insists that Li Qingzhao wrote the piece and goes so far as to say that she is the only person who could have written this composition.[37]

What could account for such an extreme position? Once again, the power of the idealization of the Li-Zhao marriage lies behind it, enforced by the enthusiasm of the discovery that the piece can, with ingenious scholarly manipulation, be set into a particular moment of Li Qingzhao's life that seems to explain and, indeed, to enliven it.

The commentator who would perform this action seizes upon a few phrases in the poem and weaves them into a narrative that seems to fit a biographical occasion in Li Qingzhao's life. The speaker, assumed to be female, is alone and remembering the companion that she used to have. She is somewhere on the Yangzi River. When was Li Qingzhao alone on the Yangzi? In 1129, shortly after Zhao Mingcheng had died in Jiankang (Nanjing), and she, following Gaozong and his court, was fleeing eastward down the river from the advancing Jurchen armies. For the critic determined to read the poem this way, other elements, then, fall into place. Lines 4 and 5 are then said to be recollections of the happier times Li Qingzhao spent with Zhao Mingcheng during the Qingzhou period (that is, the period she described so memorably in her afterword). But line 5 is read as an ominous image, portending Zhao Mingcheng's untimely death earlier in 1129 ("seal character" is the incense itself, formed in the shape of a character in archaic seal script, which would

---

33. The attributions given in various Ming and Qing sources are summarized in *Jianzhu* 1.121 and Wang Zhongwen, *Li Qingzhao ji jiaozhu* 1.85–86.

34. Wang Zhongwen, *Li Qingzhao ji jiaozhu* 1.85–86.

35. Xu Beiwen, *Li Qingzhao quanji pingzhu*, pp. 155–56.

36. Zhuge, *Li Qingzhao shici xuan*, pp. 54–56, where there is no indication of any question of the work's attribution to Li Qingzhao. In his earlier study, *Li Qingzhao yu Zhao Mingcheng*, pp. 152–54, Zhuge is somewhat more cautious, noting that scholars have doubts about this piece. But he goes on to present a reading of the piece that roots it in Li Qingzhao's life.

37. *Jianzhu* 1.122.

eventually be consumed by the fire). Once it has been decided that this poem was written soon after Zhao Mingcheng's death, the closing lines are taken as referring simultaneously to the desire to communicate with her late husband and the impossibility of communicating with him any longer. That accounts for the touching but futile thought of entrusting her tears of former days to the geese in the sky. The phrase "purple-gold peak" 紫金峰 was at first something of a problem. Wang Zhongwen had noted that no such place is attested in Song sources, specifically noting that Purple-Gold Mountain 紫金山 in modern-day Nanjing (another name for Zhong Mountain 鍾山) is not referred to in Southern Song gazetteers of the region.[38] But his warning went unheeded by other scholars, two of whom claim to have found a pre-Tang reference, in an obscure poem, to a mountain in Jiankang by that name.[39] Locating Purple-Gold Peak in Jiankang appears to cement the argument: Li Qingzhao is not only thinking of her late husband, commemorating him in her poem; she is gazing back toward the city in which he died. When Xu Peijun says that only Li Qingzhao could have written this piece, he is finding particular emotive power and excellence in its lines because he is already convinced that she did, in fact, write it. Once the song lyric has been situated at a heart-rending moment in Li Qingzhao's life, when her past happiness had just been taken from her so abruptly and her future was suddenly so uncertain and dangerous, the lines seem all the more poignant and beautiful.

This makes for a good story, but it is not the only way the poem might be read and not even the most obvious way of reading it. First, bear in mind that the earliest sources that present this poem, which date from four hundred years after Li Qingzhao's death, contradict each other on its authorship. Even the Ming period assertion, repeated in various anthologies, that an early source attributes the piece to Liu Yong, though itself in error, serves to show how arbitrary is the reading that credits the piece to Li Qingzhao.

Furthermore, it is not certain that the speaker is a woman. The mention of tears cried over lost love is found repeatedly in Liu Yong's song lyrics, even when the speaker is unambiguously male. The motif of lovelorn tears falling

---

38. Wang Zhongwen, *Li Qingzhao ji jiaozhu* 1.86.

39. Li Hanzhao and Liu Yaoye, "Li Qingzhao 'Lang taosha' jiexi"; also widely reproduced on other Internet sites. The authors have found the phrase *zijin feng* in a poem by Xu Xiaoke 徐孝克 (6th c.), "Yangtong lingjun Sheshan Qixia si shanfang yezuo liuyun shi" 仰同令君攝山棲霞寺山房夜坐六韻詩, *Chenshi* 6.2562. Unfortunately for their argument, it is not at all clear that the phrase in that poem is a place-name rather than a description of "purple-gold peaks."

on the lapel or neck lining of a man's robe is found twice in Liu Yong's compositions.[40] So it is entirely plausible to "hear" the lines of the song as spoken
by a man. In fact, the song sounds like many of Liu Yong's pieces set in a
male voice, pieces that feature a man who is traveling in the south and recalling a woman he loved back up north in the capital. But since the season is
spring, the "migrating geese" should be flying northward rather than westward (toward Jiankang). And if the speaker is thinking of using the geese to
"send" his tears, he should be sending them to someone capable of receiving
them, not someone who is deceased. *Jiang* 江 could be any river in the south
and need not be the Yangzi. As for "purple-gold peak," not only does it seem
not to be a Song period mountain in Jiankang; it need not be a place-name at
all: it could just as well be a descriptive phrase: "I look back to the purple-
gold peaks." The claim that there was such a place-name in Jiankang before
the Song (before the Tang, actually) counts for little, even if it is true.
Nowhere in Tang poetry and nowhere in Song poetry (*shi* or *ci*) is the phrase
"purple-gold peak" used at all, much less used to specify a particular mountain peak in Jiankang (this is apparent by searching the two corpuses of
poetry electronically). The understanding of those who insist on Li Qingzhao's authorship is that she uses the phrase to evoke Jiankang, where her late
husband had died. But the phrase cannot do that if there is no conventional
association between the peak name and Jiankang, and to judge from the voluminous surviving literature, there was none. Finally, it sounds like the speaker,
whoever he or she is, is stationary somewhere in the south rather than on the
move, and certainly is not frantically fleeing (i.e., before invading armies).
Otherwise how could we explain line 3: "Again I climb the painted tower"?

What is it that causes Ming and Qing anthologists to attribute these poems,
whose provenance is unknown, to Li Qingzhao and then causes critics to
effuse over what "she" expresses in them? A primary cause is the conviction
that the essence of Li Qingzhao's identity as a woman is her devotion to
Zhao Mingcheng and her emotional dependence on him, and that consequently the essence of her work as a poet is the expression of such devotion
and dependence, both of which they discern in such poems. It is only certain
kinds of song lyrics that gravitate in Ming-Qing times toward Li Qingzhao.
They are those of loneliness and longing (which may be combined with grief

---

40. Liu Yong, "Dijia nong" 笛家弄 and "Yan guiliang" 燕歸梁, *Quan Songci* 1:21 and 1:49.
The first of these is translated in Hightower, "The Songwriter Liu Yong," p. 220.

over a death), as in the two pieces just above, or they may be vignettes depicting the woman together with her man, as in the flirtatious pieces discussed earlier, read in a particular way. Song lyrics on other themes, including many attested in Li Qingzhao's most reliable compositions, such as the passing of the seasons, outings into nature, boating, and frustration for undisclosed reasons, do not attach themselves to her in the Ming and Qing periods.

How can it be that even mediocre poems come to be associated with Li Qingzhao in this process? Because they are no longer perceived as mediocre once they are believed to come from Li Qingzhao's hand. It is not so much that readers consciously think that if Li Qingzhao wrote a poem, it cannot be of average quality. Rather, the attribution to Li Qingzhao transforms the work in question, endowing even conventional lines in it with new power and intensity. The resultant reading is no longer primarily a literary approach or reaction to the poem. It is more of a pseudohistoricist or biographical reading of the work, in which the lines are perceived as being infused with the thoughts and feelings of the great woman poet. If the poem is actually well-written and inherently interesting in its own right, as with the second example above, so much the better. It too is enhanced by being attached to Li Qingzhao, and becomes further evidence of her special talent. Chen Tingzhuo's comments on that poem are apropos: "It is so sad and beautiful, I can hardly read it to the end. Must it not have been written for Defu [Zhao Mingcheng]?"[41] Elsewhere he adds, "The feelings and words are indescribably sad; how many blood-stained tears must have been shed!"[42]

Contours of Affection and Preconceptions

In chapter 10 we examined a group of song lyrics, including many of Li Qingzhao's best known pieces, marked by their insistence on a dismal state of mind. It is often impossible to know exactly what shade of displeasure the speaker is experiencing (bitterness, anxiety, anger, hopelessness, loneliness, or some combination) or its exact cause, but the general mood is clear enough.

So long as one comes to Li Qingzhao with the traditional preconceptions about her life and works, it is easy to assume that the poems of distress represent the only mood she worked in as a song lyrics poet, overlooking entirely works that present other affections. Once we question or even put aside

---

41. Chen Tingzhuo, *Baiyu zhai cihua zuben jiaozhu* 2.220; also in *Jianzhu* 1.123.
42. Chen Tingzhuo, *Yunshao ji* 10, *Jianzhu* 1.123.

conventional images of her, however, it becomes easier to give attention to other moods expressed in her work and view them as significant parts of her output. Some of the outdoor excursion compositions discussed in the preceding chapter constitute one exception to her poetry of despair. In other pieces she likewise explores a range of emotions among her female subjects. Several of them are early attributions, from my groups 1 and 2.

There are poems that explore a shifting complex of emotions, as in the following:

念奴嬌   *To the tune "Recalling Her Charm"* (no. 30)

蕭條庭院	So deserted, the courtyard,
又斜風細雨	And a fine drizzle is blown by slanting winds.
重門須閉	The double doors must be closed,
4　寵柳嬌花寒食近	Oh, the beloved willows and lovely flowers, as Cold Food Day approaches,
種種惱人天氣	It's the season that's unsettling in so many ways.
險韻詩成	My poem set to a difficult rhyme is finished,
扶頭酒醒	I sober up from head-holding wine,
8　別是閑滋味	To a special flavor of idleness.
征鴻過盡	The migrating geese fly past,
萬千心事難寄	Impossible for them to convey the myriad concerns on my mind.
樓上幾日春寒	Several days of spring chill in my upper-story room,
12　簾垂四面	The blinds have stayed down on all four sides.
玉闌干慵倚	Too languid to lean on the jade balustrade,
被冷香消新夢覺	My blanket is cold, the incense burned out, just awake from my dream,
不許愁人不起	It's impossible with such sadness not to get up.
16　清露晨流	Pure dewdrops drift down in the morning air,
新桐初引	New paulownia leaves are putting forth buds,
多少游春意	How I long to go for a springtime outing!
日高煙斂	As the sun rises and the mist burns off,
20　更看今日晴未	Let me look again to see if the sky will be clear today.[43]

The speaker's emotional state is the subject of this poem, and that state is complicated and varies through the course of the work. The speaker is alone and beset by nagging sadness. What weighs on her mind seems mostly to be

---

43. *Jianzhu* 1.75; *Quan Songci* 2:1208.

separation from home (rather than the absence of the man in her life), as suggested by the reference to the migrating geese. It is spring, so the birds would be flying north. The speaker would like to have the geese bear her letters to loved ones up north but cannot do so; is it because she has too many concerns to put into letters? It sounds that way.

As lonesome as she feels, the speaker is also keenly aware of the beauty of nature in the spring. The courtyard she looks out on may be deserted and the double doors to her residence closed, but still she senses, if she cannot see, the attractiveness of the willows and the flowers of the season. The season has an unsettling, vexing (*naoren* 惱人) effect, which is to say it is disquieting, in both welcome and unwelcome ways.

In the second stanza, the chill and isolation that pervades the speaker's room, with blinds hanging down on all sides, becomes unbearable, especially when she thinks of how attractive the natural setting is outside. Lines 16 and 17 present comely images of nature's purity and rejuvenation. They are intended to describe the beauty of what the speaker sees (or vividly imagines); they are also drawn word for word from an anecdote in *A New Account of Tales of the World*, where they are not literal description at all but rather metaphors used to evoke the purity, freshness, and goodness of a former friend, who had lately become estranged but is still remembered fondly.[44] Is the speaker in the song lyric appropriating the lines merely as nature description, or does she use them also to signal her hope that a damaged relationship might be salvaged? We cannot know. We do know that in the closing couplet she is eager to see what the weather will be like this new day, evidently planning to fulfill her desire to venture out into the spring scene if the sky has cleared. The poem ends with eager expectation: will the weather finally cooperate today so that she can go out to enjoy the spring scenery that has been filling her thoughts?

There are also compositions in which the speaker remains aloof and refrains from expressing any strong emotion.

浣溪沙   *To the tune "Sands of the Washing Stream"* (no. 11)

淡蕩春光寒食天	The spring sunlight is warm and gentle in Cold Food Day season.
玉爐沉水裊殘煙	Aloeswood burns in the jade censer, a waving trail of lingering smoke.

---

44. Liu Yiqing, *Shishuo xinyu jianshu* 8/153/496–97; trans. Mather, *Shih-shuo Hsin-yü*, p. 246.

夢回山枕隱花鈿	Awake from a dream, the pillow hides my inlaid flower hairpin.
海燕未來人鬭草	The coastal swallows have not returned, people play the stalk guessing game.
江梅已過柳生綿	The southern plum has faded, willows send forth their cottony fluff.
黃昏疏雨濕鞦韆	A light rain at sunset moistens the garden swing.[45]

There is barely a persona in this poem at all. But she is there, almost entirely hidden, with her inlaid hairpin, at the close of the first stanza. Realizing that she is there, we understand that all the other lines are not omniscient description, as they may first seem, but are rather her observations of the setting and circumstances in which she finds herself. We see, then, that the first stanza mostly concerns her room, and in the second stanza her attention moves away from her room to what is happening outside but close at hand. This is exactly the opposite of the movement in countless song lyrics by other authors (all male), in which we, as onlookers, are brought closer and closer to a woman alone in her room as the song progresses until, in the closing lines, the focus is entirely on her and her emotions.

We expect some revelation, somewhere in the composition, of the speaker's emotional condition, but it never comes. Instead, the entire second stanza is given over to observations about the scene outside. It is a comely spring scene, a pleasant scene. The guessing or gambling game mentioned is one associated with spring and springtime outings. Playing on garden swings is an amusement for girls or women in song lyrics. No one is amusing herself on the swing now, because a fine rain is falling. But even that image, of the vacant swing moistened in rain at sunset, is crafted to sound attractive. There is no reason to think that the speaker is complaining. It sounds more like she is intently observing, with interest, the sounds and sights of the setting outside.

A similar reticence is evident in this poem that we considered in chapter 3 with reference to the autobiographical reading problem:

---

45. *Jianzhu* 1.116; *Quan Songci* 2:1203–4.

浣溪沙　*To the tune "Sands of the Washing Stream"* (no. 10)

小院閑窗春色深	A small courtyard and lattice window, the spring colors are vivid.
重簾未捲影沈沈	The double blinds are not lifted, shadows gather deep inside.
倚樓無語理瑤琴	She leans against the building, saying nothing, plucking a jeweled zither.
遠岫出雲催薄暮	A distant cave emits clouds, hurrying the onset of dusk.
細風吹雨弄輕陰	A light wind brings rain, jostling the sparse shade.
梨花欲謝恐難禁	The pear blossoms are about to wither, there's no preventing it, I'm afraid.[46]

This is usually read, as we have seen, with a set of assumptions regarding how Li Qingzhao wrote about longing for her absent husband fully in place. It need not be read that way at all. If we look at it afresh, we discover here a poem about a spring scene and a woman looking out at it, enjoying it, while keenly aware that it will not last much longer. She is evidently alone, that is true, but there is no explicit mention of unhappiness. She is looking out at the scene ("leaning against a building" in song lyrics usually implies gazing afar while standing on a balcony, leaning on a railing or back against the building itself), playing an instrument, and largely keeping her thoughts to herself. This could as well be a portrait of self-sufficiency as one of loneliness. The first two lines of the second stanza suggest an appreciation of the beauty of the scene. They both contain conceits: the cave sends forth clouds, and the clouds quicken the sunset; the wind brings the rain (not just "blows it" but "blows it here" because of the parallel with the preceding line), and the wind and rain together toss or play with the sparse shade. The conceits impart a tone of playfulness to the lines. This is nature enhanced by imaginative representation. The concluding line need not be read as ominous (i.e., spring's beauty is about to end, and I have no one to enjoy it with). It can instead be taken as fanciful and slightly jocular: a reference to the anticipated fading of the blossoms as if it were not inevitable. These are the words of someone who is kidding herself while knowing that she is doing so. The logical implication of this line would be to resolve to enjoy what one can of the season, since one knows it will soon be over.

---

46. *Jianzhu* 1.67, *Quan Songci* 2:1203.

It is interesting to see how the readings of certain pieces change once we free ourselves from the traditional assumptions. Consider this piece:

玉樓春   *To the tune "Spring in the House of Jade"* (no. 28)

紅酥肯放瓊苞碎	Red cream allows jade buds to break open,
探著南枝開遍未	I'll go see if the south branches are fully in bloom.
不知醞藉幾多香	I don't know how much fragrance they hold inside,
但見包藏無限意	But I see they contain unlimited meaning.
道人憔悴春窗底	They know a person is haggard, sitting beneath a springtime window,
悶損闌干愁不倚	Beset by boredom, too sad to lean on the railing.
要來小酌便來休	"If you want to come drink a little, come on then.
未必明朝風不起	There's no guarantee a wind won't arise tomorrow morning."[47]

This is one of the pieces in the *Garden of Plums* anthology, and so the attribution is problematic. If the piece is authentic, it is another example of a sudden change of sentiment within a song, and (in this reading, at least) one that leads to a manner of thinking seldom associated with Li Qingzhao.

The traditional way of reading this song, which still dominates in the most recent scholarship on Li Qingzhao, is that the poet is the haggard person who is referred to, and the closing lines are addressed to Zhao Mingcheng. She is imploring him to come spend time with her, to come drink and enjoy the plum blossoms before they are blown off the tree by the wind.[48] But this reading disregards some interesting phrases earlier in the poem that point to an entirely different interpretation. Lines 3 and 4 imply this: the speaker cannot vouch for the blossoms being very fragrant (a reference to the lack of scent for which plum blossoms are known), but she is sure that their *yi* 意 is abundant. *Yi* could be rendered different ways (meaning, intent, significance), but clearly the lines imply a relationship between the blossoms and the

---

47. *Jianzhu* 1.27; *Quan Songci* 2:1201.

48. For this reading, see Xu Beiwen, *Li Qingzhao quanji pingzhu*, p. 27; Zhuge, *Li Qingzhao shici xuan*, p. 15; and Deng, *Li Qingzhao xinzhuan*, p. 68. Chen Zumei (followed by Xu Peijun) has a different, political reading: she dates the piece to the period of factional struggle of 1103–5, when the Yuanyou Party was condemned and Zhao Tingzhi was in and out of high office, and thinks that the concluding lines refer to the precariousness of Li Qingzhao's situation, fearing another imminent "fall" of her father, who had Yuanyou connections, and her father-in-law. See Chen's *Li Qingzhao ci xinyi jiping*, p. 63; and *Jianzhu* 1.27–28.

speaker. Several commentators explain *dao* 道 in line 5 as "to know" or "to say," glossing it with reference to uses of the word in other song lyrics, and take its grammatical subject to be the blossoms.[49] The blossoms, personified, are aware of the speaker's unhappy condition. In that case it is tempting to take *yi* also to refer to the flowers' "concern" or "consideration" for the speaker, which the speaker senses or is confident about. With the relationship between blossoms and speaker established, the blossoms being described as the speaker's understanding friend, it becomes plausible, as at least one recent scholar has argued, to take the closing lines as the blossoms' invitation to the speaker (as I have translated).[50] The blossoms know how transient they are and hope the lady will give them a chance to cheer her up before they depart. Song lyrics on flowers (whether by Li Qingzhao or by her contemporaries) are full of personification, and while the flowers do not often speak, there is no reason they might not. If this reading is right, the standard readings of the poem do an injustice to its cleverness and originality. By clinging to preconceptions about what "Li Qingzhao" must be saying in a poem, the conventional reading misconstrues what she actually says.

We look now at one last song lyric, which similarly raises questions about the wisdom of traditional assumptions about how Li Qingzhao expresses herself in song lyrics.

小重山　　*To the tune "Low Rows of Hills"* (no. 17)

春到長門春草青	Spring comes to Long Gate, spring vegetation is verdant.
紅梅些子破	Red plum blossoms are beginning to open,
未開勻	But are not yet in full flower.
4　碧雲籠碾玉成塵	Emerald clouds cover the grinder, jade slivers lie piled like dust,
留曉夢	My lingering dream from dawn
驚破一甌春	Is abruptly broken by a pot of spring.
花影壓重門	Blossom shadows press down upon double doors,
8　疏簾鋪淡月	The spaced blinds are covered with pallid moonlight.
好黃昏	What a fine evening it is!

---

49. *Jianzhu* 1.28; Chen Zumei, *Shuyu ci zhu*, p. 16.
50. Wang Yingzhi, *Li Qingzhao ji*, pp. 21–22.

二年三度負東君   Three times in two years I've been untrue to the Lord
                                    of the East,

歸來也   .   .   .   .

12 著意過今春   .   .   .   .[51]

Line 1: Long Gate is the palace in which Empress Chen was confined after she lost the favor of her husband, Emperor Wu of the Han (r. 141–87 BCE).

Line 4: "Emerald clouds" are tea leaves, which were ground up before infusing in hot water. The "jade slivers" are the ground tea powder.

Line 5: "Pot of spring" is a pot of tea.

Line 10: The Lord of the East is the god of spring.

For the time being, I leave the last two lines untranslated. There are two main readings of this song lyric in recent scholarship. The primary one, which is also the traditional one, is that the poem was written to express Li Qingzhao's fond wish that Zhao Mingcheng, who has been separated from her for two or more years, return home to spend the current spring with her. In that case, the last two lines should be taken as an injunction: "Come back home / So I [or we] can concentrate on passing this spring [i.e., not wasting it again]." There are problems with this interpretation, however. It necessitates creating a separation of husband and wife for two or three years, and none is supported by the sources. Scholars thus speculate that such a separation existed (there is a marked disagreement among the different scholars about when it occurred, which is hardly surprising since it is, in fact, a speculation).[52] Another problem is purely linguistic: line 11 does not sound like an injunction. The particle *ye* 也 at the end of a line does not form an injunction; other particles do that (e.g., *xiu* 休, which we saw used this way in the preceding song). This line reads like a declarative statement: "[Subject] has come

---

51. *Jianzhu* 1.94; *Quan Songci* 2:1205.

52. Xu Peijun says that it refers to the separation of 1127–28, when Zhao Mingcheng first went south to Jiankang for his mother's funeral, and Li Qingzhao joined him in the following year. But husband and wife were, in fact, separated for less than twelve months, not two years. *Jianzhu* 1.94–95. Noticing, probably, the weakness of Xu's argument, Zhuge Yibing says that it refers to a separation in 1117–19, after Zhao Mingcheng left Qingzhou and his wife behind to take up office elsewhere. *Li Qingzhao yu Zhao Mingcheng*, pp. 35–36. But there is no textual support for this separation either. Xu Beiwen avoids these problems by saying that the piece refers to a long separation of husband and wife without specifying when it occurred (except to say that it was before the Jurchen invasion). *Li Qingzhao quanji pingzhu*, p. 8. For yet another suggested period of separation, see the discussion of Chen Zumei's interpretation that follows.

back." The reference to the Han palace in line 1 is generally taken as a sign that Li Qingzhao felt she had lost her husband's favor.

A secondary interpretation has been offered by Chen Zumei, probably because she sees the shortcomings of the primary one, and adopted by Deng Hongmei and Wang Yingzhi.[53] This is a political reading of the poem (similar to Chen's reading of the preceding song lyric, see note 48). She dates the poem to 1106, when the ban on the Yuanyou Party was lifted and Zhao Ting-zhi (Li Qingzhao's father-in-law) was returned to favor. Chen believes that in 1103, because of the Yuanyou Party's ban, Li Qingzhao had been forced to return to her natal home in Shandong, but three years later, with the end of the Yuanyou ban, she was able to return to the capital. As discussed in chapter 3, this too is sheer speculation; there is no textual support for Li Qingzhao's three-year absence from the capital at this time. In this reading, Long Gate Palace in line 1 does not evoke a woman who has lost the favor of her husband; it is instead used figuratively, in the "beautiful lady and fragrant plant" 美人香草 tradition of poetic allegory, to refer to an official who is out of favor. But to say that "spring has returned" to Long Gate is to say that he (or they) who were rejected have been restored to imperial favor. And with that development, Li Qingzhao has been allowed to return to the capital from her seclusion in her native place. That is what the phrase *guilai* 歸來 means in line 11, in this interpretation. Thus the ending should be understood this way: "Now I have come back / And am determined to pass this spring well." In this interpretation, Li Qingzhao is no longer imploring Zhao Mingcheng to come back to her. She is saying that she has come back to him and is looking forward to spending a pleasant springtime with him. Li Qingzhao's identity as wife and her devotion to Zhao Mingcheng is still key. Her longing for an absent husband has been replaced by her joy at being reunited with him.

To the uninitiated, it may seem odd that the life history of a person is altered in order to make sense out of lines in a poem she wrote, but that sort of biographical "adjustment" is done with Li Qingzhao all the time. Aside from necessitating a three-year absence from the place we have every reason to believe she was (based on what she says in her afterword), the political reading of the song lyric is strained and unconvincing.

---

53. Chen Zumei, *Li Qingzhao ci xinyi jiping*, p. 72; Deng, *Li Qingzhao xinzhuan*, pp. 55–56; Wang Yingzhi, *Li Qingzhao ji*, p. 28.

There is another way of reading this poem, which is offered here as an alternative to the two described so far. This reading takes its cue from the opening line, which is borrowed word for word from the opening line of a song lyric by Xue Zhaoyun 薛昭蘊 (10th c.) found in the well-known anthology *Among the Flowers*.[54] That the line is lifted from that earlier poem is not my discovery; the borrowing has long been recognized as such. But most commentaries on Li Qingzhao's poem simply note the source of her line and do not explore the ramifications of the borrowing. This is Xue Zhaoyun's complete poem:

小重山　　*To the tune "Low Rows of Hills"*

春到長門春草青	Spring comes to Long Gate, spring vegetation is verdant.
玉階華露滴	Onto jade steps dewdrops fall,
月朧明	The moon shines brightly.
東風吹斷玉簫聲	The east wind blows away the melody of a jade flute,
宮漏促	The palace water-clock hurries the night,
簾外曉啼鶯	Beyond the blinds an oriole calls at dawn.
愁極夢難成	Her sadness extreme, it is hard to form a dream.
紅妝流宿淚	Rouge make-up is streaked with last night's tears,
不勝情	She cannot control her feelings.
手挼裙帶繞花行	She fingers the belt of her skirt as she circles around inside the palace.
思君切	Her longing for her lord is intense,
羅幌暗塵生	Dark dust gathers on the silken curtains.

This poem is not necessarily about Empress Chen of the Former Han (because the palace mentioned in the opening line could stand for any palace), but it is about the stereotype of the neglected palace lady. It is likely that the flute mentioned in line 4 is intended to suggest entertainment taking place in another nearby palace, where the husband of the woman is enjoying himself with other women. She waits through the night for him to come to her, but he never does, and before she knows it, night has given way to dawn. She has been weeping through the night, and even after dawn she cannot get to sleep and walks aimlessly about inside her palace, thinking about her lord and master. The dust that gathers on her curtains evokes the hopelessness of her situation: nothing is going to happen, this springtime, in her palace. No

---

54. Xue Zhaoyun, "Xiao chongshan" 小重山, *Huajian ji zhu* 3.90.

one is going to come to break up the loneliness; she is an abandoned woman living in an abandoned place.

Song lyric 19 by Li Qingzhao (discussed in chapter 10) also opens with a line borrowed from another poet's song. In a preface, Li Qingzhao remarks that she so liked the song that she wrote "several" of her own all starting with that same borrowed opening line. After repeating the same opening line, Li Qingzhao went on to change the content and tone of the rest of the song, compared with the earlier one.

In poem number 17 above, Li Qingzhao is, again, recasting the piece that provided her with her opening line. This time the relationship with the earlier song is even closer because she sets her composition to the very same tune. Moreover, there are several shared elements common to the two songs: the moonlight, a dream, blinds, and a "lord" mentioned in the closing lines. Yet the mood and substance of Li Qingzhao's piece stands in sharp contrast to Xue Zhaoyun's song. In Xue's composition, the loveliness of the spring night only intensifies the loneliness of the woman in her room. What she notices, on this pleasant night, is the sound of the flute melody that she can no longer hear. Then it is suddenly dawn (too late for her lord to come to her). The second stanza presents a sustained account of her misery and listlessness.

The distinctive trait of Li Qingzhao's poem is how attractive everything is, both inside and outside. The persona's attention is focused on minute physical details, and they are all pleasing. The plum blossoms have just begun to open but are going to become even more beautiful. The ground-up tea leaves are like a pile of shaved jade chips. This woman has no trouble dreaming; in fact she needs to drink tea to clear her head and dispel her dream once and for all. The opening lines of the second stanza show that although this lady is also cooped up indoors, the beauty of the springtime evening manages to convey itself to her nevertheless. The barrier of double doors is overcome by the shadows of blossoms that overlay them, and moonlight presents itself to her, appearing on her blinds. All this leads to her exclamation, the kind of line rarely encountered in song lyrics about solitary women: "What a fine evening it is!" There is, so far, no hint of loneliness.

Now we come to the closing lines. The Lord of the East is the god that governs spring and controls its arrival and departure. He is a personification of spring and the wondrous effects it has on nature. He is abundantly referred to in song lyrics about springtime. His comings are longed for, his arrival is celebrated, his delay in coming railed against; his hasty departure is regretted, methods to detain him are contemplated, and he is criticized as a "traveler on the go" who is fickle and will not tarry. Verbs of arrival and departure are frequently applied to his movements: "The Lord of the East has purposefully come to the western garden" 東君著意到西園;[55] "They vie to spy out the Lord of the East / Where will he first arrive?" 爭探得東君，何處先到;[56] "May the Lord of the East soon devise a plan to return" 東君早作歸來計;[57] "[They try] to detain the Lord of the East" 留住東君;[58] "Ever since the Lord of the East departed" 自東君別後;[59] "[The orioles] seem to be telling the Lord of the East to stay" 似叫住東君;[60] "She resents the Lord of the East / For being in such a hurry, / He's just like a traveler among men" 怪東君，太匆匆，亦是人間行客.[61]

Given such conventions of usage as well as the tone and direction of the preceding lines in Li Qingzhao's poem, it is plausible to take the closing lines as referring to the "return" of the Lord of the East and the speaker's resolve to take full advantage of his return this year, not being "unfaithful" to him again. Thus:

二年三度負東君	Three times in two years I've been untrue to the Lord of the East,
歸來也	Now that he has returned,
12　著意過今春	I will set my mind on enjoying this spring.

The lines complete the recasting of Xue Zhaoyun's poem. Lacking an ordinary companion, the speaker is determined to enjoy the season anyway, thinking of it as the embodiment of the "lord" who brought it back with him. Her Lord of Spring is the perfect alternative to the "lord" in Xue Zhaoyun's poem, who does not return to that lady.

If only we put aside the assumptions that are regularly brought to the song lyrics of Li Qingzhao, which condition us to think she is only capable of a certain kind of composition and affection, we will discover a new variety of expression in what she writes. We will find that, apart from the most celebrated of her compositions, she is also capable of producing works that are completely at odds with traditional images of her.

---

55. Shi Xiaoyou 石孝友, "Yulou chun" 玉樓春, *Quan Songci* 3:2631.
56. Tian Wei 田爲, "Tan chun" 探春, *Quan Songci* 2:1053.
57. Shen Tang 沈唐, "Shuangye fei" 霜葉飛, *Quan Songci* 1:219.
58. Ge Lifang 葛立方, "Yuzhong hua" 雨中花, *Quan Songci* 2:1744.
59. Chen Dewu 陳德武, "Mulan hua ling" 木蘭花令, *Quan Songci* 5:4375.
60. Li Angying 李昂英, "Mo yuer" 摸魚兒, *Quan Songci* 4:3638.
61. Chen Ji 陳紀, "Juan xunfang" 倦尋芳, *Quan Songci* 5:4291.

Conclusion

Li Qingzhao's story has much to teach us about what life was like for elite women in twelfth-century China. If we think for a moment not about the literary qualities and literary issues that surround her writings, but about the biographical and historiographical interest they hold, we perceive at once how rare and valuable she is in this regard. Her biography instructs us about what women of her time faced in marriage, widowhood, remarriage, and divorce. Likewise, the ways "Li Qingzhao" was formulated and re-created time and again in the centuries after her death informs us about later social, legal, and literary history, and specifically about changing attitudes toward women, widowhood, and women's writing in the later imperial period and on into the modern age.

Beyond such significance, Li Qingzhao's life as the story of the challenges one woman faced and the difficult decisions she made has special meaning. That is, if we can separate the import of individual lives from what role they may play as data in the service of general cultural history, hers surely has a unique place. It is not that the experiences that befell her were unique, although the combination of so many trying circumstances could not have been commonplace (including fleeing from an invasion, the death of her husband during that flight, widowhood close to the age of fifty without any grown children to rely on, the burden of a cumbersome collection of books and artworks, an opportunistic remarriage proposal, abuse at the hands of her second husband, bringing suit against him, trial and imprisonment, humiliation, and public mockery). What makes her story unique is that she recorded her experiences and reactions to them in writing. The richness of her output in writing, in a range of forms and styles, is unmatched by any woman of her day. To have her own reflections on her life and those of the literary personas she created gives her writing interest and value unlike that of any other woman of her time and like few before or after her in imperial Chinese history.

There is no need to exaggerate Li Qingzhao's suffering, wifely devotion, courage, "patriotism," or other virtues. That has already been done too often in the past (and continues to be done today). Biographers should be content to note that she had the gumption to write candidly about so much that happened to her and to forge her thoughts and feelings into poetry. Directly or indirectly, she describes what she faced and expresses her feelings about it. Particularly memorable are what she reveals about the early years of her marriage to Zhao Mingcheng, his growing obsession with his collection, how utterly alone she felt upon being reunited with him in Laizhou, how on his deathbed he failed to make arrangements for her after he was gone, how the collection she was charged to keep intact attracted thieves and other unscrupulous men who sought to exploit her situation, and how complete was her humiliation after she decided to incriminate her second husband just weeks after marrying him, thereby dissolving their union. Unforgettable too is how she conducted herself after that divorce: she went back to what she knew and did best, resolved to write her way back to respectability in a very public way. Running through all the tumult of these years, stretching from before to after them, was a steady output of poetry in the song lyric form that readers of her day already recognized as outstanding, reluctant as they were to acknowledge that such literary talent could reside in a woman. It was a remarkable woman and remarkable writer who expressed herself in these ways. In doing so she gave to posterity a corpus of texts that has an intense and enduring luster all its own.

Concerning literary issues, I wish first to return to the ramifications that Li Qingzhao's identity as a woman writer have for her work in the song lyric form. Here I want to consider the matter briefly from her point of view as a writer, rather than from our point of view as readers. We know that in a patriarchal society when a woman, any woman, decides to enter into a literary arena dominated by men, she is violating assumptions about what she can and should do. The issue I wish to raise here is what problems arise when the woman is venturing to compose in a form in which men had long before appropriated the female voice and placed the focus on women. How is the woman writer to find a voice when the voices already present in the form are those of men speaking as women? In addition to all the difficulties that any woman would have producing writing when all the other writers are male, to compose in the song lyric form necessarily entailed this additional complication. The female voice was already prevalent in the form, since many of the male writers were writing with female singers in mind to perform their works. How then could a woman writer "speak" in the form without sounding like yet another man writing in the guise of a woman?

In her essay "On Song Lyrics" Li Qingzhao adopts unusual strategies in writing about the form. On the one hand, she does not deny its low stature. She sets up an opposition between the song lyric and "learning" and other high-minded pursuits. On the other hand, she insists on the unique prosodic requirements of the form, to which she says many writers have failed to attend. She likewise insists that those who truly understand the form and all of its intricacies are very few. She also presents images of men making fools of themselves by attempting to compose song lyrics when they are, by training and temperament, particularly unqualified to do so.

It is unlikely, nevertheless, that Li Qingzhao hoped to claim the song lyric as a genre of women's own. She came too late in the history of the form for that to be a possibility; besides, she was only one woman writer. Yet there is no question that she felt specially knowledgeable and capable as a song lyrics writer. What she wanted—recall the Li Balang anecdote—was to be given a chance in this male domain and to be judged on the quality of what she produced rather than on her identity as a woman and thus an outsider. Her boldness or brazenness in reciting, one by one, the weaknesses of the leading male practitioners of the form is an indication of how eager she was to show her special understanding and probably how irritated she felt at constantly encountering male condescension or dismissal of her efforts.

We have seen ample evidence of Li Qingzhao's competitiveness with her husband and, as a writer of *shi* poetry, with other men. One explanation of why so many of her surviving *shi* compositions, or fragments, sound so unlike what we expect from women writing at the time is that when writing *shi,* she deliberately adopted the subjects and themes of the dominant, male tradition, and that she did this in part to show that she could produce works that take their place alongside those by men. Her youthful compositions on the Tang restoration tablet already show this tendency, and an early admirer of those poems says precisely that her compositions hold their own beside other pieces on the theme written by men. Subsequently, the Jurchen invasion and the willingness of Gaozong's court to remain south of the Yangzi River gave her plenty of opportunities in other poems to disparage the Southern Song leaders for their lack of resolve and "manliness."

Unlike with *shi* poetry, with song lyrics Li Qingzhao did not have to affect a male voice to produce works that fit within the dominant tradition. Yet this did not mean there was no problem or challenge awaiting her. If she was going to establish herself as a song lyrics writer, she still had to find a voice different from those of the men writing about or as women. She evidently sensed she had an advantage here, even though she came late to the form, that is, well after men had already appropriated the female subject, language, and personas, making them their own. The feeling that she had an advantage is evident throughout "On Song Lyrics" between the lines. Yet confidence in this regard did not necessarily mean that she was also confident that her works, coming from a woman, would be given a fair and unbiased hearing. That must be why she opens her essay with the Li Balang story, deftly recast to suit her own predicament.

Did she find a distinctive voice in the song lyric? Centuries of readers and critics have felt that she did. The view advanced here concurs with this assessment, even as it would introduce modifications of the traditional view. In this book we have seen time and again how the women and women's voices in her compositions differ from those that had become conventional in song lyrics composed by men. In subtle and sometimes not-so-subtle ways, the women in Li Qingzhao's songs are different. They are, as we have discussed, consistently more independent, unconventional, and unpredictable. Sometimes they are more outspoken; more often they are more insistent about refusing to speak. They are occasionally more self-sufficient than we find in the works of other writers; and when they are lonely and bitter, those emotions have a depth uniquely their own.

As observed earlier, we will never be able to pin down the exact relationship between the woman or female speaker in Li Qingzhao's song lyrics and Li Qingzhao the person. A prudent way to proceed is to assume that, as with virtually any poet, her writing combines invention with personal experience. But it seems only fair to acknowledge the possibility that she was capable of crafting literary voices and personas in her poetry, just as we acknowledge that possibility with male writers.

Another key feature of the foregoing analysis of Li Qingzhao's song lyrics is attention to when and how individual pieces are first attested, and the considerable divergence, consequently, between the more credible and less credible attributions. To treat indiscriminately all or most all of the works that have ever been attributed to her, the highly likely with the highly unlikely, results in an extremely mixed collection that almost certainly obscures and distorts her genius as a poet. We should be especially wary of the uncritical and even enthusiastic acceptance of late-appearing works (which surfaced four centuries or longer after her death) if for no other reason than that they reinforce the conventional image of the Li-Zhao marriage that evolved over the centuries, which is itself a cultural construction.

Beyond the goal of pushing forward our understanding of Li Qingzhao's song lyrics, the chapters in this volume lead to other related findings. It is interesting to see how quantity of output affects our understanding of writers. Compared with works by other major writers of her day, the quantity of works we have by Li Qingzhao is extremely small. This may be partly because her output was just a fraction of her male counterparts—though we do not know this for sure—but it was also because her two collections (her song lyrics collection and the literary collection of everything else she wrote) were lost. This loss itself must have been linked to her identity as a woman writer, for a parallel case would be hard to find among male writers who were already famous in their lifetimes. The point here is how the small number of works by her makes so difficult any attempt to develop a comprehensive picture and critical account of her life and writings. The men of her day who are major writers left thousands of poems (Lu You's poetry collection totals nearly ten thousand pieces), not to mention vast amounts of formal and informal prose writings, including memorials, essays, inscriptions, letters, notes, and colophons. Consequently, with men like Su Shi, Lu You, and Fan Chengda, we can reconstruct where they were, what they were doing, who they were with, and what they were thinking about and writing about during virtually every week of their lives. The paucity of surviving writings by Li Qingzhao makes it impossible to do the same for her. In her case, what has come down to us is a few dozen compositions (cumulatively, in all genres of poetry and prose) rather than thousands or tens of thousands. This should be a humbling thought for anyone who aspires to write a biography or critical account of her literary works. We know very little about her because of the paucity of what she left and also, because she was a woman, the near complete silence of contemporary sources regarding her. The sources are full of gaps, and the gaps raise questions we cannot answer. Any reconstruction of her life or discussion of her literary work is thus highly contingent upon what happened to survive. We can only guess how our impression of her might change if we did have all her writings or a fuller record of her life in early sources.

One aspect of her legacy that is clear is how difficult it was for elite culture, constituted entirely in her day by men, to accommodate her. This difficulty lasted through the Ming and Qing, as critics struggled to fashion an image of her that they could live with. From the point of view of the guardians of elite culture and its value, Li Qingzhao was a great anomaly. A writing woman, that is, a woman writing anything at all, was already a rarity. But she was a woman who wrote *shi* poetry addressed to court officials, who belittled the weakness of the male leadership, and who openly flaunted her fondness for and aptitude at a gambling game modeled on military strategy. More shocking still, she wrote a critical essay about the song lyric in which she claimed to have special knowledge about the form and then proceeded to enumerate, one by one, the shortcomings of the song lyrics composed by most prominent male writers of the generations preceding her own.

To be sure, there were exceptional men who allowed themselves to express their admiration for her talent. And there were readers, male and female, who enjoyed reading her compositions as well as anthologists who made sure to include works by her in their compilations. But elite culture as a whole was as discomforted by the prospect of such a woman as some of its members were intrigued by her.

Her willingness to remarry after Zhao Mingcheng's death and the dissolution of that second marriage soon thereafter provided those who were only too eager to dismiss and condemn her with a way of doing so that would be difficult to gainsay. In her remarriage and divorce they discerned evidence of the headstrong and unwomanly nature that accounted for the exceptional qualities of her poetry. At the same time, a more subtle process was at work that would provide a less strident means of dealing with her by corralling her unorthodox talent, domesticating her, and making her more acceptable to dominant cultural expectations and values. Through the exploitation of one unique piece of writing from her own hand (for what better to use than something she herself had written?), conveniently disregarding the context in which it was written or what unarticulated motives she may have had in writing it, she was recast as devoted wife and forlorn widow. She was infinitely less of a problem, less threatening to the men who could be jolted by her opinions and behavior, if her inspiration could be shown to flow from her devotion to her husband when he was alive and her fond memory of him after he died. With the lead provided by her celebrated afterword, then, her song lyrics were viewed entirely through the prism of her idealized marriage to Zhao Mingcheng and her inconsolable longing for him during his absences or after his passing. It thus followed that everything she wrote was a direct outpouring of her love for him; it was all "genuine" and intensely autobiographical. Read that way, her song lyrics acquired new meaning and depth.

Even conventional lines were enriched by discerning heartfelt emotion behind them.

Yet a problem remained, and that was Li Qingzhao's conduct as a widow. Once her literary output came to be seen as revolving entirely around her devotion to Zhao Mingcheng, it was more troubling than ever to recall that she had remarried (at the advanced age of forty-nine), only to bring suit against her new husband a mere three months later. The problem was made more serious by growing intolerance of widows' remarriage in Ming-Qing times just as the new acceptance of women's writing retroactively lent new significance to Li Qingzhao as the precursor to aspiring literary women. The conflict between the exemplary Li Qingzhao and the unprincipled Li Qingzhao became so acute that it could no longer be ignored or tolerated. Something had to give way. The easiest course was to deny her remarriage, to claim that it had no basis in historical fact. Yet this was no easy argument to make because of the substantial number of Song period sources that document it, not to mention a letter by Li Qingzhao herself that clearly refers to it. A concerted scholarly effort had to be launched to make the denial seem credible. That effort eventually won out, in time for the thoroughly refashioned Li Qingzhao, woman poet of wifely devotion who never would have considered remarriage (and also a victim of vicious slander concerning the same), to be written into the first histories of Chinese literature that appeared in the twentieth century and were part of the modern history of nation building and modernization. It was not until the late 1950s that the late Qing re-creation of Li Qingzhao was challenged. That challenge, in turn, sparked a scholarly controversy that took nearly fifty years to run its course, with a new consensus that overturned the Qing denial emerging only in recent years. Despite the reversal on this one point—the remarriage—in Li Qingzhao's biography, traditional ways of thinking about her, in place since late imperial times, have been slow to change. Conventional images and ways of reading her works have become so ingrained that they have proved difficult to put aside.

The advent of feminism in Chinese studies provided a new orientation and theoretical basis for challenging the traditional treatments of Li Qingzhao. It may not have been feminist theory per se, but new ways of thinking about old issues, now informed by feminist scholarship, helped to provide an impetus for rethinking Li Qingzhao. Feminist scholarship on women writers of early modern England and America provided the model for a new understanding of the controversies that swirled around Li Qingzhao. Much of the credit for initiating the reappraisal process of Li Qingzhao goes to scholars of the younger generation in the People's Republic of China, who have been open to reconsidering received notions about the harmony of the Li-Zhao marriage and to entertaining the likely prospect of a concubine complicating that relationship. It has nevertheless proved difficult for scholars and critics to break free of the old stereotypes or to see how thoroughly they have conditioned our understanding of the great poet. It is not enough simply to point to a few pieces, discovering frustration and bitterness in them rather than love and longing, while continuing to read the bulk of her work in a traditional way.

Ultimately, it is a testament to Li Qingzhao's singularity as poet and person that her legacy has so often been contested and her work recast and reinterpreted. She did not conform to assumptions about what a woman should write or how she should conduct herself. It is little wonder that scholars and critics have had difficulty knowing what to make of her. Their puzzlement before her helps to explain the radically different ways she has been represented, positively and negatively.

Her greatest achievement, it could be argued, was her dualistic accomplishment as a writer. Living centuries before the arbiters of elite culture became even reluctantly accepting of women as writers, she entered into the domain of writing as a lone woman, without a community of literate women around her and surely facing a wall of skepticism and discouragement. First, she showed that she could write on the subjects men wrote on, in a range of genres, and produce work that did not pale before the best of what was written by poets wearing "the cap and robe" of officialdom (as Yang Shen observed). To do this much was already unprecedented. To say that she thus showed she could write "as a man" was expected to write is a simplification. She did this as a woman—with all that that gender identity entailed and excluded her from—and so her work was both comparable to what men wrote and very distinct at the same time. Second, in the song lyric form she proceeded to produce works of intrinsic and enduring interest with characteristics distinct from the best compositions by male writers. In so doing she established an important precedent, showing later centuries of literate women and men in China that women's writing could explore modes of experience and expression recognizably distinct from those in writing by men. This second accomplishment was one that male critics in premodern times were less likely to acknowledge, much less to reflect upon. But the enthusiasm readers of both genders through the ages have shown for Li Qingzhao's poetry, which continues today, suggests that this accomplishment was often sensed even if seldom critically discussed.

Song Lyric Piece Numbers and Finding List

My no.	Tune title	Page in Xu Peijun, *Jianzhu*	Page in *Quan Songci*	Page(s) discussed in this volume
1	南歌子：天上星河轉	35	1201	341, 345
2	轉調滿庭芳：芳草池塘	146	1202	
3	漁家傲：天接雲濤	127	1202	49, 402
4	如夢令：常記溪亭	40	1202	337
5	如夢令：昨夜雨疏	14	1202	232, 327, 342
6	多麗：小樓寒	36	1202	315, 397
7	菩薩蠻：風柔日薄	131	1203	342, 346
8	菩薩蠻：歸鴻聲斷	102	1203	
9	浣溪沙：莫許杯深	6	1203	
10	浣溪沙：小院閑窗	67	1203	105, 377
11	浣溪沙：淡蕩春光	116	1203	375
12	鳳凰臺上憶吹簫：香冷	59	1204	127, 342, 398
13	一剪梅：紅藕香殘	20	1204	114, 118, 226–27, 331, 338
14	蝶戀花：淚搵征衣	86	1204	312, 399
15	蝶戀花：暖雨晴風	84	1204	
16	鷓鴣天：寒日蕭蕭	101	1205	235
17	小重山：春到長門	94	1205	379, 396
18	怨王孫：湖上風來	540	1205	234, 336
19	臨江仙：. . . 常扃	105	1205	329, 401
20	醉花陰：薄霧濃雲	52	1205	222, 233, 262, 342
21	好事近：風定落花	132	1206	341, 345
22	訴衷情：夜來沉醉	111	1206	322, 401
23	行香子：草際鳴蛩	32	1206	
24	清平樂：年年雪裏	126	1201	93
25	漁家傲：雪裏已知	8	1201	93
26	孤雁兒：藤床紙帳	123	1201	93
27	滿庭芳：小閣藏春	113	1200	93, 397
28	玉樓春：紅酥肯放	27	1201	93, 378
29	玉燭新：溪源新臘		1211 存目	93
30	念奴嬌：蕭條庭院	75	1208	374, 399
31	聲聲慢：尋尋覓覓	161	1209	319, 353, 400

Recent Interpretations of Particular Poems on the Concubine Issue

Song/poem title	Chen Zumei, *New Biography* 新傳 (2001)	Deng Hongmei, *New Biography* 新傳 (2005)	Zhuge Yibing, *Li Qingzhao and Zhao Mingcheng* 李清照與趙明誠 (2004)
"Dawn Dream" 《曉夢》	Written in 1105 or 1106. This piece is not about marital estrangement. It is about Li Qingzhao's apprehensions over the political factionalism that her father and father-in-law were caught up in. Pp. 74–75.	Written during Li Qingzhao's stay in Laizhou (1121–24). Joyful scene in the poem is inspired by her recollection of life together with Zhao Mingcheng in Qingzhou, which is a far cry from her current neglect and unhappiness, because Zhao's affection has turned to a concubine or another woman. Pp. 97–98.	Similar to Deng's interpretation. Pp. 121–22.
no. 17, 《小重山：春到長門》	The song, written around 1106, when Li Qingzhao was traveling back and forth between the capital and her native Zhangqiu, expresses her feeling that Zhao Mingcheng is neglecting her for another woman or concubine. The Long Gate allusion in line 1 is the key. P. 77.	The song expresses Li Qingzhao's relief at being able to return to the capital in 1106, after a period of forced separation. She was abandoned, but now the ban on Yuanyou partisans has been lifted, "spring" has returned to Long Gate, and she is back together with Zhao Mingcheng again. P. 55.	The song was written around 1119, when Zhao Mingcheng had already left Qingzhou for a post for two years. Li Qingzhao is begging him to come back to her. No mention of another woman being the problem. P. 88.

Song/poem title	Chen Zumei, *New Biography* 新傳 (2001)	Deng Hongmei, *New Biography* 新傳 (2005)	Zhuge Yibing, *Li Qingzhao and Zhao Mingcheng* 李清照與趙明誠 (2004)
no. 6, 《多麗：詠白菊》	Date and intent are similar to no. 17 above. Keys are allusion to Zheng Jiaofu's encounter with goddesses at Han'gao (i.e., Zhao Mingcheng has outside affair) and Concubine Ban's fan poem (Li Qingzhao has been shunted aside) as well as references to Qu Yuan and Tao Qian as rejected ministers. P. 77.	Similar to Chen's interpretation, but the two second stanza allusions are understood differently. They are allusions to stories of love that was not fulfilled or ended unhappily. The Han'gao goddesses and Concubine Ban are Li Qingzhao herself: rare, talented, beautiful, but unfulfilled in love. Pp. 57–59.	This is a brilliant example of a "song lyric on an object" 詠物詞, the product of the happy period of Li Qingzhao's life together with Zhao Mingcheng in Qingzhou. Elegant, clever, learned, subtle, this piece fulfills the high standards Li Qingzhao refers to in "On Song Lyrics." The cleverness of the lines shows how she and Zhao Mingcheng must have competed in poetry composition. This piece is very unlike her melancholy song lyrics from other periods. Pp. 62–63.
no. 27, 《滿庭芳：小閣藏春》	A song on plum blossoms, written close in time to the two above. The "person" who fails to come in the song is really Zhao Mingcheng. There's no need for Li Qingzhao to "climb the tower" and write a *fu* like Wang Can because her situation is utterly different. Likening herself to He Sun in Yangzhou is likening herself to the abandoned women Sun refers to in the plum blossom poem he wrote there: Chen Ajiao and Zhuo Wenjun. Pp. 79–80.	General interpretation similar to Chen's, but instead of being an allusion to Wang Can (and herself), the lines about there being no need to climb a tower are "bitter words" about Zhao Mingcheng and his conduct (i.e., the plum blossoms we planted are beautiful enough; why need you look elsewhere for others?). Although the general intent is interpreted similarly, the details—the way the intent is conveyed—are read utterly differently. P. 90.	This is a song about Li Qingzhao's loneliness for Zhao Mingcheng, written about 1117, when Zhao has left Li Qingzhao alone in Qingzhou and gone off to take up a new post. It is not about being abandoned for another woman. In the lines about not needing to climb the tower, she is telling herself not to go up and look for her returning husband; that would only upset her even more. Pp. 79–80.

Song/poem title	Chen Zumei, New Biography 新傳 (2001)	Deng Hongmei, New Biography 新傳 (2005)	Zhuge Yibing, Li Qingzhao and Zhao Mingcheng 李清照與趙明誠 (2004)
no. 12, 《鳳凰台上憶吹簫：香冷金猊》	Written after Zhao Mingcheng has left Li Qingzhao in Qingzhou to take up a new assignment (ca. 1117). The song title refers to the love story of Xiao Shi and Nongyu (as does later reference to Qin Tower), not in the obvious sense (which would not be fitting) but in the sense evoked in Li Bai's poem about Qin Tower being forlorn now because the lovers have left. Thus the great irony here is that Zhao Mingcheng has changed, in this song, from Xiao Shi to "the man of Wuling," i.e., Ruan Zhao, who proceeded to have a love tryst at Tiantai! So Li Qingzhao through these references is unmistakably expressing her anxiety that the distant Zhao Mingcheng is having love affairs. Pp. 96–98 and 216; cf. Chen's *Critical Biography* 李清照評傳 pp. 65–67.	The song is about Li Qingzhao feeling rejected by Zhao Mingcheng for another lover he took in Laizhou (ca. 1121). But the Wuling allusion works differently. The references to Xiao Shi/Nongyu and to Wuling (i.e., Peach Blossom Spring) are meant to suggest that their formerly idyllic marriage (in Qingzhou) has given way to abandonment. Li Qingzhao is saying that she used to be married to a "Wuling man," but he's not with her anymore. Pp. 85–87.	The song, written about 1119, is a plea by Li Qingzhao for Zhao Mingcheng to come home from an assignment. There is no suggestion of anxiety about him having taken a new love. The references to Xiao Shi/Nongyu and Wuling (i.e., Ruan Zhao and Liu Chen) invoke idyllic love relationships (not an extramarital affair). This is what we had, Li Qingzhao, is saying, and she wants it to be restored. Pp. 91–93.

Song/poem title	Chen Zumei, New Biography 新傳 (2001)	Deng Hongmei, New Biography 新傳 (2005)	Zhuge Yibing, Li Qingzhao and Zhao Mingcheng 李清照與趙明誠 (2004)
no. 30, 《念奴嬌: 蕭條庭院》	Similar to reading of no. 12 above. Li Qingzhao is hoping to persuade her wayward husband to come home; hoping to regain his affections. Pp. 99–100.	Similar to Chen's interpretation. The lines about her inability to entrust her thoughts to the passing wild geese refer to her frustrations with Zhao Mingcheng's neglect of her in favor of another. P. 91.	A song written near the end of Li Qingzhao's life, when she felt alone. It has nothing to do with feelings of betrayal by Zhao Mingcheng. Pp. 205–6.
no. 14, 《蝶戀花: 淚揾征衣》	Why is there so much emotion in this song, when Li Qingzhao is going to be reunited with Zhao Mingcheng in Laizhou in 1121? Because she's so apprehensive about her reception there. Laizhou is not far or cut off by mountains (as the song suggests). These are metaphors for how "distant" she feels Zhao Mingcheng has become. Also Penglai in the closing line is like Wuling in the previous song; a reference to Zhao Mingcheng's love affairs in Laizhou. Pp. 103–5; cf. Critical Biography, pp. 70–72.	General agreement with Chen about the nature of this song but no such reading of "Penglai." Pp. 92–93.	A similar general reading. Pp. 106–16.

Song/poem title	Chen Zumei, *New Biography* 新傳 (2001)	Deng Hongmei, *New Biography* 新傳 (2005)	Zhuge Yibing, *Li Qingzhao and Zhao Mingcheng* 李清照與趙明誠 (2004)
no. 31, 《聲聲慢：尋尋覓覓》	Written right before or during the Laizhou period. Chen insists on the textual variant *xiaolai* 曉來 for *wanlai* 晚來 then finds an allusion in that phrase to *Classic of Poetry* pieces said to have been written by a wife who was abandoned because she was childless, in favor of a concubine. Li Qingzhao is protesting her own rejection and hoping Zhao Mingcheng will be persuaded to change his heart. A highly idiosyncratic reading of this song lyric. Pp. 105–8; cf. *Critical Biography*, pp. 68–69.		Written in her later years, long after Zhao Mingcheng's death and also after her remarriage and divorce. The song has nothing to do with jealousy over another woman. Pp. 200–203.
"Stirred by Emotions" 《感懷》	Chen reads the poem as an expression of anguish when Li Qingzhao arrives in Laizhou and discovers that Zhao Mingcheng has no interest in her. He puts her in a room by herself while he devotes himself to a new love. Pp. 108–10; cf. *Critical Biography*, pp. 72–76.	Similar to Chen interpretation. Pp. 94–95.	Similar. Pp. 107–15.

Song/poem title	Chen Zumei, New Biography 新傳 (2001)	Deng Hongmei, New Biography 新傳 (2005)	Zhuge Yibing, Li Qingzhao and Zhao Mingcheng 李清照與趙明誠 (2004)
no. 22, 《訴衷情：夜來沉醉》	Dates this song to about 1127, when Li Qingzhao is distressed by Zhao Mingcheng's attention to other women. The opening stanza recalls the "Cypress Boat" 柏舟 poem in the Classic of Poetry, which many (including Zhu Xi) believed was written by a spurned woman. It is late at night, and Li Qingzhao is alone in her room because Zhao Mingcheng is pursuing other romantic interests. Pp. 127–28.	Dates song to 1108, when Zhao Mingcheng is on his long trip to fetch his mother in the south, and Li Qingzhao is left alone in the capital. But no sense here of distress over another woman. P. 64.	Dates song to around 1118, when Zhao Mingcheng left Li Qingzhao by herself in Qingzhou. No sense of distress over another woman. P. 76.
nos. 19 and 61, 《臨江仙：…常扃》,《臨江仙：…春遲》	The reason Li Qingzhao was so moved by what she thought was Ouyang Xiu's song is because it is about a woman whose man has left her for the pleasure quarters. That is why Li Qingzhao felt an affinity for that song and borrowed its opening line in her songs. Pp. 216–17.	Similar to Chen's reading of both songs. Pp. 125–26.	The songs, written in 1129, express Li Qingzhao's sadness at having to flee south during the invasion. They have nothing to do with marital unhappiness. Pp. 137–41.
no. 33, 《憶秦娥：臨高閣》	Written soon after Zhao Mingcheng's death in 1129, a lament for him. Pp. 139–40.		Judging from the mood of this piece, it must reflect Li Qingzhao's sense of alienation from Zhao Mingcheng during the Laizhou period. P. 118.

Song/poem title	Chen Zumei, New Biography 新傳 (2001)	Deng Hongmei, New Biography 新傳 (2005)	Zhuge Yibing, Li Qingzhao and Zhao Mingcheng 李清照與趙明誠 (2004)
no. 3, 《漁家傲：天接雲濤》	Written during 1130, during the turmoil of her flight from the new Jurchen invasion. Has nothing to do with marital estrangement. Pp. 147–48.	Written during the Laizhou period. Li Qingzhao writes of Heaven questioning her this way because she feels alienated from Zhao Mingcheng and is wondering what will, after all, become of her now that she has lost his affection. Pp. 98–99.	Similar to Deng, although this reading of this poem is more positive. It shows her pride and self-esteem, even as she is feeling estranged from Zhao Mingcheng. Could not have been written earlier (when marriage was happier) or after flight south, when she was not so secure in her vision of herself. Pp. 120–21.
"What Is Left of Spring" 《春殘》		The poem was written in 1135, after Li Qingzhao's divorce, when she was in Jinhua. It has nothing to do with estrangement from Zhao Mingcheng. P. 163.	This poem must also date from the Laizhou period. Why else would Li Qingzhao be homesick in spring? The reference to being bothered about combing her hair alludes to Zhao Mingcheng's lack of interest in her—so why should she make herself pretty? Similarly, the reference to the swallows suggests a contrast between their pairing and her marital estrangement. P. 119.

Works Cited

Analects (*Lunyu* 論語). Standard book and paragraph numbers.

Baibu congshu jicheng 百部叢書集成. Taipei: Yiwen yinshuguan, 1965–69.

Bamanzi 巴蔓子. "Guanyu Zhang Fei qizi" 關於張飛妻子. *Zhonghua dushu bao* 中華讀書報, December 14, 2005. http://big5.xinhuanet.com/gate/big5/news.xinhuanet.com/book/2005-12/20/content_3945369.htm.

Barlow, Tani E. "The Direction of History and Women in China." *Journal of Colonialism and Colonial History* 4.1 (2003): 1–9.

Bian Yongyu 卞永譽 (1645–1712). *Shigu tang shuhua huikao* 式古堂書畫彙考. In *Siku quanshu* (q.v.).

Birge, Bettine. *Women, Property, and Confucian Reaction in Sung and Yüan China (960–1368)*. Cambridge: Cambridge University Press, 2002.

Bossler, Beverly. *Courtesans, Concubines, and the Cult of Female Fidelity*. Cambridge, MA: Asia Center, Harvard University, 2013.

———. "Shifting Identities: Courtesans and Literati in Song China." *Harvard Journal of Asiatic Studies* 62.1 (2002): 5–37.

Cai Yijiang 蔡義江. "Liang sheng zhendian leihen zi" 涼生枕簟淚痕滋. In *Li Qingzhao ci jianshang* 李清照詞鑑賞, pp. 148–51. Ji'nan: Qilu shushe, 1986.

Cao An 曹安 (fl. 1444). *Lanyan changyu* 讕言長語. In *Siku quanshu* (q.v.).

Cao Xueqin 曹雪芹 (ca. 1717–64). *Honglou meng* 紅樓夢. Hong Kong: Zhonghua shuju, 2001 reprint of 1996 edition.

Cao Xuequan 曹學佺 (1574–1647). *Shuzhong guangji* 蜀中廣記. In *Siku quanshu* (q.v.).

Caotang shiyu 草堂詩餘 (ca. 1195). Anon. In *Tangsong ren xuan Tangsong ci* (q.v.).

Carlitz, Katherine. "Shrines, Governing-Class Identity, and the Cult of Widow Fidelity in Mid-Ming Jiangnan." *Journal of Asian Studies* 56.3 (1997): 612–40.

Chang, Kang-i Sun. *The Late-Ming Poet Ch'en Tzu-lung*. New Haven, CT: Yale University Press, 1991.

———. "Ming-Qing Women Poets and the Notions of 'Talent' and 'Morality.'" In *Culture and the State in Chinese History: Conventions, Accommodation, and Critiques*, edited by Theodore Huters, R. Bin Wong, and Pauline Yu, pp. 236–58. Stanford, CA: Stanford University Press, 1997.

Chang, Kang-i Sun, and Haun Saussy. *Women Writers of Traditional China: An Anthology of Poetry and Criticism*. Stanford, CA: Stanford University Press, 1999.

Chao Buzhi 晁補之 (1053–1110). *Jilei ji* 雞肋集. In *Siku quanshu* (q.v.).

Chao Gongwu 晁公武 (fl. 1151). *Junzhai dushu zhi jiaozheng* 郡齋讀書志校證. Edited by Sun Meng 孫猛. 2 vols. Shanghai: Shanghai guji chubanshe, 2005 reprint of 1990 edition.

Chen Donghui 陳東輝. "Zhongguo jindai qimu qianxi de yiwei renjie: Du Yu Zhengxie quanji you gan" 中國近代啓幕前夕的一位人傑：讀《俞正燮全集》有感. *Anhui shixue* 安徽史學 2007.1:124–28.

Chen Hu 陳鵠 (early 13th c.). *Qijiu xuwen* 耆舊續聞. In *Siku quanshu* (q.v.).

Chen Jingyi 陳景沂 (fl. 1225–64). *Quanfang beizu* 全芳備祖. In *Siku quanshu* (q.v.).

Chen Jiru 陳繼儒 (1558–1639). *Guwen pin wailu* 古文品外錄. In *Siku quanshu cunmu congshu* (q.v.).

Chen Kui 陳騤 (1128–1203). *Nan Song guan'ge lu* 南宋館閣錄. In *Siku quanshu* (q.v.).

Chen Shangjun 陳尚君. "Tang nü shiren zhenbian" 唐女詩人甄辨. *Wenxian* 文獻 2010.2:10–25.

Chen Shidao 陳師道 (1053–1102). *Houshan ji* 後山集. In *Siku quanshu* (q.v.).

Chen Shou 陳壽 (233–97). *Sanguo zhi* 三國志. Beijing: Zhonghua shuju, 1959.

Chen Tingzhuo 陳廷焯 (1853–92). *Baiyu zhai cihua zuben jiaozhu* 白雨齋詞話足本校注. Edited by Qu Xingguo 屈興國. Ji'nan: Qilu shushe, 1983.

Chen Yaowen 陳耀文 (*jinshi* 1550). *Huacao chuibian* 花草粹編 (1583). Taofeng lou 1933 reprint of 1583 edition.

Chen Yu 陳郁 (fl. 1245–53). *Cangyi huayu* 藏一話腴. In *Siku quanshu* (q.v.).

Chen Yuanjing 陳元靚 (13th c.). *Zuantu zengxin qunshu leiyao Shilin guangji* 纂圖增新群書類要事林廣記. Beijing: Zhonghua shuju, 1999.

Chen Zhensun 陳振孫 (fl. 1211–49). *Zhizhai shulu jieti* 直齋書錄解題. Shanghai: Shanghai guji chubanshe, 2005 reprint of 1987 edition.

Chen Zumei 陳祖美. "Guanyu Yi'an zhaji erze" 關於易安札記二則. *Zhonghua wenshi luncong* 中華文史論叢 1985.4:87–98.

———. *Li Qingzhao ci xinyi jiping* 李清照詞新釋輯評. Beijing: Zhongguo shudian, 2003.

———. *Li Qingzhao pingzhuan* 李清照評傳. Nanjing: Nanjing daxue chubanshe, 1995.

———. *Li Qingzhao xinzhuan* 李清照新傳. Beijing: Beijing chubanshe, 2001.

———. *Shuyu ci zhu* 漱玉詞注. In Chen Zumei, Deng Hongmei 鄧紅梅, et al., *Shuyu ci zhu, Jiaxuan ci zhu* 漱玉詞注，稼軒詞注. Ji'nan: Qilu shushe, 2009.

Ch'en, Hsiao-lan, and F. W. Mote. "Yang Shen and Huang O: Husband and Wife as Lovers, Poets, and Historical Figures." In *Excursions in Chinese Culture: Festschrift in Honor of William R. Schultz*, edited by William R. Schultz et al., pp. 1–32. Hong Kong: Chinese University Press, 2002.

Cheng Yi 程頤 (1033–1107). *Henan Chengshi wenji* 河南程氏文集. In Cheng Hao 程顥 and Cheng Yi, *Er Cheng ji* 二程集. Beijing: Zhonghua shuju, 1981.

———. *Henan Chengshi yishu* 河南程氏遺書. In Cheng Hao and Cheng Yi, *Er Cheng ji*. Beijing: Zhonghua shuju, 1981.

Chenshi 陳詩. In *Xian Qin Han Wei Jin Nanbei chao shi* (q.v.).

Chu Binjie 褚斌杰 et al. *Li Qingzhao ziliao huibian* 李清照資料彙編. Beijing: Zhonghua shuju, 1984.

Chunqiu Zuozhuan zhushu 春秋左傳注疏. In *Shisan jing zhushu fu jiaokan ji* 十三經注疏附校勘記, edited by Ruan Yuan 阮元 (1764–1849). Nanchang, 1814.

Chunqiu Zuozhuan zhuzi suoyin 春秋左傳逐字索引. In *ICS Ancient Chinese Texts Concordance Series* (q.v.).

Classic of Documents 尚書. Standard chapter and paragraph numbers.

Classic of Poetry 詩經. Standard (Mao) poem numbers.

Cui Lingqin 崔令欽 (fl. 749). *Jiaofang ji* 教坊記. In *Siku quanshu* (q.v.).

Deng Hongmei 鄧紅梅. *Li Qingzhao xinzhuan* 李清照新傳. Shanghai: Shanghai guji chubanshe, 2005.

————. *Nüxing cishi* 女性詞史. Ji'nan: Shandong jiaoyu chubanshe, 2002 reprint of 2000 edition.

————. "Zhu Shuzhen shiji xinkao" 朱淑眞事迹新考. *Wenxue yichan* 1994.2: 66–74.

Dou Yi 竇儀 (904–67). *Song xingtong* 宋刑統. Edited by Xue Meiqing 薛梅卿. Beijing: Falü chubanshe, 1999.

Du Fu 杜甫 (712–70). *Dushi xiangzhu* 杜詩詳註. Edited by Qiu Zhao'ao 仇兆鰲 (1638–1717). 5 vols. Beijing: Zhonghua shuju, 1979.

Du Mu 杜牧 (803–ca. 853). *Fanchuan wenji* 樊川文集. Shanghai: Shanghai guji chubanshe, 1978.

Ebrey, Patricia Buckley. *The Inner Quarters: Marriage and the Lives of Chinese Women in the Sung Period*. Berkeley: University of California Press, 1993.

Egan, Ronald. *The Literary Works of Ou-yang Hsiu (1007–72)*. Cambridge, England: Cambridge University Press, 1984.

————.*The Problem of Beauty: Aesthetic Thought and Pursuits in Northern Song Dynasty China.* Cambridge, MA: Asia Center, Harvard University, 2006.

————. "Why Didn't Zhao Mingcheng Send Letters to His Wife, Li Qingzhao, When He Was Away?" In *Hsiang Lectures on Chinese Poetry*, edited by Grace Fong, pp. 57–77. Montreal: Center for East Asian Research, McGill University, 2010.

————. *Word, Image, and Deed in the Life of Su Shi*. Cambridge, MA: Council on East Asian Studies, Harvard University, 1994.

Fan Ye 范曄 (398–445). *Hou Hanshu* 後漢書. Beijing: Zhonghua shuju, 1965.

Felski, Rita. *Literature after Feminism.* Chicago: Chicago University Press, 2003.

Feng Menglong 馮夢龍 (1574–1646). *Qingshi* 情史. In *Feng Menglong quanji* 馮夢龍全集, edited by Wei Tongxian 魏同賢, vol. 7. Nanjing: Fenghuang chubanshe, 2007.

————. "Su Xiaomei san nan xinlang" 蘇小妹三難新郎. In *Xingshi hengyan* 醒世恆言, *Feng Menglong quanji* 3:212–25.

Fenmen zuanlei Tang Song shixian qianjia shi xuan jiaozheng 分門纂類唐宋時賢千家詩選校證. Compiled by Sun Shouzhai 孫壽齋 (fl. 1202); edited by Li Geng 李更 and Chen Xin 陳新. Beijing: Renmin wenxue chubanshe, 2002.

Fong, Grace. "Gender and the Failure of Canonization: Anthologizing Women's Poetry in the Late Ming." *Chinese Literature: Essays, Articles, Reviews* 26 (2004): 129–49.

————. *Herself an Author: Gender, Agency, and Writing in Late Imperial China*. Honolulu: University of Hawai'i Press, 2008.

Furth, Charlotte. "Poetry and Women's Culture in Late Imperial China: Editor's Introduction." *Late Imperial China* 13.1 (1992): 1–8.

Gu lienü zhuan zhuzi suoyin 古列女傳逐字索引. In *ICS Ancient Chinese Texts Concordance Series* (q.v.).

Han Yu 韓愈 (768–824). *Han Changli wenji jiaozhu* 韓昌黎文集校注. Edited by Ma Maoyuan 馬茂元. Shanghai: Shanghai guji chubanshe, 1986.

Hawkes, David, and John Minford, trans. *The Story of the Stone.* 5 vols. London and New York: Penguin Books, 1973–86.

He Guangyan 何廣棪. *Li Qingzhao gaijia wenti ziliao huibian* 李清照改嫁問題資料彙編. Taipei: Jiusi wenhua shiye, 1990.

Hightower, James R. "The Songwriter Liu Yong." In Hightower and Florence Chia-ying Yeh, *Studies in Chinese Poetry*, pp. 168–268. Cambridge, MA: Asia Center, Harvard University, 1998.

Hong Mai 洪邁 (1123–1202). *Rongzhai suibi* 容齋隨筆. Edited by Kong Fanli 孔凡禮. Beijing: Zhonghua shuju, 2005.

————. *Yijian zhi* 夷堅志. 4 vols. Beijing: Zhonghua shuju, 1981.

Hong Kuo 洪适 (1117–84). *Li shi* 隸釋. In *Siku quanshu* (q.v.).

Hu, Pin-ching. *Li Ch'ing-chao*. *Twayne World Author Series*. New York: Twayne, 1966.

Hu Shi 胡適. *Guoyu wenxue shi* 國語文學史. Hefei: Anhui jiaoyu chubanshe, 1999 reprint of 1927 edition.

Hu Wenkai 胡文楷. *Lidai funü zhuzuo kao* 歷代婦女著作考. Revised edition. Edited by Zhang Hongsheng 張宏生. Shanghai: Shanghai guji chubanshe, 2008.

Hu Yinglin 胡應麟 (1551–1602). *Shaoshi shanfang bicong* 少室山房筆叢. Taipei: Shijie shuju, 1963.

Hu Yunyi 胡雲翼. *Li Qingzhao yu qi Shuyu ci* 李清照與其漱玉詞. 1928; rpt. Beijing: Yaxiya shuju, 1931. Later reprinted in 1947 and 1967 as *Li Qingzhao ci* 李清照詞 in Hu Yunyi's *Cixue xiao congshu* 詞學小叢書 (n.p.).

Hu Zi 胡仔 (1082–1143). *Tiaoxi yuyin conghua* 苕溪漁隱叢話. 2 vols. Beijing: Renmin wenxue chubanshe, 1984.

Huajian ji zhu 花間集注. Edited by Hua Zhongyan 華鍾彥. Suchang, Henan: Zhongzhou shuhuashe, 1983.

Huang Dayu 黃大輿 (early 12th c.). *Meiyuan* 梅苑. Author's preface 1129. In *Siku quanshu* (q.v.).

Huang Mogu 黃墨谷. *Chongji Li Qingzhao ji* 重輯李清照集. Zhangqiu: Qilu shushe, 1981.

———. "'Tou neihan Qigong Chongli qi' kao—wei Li Qingzhao gaijia bianwu" 《投內翰綦公崇禮啓》考—為李清照改嫁辨誣. *Wen shi zhe* 文史哲 1981.6:56–60.

———. "Wei Li Qingzhao gaijia zai bianwu" 為李清照改嫁再辨誣. *Qilu xuekan* 1984.6:104–10.

———. "Weng Fanggang 'Jinshi lu' ben duhou—jian ping Huang Shengzhang 'Li Qingzhao shiji kao' zhong 'gaijia xinkao'" 翁方綱《金石錄》本讀後—兼評黃盛璋《李清照事迹考》中《改嫁新考》. *Qilu xuekan* 齊魯學刊 1980.6: 56–60.

Huang Sheng 黃昇 (fl. 1240–49). *Tang Song zhuxian juemiao cixuan* 唐宋諸賢絕妙詞選. 1249. In *Tangsong ren xuan Tangsong ci* (q.v.).

———. *Zhongxing yilai juemiao cixuan* 中興以來絕妙詞選. 1249. In *Tangsong ren xuan Tangsong ci* (q.v.).

Huang Shengzhang 黃盛璋. "Li Qingzhao shiji kaobian" 李清照事迹考辨. *Wenxue yanjiu* 文學研究 1957.3. Reprinted in *Li Qingzhao yanjiu lunwen ji* 李清照研論文集, edited by Ji'nan shi shehui kexue yaojiusuo, pp. 311–58. Beijing: Zhonghua shuju, 1984.

———. "Zhao Mingcheng Li Qingzhao fufu nianpu" 趙明誠李清照夫婦年譜. *Shandong shengzhi ziliao* 山東省志資料 1957.3. Reprinted in *Li Qingzhao yanjiu huibian* 李清照研究彙編, edited by Zhou Kangxie 周康燮, pp. 132–87 (using the bottom-of-page pagination, not the side margin pagination). Hong Kong: Chongwen shudian, 1974.

Huang Tingjian 黃庭堅 (1045–1105). *Huang Tingjian shiji zhu* 黃庭堅詩集注. Edited by Liu Shangrong 劉尚榮. 5 vols. Beijing: Zhonghua shuju, 2003.

———. *Shangu shiji zhu* 山谷詩集注. In *Huang Tingjian shiji zhu* (q.v.).

Huang Yanli 黃嫣梨 and Wu Xihe 吳錫河. *Duanchang fangcao yuan: Zhu Shuzhen zhuan* 斷腸芳草遠：朱淑真傳. Shijiazhuang: Huashan wenyi chubanshe, 2000.

Huang Youqin 黃友琴 (19th c.). "Shu Yayu tang chongkan 'Jinshi lu' hou" 書雅雨堂重刊《金石錄》後. In Yun Zhu 惲珠, *Guochao guixiu zhengshi ji* 國朝閨秀正始集. Hongxiang guan 紅香館 edition, 1831. In Ming Qing Women's Writing Electronic Database (q.v.).

Huang Zhongzhao 黃仲昭 (1435–1508). *Bamin tongzhi* 八閩通志. In *Beijing tushuguan guji zhenben congkan* 北京圖書館古籍珍本叢刊, vols. 33–34. Beijing: Shumu wenxian chubanshe, 1988.

Huibian. See Chu Binjie et al.

Hummel, Arthur W. *Eminent Chinese of the Ch'ing Period*. 1943. Taipei: Ch'eng-wen Publishing Co., 1972 reprint.

ICS Ancient Chinese Texts Concordance Series. Edited by D. C. Lau et al. Hong Kong: Institute for Chinese Studies, Chinese University of Hong Kong, 1992–2002.

Idema, Wilt. "Male Fantasies and Female Realities: Chu Shu-chen and Chang Yu-niang and their Biographers." In *Chinese Women in the Imperial Past: New Perspectives*, edited by Harriet T. Zurndorfer, pp. 19–52. Leiden: Brill, 1999.

Idema, Wilt, and Beata Grant. *The Red Brush: Writing Women of Imperial China*. Cambridge, MA: Harvard University Asia Center, 2004.

Ji Huang 嵇璜 (1711–94) et al. *Qinding xu tongdian* 欽定續通典. In *Siku quanshu* (q.v.).

Ji'nan fu zhi 濟南府志. 1841. Compiled by Wang Zengfang 王贈芳 et al. Reprinted in *Xinxiu fangzhi congkan* 新修方志叢刊. Taipei: Taiwan xuesheng shuju, 1968.

Ji Yun 紀昀 (1724–1805) et al. *Siku quanshu zongmu tiyao* 四庫全書總目提要. In *Heyin Siku quanshu zongmu tiyao ji siku weishou shumu jinhui shumu* 合印四庫全書總目提要及四庫未收書目禁燬書目. 5 vols. Taipei: Commercial Press, 1978.

Jiang Shaoyu 江少虞 (fl. 1145). *Shishi leiyuan* 事實類苑. In *Siku quanshu* (q.v.).

Jianzhu. See Xu Peijun.

Jin Qihua 金啓華 et al. *Tang Song ciji xuba huibian* 唐宋詞集序跋匯編. Jiangsu: Jiangsu jiaoyu chubanshe, 1990.

Jingde chuandeng lu 景德傳燈錄. In *Taishō Tripitaka* (q.v.), vol. 51, no. 2076.

Jinshu 晉書. Beijing: Zhonghua shuju, 1974.

Jiu Tangshu 舊唐書. Beijing: Zhonghua shuju, 1975.

Judge, Joan. *The Precious Raft of History: The Past, the West, and the Woman Question in China*. Stanford, CA: Stanford University Press, 2008.

Knechtges, David, trans. and annot. *Wen xuan, or Selections of Refined Literature*, vol. 1: *Rhapsodies on Metropolises and Capitals*. Princeton, NJ: Princeton University Press, 1982.

Ko, Dorothy. "Pursuing Talent and Virtue: Education and Women's Culture in Seventeenth- and Eighteenth-Century China." *Late Imperial China* 13.1 (1992): 9–39.

———. *Teachers of the Inner Chambers: Women and Culture in Seventeenth-Century China*. Stanford, CA: Stanford University Press, 1994.

Kongzi jiayu zhuzi suoyin 孔子家語逐字索引. In *ICS Ancient Chinese Texts Concordance Series* (q.v.).

Lang Ying 郎瑛 (1487–1566). *Qixiu leigao* 七修類稿. Beijing: Zhonghua shuju, 1959.

Lee, Hui-shu. *Empresses, Art, and Agency in Song Dynasty China*. Seattle: University of Washington Press, 2010.

Levine, Ari Daniel. "The Reigns of Hui-tsung (1100–1126) and Ch'in-tsung (1126–1127) and the Fall of the Northern Song." In *The Cambridge History of China*, vol. 5, part 1: *The Sung Dynasty and Its Precursors, 907–1279*, edited by Denis Twitchett and Paul Jakov Smith, pp. 556–643. Cambridge: Cambridge University Press, 2009.

Li Chuo 李綽 (9th c.). *Shangshu gushi* 尚書故實. In *Siku quanshu* (q.v.).

Li Guowen 李國文. "'Hua zi piaoling shui ziliu'—Zhongguo nüxing wenrenzhong zuiwei yiyi faguang de xing"《花自飄零水自流》—中國女性文人最爲熠熠發光的星. In *Zhongguo wenrende huofa* 中國文人的活法, pp. 215–24. Beijing: Renmin wenxue chubanshe, 2004.

Li Hanchao 李漢超 and Liu Yaoye 劉耀業. "Li Qingzhao 'Lang taosha' jiexi" 李清照《浪淘沙》解析. Revised edition. In Chinese Poetry Web 中華詩詞網. http://www.zhsc.net/Item/6809.aspx.

Li Hu 酈琥 (fl. 1552). *Gusu xinke tongguan yibian* 姑蘇新刻彤管遺編. 1567. In *Siku weishou shu jikan* (q.v.).

Li Jun 李浚 (fl. 713–27). *Songchuang zalu* 松窗雜錄. In *Siku quanshu* (q.v.).

Li Qingzhao 李清照. For modern editions of her *Complete Works*, see Wang Zhongwen, Xu Peijun, and Xu Beiwen.

———. *Shuyu ci* 漱玉詞. (1) In Mao Jin's 毛晉 (1599–1659) *Shici zazu* 詩詞雜俎 (1630), said to be based on a 1370 manuscript, containing 17 pieces; (2) in Mao Jin's *Jigu ge weike ci* 汲古閣 未刻詞, containing 49 pieces; (3) in *Siku quanshu* 四庫全書, reproducing no. 1; (4) in Wang Pengyun's 王鵬運 *Siyin zhai suoke ci* 四印齋所刻詞 (1881, rev. ed. 1889), containing 57 pieces; (5) in Zhao Wanli's 趙萬里 *Jiaoji Song Jin Yuanren ci* 校輯宋金元人詞 (1931), containing 43 "authentic" pieces, 9 "questionable," and 8 "misattributions."

Li, Wai-yee. "The Late Ming Courtesan: Invention of a Cultural Ideal." In *Writing Women in Late Imperial China*, edited by Kang-i Sun Chang and Ellen Widmer, pp. 47–73. Stanford, CA: Stanford University Press, 1997.

Li, Xiaorong. "'Singing in Dis/Harmony' in Times of Chaos: Poetic Exchange between Xu Can and Chen Zhilin during the Ming-Qing Transition." *Jindai Zhongguo funü shi yanjiu* 近代中國婦女史研究 19 (2011): 215–54.

Li Xinchuan 李心傳 (1166–1243). *Jianyan yilai xinian yaolu* 建炎以來繫年要錄. 3 vols. Beijing: Zhonghua shuju, 1988.

Li Yu 李攸 (early 12th c.). *Songchao shishi* 宋朝事實. In *Siku quanshu* (q.v.).

Li Zhao 李肇 (fl. 806–20). *Xinjiao Tang guoshi bu* 新校唐国史補. In *Tang guoshi bu deng bazhong* 唐国史補等八种. Taipei: Shijie shuju, 1968.

Liangshi 梁詩. In *Xian Qin Han Wei Jin Nanbei chao shi* (q.v.).

Liji zhuji suoyin 禮記逐字索引. In *ICS Ancient Chinese Texts Concordance Series* (q.v.).

(Xianchun) Lin'an zhi 咸淳臨安志. Compiled by Qian Shuoyou 潛説友 (ca. 1200–1280). Qiantang, 1830. Taipei: Chengwen chubanshe, 1970, reprint.

Ling Xuan 伶玄 (1st c. BCE). "Xu" 序. In *Zhao Feiyan waizhuan* 趙飛燕外傳, *Yangshan Gushi wenfang* 陽山顧氏文房. In *Baibu congshu jicheng* (q.v.).

Liu Kezhuang 劉克莊 (1187–1269). *Houcun shihua* 後村詩話. In *Siku quanshu* (q.v.).

Liu Ruilian 劉瑞蓮. *Li Qingzhao xinlun* 李清照新論. Taiyuan: Shanxi renmin chubanshe, 1990.

Liu Yiqing 劉義慶 (403–44). *Shishuo xinyu jianshu* 世說新語箋疏. Edited by Yu Jiaxi 余嘉錫. Beijing: Zhonghua shuju, 1983.

Liu Yixuan 劉憶萱. "Li Qingzhao yanjiu zhong de wenti: yu Huang Shengzhang tongzhi shangque" 李清照研究中的問題：與黃盛璋同志商榷. *Qilu xuekan* 1984.2: 101–5.

Liu Yupan 劉毓盤. *Cishi* 詞史. Shanghai: Shanghai shudian, 1985 reprint of 1930 edition.

Liu Zongyuan 柳宗元 (773–819). *Liu Hedong ji* 柳河東集. Hong Kong: Zhonghua shuju, 1972.

Lo, Winston W. *An Introduction to the Civil Service of Sung China*. Honolulu: University of Hawai'i Press, 1987.

Lou Yao 樓鑰 (1137–1213). *Gongkui ji* 攻媿集. In *Siku quanshu* (q.v.).

Lu Kanru 陸侃如 and Feng Yuanjun 馮沅君. *Zhongguo shishi* 中國詩史. 3 vols. Shanghai: Dajiang shupu, 1930.

Lu You 陸游 (1125–1210). *Laoxue an biji* 老學庵筆記. In *Song Yuan biji xiaoshuo daguan* (q.v.), vol. 4.

———. *Weinan wenji* 渭南文集. In *Siku quanshu* (q.v.).

Lu Yuan 魯淵. "Jin bainian Li Qingzhao yanjiu zongshu" 近百年李清照研究綜述. *Haerbin xueyuan xuebao* 哈爾濱學院學報 2007.9: 91–95.

Lunyu. See *Analects.*

Luo Dajing 羅大經 (*jinshi* 1226). *Helin yulu* 鶴林玉露. In *Song Yuan biji xiaoshuo daguan* (q.v.).

Mann, Susan. *Precious Records: Women in China's Long Eighteenth Century.* Stanford, CA: Stanford University Press, 1997.

Mao Chenglin 毛承霖. *Minguo xuxiu Licheng xianzhi* 民國續修歷城縣志. Reprinted in *Zhongguo difangzhi jicheng* 中國地方志集成. Nanjing: Fenghuang chubanshe, 2004.

Mao Jin 毛晉. See Li Qingzhao, *Shuyu ci.*

Mao Ying 茅暎 (*jinshi* 1595). *Cidi* 詞的. In *Siku weishou shu jikan* (q.v.).

Mather, Richard B. *Shih-shuo Hsin-yü: A New Account of Tales of the World.* Minneapolis: University of Minnesota Press, 1976.

McKnight, Brian E., and James T. C. Liu, trans. *The Enlightened Judgments: Ch'ing-ming Chi, The Sung Dynasty Collection.* Albany: State University of New York Press, 1999.

Mencius 孟子. Standard book and paragraph numbers.

Mengzi. See *Mencius.*

Ming Qing Women's Writing Electronic Database. McGill University and Harvard-Yenching Institute. http://digital.library.mcgill.ca/mingqing/english/index.htm.

Nangong Bo 南宮搏. *Li Qingzhao de hou bansheng* 李清照的後半生. Taipei: Commercial Press, 1971, reprinted in 1996.

Nanshi 南史. Beijing: Zhonghua shuju, 1975.

Ouyang Xiu 歐陽修 (1007–72). *Jushi ji* 居士集. In *Ouyang Xiu quanji* 歐陽修全集, edited by Li Yi'an 李逸安. 5 vols. Beijing: Zhonghua shuju, 2001.

Owen, Stephen. *Remembrances: The Experience of the Past in Classical Chinese Literature.* Cambridge, MA: Harvard University Press, 1986.

Pan Yongyin 潘永因 (fl. 1666). *Songbai leichao* 宋稗類鈔. In *Siku quanshu* (q.v.).

Peng Cheng 彭乘 (fl. 1087). *Moke huixi* 墨客揮犀. In *Siku quanshu* (q.v.).

Qian Jianzhuang 錢建狀. "Weirao Zhao Mingcheng 'zhuzi' yu Li Qingzhao shengping chuangzuo de jige wenti" 圍繞趙明誠'諸子'與李清照生平創作的幾個問題. Paper presented at the International Conference on Song Lyric Studies 國際詞學研討會, Hohhot, Inner Mongolia, August, 2008.

Qian Jibo 錢基博. *Zhongguo wenxue shi* 中國文學史. 3 vols. Beijing: Zhonghua shuju, 1993.

Qian Yi 錢易 (968–1026). *Nanbu xinshu* 南部新書. In *Quan Song biji* (q.v.), series 1, vol. 4.

Qian Zhongshu 錢鍾書. *Songshi xuanzhu* 宋詩選註. Beijing: Renmin wenxue chubanshe, 1979.

Qian Zhongxia 錢鍾霞, "Houji" 後記, no. 3. In Qian Jibo, *Zhongguo wenxue shi* (q.v.) 3:1144–45.

Quan Song biji 全宋筆記. Edited by Shanghai shifan daxue guji zhengli yanjiu suo 上海師範大學古籍整理研究所. Series 1–5. Zhengzhou: Daxiang chubanshe, 2003–11.

Quan Songci 全宋詞. Revised edition. Edited by Tang Guizhang 唐圭璋 et al. 5 vols. Beijing: Zhonghua shuju, 2005.

Quan Songshi 全宋詩. Edited by Fu Xuanzong 傅璇琮 et al. 72 vols. Beijing: Beijing daxue, 1991–98.

Quan Songwen 全宋文. Edited by Zeng Zaozhuang 曾棗莊 et al. 360 vols. Chengdu: Bashu shushe, 1988–94.

Quan Tangshi 全唐詩. Edited by Peng Dingqiu 彭定求 (1645–1719) et al. 12 vols. Beijing: Zhonghua shuju, 1960.

Quan Tangwen xinbian 全唐文新編. Edited by Zhou Shaoliang 周紹良 et al. 22 vols. Changchun: Jilin wenshi chubanshe, 2002.

Quan Tang Wudai ci 全唐五代詞. Edited by Zeng Zhaomin 曾昭岷 et al. 2 vols. Beijing: Zhonghua shuju, 1999.

Rao Zongyi 饒宗頤. *Ci ji kao* 詞籍考. Hong Kong: Hong Kong University Press, 1963.

Rexroth, Kenneth, and Ling Chung. *Li Ch'ing-chao: Complete Poems*. New York: New Directions, 1979.

Rong Bin 榮斌. "'Qingzhao gaijia' nanyi fouren" "清照改嫁" 難以否認. *Qilu xuekan* 1984.2: 111–15, 122.

Ruan Yue 阮閱 (*jinshi* 1085). *Shihua zongguii* 詩話總龜. Edited by Zhou Benchun 周本淳. 2 vols. Beijing: Renmin wenxue chubanshe, 1987.

Shangshu. See *Classic of Documents*.

Shen Kuo 沈括 (1031–95). *Mengxi bitan* 夢溪筆談. In *Quan Song biji* (q.v.), series 2, vol. 3.

Shields, Anna. "Defining Experience: The 'Poems of Seductive Allure' (*yanshi*) of the Mid-Tang Poet Yuan Zhen (779–831)." *Journal of the American Oriental Society* 122.1 (2002): 61–78.

Shijing. See *Classic of Poetry*.

Shu Jingnan 束景南. *Zhu Xi nianpu changbian* 朱熹年譜長編. 2 vols. Shanghai: Huadong shifan daxue chubanshe, 2001.

Shu Xilong 舒習龍. "Lichu xuepai de lishi dili yanjiu: Yi Yu Zhengxie, Cheng Enze wei li" 理初學派的歷史地理研究：以俞正燮，程恩澤爲例. *Hunan wenli xueyuan xuebao* 湖南文理學院學報 33.4 (July 2008): 73–77.

Shuo fu 說郛. 100 *juan* edition. In *Shuo fu sanzhong* 說郛三種. Shanghai: Shanghai guji chubanshe, 1988.

Siku quanshu 四庫全書. Wenyuange edition. Shanghai: Shanghai guji chubanshe, 1987.

Siku quanshu cunmu congshu 四庫全書存目叢書. Ji'nan: Qilu shushe, 1999.

Siku weishou shu jikan 四庫未收書輯刊. Beijing: Beijing chubanshe, 1997–2000.

Sima Guang 司馬光 (1019–86). *Jia fan* 家範. In *Siku quanshu* (q.v.).

Sima Qian 司馬遷 (ca. 145–ca. 86 BCE). *Shiji* 史記. Beijing: Zhonghua shuju, 1959.

Song huiyao jigao 宋會要輯稿. Taipei: Shijie shuju, 1974.

Songshi 宋史. Beijing: Zhonghua shuju, 1977.

Songshu 宋書. Beijing: Zhonghua shuju, 1974.

(Shunzhi) Songyang xianzhi (順治)松陽縣志. Compiled by Tong Qingnian 佟慶年. In *Zhongguo difangzhi jicheng* 中國地方志集成, 5th series, vol. 67: *Zhejiang fuxian zhi ji* 浙江府縣志輯. Shanghai: Shanghai shudian, 1993.

(Guangxu) Songyang xianzhi (光緒)松陽縣志. Compiled by Zhi Hengchun 支恆春. In *Zhonghua fangzhi congshu*, vol. 190: *Huazhong difang* 中國方志叢書，華中地方. Taipei: Chengwen chubanshe, 1975.

Song Yuan biji xiaoshuo daguan 宋元筆記小說大觀. Edited by Shanghai guji chubanshe 上海古籍出版社. 6 vols. Shanghai: Shanghai guji chubanshe, 2001.

Spencer, Jane. "Imagining the Woman Poet: Creative Female Bodies." In *Women and Poetry, 1660–1750*, edited by Sarah Prescott and David E. Shuttleton, pp. 99–120. Basingstoke: Palgrave Macmillan, 2003.

Suishu 隋書. Beijing: Zhonghua shuju, 1973.

Su Shi 蘇軾 (1037–1101). *Su Shi wenji* 蘇軾文集. Edited by Kong Fanli 孔凡禮. 6 vols. Beijing: Zhonghua shuju, 1986.

Taiping guangji 太平廣記. Compiled by Li Fang 李昉 (925–66). 10 vols. Beijing: Zhonghua shuju, 1994.

Taiping yulan 太平御覽. Compiled by Li Fang 李昉 (925–66). 4 vols. Beijing: Zhonghua shuju, 1985.

Taishō Tripitaka (Taishō shinshū daizōkyō 大正新修大藏經). Tokyo: Daizō Shuppansha, 1924–32.

Tang Guizhang 唐圭璋. "Duci zhaji" 讀詞札記. *Shehui kexue zhanxian* 社會科學戰線 1983.3:255–59.

———. "Du Li Qingzhao ci zhaji" 讀李清照詞札記. *Nanjing shida xuebao* 南京師大學報 1984.2:2–4.

———. "Li Qingzhao pingzhuan" 李清照評傳. In *Tang Song cixue lunji* 唐宋詞學論集, edited by Tang Guizhang, pp. 126–27. Ji'nan: Qilu shushe, 1985.

———. "Lun Li Qingzhao de houqi ci" 論李清照的後期詞. *Jianghai xuekan* 江海學刊 1961.8; reprinted in Tang Guizhang, *Tang Song cixue lunji*, pp. 133–45.

Tangsong ren xuan Tangsong ci 唐宋人選唐宋詞. Edited by Shanghai guji chubanshe. 2 vols. Shanghai: Shanghai guji chubanshe, 2004.

Tao Hongjing 陶弘景 (452–536). *Zhen'gao* 真誥. In *Congshu jicheng jianbian* 叢書集成簡編. Taipei: Commercial Press, 1965.

Tao, Jing-shen. "The Move to the South and the Reign of Kao-tsung." In *The Cambridge History of China*, vol. 5, part 1: *The Sung Dynasty and Its Precursors, 907–1279*, edited by Denis Twitchett and Paul Jakov Smith, pp. 644–709. Cambridge: Cambridge University Press, 2009.

Tao Zizhen 陶子珍. *Mingdai cixuan yanjiu* 明代詞選研究. Taipei: Xiuwei zixun keji, 2003.

Tao Zongyi 陶宗儀 (fl. 1360–68). *Shushi huiyao* 書史會要. In *Siku quanshu* (q.v.).

Theiss, Janet M. *Disgraceful Matters: The Politics of Chastity in Eighteenth-Century China*. Berkeley: University of California Press, 2004.

Tian Rucheng 田汝成 (*jinshi* 1526). *Xihu youlan zhiyu* 西湖遊覽志餘. Shanghai: Shanghai guji chubanshe, 1998.

Tian Yiheng 田藝蘅 (fl. 1557). *Shinü shi* 詩女史. In *Siku quanshu cunmu congshu* (q.v.).

T'ien Ju-k'ang. *Male Anxiety and Female Chastity: A Comparative Study of Chinese Ethical Values in Ming-Ch'ing Times*. Leiden: Brill, 1988.

Uchiyama Seiya 內山精也. "Liang Song yinkuo cikao" 兩宋檃括詞考. Translated by Zhu Gang 朱剛. *Xueshu yanjiu* 2005.1:128–35.

Wang Chong 王充 (27–91). *Lunheng zhuzi suoyin* 論衡逐字索引. In *ICS Ancient Chinese Texts Concordance Series* (q.v.).

Wang Cicheng 王次澄. "Zhang Yuniang jiqi 'Lanxue ji'" 張玉娘及其《蘭雪集》. In *Songdai wenxue zhi huitong yu liubian* 宋代文學之會通與流變, edited by Zhang Gaoping 張高評, pp. 400–447. Taipei: Xin wenfeng chuban gongshe, 2007.

Wang Fan 王璠. *Li Qingzhao yanjiu conggao* 李清照研究叢稿. Hohhot: Nei Menggu renmin chubanshe, 1987.

Wang Kean 王克安. "Jin 50 nian Li Qingzhao yanjiu zongshu" 近50年李清照研究綜述. *Shandong shida xuebao (Shehui kexue ban)* 山東師大學報 (社會科學版) 1999.5:83–87.

Wang Mingqing 王明清 (b. 1127). *Huizhu lu* 揮麈錄. In *Song Yuan biji xiaoshuo daguan* (q.v.), vol. 4.

Wang Pengyun. See Li Qingzhao, *Shuyu ci*.

Wang Shizhen 王士禛 (1634–1711). *Yanbo ci* 衍波詞. In *Wang Shizhen quanji* 王士禛全集, edited by Yuan Shishuo 袁世碩. 6 vols. Ji'nan: Qilu shushe, 2007.

Wang Shizhen and Zou Zhimo 鄒祗謨. *Yisheng chuji* 倚聲初集. In *Xuxiu Siku quanshu* (q.v.).

Wang Xiaoli 王曉驪. "Li Qingzhao weishenme zhi ruyu jiutian? Li Qingzhao ruyu wenti xintan" 李清照爲什麼只入獄九天？李清照入獄問題新探. Unpublished paper, 2011.

Wang Xuechu. See Wang Zhongwen.

Wang Yi 王易. *Ciqu shi* 詞曲史. Beijing: Dongfang chubanshe, 1996 reprint of 1930 edition.

Wang Yingzhi 王英志. *Li Qingzhao ji* 李清照集. Nanjing: Fenghuang chubanshe, 2007.

Wang Zhao 王詔 (fl. 1522–66). "Zhang Yuniang zhuan" 張玉娘傳. In *Zhang Yuniang Lanxue ji erjuan* 張玉娘《蘭雪集》二卷. Nancheng: Yiqiu guan 宜秋館, 1920.

Wang Zhongwen 王仲閒 (Wang Xuechu 王學初). *Li Qingzhao ji jiaozhu* 李清照集校註. Beijing: Renmin wenxue chubanshe, 1979.

———. "Li Qingzhao shiji zuopin zakao" 李清照事迹作品雜考. *Wenshi* 文史 2 (1963): 171–92.

Wang Zhuo 王灼 (fl. 1149). *Biji manzhi* 碧雞漫志. In *Cihua congbian* 詞話叢編, edited by Tang Guizhang 唐圭璋. Beijing: Zhonghua shuju, 1986 (1993 printing).

Wei Qingzhi 魏慶之 (fl. 1240–44). *Shiren yuxie* 詩人玉屑. Shanghai: Shanghai guji chubanshe, 1978.

Weigong bingfa 衛公兵法 (Tang dynasty?). Quoted in Chen Ying 陳英 (1637–1708), *Yuanjian leihan* 淵鑑類函, in *Siku quanshu* (q.v.).

Weishi 魏詩. In *Xian Qin Han Wei Jin Nanbei chao shi* (q.v.).

Wenxuan 文選. Compiled by Xiao Tong 蕭統 (501–31). Taipei: Huazheng shuju, 1994 reprint of Hu Kejia's 胡克家 1809 edition.

Widmer, Ellen. *The Beauty and the Book: Women and Fiction in Nineteenth-Century China.* Cambridge, MA: Asia Center, Harvard University, 2006.

———. "Xiaoqing's Literary Legacy and the Place of the Woman Writer in Late Imperial China." *Late Imperial China* 13.1 (1992): 111–55.

Wu Chengxue 吳承學. "Lun Songdai yinkuo ci" 論宋代檃括詞. *Wenxue yichan* 2000.4:74–83.

Wu Mei 吳梅. *Cixue tonglun* 詞學通論. Hong Kong: Taiping shuju, 1964 reprint of 1930 edition.

Wu, Shengqing. "Gendering the Nation: The Proliferation of Images of Zhen Fei (1876–1900) and Sai Jinhua (1872–1936) in Late Qing and Republican China." *Nan nü* 11 (2009): 1–64.

Wu Zeng 吳曾 (d. after 1170). *Nenggai zhai manlu* 能改齋漫錄. Shanghai: Zhonghua shuju, 1960.

Xia Chengtao 夏承燾. "Houyu er" 後語二. Appended to "'Yi'an jushi shiji' houyu" 《易安居士事輯》後語, in *Tang Song ci luncong* 唐宋詞論叢, revised edition, edited by Xia Chengtao, pp. 222–23. Shanghai: Zhonghua shuju, 1962.

Xian Qin Han Wei Jin Nanbei chao shi 先秦漢魏晉南北朝詩. Edited by Lu Qinli 逯欽立. 3 vols. Beijing: Zhonghua shuju, 1983.

Xie Ji 謝伋 (fl. 1141). *Siliu tanzhu* 四六談麈. In *Siku quanshu* (q.v.).

Xie Wuliang 謝無量. *Zhongguo funü wenxue shi* 中國婦女文學史. Shanghai: Zhonghua shuju, 1916.

Xin Tangshu 新唐書. Beijing: Zhonghua shuju, 1975.

Xu Beiwen 徐北文. *Li Qingzhao quanji pingzhu* 李清照全集評注. 2nd edition. Ji'nan: Ji'nan chubanshe, 2005.

Xu Mengxin 徐夢莘 (1124–1205). *Sanchao beimeng huibian* 三朝北盟會編. Taipei: Wenhai chubanshe, 1962 reproduction of 1878 edition.

Xu Peijun 徐培均. *Li Qingzhao ji jianzhu* 李清照集箋注. Revised edition. Shanghai: Shanghai guji chubanshe, 2009.

Xu Qiu 徐釚 (1636–1708). *Ciyuan congtan* 詞苑叢談. In *Siku quanshu* (q.v.). Also contained in *Haishan xianguan congshu* 海山仙館叢書, in *Baibu congshu jicheng* (q.v.).

Xu Shiduan 徐適端. "Yu Zhengxie de renquan yishi jiqi funüguan pingshu" 俞正燮的人權意識及其婦女觀評述. *Xi'nan shifan daxue xuebao (renwen shehui kexue ban)* 西南師範大學學報 (人文社會科學學院版) 32.6 (Nov. 2006): 140–44.

Xuxiu Siku quanshu 續修四庫全書. Shanghai: Shanghai guji chubanshe, 2002.

Yang Shen 楊慎 (1488–1559). *Cilin wanxuan* 詞林萬選. In *Yang Sheng'an congshu* 楊升庵叢書. Chengdu: Tiandi chubanshe, 2002.

Yang Weizhen 楊維楨 (1296–1370). *Dong Weizi ji* 東維子集. In *Siku quanshu* (q.v.).

Yang Zhaoying (fl. ca. 1244). "Yangchun baixue" 陽春白雪. In *Yueya tang congshu* 粵雅堂叢書, in *Baibu congshu jicheng* (q.v.).

Yang Zhongliang 楊仲良 (13th c.). *Xu zizhi tongjian changbian jishi benmo* 續資治通鑑長編紀事本末. Beijing: Beijing tushuguan chubanshe, 2003.

Ye Mengde 葉夢得 (1077–1148). *Yanxia fangyan* 巖下放言. In *Quan Song biji* (q.v.), series 2, vol. 9.

Ye Ziqi 葉子奇 (fl. 1378). *Caomu zi* 草木子. In *Mingdai biji xiaoshuo daguan* 明代筆記小説大觀, vol. 1. Shanghai: Shanghai guji chubanshe, 2005.

Yi Shizhen 伊世珍 (14th c.). *Langhuan ji* 瑯嬛記. In *Huibian* (q.v.), pp. 28–29.

You Huiyuan 游惠遠. *Song Yuan zhiji funü diwei de bianqian* 宋元之際婦女地位之變遷. Taipei: Xin wenfeng, 2003.

Yu Zhengxie 俞正燮 (1775–1840). "Yi'an jushi shiji" 易安居士事輯. *Guisi leigao* 癸巳類稿 15, in *Yu Zhengxie quanji* 俞正燮全集, edited by Yu Shi 于石 et al., vol. 1, pp. 763–79. Hefei: Huangshan shushe, 2005. Cf. *Huibian*, pp. 107–20.

Yu Zhonghang 于中航. *Li Qingzhao nianpu* 李清照年譜. Taipei: Commercial Press, 1995.

Yue Ke 岳珂 (1183–1234). "Baozhen zhai fashu zan" 寶眞齋法書贊. In *Zhongguo shuhua quanshu* 中國書畫全書, edited by Lu Fusheng 盧輔聖. Shanghai: Shanghai shuhua chubanshe, 2000.

Zeng Zao 曾慥 (1091–1155). *Yuefu yaci* 樂府雅詞. In *Tangsong ren xuan Tangsong ci* (q.v.).

Zhang Duanyi 張端義 (1179–ca. 1235). *Guier ji* 貴耳集. In *Song Yuan biji xiaoshuo daguan* (q.v.), vol. 4.

Zhang Hongsheng 張宏生. "Jingdian queli yu chuangzuo jian'gou: Ming Qing nü ciren yu Li Qingzhao" 經典確立與創作建構：明清女詞人與李清照. *Zhonghua wenshi luncong* 中華文史論叢 2007.4:279–313.

Zhang Shinan 張世南 (13th c.). *Youhuan jiwen* 游宦紀聞. In *Siku quanshu* (q.v.).

(Daoguang) Zhangqiu xianzhi (道光)章邱縣志. Compiled by Wu Zhang 吳璋 and Cao Maojian 曹楙堅. 1833 edition. In *Zhongguo difangzhi jicheng* 中國地方志集成. Nanjing: Fenghuang chubanshe, 2004.

(Kangxi) Zhangqiu xianzhi (康熙)章邱縣志. Compiled by Zhong Yuntai 鍾運泰. 1691 edition. In *Qingdai guben fangzhi xuan* 清代孤本方志選. Beijing: Xianzhuang shuju, 2001.

(Qianlong) Zhangqiu xianzhi (乾隆)章邱縣志. Compiled by Zhang Wanqing 張萬青. 1775 edition. Microfilm copy.

(Wanli) Zhangqiu xianzhi (萬歷)章邱縣志. Compiled by Dong Fuheng 董復亨. 1596 edition. Microfilm copy.

Zhao Mingcheng 趙明誠 (1081–1129). *Jinshi lu jiaozheng* 金石錄校證. Edited by Jin Wenming 金文明. Guilin: Guangxi shifan daxue chubanshe, 2005.

Zhao Wanli. See Li Qingzhao, *Shuyu ci*.

Zhao Wenli 趙聞禮 (fl. ca. 1244). *Yangchun baixue* 陽春白雪. In *Tangsong ren xuan Tangsong ci* (q.v.).

Zhao Yanwei 趙彥衛 (1140–1210). *Yunlu manchao* 雲麓漫鈔. 1206. Beijing: Zhonghua shuju, 1996.

Zhen Dexiu 真德秀 (1178–1235). *Xishan dushu ji* 西山讀書記. In *Siku quanshu* (q.v.).

Zheng Chuhui 鄭處誨 (*jinshi* 834). *Minghuang zalu* 明皇雜錄. Beijing: Zhonghua shuju, 1994.

Zheng Guobi 鄭國弼. "Li Qingzhao gaijia bianzheng" 李清照改嫁辨正. *Qilu xuekan* 1984.2:105–11.

Zheng Juzhong 鄭居中 (1059–1123). *Zhenghe wuli xinyi* 政和五禮新儀. In *Siku quanshu* (q.v.).

Zheng Wenang 鄭文昂 (Ming dynasty). *Mingyuan huishi* 明媛彙詩. Zhang Zhengyue 張正岳, 1620 edition. In Ming Qing Women's Writing Electronic Database (q.v.).

Zheng Wenbao 鄭文寶 (953–1013). *Nantang jinshi* 南唐近事. In *Quan Song biji* (q.v.), series 1, vol. 2.

Zheng Zhenduo 鄭振鐸. *Chatu ben Zhongguo wenxue shi* 插圖本中國文學史. 1932. In *Zheng Zhenduo quanji* 鄭振鐸全集, edited by Liu Yingmin 劉英民 et al., vol. 6. Shijiazhuang: Huashan wenyi chubanshe, 1998.

———. "Li Qingzhao" 李清照. *Xiaoshuo yuekan* 小說月刊 14.3 (1923). In *Zheng Zhenduo quanji*, vol. 6, p. 170.

Zhou Hui 周煇 (b. 1126). *Qingbo biezhi* 清波別志. In *Quan Song biji* (q.v.), series 5, vol. 9.

———. *Qingbo zazhi* 清波雜志. In *Song Yuan biji xiaoshuo daguan* (q.v.), vol. 5.

Zhou Mi 周密 (1232–1308). *Haoranzhai yatan* 浩然齋雅談. In *Siku quanshu* (q.v.).

———. *Juemiao haoci* 絕妙好詞. In *Tangsong ren xuan Tangsong ci* (q.v.).

———. *Qidong yeyu* 齊東野語. In *Song Yuan biji xiaoshuo daguan* (q.v.), vol. 5.

———. *Wulin jiushi* 武林舊事. In *Siku quanshu* (q.v.).

Zhou Ming 周銘 (fl. 1670). *Linxia cixuan* 林下詞選. 1670. In *Xuxiu Siku quanshu* (q.v.).

Zhou Ruchang 周汝昌. "Xu" 序. In Liu Ruilian, *Li Qingzhao xinlun* (q.v.), p. 3.

Zhou Xunchu 周勛初. As quoted in the unsigned article "Yunshan cangcang, jiangshui yangyang, xiansheng zhifeng, shangao shuichang—Tang Guizhang xiansheng danshen yibai zhounian jinianhui zhaiyao" 雲山蒼蒼，江水泱泱，先生之風，山高水長—唐圭璋先生誕辰一百週年紀念會摘要. *Nanjing shida bao* 南京師大報, Nov. 30, 2001, section 4.

Zhu Bian 朱弁 (d. 1154). *Fengyue tang shihua* 風月堂詩話. In *Siku quanshu* (q.v.).

Zhu Jinghua 朱靖華. "Wujing yu xinjing jiaohu ranse: 'Shengsheng man' shangxi" 物境與心境交互染色：《聲聲慢》賞析. In *Li Qingzhao ci jianshang* 李清照詞鑑賞, pp. 120–27. Ji'nan: Qilu shushe, 1986.

Zhu Shangshu 祝尚書. *Songren bieji xulu* 宋人別集敘祿. 2 vols. Beijing: Zhonghua shuju, 1999.

Zhu Shuzhen 朱淑真 (11th c. ?). *Zhu Shuzhen ji zhu* 朱淑真集注. Ed. Ji Qin 冀勤. Beijing: Zhonghua shuju, 2008.

Zhu Xi 朱熹 (1130–1200). *Zhu Xi ji* 朱熹集. Edited by Guo Qi 郭齊 and Yin Bo 尹波. 10 vols. Chengdu: Sichuan jiaoyu chubanshe, 1996.

———. *Zhuzi yulei* 朱子語類. Edited by Wang Xingxian 王星賢. 8 vols. Beijing: Zhonghua shuju, 1986.

Zhu Yu 朱彧 (fl. 1110). *Pingzhou ketan* 萍州可談. As quoted in Wang Zhongwen, "Fulu: Cankao ziliao" 附錄:參考資料, in *Li Qingzhao ji jiaozhu* (q.v.), p. 310.

Zhuangzi zhuzi suoyin 莊子逐字索引. In *ICS Ancient Chinese Texts Concordance Series* (q.v.).

Zhuge Yibing 諸葛憶兵. *Li Qingzhao shici xuan* 李清照詩詞選. Beijing: Zhonghua shuju, 2005.

———. *Li Qingzhao yu Zhao Mingcheng* 李清照與趙明誠. In *Wenren qinglü congshu* 文人情侶叢書. Beijing: Zhonghua shuju, 2004.

Index

Harvard-Yenching Institute Monograph Series
(titles now in print)